The Complete Guide to

AND HOME MAINTENANCE

Edited by MIKE LAWRENCE

The material in this book has previously
appeared in *Know How* with the exception of
the illustrations which were kindly provided by
the following: p.29 Stirling Roncraft;
p.230 Dulux; p.231 and p.316 Osram-GEC;
p.398 Aga-Rayburn.

© Orbis Publishing Limited 1979, 1987

This edition © Macdonald & Co (Publishers) Ltd,
1987

ISBN 0-356-15188-3

Printed and bound in Barcelona, Spain by Cronion, S.A.

CONTENTS

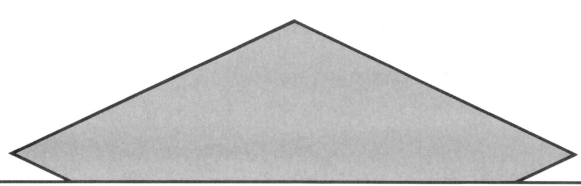

INTRODUCTION

Making the home a pleasant, comfortable, good-looking and weatherproof place to live in – and keeping it that way – takes up quite a lot of the average householder's time. It can also use up a fair amount of money, although the free labour element is what makes doing your own home improvements and maintenance especially worthwhile. It's now easier than ever before to buy tools, equipment and materials, and manufacturers in the industry keep on introducing new products designed not only to make do-it-yourself jobs easier but to guarantee better results into the bargain.

The one thing that you need, alongside your toolkit and the raw materials you've bought, is know-how. That's where this encyclopaedia comes in. It's a comprehensive guide to looking after your home that's clearly written and fully illustrated with comprehensive stage-by-stage instructions, so you can find your way through even the most daunting projects.

The first section starts off with a look at the tools you'll need, and deals with products like fixing devices and fillers which you'll find yourself using time and again. It goes on to cover a huge range of maintenance and repair jobs indoors – on walls, ceilings, floors, fireplaces, doors and windows – and outside – roofs, chimneys, gutters and downpipes, and so on. It also includes valuable advice on dealing with the householder's biggest enemies – damp, woodworm and rot – and finishes up with a look at the vital question of home security.

The second section is all about making your home look good. It starts by dealing with painting, paperhanging, tiling walls and laying floorcoverings of all types, and then goes on to cover all the skills you need to get professional results with soft furnishings – upholstery and curtains – too. Then there's helpful advice on one of the most popular do-it-yourself jobs: putting up shelves.

The last three sections deal with your home's services – the electricity supply, the plumbing system and the central heating. Here you'll find clear explanations of how things work – the first and most important requirement, whether you're improving facilities or just mending things that have gone wrong – followed by detailed advice on how to carry out a wide range of repairs and improvements.

A book of this size cannot possibly cover everything you need to know about maintaining and improving your home, but we hope that it will help you to widen your knowledge, improve your skills and give yourself a better home.

1

MAINTENANCE AND REPAIRS

Basic tool kit

When you start to stock up your workshop with a selection of basic tools, don't rush into buying the first ones you see. The real craftsman never blames the tools – and that surely is a good enough reason for buying the best you can afford

Most of the jobs tackled by the DIY novice involve simple techniques such as screwing fitments to walls, making shelves, laying floor coverings and so on. And you do not need a vast range of tools to take care of these everyday tasks.

The tools shown here and on the following pages are all useful but you do not have to buy all of them at once. So if you already have an electric drill you can get by without a hand one. A cross pein hammer and veneer tenon saw are not essential, while a vice will keep you going until you invest in a proper workbench. And you can always hire specialist tools (or if you are lucky borrow them from friends) as and when the need arises.

As your experience grows you will learn how to get the best out of your existing tools, when to make do with substitutes and when to acquire new ones. Top quality tools are expensive and it is a temptation to balance your budget by going for cheaper ones. But this policy usually proves more expensive in the long run and our advice is to buy the very best tools you can afford and to maintain them well.

1 Electric drill Go for a two-speed model which has a 12mm ($\frac{1}{2}$in) capacity chuck and also incorporates a hammer action. When drilling into different materials – wood, metal and so on – speeds from slow to fast are needed and variable speed facility allows for this. The 12mm ($\frac{1}{2}$in) chuck will enable you to bore large diameter holes and the hammer action to drill into really hard materials, such as the concrete lintel above a window to fix a curtain rail which can be extremely difficult to penetrate with ordinary power drills.

2 Hand drill (wheel brace) and countersink bit You can drill holes with it in a variety of materials using wood or masonry twist drills. It is usually supplied with a removable handle so you can work in tight corners often inaccessible to a power drill. Countersink bits make a neat, perfectly round recess for countersunk screws. Screw sinks can also be used to drill pilot and clearance holes in one operation. 0–8mm/0–$\frac{5}{16}$in, countersink bit 137, 12mm/$\frac{1}{2}$in)

3 Steel measuring tape A 3m (10ft) length will be enough to cover all normal measuring jobs. Dual markings enable you to work in metric or Imperial units. Plastic window at top of case gives instant, accurate measures of internal recesses, drawer interiors and so on.

4 Combination square Version illustrated incorporates inside/outside try square (for measuring angles), straight-edge/marking edge, depth gauge, mitre square, small spirit level, scriber, protractor and screw gauge for screws Nos 4–12. The stock slides along a 305mm (12in) steel rule and can be locked in place anywhere along it. The rule can also be used on its own as a straightedge.

5 Try square Simpler alternative to combination, 229mm (9in) long blade.

6 Cutting knife Multi-blade 127mm (5$\frac{1}{4}$in) long tool with range of blades to tackle cutting of a wide variety of materials from vinyl floor-coverings to plastic laminates. It's useful for accurate marking-out jobs too.

7 Steel (cabinet) scraper This type gives a fine finish to hardwood surfaces, veneers and laminate edgings, shaving rather than scraping the surface.

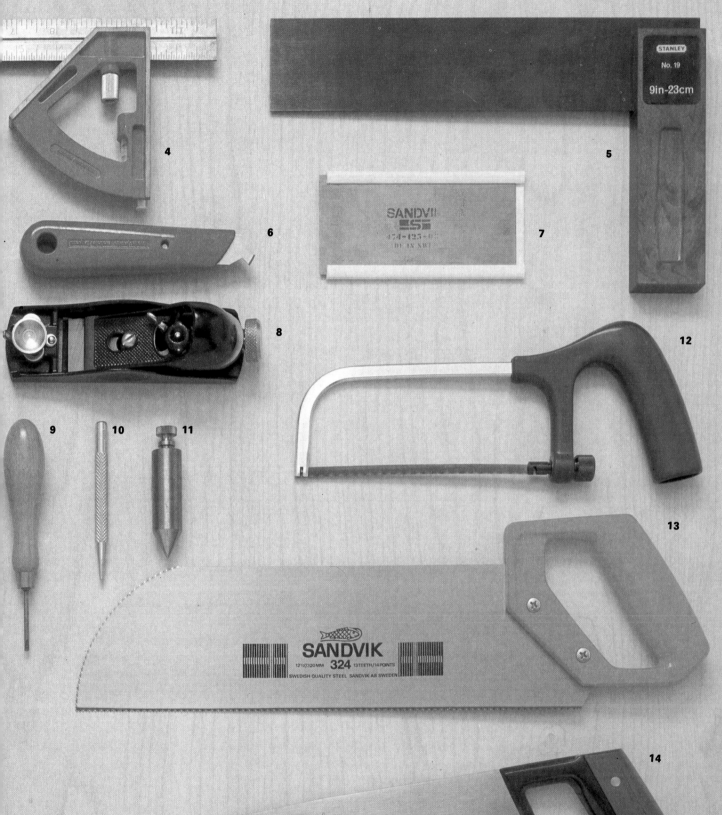

4

5

STANLEY
No. 19
9in-23cm

6

7

SANDVIK

8

12

9

10

11

13

SANDVIK
324
12½"/320MM 13 TEETH/14 POINTS
SWEDISH QUALITY STEEL · SANDVIK AB SWEDEN

14

2000

SANDVIK AB · SWEDEN

SANDVIK
22" / 550 mm
7 TEETH / 8 POINTS

Swedish Quality Steel · Super-Cut · Hard-Point

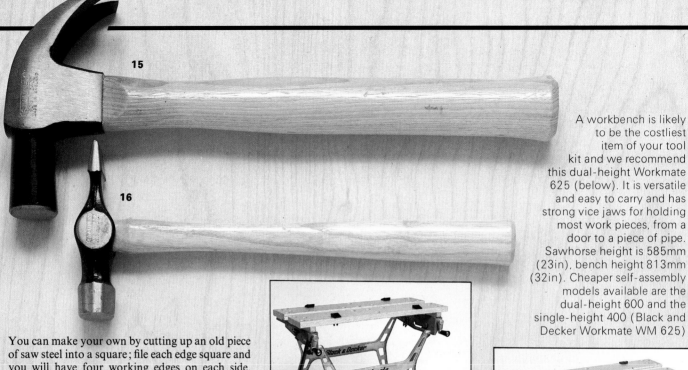

A workbench is likely to be the costliest item of your tool kit and we recommend this dual-height Workmate 625 (below). It is versatile and easy to carry and has strong vice jaws for holding most work pieces, from a door to a piece of pipe. Sawhorse height is 585mm (23in), bench height 813mm (32in). Cheaper self-assembly models available are the dual-height 600 and the single-height 400 (Black and Decker Workmate WM 625)

You can make your own by cutting up an old piece of saw steel into a square; file each edge square and you will have four working edges on each side. Sharpen it each time you use it.

8 Block plane For a range of trimming jobs a model such as the one illustrated is most useful. The depth of cut is adjustable for coarse or fine work, including plastics. If you progress to more sophisticated woodwork you can buy a smoothing plane later, and also add a longer jack plane for producing perfectly true long straight edges.

9 Bradawl Essential for marking timber and other soft materials prior to drilling. It is pressed into the surface to provide an accurate guide for the drill bit. You can use a small worn screwdriver instead; file the blade to a chisel edge.

10 Nail punch For sinking pin and nail heads below the surface of timber without the hammer head bruising the work. You could start off with a 152mm (6in) nail with the point blunted.

11 Plumb bob Essential for establishing true verticals. You can make one yourself by tying a weight to a length of string.

12 Hacksaw A smaller type such as the one illustrated is useful for cutting through metal, sawing through rusty nuts, bolts, screws and nails. The blades are simply replaced when blunt.

13 Veneer tenon saw A fine tooth saw for small jobs where the larger panel saw with its coarser tooth setting would be impractical. Ideal for laminates, mitring and dowelling, it does not have the hard spine (back) common to most traditional tenon saws and so is more useful for jobs such as accurate cutting of thin sheet materials.

14 Panel saw Although there is a vast range of saws, each designed to do different work, the panel saw will cope with most straightforward sawing jobs. It is worth buying a hardpoint version as it will last longer than a conventional saw before the teeth blunt. 550mm (22in) long with seven teeth (eight points) per 25mm (1in) is the ideal size for a wide range of cutting jobs.

15 Claw hammer Dual purpose type, one side of the head for normal banging, the other shaped like a claw for extracting nails. Various head weights are available; choose one that feels comfortable.

16 Warrington cross pein hammer For driving home small nails and pins, either side of the head can be used. The cross pein (narrow rectangular side) is useful when working in confined spaces or where the size of nail head restricts normal holding. Smaller versions are known as pin hammers.

17 General purpose flat file Select a file that is coarse cut on one side for rough filing and fine cut on the other for smoothing and finishing metal. Apart from keeping your scraper sharp, this file will help with a variety of smoothing jobs. Never use it as a lever, though: it will break.

18 Yankee screwdriver Range of interchangeable bits makes this several screwdrivers in one, coping with various screws from electrical equipment sizes right up to large No 12s, including Pozidriv screws with cross slot heads. Its pump action makes work easier. You can also use it as a push drill to make pilot holes for screws if you fit special miniature twist drill bits into the chuck.

19 Bevel edge chisel Basically intended for light work, this sloping-side chisel can reach into tight corners. With a plastic-handled type you can use a hammer without fear of the handle breaking. Start with a 12mm (½in) size, adding 6mm (¼in) and 25mm (1in) sizes as you need them.

Care of basic tools

DON'T leave steel measuring tape extended, especially with blade on edge, on workbench or floor in case something falls onto it; damaged tape will be virtually useless

DO hang up saws by handle or frame when not in use and put blade guard over cutting edge; if left lying about teeth may get damaged. Lightly oil blade to prevent rust. Sharpen teeth, or replace blade, regularly.

DO tie chuck key of electric drill to lead with string, but allow enough length to turn key without having to untie it. Service drill regularly as worn parts will impair efficiency.

DO keep hammer heads clean and free of any traces of adhesive; rub hammer face squarely with fine glasspaper round block of wood. Bang loose heads back into place and/or use wedging pins.

DON'T use hammer on wood-handled chisels; side of hammer head can be used on plastic handles. Ideally use mallet to prevent damaging handle. Never use chisel as screwdriver or you will ruin edge. Maintain good cutting edge by regular sharpening.

DON'T use screwdrivers as levering devices or for raking, chipping or digging holes. If shafts are bent or blade ends not squarely cut they will not turn screws efficiently.

DO check plane blades are correctly adjusted. Hold bottom of plane squarely up to light; blade should be parallel to bottom so it cuts evenly across its full width

DO rest planes on their side to avoid damaging blade or bottom and keep regularly sharpened. After use, store in dry place to avoid rusting.

Steel measuring tape
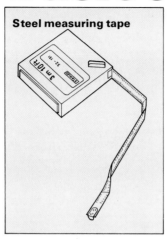

Saw
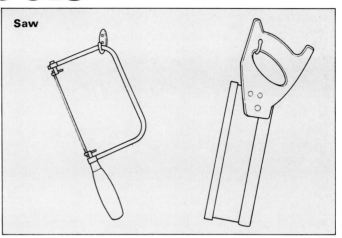

Electric drill
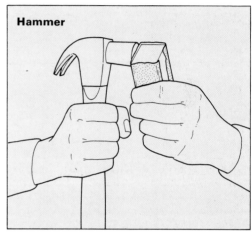

Hammer
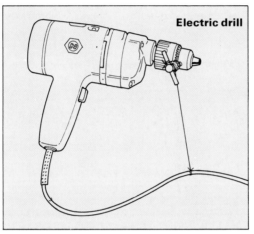

Chisel
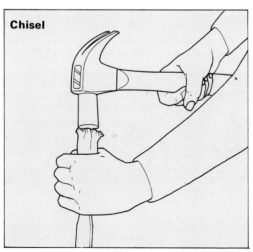

Screwdriver
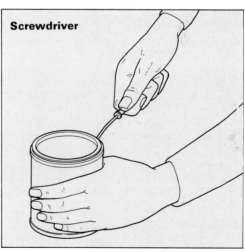

Plane
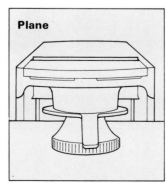

Plane
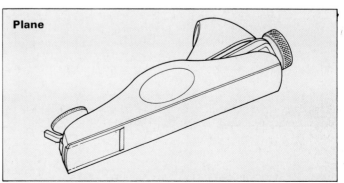

Fix it up to stay up

When you fix something up, you want to make sure it's not going to fall down as soon as your back is turned. So it's important you use the right type of fixing for the material on which you plan to put your fitments.

The correct fixing method depends not only on the construction of the wall but also on the weight and nature of the object to be supported.

There are two basic types of wall – solid (brick or block built) or hollow partition. From the point of view of wall fixings cavity construction can be regarded as solid brickwork. If you tap the surface of your wall you will get either a solid or hollow response depending on the construction. Remember where a thick plaster coating is applied to brickwork it is important to get your fixing securely into the brickwork for maximum support. Hollow types consist of sheets of plasterboard or laths and plaster fixed to a timber framework and are mainly used for partitioning.

Decide exactly where you want to place the fitment on the wall and then mark the fixing holes accordingly. Drill holes in the fitment first, if not already made. Don't attempt to fix heavy items on partition walls unless you can drill into the framework of the partition.

Drilling into a wall

For this job you will need a tungsten carbide-tipped masonry drill bit fitted into the chuck of an electric or hand drill. The tough carbide tip ensures a long life for the drill bit even with the rapid wear and tear involved in drilling masonry. If your drill has more than one speed, operate it as slowly as possible.

If you find a section is extremely hard, such as a concrete lintel above a door or window, you may need a hammer action electric drill or a drill fitted with a hammer attachment. The hammer drill bit is driven into the wall by turning and hammering simultaneously.

If a power or hand drill is not available then a hole can be made with a jumping bit (such as the Rawldrill or Stardrill) and a club hammer (a heavy duty hammer with a large striking face).

Rawldrill Used for punching holes in all types of masonry. This bit is made from a high quality steel for toughness and durability. The bit is fitted into a special holder through its tapered shank; it is fluted so that debris from the hole is cleared out as work progresses.

Fit a bit of the correct diameter into the tool holder. Mark clearly with a pencil where the hole is to be made, place the bit on the mark and gently tap the holder with a hammer. Turn the holder slightly between blows and continue until you reach the required depth. Use the special ejector tool to remove the bit from the holder.

1 Nylon wall plugs with helical wings
2 Nylon collapsible anchors
3, 4 Spring toggles with hook or washer
5, 6 Spring toggles
7, 8 Gravity toggles
9 Fibre wall plugs

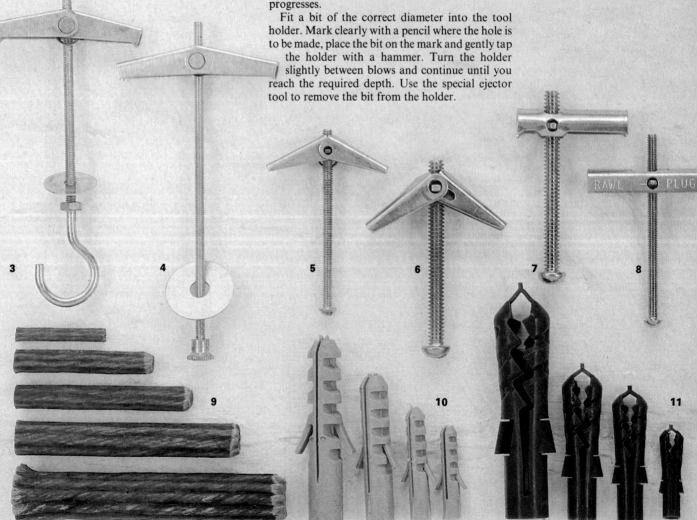

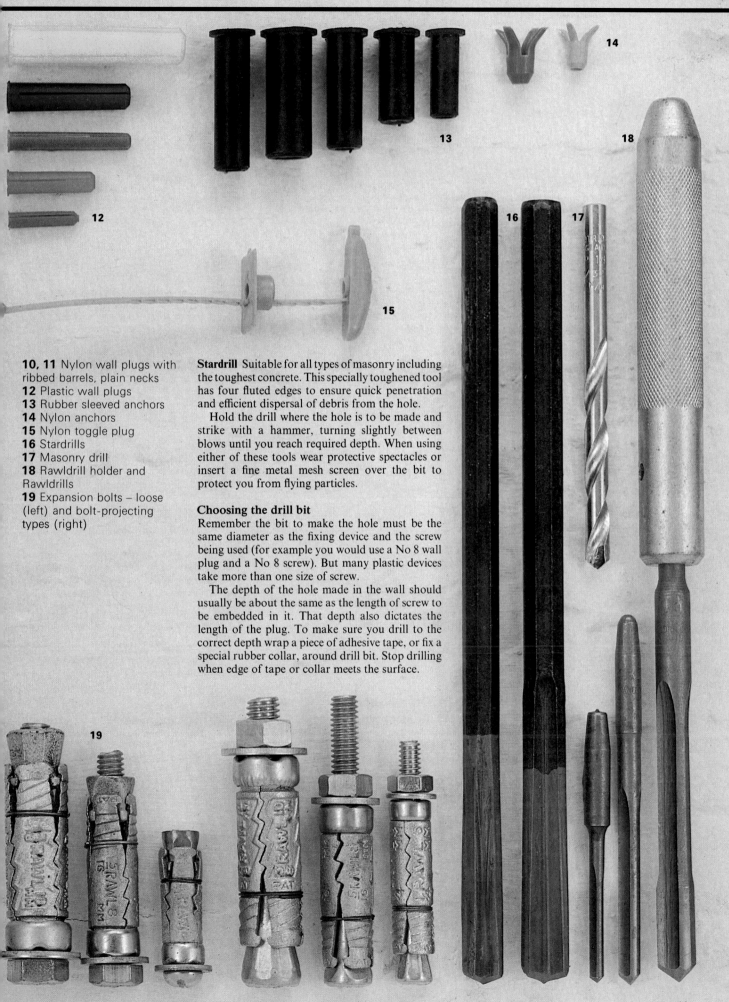

10, 11 Nylon wall plugs with ribbed barrels, plain necks
12 Plastic wall plugs
13 Rubber sleeved anchors
14 Nylon anchors
15 Nylon toggle plug
16 Stardrills
17 Masonry drill
18 Rawldrill holder and Rawldrills
19 Expansion bolts – loose (left) and bolt-projecting types (right)

Stardrill Suitable for all types of masonry including the toughest concrete. This specially toughened tool has four fluted edges to ensure quick penetration and efficient dispersal of debris from the hole.

Hold the drill where the hole is to be made and strike with a hammer, turning slightly between blows until you reach required depth. When using either of these tools wear protective spectacles or insert a fine metal mesh screen over the bit to protect you from flying particles.

Choosing the drill bit
Remember the bit to make the hole must be the same diameter as the fixing device and the screw being used (for example you would use a No 8 wall plug and a No 8 screw). But many plastic devices take more than one size of screw.

The depth of the hole made in the wall should usually be about the same as the length of screw to be embedded in it. That depth also dictates the length of the plug. To make sure you drill to the correct depth wrap a piece of adhesive tape, or fix a special rubber collar, around drill bit. Stop drilling when edge of tape or collar meets the surface.

Types of wall fixings and how to use them

Situation	Type of fixing	How to use
Masonry, brickwork and concrete 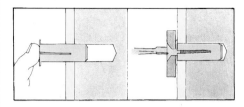	**Plastic wall plugs** The variety of plug lengths available makes these convenient when large number of fixings has to be made. The plug is tapered internally to centre screw correctly, making it easier to use than fibre plug. The range is coded in seven colours, each taking variety of screws. (To fit screws Nos 4–20)	Drill hole to same depth as wall plug. Push plug into hole, slip screw through fitment into plug and tighten.
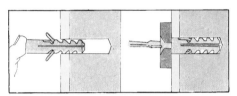	**Fibre wall plugs** Screws can be withdrawn and replaced if necessary without removing plugs. Cut to exact length as required. (Range to fit screws Nos 6–26; coach screws 6mm/¼in and 12mm/½in diameter)	Drill hole and insert plug to just below wall surface. Turn screw into plug up to shank and then withdraw it. The plug expands to fit hole tightly making it easier to find centre of plug when fixing fitment into place and to drive screw home firmly. Note that plug should be as long as threaded part of screw.
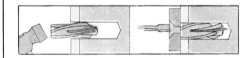	**Nylon wall plugs with ribbed barrel and plain neck.** Ribbed barrel gives a really tight fit. Each plug takes a variety of screws, also shank of screw.	Drill hole slightly deeper than wall plug being used. Push plug into hole, slip screw through fitment into plug and tighten.
Soft materials, such as lightweight building blocks	**Nylon wall plugs with ribbed barrel and plain neck.** As for **Masonry etc.**	Drill hole slightly deeper than wall plug being used. Push plug into hole, slip screw through fitment into plug and tighten.
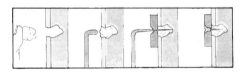	**Nylon wall plugs with helical wings to grip hole sides.** The helical wings grip contours of hole, giving very strong fixing. (To fit screws Nos 10–18)	Drill hole of same diameter as plug body. Overall diameter of plug will be twice drill hole, so you must hammer plug into wall. Slip screw through fitment into plug and tighten.
Irregular or oversize holes 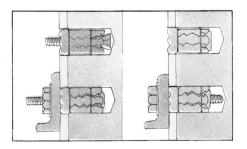	**Compound fillers** These come in powder form in packets or tubs, and have to be mixed with water before use. Recent types are asbestos-free.	Moisten sufficient amount of powder with water and ram into hole either with special tool (often provided with filler) or any flat piece of metal about same size as hole. When filler is still moist make indentation with sharp tool where screw is to go.
High temperature areas	**Fibre wall plugs** As for **Masonry etc.**	Drill hole and insert plug to just below wall surface. Turn screw into plug up to shank and then withdraw it. The plug expands to fit hole tightly making it easier to find centre of plug when fixing fitment into place and to drive screw home firmly. The plug should be as long as threaded part of screw.
	Expansion bolts Projecting type (when bolt cannot be removed) is suitable when fixture can be suspended before being screwed into place. With loose type, fixing bolt can be removed at any time. The anchoring unit comprises shield with expander nut. Loose type allows bolt to be inserted after shield is in place	Drill required hole. If using projecting type insert it, position fitment on bolt end and tighten nut. With loose type, insert shield and position fitment over it; pass bolt or stud through fitment into shield and tighten.

Types of wall fixings and how to use them

Situation	Type of fixing	How to use
Extra hard walls 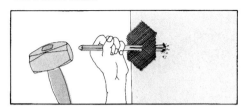	**Nylon wall plugs with ribbed barrel and plain neck.** As for **Masonry etc**.	Drill hole slightly deeper than wall plug being used. Push plug into hole, slip screw through fitment into plug and tighten. You cannot make hole with a standard hand drill when surface is very hard. Use jumping bit (Rawldrill; Stardrill) or hammer drill to make hole. You must wear protective spectacles or insert fine metal mesh screen over drill bit to protect you from flying particles.
Plasterboard, hardboard, lath and plaster 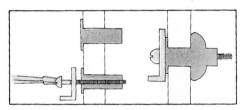	**Rubber-sleeved anchors** Generally used in thin cavity walls and especially useful in thin sheets of metal or plastic because fixing is vibration-proof. When screw is tightened, rubber sleeve is compressed against reverse side of wall. The anchor will remain in place if retaining screw removed. (Variety of sizes available; screws supplied with anchors)	Drill hole of same diameter as rubber sleeve and insert anchor until flange touches wall surface. Slip screw through fitment into anchor and tighten.
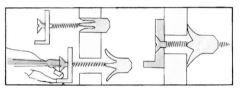	**Nylon anchors** Very useful when cavity in hollow wall is particularly small. If screw is removed anchor is lost. The screw should be at least equal in length to thickness of fitment plus thickness of wallboard and length of anchor. (Three anchor sizes to fit screws Nos 6, 8 and 10)	Drill required hole. Insert screw through fitment into anchor, with two or three turns only, before pushing it through hole into wall cavity. Pull fitment towards you to compress anchor tongue against wall and tighten screw at same time.
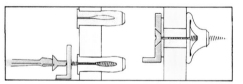	**Nylon collapsible anchors** As screw is tightened, body expands; device remains in place if screw is removed.	Drill required hole and push anchor through until flange touches wall surface. Slip screw through fitment into anchor and tighten.
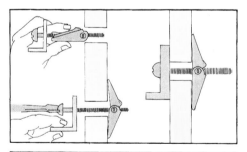	**Spring toggles** Metal thread screw and two spring-loaded metal arms which spread load over wide area on reverse side of wall cavity. Toggle is lost if screw removed.	Drill hole just big enough to allow toggle to be passed through with its spring-loaded arms squeezed together. Pass fixing screw through fitment into toggle. Push toggle through hole until arms spring apart, pull fitment towards you and tighten screw.
	**Gravity toggles** When toggle is passed through hole, bar drops down at right-angles to fixing screw. The toggle is lost if screw is removed. These can only be used when fixing to vertical surfaces. (Three sizes, with or without screws)	Drill hole just big enough to allow toggle to be passed through when bar is parallel to fixing screw. Pass fixing screw through fitment into toggle and push toggle through hole until bar drops. Pull fitment towards you and tighten screw until fitment is firm.
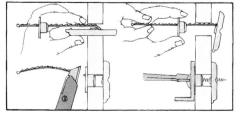	**Nylon toggles** The ingeniously-notched nylon strip makes it possible to use device on any thickness of wall or board as plugs are easily adjusted. The toggle remains in place if screw is removed. (Toggle 32mm/$1\frac{1}{4}$in or 57mm/$2\frac{1}{4}$in long, both take No 8 screw)	Drill required hole so toggle collar fits neatly into it with flange touching surface of wall. Push toggle through hole, fit collar in place and pull notched nylon strip towards you until device is tightly in place. Cut off any surplus from strip. Slip screw through fitment and collar into toggle and tighten.

Fillers and fillings

Fillers are used to make good any defective area in wood, concrete, brick, plaster, metal or any other material. In wood and metal where rot or rust has been removed, leaving an irregular indentation, a filler can be worked into the recess and then shaped to blend in with the surface of the work.

There are certain circumstances in which fillers should not be used. Large holes in sheet materials such as metal, plywood and laminates cannot be filled since there is no proper key, base or reinforcement. It is also inadvisable to try to make good any weakness in the structure of any work since a filler will only provide a temporary remedy and will undoubtedly break or collapse at some future date.

The chief disadvantage of fillers is they cannot easily be made to match in appearance or colour the original work and therefore require a paint or rendered finish. If the final appearance is critical and paint or rendering is not applied, fillers should not be used and replacement parts or sections will have to be fashioned out of the original material and grafted on – an extremely difficult and time-consuming task. Fortunately this rarely arises and a paint or rendered finish is perfectly adequate.

Types of filler

Fillers used for repair work around the home are available in two forms. Both contain a mixture of filling substances and chemicals as well as a bonding agent to help them retain their form when set. Some brands of filler are described as elastic, which means they can absorb a small amount of movement without working loose and falling out.

One-part These general-purpose fillers come in a powder or ready-mix form and are used mainly for wood, plaster, brickwork and masonry. Some brands are water and weather-resistant, which makes them suitable for exterior as well as interior use.

Two-part These fillers are used almost exclusively for repairing metal, such as car bodywork, and begin to harden immediately they are mixed.

Interior fillers

These are all of the one-part type and should be used for the materials specified by the manufacturer; these chiefly include wood, plaster and some plastics. The most popular are ready-mix, although the unmixed varieties are a little cheaper. All are said to be 'shrink' or 'sink' resistant and most can be dyed, stained or painted. Some are claimed to be heatproof, which means they will maintain their form even when exposed to above normal temperatures – as when used near fires or cookers. All interior fillers will tolerate the normal range of domestic temperatures including those created artificially by central heating or air conditioning.

Above Various fillers in powder, ready-mixed and two-part form. Some types are more suited to a particular job than others, so before you buy always check the manufacturer's instructions to ensure you choose the right type of filler for the work in hand

Above With powder filler, you will need a mixing board or hawk and a filling knife
Top right To mix filler, form it into a heap and make a well in the centre; add water and mix until smooth
Above right Spread filler as evenly as possible to avoid rubbing down later

Exterior fillers
These fillers have been developed to resist all weathering without shrinking, cracking or working loose. The toughest type are cement-based and are best suited for use with concrete, bricks, masonry, asbestos and glass fibre (wood requires a more flexible filler which can tolerate the movements that take place in exterior woodwork). Some of the fillers are suitable for use on marine structures, although none is suitable for surfaces which are constantly under water.

Wood fillers
These fillers are used in joinery and carpentry before the final finish is applied to a particular item. They fall into two general categories – those used for filling cracks and abrasions and those used for filling the grain.

The former are supplied in many shades and with specifications by the manufacturers as to which finishes (eg oil, polish, polyurethane) they can be used with. The latter are available ready-mixed (or as powders which are mixed with water into a fine slurry) to fill the grain and seal the surface of porous woods such as oak and ash.

Metal fillers
These fillers are mostly of the two-part type. They are of a thick paste consistency and can be quite difficult to work with, since they are relatively quick-setting. But once rubbed down and painted they are almost impossible to detect. When set, they maintain their form under all conditions, including vehicle vibration and bad weather.

Application and storage

The method of application is simple and usually all that is required in the way of equipment is a filling knife and board. Tins or containers should be resealed after use to prevent drying out and care should be taken to use up all the filler well within the manufacturer's stated drying time before any more is mixed for use or taken out. Partly set filler and fresh filler should never be mixed since the stated drying time will be shortened. Regular cleaning of your filling knife is very important.

Spread the filler as evenly as possible to avoid any extra work in rubbing down afterwards. This can be achieved when using water-based fillers by dipping the knife in cold water at regular intervals during use. With large cavities build up the filler in layers and always work carefully and slowly, otherwise air bubbles may be trapped round the bottom of the hole which can result in the filler working loose at some later stage. Always read the manufacturer's instructions and never use fillers when proper repairs are required.

Few homes will escape damage to wall plaster. Settlement of the main structure over the years, penetration by damp, excessive heat or just general wear and tear will all lead to damaged plaster surfaces. Not only do imperfect patches look unsightly, they can also grow into a major problem if they are not dealt with promptly. By tackling the job at an early stage, both time and expensive will be saved in the long run: reason enough to get cracking.

The thought of repairing damaged or flaking plaster may be fairly daunting to some people, but tackled in the right way with the right materials it is a relatively straightforward operation. Obviously it is quite a different matter if you have to replaster an entire wall or ceiling, in which case this is probably best left to the professional. But most of the small repairs normally required in the home are well within the capabilities of the DIY enthusiast.

Ceiling cracks These are caused by the movement in roofing and flooring joists, leading to the plasterboard (where fitted) parting at the joints. Repairs, which are quite simple, are discussed later in the book.

Wall cracks These are more likely to occur in new houses and are caused by the settlement of the main structure. The area most likely to be affected is the angle between the wall and the ceiling. Apart from filling in these cracks, which are likely to reopen later, one of the most effective methods is to fix cove over the gaps round the room. Plaster cove can be bought from DIY suppliers.

Unsightly cracks across the wall may also be caused by settlement and normally only affect the plaster. If, however, you get a wide diagonal crack appearing not only in the plaster but also in the wall, this could be a major problem and professional advice should be sought immediately. When this happens it is usually on external walls and is clearly visible from the outside as well.

Filling cracks

Common hairline cracks can be repaired simply and quickly. Rake out the affected area with a sharp knife or the edge of a paint scraper. Cut a 'V' shape into the wall along the crack so that it is widest at the deepest point of the crack. This allows you to push the filler into the cavity dovetail fashion to prevent it falling out on drying. Apply cellulose filler with a flexible steel filling knife. Use either a 75 or 100mm (3 or 4in) filling knife, the larger size being preferred since you can work quickly over large areas. Don't confuse this knife with a paint stripping knife, which looks similar, but must not be used as a substitute. The blade, which will bend about 90 degrees, should be perfectly straight and undamaged. Correctly used the knife can be used to give a smooth finish and make the job of rubbing down later unnecessary. Otherwise rub down with medium fine, then fine, glasspaper when the filler has completely dried, before redecorating.

Replacing loose plaster

Plaster often comes away from the surface around fireplaces. It can work loose due to vibration such as excessive hammering near the affected area – possibly when fitting a door or window frame. One simple test for loose plaster is to tap the suspect surface with the handle of a knife or a small blunt instrument. A hollow sound indicates poor adhesion between the plaster and substrate. Lift all the loose pieces with a broad knife and clean the surface beneath with a soft brush.

Repairing plaster

Filling cracks
sharp knife or paint scraper
cellulose filler
flexible filling knife
medium fine and fine glasspaper

Replacing loose plaster
knife or blunt instrument
broad knife and soft brush
undercoat plaster
finishing plaster
wood float, plasterer's trowel
cellulose filler and flexible filling
    knife (if needed)

Repairing external corners
cellulose filler, flexible filling
    knife and medium fine
    glasspaper (if needed)
undercoat plaster
finishing plaster
soft brush, timber batten
plasterer's trowel or wood float

Recessing fittings and cables
cold chisel
brick bolster
plaster or cellulose filler

equipment

Filling deep cavity

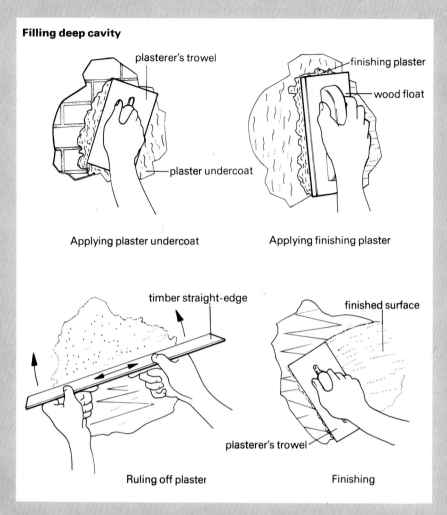

Applying plaster undercoat

Applying finishing plaster

Ruling off plaster

Finishing

If you are dealing with only a small cavity you will probably get away with filling the area with fresh finishing plaster. In the case of a deep cavity, first apply a plaster undercoat. Wet the wall thoroughly, then roughly fill the cavity to within about 3mm (⅛in) of the original plaster surface, applying the undercoat with a plasterer's trowel. The undercoat will dry with a rough texture which will provide a key for the finishing plaster. You will find a small 'hawk' useful to carry the plaster to the wall area after mixing it; make one by nailing a square of plywood to a short length of broom handle.

When the undercoat is quite dry, mix up enough finishing plaster to a creamy consistency to complete the job. In powder form it does not keep that long and old plaster will often set too quickly to enable you to spread it properly; in this case the application will just crack and fall away. If you find the plaster is hardening before you have a chance to use it, take it back to your supplier for replacement.

To complete filling, go over the undercoat surface with a dampened brush, put a generous amount of plaster onto the bottom of a wood float or plasterer's trowel and apply it into the remaining cavity. When the cavity is filled you can rule off the plaster. Using a timber straight-edge, which must be longer than the area being repaired, start from the bottom and work upwards over the new plaster with a sawing action, making sure both ends of the timber keep in contact with the surface of the existing plaster. This method ensures high spots are removed and low spots are built up as excess plaster is pushed up the wall, giving a level finish. When the plaster has almost set, rub a plasterer's trowel over the new surface to give a smooth, polished finish. Lift the front edge of the trowel away from the wall

Repairing external corner

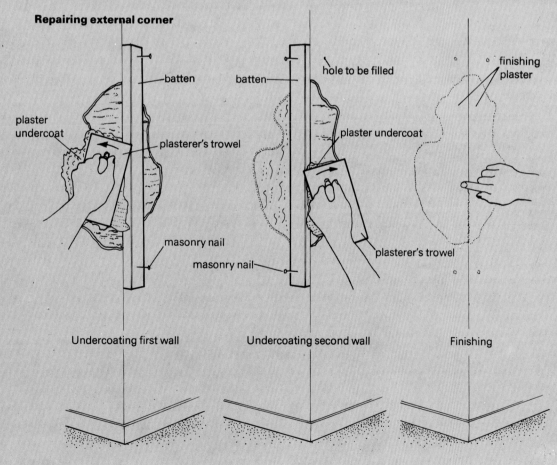

Undercoating first wall

Undercoating second wall

Finishing

so only the back edge is in contact; this will prevent the trowel cutting into the new plaster. Alternatively wait until the plaster has set completely and apply a layer of cellulose filler over the fresh plaster using a filling knife.

Repairing external corners

In any room it is the plaster on external corners that is the most vulnerable to damage. You can repair small holes and chips with cellulose filler as described earlier. When making good these small areas, apply the filler with a flexible filling knife working in each direction away from the corner. When dry the filler can be rubbed down lightly to form an edge to match the rest of that corner.

With a badly damaged corner you will make the best repair by building up the corner with a plaster undercoat, then applying a layer of finishing plaster. Remove any loose plaster and clean back the area with a soft brush. Fix a batten, which must be longer than the affected area, to the wall so its edge is in line with the existing front wall plaster – and flush to the corner. Either hold the batten in position as you work or tack it lightly to the wall with masonry nails, knocking the points of the nails through the batten before fixing. You can screw it into position by drilling the necessary holes in the batten and the wall, plugging the wall and inserting screws through the batten. Make sure you fix the batten well clear of the affected area or you may cause further damage.

Build up the level by applying the undercoat plaster with a trowel or float, always working away from the corner. On one side, plaster the area to within about 3mm ($\frac{1}{8}$in) of the original surface, then move the batten to the other wall to complete the undercoating. When this is dry, complete the repair with finishing plaster, using the batten on each wall as before.

If you nailed or screwed the batten to the wall, fill the holes with any plaster you have left over or with cellulose filler. Before the plaster sets hard, round off the corner by rubbing your fingers over the plaster to form an edge to match that on the rest of the corner. Use glasspaper if the plaster has set really hard.

Recessing fittings and cables

When new socket outlets have to be fitted or wiring extended along walls or ceilings, you will have to cut a channel in the plaster to conceal the cable. You will also have to chop out some of the brickwork to house the steel box for the socket.

Cut through the plaster cleanly with a sharp cold chisel (or fit a specially designed router to an electric drill and work at slow speed), making the grooves and openings as wide as necessary. Chop through the brickwork with a sharp brick bolster, making the hole deep enough for the front edge of the box to lie flush with the wall surface. Screw the box into position, feed in the cable and fill any surrounding gaps with plaster or cellulose filler, finishing the surface as before. When you have made the necessary repairs you can then connect up the socket and screw it onto the box.

Plastering large areas is physically demanding work best left to a skilled professional, who can apply large amounts of plaster before the mixture begins to harden. If you employ a contractor to insert a new damp proof course, an estimate for replastering internal walls should be included if hacking away old plaster is involved.

Cutting recess for socket
Chanelling plaster

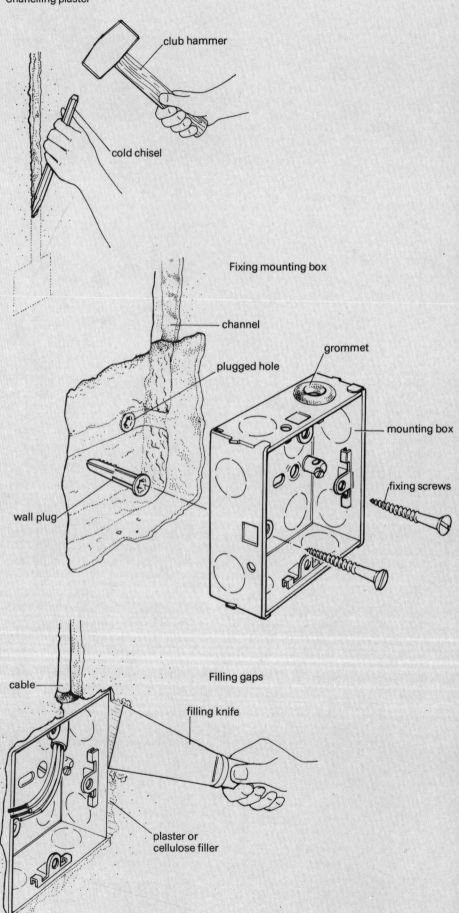

club hammer

cold chisel

Fixing mounting box

channel

plugged hole

grommet

mounting box

wall plug

fixing screws

cable

Filling gaps

filling knife

plaster or cellulose filler

Ceiling problems

Patchy ceilings are not just an eyesore; the smallest defect may eventually grow into a major problem. Never try to hide them or they'll soon become expensive headaches. There are lots of small repair jobs you can do yourself, so start now while it still involves just filling in cracks and removing bubbles in the plaster.

There are two main types of ceiling: plasterboard or lath and plaster. Most ceilings in modern properties are composed of plasterboard sheets butted closely together and nailed to the joists above, covered with a skim or thin coat of plaster. The lath and plaster type of ceiling is no longer constructed, so will only be found in older buildings. The laths (thin strips of timber) were nailed to the joists with narrow gaps between them. Plaster was pressed onto the laths and forced up between (and above) them; when set, this formed the ceiling. A setting coat of plaster was sometimes applied to give a smooth finish.

If you are not sure which type of ceiling you have, look in the loft to see whether there is a plain surface of plasterboard or plaster keyed between the laths. And before you make any repairs to a top floor ceiling make sure there is nothing wrong with your roof. If it leaks, any repair work will be wasted.

Types of ceiling filler

Cellulose filler and plaster are the main types of material used in repairing ceilings.

Cellulose Comes in powder form for mixing with water to a workable consistency, or ready-mixed in tubs and tubes. When filling really deep cracks you may have to build up the surface gradually. Leave each layer to dry thoroughly before making the next application. If you have not done this job before you may find you have to use fine glasspaper on the final layer to obtain a really smooth flush finish.

Plaster More economical than filler when making large repairs. To achieve a smooth finish either level the plaster with a timber straight-edge or, much easier, fill the bulk of the hole with plaster and finish with cellulose filler.

Repairing general damage

Before you start work on any type of ceiling make sure you have a secure platform on which to stand to make the job less tiring and to reduce the risk of accident. If only a small area is involved a step ladder is sufficient. For large repairs use a scaffold board supported both ends on step ladders, trestles or stout boxes. You will be able to move around freely and adjust the height to suit your needs.

Protect all floor coverings and furniture preferably with polythene dust sheets but take care not to spill liquids on the polythene, making it slippery. If you are dealing with a large area, it is best to clear the room completely or stack the furniture well away from the working area.

Bubbles in ceiling paper These often occur when emulsion has been applied over ceiling paper. To remove one or two bubbles, cut them with a sharp knife, daub wallpaper paste on the ceiling and push the flaps back into place. Once repainted the cuts should be invisible.

Bubbles and loose areas may also appear through insufficient pasting of the paper or, particularly in older houses, papering over soft distemper. Temporary repairs are unlikely to be satisfactory and you will do better to repaper the whole ceiling. Soak the paper with water and pull it off, using a flat wallpaper scraper on stubborn areas. To find out if the surface has originally been distempered, rub wet fingers over the ceiling; if you find heavy deposits of white powder on your hand then the ceiling has been distempered. Remove thin layers of distemper with a coarse cloth and plenty of water; thick layers will need to be well soaked before they can be scraped off. To reduce mess, catch as much as possible of the old distemper in a dustpan as it falls. Rinse the ceiling with clean water and, when dry, apply a sealer or size before repainting or papering the surface.

Stains Most ceiling stains are caused by water from leaking pipes or overflowing tanks. Once you have rectified the plumbing fault and the ceiling has dried out, cover the area with aluminium primer to prevent the stain showing through and redecorate as usual.

Tobacco smoke can leave a yellowish film on a painted ceiling. Wash the area thoroughly with a solution of water and sugar soap and rinse well.

Narrow cracks Cut along to form 'V' shape in the surface (this is known as undercutting). The point of the 'V' should be at the surface so the cut is widest at its deepest point. Clear the crack of dust and force filler into the cavity, using a flexible filling knife for a smooth, flush finish.

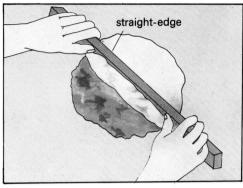

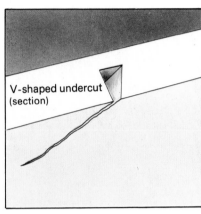

Repair major damage to ceiling with layers of plaster and go over surface with timber straight-edge to ensure smooth finish

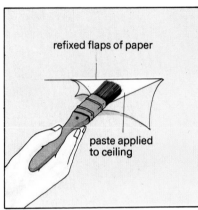

Cut bubbles in ceiling paper with sharp knife. Lightly paste ceiling and smooth paper back into place

Cut back surface of shallow cracks in 'V' shape and apply enough filler to ensure strong repair

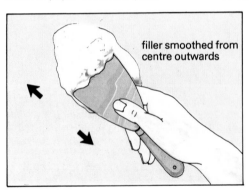

Pack wide shallow cracks with filler. Use knife in both directions, working outwards from centre, for smooth flush finish

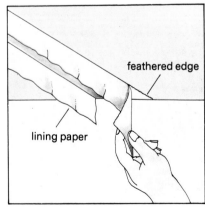

Thin springy blade of flexible filling knife draws filler smoothly over surface

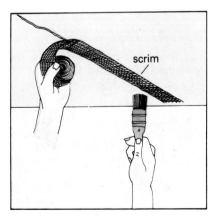

To repair reopened cracks in plasterboard ceilings, fill cavity and paste scrim over length of crack

Paste lining paper over scrim; leave sides free. Tear off sides to give feathered edge. Mask with filler

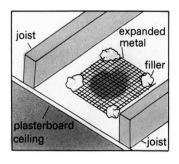

Before filling, support large holes with expanded metal

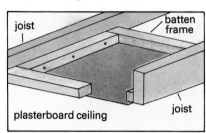

Repair major damage with new section of plasterboard fixed to batten framework and nailed to joists

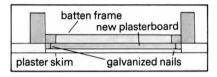

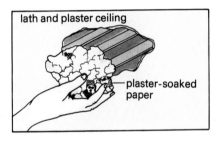

For backing support, line large holes in lath and plaster ceilings with wedges of plaster-soaked paper

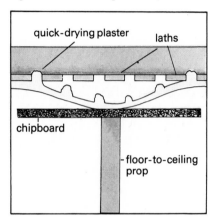

To remove bulges from lath and plaster ceiling, prop up ceiling and apply new plaster from above

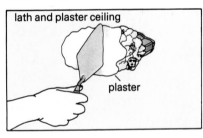

Build up repair with layers of plaster. When set, dampen edges and apply last coat of plaster or filler

Wide, shallow cracks Apply the filler and smooth the surface by drawing the knife outwards from the centre of the cavity, working in alternate directions.

Plasterboard ceilings

Certain types of damage are found specifically with plasterboard and can be made good by using the following methods.

Reopened cracks These are usually caused by seasonal movement of the ceiling joists supporting the plasterboard. If you use just filler the cracks are likely to recur; so you must make a stronger re-inforced repair with a build-up of filler, scrim and lining paper. Scrim resembles a coarse bandage and acts as a keying material to prevent the cracks re-opening. Lining paper provides a good surface for repainting.

Fill the crack in the usual way and, with wall-paper paste, fix a strip of scrim along the crack. Cut a piece of lining paper to the same length as the crack and about 300mm (or 12in) wide. Paste the middle section of the paper and brush it over the filled crack, leaving the unpasted edges hanging. When the paste is dry, tear off the hanging paper to give a fine feathered edge. Apply a thin film of filler to the edges to mask the paper and finish off with two coats of emulsion.

Sizeable holes Here you will have to gain access from above. This will be simple enough if you are working in an upstairs room with a loft space above; but if the room is downstairs, you will have to lift the relevant floorboards from the room above.

Strengthen the hole with a piece of expanded metal (a type of wire mesh), fixing it to the back of the plasterboard above with dabs of filler. From below, fill the cavity with plaster, building it up in two or three layers. Finish off by applying filler with a flexible filling knife.

Major damage The only way to repair major damage is to insert a new section of plasterboard the same thickness as the existing board.

Cut back around the damaged area to the joists above. Nail softwood battens to the insides of the joists to form a support framework, making sure the bottom edge of the joists and framework are flush. Cut the replacement board to the size of the hole and use galvanized nails to fix it to the frame-work, sinking the nail heads below the surface with a nail punch. Cover the nail holes and the edges of the new plasterboard with filler. You may need to apply a skim of board-finish plaster to the repair to make up the level to the surrounding ceiling.

Lath and plaster ceilings

For removing bulges and repairing major damage with this type of ceiling use the following methods.

Bulges These are caused when the plaster keying the ceiling to the laths cracks up and no longer pro-vides any support. It may occasionally be possible to make a temporary repair by pushing the bulge into place from below with a square of wood sup-ported by a floor-to-ceiling prop and screwing through the bulge into the laths. But we recommend you cut out the bulge and repair as for holes.

With access to the ceiling from above there is another method of repair. Push the bulge into place and prop up from below with a piece of chip-board or plywood as before, rake out the blobs of plaster from the laths and pour in some quick-setting plaster (like plaster of Paris) so ridges are formed above the laths. Don't remove the prop until the plaster has set.

Major damage Repair small holes just with plaster or cellulose filler, but for holes more than 75mm (3in) wide you will need to provide a backing sup-port before filling. Either nail expanded metal to the laths or wedge plaster-soaked paper into the hole. Fill the bulk of the cavity with plaster using a trowel, gradually building up the layers to within 6mm ($\frac{1}{4}$in) of the surrounding area. Leave this to set, dampen the surface with water and apply a last layer of plaster or filler. Finally, go over the edges of the repair with a dampened brush to give the necessary smooth finish.

Basic items	For plasterboard ceilings
step ladders or scaffold board supported on ladders, trestles or stout boxes polythene dust sheets	cellulose filler, wallpaper paste and brush, scrim, lining paper (for reopened cracks) filler, expanded metal, plaster, flexible filling knife (for sizeable holes)
For bubbles in paper sharp trimming knife wallpaper paste and brush flat wallpaper scraper coarse cloth, sealer or size (for distempered ceilings)	softwood batten framework, plasterboard, galvanized nails 38mm (1½in) long, nail punch, hammer, board-finish plaster (for major damage)
For stains aluminium primer sugar soap (for smoke stains)	**For lath and plaster ceilings** square of wood, floor-to-ceiling prop, filler, quick-setting plaster (for bulges)
For cracks cellulose filler flexible filling knife	expanded metal or plaster-soaked paper, plaster, plastering trowel (for major damage)

equipment

Repairing timber floors

Most homes have timber floors in upstairs rooms, but in houses built in Britain since 1945 – and in recent extensions to older houses – you will often find that the ground floor rooms have solid floors. As both timber and solid floors can be covered with wood blocks or plastic tiles it may not be immediately obvious which type you are dealing with. So always check first what sort of floor you have.

Timber floors downstairs consist of boards or sheets of chipboard nailed over sturdy timber joists, which are often supported on low walls (called sleeper walls). Upstairs the joists may be built into opposite walls or supported in galvanized steel brackets (joist hangers).

As they are supported on joists, timber floors are also called suspended floors. Unlike solid floors, they make a hollow sound when stamped on and also have a certain amount of bounce. Another means of recognizing a timber floor downstairs is the presence of airbricks on the outside walls just above soil level. These bricks allow air to circulate beneath the floor to keep it dry and free of rot. Solid floors at ground level do not have airbricks.

Fixing loose and squeaky boards
Loose boards move when you walk on them and will increase wear on any floor coverings laid over them. They may also develop annoying squeaks and creaks as two faces of timber rub together. To cure this, refix the boards by nailing them down properly. Possibly not all the nails were replaced the last time the boards were lifted; more likely the nails are loose. Renailing with cut floor brads or round head nails slightly to one side may solve the problem, but there is a danger this will cause the end of the board to split. It is better to drill small pilot holes and refix the boards, using No 10 countersunk screws 38mm (1½in) long. The screws must pass into the joists, the position of which can be seen by the line of nail heads on the surface of the boards.

If the boards are properly fixed but still squeak because they are flexing, the problem can be temporarily overcome by dusting the crack between the boards with French chalk or talcum powder. If the squeak returns, one of the boards must be lifted and the edge planed to give slight clearance.

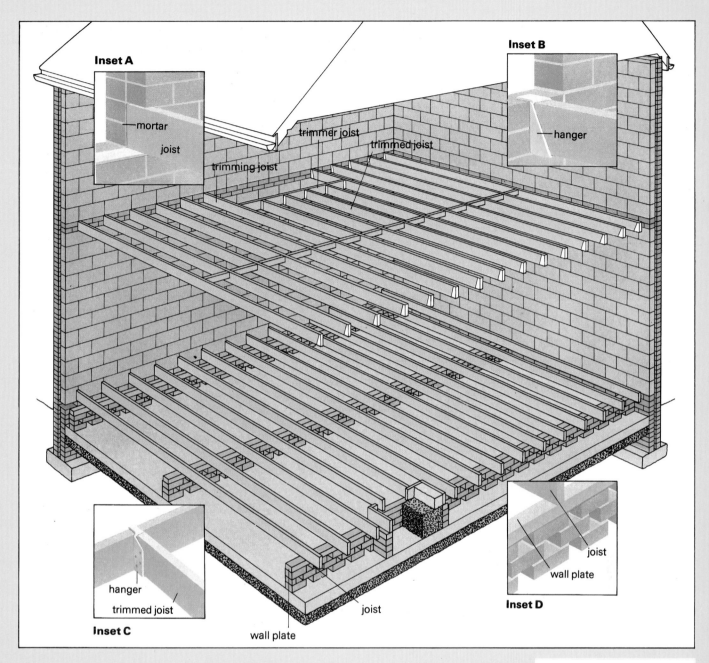

Inset A

mortar

joist

Inset B

hanger

trimmer joist

trimmed joist

trimming joist

hanger

Inset C

hanger

trimmed joist

joist

wall plate

joist

wall plate

Inset D

Sometimes boards which have been properly fixed to the joists still spring up and down, usually because the joists themselves are not properly secured. The only way to check this is to lift some boards in the affected area and examine the joists.

Lifting floorboards

Because of the way floors are made, lifting a floorboard is not always as straightforward as it may appear. Older houses usually have square-edged boards (**see 1**). These are not too difficult to lift, although some force may be needed.

Square-edged floorboards To lift these, check the surface of the board to see if it is secured with nails or screws; the screw slots may be filled with dirt, so look carefully. If it is held with screws, the board will come up easily once the screws are removed; if nailed, it must be levered up.

Start near the end of a conveniently placed board and insert a strong lever, such as a long cold chisel, car tyre lever or flooring chisel, into the gap between the boards (**see 2a**). Hammer the chisel to prise up the end until another lever, for example a

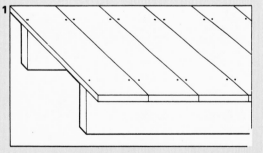

1

claw hammer, can be inserted under the board (**see 2b**). Work the two levers along the board until it is free. Alternatively, put a batten under the board, resting on boards either side, and hammer it along to avoid splitting the board or marking the next.

Another method is to slip a length of steel pipe or rod under the end which has been lifted. Stand on the loose end and the leverage of the rod will force up the board further along its length. Keep moving the rod forward until the entire board comes up (**see 2c**).

Above Example of timber floor construction in two-storey house, with joists and struts exposed
Inset A End of joist embedded into wall with mortar
Inset B End of joist supported by hanger in wall
Inset C Trimmed joist supported on trimmer joist by hanger
Inset D Joist supported by wall plate on sleeper wall
1 Square-edged floorboards

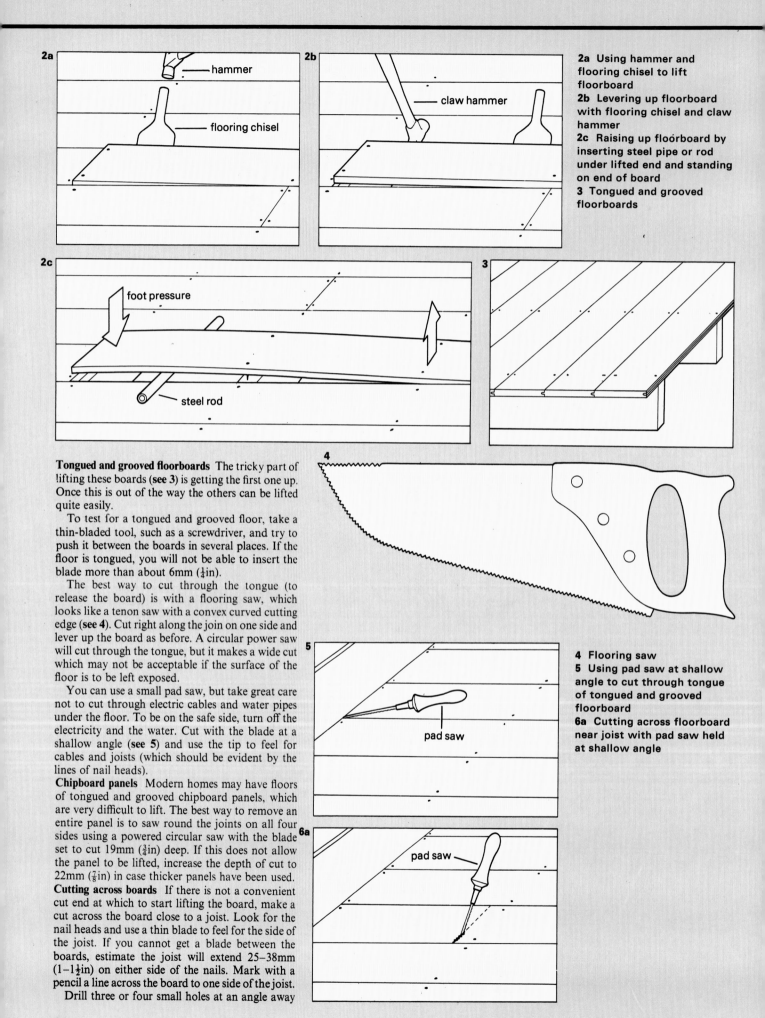

2a Using hammer and flooring chisel to lift floorboard
2b Levering up floorboard with flooring chisel and claw hammer
2c Raising up floorboard by inserting steel pipe or rod under lifted end and standing on end of board
3 Tongued and grooved floorboards

2a hammer — flooring chisel
2b claw hammer
2c foot pressure — steel rod

Tongued and grooved floorboards The tricky part of lifting these boards (**see 3**) is getting the first one up. Once this is out of the way the others can be lifted quite easily.

To test for a tongued and grooved floor, take a thin-bladed tool, such as a screwdriver, and try to push it between the boards in several places. If the floor is tongued, you will not be able to insert the blade more than about 6mm ($\frac{1}{4}$in).

The best way to cut through the tongue (to release the board) is with a flooring saw, which looks like a tenon saw with a convex curved cutting edge (**see 4**). Cut right along the join on one side and lever up the board as before. A circular power saw will cut through the tongue, but it makes a wide cut which may not be acceptable if the surface of the floor is to be left exposed.

You can use a small pad saw, but take great care not to cut through electric cables and water pipes under the floor. To be on the safe side, turn off the electricity and the water. Cut with the blade at a shallow angle (**see 5**) and use the tip to feel for cables and joists (which should be evident by the lines of nail heads).

Chipboard panels Modern homes may have floors of tongued and grooved chipboard panels, which are very difficult to lift. The best way to remove an entire panel is to saw round the joints on all four sides using a powered circular saw with the blade set to cut 19mm ($\frac{3}{4}$in) deep. If this does not allow the panel to be lifted, increase the depth of cut to 22mm ($\frac{7}{8}$in) in case thicker panels have been used.

Cutting across boards If there is not a convenient cut end at which to start lifting the board, make a cut across the board close to a joist. Look for the nail heads and use a thin blade to feel for the side of the joist. If you cannot get a blade between the boards, estimate the joist will extend 25–38mm (1–1$\frac{1}{2}$in) on either side of the nails. Mark with a pencil a line across the board to one side of the joist.

Drill three or four small holes at an angle away

4 Flooring saw
5 Using pad saw at shallow angle to cut through tongue of tongued and grooved floorboard
6a Cutting across floorboard near joist with pad saw held at shallow angle

5 pad saw
6a pad saw

from the joist, just inside the pencil line, to enable **6b**
you to insert a saw blade. Using a pad saw or
powered jig saw cut across the board (**see 6a**),
keeping the handle of the saw tilted towards the
middle of the joist so the board will be supported
when it is replaced. Give the board some additional
support when you replace it by gluing and nailing a
piece of scrap wood (50 × 25mm/2 × 1in) to the side
of the joist with clout nails 38mm (1¾in) long so its
top is flush with the top of the joist (**see 6b**).

Securing loose joists
When floorboards have been lifted, the exposed
joists can be tested for movement. If the ends have
rotted, it is best to check with a flooring expert to
remedy the problem. Dampness in the supporting
walls is the usual cause – or blocked or insufficient
airbricks.

    If the joists and floorboards show signs of wood-
worm attack (neat round holes surrounded by fine
sawdust), brush them free of dust and cobwebs and
spray with woodworm killer applied with a
garden-type insecticide sprayer. If the attack is
widespread, you should get professional advice.

    The joists may be loose because the mortar which
holds them firmly in place in the wall has dropped
out (**see floor construction diagrams**). In this case the
joist should be repacked with new mortar.

    If the joist end is supported on a wall plate or in
a metal joist hanger (**see floor construction diagrams**), you may be able to secure it by wedging it
in place with a piece of scrap wood or by packing
pieces of slate under it.

    If the joists bounce, it is because they are fitted
across too wide a span. They can be stabilized with
timber struts fitted between them midway from the
support points. Lengths of floorboard about 125 ×
25mm (5 × 1in) nailed into the joists are the easiest
to fit (**see 7**).

Levelling boards
Uneven surfaces of old floors result in extra wear
on floor coverings and could be a hazard, causing
people to trip over raised sections.

Correcting surface levels If the floor surface is
uneven in only a few places and is to be covered, lift
the offending boards and pack them with pieces of
scrap hardboard or plastic laminate to the correct
level.

    When the boards are high, the securing nails
should be punched well below the surface, tacks
should be pulled out and the surface of the boards
levelled with either a plane or a coarse sanding disc
attached to an electric drill.

    Alternatively you can cut a rebate in the under-
side of the offending floorboard where it sits on the
joists. Measure the depth of board to be trimmed,
lift and hold it at right-angles to the floor. Mark on
the underside the exact position of the joists, allowing 12mm (½in) on either side of each joist (**see 8a**).
With a try square complete your marks across the
width of the board and shade in the rebate area.
Measure and mark the depth of the rebate on both
edges of the board (**see 8b**) and tenon saw along the
pencil lines to the depth marked on the edges (**8c**).
Clamp the board and chisel out the rebate area,
taking care not to chisel below the required depth
(**see 8d**). Replace the floorboard, check it is the
same level as the other boards (**see 8e**) and nail it
to the joists with 63mm (2½in) cut floor brads or
round head nails.

Warning Floorboards are usually 22mm (⅞in)

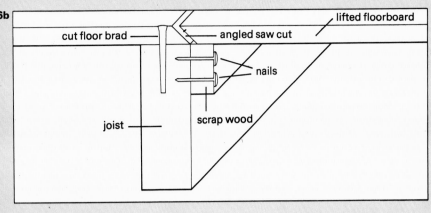

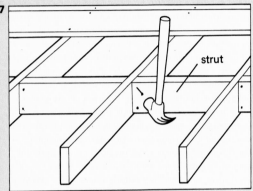

6b Section of lifted board
replaced and supported
7 Fixing plain struts between
joists

Below Levelling a thick
floorboard **8a** Marking
rebate on underside of
floorboard. **8b** Measuring
and marking depth of rebate.
8c Sawing rebate depth.
8d Chiselling out rebate.
8e Thicker board now lies at
correct level

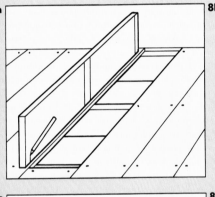

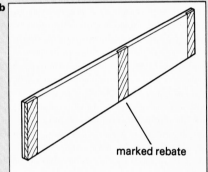

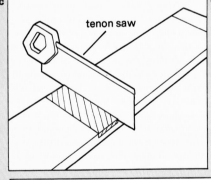

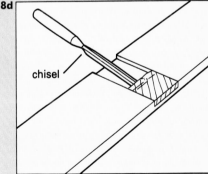

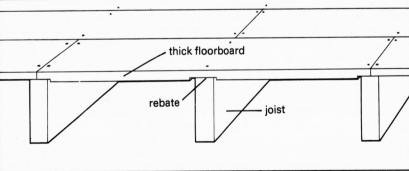

thick. It is dangerous to remove more than 3mm ($\frac{1}{8}$in) from the thickness of the board. Pay special attention to this when making the saw cuts.

Resurfacing Where a number of boards are uneven, resurface the entire floor by sanding it with an industrial-type electric floor sander, which can be hired. This has a large drum covered with a belt of tough abrasive paper.

The machine will remove about 3mm ($\frac{1}{8}$in) of the surface without difficulty, but nail heads must first be sunk well below the surface or they will tear the abrasive paper. Move the sander up and down the length of the floorboards or slightly at an angle. Most of the dust is collected in a bag, but some will escape into the air so you must wear a mask when sanding.

The alternative to sanding is to lay sheets of hardboard on the floor surface. If there are any serious undulations, these should first be corrected by lifting and relaying the offending boards.

Usually 3mm ($\frac{1}{8}$in) standard hardboard is suitable for resurfacing, but use 5mm ($\frac{3}{16}$in) board if the floor is in a very poor state and there are gaps of more than 6mm ($\frac{1}{4}$in) between the boards. If the hardboard is to be laid in a kitchen, bathroom or where it could be subjected to damp, tempered hardboard should be used since it is resistant to moisture.

Conditioning hardboard To avoid buckling, hardboard must be conditioned before it is laid. Separate the boards and stand them on edge in the room where they will be fixed for up to 72 hours before laying. In new houses, and in kitchens and bathrooms, where there is likely to be more moisture, sprinkle the rough side with water – about 1 litre per 2440 × 1200mm sheet (2 pints per 8 × 4ft sheet). Stack the boards flat, back to back, and leave for 48 hours (standard hardboard) or 72 hours (tempered).

Laying hardboard sheets The boards should be laid as soon as they have been conditioned. If working with full 2440 × 1200mm (8 × 4ft) sheets, cut each one in half or quarters with a fine tooth saw since smaller sheets are much easier to handle. Either get someone to help hold the sheet or clamp and support where possible to keep the sheet firm when cutting.

If varnishing the hardboard and using it as a decorative surface (or if laying thin vinyl floor tiles on it) lay the shiny side uppermost; for any other decorative floor covering lay the rough side upwards.

The hardboard sheets should be laid, as far as possible, in staggered brickwork fashion so the joints do not align. Fix down the boards with hardboard nails 25mm (1in) long at 100mm (or 4 in) intervals along the edges and at 150mm (or 6in) intervals over the whole board surface (**see 9**).

Where floorboards may have to be lifted from time to time to give access to cables and pipes, the hardboard should be fixed in small panels with No 6 countersunk screws.

Relaying a floor
If the boards are badly worn and there are a lot of wide gaps between them, it is best to relay the floor. You can then refix worn boards upside down to give a new surface. It is possible to fill gaps between boards with papier mâché, wood filler or wood strips, but this is generally too time-consuming except where there are only a few gaps to fill.

If you are relaying the floor, it is a good oppor-

tunity while the boards are lifted to check for damp, rot and woodworm – and carry out treatment if necessary. You may also decide it is worth while insulating under the floor, if working downstairs.

Normally gaps between boards can be eliminated by pushing the boards together as they are renailed. If they are warped, however, you will have to fill the gaps with wedges or plane the edges level.

Nail the first board into place with 63mm (2$\frac{1}{2}$in) cut floor brads or lost head nails, then position four or five boards together. Place folding wedges at intervals against the boards and nail pieces of scrap timber to the joists against the wedges to stop them moving. Hammer the wedges together to close the gaps in the boards, then nail the boards to the joists when the boards are in the correct position (**see 10**).

Replace damaged boards with new timber or with second-hand floorboards, which are usually available from demolition yards. All second-hand timber should be carefully examined for rot and woodworm damage. It is advisable to take a sample of the existing floorboards to compare for width and thickness.

You can make a very hard and smooth floor by replacing the timber floorboards with flooring grade chipboard panels. The tongued and grooved type makes an exceptionally smooth floor, but because it is difficult to lift make sure to leave small, screwed down access panels over cables and pipes which may have to be reached from time to time.

9 Order of laying cut hardboard sheets to level uneven floor surface
10 Using folding wedges and nailed blocks to close gaps between boards when relaying timber floor

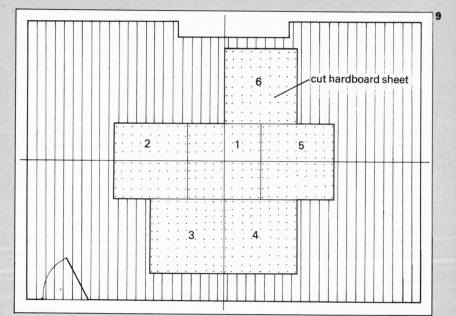

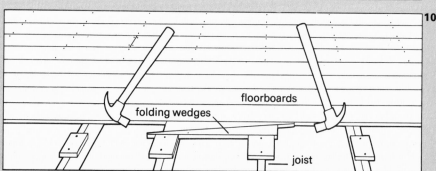

Use 19mm ($\frac{3}{4}$in) chipboard for joists up to 450mm (or 18in) apart and 22mm ($\frac{7}{8}$in) chipboard for joists from 450–600mm (or 18–24in) apart. Fit the panels together and nail in place through the tongues with round head nails.

Levelling a solid floor

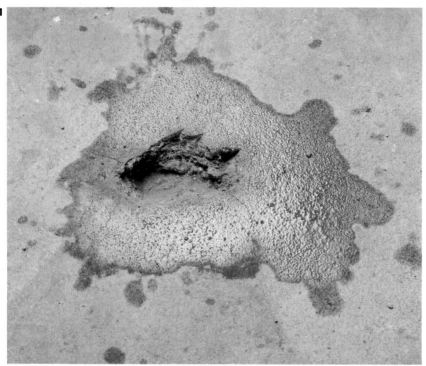

How you deal with an uneven or sloping solid floor depends on the degree to which it is out of true. Check this with a spirit level placed on a long straight board, using it over different areas of the floor and pointing in a number of directions. If the floor slopes more than about 6mm (or $\frac{1}{4}$in) you will have to level it with a sand and cement surfacing layer, or screed. Where the irregularity is no more than 6mm (or $\frac{1}{4}$in) you can make the floor level with one or two layers of a self-smoothing screeding compound. This is a mixture like runny cement which sets in a few hours to form a hard surface suitable as a base for any type of floor covering.

If the floor is old it may be badly cracked and very uneven and it is best to remove it and lay a new concrete floor with a damp proof membrane. (You can use the same method to replace a downstairs timber floor which has rotted.) Where the floor is damp but otherwise sound, you do not need to replace it; simply paint the floor with a damp-proofing sealer.

1 Fill any holes in the floor. **2** Pack with cement mortar and trowel smooth. **3** If necessary brush on a liquid damp proof membrane. **4** Pour on the levelling compound, mixed to a creamy paste

Laying a self-smoothing screed

Clean, dust-free concrete is the ideal surface for a self-smoothing screed and it is best to remove any existing floor covering before starting treatment. You should always remove wood blocks or any type of sheet covering (vinyl, carpet etc.), but you can use screeding compounds on quarry tiles, flagstones, slate and bricks. Some compounds are suitable for application over hard surface vinyl tiles provided these are securely fixed and properly prepared.

Preparing the surface Remove any flaking or crumbling sections with a metal scraper. Sweep the floor and wash it thoroughly with a strong sugar soap solution. Remove stubborn oil and grease patches with caustic soda or a proprietary floor cleaner and take off polish with medium grade wire wool and cleaning powder. Rinse with clean water and, when dry, sweep the floor again.

Indentations more than 6mm (or ¼in) deep must be filled with cement mortar (one part Portland cement to three parts clean, coarse sand). To make sure the mortar adheres firmly in these hollows paint the affected area with a PVA bonding agent diluted according to the manufacturer's instructions. Allow this to dry before applying another coat and, before the second coat dries, trowel on the cement mortar.

Prepare reasonably absorbent surfaces, such as cement mortar or concrete, by lightly dampening the surface with water using a garden syringe or spreading with a wide brush. Prime quarry tiles and other non-absorbent surfaces – and very dusty ones such as sandy screeds – with a PVA bonding agent; allow this to dry before applying the compound.

Vinyl tiles These need special preparation: wash them thoroughly with a proprietary floor cleaner or with sugar soap. Don't use abrasive or solvent-based cleaners. Fill small depressions in the surface with a mixture of two parts of a special water-mixed screeding compound and one part clean sharp sand.

Vinyl tiles also need special priming treatment: use an acrylic floor primer mixed with water (one part primer to one part water). When the primer has dried, brush a thin coat of a suitable bonding agent over the floor (never a PVA bonding agent). Allow the bonding agent to set for up to two hours or until you can walk on it without it sticking to your feet.

Applying the compound Screeding compounds are usually supplied in powder form, which you mix with water to a creamy paste. Pour a little of the paste onto the floor and spread it out as evenly as possible with a steel float. No finishing off is needed since the marks made by the float disappear within a few seconds. Work from the corner farthest from the door to allow an easy exit. You can use the compounds in layers from 1.5 to 3mm (or $\frac{1}{16}$ to $\frac{1}{8}$in) thick, making one or two applications. If two coats are necessary, apply the second as soon as the first has dried hard enough to walk on. The screed sets quickly and can be walked on usually after about one or two hours. You can lay the floor coverings the following day, although the screed does not harden thoroughly for a week.

5 Smooth the levelling compound with a steel float; no finishing is needed
6 Before laying a sand and cement screed, position battens over the floor
7 Draw a levelling board across the screed using the battens as a guide

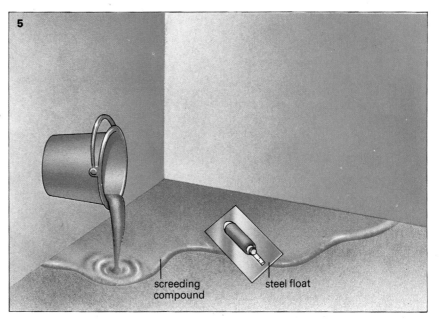

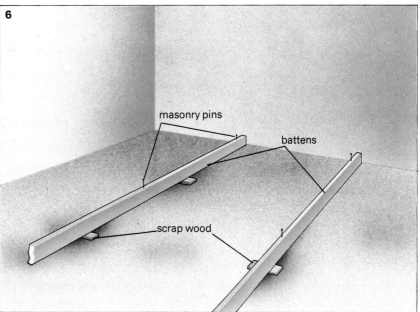

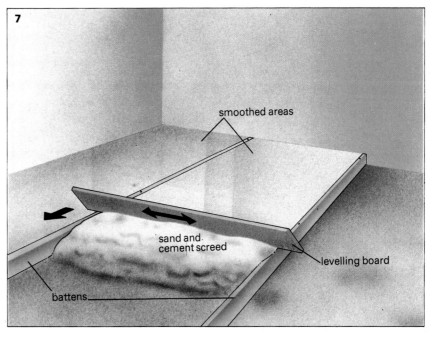

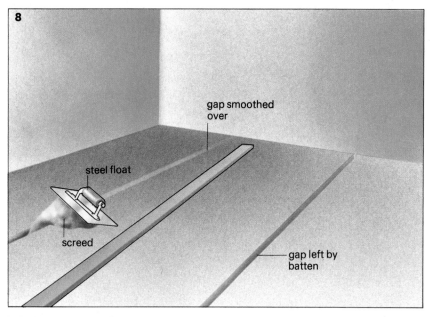

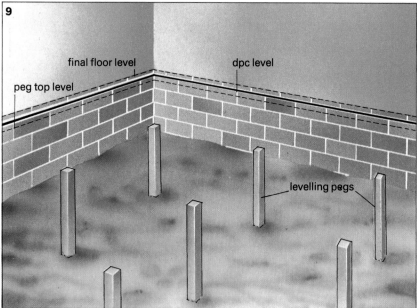

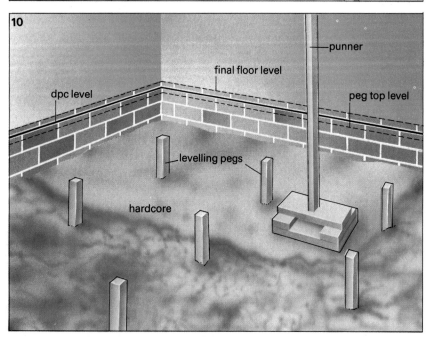

Laying a sand and cement screed

The technique you use for laying a sand and cement screed is very similar to laying a self-smoothing screed, but this type is thicker and it takes more effort and skill to get a smooth level surface. Since the finished surface will be slightly higher than before, it will be necessary to plane a small amount from the bottom of doors and perhaps refix skirting boards.

Preparing the floor Clean the floor as previously described, then apply a PVA bonding agent and allow it to dry. To ensure the new floor surface will be smooth and level, you will have to lay battens on the floor; the screed is spread between these battens and levelled off by drawing a board along them. The thickness of the battens will govern the thickness of the screed which, for maximum strength, should be 25 to 50mm (1 to 2in) – and no less than 6mm (or $\frac{1}{4}$in) – thick.

Lay the battens a convenient distance apart: about 1m (or 3ft) is ideal because it allows you to place the screed in strips. Use a spirit level and a straight-edge to get the battens level in all directions and position pieces of scrap wood to pack them out at the low spots. Fix the battens temporarily to the floor with masonry pins and apply another coat of slightly diluted bonding agent, allowing it to dry partially.

Applying the screed Mix the cement screed (one part Portland cement to three parts clean coarse sand), making sure the mixture is not dry or crumbly nor too wet so puddles form on the surface when the screed is smoothed over. If the screed will be less than 25mm (1in) thick, add a bonding agent to the mix according to the manufacturer's instructions.

Roughly spread the screed between the battens with a steel float. Pull the edge of the levelling board, which should be long enough to rest easily on the battens, over them to give a level finish and smooth the screed with the steel float, checking the surface frequently with your spirit level.

When the surface of each strip of screed is slightly firm, prise up the battens and fill the resulting gaps with screed mixture, smoothing it out to maintain the level surface. Leave the finished screed to cure for at least three days before walking on it. If it is essential to cross the floor before this time, lay duckboards of timber planks or chipboard or plywood sheets.

Warning It is essential thin section screeds do not dry out too rapidly or the cement will not cure and harden properly. Cover them with polythene sheets or wet newspapers or sacking during curing.

Laying a new solid floor

Putting down an entirely new floor allows you to control exactly the height of the finished floor surface. It can line up with existing floors, or be at a lower level to give extra height to the room. Always consult your local building control officer before making a new floor to ensure the work complies with current regulations.

8 When the surface is firm, remove the battens and fill the gaps with more screed
9 Set out levelling pegs for a new floor
10 Compact the hardcore with a punner

Preparing the surface Remove the old floor by breaking it up with a sledgehammer and pickaxe or a heavy duty electric hammer, all of which you can hire. Dig out the base to a depth of 300mm (or 12in) below the finished floor level. Remove plaster from the walls until you find the level of the damp proof course.

Insert a series of stout levelling pegs made from 50 × 50mm (or 2 × 2in) timber at regular intervals over the entire area. The tops of the pegs should be level and 50mm (or 2in) below the finished floor surface. Use a long straight-edge and a spirit level to set the pegs accurately.

Constructing the floor Place a layer of hardcore (the broken segments of the old floor can be used for this) about 100mm (4in) thick between the pegs. Ram it well down and bind the surface with a layer of sand. Then spread concrete to the top of the levelling pegs to give a concrete depth of about 150mm (6in). A suitable concrete mix is one part Portland cement, two-and-a-half parts concreting sand and four parts coarse aggregate. You can use ready-mixed concrete if a large area is involved.

Damp proof membrane Most local authorities will accept a damp proof membrane consisting of two coats of a heavy damp-proofing liquid, but some may prefer a plastic membrane sheet. A plastic membrane sheet is usually laid over the concrete before the finishing screed. Fold it up the walls to link with the existing damp proof course.

A liquid bitumen rubber damp proof membrane is brushed over the surface after the concrete has hardened. Start in the corner furthest from the door and apply an even coat, taking care not to miss any areas. Again, make sure you take the membrane up the wall to link with the damp proof course. When the first coat has dried apply a second one and cover it with clean coarse sand while it is still wet to provide a good key for the screed (which you will lay next) and to protect the membrane when it is walked on.

Laying the screed Finish the floor by laying a 50mm (or 2in) thick sand and cement screed (one part cement to three parts sharp, washed sand) over the damp proof membrane.

Because the concrete sub-floor is level and smooth you do not need to nail guide battens over the surface in the same way as when a screed is laid on an uneven floor. Instead, make two guide battens 2m (or 6ft) long and 50mm (2in) thick and lay them fairly close to each side of the room with a levelling board placed across them. Spread the screed mix around the battens using the levelling board as a guide.

Smooth the surface with a steel float and check with a spirit level to make sure the surface is level. Draw back the battens and make good the surface before laying another screed strip. Work backwards to the doorway, changing the direction of work if necessary.

To avoid damage to the screed before curing is complete, it is advisable to allow a three-day curing period before you walk on the floor.

If walking over a freshly laid screed is unavoidable, it should be protected by laying duckboards or planks or boards to spread the load over as wide an area as possible.

11 Put a plastic membrane sheet over the newly laid concrete
12 Apply screed on top of the sheet
13 Remove the battens and fill the gaps

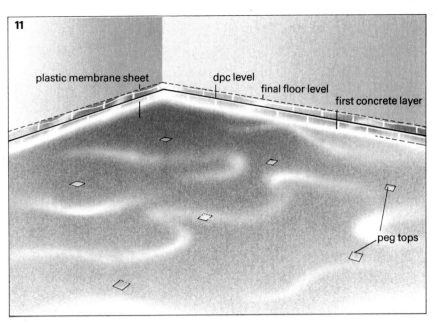

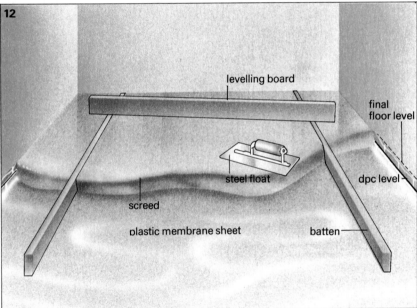

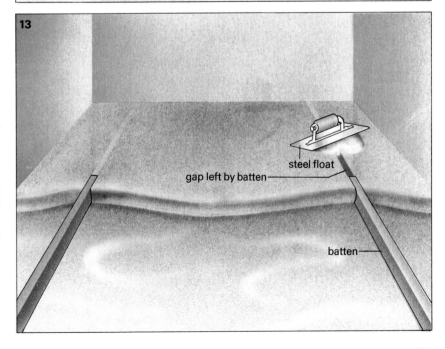

Repairing a fireplace

An open fire provides real comfort in cold weather; if not being used, a screen or large plant placed there can provide an attractive focal point for the room. If your fireplace is showing signs of wear or damage, you can carry out repairs quite easily.

Repairing hearth and surround

Heat and smoke from an open fire can cause tiles in the hearth and surround to crack or the pointing between bricks to deteriorate. If a tile becomes damaged and you manage to find a suitable replacement, remove the old tile by chipping it out with a cold chisel and hammer, starting at the centre and working outwards. Fix the replacement tile with mortar, making sure it lies flush with the existing ones.

Brickwork For repointing, rake out the old mortar to a depth of about 13mm (½in), remove dust and

1a When replacing a brick, insert small pieces of wood at each corner to hold it in position
1b Use a straight-edge to check the brick is in line with the existing bricks
2 Use fireclay cement to repair a cracked fireback
3 To remove a fireback, break it up with a club hammer and bolster chisel

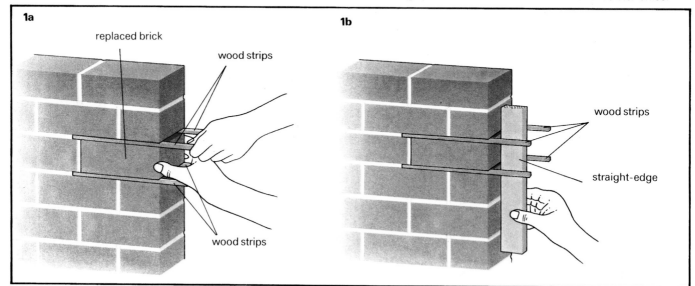

1a

replaced brick

wood strips

wood strips

1b

wood strips

straight-edge

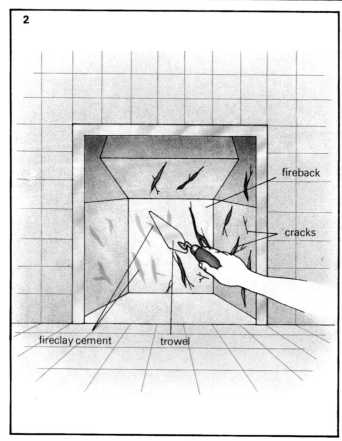

2

fireback

cracks

fireclay cement   trowel

3

bolster chisel

club hammer

debris, brush water over the bricks and fill the joints with a new mortar mix of one part Portland cement, three parts hydrated lime and ten parts silver (heat-resistant) sand; if the fireplace is no longer in use, a mix of one part cement to three parts clean builder's sand is suitable. It is best to repoint the whole fireplace to ensure a uniform effect. To replace a loose brick, use a bolster chisel and club hammer to remove the brick and clean mortar from the cavity and any adjoining bricks. Soak the brick in clean water and apply a layer of mortar (three parts sand to one part cement) to the back and sides. Replace the brick, using small wood strips of equal size top and bottom to hold it in line with the existing bricks. Once the cement has set, remove the strips of wood and repoint.

Repairing fireback

Cracks sometimes develop in firebacks and the chimney structure may eventually be weakened due to the penetration of heat and smoke. Repair work is easy, using fireclay cement (available from builders' merchants). The surround should be cold when the work is done, so don't light a fire for at least 24 hours beforehand. Clean away any soot or dirt from the surface with a stiff brush. Undercut the crack slightly, using a bolster chisel and a club hammer, to ensure the filling is well anchored and rake out any loose material. Soak the cracks thoroughly with water and, before the water dries, trowel in the fireclay cement, making sure the crack is well filled and levelling off as the work proceeds. Allow at least 24 hours before lighting a fire.

Replacement When a fireback is badly cracked or otherwise damaged it must be removed and a replacement unit fitted. Lever out the fireback with a crowbar or use a club hammer and bolster chisel to break it up. Remove the rubble from behind the base section and hack off the cement, on which the base was bedded, to the concrete below.

On many old firebacks, there will be a manufacturer's name or reference code which will help when ordering a new unit. The traditional fireback has a central protruding portion called a 'knee'; on some the knee is too low and causes problems in the final stages of installation when shaping the area which forms the throat to the flue of the chimney. When ordering your new fireback, ask for one which complies with British Standards – this will ensure the unit supplied has a high knee and is made to modern dimensions to suit a modern open fire. The quality of the fireback is another important factor. The old unit may have cracked or suffered general deterioration through age.

Although single-piece firebacks are available, they are best avoided because the fireplace surround must be removed to fit them and they are heavy and awkward to handle. Also, cracking is often caused by heat expanding the lower part of the fireback while the cooler upper part does not expand; in a single-piece unit without space for expansion, cracks will develop. Two-piece units are the most popular, although there are four and six-piece versions. With the two-piece unit, the lower half is free to expand without the rest of the fireback being affected.

Check if there is asbestos rope clipped to the back edges of the fireplace surround. If not, hold two lengths of 13mm (½in) asbestos rope, equal to the height of the lintel above the hearth, against the back edges of the surround and place the lower half of the fireback squarely and centrally in the open-

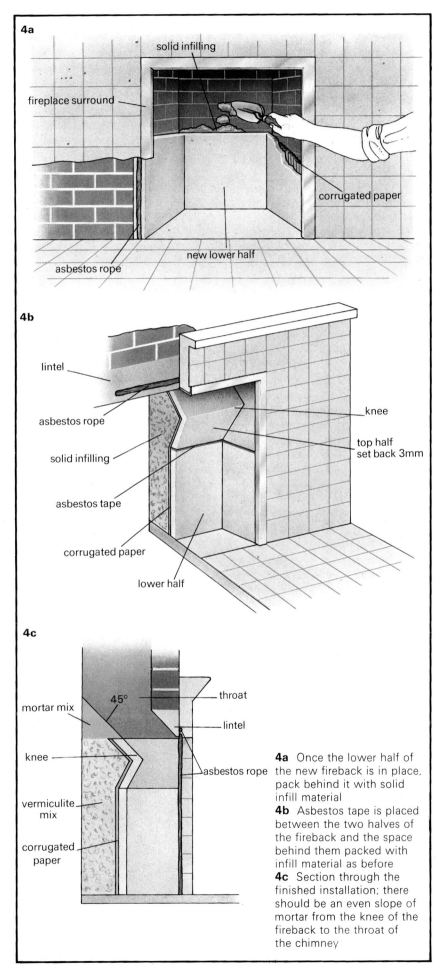

4a Once the lower half of the new fireback is in place, pack behind it with solid infill material

4b Asbestos tape is placed between the two halves of the fireback and the space behind them packed with infill material as before

4c Section through the finished installation; there should be an even slope of mortar from the knee of the fireback to the throat of the chimney

35

ing so the asbestos rope is slightly compressed and held in position. To allow for a small amount of expansion, line the back of the new fireback by pushing corrugated paper or thin strawboard up against it and pack infill material behind it to provide insulation between the fireback and the wall. You will need a solid infilling, not loose rubble; a mix of one part lime, two parts sand and four parts broken brick is suitable. (Don't use cement in the mix since it would be too strong for this function.) Alternatively use a mix of six parts vemiculite and one part lime, mixed to a paste with water; this has better insulating qualities and is especially useful against an outside wall, through which you could otherwise lose an excessive amount of heat.

Place a length of flat asbestos tape along the top edge of the lower half of the fireback. Unlike fire cement, which is sometimes used to make the joint between the top and bottom pieces of the fireback, asbestos tape will not fall out and it allows for the expansion difference between the two halves. Hold the asbestos rope in place against the back of the fireplace surround, check there is a third length across the top of the fire opening between the lintel and the back of the fireplace and place the top half of the fireback flush on the lower portion or set it back by 3mm (⅛in) to avoid its lower edge being burned. On no account should it protrude forwards. Fill in behind the top half with the same mix as before, smoothing the filling level with the top. Fill the space all round the top of the fireback within the chimney with a mortar mix of four parts sharp sand to one part cement (using broken brick as a filler if the space is large) to give an even slope of at least 45 degrees from the knee to the throat – you should end up with a smooth line running from the knee to the back of the flue. You can leave the asbestos rope exposed or hide it by applying a very thin layer of fire cement to smooth out the surface.

Lining the fireplace opening
At a time when electricity supplies can be cut off with little advance warning, it is useful to keep those old fireplaces in good repair for use in an emergency. However, if you decide to abandon coal fires, there is an alternative to briking it up.

If your fireplace is disused, instead of filling it in with bricks or a panel you can turn it into an attractive alcove by providing a panelled lining. For this, tongued and grooved panels, veneer plywood, melamine faced boards or plasterboard are suitable materials.

To prevent dust and soot falling into the alcove, you should block off the chimney. Since this cuts off ventilation to the chimney, knock out a brick in the fireplace above the lintel, replace it with an airbrick and screw on a fixed ventilation grille. Use plugs and screws to fix 50 × 25mm (2 × 1in) battens to the sides and back of the fireplace opening so the bottom edges of the battens are flush with the bottom of the fireplace lintel, and screw a piece of resin-bonded plywood to the battens to seal off the chimney. Install a framework of 50 × 25mm (2 × 1in) battens (using plugs and screws) in the fireplace opening and fix decorative panels to the framework with impact adhesive.

Warning Don't attempt to leave out the timber framework and glue the panels directly to the bricks, since the sooty surface of the bricks prevents secure fixing and the panelling in the recess will not stay in place.

Basic items
bolster and cold chisels, club hammer
mortar mix, wood strips (for replacing brick)
stiff brush, crowbar, fireclay cement (for repairing cracked fireback)
asbestos rope, corrugated paper or thin strawboard, infill material, asbestos tape, mortar mix (for replacing fireback)
airbrick, 50 × 25mm (2 × 1in) battens, plugs and screws, resin-bonded plywood, decorative panels, impact adhesive (for lining opening)

equipment

5a When lining a disused fireplace with decorative panels, first block off the chimney by fixing resin-bonded plywood to a timber batten framework
5b Screw a batten framework to the walls of the fireplace opening and fix the decorative panels to this with impact adhesive; remember to install an airbrick above the lintel to provide ventilation to the chimney. If you don't, damp may set in and spoil wall decorations

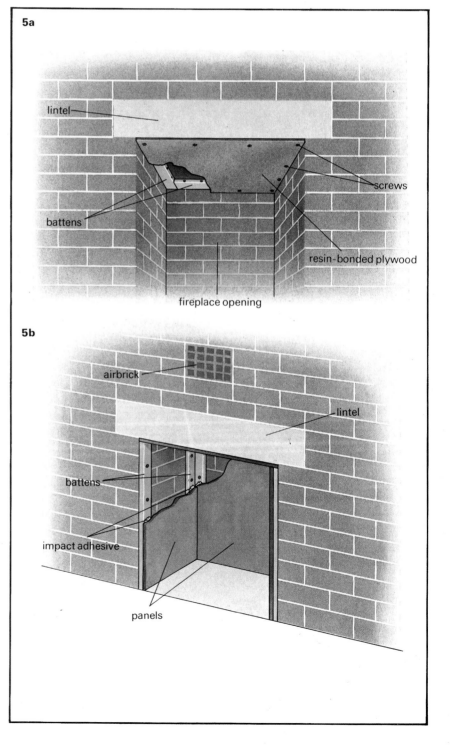

5a

lintel

screws

battens

resin-bonded plywood

fireplace opening

5b

airbrick

lintel

battens

impact adhesive

panels

Boxing in pipes

Plumbing means pipes, which can be unsightly if left exposed. Boxing them in will tidy up the look of the home.

Whichever method you choose to conceal pipes, the first task is to strip the wall around the pipes so a supporting frame can be securely fixed. Make sure the pipes are in good condition and that the joints are well made. Check compression joints for tightness and, if there is any corrosion, remake the joints. Before boxing in make sure the pipes are fixed securely to the wall with pipe clips. Where pipes come through the floor from a room below, seal the gap between the pipes and the floor with a shaped piece of 12 or 18mm ($\frac{1}{2}$ or $\frac{3}{4}$in) chipboard to reduce the risk of fire spreading. Pipes on an outside wall should be insulated with a glass fibre blanket or with shaped foam secured with tape.

Making the box
Using plugs and screws fix 25×19mm ($1 \times \frac{3}{4}$in) timber battens vertically to the wall on each side of the pipes; check with a plumb line to ensure accurate positioning. Where the pipes are on an open wall, glue and screw or pin 12mm ($\frac{1}{2}$in) thick plywood or chipboard to the sides of the battens (the width of the timber side pieces depends on the depth required for the box). Where the pipes are in a corner you will need only one side piece and, if the pipes protrude less than 50mm (2in) from the wall, you may not need side pieces at all. In this case use 25mm (1in) battens, wide enough to clear the pipes, as side pieces.
Front panel Cover the pipes with 3 or 5mm ($\frac{1}{8}$ or $\frac{3}{16}$in) hardboard or plywood; if you want a more solid panel, use 12mm ($\frac{1}{2}$in) chipboard. Don't glue the front panels in place because you must have access to the pipes in case of leaks. Fix hardboard or plywood with panel or hardboard pins and

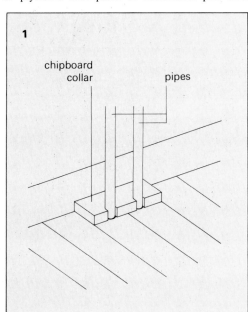

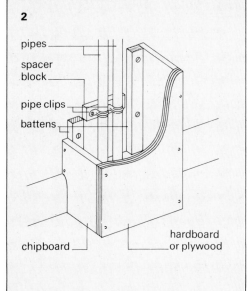

Above You can conceal awkward fittings such as this by building an L-shaped frame; simply follow the principles for boxing in straight runs of pipe
1 If pipes come through the floor from the room below, fit a piece of chipboard round them to seal the gap in the floorboards
2 Boxing in pipes on an open wall: shape the sides of the box so they fit neatly over the skirting

secure chipboard with countersunk screws. You will achieve a better finish if you cut your front panel slightly oversize and trim it back with a plane once it is fixed in position.

Use a cellulose filler to fill any cracks and countersunk screw heads, except where these provide access. Give the box a coat of primer before decorating as required. When decorating, make sure you do not cover the join or your decorations will be spoiled when you need to remove the box.

Stopcocks and draincocks Where there are stopcocks or draincocks in the pipe runs you must cut holes in the front panel to allow the handles to protrude, unless you fit access covers in the boxes. Alternatively construct a box which can be easily removed. Make up a hardboard box of the required size, using 25mm (1in) square battens at the front corners to give it form. On the inside face of the front panel glue 19mm ($\frac{3}{4}$in) wide battens at approximately 1m (or 3ft) intervals and secure them with panel pins hammered through from the outside. Screw Terry clips of the required size,

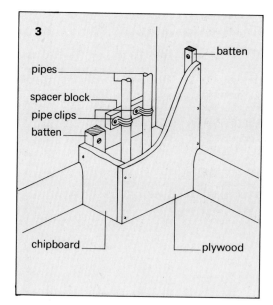

3

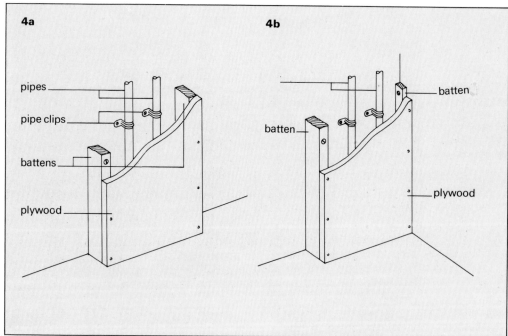

4a

4b

3 Where the pipes are in a corner, you will need only one side piece
4a With small diameter pipes you may be able to use timber battens as side pieces
4b If the pipes are against a corner, you can use a thinner batten on the side wall
5 If you need to gain access to the pipes, make a box which can be easily removed: screw battens to the inside face of the front panel and fix Terry clips to the battens; the clips fit over the pipes and hold the panel in place (**inset**)

according to the pipe dimensions, to the battens; these will snap over the pipes and secure the panel.

Disappearing pipes
Where pipes disappear into a wall, the bottom or top (as applicable) of the box can be finished at an angle. Cut the side pieces and/or battens at 45 degrees, pin a small piece of hardboard or plywood to the sloping part and plane across the front panel until it forms a neat joint.

Alcove pipes
When you wish to conceal pipes in an alcove it is often best to cover the entire wall area with a full width panel; this robs you of little space and does not affect the look of the wall line. Fix timber battens on each side of the pipes, as previously explained. Plug and screw a piece of batten on each side of the alcove level with the front of the battens on each side of the pipes. Use 9mm ($\frac{3}{8}$in) chipboard, fixed with countersunk screws, to conceal the pipes and to provide easy access and nail 9.5mm ($\frac{3}{8}$in) plasterboard either side of the chipboard.

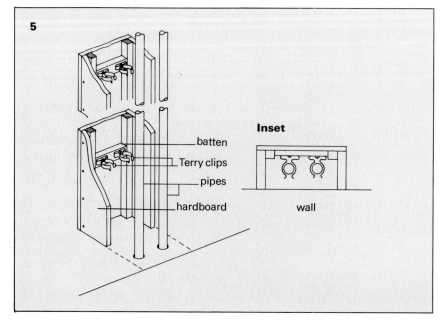

5

You can use the same method, but with a stronger framework, to conceal cisterns and soil and water pipes.

Skirting board pipes

Nail a 25 × 19mm (1 × ¾in) batten to the floor with its face just in front of the maximum projection of the pipes. Glue and nail a 12mm (½in) facing board to the batten, then glue and nail scotia moulding to the top of the facing board. Finally glue and pin a strip of hardboard or plywood between the moulding and the top of the skirting.

If you want a round edge finish, use a facing board of the same height as the skirting; glue and pin a length of 12mm (½in) board to the top of the facing board and skirting and round the front edge with a plane.

Although a certain amount of time, effort and money is involved, you will be surprised how much neater rooms will look when the pipes have been boxed in. You can paint or wallpaper the covering.

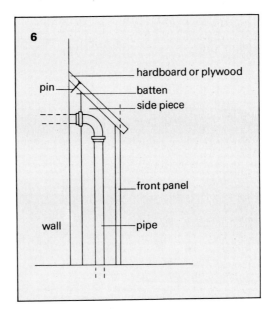

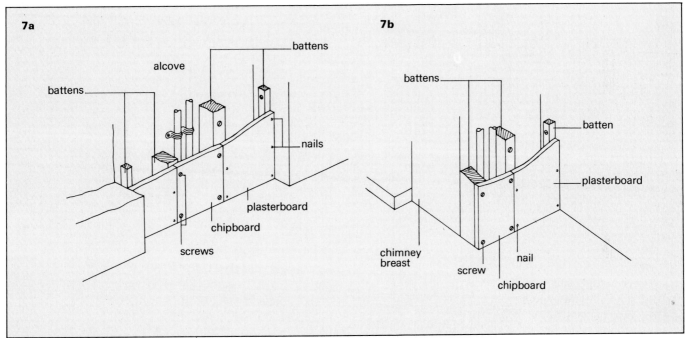

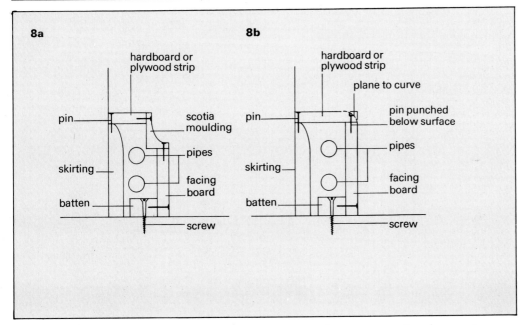

6 Making an angled box to conceal pipes which disappear into a wall: plane the top flush with the front panel for a smooth finish
7a Where the pipes are in an alcove, fit panels across the whole width of the recess to make it look neater
7b If the pipes are beside the chimney-breast, make the box the full depth of the projecting wall and flush with the front edge to avoid awkward corners
8a When concealing pipes running along the skirting, you can give shape to the box by using scotia moulding
8b Alternatively use facing board the same height as the skirting and round off the front edge with a plane

Rehanging internal doors

The way a door opens can play an important part in a successful room layout and often builders fail to pay enough attention to this fact when the doors are originally positioned. You may, for example, decide you want a door to open out of a room rather than into it – or that it is more convenient to have the door opening from left to right and not the other way round. There are also occasions when you may have to adjust the position of the door frame, particularly if you are insulating the walls of a room with boards or panels fixed to battens. Rehanging a door or repositioning it is not a difficult job – and one you can do yourself.

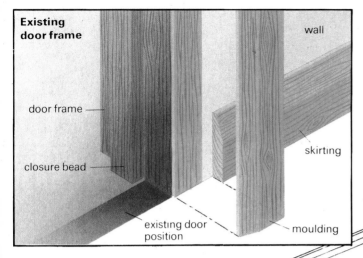

Existing door frame

- door frame
- closure bead
- existing door position
- wall
- skirting
- moulding

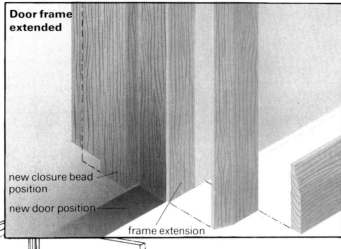

Door frame extended

- new closure bead position
- new door position
- frame extension

Repositioning doors

If you wish to reposition a door when you are lining your walls with board, the door must be removed and the frame extended into the room before you start lining the walls around the door. But measure carefully the total thickness of the lining so you know how far to extend the frame and where to reposition the door.

Removing the door Open the door to its full extent and support it by pushing wedges underneath. Release it from the frame by removing the screws in the door frame hinges. These screws may be difficult to loosen if they have been in place for some time, particularly if there is a build-up of old paint over the screw heads. Clean the paint from the slots with a sharp, pointed instrument or an old, small square-ended screwdriver. Use the correct size screwdriver to get the maximum grip on the screw – or use an impact screwdriver. To release a stubborn screw, it often helps to tighten the screw slightly before trying to unscrew it. If this fails to move the screw, as a last resort put the edge of the screwdriver blade against the lower half of the slot head and tap it gently in an anti-clockwise direction. This will not do either the screw or the screwdriver any good, but it should bring results.

Having taken out the screws and removed the hinges from the frame, unscrew the striking plate. Cut pieces of softwood or hardboard to fit exactly into the recesses in the frame and glue and pin them into position.

Next lift away the frame moulding with a broad chisel and mallet. If you do this carefully, the small nails which hold the moulding in place will stay in position and you will be able to use them again when you come to fix the moulding back in position. Try not to damage the moulding or it will have to be replaced.

Extending the frame

The door frame can be extended to the required distance by nailing or screwing the same thickness timber to the sides and top of the existing door frame. Measure and cut these new pieces carefully so the extended frame will be flush with the new wall surface. Always extend the frame before relining the wall or you could damage the frame moulding when trying to remove it. Having extended your door frame, fix the wall lining before continuing work on the door, checking again that the new wall and frame surfaces are flush. You can now nail back the moulding on the frame.

door

wedges

The door will have to be brought forward to line up with the frame, which means cutting new recesses for the hinges and striking plate, depending on how you want the door to hang. When you have decided on the new position for the door, mark it on the frame. Remove the door closure bead with a broad chisel and mallet, starting at the bottom of one of the side pieces. Remember to lift it away carefully to avoid damage to the bead and so you can use the existing nails again, then refix it against the new position of the external face of the door.

Rehanging a door

If you want to change the way the door opens into the room, first label the two faces of the

Changing hinge recess

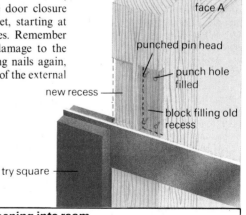

- face B
- face A
- punched pin head
- punch hole filled
- new recess
- block filling old recess
- try square

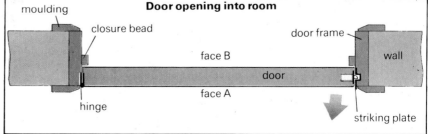

Door opening into room

- moulding
- closure bead
- face B
- hinge
- face A
- door
- door frame
- wall
- striking plate

41

door A and B. A will be the face of the existing door on the room side and B the external face.

Changing sides If you are moving the hinges so the door still opens into the room but from the opposite side of the frame, you must patch the old hinge recesses on the door. If your door has a natural finish which you want to keep, you will have to match up the wood carefully. If you are going to paint over the door, any softwood will do.

Cut the filling pieces slightly larger than the recesses and glue and pin them firmly into place, driving the pin heads below the surface with a nail punch. Fill the punch holes with cellulose filler or matching plastic wood, depending on whether you are painting the door or leaving a natural finish. For a really flush surface, plane down the filled edge and face A of the door and rub smooth with medium glasspaper.

With a try square and pencil continue the top and bottom lines of the old hinge positions across the edge of the door and mark out the new hinge positions from the B side of the door, then cut out the recesses with a sharp chisel and mallet. Unscrew the striking plate from the door frame; this must be placed on the opposite side later.

Fill the plate recess in the frame with softwood or hardboard in the same way as before if the frame is to be painted; match the wood carefully if you want to keep a natural finish. Complete the patching up by filling the hinge recesses on the other side of the frame. Then screw the hinges into the new recesses in the edge of the door.

Turn the door round so the side B faces into the room. Push it tightly into the frame, using the wedges to raise the door to its original clearance height above the ground. Mark the top and bottom positions of the new hinges onto the door frame and then take away the door from the frame. Cut out these recesses and screw in the unattached leaves.

You will now have to reverse the spring-loaded door catch, since this will be facing the wrong way to engage the striking plate. (If the door has a ball catch, there is no need to transpose its position.) Remove the door handles and cover plates from either side, pull out the connecting rod and remove the catch assembly fixing screws. Using a screwdriver ease out the catch assembly housing, replace it upside down and screw back all the fittings.

To find the correct position for the striking plate, dab paint on the catch and push the door closed. The paint mark left on the door frame will indicate the area for the striking plate. Position the plate to fit correctly over this mark and trace the outline of the plate on the frame. Chisel out the recess to the required depth and screw the striking plate into position.

Changing direction After removing the door, lift the closure bead away from the frame and patch the existing hinge recesses, cutting new ones on the same edge of the door but flush to the B face, as described before. Patch up the hinge and striking plate recesses on the frame in the same way. Reverse the catch assembly housing as before, cut out new recesses for the hinges on the outer side of the frame and also a new striking plate cavity. Tack back the door closure bead close to the A face of the door on the room side. If the door closure bead is formed as a solid recess, as it is in some older properties, you will have to cut about 13mm ($\frac{1}{2}$in) from each side of the door with

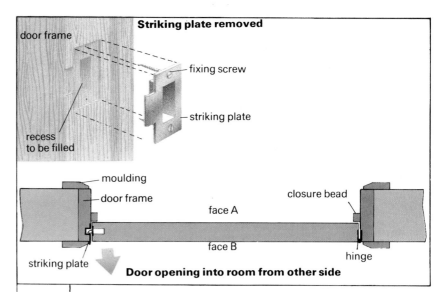

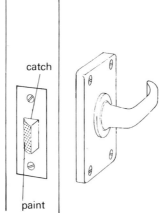

Finding striking plate position

a panel saw and tack on a new closure bead.

Changing sides and direction Remove the door closure bead, door and striking plate, leaving the hinges on the door and patch up the recesses on the frame. Reverse the door so face A is on the outside, mark and cut out new hinge and striking plate recesses on the door frame and screw the striking plate into its new position. Fix the door in place and tack the closure bead down close to face B of the door, now on the room side.

Warning Whenever you reposition and hang a door, to fix the hinges always insert the centre screw only into each hinge and check the door opens and closes properly before inserting the remaining screws. This saves a lot of time and trouble drilling unnecessary holes in the door frame. If the screws do not tighten, plug the holes and insert the screws again.

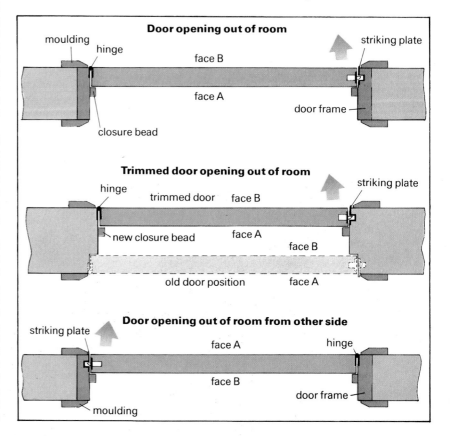

Internal window sills

Internal window sills were traditionally made of timber, although many modern houses now have quarry tiled sills. Their obvious advantage is that they will stand up to far greater wear and tear and do not suffer from the same deterioration as their timber counterparts. However most of the problems surrounding timber sills stem from the fact that they are now made from inferior quality timber.

Timber sills

The depth of the average window sill recess is 150–225mm (6–9in) and a length of 25mm (1in) thick timber is commonly used. In houses built before 1939 the material was of a high standard and has mainly stood the test of time. Properly maintained, these sills will remain sound for many more years.

The growing trend for central heating has, however, highlighted the problems of timber sills, especially those in newer houses where inferior quality material has been fitted. The sills dry rapidly, causing splits and warping along the timber, faults often accelerated by priming and painting on the top, visible surface only. These cracks and splits are then vulnerable to moisture resulting from excessive condensation from the windows.

Any attempts to repair a sill in this condition and keep it in a reasonable state of decoration are eventually doomed to fail and the only certain remedy is to remove the offending timber and replace it with good quality material.

Removing old sill

Timber sills are often nailed into timber blocks in the masonry below them and into the base of the

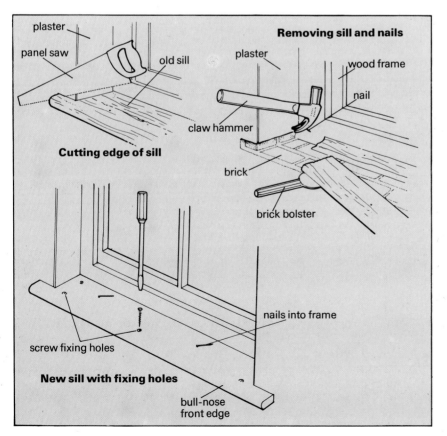

Cutting edge of sill

plaster
panel saw
old sill

Removing sill and nails

plaster
wood frame
nail
claw hammer
brick
brick bolster

New sill with fixing holes

screw fixing holes
nails into frame
bull-nose front edge

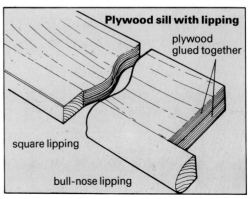

Plywood sill with lipping

plywood glued together
square lipping
bull-nose lipping

window frame. The ends of the sill are also secured – by the plaster which is laid tight to the sill when it is in position.

It is quite a simple operation to remove the sill. With a sharp chisel and hammer chop through the ends and then drive a brick bolster under the front edge to lever the sill up. You may find it easier to lever the overlap onto the wall surface at either end of the sill using a chisel; alternatively you can free the timber from the plaster with a small saw. Make sure you remove any nails that are left, levering them up with a claw hammer, and clean out any ragged corners with the chisel so the new piece of timber will sit flush in position.

Making new sill
When you fit a new piece of timber, make sure it is well seasoned and of good quality. Measure carefully the area left by the old sill – depth, thickness and length; it is safest to buy the timber slightly over-sized and trim for an exact fit, in case you make a mistake and otherwise find your new sill is too small. Mark up the new timber carefully with a pencil and straight-edge and cut just to the waste side of these lines with a tenon saw. Smooth down the cut edges with medium, then fine, glasspaper until the timber fits exactly. If you want a half-rounded bull-nose finish on the front edge, plane the area carefully with a small block plane and rub smooth with medium, then fine, glasspaper. Alternatively you can buy bull-nose lipping which should be glued and pinned into position on the front edge.

If there are already fixing points in the masonry, mark accurately corresponding positions on the new sill and drill clearance holes ready for fixing later. Alternatively drill a set of clearance holes in the new sill at about 400mm (or 15in) intervals along the front and back edges of the sill and, laying the sill in position, mark through these holes where to drill into the masonry to take plugs and countersunk screws. Remove the sill and complete these fitting points in the masonry. Before fitting the new sill make sure all faces and edges are well-primed. Apply two coats of proprietary wood primer to the back edge where it meets the window frame, since this is one area particularly prone to attack from moisture.

Fitting new sill
To secure the new piece of timber, countersink the clearance holes and screw through these into the masonry fixing points. For extra strength hammer in two or three nails at an oblique angle into the window frame. All nail and screw heads must be primed with a rust-resistant primer before they are filled in with cellulose filler, or matching plastic wood if you want a natural finish. When fitted, the sill can be decorated as you want in the usual way, either painted or given a natural finish.

Using plywood
The best alternative to natural timber is a good quality plywood. To get the required thickness for the sill you may find it easier to glue together two 9 or 12mm ($\frac{3}{8}$ or $\frac{1}{2}$in) thicknesses. For added protection it is worth sticking a timber lipping to the outer edge of the plywood – and if you want the edge shaped you can pin and glue on bull-nose lipping. Prime all the edges carefully and fix using the same method as for timber. Then complete the decoration. A good resin-bonded plywood will give

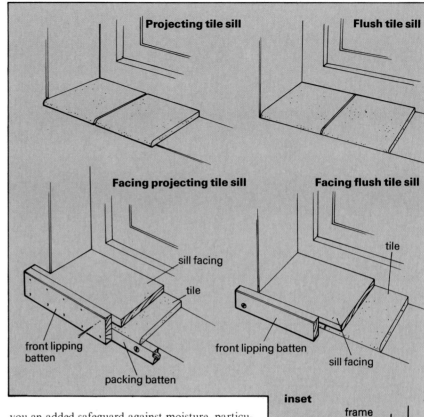

you an added safeguard against moisture, particularly along the back edge.

Extending sill
If you are lining the walls around a window for insulation, you will probably have to extend the existing sill (or make the new one) to sit flush with or, if you prefer, overhang the new wall surface. If cutting out a new sill, allow for the extra when measuring the new piece of timber. If your old sill is in good condition you can simply fix on a new piece of lipping of the correct thickness and length as the original timber and of the width required. All you have to do is glue and pin the lipping into position, but make sure the edge of the old sill is trimmed square for a flush fitting and that all paint or other covering is cleaned off to ensure a firm bond.

Tiled sills
Because of the problems already described with timber sills, many builders have tended to favour quarry tiles on sills in new houses. Although hard-wearing and needing little maintenance, they can be chipped or work loose, in which case you will have to refix them with a tile adhesive, if necessary clearing away the surface below to ensure a flush finish – or replace them with new tiles. If you think quarry tiles do not suit the room decoration, you can face over the tiles and have a painted or laminate finish.

Facing tiles
If you want a painted finish, the best facing to use over tiles is either plywood or blockboard.
For painted finish The plywood or blockboard facing should be approximately 13mm ($\frac{1}{2}$in) thick and taken to the front edge of the tiles. If the tiles are flush to the wall, a lipping batten should be fixed to the front edge of the new facing so a strong fixing can be made into the wall below the tile line.

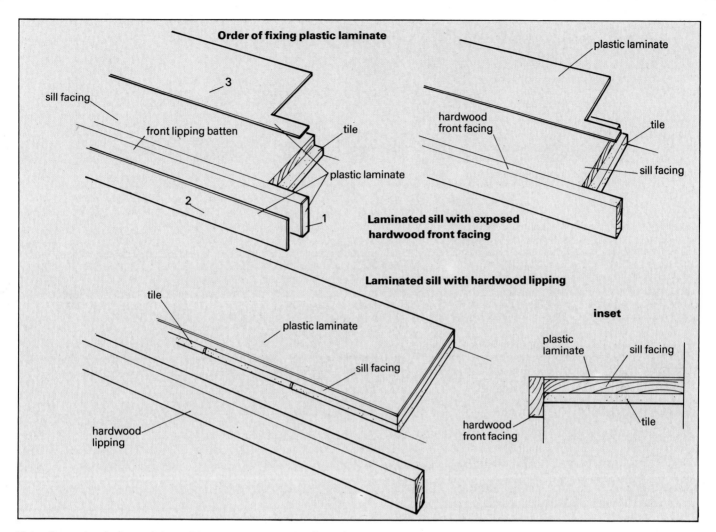

Order of fixing plastic laminate

sill facing

front lipping batten

3

2

1

tile

plastic laminate

Laminated sill with exposed hardwood front facing

plastic laminate

hardwood front facing

tile

sill facing

Laminated sill with hardwood lipping

tile

plastic laminate

sill facing

hardwood lipping

inset

plastic laminate

sill facing

hardwood front facing

tile

If the tiles project in front of the wall line, you will have to fix a packing batten below them to make up the level. This batten must be screwed into the wall with countersunk screws at 400mm (or 15in) intervals; the facing batten can then be glued and pinned to the packing batten and the edge of the sill facing board above. The packing batten is not needed if the tiles are flush to the wall line, since the facing batten can be fixed (in the same way) to the wall below the tiles and glued and pinned to the edge of the facing board as before.

For laminate finish Chipboard can be used here as the facing board, one advantage being that it is cheaper than plywood or blockboard. It is, however, extremely vulnerable; if you do use it, make sure all edges and faces not being covered with laminate are thoroughly sealed with two or three coats of a proprietary wood primer. If you do use laminate on all the surfaces, it has the advantage of concealing the fixings.

Having assembled the facing boards, cut out strips of laminate to cover the areas you want. If covering the whole facing, first stick the laminate with an impact adhesive onto the underside and ends of the front lipping batten, then the face of this batten and finally the top of the sill facing board, including the top edge of the lipping batten. If using hardwood on the front facing and leaving it exposed, fix it with the same adhesive, which will save you having to plug it to the board facing.

When lipping with hardwood, fix the top edge as flush as possible to the laminate surface on the sill to cut down the need for trimming afterwards; a

really flush finish can be achieved by carefully planing the top edge. To protect the hardwood, treat it with teak oil or apply a thin coat of clear polyurethane with a lint-free rag. One advantage of hardwood as lipping is that if the edge of the sill is damaged, you can plane the hardwood smooth again. The only way to repair laminate-covered lipping is to strip away the damaged material and reface with a new piece.

Extending sill

It is a very difficult job to extend a quarry-tiled sill, since the tiles are difficult to lift and you will have great trouble trying to make rows of even-shaped tiles. The best way is to face the tiles, as described above, making sure the new facing extends far enough out to sit flush or overlap the new wall surface if you are lining your walls for insulation. Fit the facing as before.

Fixing faulty windows

Windows may crack or stick, the frames warp or let in water and sash cords break. These common faults in windows are relatively easy to correct and it is worth doing so at the earliest possible stage to avoid prolonged inconvenience or further damage. But make sure any repairs are done thoroughly or the problem is likely to reoccur.

Broken sash cords

Sash windows are commonly found in older houses and the sash cords on which the windows hang are likely to wear and break with age. When replacing sash cords there are several points which you should bear in mind. You will have to lever out the beads on either side of the window inside the room and it is important to keep the wood intact; start at the centre point of each bead to avoid damaging the mitre joints at the top and bottom.

You should replace all cords even if only one is broken. For replacement use terylene cord since this is much more durable than the old-fashioned wax type. You can prevent the cord fraying by heating the end with a lighted match to melt the fibres into a solid lump.

Sticking windows

There are various reasons why sliding sashes and hinged casement windows in both timber and metal start to stick. In some cases new paint may have gummed up the window. Cutting round the opening faces with a sharp trimming knife will usually alleviate the problem, but sometimes you may have to force the faces apart by inserting the blade of a broad filling knife between them. If the trouble is caused by a gradual build-up of paint over the years, use paint stripper to get back to the bare wood or metal; alternatively use a blowtorch to remove the paint from the wood. Make sure there is adequate clearance between the fixed and moving parts of the frame – in most cases 1.5mm ($\frac{1}{16}$in) clearance is sufficient – and repaint.

Poor paintwork and cracked glass can allow damp to get at the frame causing wood to swell and metal frames to rust. Use a wire brush to get rid of rust, treat the frame with rust killer and apply metal primer, undercoat and gloss paint. With a swollen timber frame it is best to strip off the paint with a blowtorch, taking care not to damage the glass, and gently play the blowtorch flame over the

1a When replacing sash cords use a chisel to remove the staff beads. Start at the centre of each bead to avoid damaging the mitre joints at top and bottom

1b With the bottom sash closed, cut any sound cord close to the top of the sash, after tying a length of string to the cord above where it is to be cut. (For a broken cord, tie string to the upper end of the cord.) Holding onto the strings, slowly lower the balance weights until they are at the bottom of the pockets and then remove the bottom sash. Leave the strings in position to pull the new cords through. Remove the parting beads in the same way as for the staff beads and the top sash in the same way as for removing the bottom sash. Use pincers to pull out the nails which attach the ends of the cords to the sashes

1c Remove the pockets and then the balance weights with the old cords attached. Mark which weights are for which sash – upper sash ones are heavier – and measure the old cord to get the new cord length

1d Where a cord is broken, rethread it using a small nail, or mouse, tied to a length of string. Feed the mouse over the pulley and retrieve it through the pocket. Replace the top sash first

1e Tie string to the new cord and draw it up over the pulley

1f Pull the cord through the pocket and attach the balance weight with a double knot. Heat the cut end with a match to melt the fibres into a lump to prevent fraying. Repeat for all the cords and replace the weights in the pockets

1g Measure the distance from the top of the sash to the bottom of the groove and mark on the frame this distance down from the top. Pull the cord so the weight is about 50mm from the bottom of the box and cut the free end level with the mark

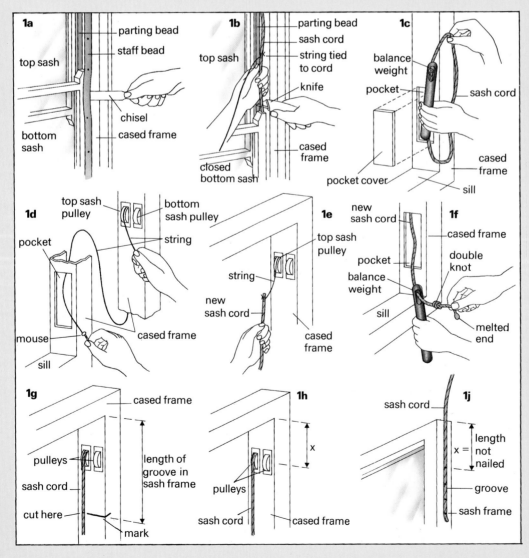

46

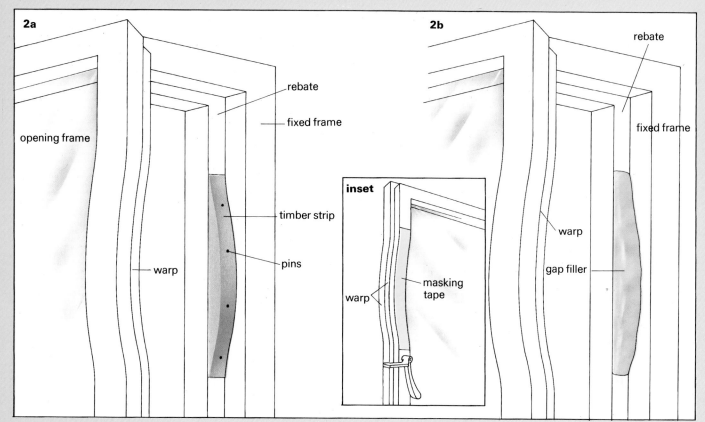

2a

opening frame

warp

rebate

fixed frame

timber strip

pins

inset

warp

masking tape

2b

rebate

fixed frame

warp

gap filler

1h To decide the nailing position, measure the distance X from the mid-point of the pulley to the inside of the top of the frame
1j Pull the cord so the weight is at the top of the pulley, wedge a piece of wood between the frame and the pulley to prevent slipping and secure the new cord with galvanized 25mm broad head nails the distance X down from the top of the groove. Do not nail above this point or the window will not close. Replace the parting beads, fit the bottom sash in the same way and replace the staff beads
2a To seal the gap in a warped window, tack a shaped timber strip into the rebate of the fixed frame
2b Alternatively apply silicone rubber gap filler to the fixed frame. Fix masking tape on the inside face of the opening frame (**inset**) to protect this frame from the filler. Leave the filler to set with the window closed
3a Overhanging lips and drip grooves prevent rainwater ingress in a casement window
3b Where there is no overhanging lip, screw hardwood weatherstrips along the bottom of the opening casements or top vents

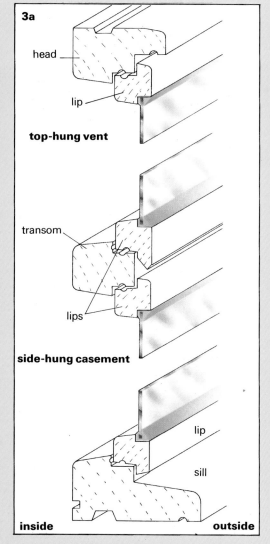

3a

head

lip

top-hung vent

transom

lips

side-hung casement

lip

sill

inside

outside

timber to dry it out. In hot weather you can leave the frame unpainted for a few days; this will help to get rid of damp. When the wood is dry, rub it down with glasspaper or use a plane to give a 1.5mm ($\frac{1}{16}$in) clearance round the frame. Make sure the putty is sound and, after priming any areas of bare wood, cover the frame with at least three coats of paint to ensure the timber is sealed against damp. Remember to take about 3mm ($\frac{1}{8}$in) of paint onto the glass to form a seal between the glass and the putty and prevent water seeping down into the frame.

Sash windows which stick may often be freed by opening the sash to its fullest extent and sanding the channel with coarse glasspaper wrapped round a block of wood. Where the trouble has been brought about by paint building up in the channel, you may find it necessary to strip the surface back to bare wood and repaint. If the wood has swollen, you should take the sash out of its channel and plane it on each side where the sash cord is fixed.

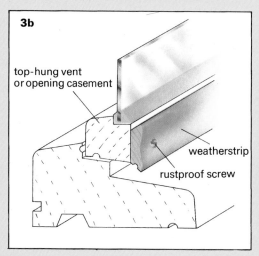

3b

top-hung vent or opening casement

weatherstrip

rustproof screw

With hinged timber windows, sticking may be caused by incorrectly fitted hinges. If the window is binding hard up against the side where the catch is fitted and there is a gap on the hinge side, the hinge flaps should be sunk deeper into the wood. On the other hand, if the window is binding hard up to the frame on the hinge side while there is a gap on the catch side, pack thin pieces of card under the hinge flaps to prevent the window sticking.

Warped windows

The opening frames of casement and vent windows often become warped and ill-fitting. It is usually possible to compensate for the warp and eliminate or minimize the gap by adjusting the position of the hinges. If the gap is not completely closed, you can seal a timber window with a suitably shaped timber strip; fix it with panel pins, at about 50mm (2in) intervals, into the rebate of the fixed frame. Alternatively, for both timber and metal windows use a flexible silicone rubber gap filler. Make sure the gap is thoroughly clean and dry; then apply self-adhesive masking tape to the inside face of the opening frame to prevent the filler adhering in this area. Squeeze the filler out of its tube into the gap and leave it to set overnight; the window can then be opened and the tape removed.

Warning Never try to force an ill-fitting frame back into the right position since the glass is likely to break under the strain.

Dampness around windows

Damp patches on a wall around a window may indicate an external gap between the brickwork and the frame. To seal the gap, use a bead of non-hardening flexible mastic, applying it with an applicator which injects the mastic through a plastic nozzle.

Check the frame has drip grooves incorporated to prevent rainwater being drawn between the opening and fixed parts of the frame and make sure the grooves have not been filled with layers of paint. If necessary, scrape them out and repaint. Modern casement windows are designed with overhanging lips as well as drip grooves to prevent water ingress. Old casements may not have this lip; if they are letting in water, it is a good idea to screw hardwood weatherstrips along the bottom of the opening casements and top vents. If French doors are letting in water, screw weatherboards to the bottom of the doors to throw water clear of the sill. In both cases use rustproof screws at approximately 100mm (4in) intervals.

Leaded lights

Leaded light windows are found in an ever-decreasing number of properties. They are only rarely used in new housing schemes, and over recent years large numbers of leaded lights have been replaced by modern picture windows. However, many people still find a period appeal in leaded windows, particularly when employed to create a design with panes of different colours, for example in the front door. Repairs will occasionally be necessary. Replacing glass pane in a leaded light window requires a technique rather different from that already described for standard windows. In leaded lights, the panes are secured in H-section strips of lead, called cames. To release a broken pane, cut the cames at each corner with a sharp knife and lever up the lead flanges at the sides and bottom with a wide chisel.

Either use the old pane as a template to cut a new pane or make a card template to fit in the cames and cut a new piece of glass about 1mm (or $\frac{1}{32}$ in) smaller than the template.

Traditionally gold size putty, obtainable from builders' merchants, is used to bed the glass in the cames; but you can bed the glass on a thin strip of grey mastic. Insert the new glass under the top flange and then carefully fit it at the sides and bottom; use a wood stick to press down the edges of the cames. Clean lead with medium glasspaper; resolder each corner with soft, resin-cored solder applied with a hot soldering iron.

Leaks If a leaded light leaks, scrape dirt away from the flanges of the cames and brush under the edges with clear polyurethane varnish. Make sure the flanges are well pressed down and use a razor blade to clear away varnish from the glass after it has set. If this does not stop the leaks, you should cut the came corners and use a chisel to fold back the lead in the affected areas so you can fit a thin strip of mastic or gold size putty under the flange.

4a The pane of a leaded light is held in H-section strips of lead, or cames
4b To remove a broken pane, use a sharp knife to cut the corners of the cames
4c Using a wide chisel, lever up the lead flanges at the sides and bottom to release the pane
4d Bed the new pane in gold size putty, fitting it at the top first and then the sides and bottom

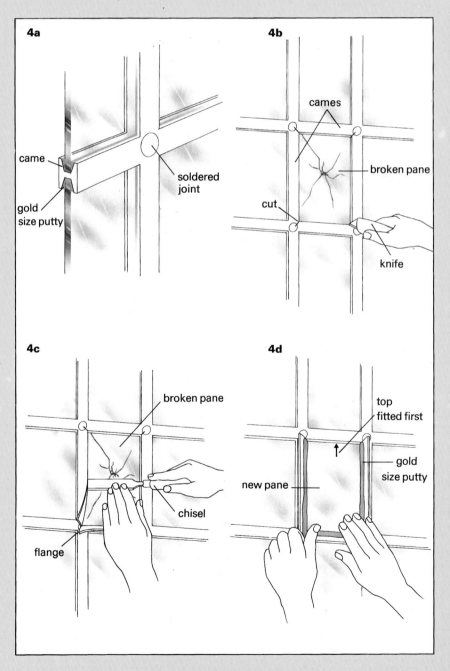

Replacing broken glass

Emergency repair

If you break a window and cannot get replacement glass immediately, as a temporary measure fix a sheet of polythene to the inside of the window.

With a wood frame either fix the polythene with adhesive tape or, for a stronger fixing, secure the top of the polythene to the window with drawing pins, nail a batten along the top and then secure each side and bottom edge with battens (**see 1**). Stretch the polythene to smooth out wrinkles as you work. You will not be able to nail through a metal frame, however, so use heavy duty polythene secured with strong adhesive tape.

Wood frames

Clear up the glass left on the ground and remove the fragments in the frame. These should pull away easily, but if the putty or wood beading keeping the glass in place is firmly fixed you may have to remove the holding material first.

Take out the glass from the top of the frame, then work down the sides and along the bottom edge. To remove stubborn pieces run a glass-cutter round the perimeter of the glass and close to the rebates (**see 2**). Tap out the pieces with the handle of a light hammer, holding each piece until it is free.

If the holding material is putty chop away with a hacking knife or old chisel (**see 3**). This will reveal a series of small headless nails (sprigs) which do the real job of holding the glass. Carefully remove the sprigs with pincers (**see 4**). If they are still straight, you can re-use them; if not, buy new ones 16mm ($\frac{5}{8}$in) long.

Sometimes the glass will have been secured by wood beading fixed with panel pins. Prise away the beading and remove the pins (**see 5**). Take care when removing since the beading will have mitred

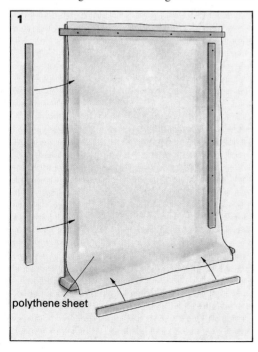
polythene sheet

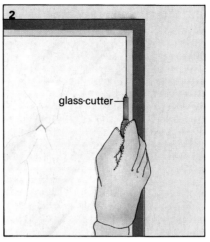
glass-cutter

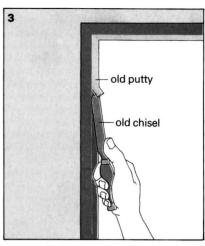
old putty
old chisel

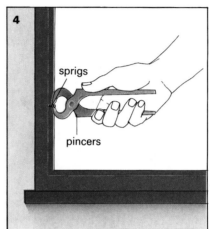
sprigs
pincers

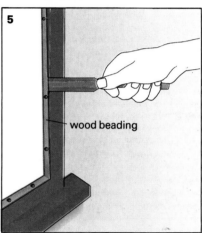
wood beading

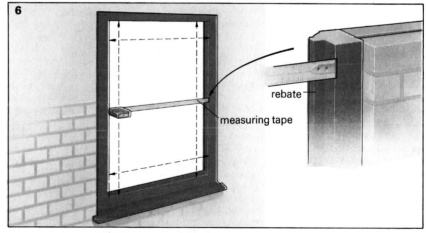
rebate
measuring tape

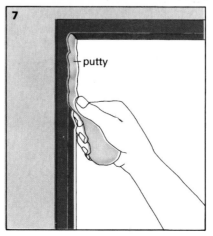
putty

sprig

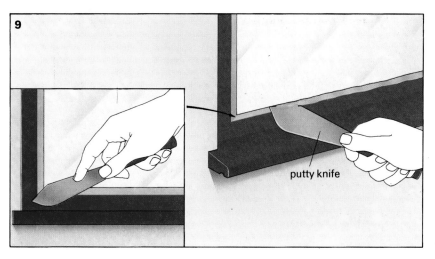

putty knife

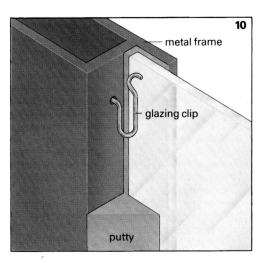

metal frame

glazing clip

putty

1 Make a temporary repair to a broken window by covering it with polythene sheet
2 Use a glass-cutter close to the rebates to remove every piece of glass from the frame
3 Hack out all the old putty from the rebates
4 Remove the holding sprigs with pincers
5 If wood beading holds the glass in place, prise it away with an old chisel
6 To find the dimensions for the new glass always take three measurements across the width and over the length of the frame to ensure accuracy
7 Press soft putty in a continuous layer round the rebates
8 Refit the sprigs, tapping them in flush with the glass
9 Smooth out the final layer of putty shaping it to form mitres at the corners
10 When fitting glass in a metal frame use glazing clips and metal casement putty

When handling broken glass, wear protective spectacles and a pair of old, preferably leather, gloves. Keep children and pets well away until you have finished the job and every piece of glass has been cleared up. Wrap the glass in newspaper and put it straight into the dustbin to avoid accidents.

safety

ends to form neat corner joints and if you damage these you will have to buy more beading and shape the mitres yourself.

Brush out all the dust from the rebates and rub the timber smooth with medium coarse glasspaper. Apply a coat of wood primer and leave to dry.

Measuring up
Accurate measuring for the new sheet of glass is vital. Measure the full width of the opening between the side rebates at the top, centre and bottom of the frame (**see 6**). These should be the same, but if there is a slight difference work on the smallest measurement. Next measure between the other two rebates, top to bottom, again if necessary noting the smallest measurements. Deduct 3mm ($\frac{1}{8}$in) from these dimensions (this is to allow for the glass expanding and contracting in the frame). These are the dimensions to use when ordering your glass.

If your window frame is badly out of square or an awkward shape, such as curved, make a template (pattern) of the frame from card or stiff paper so the glass can be cut to the exact size.

For normal domestic use you will need 3mm ($\frac{1}{8}$in) sheet glass. Take some old newspapers to wrap round the glass or wear gloves to protect your hands from the edges when carrying it.

Fitting the glass
Hold the new glass up to the frame to check it is the right size. Knead some linseed oil putty into a ball in your hands to make it soft and pliable and if necessary add a little linseed oil to make the putty more workable. (Putty has an irritating habit of clinging to dry surfaces when you do not want it to, so keep both hands and the putty knife wet.)

Run a continuous layer of putty about 3mm ($\frac{1}{8}$in) thick round the rebates and press well in with your thumb (**see 7**). Carefully lift the glass into position, allowing for the 3mm expansion gap, and press it into the layer of putty pushing only on the edge of the glass, never in the middle.

Refit the sprigs, spacing them at intervals of about 150mm (6in) around the glass. They must be flat against the glass to hold it securely, so tap them in carefully. The flat edge of a wide chisel could be used for this (**see 8**). Run another layer of putty around the front of the glass, pressing it in with your thumb. With a putty knife smooth out the layer, shaping it to match the angle on your other windows, and form mitres at the corners (**see 9**). Use the edge of the knife to trim off surplus putty from the glass.

Run over the putty with a paint brush dampened with water to make sure it adheres firmly to the glass to give a tight, water-resistant seal. Leave the putty for one to two weeks to dry out before painting or the paint surface will crack.

Metal frames

To fit a new pane of glass into a metal frame adopt basically the same method as for a wood one except you must use metal casement putty, since linseed oil putty is not suitable for metal. The glass is held in place by special glazing clips rather than sprigs – one arm of the clip slots into a hole in the rebate, while the other arm of the clip clamps onto the face of the glass (**see 10**).

Hack away the old putty and note the positions of the glazing clips so you will know where to refit them. Remove the clips from the frame (if you do this carefully, you will be able to use them again). Brush the rebates clean, apply a coat of metal primer and leave to dry for a few hours.

Spread a layer of putty in the rebates and fit the new pane of glass into the frame on the putty. Replace the clips in their original positions and finish off as for a wood frame.

Basic items
protective spectacles and old leather gloves
glass-cutter, light hammer
hacking knife or old chisel
putty knife, small paint brush
measuring tape
card or stiff paper (for template)

For emergency repair
polythene sheet
adhesive tape or drawing pins
four 25 × 12mm (1 × $\frac{1}{2}$in) battens and
   round wire nails, 25mm (1in) long
   (for wood frames)

For wood frames
pincers
medium coarse glasspaper
wood primer
linseed oil putty
linseed oil (to soften hard putty)

For metal frames
metal primer
metal casement putty

equipment

Working with glass

Glass is such a fragile and potentially dangerous material that most people understandably prefer to have it cut to size and delivered by their supplier. It can be difficult to manoeuvre a large sheet of glass from the supplier's to your home without the aid of the glazier's specially adapted van. However, it is often impossible to give the supplier complete instructions for cutting and drilling before the glass is delivered. Once you understand the elementary procedures for working with glass, you will find there are many jobs you can handle with both confidence and safety.

Cutting the required size from a large piece of glass presents problems and there is little that can be done with offcuts – unlike timber and similar sheet materials. But there are occasions when it is useful to know the basic techniques of working with glass, whether you want to cut a straight or curved line, to finish edges or to drill holes in glass.

Warning Always wear thick, preferably leather, gloves when handling glass and put on protective spectacles before cutting. When you carry glass hold it either vertically or horizontally midway along the long edges.

Cutting straight edges

Glass is cut by scoring a line on the surface with a glass-cutter and applying pressure on each side of the line to make a clean break. A glass-cutter is a delicate instrument and must be stored carefully when not in use. Hardened steel cutters are suitable for most types of glass, but you need a diamond cutter for harder high-silica glass. Before use, wet the cutter with a light oil or paraffin.

Place the sheet of glass on a level surface covered with a thick layer of clean felt. Score a line along the surface of the glass by drawing the cutter across it under pressure. Patterned and rolled glass should always be cut on the smooth side. Use a try square to ensure you score at right-angles to the edge of the sheet. To cut irregular shapes, make an accurately shaped template and run the cutter against this.

There are various ways of breaking the glass along the scored line. One is to tap the underside of the glass with the cutter along the scored line and then place your fingers under the glass – with the thumbs on top – and press down firmly. Alternatively you can lay the glass over a straight edge with the scored line immediately above it and apply gentle pressure. Too much pressure may cause the surface of the glass to splinter or flake as it breaks.

Cutting holes

A special cutting tool is used to score a circle. It consists of a suction pad, a cutting edge that rotates on a pivot and a radius scale. First establish the

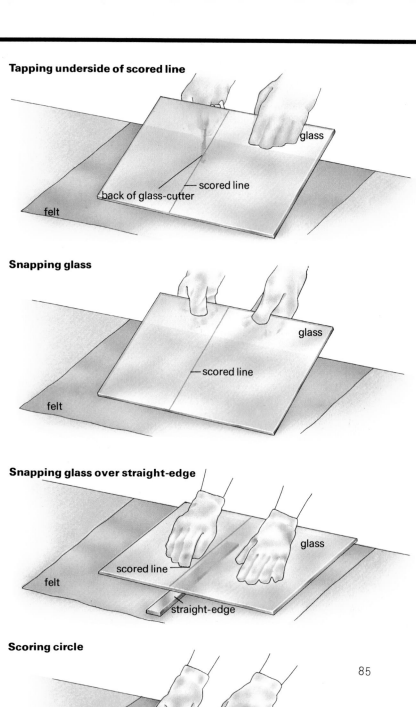

Tapping underside of scored line

glass — scored line — back of glass-cutter — felt

Snapping glass

glass — scored line — felt

Snapping glass over straight-edge

glass — scored line — felt — straight-edge

Scoring circle

circular glass-cutter — glass — score — felt

85

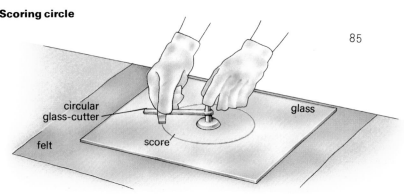

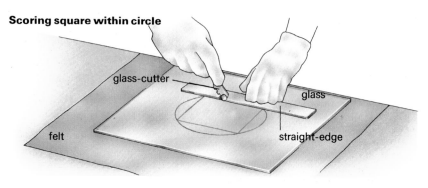

Scoring square within circle

glass-cutter — glass — felt — straight-edge

51

centre of the circle you intend to cut. Set the cutting edge at the correct radius and rotate it to score the circle outline. Lightly tap the underside of the glass and, unless you are cutting a fixed piece of glass, lay it on a flat, felt surface. Score the largest possible square within the circle, then score several smaller squares within each other. Finish scoring with a series of criss-cross lines within the area of the circle. This will help to provide a clean break when the glass is tapped out from the underside (or the outside of a pane already in a window). Start tapping out from the centre and work outwards towards the circumference in all directions.

This method is only suitable if you are working on a small area of glass. If you do break the glass, it will not cost too much to replace and the supplier can also cut out the circle for you.

Finishing edges

Straight cut edges can be smoothed by placing the glass on the bench with a slight overhang and rubbing a wet smooth emery block along the entire length of glass. Fine glasspaper can also be used but it must be wrapped round a support block for safety. Curved cut edges can be smoothed in a similar manner.

Drilling holes

Never use a masonry bit to drill holes because it could easily shatter the glass. Use a special spear bit and try to keep the holes at least 25mm (1in) from the edge, since the chances of the glass breaking are increased the closer to the edge you drill. The absolute minimum distance is 13mm ($\frac{1}{2}$in).

Having decided on the position of the hole, place a ring of putty or plasticine around it to form a well and place a few drops of white spirit or paraffin in the middle. If you are drilling a mirror, use water to prevent the silvering from staining.

Ideally use a multi-speed drill because it is important to start drilling as slowly as possible to prevent the bit skating across the surface. Maintain light pressure and continue drilling as slowly as possible to keep the point of the bit cool.

Start drilling mirrors from the back to make a clean cut through the backing and silvering. Once the drill makes a pinhole on the other side, turn over the mirror to complete the drilling from the front and ensure you have a clean hole on both surfaces.

When drilling bottles, fill the bottle with sand and place it in a bed of sand to keep it in position. Drill slowly through the glass, stopping frequently to lubricate the glass with a brush or dropper and white spirit or paraffin. Alternatively lubricate the bit from time to time.

Basic items
thick gloves, protective spectacles
glass-cutter
circle glass-cutter
try square
carborundum stone, smooth emery block or fine glasspaper
multi-speed electric drill, spear bit
putty or plasticine
paraffin, white spirit or light oil
sand (if drilling bottles)

equipment

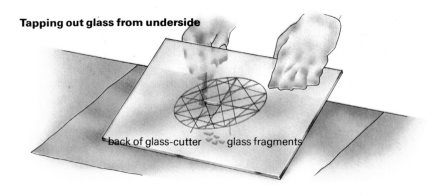

Tapping out glass from underside

back of glass-cutter — glass fragments

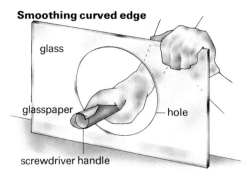

Smoothing glass edge

carborundum stone

glass

edge of bench

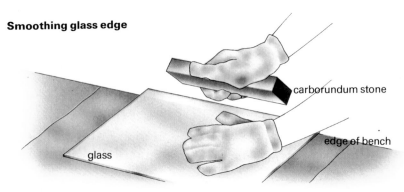

Smoothing curved edge

glass

glasspaper

hole

screwdriver handle

Drilling glass with spear bit

spear bit

paraffin

ring of putty

glass

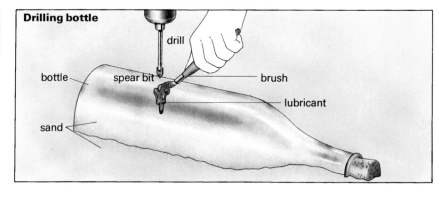

Drilling bottle

drill

bottle

spear bit

brush

lubricant

sand

Repairing external window sills

Timber window sills

Flaking paintwork is one of the first signs of rotting wood, but even an outwardly sound paint surface can, on closer inspection, be hiding a multitude of troubles. If you suspect rot in a sill strip off the paint and cut back any rotting areas until you reach sound timber. If the exposed timber looks grey it is suffering from surface decay, which you must skim away before repainting. When removing affected areas take out any nails or screws in the surface and plane down until you reach clean, healthy timber.

Don't forget to check the underside of the sill as well. Dig a sharp penknife into the wood; if it goes in easily these soft parts will have to be dug out and stripped back as before.

An important part of the sill is the drip groove, a U-shaped channel running the length of the underside. This ensures a free passage for rainwater and must therefore be kept free of dirt.

If you have discovered rot in its early stages you will have only small cavities to fill. This operation is carried out using a hard stopping such as an exterior wood filler or waterproof stopping.

Warning If you use putty instead of a hard stopping, when the sill has been repainted the oil content trapped beneath the surface of paint film could cause blistering when the paint is subjected to excessive heat.

Let the stopping set according to the manufacturer's instructions and sand smooth. Where resinous (sticky) knots are revealed apply a coat of shellac knotting and leave to dry before painting. Repaint the entire surface with primer, undercoat and top coat.

Where it has been necessary to remove a large chunk of rotten timber, to repair by filling would not only be impractical but unsound. Here you will need to make good by cutting a new piece of timber with a panel saw to the same size as that removed. Position the new piece of timber and mark a drip groove in pencil, following the line of the existing groove. Remove and tenon saw the groove to the required depth and width, gouging out the waste timber with a narrow chisel. Glasspaper smooth for a clean finish.

Fix the new piece of timber in position with exterior adhesive and galvanized nails. Sink the nail heads below the surface with a nail punch and fill the cavities with exterior filler or waterproof stopping. Repaint as before.

The most troublesome timber is oak which, because of its open grain, tends to encourage breakdown of the paint. Here strip back to bare wood and rub fine surface filler well down into the grain with a piece of clean rag. Let it set and then smooth with glasspaper, working only with the grain. Finally apply a coat of aluminium primer, then undercoat and top coats of paint.

Ideally oak is best left in its natural state and protected by coating with boiled linseed oil or a timber preservative. So when you strip the sill decide which finish you want – natural or painted.

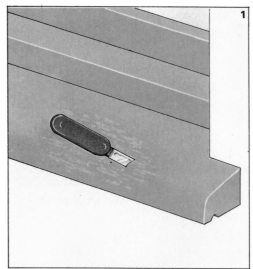

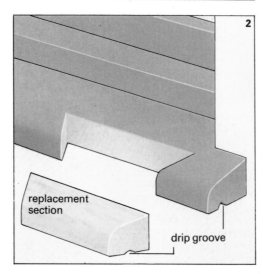

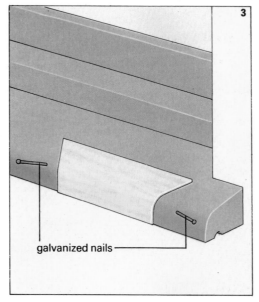

1 Checking for decay in timber window sill with sharp knife
2 Extensive rot removed and new piece of timber cut to fit gap with drip groove to match existing one
3 New timber fixed into place with exterior adhesive and galvanized nails

Overleaf
4 Badly rotted timber sill cut away to be replaced with new one cast in concrete
5a Timber shuttering box supported on batten screwed to wall below window frame. Sash cord stretched along base of box and knotted through holes in box ends gives line of drip groove (see 6)
5b Cast concrete sill is smoothed level to top edges of timbers with steel float
6 Detail of drip groove at side of sill, with knotted cord in place. Remove cord when concrete is set

replacement section

drip groove

galvanized nails

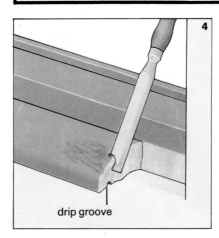
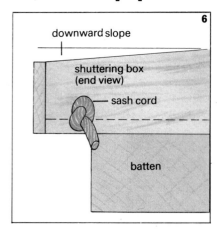
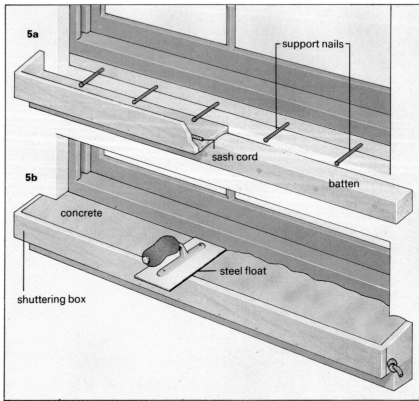

5a

support nails

sash cord

batten

5b

concrete

steel float

shuttering box

Making a concrete sill

In extreme cases of rotting, where the sill has to be removed completely, it is worth casting a new one of your own in concrete. This is not difficult or expensive and removes forever the possibility of rot.

Chisel out all remaining pieces of the old sill. Apply one coat of acrylic primer to the bare wood of the frame for protection and apply a second coat immediately prior to casting the sill. To reinforce the concrete, drive a row of 150mm (6in) nails, 150mm apart and a third of their length, into the timber along the bottom of the window frame.

You must then construct a shuttering box from 25mm (1in) thick timber, screwed together, into which you pour the concrete. The tops of the sides of the box should slope slightly downwards away from the wall to prevent rainwater from collecting on the sill and causing possible rotting of the window frame. To support the shuttering box screw a batten to the wall below the window frame, ensuring the screws are well anchored. Remember to make the top of the box the level you intend as the top surface of the sill, and that the inside measurements of the box will be the outside measurements of the sill.

For your drip groove, stretch a length of stout cord – sashcord is ideal – along the base of the box and through specially drilled holes in the side pieces, knotting at both ends to keep it taut.

Mixing the concrete

Using one part fine shingle, two parts clean sharp sand and one part cement, add water gradually until you have a buttery, rather than sloppy, consistency. Shovel the mix into the shuttering box and smooth level with the top edges of the timbers with a steel float. Care will be needed to maintain an even downward slope in the centre of the new sill. Before you remove the box frame, cord and wall batten, allow a few days for the concrete to set thoroughly. The job is completed by painting with a proprietary concrete paint.

Replacing windows in solid walls

You can remove and replace all types of window yourself as long as you adopt the right procedure. But make sure you can finish the job in a reasonable amount of time to avoid leaving openings exposed.

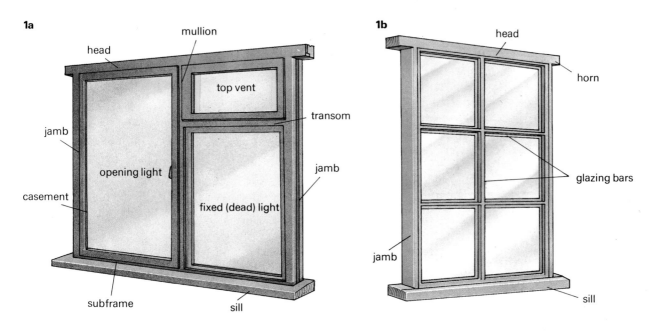

1a

head

mullion

top vent

transom

jamb

opening light

jamb

casement

fixed (dead) light

subframe

sill

1b

head

horn

glazing bars

jamb

sill

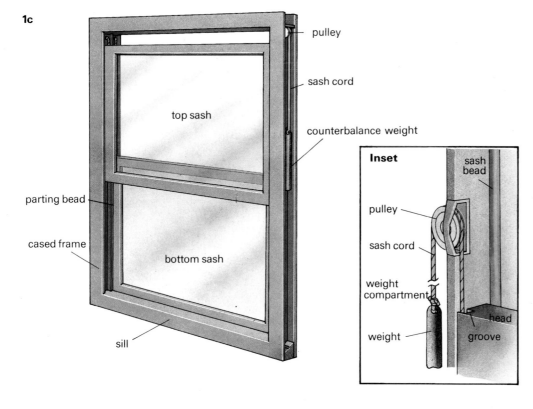

1c

pulley

sash cord

top sash

counterbalance weight

parting bead

cased frame

bottom sash

sill

Inset

sash bead

pulley

sash cord

weight compartment

weight

head

groove

Before you begin removing a window, identify the various parts from our diagrams
1a Casement window with fixed light, opening light and top vent
1b Fixed window
1c Sash window and its operating mechanism (**inset**)

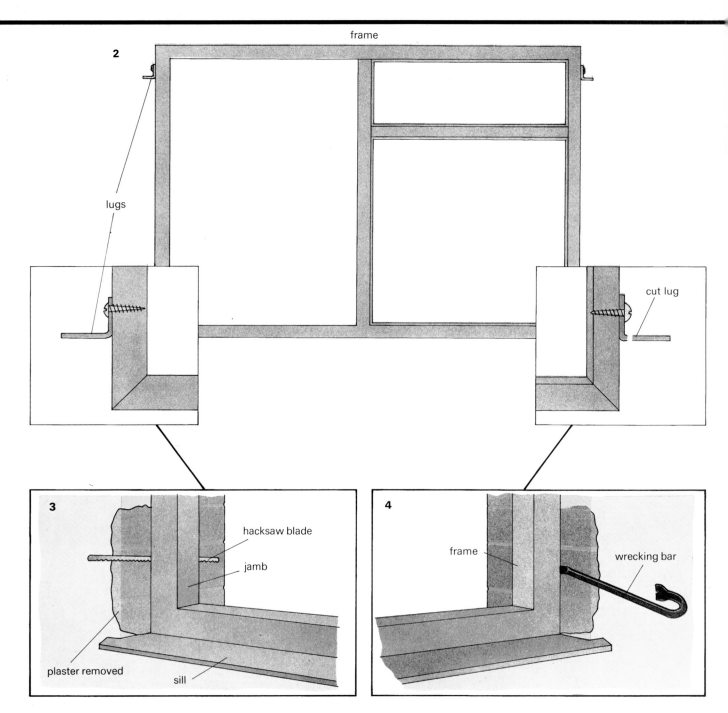

frame

2

lugs

cut lug

3

hacksaw blade

jamb

plaster removed

sill

4

frame

wrecking bar

2 The position of the fixing lugs on a casement window
3 You can remove the frame relatively intact by severing the fixings with a hacksaw blade threaded between the frame and the brickwork
4 Lever the frame away from the wall with a wrecking bar

Having decided on the style of window you want, you may need to have it made instead of simply choosing one from a catalogue. In either case, measure the size of the opening (checking all angles are 90 degrees) and deduct 6mm ($\frac{1}{4}$in) from the height and width measurements. Make sure your figures are accurate; while it is possible to trim a timber frame if it arrives over-size, there is nothing you can do about a metal one. When you take delivery, make sure the size and quality are as specified. Refuse to accept the frame if the wood is bruised, split or has developed shrinkage cracks, or if there are numerous large or loose knots, badly cut joints or the frame is out of true.

Never begin removing a window before you have the new one delivered; it is not only inconvenient to have to cover a gaping hole with polythene for a night or longer, but also a positive invitation to intruders.

Replacing timber frames

Take down window hangings and curtain tracks and remove any window fittings, including security catches. Remove the glass from the frame, preserving as much of it as possible; even if it is not suitable for your replacement window, you may be able to use it at some point in the future.

Removing casement windows

Start by removing hinged lights; when taking off the casements, it is easier to remove screws from the top hinge last – but be prepared for the weight when it comes free.

Frames are fixed with metal lugs or ties which are built into the mortar joints of the brickwork, although screws or spikes (long nails) are sometimes used. There are usually two fixings in each upright jamb. If you want to remove the frame relatively

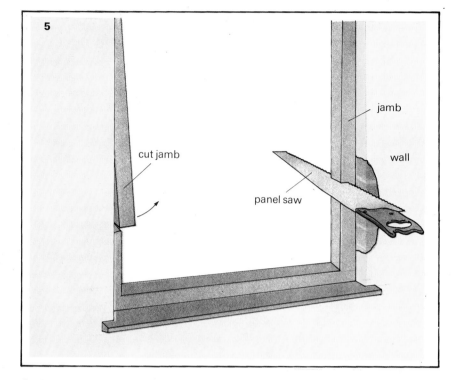

cut jamb

panel saw

jamb

wall

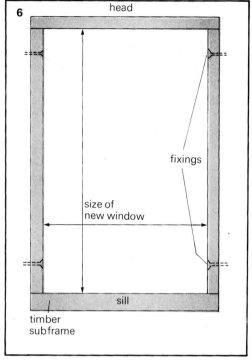

head

fixings

size of
new window

sill

timber
subframe

5 If you do not wish to keep
the frame, cut through the
jambs with an old panel saw
and lever them out with a
wrecking bar

6 If you are replacing a sash
window with another type,
you will probably have to
install a subframe first so
the new frame will fit
snugly into the opening

undamaged, try cutting through the fixings with a
general purpose saw or a hacksaw blade threaded
between the brickwork and the frame. First you
will have to remove the mastic seal between the
frame and the wall and you may need to hack away
plaster from interior walls around the window and
some exterior pointing.

Check whether there are fixings at the head and
sill of the frame (it is unlikely you will find any in
small domestic windows, but you can put them in
when installing the new frame).

After severing the fixings, use a wrecking bar to
lever out the frame. If you are dealing with a ground
floor or basement window, you can push the frame
outwards, but on upper storeys you must lever it
into the building. If you have any doubts about
which way to take the frame, remember damage to
interior plasterwork is easier to repair than brickwork. Whichever way you go, use even leverage all
round, otherwise you may jam the frame in the
opening.

If you do not wish to save the frame, you can
remove it quickly by sawing through the jambs
(using an old panel saw because the teeth are
certain to grate on the bricks). When the jambs (and
mullion, if there is one) are out of the way you can
lever out the head and sill.

Installing the new frame
Prime timber frames on all surfaces before you
install them, using a lead-based primer for best
results. Make good any damage to the brickwork
and, if you are using screws or spikes, check the
plugs in the wall (often just hardwood) are sound
and tight. You may be able to use them again by
knocking slivers of hardwood into the holes left by
the old screws.

Mark the position of the plugs on the frame, drill
fixing holes, put the frame in position and, using
packing pieces to keep it central, fix with countersunk screws or spikes. It is important to keep
checking the angles are at 90 degrees – using a
spirit level and plumb line – because screwing can
force the frame out of true and any distortion will

make it difficult to hang the opening lights. Using a
trowel or putty knife apply a non-hardening mastic
to the gaps between the frame and the walls.
Finally hang lights and casements, glaze and paint
the frame and replace fittings, security catches or
locks. Lightly oil moving parts.

Using metal lugs or ties If you are fixing the frame
with metal lugs or ties, screw them to the frame so
they coincide with mortar joints in the brickwork.
Remove the mortar from the brickwork with a
chisel and hammer, or with a masonry router bit in
an electric drill, and cement the lugs or ties into
position. Allow the cement to set before hanging
lights and casements.

Using masonry bolts Another method is to wedge
the frame into position, drill through the timber
into the brickwork and secure the frame with loose-
type expanding masonry bolts. First drill a flat-
bottomed hole with a power bore bit deep enough
to recess the bolt head and wide enough to allow it
to be tightened with a box (or socket) spanner.
Continue drilling through the frame with a twist
drill slightly larger than the expanding bolt.
Finally use a masonry bit of the same size to drill
into the brickwork to the correct depth for the
fitting.

Double-hung sash windows
With sash windows it is not always necessary to
replace the whole frame. Where the sashes themselves have become mis-shaped, it is possible to
replace only these, but it is likely the box frame
(containing the mechanism) is in the same condition. You can discard the sashes, retain the
framework and install a fixed window, a casement
or a steel sash. This involves lining the frame with
plywood and fixing your new window to this, which
may not be satisfactory because you will not know
the real condition of the bricks and mortar behind
the box. It would be better to replace the entire
frame.

Replacing sashes These will almost certainly have
to be made to order and must be of the same
specification as the originals: the same thickness

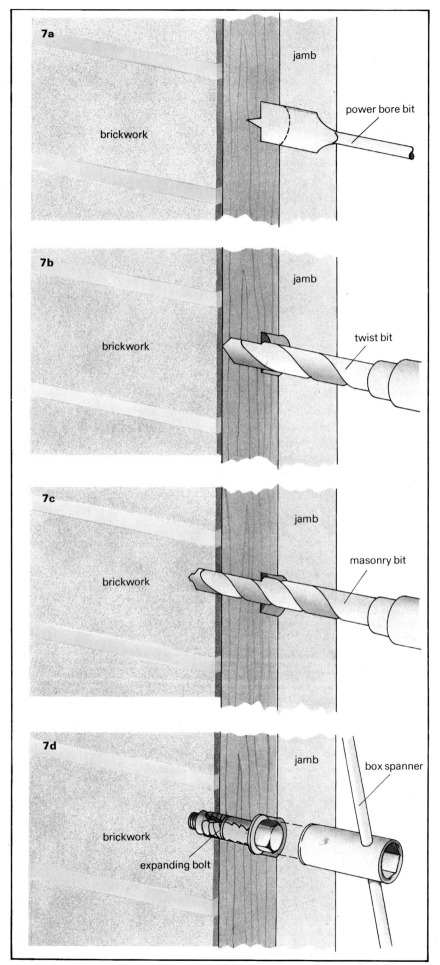

7a

brickwork

jamb

power bore bit

7b

brickwork

jamb

twist bit

7c

brickwork

jamb

masonry bit

7d

brickwork

jamb

box spanner

expanding bolt

glass and sash stuff (timber), otherwise the weights will not counterbalance the sashes.

Use a chisel to lever out the staff (or inside) bead all round the window, taking care not to damage the wood. Lower the inside window and, holding the cord in one hand, cut it with a knife close to the top of the sash and lower the weight to the bottom of the box. Repeat for the other side. Remove the inside sash then lever away the parting beads from the framework, cut the outside sash cord in the same way and remove the outside sash.

Lift the pockets on each side of the frame and remove the four weights (two for each sash) and the cord attached to them. Mark which weights are for which sash – those for the upper sash are heavier to keep it in the fully up position. Measure your pieces of cord to give the length of the new cord. Check the condition of the pulleys: if they are sound, oil them lightly to ensure they run freely. If the pulleys are rusted, unscrew them and buy new ones; take the originals with you to the dealer to ensure you buy the right size.

Reassembly Always begin replacing sashes and cords in the reverse order – the outside sash must go in first. The cord may be fixed to the sashes by nails or with a system of slots and wedges: follow the previous fixing method where possible.

Begin the reassembly by taking a length of twine and attaching one end to a cord. Attach a heavy nail to the other end of the twine and run it round one outside sash pulley into the frame box. Retrieve the nail and twine through the pocket and tie the cord end to one of the counterbalance weights, checking you have the right weight for the sash. Measure the distance between the top of the sash and the bottom of the cord position or groove and mark the frame at this distance down from the top.

Pull the cord until the weight is about 50mm (2in) from the bottom of the box and cut the free end of the cord level with the mark you have made. Pull the cord again until the weight touches the pulley and wedge a piece of wood between the frame and the pulley, making sure it will not slip. Repeat with the second cord and secure the cords to the sash grooves with nails or fixing wedges. At this stage the job will be easier if you have help, especially when dealing with large, heavy sashes. Check the sash slides properly and the weights do not hit the bottom of the box: if they do, you will have to shorten the cords.

When replacing the inner sash, follow the same method until you have inserted the weight and cord. This time, mark the frame at the lowest cord position with the sash down. Pull the weight almost to its top position and cut the cord at the mark on the frame. Then follow the procedure for fitting the outer sash. Finally replace the pockets and parting bead and the staff bead.

Replacing sash windows

If you are replacing the entire window with a new double-hung sash or with another type, remove the sashes as described above. Then, using a chisel, remove the architrave (moulding), taking care not to damage it since you may want to use it again. Lever out the whole frame and make good by cleaning up and repointing. In the case of a replacement of the same type, put the window straight in.

If you are installing a different type of window, such as a casement, shop around to see whether you can find a ready-made frame which will fit the opening; if not, you may find it cheaper in the long

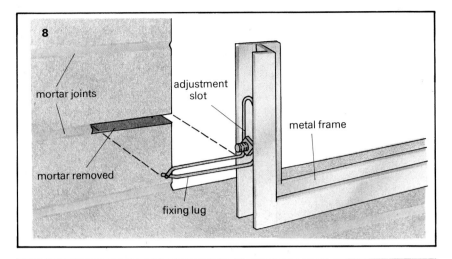

8

mortar joints

adjustment slot

metal frame

mortar removed

fixing lug

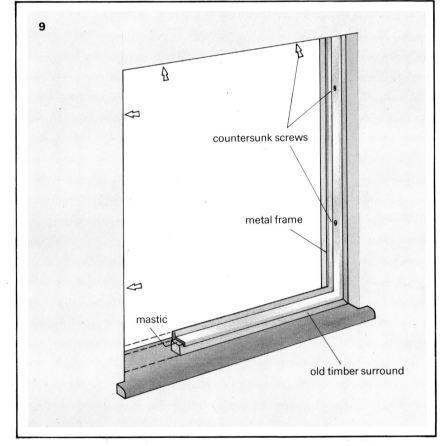

9

countersunk screws

metal frame

mastic

old timber surround

7a If you are fixing the frame with expanding masonry bolts, first drill a hole in the timber with a power bore bit
7b Change to a twist bit and continue drilling through the frame
7c To drill into the brickwork, use a masonry bit
7d Fit the bolt and tighten it with a box spanner
8 To fix a metal frame directly to brickwork, cement the lugs into the mortar joints
9 With a timber surround, set the frame in mastic and fix with countersunk screws

Basic items
screwdriver, chisel
general purpose saw or hacksaw
wrecking bar, old panel saw
electric drill
spirit level, plumb line
trowel or putty knife, trimming knife
masonry router bit or cold chisel and
 hammer (to remove mortar)
power bore bit, twist drill and masonry
 bit, box or socket spanner (for
 expanding masonry bolts)
twine, heavy nail (for replacing sashes)
centre punch, tungsten twist drill,
 protective spectacles (for metal
 frames)

equipment

run to have one made to measure, since filling in the opening so the frame fits does take a lot of time and materials. When fitting a casement window in place of a sash one, it is important to set the frame further forward in the opening so the casement will clear brickwork when you open it, otherwise there is a danger of smashing the glass.

Unless you are having a window specially made you will probably have to build and install a sub-frame first. The type of timber used will depend on the type of window, but in any case you must make the internal dimensions offer a snug fit to the actual frame. Fix the subframe as for installing timber windows: put the head and sill parts (or surround) in first, then the jambs which act as wedges and strengthen the structure. The final stage is to install the frame.

Replacing metal frames

Start by removing the opening lights; if the hinges are stiff, it is best to remove them with a hacksaw. Take the glass out of fixed lights and remove fixing screws. If the screws are rusted solid or if the heads break off, you must drill the screws out. Wear goggles as a precaution and use a centre punch and a hammer to make a starting point for a twist drill with a tungsten hardened tip (the diameter should be slightly larger than that of the screw.) Continue drilling until the screw no longer holds the frame.

If the window is not attached to a timber surround, tap all round the edge of the frame with a cold chisel and hammer to loosen the grip of the mortar and plaster. If a screw is stubborn and you do not want to drill it out, cut through the jamb with a hacksaw and lever it out with a wrecking bar.
Warning Some large windows may be made up of several standard units using coupling bars and these occasionally provide support for the lintel and are built into the structure. If this is a possibility, never hacksaw through them but seek advice from an expert.

If you are dealing with a metal frame fixed in a timber surround, remove the glass; this should reveal countersunk fixing screws. Where metal windows are fitted by lugs or ties, deal with them as for removing timber windows.

Installing the new window
If there is an old timber surround which is in good condition, you can set the frame in a bed of non-hardening mastic and secure it with countersunk screws. When fixing directly to brickwork, clean off any projections of mortar or plaster and repoint where necessary. Pay particular attention to any instructions from the manufacturer, but generally you will install the window with lugs cemented into the mortar joints, as explained for timber windows; the lugs are attached to the metal frame with screws and can be adjusted to meet the joints. Again, bed the frame on a layer of mastic before fixing.

Despite the claims made by manufacturers of the increasingly popular aluminium alloy frames, these frames are not entirely free from corrosion problems, and it may be advisable to paint them. If you do paint them, first apply a coat of zinc chromate primer, then at least three coats of paint; brush the paint well into the hinges to prevent problems with rusting and oil the hinges lightly after they have dried.

Replacing windows in cavity walls

When serious decay of a window frame makes complete replacement necessary, many people turn to the professional builder. However, if you tackle the job systematically, there is no reason why it should be beyond the skill of the handyman. Nevertheless, windows in houses with cavity walls will present the handyman with extra problems making care essential.

Replacing windows in cavity walls involves similar procedures as replacing windows in solid walls, but in this case you must take particular care not to disturb or damage the damp proof course which surrounds the frame, otherwise moisture will penetrate to the inside of the house and cause damp. In older buildings the dpc consists of strips of lead, copper or zinc; in modern buildings more flexible materials – bituminous felt or plastic – are used.

Before you remove your existing window, discover how it was installed and whether it was built into the walls or fixed after the walls were com-pleted. Built-in windows are propped into position and the walls built up on each side. This is more usual with softwood windows with a paint finish because accidental damage or repeated soaking and drying during bricklaying can be made good after the wall is finished. These windows are usually fixed by metal lugs or ties screwed or nailed to the frame and cemented into the joints.

Hardwood windows with a varnish finish are usually installed after the brickwork is finished because damage to these cannot be made good. They are usually secured by countersunk screws or spikes through the frame and into hardwood plugs built into the joints. Fixings at the heads of both types of window are often into dovetailed wood plugs cast into the concrete lintel when it is built.

Removing the frame
Begin by taking off any hinged lights and case-ments. Remove the glazing from fixed lights to

1 A window opening in a cavity wall; damp proof courses bridge the cavity horizontally top and bottom and vertically at the sides
2 If the window was built into the wall, it should be secured with fixing lugs cemented into mortar joints
3 The head of the window is usually fixed with dovetail wood plugs set in the lintel
4 If you find the vertical dpc is nailed to the frame, cut it close to the jamb before you remove the frame

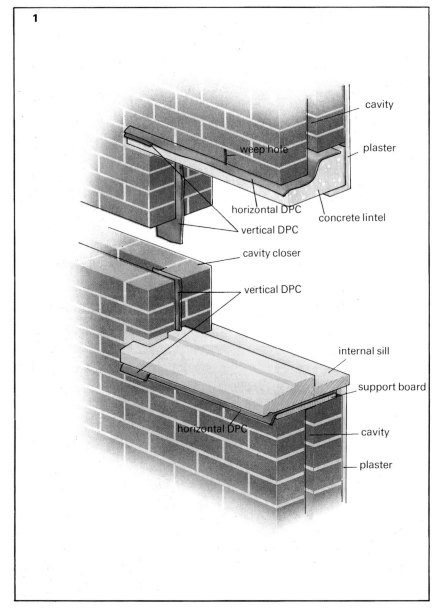

1

cavity
weep hole
plaster
horizontal DPC
vertical DPC
concrete lintel
cavity closer
vertical DPC
internal sill
support board
cavity
horizontal DPC
plaster

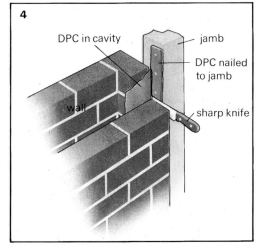

2

jamb
inner wall
vertical DPC
fixing lug
outer wall

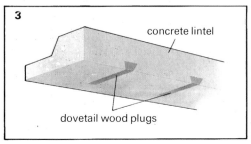

3

concrete lintel
dovetail wood plugs

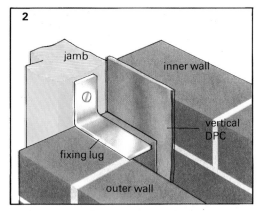

4

DPC in cavity
jamb
DPC nailed to jamb
wall
sharp knife

reveal any screw or spike fixings. You can either undo the screws or cut through them (this also applies to spikes, lugs and ties) by sliding a hacksaw blade or general purpose saw between the brickwork and the frame. It is at this point you must take great care not to damage the damp proof course or pull it out of the cavity.

A vertical dpc lines the interior of the cavity wall at each side of the frame. It is sometimes nailed to the frame itself and you should be able to see this when you begin to remove the frame. Use a sharp knife to trim the dpc as close to the jambs as possible (whatever you do, don't pull it out of the cavity), then continue removing the frame.

There should be a horizontal damp proof course under the sill unless a non-porous sill was built into the wall; the course at the head will have been laid above the lintel at the time of construction – neither needs your attention.

Fitting the new frame
Once you have made good any damage to brickwork and plaster caused by removing the frame, you can install your new window. The manufacturer may specify the type of fixing and you should always follow his instructions, but usually the window will be fixed with lugs attached to the frame and cemented into the brick joints. Clean out the required joints to a depth sufficient to slide in the frame, apply non-hardening mastic to the sides and bottom of the opening and place the frame in position. The frame must sit squarely over the wall cavity and cover the end of the vertical dpc to ensure an effective barrier against moisture penetration. Cement with a fairly dry mix of about one part cement to three parts sand.

Other methods of fixing are by nailing the frame into hardwood plugs built into the brick joints, or with screws and plugs. Position the frame on a bed of mastic as before and secure it in place with wedges between the wall and the frame. Check with a spirit level to ensure the frame sits squarely in the opening and fill any gaps between the wall and frame with more mastic. Hang any casements, glaze, replace fittings and paint with undercoat and top coats. Finally lightly oil moving parts.

5a When installing a frame which is secured with fixing lugs, first rake out the appropriate mortar joints
5b Apply non-hardening mastic to the sides and bottom of the opening so the dpcs are covered
5c Place the frame in position, sliding the fixing lugs into the raked joints; make sure the frame sits squarely over the cavity
5d Finally cement the lugs into the joints with a fairly dry mortar mix

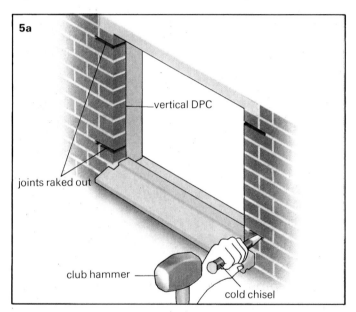

5a
vertical DPC
joints raked out
club hammer
cold chisel

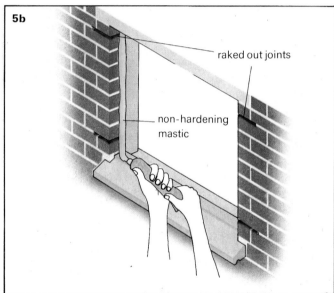

5b
raked out joints
non-hardening mastic

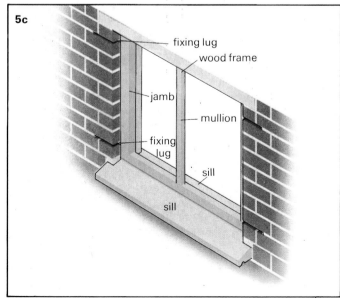

5c
fixing lug
wood frame
jamb
mullion
fixing lug
sill
sill

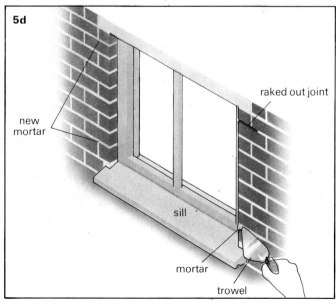

5d
raked out joint
new mortar
sill
mortar
trowel

61

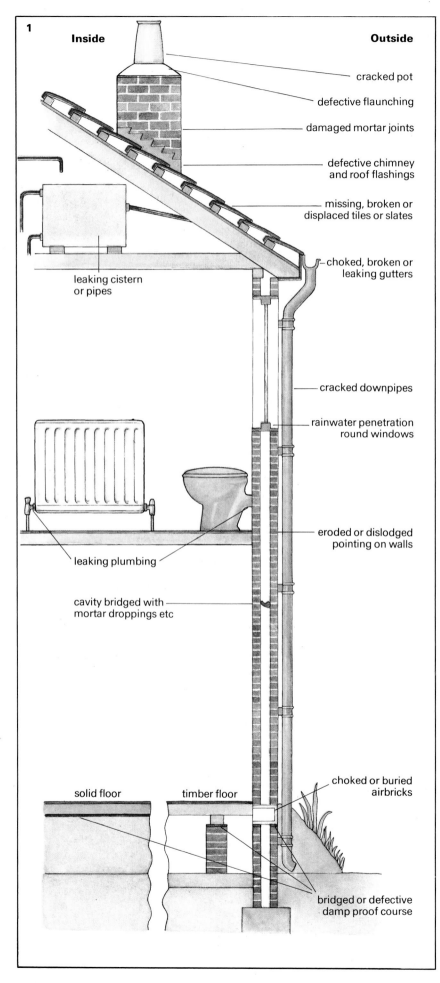

Inside   **Outside**

cracked pot

defective flaunching

damaged mortar joints

defective chimney
and roof flashings

missing, broken or
displaced tiles or slates

choked, broken or
leaking gutters

leaking cistern
or pipes

cracked downpipes

rainwater penetration
round windows

eroded or dislodged
pointing on walls

leaking plumbing

cavity bridged with
mortar droppings etc

choked or buried
airbricks

solid floor   timber floor

bridged or defective
damp proof course

Dealing with damp

Every house is prone to damp, both inside and out. Rain and snow batter the roof, walls, windows and doors, while moisture in the ground attacks the walls and floors from below. Inside the house, the plumbing pipework conveys water under floors and down walls as it travels to radiators, taps and tanks. To remain unaffected, a house must be structurally sound and well maintained; if it is not, damp will set in and bring plenty of problems with it.

The effects of damp may be manifested in relatively simple ways, such as wallpaper peeling off a wet wall or a wet patch appearing on a ceiling. In these cases, if prompt action is taken to cure the underlying cause of the problem, then all that remains to complete the repairs is a relatively straightforward decorating job. Where damp is allowed to remain untreated, more serious problems arise. There may be a dampish atmosphere throughout the house, mildew will form on clothes and a stale smell prevail. The occupants of the house may suffer ill health as a result of living in a constantly damp environment. Structural timbers such as floor joists and roof timbers may develop rot, making repair work complicated and expensive.

Protection against damp

Houses built in Britain since the 1920s are generally far less susceptible to damp than older properties since they have damp barriers incorporated into the structure which stop moisture working its way up through walls or floors (rising damp). In the concrete ground floor there is a damp proof membrane consisting of waterproof material stretched across the building from wall to wall to intercept moisture rising from the ground. The external cavity walls have a damp proof course laid in a mortar joint, usually between the second and third or third and fourth courses of bricks above ground level. This dpc, installed to prevent moisture creeping up the walls, is a strip of thin, impervious material, such as slate or bituminous felt, which stretches right round the external walls of the house to protect both the outer and inner leaves of brickwork.

Houses with suspended timber floors on the ground floor are generally far less prone to damp. Where there are problems, they are usually caused by a faulty dpc laid on the walls supporting the joists (sleeper walls) or by blocked up airbricks in the outside walls of the house. These bricks are designed to ensure a constant flow of air under the floor to keep the timber well ventilated and dry.

As well as rising damp there is also rainwater ingress or penetrating damp; this is prevented in modern houses by the air space in cavity walls. Rainwater which soaks through the outer leaf of bricks cannot cross the cavity and reach the inner

1 Faults in the house structure which can give rise to damp. Damage to chimney pots and the surrounding area should be repaired as soon as possible

leaf of bricks which form the outer walls of the rooms.

Faults in damp proofing Assuming the roof and gutters etc. of the house are sound, a modern house should remain free of damp. But problems may arise if faulty damp proof materials are used or errors occur at the building stage. For example, a split in a floor membrane or wall dpc will allow moisture through; and if mortar is allowed to fall into the cavity during building it could land on and set across one of the metal ties linking the walls to form a perfect bridge for moisture to cross over to the inner leaf of the wall.

Older houses Where there are no purpose-made damp proof barriers incorporated in the structure, the thickness of the materials used may prevent moisture creeping right through solid walls and floors. The density of some of these materials means moisture takes a long time to soak in and will dry out in settled weather without damp ever showing inside the house. On the other hand, with walls made of very porous material, moisture may well soak right through and, in severe weather conditions, tell-tale wet patches appear on interior surfaces.

Damp or condensation?

While damp is easily confused with condensation, since both produce similar wet stains on walls, it is important to differentiate between the two since remedial treatments vary. Condensation is readily recognized when it causes misting on windows or beads of moisture to drip from water pipes or the WC cistern; identification problems arise when a wet stain shows on other surfaces. Usually the weather will pin-point the problem; on a wet muggy day or during periods of prolonged rain, wet stains indicate rising damp or rainwater ingress. On a cold, dry day wet stains on walls, especially when accompanied by the more familiar signs of misty windows etc, point to condensation.

Checking for damp

Normally any wet patches caused by damp which appear inside the house can be linked to a structural fault nearby. For example, a wet patch high up on an upstairs wall could be the result of a leaking gutter or downpipe and one at skirting board level on the ground floor is probably caused by a defective or non-existent dpc. Random patches on walls point to rainwater ingress, while wet stains on ceilings could be traced back to a cracked roof tile or leaking plumbing.

Chimney stack Damp appearing on chimney-breast walls can indicate rainwater ingress in the chimney stack area. This problem is often created or accentuated by blocking off the air supply to the flue after removing a fireplace. A broken or loose chimney pot may need to be removed or replaced; if the flue is no longer used, you can fix a special capping pot which allows for ventilation but keeps out rainwater. Other common faults in chimneys are cracked flaunching (the sloping layer of mortar securing the pot), crumbling mortar joints between the brickwork of the stack, which should be re-pointed, and defective or loose flashings (the materials, usually zinc or lead, which seal the joint between the base of the stack and the roof). These can be stepped, with one edge secured in rising mortar courses of the chimney stack brickwork, or a straight band around the base of the stack, known as apron flashing.

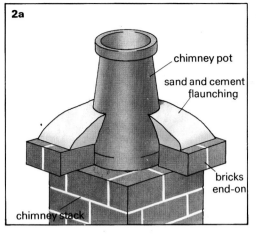

2a If damp appears on chimney-breast walls, check the condition of the chimney pots, flaunching and the chimney stack
2b Check also the flashings round the chimney stack are sound and there are no loose or missing tiles or slates

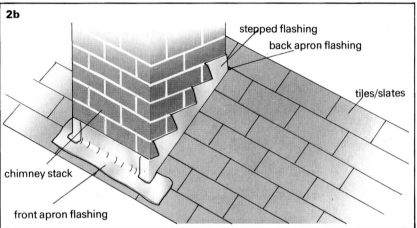

Roof Slipped or missing tiles or slates will admit rainwater to the felt beneath, which will sag, eventually split and allow water to drip onto the loft floor and show on the ceiling of the room below. Loft timbers kept constantly wet by dripping water will rot quickly so you should replace the missing roof covering as soon as possible. Fine cracks in tiles or slates will allow rainwater to seep inside; it may be difficult to spot cracks from the ground and the best way to find them is to climb into the loft during heavy rainfall and look and listen for drips. You can then trace these back to their source which could be some way from the dripping water.

Gutters and downpipes Where the rainwater drainage system is working properly, water falling off the roof is collected in the gutters from where it flows steadily into the downpipe to be discharged to the drain below. If the system fails, a large volume of water may drain onto one area of a wall, causing the brickwork to absorb an excessive amount of moisture.

Walls Where a wall has a solid covering of rendering, roughcast or pebbledash and is kept well painted with a good quality exterior paint, damp problems from rainwater ingress should never arise. However, if the wall covering is cracked or loose and the mortar joints in the brickwork behind are in poor shape or there is no decorative paint finish, then rainwater can soak through.

Treating damp

Plain unpainted solid brick walls rely completely on the density of the material and sound mortar joints to keep out rain, so any loose or crumbling joints should be repointed. If walls are in good

3a Installing a damp proof course using the liquid method is a job you can tackle yourself — as long as you are prepared for the large amount of work involved
3b With the strip method, the dpc is inserted in slots cut in the mortar with a power saw
3c Electro osmosis treatment involves inserting electrodes in the wall and linking them through a copper strip; this is connected to a terminal buried in the ground
3d With the capillary method, porous ceramic tubes are set into the wall

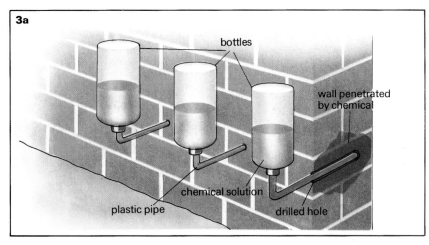

3a

bottles

wall penetrated
by chemical

chemical solution

plastic pipe

drilled hole

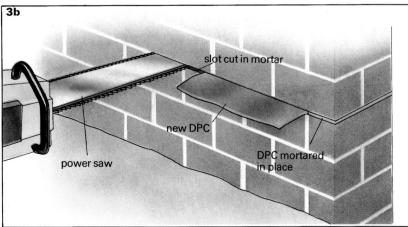

3b

slot cut in mortar

new DPC

power saw

DPC mortared
in place

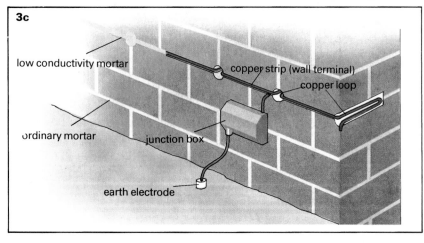

3c

low conductivity mortar

copper strip (wall terminal)

copper loop

ordinary mortar

junction box

earth electrode

3d

porous tube

grille

repair but damp shows inside, a brush coating of a silicone water repellent liquid applied to the outside of the house should cure the trouble. These colourless liquids keep out the rain but still allow moisture vapour trapped in the wall to escape. There are also liquid treatments for internal application; but these are simply sealers which prevent moisture from affecting decorative materials and are not intended to cure the damp problem. Similarly, you can apply a dry lining to walls using materials such as bitumen-backed aluminium foil or steel corrugated sheets before decorating, but again these do not cure the damp itself.

Rising damp in walls can be treated by one of four methods of installing a dpc. With one exception they are probably best left to a specialist.

Liquid treatment A chemical liquid is fed into the wall and diffuses through the brickwork to form a damp proof barrier. The liquid can be injected under pressure using special equipment or be left to soak into the wall from a number of special bottles located in a series of pre-drilled holes. This treatment is one you can carry out yourself and will be covered in greater detail later.

Dpc strip method A power saw is used to cut through a mortar course right round the outside of walls and a damp proof material such as lead, copper or polythene is slipped into the saw cut. (Slate is not normally used since saws generally do not cut a wide enough slot for this material and laborious chipping out is needed.) Fresh mortar is then inserted to complete the process.

Electro-osmosis The difference in the electrical charge between the wall and the ground causes damp to rise in the wall. The electro-osmosis system involves fitting electrodes into the wall and linking them through a copper strip which is, in turn, linked to an electrode driven into the ground. Minute electric charges in a wet wall are then discharged down the link to prevent moisture rising.

Capillary Holes are drilled into the walls, either from the inside or outside of the house, and porous ceramic tubes inserted; these are bonded into the holes with special porous mortar and then fitted with a protective evaporation cap. Moisture from the brickwork or plaster is drawn through the pores in the tube and then evaporates into the air. The installation of this process involves the minimum amount of disturbance to the structure.

Warning Before going to the trouble and expense of installing a new dpc, check that something more basic is not causing the trouble. The existing dpc may be perfectly sound but could have been bypassed by earth or a rockery piled against the wall. Paths beside a wall should be 150mm (6in) below dpc level or rainwater will constantly splash above the dpc; in times of torrential rain, water on the path could soak the wall above dpc level.

Solid floors Normally a suitable damp proof barrier can be applied by brushing or trowelling on a damp-proofing liquid such as pitch epoxy sealer or rubberized bituminous emulsion, though sometimes a plastic membrane sheet can be used instead. Remove the skirtings temporarily and take the damp proofing material up the wall to link with the wall dpc. Where the problem is more acute, a sandwich treatment is required. Apply two coats of damp proofing material, allowing the first to dry before applying the second. Sprinkle some clean, sharp sand over the second coat while it is still tacky to form a key for a finishing screed 50mm (2in) thick.

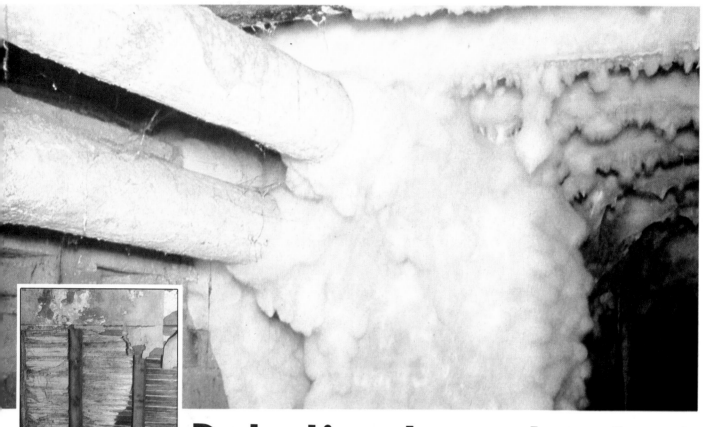

Detecting dry and wet rot

Dampness can lead to dry and wet rot which, if not properly treated, will cause a great deal of damage to the structure of a house. Dry rot, in particular, spreads rapidly and must be tackled immediately it is discovered. So it is important you can recognize the presence and extent of the problem in your home – and, where necessary, take appropriate action.

There is only one way to deal with dry and wet rot – cut out and replace the damaged timber, apply a fungicide over the nearby areas and make sure you correct the cause of the damp. Before you can treat it, however, you must diagnose what sort of rot has set in. Wet rot, caused by a combination of dampness and lack of ventilation, is symptomatic of a poorly designed and constructed building. The basic difference is that wet rot is restricted to damp timber, while dry rot can transfer itself from wet to dry timber. While wet rot is twice as likely to occur as dry rot, it is rarely as serious.

The householder can often treat both types successfully, but serious attacks affecting the structure of a building will require the advice and assistance of a specialist.

Above and left Examples of the more advanced stages of dry rot, which must be recognized and treated immediately
Top left Old timber which has been seriously affected by wet rot and must be removed and replaced wherever it is discovered

Dry rot

This is caused by a fungus which grows on damp wood then spreads – if not caught – throughout the building. The first sign is a covering of matted fungal strands on the surface of the timber. These appear with a silvery-grey skin, which could be tinged with patches of lilac or yellow.

In humid conditions the covering grows rapidly and takes on the appearance of a soft, white cushion with a cotton wool type texture. If the edges of the cushion contact drier air or become exposed to light, they will become bright yellow. In damp conditions, where the growth is still active, many globules of water will be present. The decayed wood darkens in colour, becomes lighter in weight and will crumble when rubbed between the fingers.

In advanced cases, a fruiting body or pancake will appear; it will begin as a pale grey colour, white around the edges, with the centre portion corrugated. Later a covering of rusted spore dust will appear, accompanied by a strong mushroom smell.

The dry rot fungus has an ability to produce pencil thick water-carrying roots which transport the disease to dry wood elsewhere. Simply cutting out this timber will not cure it because the strands – or roots – will have reached dampened timber elsewhere and can pass over brick, stone and metal.

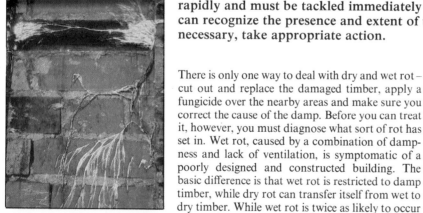

Checking for rot

Once there is an indication of dry rot, check all vulnerable parts of the house, looking for defects that allow damp to infiltrate through the roof, walls and floor. Examine the chimneys, downpipes and gutters, pointing, rendering and masonry. Check the level of soil in relation to the damp proof course and airbricks. If the house has been flooded or burst pipes have soaked timbers, be sure to check the wood has dried out.

Inside the house look for damp patches on walls, ceilings and floors. Often the problems are caused by a faulty damp proof course. By the time it becomes evident, damp patches will have penetrated structural timbers below floor level. If you suspect a defective damp proof course or blocked airbricks, it is essential to look beneath the floor. Lift the boards and look for brown discoloration of timber, cracking and 'cotton wool' or matted strands. These will reveal the extent of the problem. If fruiting bodies or rusted spore dust is present, the dry rot is of considerable maturity.

Wet rot

A number of fungi cause wet rot, which normally remains in the original area of attack although dry rot can take hold nearby. Wet rot is revealed in its early stages by discoloration around decayed wood. Look for yellowish-brown streaks or patches. Later the wood becomes lighter in weight and brownish-black in appearance. Fungal strands, thinner than those of dry rot and resembling string or twine, may grow in a fern-like shape on the surface of the timber or across damp plaster. Outdoors, a thin, olive green fungus is often seen. As wood dries, it will shrink and crack along the grain. There is sometimes cross-cracking and the individual pieces into which the wood breaks will be smaller. In severe cases, the wood becomes so brittle it crumbles between your fingers.

The difficulty in spotting wet rot is that all the damage may be taking place under what appears a sound surface – a skin of paint, for example – and will not be discovered until the skin finally collapses or is prodded with a sharp knife. Timber attacked by wet rot may also be supporting dry rot. Even wood that has dried out sufficiently to kill wet rot could still be harbouring dry rot. So always suspect the presence of dry rot.

Areas to associate strongly with wet rot are bathrooms, kitchens, the roof, cellars, fence posts, sheds and garages.

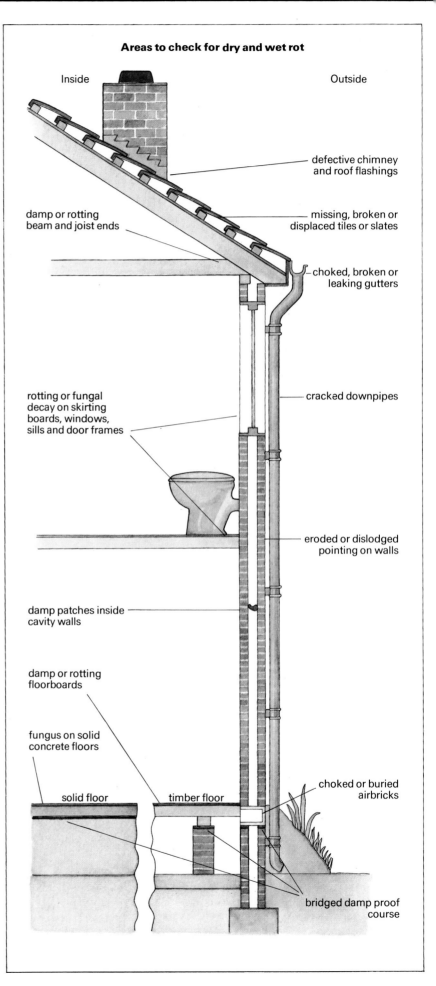

Areas to check for dry and wet rot

Inside

Outside

defective chimney and roof flashings

missing, broken or displaced tiles or slates

damp or rotting beam and joist ends

choked, broken or leaking gutters

cracked downpipes

rotting or fungal decay on skirting boards, windows, sills and door frames

eroded or dislodged pointing on walls

damp patches inside cavity walls

damp or rotting floorboards

fungus on solid concrete floors

solid floor

timber floor

choked or buried airbricks

bridged damp proof course

Treating dry and wet rot

Once you have detected wood rot (as we described previously) and have decided whether it is dry or wet rot, you must act quickly to prevent it spreading. An enormous amount of work can be involved and you will have to decide whether you have the ability and technical expertise to do it safely and efficiently or whether you need a professional.

Remember if you find evidence of rot you must regard that as being the centre of a sphere of rot and you should examine thoroughly all areas within a radius of at least 1m (or 3ft) around the discovered spot. Inspect not only timber, but also plaster, brickwork, masonry and similar materials. If you find more evidence of decay, inspect a similar size area around it and continue to do so until you have discovered the complete area of attack and

Below Clean away all traces of rot from affected areas on the wall with a wire brush

Far right Drill angled holes into the wall before inserting fluid
Right Irrigate the wall with fungicidal fluid to treat inaccessible rot

traced the structural defect causing the rot. With dry rot the defect can be a long way from the evidence of attack.

Dry rot

There are several stages involved in curing dry rot. The rotting timber has to be removed, other affec-

ted areas dealt with, surrounding areas sterilized, new timber cut in, decorations made good and the cause of the problem remedied.

Removing rot

Cut out all timber showing signs of attack for at least 1m (or 3ft) beyond the last visible evidence of fungal decay, but make sure you are not weakening the structure of the building while cutting away diseased timber. Hack away any plaster, renderings, skirtings, panellings or ceiling that have been penetrated by strands of dry rot. You must be prepared to trace the damage through or over adjacent brick, block, concrete or timber surfaces, raking out mortar joints and so on. If structural timbers – such as rafters, beams or upper floor joists – are involved, a firm of wood preservation contractors should be called in.

If the ground floor of the building is laid over an earth sub-floor and you find a covering of spore dust together with heavy growths of 'cotton wool' or matted strands, you should excavate about 100mm (4in) of soil.

In short, the entire area of concentrated dry rot attack – and beyond – must be opened up and the decayed material removed from the building by the shortest possible route. All affected timber and debris must be burned as soon as possible to prevent it being taken back into a building.

Sterilizing area

Next the affected areas should be sterilized. Using a fungicide, lightly spray all walls, partitions, sleeper walls, concrete, remaining timber and steel and pipework within a radius of 1.5m (or 5ft) from the furthest extent of suspected infection, having cleaned these areas with a wire brush and burned any dust and debris as before.

Working from the highest level downwards, apply the fungicidal fluid to all brick, block, concrete and earth surfaces until they are saturated. Refer to the manufacturer's instructions for the exact amount of fluid to use, but as a general guide apply it at a rate of 4.5 litre (1gal) to 5sq m (or 50sq ft). A coarse spray is best for this – either on a knapsack garden sprayer or a hydraulic pump.

Where dry rot strands have penetrated brickwork both sides of the wall must be treated. Using a power drill and a masonry bit, drill 13mm ($\frac{1}{2}$in) holes sloping down at 45 degrees for about 150mm (6in) at 600mm (or 2ft) staggered intervals and fill them with fluid. Irrigating the perimeter of the attacked area like this will form a 'toxic box' and any inaccessible strands inside it will die.

Replacing affected areas

Any new replacement timber must be thoroughly dry and well seasoned. Treat it with two coats of a fungicidal wood preservative (an organic solvent wood preservative or dry rot fluid complying with British Standards is ideal) and steep any sawn ends in the liquid for several minutes before fixing. If replacement timber is touching a wall, coat the wall with zinc oxychloride paint or plaster to provide an extra fungicidal barrier.

Apply two generous coats of fungicidal fluid to all timber surfaces adjacent to the area, up to 1.5m (or 5ft) from the extreme edges of cut-away timber. The second coat should be applied only when the first has been absorbed. The application rate for

timber is about 4.5 litre (1gal) to 60sq m (or 650sq ft) – but check carefully with the manufacturer's instructions. Before applying the fluid, coat any exposed rubber-covered cables with a polyurethane wood sealer to prevent the fungicide damaging the rubber.

Making good

Once the rot has been removed and new timber fitted, you can make good all decorations. Where wall plaster was hacked away, render the wall with a mix of one part cement, one part lime and six parts sand. As a precaution against further attacks you should apply a 6mm ($\frac{1}{4}$in) coat of zinc oxychloride plaster over the rendering coat to an area extending 300mm (or 12in) beyond the attacked timber. Render all surfaces adjacent to the zinc oxychloride plaster – which is now above the level of the surrounding plaster – with a further coat of the cement, lime and sand mix to level off the area.

Replace skirtings or floorboards which have been removed and repair or replace other affected areas, such as window sills or door frames.

Removing cause

You may have to repair structural defects to correct the cause of the rot. Clear blocked airbricks with an old screwdriver or insert new ones. If the damp proof course is defective or non-existent, a new one should be inserted. Always seek expert advice before attempting repairs of this nature.

Wet rot

Less drastic treatment is needed to stop the spread of wet rot. The cause of dampness must be corrected and the timber allowed to dry out. The fungus will then die off.

Treatment is in three stages. First cut out any wood that is completely rotted, protect any attacked timber that still retains adequate structural strength and, finally, treat all surrounding timber.

Work outwards from the area of badly rotting wood and test all surrounding wood with a sharp penknife until sound timber is detected. Cut out and burn all diseased timber, together with dust, dirt and debris. When replacing timber, use only well-seasoned dry wood. After cutting it to size, give it two generous coats of a proprietary rot fluid or wood preservative and immerse any end grain in the fluid for several minutes before fixing. Use wood filler for minor areas.

Treat all adjacent timbers, brick, concrete and blocks with at least two liberal coats of fluid or preservative. Ends of joists being replaced should be painted with bituminous paint (for wood) or covered with bituminous felt.

Make good any decorations in the same way as for dry rot but, if you have to replaster walls, finish them with anhydrous (wall finish) plaster.

Above Coat the ends of new timber with wood preservative for protection
Left Remove floorboards and spray the fungicidal fluid underneath

Treating damp walls internally

Various damp treatments are available for internal walls in the home; they do not cure the dampness in the wall, but they will prevent the effects of damp ruining inside decoration. Although suitable for any room, they are especially useful in cellars and basements where access for external treatment is a problem. Before carrying out treatment, always check the manufacturer's instructions carefully.

Bituminous emulsion

This rubber-rich substance adheres strongly to a smooth surface to leave a black, waterproof, elastic film. The method of treatment depends on the extent of dampness in the wall; in moderately damp conditions with reasonably sound plaster, you will first have to strip off all loose distemper, paint and dirt and repair any damaged plaster.

Before use, and occasionally during use, stir the emulsion thoroughly. Put it on with a brush, working in one direction only to give an even coating. Before starting work, dip the brush in water and shake off the moisture. When you are working it is best to immerse the bristles only halfway into the emulsion. The type of brush you should use depends on how the wall is to be finished after treatment. Where a lining paper is to be used as a base for normal decorating, you will need soft bristle brushes; where a plaster finish is required, use coconut fibre brushes. You will find you need two brushes to prevent hold-ups during the work because after five to ten minutes' use a brush should be placed in water and left to soften.

When applying the treatment, you must first dampen the affected surface with water. Put on three coats of emulsion, allowing each to dry thoroughly before applying the next. For each coat of emulsion, allow 5 litres (or 1 gal) per 11sq m (or 13sq yd). You can speed up the drying process by using a fan type electric heater. At the end of the day, suspend the brushes in creosote and next day wipe them dry and clean them off in turpentine or a proprietary equivalent.

Warning The fumes from this substance can be harmful, so make sure the room in which you are working is very well ventilated.

If the wall is very damp, a more rigorous preparation is needed. Use a cold chisel and a club hammer to hack the existing plaster back to the brickwork and spread a thin layer of cement mortar (six parts sand to one part cement and one part lime) over the brickwork. When this is dry, dampen the surface with water and apply three coats of emulsion. While the final coat is still tacky you should sand-blind it by throwing clean sharp sand at the surface with a shovel – wear protective spectacles or some other form of eye protection when carrying out this process. The sand-blinding provides a key for a plaster finish which you should apply in a layer at least 6mm ($\frac{1}{4}$in) thick.

Preparing for decoration Leave new plaster to dry out thoroughly (two to three months) before decorating, then prepare the surface to suit the kind of material you are using for decoration. For emulsion paint, allow the wall to dry then hang lining paper with heavy duty cellulose paste.

Emulsion paint can be applied direct to a plaster finish as long as the plaster is at least 6mm ($\frac{1}{4}$in) thick. You should apply a coat of plaster sealer (or a coat of emulsion thinned down with water) followed by two coats of emulsion. If you intend using oil paint, a plaster finish at least 15mm (or $\frac{5}{8}$in) thick over a sand-blinding is required. Apply two layers of plaster and allow it to dry – this can take up to six months. You can test for the degree of dryness by using a damp meter; repair the holes made by the prongs of the damp meter with cellulose filler. For wallpaper, hang lining paper horizontally over the bituminous emulsion with heavy duty cellulose paste; use the same paste to fix the wallpaper over it. For vinyl or washable paper, a 15mm (or $\frac{5}{8}$in) thick plaster surface is needed.

1a Before treating a very damp wall with bituminous emulsion, hack back the plaster to the brickwork and apply a thin layer of cement mortar
1b After dampening the mortar with water, brush on three coats of emulsion, working in one direction only; leave each coat to dry before applying the next

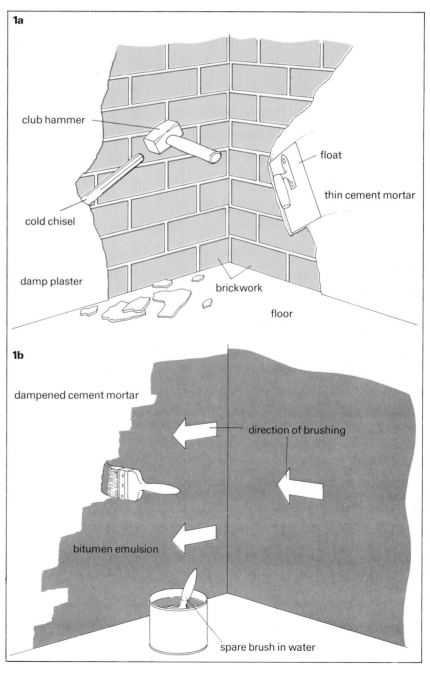

1a
club hammer
cold chisel
damp plaster
float
thin cement mortar
brickwork
floor

1b
dampened cement mortar
direction of brushing
bitumen emulsion
spare brush in water

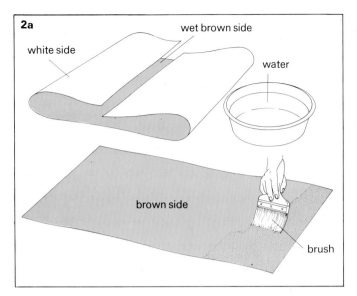

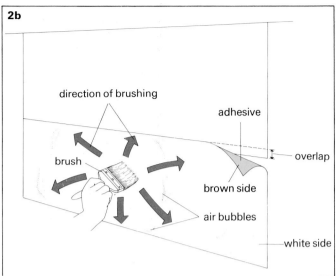

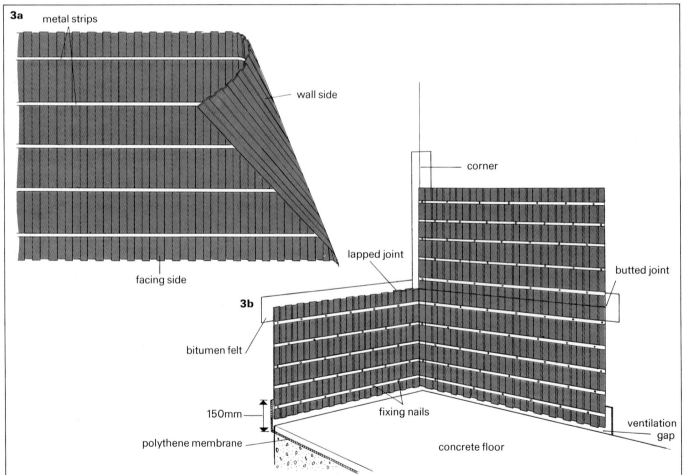

Waterproof laminate

This material comes with a special adhesive and produces a long-lasting barrier which stops both damp penetration and the appearance of efflorescent salts. It will adhere to moist surfaces.

Remove existing loose wallpaper, paint or distemper, repair damaged plaster, sand down any high spots in the wall and remove the skirting boards. Brush on a diluted coat of adhesive to prime the wall and allow this to dry for an hour. The laminate is hung in horizontal lengths, allowing a little excess for trimming. It has a white and a brown side; brush water onto the brown side of each length and fold the ends loosely to the middle with the brown surface inside. Wait an hour, then brush adhesive onto the wall to cover an area to be occupied by one length of laminate; hang the laminate immediately with the brown surface against the wall. Brush outwards over it to remove air bubbles. Even after this there may be a slightly bubbly appearance, but this will disappear in time. Hang successive lengths of laminate so the edges overlap each preceding length by 13mm ($\frac{1}{2}$in). Use a sharp knife to trim off excess laminate at the wall sides and allow 24 hours before carrying out decoration and refitting skirting boards.

2a Dampen waterproof laminate, fold it loosely and leave it for an hour
2b When hanging, place the lengths of laminate horizontally on the walls
3a With corrugated pitch-impregnated fibre base make sure the metal strips face into the room
3b When fixing to the wall, butt horizontal joints and lap vertical ones

Pitch-impregnated fibre base

Any condition of damp wall can be treated using this material. since it forms an entirely new wall surface. It is available in 5 × 1m (or 16ft 6m × 3ft 3in) rolls and is corrugated with a dovetail key to provide for plaster on one side and insulating cavities on the other.

Remove the skirting and any cove and use a cold chisel and club hammer to hack damp plaster back to the brickwork of the wall and for about 1m (or 3ft) along adjoining party or partition walls in case damp has crept into these walls as well. Using a sharp knife, cut the rolls into lengths according to the width of bare wall. You may have to trim the width of the final strip of material to fit the remaining gap at the top of the wall; where there is a solid floor, the material should stop 25–50mm (1–2in) above floor level. (This provides ventilation and the gap can be covered by skirting later). On a suspended timber floor the material should be laid between the wall and the floorboards.

Place each length in position against the wall with the corrugations vertical and the metal strips facing into the room. Nail through the corrugations at intervals of 200–300mm (or 8–12in) with galvanized clout nails or hardened masonry nails, depending on the wall surface. Alternatively, on a very hard surface, use a cartridge gun (available on hire) to shoot nails through special rectangular washers which fix into the corrugations. Any polythene damp proof membrane on a newly screeded floor should rise 150mm (6in) on to the wall and be placed behind the material.

The material is flexible and therefore can be bent round corners. Try to avoid joining lengths at corners; if this is unavoidable, place a 100mm (4in) wide strip of bitumen felt behind the joint as reinforcement to prevent the plaster finish (which is later applied over the material) being pushed through to contact the damp wall. Vertical joints must be lapped, while horizontal joints are butted up and lined with 100mm (4in) wide strips of bitumen felt. If the material has to be cut to fit round pipework, the gaps should be sealed with waterproof mastic.

When the wall is fully lined a normal three-coat plastering can be applied. If necessary, you can use a render and setting coat to leave a joint flush with any existing plaster or adjacent areas. Drying out will take longer than usual, since the damp treatment material does not absorb water; so make sure of good ventilation to speed up the process.

Alternatively you can use panel boards to finish over the material. The boards can be nailed through into the wall or fixed by applying blobs of special adhesive at 350–450mm (or 14–18in) intervals to the back of the board. This adhesive can be obtained with the damp-treatment material; a 5kg (or 10lb) tub of adhesive is sufficient for 12sq m (or 18sq yd). Rest the boards on a level 50 × 25mm (2 × 1in) timber plinth to ensure a neat joint between boards and to give the required air circulation gap at the base.

The adhesive will set in two or three days and temporary support can be provided with one or two hardened fixing pins in the middle of the panel. These can be removed or driven home later. Use brown paper tape, masking tape or cellulose filler to seal the joints between boards. You can, if you wish, apply a skim coat of plaster over plasterboard panels. Wallpaper or lining paper and emulsion paint can also be applied to the boards.

Finally replace the skirting, having checked there are no signs of rot or decay, and cover the gap between the top of the lining material and the ceiling with cove. Fix the cove to the wall and flush with the top of the lining, or to the ceiling, leaving a slight gap between the cove and the wall to provide ventilation.

Levelling wall Sometimes it may be necessary to level an uneven wall before applying the damp treatment material. You can do this by lining the wall with battens – before fixing, treat these with a wood preservative. Use a spirit level to find true horizontals and fill any low areas behind the battens with timber packing.

Arrange the battens so all the edges of the damp treatment material will be supported – one or two intermediate horizontal batten supports should also be provided. Space the battens at approximately 330mm (or 13in) intervals and place the corrugations of the material at right-angles to the battens.

3c Fix panels over the fibre base with adhesive, using timber plinths to ensure the panels are held level and to provide a ventilation gap; remove the plinths when the adhesive has set

3d On an uneven wall you will need to fix a series of battens to ensure flush fixing of the fibre base. Pack any lower areas behind the battens with pieces of scrap wood

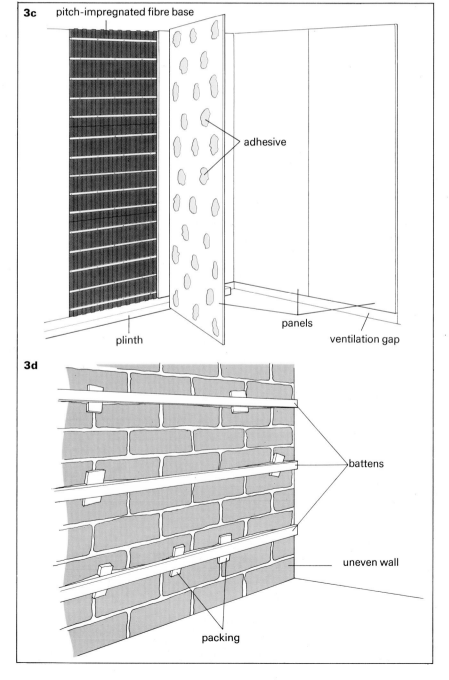

3c pitch-impregnated fibre base

adhesive

panels

ventilation gap

plinth

3d

battens

uneven wall

packing

Installing a damp-proof course

Rising damp is indicated by a tide mark just above floor level on internal walls. It does not usually rise more than about 1m (or 3ft) up the wall. Its presence means either there is no damp proof course (dpc), which is common in houses built before 1875, or that an existing dpc has failed. A dpc that is not functioning should be regarded as non-existent.

Most methods of installing a dpc should be employed only by specialists. A method which you can use yourself, however, is the infusion into a wall of a special dampcoursing solution which gels within the wall and creates a continuous chemical barrier to prevent rising damp. The system is widely used by specialists, but you should be able to achieve equally good results provided you are very thorough. If the job is skimped, the dpc will break down in places and the rising damp will return. One specialist company provides detailed working sheets and a technical advisory service.

When selecting a DIY damp proofing process, check the company supplying the materials and instructions offers a guarantee which would be acceptable for mortgage purposes.

Warning The infusion system cannot be used for walls of more than 450mm (18in) thickness, or walls constructed of materials other than brick or soft sandstone.

Inserting the dpc

The job involves three processes: drilling the holes at a selected level, carrying out a preliminary run with water to test for damaged brickwork and the infusion of the fluid.

Selecting position The level at which the dpc is to be inserted depends on whether the ground floor of the house is of suspended timber construction or solid concrete. If it is a timber floor, the dpc should be immediately below the floor level; with a concrete floor it should be adjacent to the floor.

If it is impracticable to insert a dpc below a suspended timber floor – for example, where there is a patio – it will have to be inserted at floor level. In such a case, spray the floor joists and floorboards liberally with a good timber preservative to prevent attack by rot.

Where a house is on sloping ground, step the dpc to follow the line of the ground floor. In a semi-basement install the dpc above ground level to a height of about 150mm (6in). Internal rendering, carried out after insertion of the dpc, will prevent damp rising above this level.

Drilling Use a lightweight rotary hammer drill, obtainable from a hire shop, and fit it with a 16 mm ($\frac{5}{8}$in) diameter drill bit. The length of the bit needed will depend on the depth of the holes to be drilled, which in turn will depend on the thickness of the wall. Fix a piece of adhesive tape to the drill bit at the required depth to guide you.

In all cases holes should be drilled at an angle of 30 degrees downwards from the outside face of the brickwork and at 75mm (3in) intervals horizontally; start drilling just above a mortar joint. If working from one side only, use the side most accessible and convenient. Remove the skirting board before drilling on the internal wall. If you are drilling through a party wall, let your

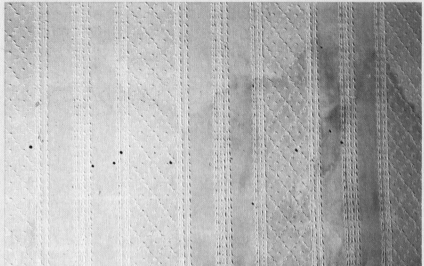

neighbours know what you are doing.

For 112.5mm ($4\frac{1}{2}$in) brickwork Drill to a depth of 100mm (4in), working from one side only.

For 225mm (9in) brickwork Drill to a depth of 200mm (8in), working from one side only.

For 337.5mm ($13\frac{1}{2}$in) brickwork Treat as for 225mm (9in) brickwork up to a depth of 330mm (13in). You may treat 337.5mm ($13\frac{1}{2}$in) brickwork from both sides if wished. In this case, drill 200mm (8in) holes one side and 100mm (4in) holes the other side.

For 450mm (18in) brickwork Treat from both sides, drilling 200mm (8in) deep holes.

For 275mm (11in) cavity brickwork Drill 100mm (4in) deep holes from both sides.

Water test If you inserted damp course liquid into a wall which was cracked or otherwise damaged, it would seep out of the cracks and be wasted. To prevent this, make a trial run with water to find out if there is any damage. Fill each hole to the brim, using a funnel. If the water disappears quickly, this indicates there are cracks. Fill the holes with a mix of two parts sand and one part cement to seal the cracks, ramming the mortar

Top The existence of damp in walls can easily be identified by the presence of mould growth

Above Rising damp will be detected inside the house when wall coverings become stained and start to peel away from the wall

1a If you are treating a wall behind which there is a suspended timber floor, the new dpc should be immediately below floor level

1b If you are working where there is a solid floor, make sure your new dpc is installed at the same level as that of the floor

1c If the area you are tackling includes floors of different levels, you will have to step the new dpc between the levels

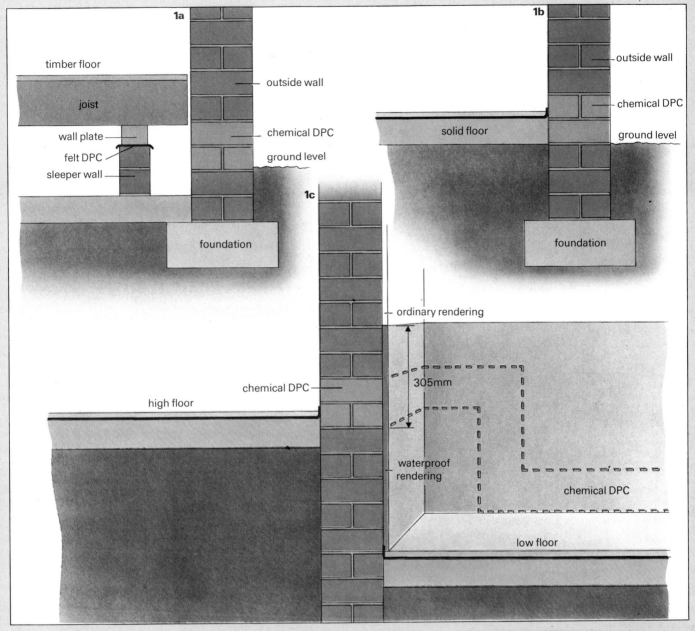

1a timber floor · joist · wall plate · felt DPC · sleeper wall · outside wall · chemical DPC · ground level · foundation

1b outside wall · chemical DPC · ground level · solid floor · foundation

1c ordinary rendering · 305mm · waterproof rendering · chemical DPC · high floor · chemical DPC · low floor

firmly into the holes with a length of dowel the same diameter as the holes; let the mortar dry before redrilling the holes in the same places.

Walls vary in porosity, so use the trial run to assess the absorption rate. This will enable you to judge how many holes you can fill at a time when you use the fluid.

Introducing the fluid Don't introduce the damp-proofing solution until at least six hours after the water test. You can hire special irrigation bottles for pouring in the fluid or use a jug and offset funnel. As a guide to the amount of fluid needed, a hole drilled in a 225mm (9in) wall will take about 190ml ($\frac{1}{3}$pt), which is about the same as filling each hole four and a half times. So use a jug holding 570ml (1pt) and allocate one jugful to three consecutive holes.

It is important not to allow a hole to empty or the liquid will start to cure at the mouth of the hole and prevent further saturation. If the absorption is particularly speedy, do not tackle too many holes at a time.

Fill the first three holes to the brim and keep the remaining liquid for topping up, doing this

progressively and methodically until all the holes have been filled.

Leave the holes for a few weeks while the solution is drying out. Then fill with a mix of three parts sand to one part cement.

Finishing treatment

When the dpc has been installed, rising damp will cease but there will still be dampness in the walls due to the action of hygroscopic (moisture absorbent) salts, general condensation or water penetration. The finishing process stops the damp and eliminates the effects.

First remove the skirting boards so the walls can be treated down to skirting level. Where dampness has existed for a few years, hack off the plaster to bare brick; work to a point about 450mm (18in) above the highest damp patch.

Porous brickwork Where the brickwork is porous, you need to treat it to prevent water penetration. Before treating it, cut out and replace any damaged bricks and repoint defective mortar joints. Then brush or spray on two coats of a silicone-based waterproofer and sealer to the outside wall.

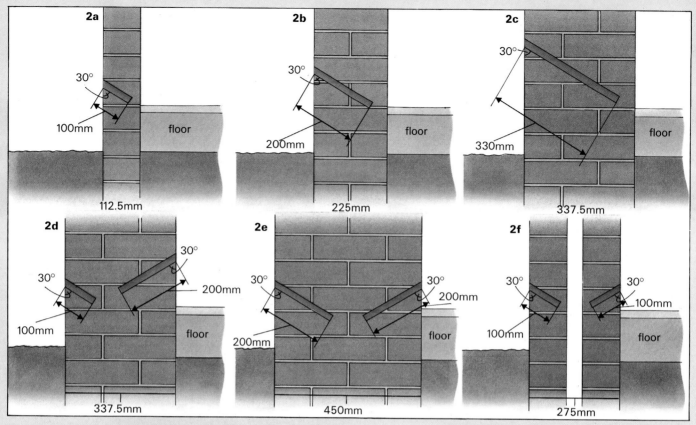

2a–f Drilling positions for different wall thicknesses. **3** Before adding damp proof liquid, pour water into the drilled holes **4** If it disappears quickly, seal the holes with mortar, ram down with dowel and redrill

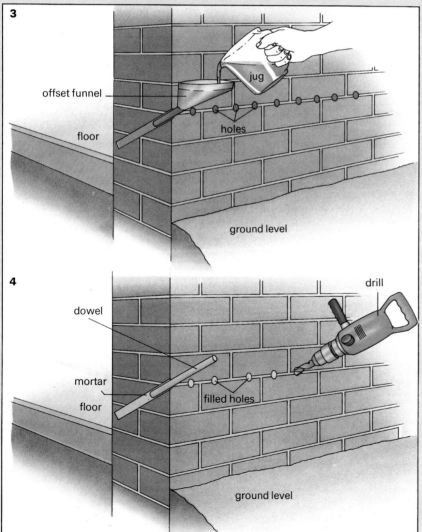

Removing mineral salts Rising damp will dissolve some mineral salts from the brickwork, which will diffuse through the wall and plasterwork in damp conditions and, on drying out on the surface, will show as a whitish chalky substance (efflorescence). These salts are hygroscopic (moisture absorbent) and if sufficient water is absorbed, they will dissolve in it forming condensation.

Use a chemical neutralizer to treat the affected area. Apply the solution to the brickwork with a 100mm (4in) paint brush. Work quickly and make sure you treat all areas where hygroscopic salt and efflorescent action was evident on the plaster. The solution penetrates up to 150mm (6in) into the brickwork and forms a barrier to the soluble salts while the wall is drying out.

Rendering After at least 48 hours, render with a sand and cement mix (eight parts sand to one part cement) containing an integral waterproofer diluted with ten parts water. Add a mortar plasticizer to make the mix more workable. Apply the render at least 10mm ($\frac{3}{8}$in) thick and finish with a lightweight plaster skim. Leave a gap of at least 38mm ($1\frac{1}{2}$in) between the render and plaster and the floor; the gap will be concealed when you replace the skirting.

Where a high ground level was involved (for example, a semi-basement) and the dpc was installed 150mm (6in) above ground level, a slightly different treatment is required at the base of the wall. From a point 300mm (or 12in) above ground level down to floor level apply three coats of rendering. When refixing the skirting, use impact adhesive so there is no danger of the rendering being punctured by nails.

Repointing bricks

Good quality brickwork is generally a maintenance-free structural material; but as a building ages the exposed surfaces of the mortar joints may show signs of decay and need repointing. There are a number of reasons why this may happen.

Poor mix The original mortar mix may have been of incorrect proportions.

Moisture Driving rains, a faulty damp proof course or leaking gutters and downpipes may have allowed water to penetrate the mortar.

Frosts Any moisture in the mortar or bricks will freeze, expand and break up the surface if subjected to heavy frosts.

Pollution In heavy industrial areas, sulphates in the atmosphere will cause deterioration.

Structural movement Inadequate foundations or a poor standard of building will break up the stability of the mortar.

Where the cause of mortar failure can be diagnosed, it should be remedied, if possible, before repointing, which itself should not be carried out during cold weather because of the possibility of frost affecting the new mortar before it has dried. If winter working is unavoidable, you must use plenty of waterproof sheeting to keep off icy winds, rain and frosts.

1 Raking out old mortar. **2** Repointing tools: cold chisel for removing old mortar **(top)**; plugging chisel, with groove same width as mortar, ideal for raking out **(centre)**; frenchman made by bending end of old kitchen knife **(bottom)**

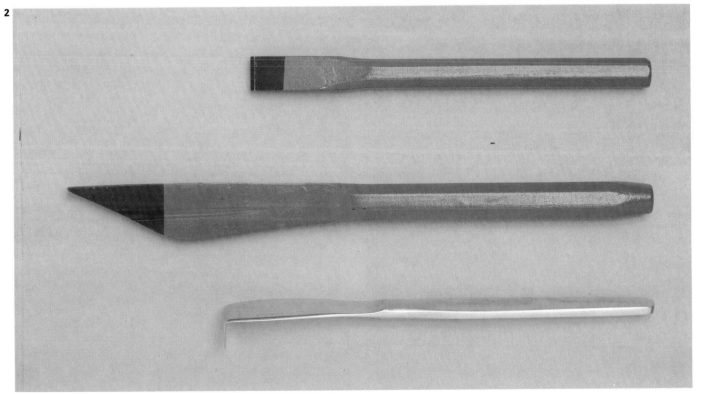

How to repoint

You should always start repointing at the top of the brickwork and work downwards, covering about two square metres (21sq ft) at a time. Scrape any moss or lichen from the surface and then rake out mortar joints to a depth of about 15mm (or ½in), taking care not to damage the brickwork. The recess must be left square (otherwise the mortar may fall out); this can be done with a cold chisel or with a tool you make yourself by filing one end of a square section length of steel. After raking out, ensure the brick edges are free from old mortar and brush out all traces of dust with a fibre bristle brush.

Dry brickwork should be dampened, not soaked, with clean water before repointing; this is important in hot weather when bricks store heat. Water will reduce any suction from the old mortar and brickwork, but too much on the surface could cause the freshly applied mortar to run down the face of the bricks. An old distemper brush is ideal for dampening.

What mix to use

The mortar should be chosen carefully to suit the existing brickwork and the amount of exposure it is likely to undergo. A general mix, suitable for most brickwork, consists of one part cement, one part lime and six parts of washed builder's sand. For a soft facing brick a mix of one part cement, two parts lime and nine parts sand would be satisfactory. Where hard, dense bricks are used in situations of extreme exposure a mix of one part cement, a quarter part lime and three parts sand should be used. This richer cement mix is more likely to

3 Brushing away dust after raking out mortar. **4** Dampening brickwork with distemper brush. **5** Applying mortar with pointing trowel. **6** Forming weathered joint with frenchman and timber straight-edge. **7** Mortar levelled with face of bricks above and below. **8** Making rounded or tooled joint. **9** Forming recessed joint with square timber

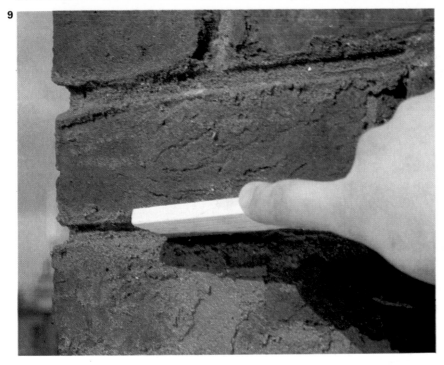

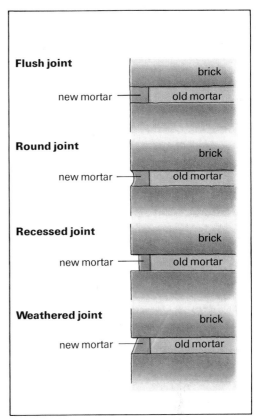

Flush joint	
new mortar	brick
	old mortar

Round joint	
new mortar	brick
	old mortar

Recessed joint	
new mortar	brick
	old mortar

Weathered joint	
new mortar	brick
	old mortar

shrink and there is a possibility of hairline cracks forming between the bricks and mortar.

As each batch is used, the joints already filled should be tooled or cut and loose material brushed away. When the colour of mortar is important, a ready-mixed coloured mix should be used to maintain consistency.

Warning Make small amounts of mortar at a time and discard it as soon as it begins to dry.

Types of pointing

Different pointing effects can be employed, depending on the type of brickwork and the style of joint used when the house was built.

Weathered The most effective way of shedding rain away from the bricks. Apply the mortar firmly with a small pointing trowel. Push the blade edge at the top of the joint to form a slight recess that slopes forward to meet the top edge of the brick below. You can form this angle using a straight-edge with the edge of the trowel or use a small tool called a 'frenchman' together with the straight-edge; this tool can easily be made by bending the end of a long thin kitchen knife.

Flush Usually employed when matching old brickwork, it is formed by applying the new mortar level with the face of the bricks above and below.

Round or tooled joint A variation on a flush joint, it is also used mainly when matching old brickwork. First form the flush joint and then run a thin rounded piece of timber along the mortar face.

Recessed joint Used solely when matching existing recessed joints in brickwork. After forming a flush joint, the recess is raked back by using a square section piece of timber of the exact width of the mortar joint.

Having finished pointing, remember to remove carefully any remaining deposits of mortar from the face of the brickwork – before the mortar is thoroughly dry – with a fibre bristle brush.

Types of roof tile

Before attempting repairs to a tiled roof, you need to know what sort of tiles have been used and how they are laid out on the roof. Tiles are made of either clay or concrete, with a variety of designs to choose from.

Types of concrete tile: **1** Bonnet hip; **2** Valley; **3** 90 degree angle — right; **4** 90 degree angle — left; **5** Baby ridge; **6** Ridge; **7** Tile-and-a-half tiles; **8** Plain tiles; **9 & 10** Plain tiles with arrowhead and bullnose; **11** Modern interlocking; **12** Bold roll interlocking; **13** Wessex interlocking; **14** Plastic rooflight; **15** Ludlow Major interlocking; **16** Mendip interlocking **Opposite page 1** English pantiles. **2** Single Roman. **3** Double Roman. **4** Spanish. **5** Italian. **6** Interlocking Somerset. **7** Interlocking concrete. **8** Interlocking vertical joint concrete. **9** Monopitch ridge. **10** Rooflight

There are specially shaped tiles designed for use on specific areas of the roof, but there are basically two types of roofing tile – double lap (or plain), and single lap.

Double lap tiles

Double lap, or plain, tiles are slightly curved with two holes for fixing nails and usually two nibs, or projections, on the underside at the top edge; some tiles, however, are continuously nibbed along the top edge. The tiles are normally fixed to battens with aluminium alloy nails and the nibs hook over the battens for extra security. The camber, or curve, to each tile provides air spaces between tiles and battens for ventilation and to prevent water ingress by capillary action.

Once made by hand, plain tiles are now mainly machine-made from clay or concrete. Many clay tiles are smooth-faced, although they are also available with a sand face. Concrete tiles are becoming increasingly popular because they are slightly cheaper than many clay tiles; they are also not so likely to laminate (or flake) and are available in a wide range of colours, including brown, red, grey, green and buff. In some cases the colour is confined to the granule facing, although often the tiles are coloured throughout. Because there are many types, sizes and colours of plain tiles, take a sample as a pattern when ordering replacements to make sure you get the right ones.

In plain tiling, the tiles hook over roofing battens so each course overlaps the tiles in the course-but-one below it; this amount of overlap (called the lap) should not be less than 65mm (2½in). Tiles in each course are butted together side by side and do not overlap. In this way there are at least two thicknesses of tile in every part of the roof – and three thicknesses in most places.

The usual size of plain tiles is 265 × 165mm (10½ × 6½in), although some hand-made tiles are 280 × 178mm (11 × 7in). In addition there are special tiles to maintain the lap and weatherproof the roof at the verge (the side of the roof), eaves (gutter level) and ridge (the apex of the roof).

Verge tiles   At the verges special tile-and-a-half tiles, usually 265 × 248mm (10½ × 9¾in), are used in alternate courses. These tiles are normally bedded on an undercloak of plain tiles, laid face downwards and projecting 38–50mm (1½–2in) over the gable walls or bargeboards. Sometimes the verge is finished with a clip-on plastic verge channel which holds the end tiles firmly and stops water penetration.

Eaves tiles   These usually measure 190 × 165mm (7½ × 6½in) and are used as an undercourse at the eaves and as a top course just below the ridge tiles.

Ridge tiles   Half-round ridge tiles, bedded with mortar along their edges and at the joints between tiles, are used to weatherproof the ridge. Hog back, segmental (or third-round) and angle ridge tiles are also used. It is most important the bedding mortar is placed only along the edges and joints between the ridge tiles, since cracking can occur if the ridge tiles are filled with bedding mortar.

Hip tiles   There are several ways in which hips (the junction of two sides of the roof) may be finished. It is common to use third-round ridge tiles bedded on mortar in a similar fashion to the way a ridge is formed. Because third-round tiles are not secured by nailing, a galvanized hip iron is screwed to the foot of the hip rafter before the hip tiles are laid to give them support.

Hip irons are not necessary when bonnet hip or angular hip tiles are used. These are nailed to the hip rafter and are bedded on mortar at the tail; they should be fitted so they lie snugly against the plain tiling at each side.

Valley tiles   In plain tiling, valleys are often formed with purpose-made valley tiles of similar colour and texture to the main roof tiles. Valley tiles butt against plain tiles on each side and are usually fixed by nailing or bedding in mortar.

Single lap tiles

Single lap tiles are designed to overlap, or be overlapped by, adjacent tiles in the same course and in the course above and below. In most parts of the roof there is only a single thickness of tile – except at overlaps, when there is a double thickness.

Clay single lap tiles have been in use for many years, but are being replaced by interlocking concrete tiles which are cheaper. Although some clay patterns are still made, it may be difficult to buy replacements; if they are not stocked by your local builders' merchant, try specialist roofing contractors or local demolition firms – but ensure second hand tiles are not flaking or cracking.

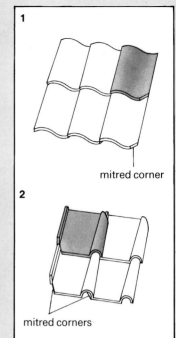

1

mitred corner

2

mitred corners

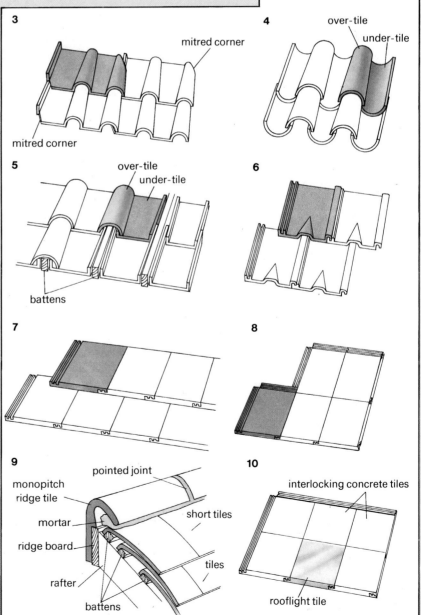

3   mitred corner

mitred corner

4   over-tile

under-tile

5   over-tile

under-tile

battens

6

7

8

9   pointed joint

monopitch
ridge tile

mortar

ridge board

rafter

battens

short tiles

tiles

10   interlocking concrete tiles

rooflight tile

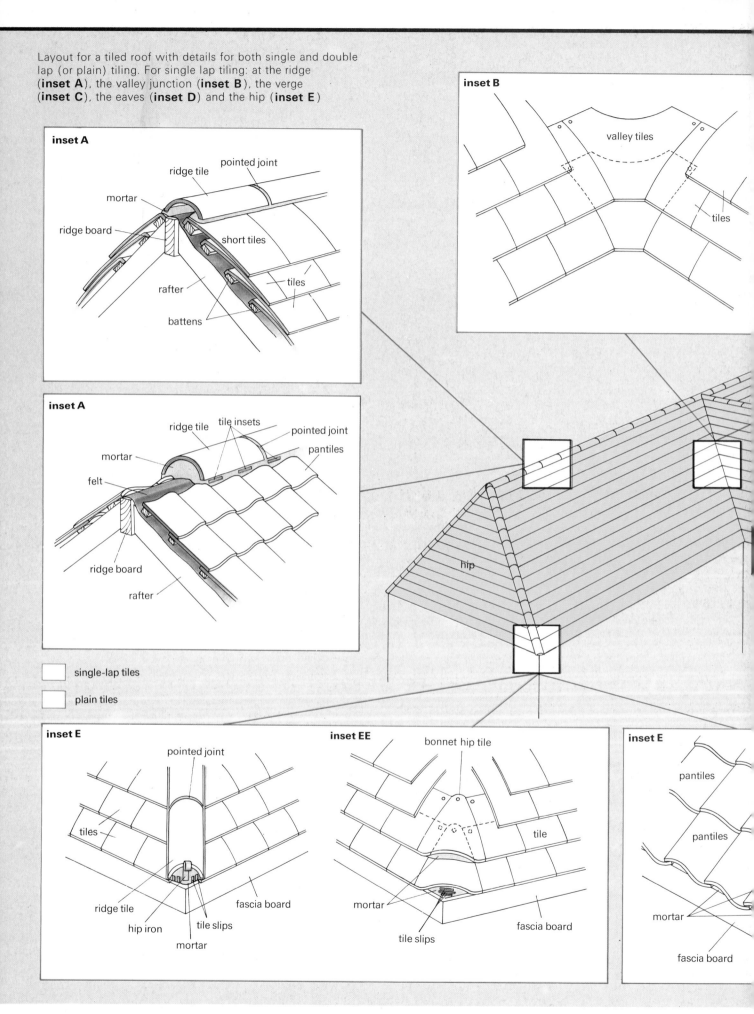

Layout for a tiled roof with details for both single and double lap (or plain) tiling. For single lap tiling: at the ridge (**inset A**), the valley junction (**inset B**), the verge (**inset C**), the eaves (**inset D**) and the hip (**inset E**)

inset B

valley tiles

tiles

inset A

pointed joint

ridge tile

mortar

ridge board

short tiles

rafter

battens

tiles

inset A

ridge tile

tile insets

pointed joint

mortar

pantiles

felt

ridge board

rafter

single-lap tiles

plain tiles

hip

inset E

pointed joint

tiles

ridge tile

hip iron

tile slips

mortar

fascia board

inset EE

bonnet hip tile

tile

mortar

tile slips

fascia board

inset E

pantiles

pantiles

mortar

fascia board

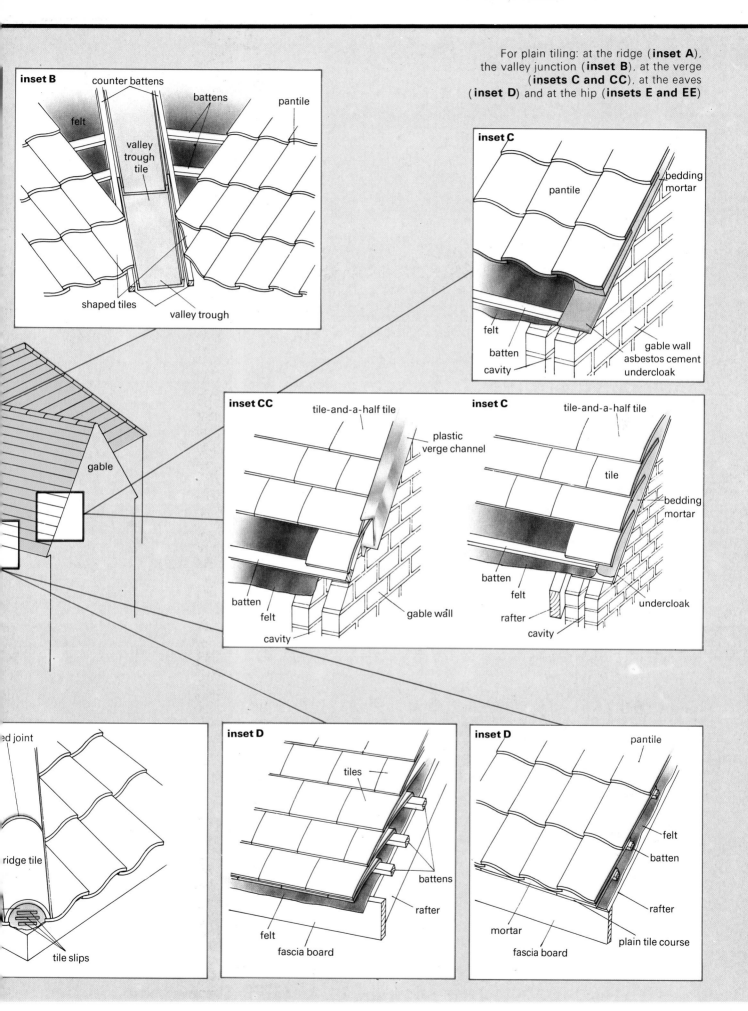

For plain tiling: at the ridge (**inset A**),
the valley junction (**inset B**), at the verge
(**insets C and CC**), at the eaves
(**inset D**) and at the hip (**insets E and EE**)

inset B

counter battens

battens

pantile

felt

valley
trough
tile

shaped tiles

valley trough

gable

inset C

pantile

bedding
mortar

felt

batten

cavity

gable wall
asbestos cement
undercloak

inset CC

tile-and-a-half tile

plastic
verge channel

batten

felt

cavity

gable wall

inset C

tile-and-a-half tile

tile

bedding
mortar

batten

felt

rafter

cavity

undercloak

...ed joint

ridge tile

tile slips

inset D

tiles

battens

felt

fascia board

rafter

inset D

pantile

felt

batten

rafter

mortar

fascia board

plain tile course

A selection of some of the many types of clay tile available; it should help you to recognize the tiles on your roof. Try builders' merchants for replacements; they should be able to order tiles for you if they do not have them in stock

1 Hawkins half-round ridge
2 Dreadnought half-round ridge
3 Half-round baby ridge
4 Pascall roll ridge
5 Hawkins machine-made tile-and-a-half
6 Rosemary machine-made tile-and-a-half
7 Dreadnought hand-made tile-and-a-half
8 Keymer hand-made tile-and-a-half
9 Keymer 265 × 165mm hand-made and sand-faced
10 Dreadnought 280 × 178mm hand-made
11 Hawkins 265 × 165mm machine-made, sand-faced
12 Keymer hand-made eaves
13 Dreadnought hand-made eaves
14 Angle ridge
15 Round ridge
16 Hawkins machine-made valley
17 Rosemary machine-made valley
18 Dreadnought hand-made valley
19 Six patterns of interlocking tiles, glazed and unglazed
20 Dreadnought machine-made bonnet hip
21 Rosemary machine-made bonnet hip
22 Rosemary machine-made arris hip
23 Rosemary machine-made 90 degree angle

A commonly found single lap tile is the English pantile; you can also buy interlocking clay pantiles which are available in a range of colours and with a glazed or matt finish. In some situations only alternate pantiles are nailed to the roofing battens but, if you have to replace this type of tile, it is a good idea to fix each one with rustless aluminium alloy nails (you may have to drill fixing holes at the top of the tiles using a masonry drill bit).

Other common single lap clay tiles are double and single Roman tiles, interlocking Somerset tiles, Spanish tiles which have concave under-tiles, and Italian tiles which have flat under-tiles.

Interlocking concrete tiles are available in a wide range of designs and colours and in smooth and granule finishes. Some have an acrylic finish which gives the roof a lustre as well as promoting rainflow off the roof and inhibiting the growth of fungi and moss. Concrete tiles imitate many of the clay tile designs and some are patterned to look like roofing slates.

Some single lap tiles have interlocking head and tail joints as well as interlocking side joints; this enables them to be used on roofs with very low pitches (or slopes) – down to 15 degrees in some cases. (Compare this with the minimum pitch for a plain roof tile which is 35 degrees.)

Fittings Fittings for use with interlocking concrete tiles include angle, half-round and third-round ridge tiles, as well as monopitch ridge tiles for monopitch roofs.

Rooflight tiles To give light in the roof space, rooflight tiles made from translucent reinforced plastic are available in the contours of the single lap roof tile patterns.

Valley trough tiles Valleys can be formed with special valley trough tiles, with adjacent tiles neatly cut and bedded on mortar.

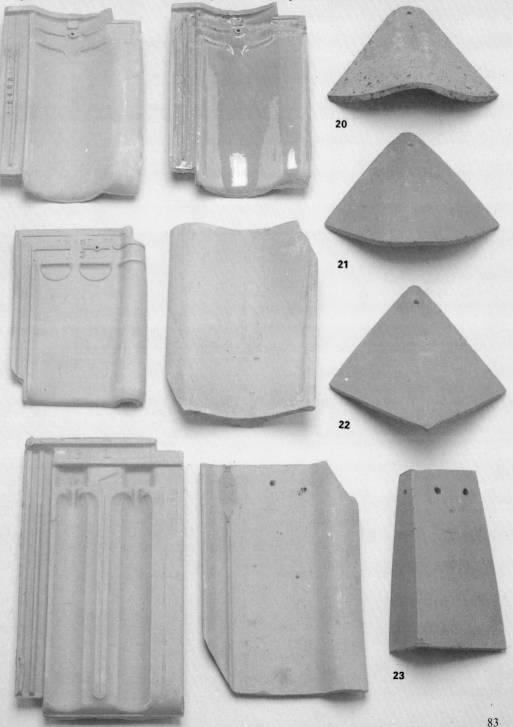

19

20

21

22

23

Repairing a tiled roof

While most roof repair jobs are easy and straight-forward, difficulties arise because the work has to be done at height; this may well deter some people from tackling them. Make safety the number one priority: whenever possible use a scaffold tower to reach the roof and to give a working platform at gutter level; always use roof crawling boards to enable you to climb on the roof.

Double lap (plain) tiles Any remaining parts of broken or crumbling plain tiles must be removed before new tiles can be fitted. To release the tile-holding nibs from the roofing battens, use small pieces of timber to lift up the tiles in the course above the tiles to be replaced; then lift the broken tile over the batten with a bricklayer's trowel. If the tile is held by nails, it may be possible to work it loose by moving the tile from side to side while prising up the tile with the tip of a trowel. Should this method fail, use a slate ripper to cut the heads off the nails; hook the blade of the ripper round the nail and pull to cut through it. Normally only the tiles in every fourth course are nailed, but in particularly exposed positions all the tiles may be nailed to prevent them being lifted by the wind.

Fit the replacement tile under the tiles in the row above, pushing it upwards until the nibs hook over the batten. Again, a trowel under the tile will help you to position it accurately. A tile without nibs can be held in place with a gap-filling adhesive applied from a special gun.

Single lap tiles These are fairly easily displaced, so where possible fix each tile with one or two 32mm (1¼in) aluminium alloy nails into the roofing batten or secure the tile with a clip nailed onto the batten, where this system is used on your roof.

Clay pantiles This type is often simply hung on battens. If they become dislodged, it is best to drill holes at the top of the tiles, using a masonry drill bit, and refix them with aluminium alloy nails.

Ridge tiles If the joints between ridge tiles have cracked but the tiles themselves are still firmly bedded, you can repair the joints with beads of non-hardening mastic applied with a mastic gun, or with thick bitumen mastic trowelled into the joints.

Loose ridge tiles must be lifted and rebedded on a mortar mix of one part Portland cement to four parts sharp, washed sand. Soak the tiles in water and place the mortar along the edges of the tiles

Above Replacing ridge tiles on a roof: always handle the tiles with care and remember they are much heavier than they look

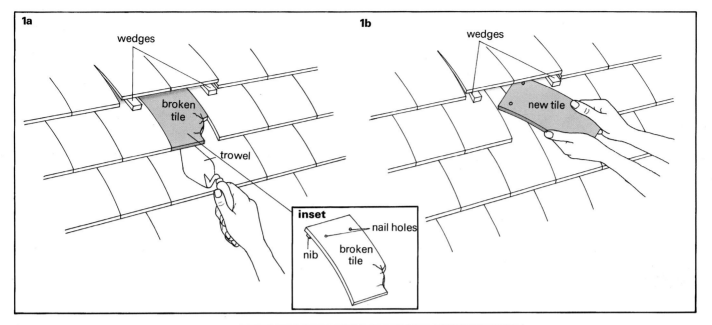

1a

wedges

broken tile

trowel

inset

nail holes

nib

broken tile

1b

wedges

new tile

2

batten

felt

nib

tile clip

interlocking concrete tiles

rafter

nib

tile clip

batten

inset

clip

tile

batten fixing nail

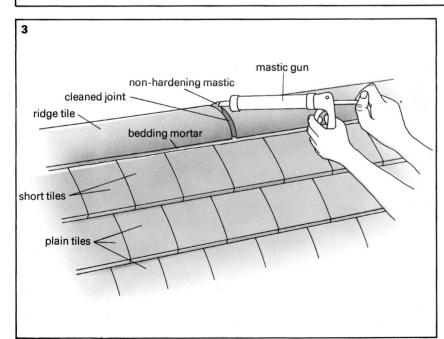

3

mastic gun

non-hardening mastic

cleaned joint

ridge tile

bedding mortar

short tiles

plain tiles

1a To remove a damaged tile, use timber wedges to raise the tiles in the row above and lift the tile with a trowel until the holding nibs are clear of the roofing batten

1b Fit the replacement tile under the tiles in the row above, pushing it up until the nibs hook over the roofing batten

2 Some single lap interlocking tiles are held in place with clips; the clip hooks over the tile and is nailed to the batten (**inset**)

3 To repair cracked joints between ridge tiles, rake out the old mortar and replace it with beads of non-hardening mastic applied from a mastic gun

and at the joints. It is important not to fill the tiles completely with mortar because the cavity allows air to circulate under the tiles, helping them to dry out quickly after rainfall and reducing cracking.

To close the cavity at each end of the ridge, use flat pieces of tile (called tile slips) set in mortar – any pieces of scrap tile will serve this purpose.

Hip tiles These are usually bedded on mortar in the same way as ridge tiles; repairs are the same as for ridge tiles except hips are usually prevented from slipping down the roof by a hip iron. If this has corroded, it should be replaced; new galvanized hip irons are obtainable from builders' merchants. Carefully lift the hip tile adjacent to the hip iron, remove the old bedding mortar and the remains of the hip iron. Screw the new iron to the foot of the hip rafter using rustproof screws and rebed the hip tiles on cement mortar, filling the open end with small pieces of tile set in mortar.

Bonnet hip tiles are fixed at the top with aluminium alloy nails, while the tail (exposed part) is bedded on cement mortar. If only one bonnet hip tile has to be replaced, it may be possible to fix it without disturbing the other hip tiles by using a

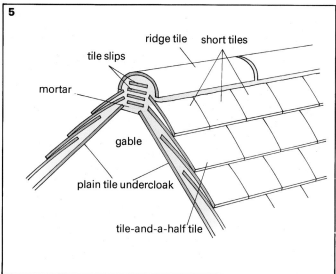

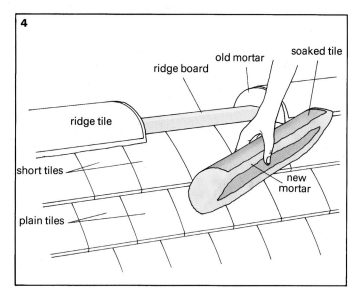

mortar mix of one part fine sand to one part cement. If you cannot do this, you will have to strip off all the tiles and renail them, working from the eaves towards the ridge.

Verge and eaves tiles The tiles on a verge are usually nailed and bedded on mortar; eaves tiles are sometimes similarly bedded, but modern practice is simply to nail them. Cracks can usually be filled with mastic, as described for ridge tiles; where damage is more severe, the tiles can be repointed with a mix of one part cement and four parts sand.

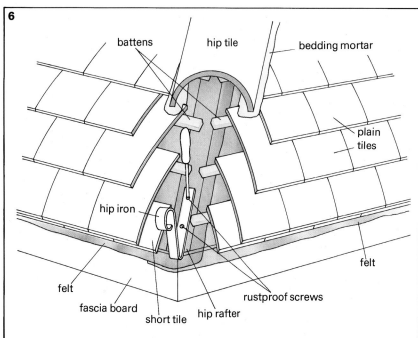

4 When replacing a ridge tile, soak it with water and apply mortar along the edges and at the joints. **5** Set tile slips in mortar to close the cavity at the end of a ridge. **6** You will have to lift the first hip tile to gain access to the hip iron. **7** You should be able to replace a single bonnet hip tile by bedding it in mortar. **8** Repair crumbled joints between verge tiles by repointing them with fresh mortar mix

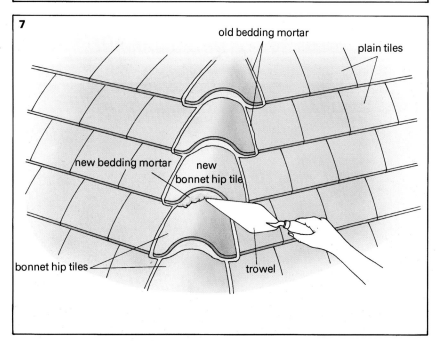

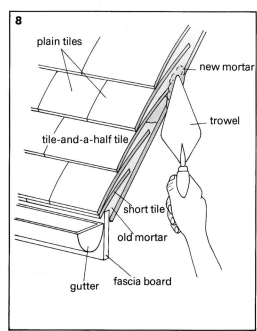

Repairing a slate roof

A sound roof keeps out water – and thus helps prevent problems caused by damp. In this section on roof repairs, we describe how to deal with the most common types of roof damage and look first at slate roofs.

Roof slates deteriorate over a period of time as a result of weathering and movement of the roof structure. If you have slates, check the roof regularly so you can make repairs before the damage lets in water. The first sign of wear may be a hairline crack, or flaking may occur along the edges or round the fixing holes. You should also check for loose slates.

Slates vary in size, shape, thickness and colour, so note your requirements carefully before ordering new slates. It is a good idea to take one of your slates to a builders' merchant to match it up. You can buy second-hand slates from a builders' yard or demolition site, but examine them carefully to make sure they are undamaged. If you cannot get a replacement of the exact size, choose a larger one of the same thickness and cut it to size.

Roof layout Slates are laid from the eaves upwards and each row, known as a course, is overlapped by the one above. The vertical joints of the slates are staggered, so each slate partially covers the two below. The slates are nailed to battens, spaced according to the pitch (or slope) of the roof.

The slates on the first row, at the eaves, and those on the last row, at the ridge, are shorter than those used on the rest of the roof. At the end of every alternate row a wider slate, called a tile-and-a-half, is used to fill the gap left on a straight edge. If the roof is angled at the edge, slates have to be cut to fit. On the edge of a gable roof there may be a narrow slate, known as a verge or creasing slate, which is laid under the slates at the end of each row; these slates give the roof a slight tilt and prevent rainwater running down the wall. V-shaped slates are used for the ridge of the roof.

Drilling and cutting slates

Roof slates may be nailed in the centre or at the top. When replacing slates, use the same nailing position as that of existing slates; to make nail holes, place the old slate over a new one and mark the position of the holes with a nail. Lay the new slate on a piece of wood and make the holes by hammering a nail through or by drilling, using a bit to match the size of the nail to be used.

Above Make regular checks on the condition of your roof. Here not only the slates, but also the roofing battens, have deteriorated badly; both will have to be replaced

1 Layout of a slate roof with details of the ridge (**inset A**), valley (**inset B**), gable end (**inset C**), eaves (**inset D**) and hip (**inset E**)

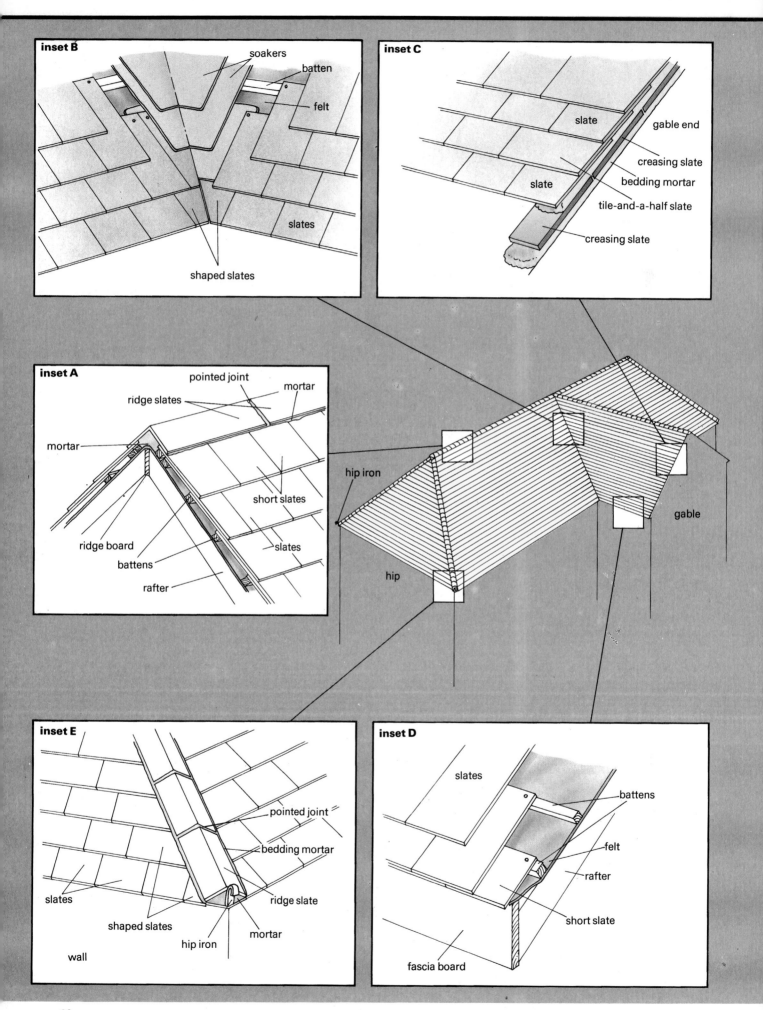

inset B
soakers
batten
felt
slates
shaped slates

inset C
slate
gable end
creasing slate
bedding mortar
tile-and-a-half slate
slate
creasing slate

inset A
pointed joint
ridge slates
mortar
mortar
short slates
ridge board
battens
slates
rafter

hip iron
gable
hip

inset E
pointed joint
bedding mortar
ridge slate
slates
shaped slates
hip iron
mortar
wall

inset D
slates
battens
felt
rafter
short slate
fascia board

If you need to cut a slate, score the cutting line on both sides with the point of a trowel. If you are cutting a large slate down to a smaller size, use an old slate as a guide. To mark out a shape – for example, to fit the angled edge of a roof – use the old slate as a guide (if it is not too badly damaged) or make a template. Place the marked slate on a firm, flat surface with the waste section overhanging. Chop halfway along the cutting line with the sharp edge of a trowel, then turn the slate over and work in from the other end so the cuts meet in the middle. Never try to snap the slate along the cutting line.

Replacing a damaged slate

When removing a single slate, take care not to damage surrounding slates. If the fixing nails have corroded through, you will be able to pull the slate away quite easily. To remove a securely nailed slate, use a slate ripper. Slide the claw of the ripper under the damaged slate and hook it round the nails. Pull the ripper to break the nails and carefully take out the old slate, making sure you do not dislodge adjacent slates.

You cannot nail down a single replacement slate, since the fixing holes will be overlapped by the slates above. To fix it you need a strip of lead about 250mm (10in) wide; nail one end of the strip to the batten between the nails of the two exposed slates. You will need to lift the edge of the slate above; be careful not to crack it. Slide the new slate into position under the overlapping ones, lining up the edge with adjacent slates, and bend up the free end of the lead strip to hold the slate in place.

Ridge slates These are bedded down in mortar. Remove any loose ridge slates for refitting and take away any damaged ones. If you need access to the top batten for fixing the top row of replacement slates, remove the relevant ridge slates. To remove securely fixed ridge slates, loosen the mortar under the slates with a sharp brick bolster. Hold the bolster parallel to the slate and tap it with a club hammer. Clean away old mortar from the top course of slates in the same way and chip away mortar from any ridge slates which are to be relaid.

For relaying ridge slates, mix a mortar of one part cement to three or four parts sand. Lay the fresh mortar along the ridge with a trowel and roughen the surface. Place the ridge slates on the mortar and tap them level with adjacent slates. Fill the joints between the slates with mortar and also press mortar along the bottom of the slates; then smooth off with a trowel. If you have to fit a whole new ridge, you may find it cheaper to use clay ridge tiles rather than slate ones.

Repairing large areas

Rotten battens may cause damage to a large area of slates. If you have to carry out major repairs, erect scaffolding and secure crawling boards to the working area to ensure safety and avoid damage.

2a Use a hammer and a nail to make fixing holes in a new slate
2b Alternatively use an electric drill
3a When cutting a large slate to size, use an old slate as a guide
3b To shape slates, make a card or hardboard template; again use an old slate (**inset**) as a guide

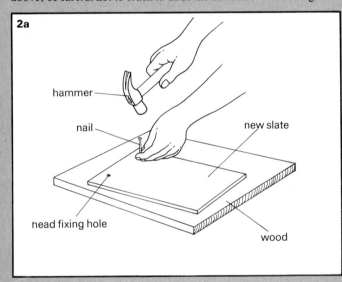

2a

hammer

nail

head fixing hole

new slate

wood

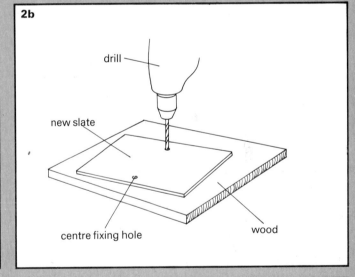

2b

drill

new slate

centre fixing hole

wood

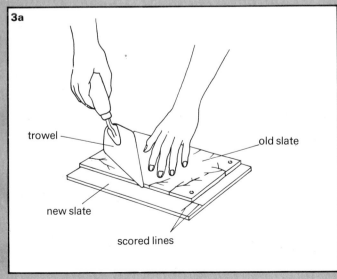

3a

trowel

old slate

new slate

scored lines

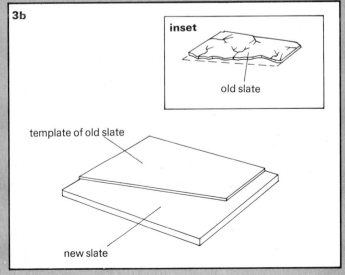

3b

inset

old slate

template of old slate

new slate

4a

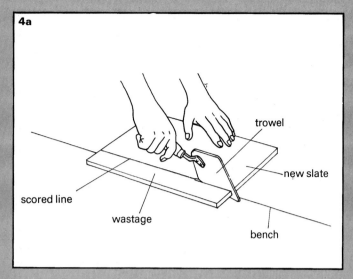

trowel

new slate

scored line

wastage

bench

4b

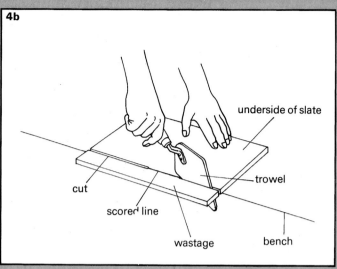

underside of slate

cut

trowel

scored line

wastage

bench

5

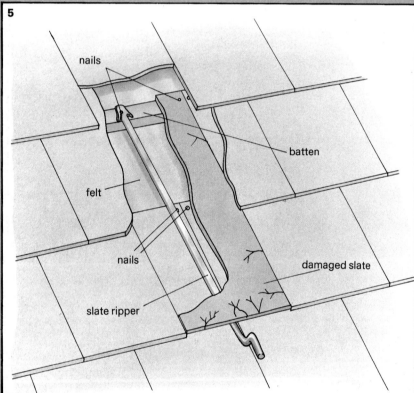

nails

batten

felt

nails

slate ripper

damaged slate

6a

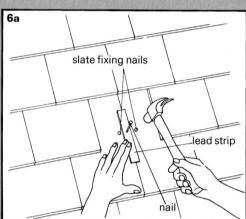

slate fixing nails

lead strip

nail

6b

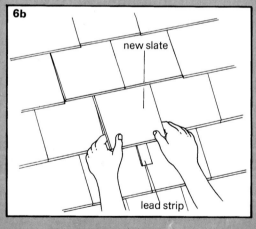

new slate

lead strip

6c

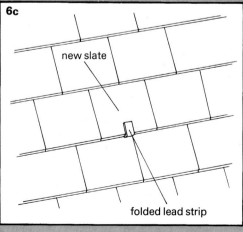

new slate

folded lead strip

4a Cut slates with a trowel; work from one end to the centre; **4b** Turn the slate over and work from the other end to finish the cut. **5** Remove slates with a slate ripper. **6a** To replace a single slate, first fix a lead strip to the batten between the nails of the two exposed slates; **6b** Lift the slates immediately above and slide the new slate into position; **6c** Bend the end of the lead strip over the slate to hold it in place. **7** Loosen the bedding mortar of ridge slates with a bolster. **8** Saw through rotten battens where they cross the rafters

Remove all the slates from the damaged area and stack the undamaged ones carefully. Remove any unsound battens by sawing through them diagonally where they cross the rafters.

Cut new lengths of the same size softwood as the existing battens – usually 50 × 25mm (2 × 1in) – at a matching angle to provide a tight fit; fix the new battens with a 50mm (2in) nail at each end. If there is any bituminous felt which is damaged, repair it before you fit the battens in place. Cut the torn piece to a neat rectangle, fit a larger rectangle of new felt over it and stick it down with bitumen adhesive. Coat all new timber and the surrounding old structure with a wood preservative before replacing the slates.

Fixing slates Start at the eaves with a row of short slates. If you are making the repair in the middle of an existing row, slide the first new slate under the last overlapping slate, placing the holes over the centre of the batten. Secure the exposed part

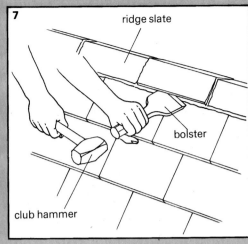

7 ridge slate · bolster · club hammer

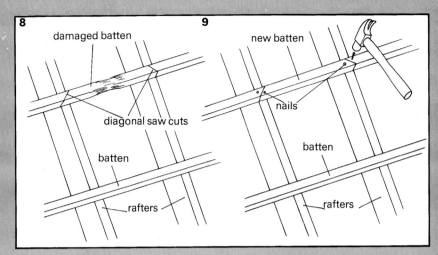

8 damaged batten · diagonal saw cuts · batten · rafters

9 new batten · nails · batten · rafters

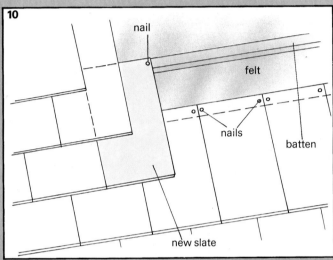

10 nail · felt · nails · batten · new slate

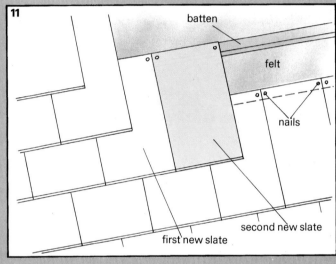

11 batten · felt · nails · second new slate · first new slate

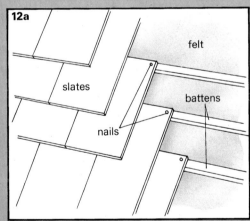

12a felt · slates · battens · nails

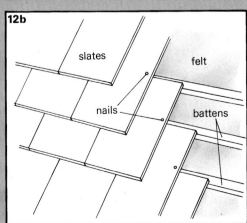

12b slates · felt · nails · battens

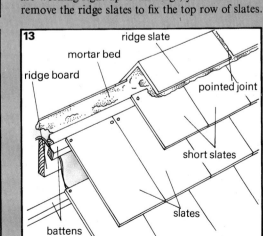

13 ridge slate · mortar bed · ridge board · pointed joint · short slates · slates · battens

of the slate with a nail driven into the batten. Butt-join the remaining slates in the row and fix each one with two nails, lining up the upper edges.

The second row will completely cover the row of short slates (this gives extra protection against damp). Fix the slates as for the first row, covering the vertical joins of the slates below. Continue fixing the slates, moving up the roof one course at a time. All vertical joins should be covered and each course should overlap the one below.

Unless you are reslating to the ridge of the roof, the nail holes of the last few slates will be covered by the overlapping slates above, so use lead strips to fix these in position, as described earlier. If you are working right up to the ridge, you will have to remove the ridge slates to fix the top row of slates.

9 Fix replacement battens with a nail at each end
10 To replace slates in the middle of an existing row, slide the first new slate under the last overlapping one; place the holes over the centre of the batten and secure with a nail
11 Butt-join the second slate and secure it with two nails; fix the remaining slates in the course in the same way
12a When replacing head-nailed slates, line up the top of the slates with the top of the battens
12b For centre-nailed slates, position the top edge of the slates in the centre of the batten above
13 Ridge slates will have to be removed when replacing the top row

Repairing chimneys

When making repairs to the roof, it is always a good idea to check the condition of the chimney as well. Loose pots, cracked flaunching and crumbling mortar joints in the chimney stack are not only unsightly; they can also lead to damp inside and, if left to deteriorate, can become dangerous.

Repairing flaunching

Flaunching is the sloping cement mortar which holds the chimney pots in place and seals the top of the chimney stack. It is quite common for the flaunching to develop cracks, especially round the base of the pots. You can repair narrow cracks with a bead of non-hardening mastic applied from a cartridge with a mastic gun or with thick bitumen mastic pressed into cracks with a flat filling knife.

Wider cracks can be repaired temporarily with a cement filler paste; for a lasting repair the flaunching should be renewed. Use a club hammer and cold chisel to remove the old flaunching, taking care not to let large lumps of debris fall from the roof; collect the pieces in a bucket and lower them carefully to the ground. (It is also a good idea to cover fireplaces inside the house to prevent dust and dirt filtering into the rooms.)
Warning Chimney pots are larger and heavier than you might expect, so handle them carefully and, if the pots are sound, take care not to crack them as the flaunching is chipped away. In old houses it is not unknown for the chimney pots to drop into the flue when the flaunching is removed; rope them to the chimney stack in case they become dislodged.

Rake out and brush all loose material from the bricks at the top of the stack; if there are any loose bricks, refix them with new mortar. Thoroughly wet the base of the pot and the surface of the bricks with water, then place the pot centrally over the flue. The base of the pot should fit the flue exactly; if there are any gaps which would allow the flaunching mortar to fall into the flue, cover them with pieces of roofing slate or asbestos cement.

Spread the flaunching mortar (a mix of one part Portland cement and three or four parts sharp, washed sand) over the top of the chimney so it is about 60mm (or 2½in) thick against the base of the pots and slopes down to about 20mm (or ¾in) thick round the edge of the stack; form a gentle curve all round to throw water away from the pots.

Replacing pots

Cracked or broken pots must be replaced since they may be displaced in a gale and cause damage to the roof or injure people below. To find the size of the pot required, remove part of the bedding mortar and measure from top to bottom and the internal diameter at the top; if possible, the replacement pot should have a square base so it fits exactly over the flue opening in the stack. To replace a pot, remove all the flaunching as previously described, place the new pot over the

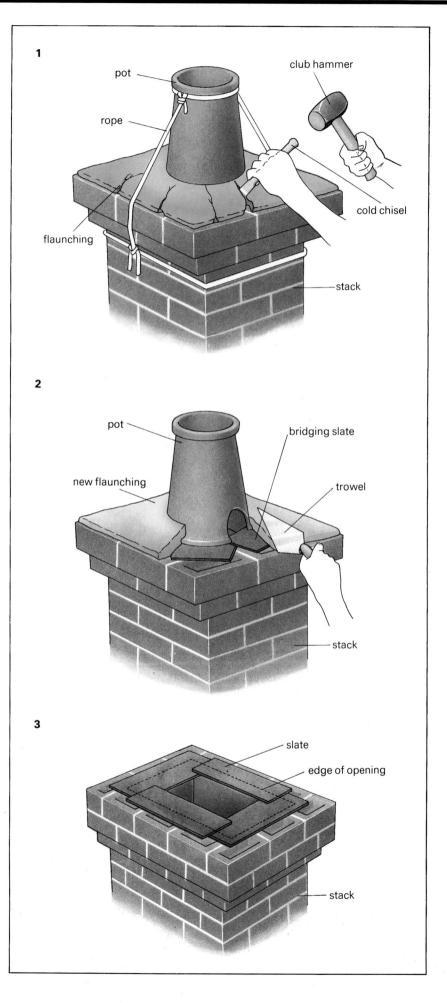

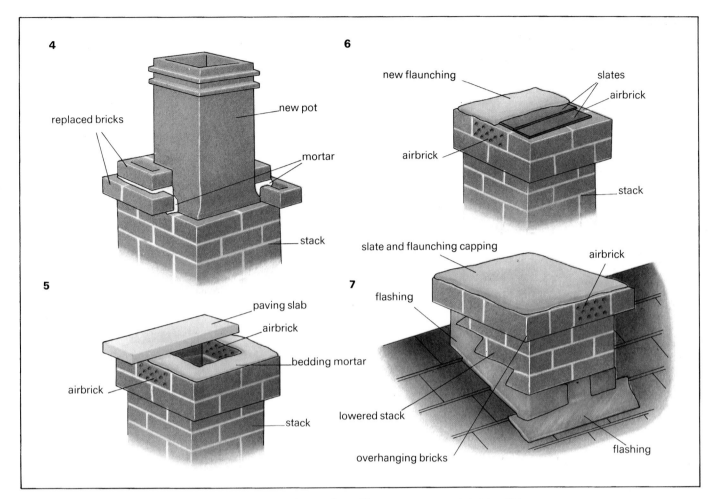

4
replaced bricks
new pot
mortar
stack

6
new flaunching
slates
airbrick
airbrick
stack

5
paving slab
airbrick
bedding mortar
airbrick
stack

7
slate and flaunching capping
airbrick
flashing
lowered stack
overhanging bricks
flashing

1 Remove cracked flaunching with a club hammer and cold chisel; before starting work, rope the pot to the stack
2 Set the pot centrally over the flue, covering any gaps with slate or asbestos cement; apply flaunching to the top of the stack and around the base of the pot
3 If a new pot is too narrow to rest over the flue, bridge the edges of the opening with pieces of slate and place the pot on these
4 Where a pot is built into the brickwork of the flue, release the pot by removing the bricks around its base; fit the new pot and replace the bricks so they overhang
5 To seal a disused flue, replace two of the bricks in the top row with airbricks and cover the opening with paving slabs bedded on mortar
6 Alternatively lay slates instead of paving slabs and cover with flaunching
7 You can reduce the height of the stack if the chimney will never be used again; lay a course of bricks on top of the lowered stack and cap with slate and flaunching

flue opening and apply new flaunching mortar.

If you are working on an old house, you may find the base of the new pot is too narrow to rest over the flue opening. In this case straddle the edges of the opening with pieces of roofing slate to restrict its size to a suitable width and support the pot on these. Where the base of the pot is built into the brickwork of the flue, you will have to remove bricks to release the pot; fit the new pot by replacing the bricks around it.

Sealing the stack
If the chimney is no longer used, you can cap the flue to make it weatherproof, but it should not be tightly sealed or the flue will become damp and spoil wall decorations in rooms through which it passes. Metal and clay capping cowls are available. The metal type simply clips into the top of the chimney pot; the clay ones, which are longer lasting and less obtrusive, are secured with cement mortar between the cowl and the inside of the pot.

When a disused flue has cracked pots or flaunching, it is best to remove the flaunching and pots and seal the flue with one or two paving slabs. Before fitting the slabs, knock out at least two bricks from the sides of the flue and replace them with airbricks. Bed the slabs on mortar so they are level and overhang the sides of the stack by at least 25mm (1in) all round. Alternatively you can lay slates over the flue after fitting the airbricks and cover the entire surface with new flaunching.

Lowering the stack
As long as you will never use the chimney again you can reduce the height of a chimney stack if you

feel this will improve the appearance of the house or if the stack is dangerous and in need of repair. It is essential to erect scaffolding round the chimney or to work from a scaffold tower when possible.

Use a club hammer and bolster chisel to remove the bricks course by course from the top down to the required height, taking care to prevent rubble falling down the flue. It is a good idea to tie a long length of stout string to the handles of the tools and tie the string firmly round the base of the stack; if you drop the tools down the flue, you can then retrieve them easily. Place the bricks in a bucket and lower them to the ground as work proceeds. At the top of the lowered stack, relay one or two courses of bricks to overhang the general brickwork surface slightly; this will help to throw water clear of the stack. Finally cap the flue.

Repairing brickwork
If the mortar joints between the bricks of a chimney are crumbling, they must be repointed using the same technique as for repointing walls. After repointing or sealing a stack, it is a good idea to paint the brickwork with a clear silicone water repellant to prevent rainwater penetration.
Cracked bricks These can often indicate serious faults and you should seek the advice of a builder or roofing specialist. Bulging brickwork or cement rendering should also be referred to a specialist.

Repairing flashings and valleys

If flashings (weatherproofing where the roof joins walls, chimney stacks or roof windows) or valley linings (weatherproofing at the junction of two sloping roof surfaces) become defective, the first signs of trouble may be spoiled ceiling decoration or damp patches on chimney-breast walls due to rainwater penetration. Check these areas of the roof regularly, making any repairs as soon as possible, and you should be able to stop the trouble before it gets too bad. Many repairs are simple and ones you can do yourself.

Flashings

Traditionally flashings are made from sheets of lead or zinc; but other corrosion-resistant materials, such as aluminium alloy, copper, bituminous felt and rigid bitumen-asbestos, are also used. A fairly recent development is the self-adhesive flashing strip; this is available in various widths and is cheaper and easier to fit than most traditional materials. These flashing strips usually consist of heavy duty reflective aluminium foil, coated on one side with a thick layer of specially formulated pressure-sensitive bitumen adhesive. The adhesive surface is protected with a siliconized release paper which you peel off just before applying the flashing. In some cases the aluminium foil is coated with a grey vinyl lacquer, so it looks like lead.

Making repairs

If flashings are torn or cracked, clean the damaged area thoroughly with a wire brush and go over it with emery paper. You can then cover the crack or tear with a patch of self-adhesive flashing strip: simply peel off the paper backing and smooth the strip firmly into place. Alternatively press thick bitumen mastic into each crack so there is about 1.5mm ($\frac{1}{16}$ in) of mastic over the crack and overlapping it by about 1.5mm ($\frac{1}{16}$ in) all round. Lay a piece of aluminium foil or thin roofing felt over each repair and press the edges into the mastic. Apply another layer of mastic and brush liquid bitumen proofing over the entire flashings.

Repointing Along its top edge, metal flashing is tucked into the mortar joints of the brickwork; if the joints are defective and the flashing comes away from them, rainwater will trickle behind and eventually seep through the roof. To repoint the joints, first rake out the old mortar with a cold chisel and club hammer, then tuck the flashing back in place, wedging it at intervals with scraps of lead or small pieces of timber. Dampen the joint with water and fill it with a mix of four parts sand to one part cement.

Replacing flashings

Flashings which are badly corroded are best replaced with new material; the method of replacement varies with the type of flashing and the material used.

Stepped flashing With a single lap tiled roof (and some slate roofs) the flashing at the side of the chimney is usually stepped and dressed (pressed down) over the tiles. Stepped flashing is inserted in the mortar joints all the way down the side of the chimney and it is difficult to replace in the same way. However, you can apply a self-adhesive flashing

1a Rainwater will seep through your roof if flashings are damaged; having cleaned the area, press mastic into the damaged area and push on a piece of foil or roofing felt
1b Apply another layer of mastic over the patch and brush liquid bitumen over the whole flashing
2 If flashings come away from the brickwork, rake out the old mortar and wedge the flashing back into the wall with timber pegs; refill with fresh mortar

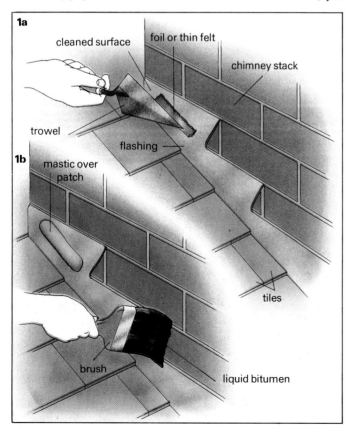

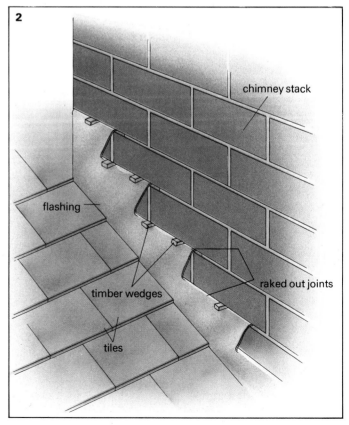

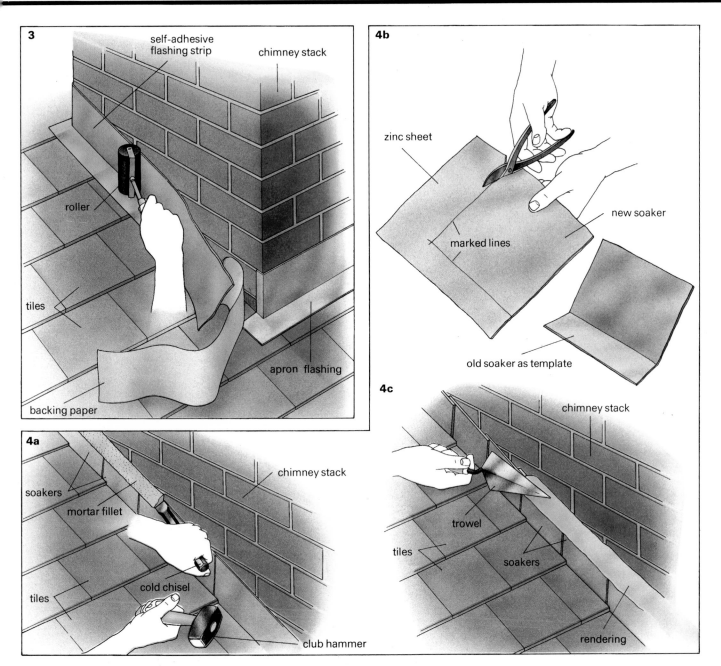

3 self-adhesive flashing strip

chimney stack

roller

tiles

backing paper

apron flashing

4b zinc sheet

marked lines

new soaker

old soaker as template

4a soakers

mortar fillet

chimney stack

tiles

cold chisel

club hammer

4c chimney stack

trowel

tiles

soakers

rendering

strip which does not need stepping or inserting in the mortar joints. Carefully lever out the old flashing and thoroughly clean the area with a wire brush; you can then apply a primer as recommended by the manufacturer – this is not essential, but it does ensure the strip adheres firmly to the brickwork. Cut the strip to length with a pair of scissors and carefully peel off the backing paper; press the strip into place and smooth it down with a cloth pad or a wood seam roller as used for wallpapering, making sure there are no gaps between the strip and the surface.

Soakers On a double lap (or plain) tiled roof – and again on some slate roofs – the flashing at the side of the chimney and against parapet walls usually consists of separate pieces of metal, called soakers, interleaved with the tiles. The soakers are turned up against the wall or side of the chimney and a stepped flashing or mortar fillet covers their upturned edges. To replace faulty soakers, chip away the old mortar fillet, or lever out the flashing, and rake out the joints between the bricks to about 19mm ($\frac{3}{4}$in). Remove adjacent tiles, numbering

them as you work to enable you to replace them in the correct order, and remove the damaged soakers – again numbering them as you do so. Cut pieces of zinc to the shape of the soakers, using the old ones as templates. If you intend to use self-adhesive flashing dampen the raked out joints with water, repoint, and replace the soakers, interleaving them with the tiles in the same way as they were originally fitted. You can now apply the flashing over the soakers, as described above. If you intend to apply rendering over the soakers and to the wall above, leave the mortar joints open to provide a key for the rendering. Use a mix of four parts sand to one part cement and trowel on the mortar to a thickness of 13mm ($\frac{1}{2}$in). Score the surface to ensure good adhesion, leave the render to dry and apply a second coat, again 13mm ($\frac{1}{2}$in) thick.

Straight flashings When replacing straight, horizontal flashings of traditional materials, such as lead or zinc, lever out the damaged flashing and rake out the mortar joints to about 25mm (1in). Cut the lead or zinc sheet to the required length, lay it over a batten and bend over a 20mm (or $\frac{3}{4}$in) strip

3 Replace stepped flashing with self-adhesive strip; peel off the backing paper and roll down the strip
4a When replacing faulty soakers, chip off mortar fillet
4b Cut the new soakers, with old ones as templates
4c Apply render over the soakers and the mortar joints
5a When replacing straight flashing, bend the edge of the new strip over a batten
5b Use a sliding bevel to check the required angle
5c Shape the metal to the correct angle
5d Fit the new flashing strip into the dampened mortar joint, hammering the lower half to match the roof slope
6 Seal cracks in cement fillet with non-hardening mastic

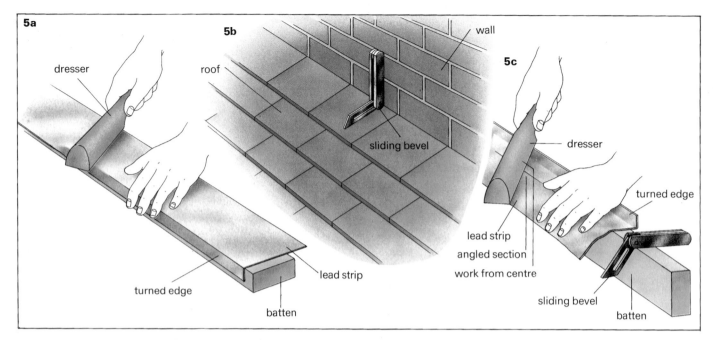

at right-angles down one long edge. Use a sliding bevel to determine the angle between the roof and the wall; turn the sheet over and shape it to match the angle on the bevel, working from the centre of the sheet outwards. Dampen the mortar joints with water and insert the angled section of the new flashing in the joint, packing with small wedges of zinc or lead at both ends and overlapping joins in the flashing by about 150mm (6in). Gently hammer the lower half of the flashing to match the slope of the roof then fill the joint with fresh mortar. Finally remove surplus mortar with the point of a trowel.

Alternatively you can replace this type of flashing with a self-adhesive strip, as described for stepped flashing.

Cement fillets Occasionally the flashing round the base of a chimney or against a parapet wall is made from a triangular fillet of cement mortar; it is quite common for this type of flashing to crack where it joins the wall. If the damage is not severe, seal the gap with a non-hardening mastic; if the fillet is in bad condition, it is best to chip the fillet away and replace it with a self-adhesive flashing strip.

Valley linings

Lead, zinc and aluminium are all commonly used for valley linings. Small cracks and holes can be repaired in the same way as for metal flashings; but after making such repairs, it is important to seal the entire valley with liquid bitumen proofing or liquid plastic coating.

Replacing valley linings

If the valley lining is severely corroded or wrinkled, it must be replaced; this involves lifting several tiles at each side of the valley, so have a tarpaulin or heavy duty polythene sheeting ready to cover the roof in case of rain. You can replace the lining with zinc or lead sheet or use roofing felt; but the simplest method is to apply a wide self-adhesive flashing strip.

Zinc or lead lining Remove the tiles covering the valley edge at each side, numbering them so you can replace them in the correct order. Lever up the old lining and lower it carefully to the ground, then remove the fixing nails with pincers. Check the

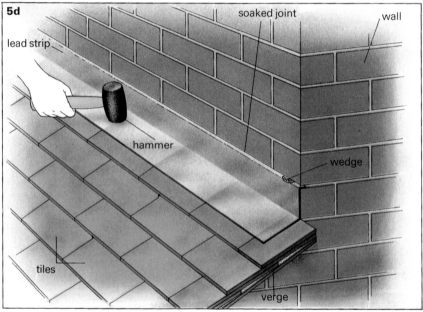

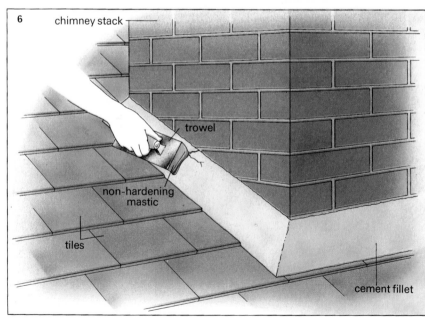

timber underlining is securely fixed and coat it with creosote for protection. Cut the replacement zinc or lead to length, allowing for a 50mm (2in) overlap at the eaves, and place it over the underlining; press the lining down firmly to fit the angle of the valley and hold it in place with galvanized nails. If you have to use more than one sheet of metal, make sure the sheets overlap by about 225mm (9in). Where the lining meets the junction of the roof and wall, shape the end to match the junction, allowing a 75mm (3in) turning against the wall. Fix the sheet to the battens at both sides using galvanized nails, then relay the tiles; work from the eaves upwards and make sure you replace the tiles in the correct order. Finally apply self-adhesive flashing strip at the junction of the roof and wall to guard against rainwater penetration.

Felt lining You can replace an old metal lining with three layers of roofing felt. Remove the tiles and old lining as before and cut the felt to length. Fix the first layer of felt to the valley underlining, using galvanized nails, and fix the second and third layers with felt adhesive. Then replace the tiles in their original positions.

Valley tiles The major concrete roof tile manufacturers now produce special valley tiles which can be used as a cheaper alternative to the traditional lining materials. However, the method of fixing these tiles involves modifying the tile battening on each side of the valley, and the financial saving on materials may therefore be more than offset by the loss of time involved in carrying out the necessary modifications to the structure before the tiles can be positioned.

7a When replacing valley linings, remove the tiles on each side and fit felt onto the battens
7b Cover the felt with lead sheet nailed to alternate battens
7c Shape the lead sheet to fit the corner of the walls
7d Replace tiles from the eaves upwards
7e Apply self-adhesive flashing at the wall joins
8 Three layers of felt can be used instead of lead; nail the first layer and glue the other two

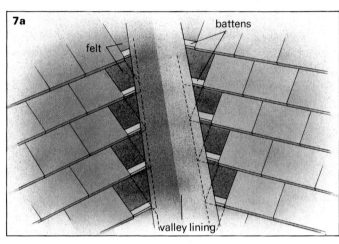

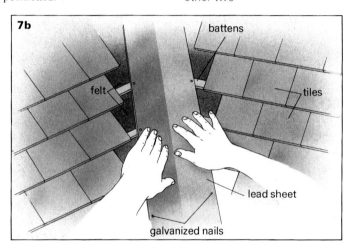

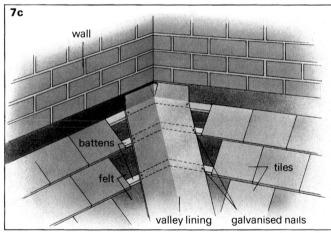

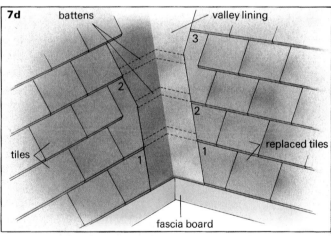

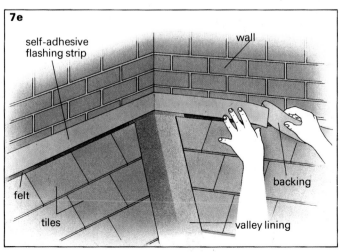

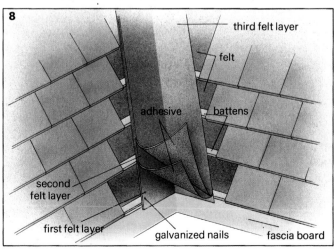

Repairing roof boards and snowguards

Where you are repairing a roof covering you should check the structure around it is in sound condition; damage in this area will shorten the life of the covering. Sometimes it may be sufficient to patch the damaged areas. Barge boards, fascias and soffits, for example, which have only slightly rotted can be temporarily repaired by scraping away the rotten timber, filling the cavity with an exterior grade filler and painting thoroughly with a water-proof paint. In slightly more serious cases the affected section should be cut out and replaced with a new piece of timber. For a lasting repair and where the damage is too bad for patching, the boards should be replaced.

Replacing boards

Before you begin, remember these boards are heavier than they look from the ground and you should attempt replacement only if you can work from a scaffold.

Fascias and soffits Fascia boards, to which the gutters are fixed, cover the ends of rafters and a soffit board seals the gap underneath, between the wall and the fascia. To replace fascias and soffits, take off the gutters and gutter brackets and remove

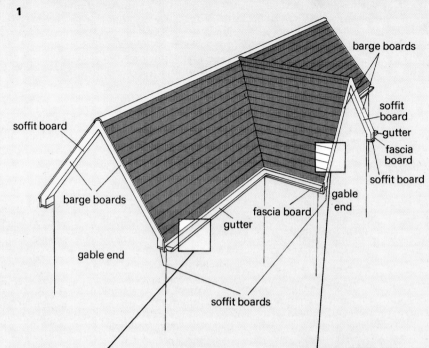

1

barge boards

soffit board

soffit board

gutter

fascia board

soffit board

barge boards

gable end

fascia board

gutter

gable end

soffit boards

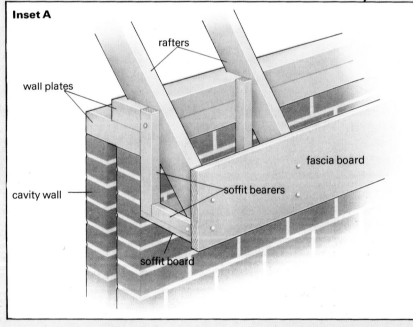

Inset A

rafters

wall plates

cavity wall

fascia board

soffit bearers

soffit board

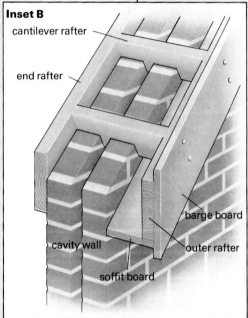

Inset B

cantilever rafter

end rafter

barge board

cavity wall

outer rafter

soffit board

the fascia by prising it away from the rafter ends with a cold chisel or wrecking bar. The soffit is nailed to the rafter ends and supported by a batten plugged and screwed to the wall or by bearers nailed to the rafters. If the soffit supports are sound, simply prise away the soffit; where the soffit is fixed to bearers you will have to remove the fixing nails partially to release the soffit. If the soffit supports are rotten, these too should be removed and replaced; where the fixings which hold these in place are too difficult to remove, you can cut out the rotten sections with a panel saw and replace them with pieces of new timber.

Where rafter ends are rotten you may be able to form new ends by bolting pieces of new timber alongside the decayed rafters. If this is impossible,

the ends should be removed and replaced.

Treat all the roof timbers with wood preservative before fixing the new boards. Cut the soffits and fascias to length; if you have to join several lengths to make up a long run, check the joints coincide with the centre lines of the rafters and make the saw cuts at an angle of 45 degrees to ensure neat joints. Hold the soffit in position; if there is a definite gap between the wall and the soffit, you will have to cut the soffit to the shape of the wall so make sure the board is wide enough. To mark the cutting line on the soffit, hold a pencil against a scrap of wood and move this along the wall, tracing the contour of the wall onto the soffit. Trim the edge of the soffit to match, making an allowance for the width of the block of wood.

1 Locating the position of soffit boards, fascias and barge boards
Inset A Detail of the fascia fixing at the eaves
Inset B Detail of the barge board fixing at the verge

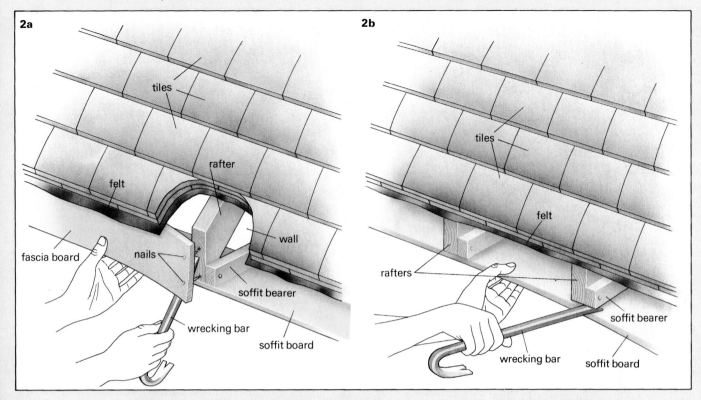

2a

tiles

rafter

felt

wall

fascia board

nails

soffit bearer

wrecking bar

soffit board

2b

tiles

felt

rafters

soffit bearer

wrecking bar

soffit board

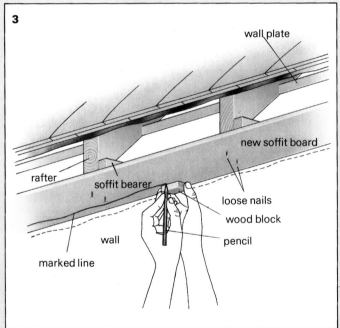

3

wall plate

new soffit board

rafter

soffit bearer

loose nails

wood block

pencil

wall

marked line

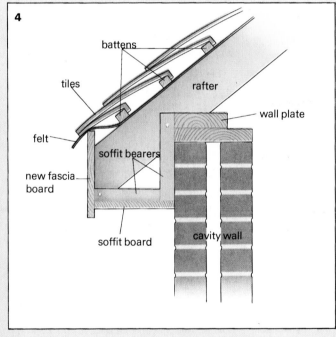

4

battens

tiles

rafter

wall plate

felt

soffit bearers

new fascia board

soffit board

cavity wall

2a Removing the fascia
2b Levering the soffit away from its bearers
3 Tracing the wall outline onto the new soffit
4 Fitting the new soffit and fascia

Treat the new boards with wood preservative and apply a wood primer. Replace the soffit by fixing it to the underside of the rafter ends and supports with galvanized nails. Fix the new fascia by nailing it to the rafter ends and through the edge of the soffit. The top edge of the fascia should tuck under the overhang of the roof slates or tiles and any underfelt should overhang the front of the fascia so it can be tucked into the gutters later. The lower edge of the fascia should protrude below the face of the soffit to protect the soffit and the walls.
Barge boards These are fitted at the gable end of the roof. They are screwed to the roof timbers and, like the fascia board, incorporate a soffit which seals the gap underneath. Lever out the old boards with a crowbar or wrecking bar, starting at the

eaves and working upwards. Use the old boards as a guide to cut the new ones to the correct angle at the ridge; alternatively make a card template of the angle before removing the boards and transfer the shape to the new boards, trimming as necessary. Treat the boards with clear wood preservative and allow this to dry, then prime all surfaces. Fix the soffit to the underside of the roof timbers, using rustproof screws, then fit the barge board over the soffit and screw it to the roof timbers. After fixing, you may find you have to seal the verge by re-pointing the tiles.

Repairing snowguards
Usually these consist of a strip of galvanized steel mesh fixed to support brackets which are screwed

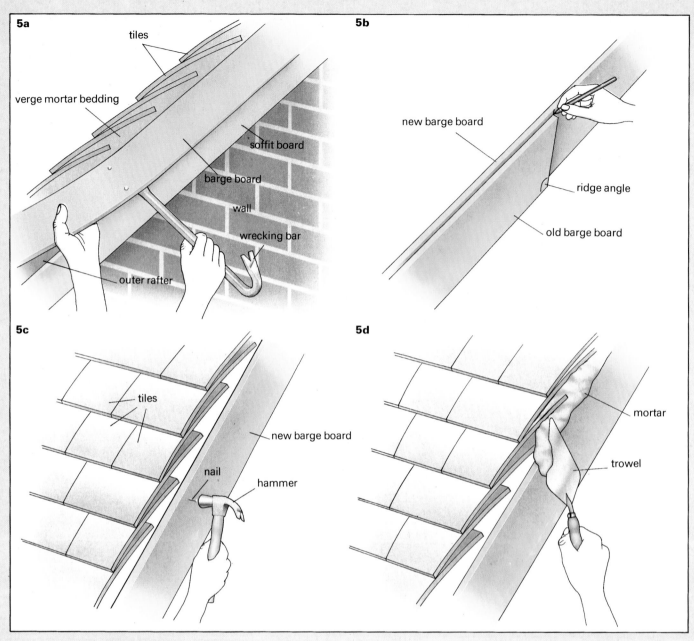

5a
tiles
verge mortar bedding
soffit board
barge board
wall
wrecking bar
outer rafter

5b
new barge board
ridge angle
old barge board

5c
tiles
new barge board
nail
hammer

5d
mortar
trowel
new barge board

to the sides of the rafters or to the fascia board. Where the mesh has come loose, refix it to the supports with twists of copper or galvanized steel wire. If the mesh has corroded, remove the fixings which hold it in place and, after lifting away the mesh, replace it with galvanized steel mesh fixed to the roof side of the support brackets with wire twists. Remove any loose brackets and refix them in a slightly different position so the fixing screws can bite into new wood. If brackets are bent, you can straighten them by using a length of strong tube as a lever, slipping it over the bracket.

Warning For safety reasons, you should always work from a secure foothold, such as a scaffold tower cantilevered over the roof or a ladder which is securely tied at the top.

5a Removing an old barge board with a wrecking bar
5b Using the old board as a guide to mark the shape of the new board
5c Nailing the new board in place
5d Repointing the tiles at the verge
6 Repositioning loose snowguard brackets

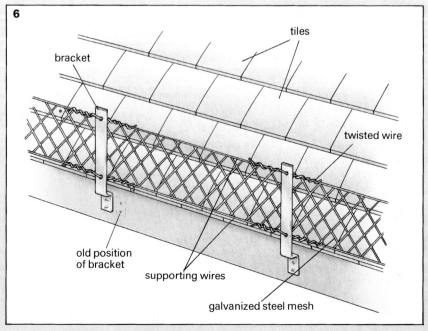

6
tiles
bracket
twisted wire
old position of bracket
supporting wires
galvanized steel mesh

Repairing gutters

Plastic or cast iron guttering comes in three shapes
1 Half-round, to rest in brackets fixed to fascia board, rafters or brickwork
2 Square, fixed as above
3 Ogee, to be screwed direct to fascia, or rest on brackets as shown here

1

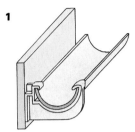

2

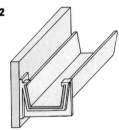

3

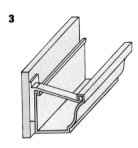

Defective rainwater systems cause all sorts of damp problems in the house structure. Water constantly pouring down an outside wall will eventually penetrate inside, ruining the decoration and causing mould growth. So it is important to keep your guttering in good repair. If you are prompted now to check your guttering for the first time, you may have a fair amount of work on hand to get it into shape. But once the repair work has been done, maintenance is a simple yearly task.

If you need an extra incentive to start immediately, remember if you allow things to deteriorate you may have to call in a professional to repair the guttering or even to replace the complete system and this would prove expensive. The best time to check the gutters is in the late autumn, once all the leaves have fallen. If you have already noticed leaks or damp patches, make the job a priority.

Working at height is not to everyone's liking. Use a secure ladder or make the job easier with a scaffolding system (available from hire shops). When working on metal gutters, wear an old pair of gloves to guard against cuts from sharp edges.

Types of gutter
In the past cast iron was the most common material for guttering, but plastic is now widely used. Today you cannot easily obtain a complete cast iron system, although you can buy replacement parts. Cast iron guttering comes in three shapes: half-round, square and ogee (a cross between half-round and square section). Half-round and square types rest in brackets fixed to the fascia board, rafters or brickwork. Ogee section can either be screwed direct to the fascia or be supported on brackets. The joints are sealed together with red lead, putty or other suitable jointing mastic and secured with bolts.

Plastic rainwater systems have a distinct advantage over cast iron ones since plastic is light, durable and needs little or no decoration. Plastic guttering is made in half-round, ogee and square sections which fit into special brackets. The lengths are joined together with clips housing rubber seals, or gaskets, to make them waterproof; a jointing cement is sometimes used instead of, or in addition to, the gasket.

Gutter blockages
Scoop out the rubbish with a trowel or a piece of card shaped to the profile of the gutter. Don't use the downpipe as a rubbish chute as it may become blocked or the rubbish sink into the drain.

Flush out the gutter with water; it should flow steadily towards the downpipe. If it overflows at the entrance then the downpipe is blocked and needs to be cleared.

If the downpipe gets blocked tie a small bundle of rags to the end of a pole and use this as a plunger to push away any obstruction. Place a bowl at the outlet on the ground to prevent rubbish sinking into the drain. If there is a 'swan neck' between the gutter and the downpipe, use a length of stiff wire to clear it of debris. To prevent further blockages, fit a cage into the entrance of the downpipe. You

---

Basic items
drill, hammer and screwdriver

For clearing blockages
trowel or piece of card
pole or stiff wire, rags and bowl
wire or plastic netting (to prevent blockages)

For realigning
string line, spirit level (if used)
nails 150mm (6in) long
No 8 chrome-plated round head screws 37mm (1½in) long
wall plugs

For treating rust
wire brush or electric drill with wire cup brush
rust killer, rust-resistant primer

epoxy repair material
fine glasspaper

For repairing joints
epoxy repair material
medium glasspaper
mastic sealer or replacement gasket

For replacing a section
nails (to locate bolt holes)
rust killer
penetrating oil or hacksaw (to remove bolts)
old chisel (to scrape off)
metal putty
rust-resistant primer
aluminium primer (over bituminous coatings)
undercoat and top coat paint

equipment

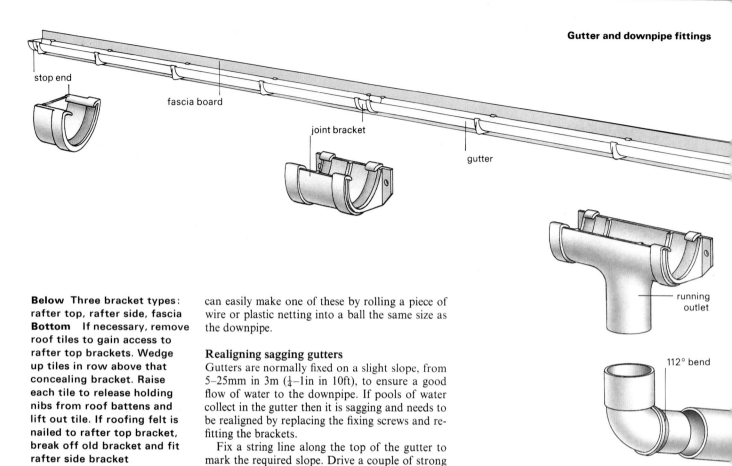

stop end

fascia board

joint bracket

gutter

running outlet

112° bend

Below Three bracket types: rafter top, rafter side, fascia Bottom If necessary, remove roof tiles to gain access to rafter top brackets. Wedge up tiles in row above that concealing bracket. Raise each tile to release holding nibs from roof battens and lift out tile. If roofing felt is nailed to rafter top bracket, break off old bracket and fit rafter side bracket

can easily make one of these by rolling a piece of wire or plastic netting into a ball the same size as the downpipe.

Realigning sagging gutters

Gutters are normally fixed on a slight slope, from 5–25mm in 3m ($\frac{1}{4}$–1in in 10ft), to ensure a good flow of water to the downpipe. If pools of water collect in the gutter then it is sagging and needs to be realigned by replacing the fixing screws and re-fitting the brackets.

Fix a string line along the top of the gutter to mark the required slope. Drive a couple of strong

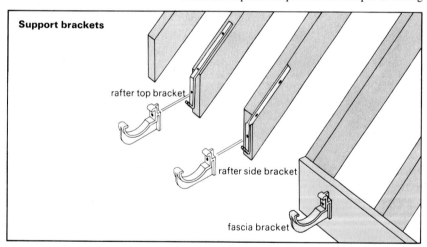

Support brackets

rafter top bracket

rafter side bracket

fascia bracket

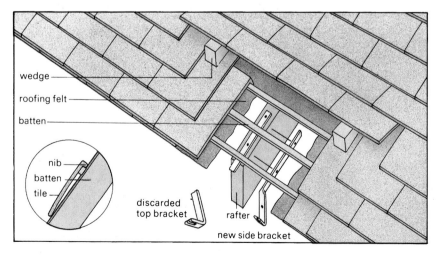

wedge

roofing felt

batten

nib

batten

tile

discarded top bracket

rafter

new side bracket

nails into the fascia about 25mm (1in) below the gutter for support while it is being refitted. Take out the old fixing screws (if these are in the edges of the rafters you may have to remove a tile from the roof to gain access to them). Now release the brackets so the gutter rests on the support nails; tap wall plugs into the old screw holes and refix the brackets using new screws. Pack the gutter up to the required height with bits of timber placed between it and the support nails. Finally remove nails and string line.

Rust and cracks

Inspect metal systems for any signs of rust and clean back with a wire brush or, if you have an extension lead, with an electric drill fitted with a wire cup brush – this saves a lot of hard work. Now treat the cleaned areas with a rust killer.

Fill hairline cracks with two coats of rust-resistant primer. Fill definite cracks or holes with an epoxy (water-resistant) repair material. Rub down with fine glasspaper.

Corrosion is always worst at the back edge of the gutter and to repair this you will have to dismantle the system and treat each section separately.

Leaking joints

Seal leaking joints in metal gutters with an epoxy repair material and rub down. If a leak develops at the joints of a plastic system, release the affected section by squeezing it at one end and lifting it clear of the adjoining length. If the gasket in the joint is sound, simply replace the section making sure the spigot end butts tightly against the socket of the adjoining piece. If the gasket is worn, scrape away all the old material and insert a replacement gasket or apply three good strips of mastic sealer in its place. Then press the two sections together again.

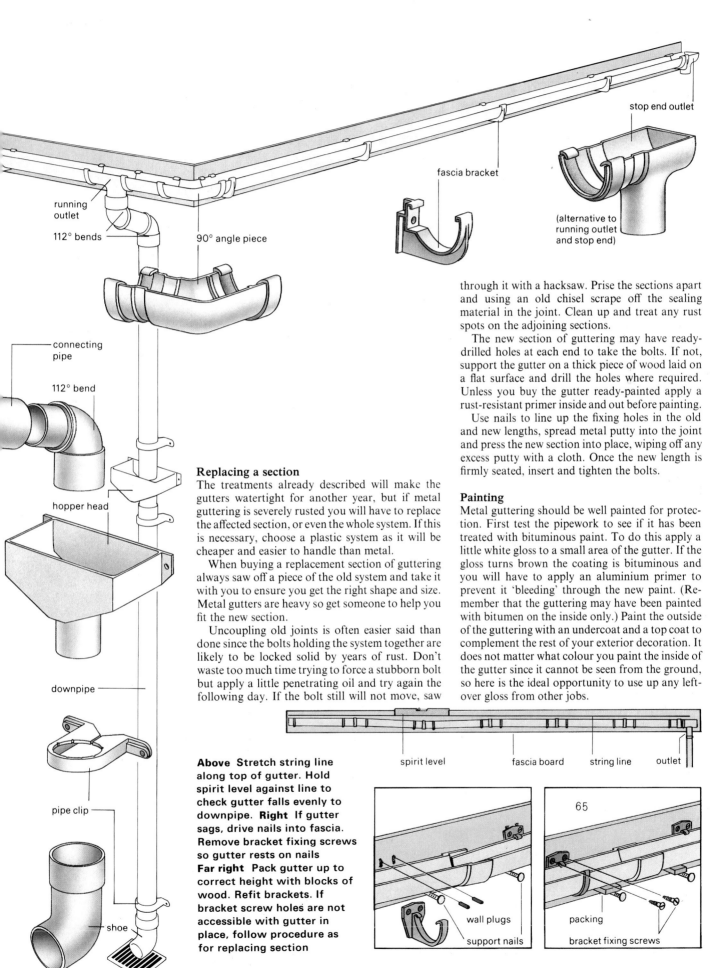

running
outlet

112° bends

90° angle piece

connecting
pipe

112° bend

hopper head

downpipe

pipe clip

shoe

fascia bracket

stop end outlet

(alternative to
running outlet
and stop end)

Replacing a section

The treatments already described will make the gutters watertight for another year, but if metal guttering is severely rusted you will have to replace the affected section, or even the whole system. If this is necessary, choose a plastic system as it will be cheaper and easier to handle than metal.

When buying a replacement section of guttering always saw off a piece of the old system and take it with you to ensure you get the right shape and size. Metal gutters are heavy so get someone to help you fit the new section.

Uncoupling old joints is often easier said than done since the bolts holding the system together are likely to be locked solid by years of rust. Don't waste too much time trying to force a stubborn bolt but apply a little penetrating oil and try again the following day. If the bolt still will not move, saw

through it with a hacksaw. Prise the sections apart and using an old chisel scrape off the sealing material in the joint. Clean up and treat any rust spots on the adjoining sections.

The new section of guttering may have ready-drilled holes at each end to take the bolts. If not, support the gutter on a thick piece of wood laid on a flat surface and drill the holes where required. Unless you buy the gutter ready-painted apply a rust-resistant primer inside and out before painting.

Use nails to line up the fixing holes in the old and new lengths, spread metal putty into the joint and press the new section into place, wiping off any excess putty with a cloth. Once the new length is firmly seated, insert and tighten the bolts.

Painting

Metal guttering should be well painted for protection. First test the pipework to see if it has been treated with bituminous paint. To do this apply a little white gloss to a small area of the gutter. If the gloss turns brown the coating is bituminous and you will have to apply an aluminium primer to prevent it 'bleeding' through the new paint. (Remember that the guttering may have been painted with bitumen on the inside only.) Paint the outside of the guttering with an undercoat and a top coat to complement the rest of your exterior decoration. It does not matter what colour you paint the inside of the gutter since it cannot be seen from the ground, so here is the ideal opportunity to use up any left-over gloss from other jobs.

spirit level   fascia board   string line   outlet

Above Stretch string line along top of gutter. Hold spirit level against line to check gutter falls evenly to downpipe. **Right** If gutter sags, drive nails into fascia. Remove bracket fixing screws so gutter rests on nails **Far right** Pack gutter up to correct height with blocks of wood. Refit brackets. If bracket screw holes are not accessible with gutter in place, follow procedure as for replacing section

65

wall plugs

support nails

packing

bracket fixing screws

Repairing flat, shed and corrugated roofs

While the most common type of house roof is pitched and covered with tiles or slates, there are other kinds of covering and you may have one on your property. The main roof can be flat rather than pitched or there may be a flat roof on a room extension, garage or other small-scale construction; some roofs are corrugated and you may have a shed with a roof covered in roofing felt. Whatever the type of roof, it is worth checking for signs of deterioration – where repairs are needed, it may be possible for you to carry them out yourself.

Flat roofs

A faulty roof may be indicated by a damp patch on a ceiling. Tracing the source of a leak in a flat roof can be difficult since water may have travelled some distance before it shows as a damp patch. Therefore looking at a roof directly above a damp patch will not necessarily show where the problem lies and you should examine the entire roof for damage.

If the roof looks in reasonable condition, it should be sufficient to apply two coats of heavy duty liquid bitumen coating to waterproof it. Alternatively you can apply an overall plastic membrane to the roof surface. Both treatments can be carried out on roofing felt, asphalt, zinc, lead or concrete.

Bitumen proofing Before applying this waterproofing liquid, remove dirt and dust with a wire brush and a knife or wallpaper scraper and sweep the roof to remove debris. If there is any moss and lichen, scrape it off and treat the roof surface with a proprietary fungicide solution, allowing this to dry before carrying out the waterproofing treatment. Bitumen proofing can be applied by brush to damp as well as dry surfaces; you will find dipping the brush in water from time to time makes it easier to spread the bitumen. Make sure the first coat is thoroughly dry before applying the second.

Where there is more serious damage to the roof

1a Before laying new felt, remove the old felt by cutting round the edges and tearing it off; trim round fixing nails as necessary
1b Nail battens to the top of the fascia boards to form drip rails. If the fascia board projects upwards at the verge, also nail an angled timber fillet to the inside of the board
1c Use nails to fix the first layer of felt, working from the centre outwards
1d Fix the second layer of felt using adhesive; make sure the joints do not coincide with the joints of the first layer

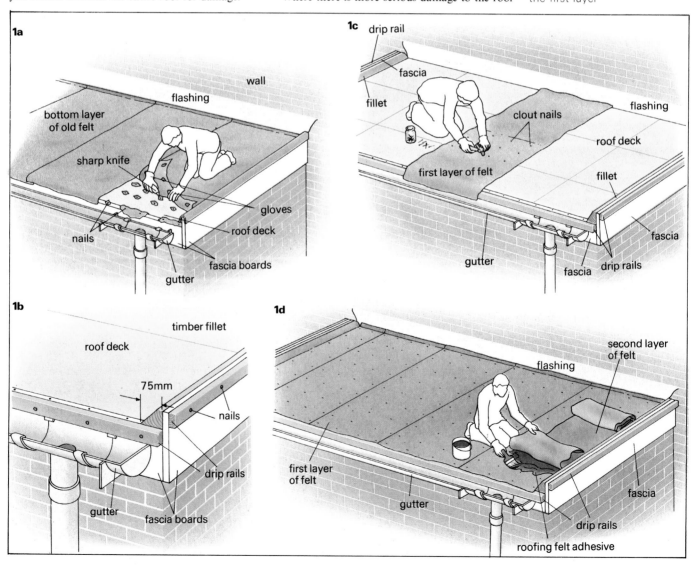

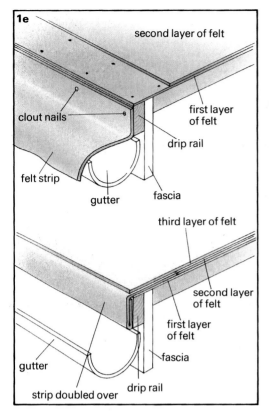

1e

second layer of felt

clout nails

first layer of felt

drip rail

felt strip

gutter

fascia

third layer of felt

second layer of felt

first layer of felt

gutter

fascia

strip doubled over

drip rail

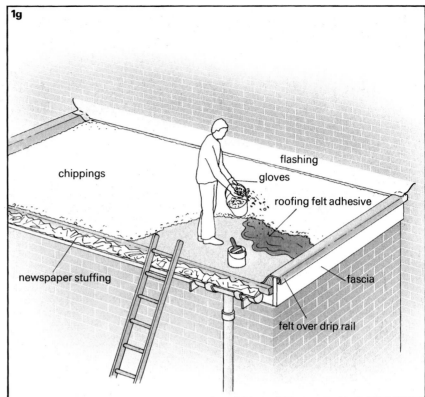

1g

chippings

flashing

gloves

roofing felt adhesive

newspaper stuffing

fascia

felt over drip rail

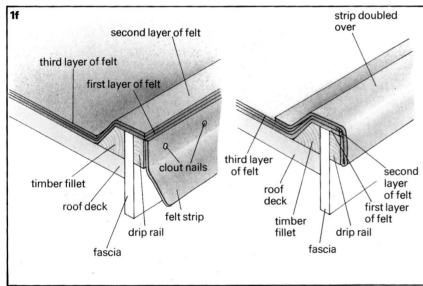

1f

second layer of felt

third layer of felt

first layer of felt

strip doubled over

clout nails

third layer of felt

roof deck

second layer of felt

first layer of felt

timber fillet

roof deck

drip rail

timber fillet

felt strip

fascia

drip rail

fascia

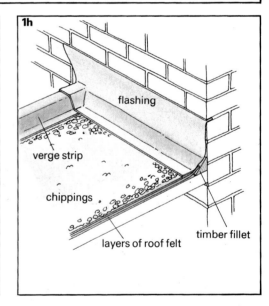

1h

flashing

verge strip

chippings

layers of roof felt

timber fillet

covering, such as severe cracks, loose areas and bad wrinkles, the roof should be stripped and the covering replaced. In the case of an asphalt roof, this work should be left to a professional. Where a concrete roof has cracked, trowel on a mortar mix to fill the cracks before treating with bitumen proofing. Where the roof has a timber base, check the timber is sound and remove and replace any unsound boards before carrying out further repairs.
Roofing felt Flat roofs covered with bituminous roofing felt are quite easy to strip and replace. On house extension or garage roofs there are usually three layers of felt fixed down over a roof deck of timber boards or chipboard sheets. Tear off the old felt, using a sharp knife to cut round the nails. It is best to wear tough gloves when doing this job since the felt is rough and may cut or scratch your hands. Remove the old fixing nails with a claw hammer or hammer them as flush with the

surface as possible. Sweep the surface clean and check it is smooth – high points can be taken off with an abrasive disc fitted to an electric drill and depressions levelled with an exterior grade filler. Nail a $50 \times 38mm$ ($2 \times 1\frac{1}{2}in$) batten along the outside edge or verge of the roof to serve as a drip rail over which felt will later be fixed to form an apron; this weatherproofs the edge of the roof and throws water clear of the walls of the building or into a gutter, if one is fitted. If the fascia board projects upwards at the verge, you should also nail a 75mm (3in) wide angled timber fillet behind the fascia.

Before you buy felt, consult your local building inspector to check that the type you have in mind complies with the current Building Regulations. Felt manufacturers make recommendations regarding the kind of felt to be fitted to suit the type of roof and will supply comprehensive fixing instructions. Where possible, cut the felt roughly to length and

1e At the eaves, nail a strip of felt to the drip rail and then double it back over to lie flush with the second layer of felt
1f At the verge, nail a strip of felt to the drip rail and then double it back to lap over the third layer of felt
1g Apply adhesive and chippings to the top layer of felt after stuffing the gutter with newspaper
1h At the parapet wall, fit a felt flashing with the end cut at 45 degrees and the top tucked into the raked-out mortar joint

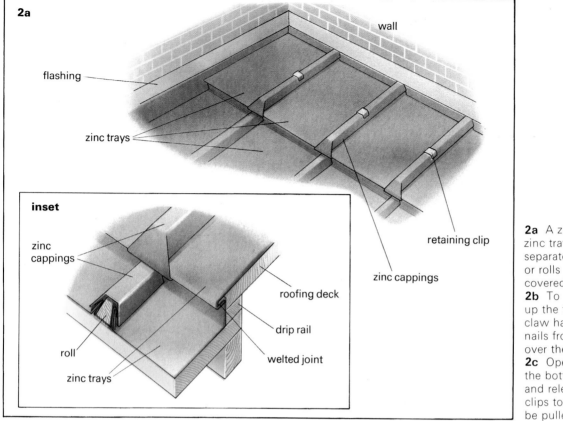

2a

wall

flashing

zinc trays

inset

zinc cappings

roll

zinc trays

roofing deck

drip rail

welted joint

retaining clip

zinc cappings

2a A zinc roof is made up of zinc trays, which are separated by timber battens or rolls (**inset**); these are covered with zinc cappings
2b To remove a tray, lever up the flashing and use a claw hammer to remove the nails from the zinc cappings over the rolls
2c Open the welted joint at the bottom edge of the tray and release the retaining clips to enable the tray to be pulled out

leave it flat for at least 24 hours before fixing to minimize the effects of subsequent curling and stretching. Usually, you will have to fix the first layer of felt to the roof boards with galvanized clout nails at 150mm (6in) intervals. Fix from the centre of the sheet outwards to prevent wrinkles and bubbles forming and secure subsequent layers of felt by brushing on roofing felt adhesive. Also apply roofing felt adhesive over the surface of the top layer of felt and sprinkle on small stone chippings to protect the felt and give a non-slip surface – or you can spread on a special chipping compound. Protect the gutter from the chippings by blocking it with newspaper or rags while you are carrying out this operation. To form the weatherproofing apron at the eaves, the middle layer of felt should be cut a little shorter than the other layers; cut a separate strip, nail it to the drip rail with galvanized clout nails and double the edge over to lie flush with, and butting against, the second layer. At the verge, a similar piece of felt is nailed to the drip rail and doubled over to form the apron and then taken over the roof to overlap the top layer of felt.

Zinc roofing Normally a zinc roof is constructed in tiers called drips and each drip is subdivided into sections or zinc trays; the trays are separated by timber battens or rolls which are also covered with zinc. While extensive repairs are probably best left to a roofing specialist, you can replace a damaged tray yourself. Where the tray meets a retaining wall there will be a flashing overlapping the tray. Lever this up and use a claw hammer or pincers to remove the nails from the zinc capping covering the rolls. Open the welted joint at the bottom edge of the tray, release the retaining clips which hold the tray in place and slide the tray free. Use the old tray as a pattern to cut the new one to size with tin snips. Repeat for the cappings, remembering to make sure

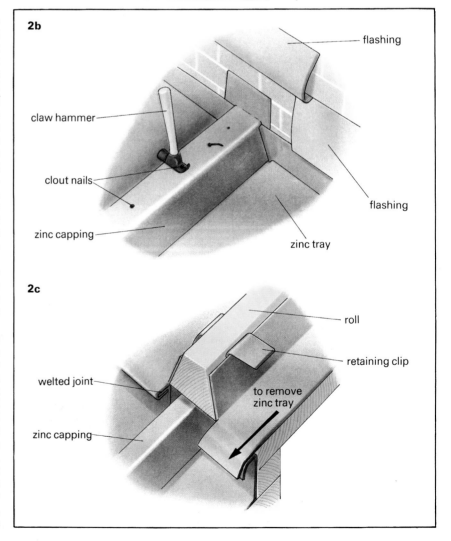

2b

flashing

claw hammer

clout nails

zinc capping

flashing

zinc tray

2c

welted joint

zinc capping

roll

retaining clip

to remove zinc tray

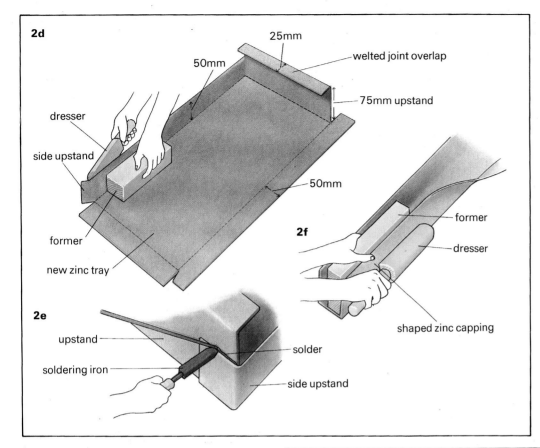

2d 25mm — welted joint overlap

50mm

dresser

side upstand

75mm upstand

former

50mm

new zinc tray

2f former

dresser

2e

upstand

soldering iron

solder

side upstand

shaped zinc capping

2d To shape the new tray, use a batten as a former and press the zinc up round it with a wood dresser
2e Solder the tray corners
2f Fold the new capping with a former and dresser
2g Position the new tray, butting the upturned sides against the rolls and leaving the bottom end open to form the welted joint
2h Solder the edges of the capping to the tray at the roll end

on both occasions you fold out the welted joint to cut the new zinc to the right size.

Using a batten of suitable length as a former, bend up the sides and end of the new zinc to form the upstands of the tray, clean all round with wire wool, and solder the corners. Fold the capping in the same way as the old capping. Place the new tray in position, lap the flashing over it and butt the upturned sides hard up against the rolls, folding the retaining clips over the upstands. Secure the new capping in place with galvanized nails and solder the edges of the capping at the roll end where they butt against the zinc tray underneath.

Alternatively you can strip the zinc covering and replace it with roofing felt. You can replace the zinc with metal-faced glass fibre bitumen sheeting, but this type of work is best left to a specialist.
Lead roofing Normally a lead roof should last for a long time; but if there are small damaged patches in a roof, you can solder on small pieces of lead to cover the damage. Buying sheets of lead for more extensive repair work is expensive and it is cheaper and simpler to strip off the lead and apply three layers of bituminous felt.

Shed roofs

A single sheet of mineral-surfaced roofing felt is normally used to waterproof a shed roof, but sometimes it may be covered with bitumen strip slates which simulate a tiled roof. In both cases, you can patch small tears and cracks with new pieces of roofing felt stuck down with roofing felt adhesive. If the covering is in very bad condition, it should be removed and replaced. Before carrying out replacement, remove any protruding nails with a claw hammer or drive them in flush with the roof.
Felt covering Lay new bituminous roofing felt in wide strips which run along the length of the roof. The strips should be cut and laid out for at least 24

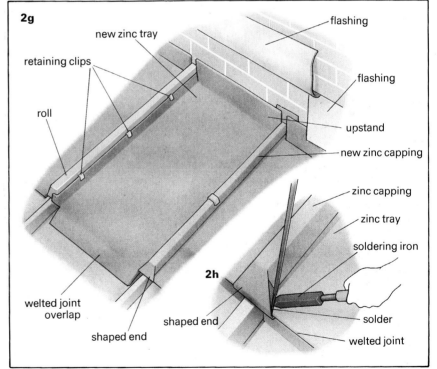

2g new zinc tray

retaining clips

roll

flashing

flashing

upstand

new zinc capping

zinc capping

zinc tray

soldering iron

solder

welted joint

welted joint overlap

shaped end

shaped end

2h

hours before fixing. Start fixing at eaves or gutter level and overlap adjacent strips by 75mm (3in), finishing off at the ridge or apex. Nail them down using 13mm (½in) galvanized clout nails at about 50mm (2in) intervals around the edges. Fold under exposed edges at the eaves and verges before nailing. For extra weather protection, secure the felt overlaps with roofing felt adhesive. Seal the ridge with a 300mm (or 12in) wide strip of felt fixed with adhesive and clout nails along the edges.

Bitumen strip slates These are fixed in place with galvanized clout nails. Start at the eaves and work up the roof to the ridge, making sure the strips are laid with staggered joints. With some types of strip slates, you should stick down the exposed part of each strip by melting the underside of the strip with a blowlamp: check the maker's instructions.

Corrugated roofs

Plastic, glass fibre, asbestos-cement, galvanized steel and aluminium are frequently used for corrugated roofing. In all cases, small cracks and holes can be repaired by patching with self-adhesive foil-backed flashing strip.

Patching Use a wire brush to clean the damaged area; cut the patch so it overlaps this area by at least 50mm (2in) all round and press it on. You should prime an asbestos-cement surface first with flashing strip primer to ensure the patch adheres firmly. As an alternative method, you can repair holes using the glass fibre matting repair kits sold for car bodywork repairs. When the repairs are complete, resurface the entire roof with two coats of heavy duty liquid bitumen proofing. This will seal pin-prick holes or porous areas on most surfaces, but cannot be used on thin plastic sheeting.

Replacing corrugated sheet Where there is extensive damage you should replace the damaged sheets. Use a claw hammer to remove the nails from an old sheet, then ease up the flashing and pull out the sheet. Cut the new sheet using the old sheet as a pattern. Put wood blocks under the third corrugation of a sheet next to the gap which the new sheet will fill and slide the new sheet under the raised sheet and over the sheet on the opposite side, checking it is properly in place. Remove the blocks and drill holes to take the fixing screws which should penetrate the high points of the corrugations, not the valleys. (Check with your supplier on the type of screw suitable for use with the material you are fixing.) If necessary, replace the flashing with self-adhesive flashing strip.

3a When covering a shed roof with felt, fix the first strip at the level of the eaves or gutter. Fold the felt at the corner and nail it in place (**inset**)

3b Make sure there is an overlap between adjacent strips of felt

3c Seal the ridge of the roof with a strip of felt. Where the felt laps over the edge of the ridge, fold and nail it

4a Use galvanized clout nails to fix trimmed bitumen strip slates at the eaves

4b Lay the rows of strips so the joints are staggered for weatherproofing

4c With some types of strip slates you will have to melt the underside of the slates with a blowtorch to stick them down

5a Use a self-adhesive flashing strip to patch small tears and cracks in corrugated roofing

5b To replace a damaged corrugated sheet, slide the new sheet under one sheet, which is raised up by a wood block, and over the sheet on the opposite side

5c Types of fixing for corrugated roofing

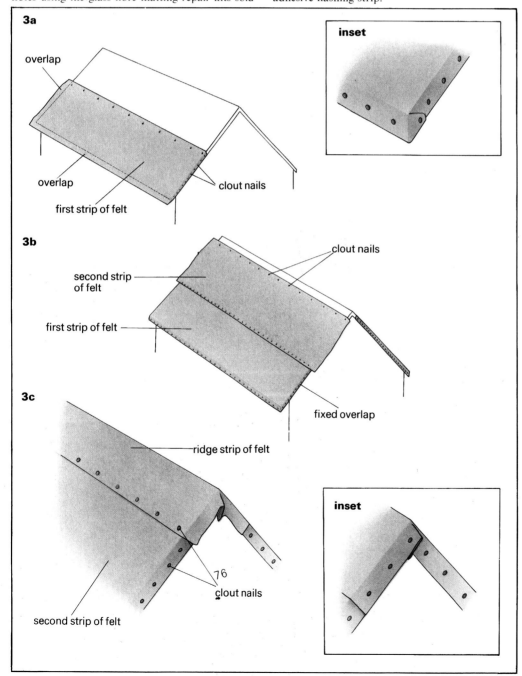

3a

overlap

overlap

first strip of felt

clout nails

inset

3b

clout nails

second strip of felt

first strip of felt

fixed overlap

3c

ridge strip of felt

76

clout nails

second strip of felt

inset

4a

clout nails

trimmed slates

gutter

metal drip

bitumen adhesive

roof deck

felt soaker

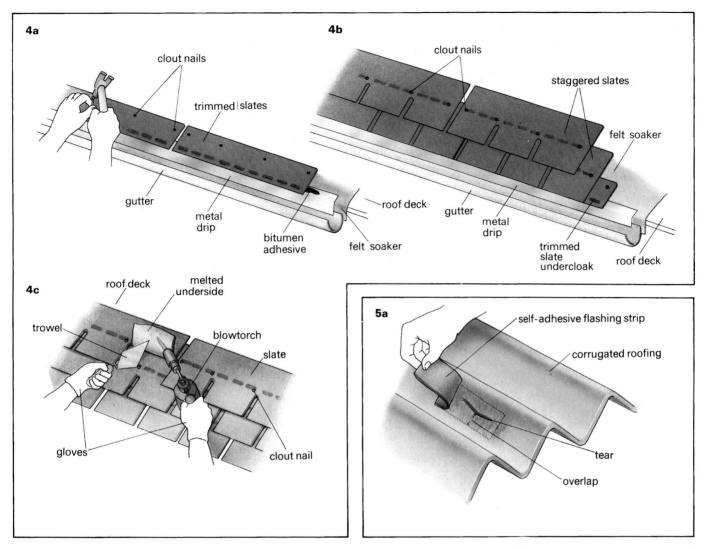

4b

clout nails

staggered slates

felt soaker

gutter

metal drip

trimmed slate undercloak

roof deck

4c

roof deck

melted underside

trowel

blowtorch

slate

gloves

clout nail

5a

self-adhesive flashing strip

corrugated roofing

tear

overlap

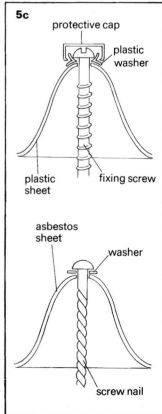

5b

roof deck

wood block

new sheet

fixings

old sheets

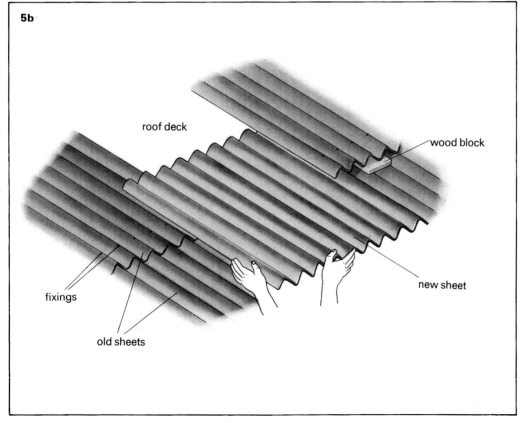

5c

protective cap

plastic washer

plastic sheet

fixing screw

asbestos sheet

washer

screw nail

Locks for doors

The average home contains at least ten doors, most of which have various functions and require different locking devices. You should fit both interior and exterior doors with good quality locks which offer proper security and do not hinder everyday life for members of the household.

When considering home security it is a good idea to start by making a floor plan of your home; take exact measurements of door thickness and door stile widths and note the condition of locks already fitted. This plan will help you to examine the cost of overall security requirements and to order the devices and fittings you will need.

Types of door

Outside doors should be at least 45mm (1¾in) thick and made of stout hardwood. There is little point in fitting expensive security devices to doors which are weak and likely to be broken down easily.

Front door This is usually the most vulnerable door since it is the one you use to leave the house and therefore cannot be bolted from the inside. Approximately 28 percent of all break-ins occur from the front of private houses. Many front doors are fitted with old fashioned rim locks (a cylinder mounted inside and through the door); you can secure the door by adding a one bolt, five or six lever mortise deadlock (a box mounted inside the door) or replace it with a rim lock and a lockable handle which has the deadlocking function. If the stile is under 75mm (3in) wide, you will have to fit the former or a special narrow rim deadlock. The door must have a minimum thickness of 38mm (1½in) for both types.

If you decide to replace the rim lock, buy one of similar dimensions so only slight modification will be needed to fit it. The standard mortise lock has two keyholes and is fitted into a mortise in the edge of the door; it is suitable for double doors if one door is locked with flush bolts. Double doors with a rebate require a rebated forend and a rebated locking plate, which must be stipulated when the lock is ordered; you should quote the hand of the lock, whether the door opens inwards or outwards and the depth of the rebate. To determine the hand of a lock, view the door from the outside; the edge on which the lock will fit is the hand. If the lock is for the edge of the door on your right, a right-hand lock is required.

Two security or mortise bolts fitted top and bottom of a front door will give additional security. A security chain will guard against unexpected intrusion if you remember to secure it before opening the door to strangers. Fit a door viewer to allow visitors to be identified before the door is opened.

Back door and side door Approximately 62 percent of break-ins take place at the back of houses. Low security locks should be replaced with a standard or two bolt mortise deadlock of at least five levers and two bolts can be added as additional security. If the door is glazed, it is better to use mortise bolts; if trades people and callers are expected you should fit a chain and door viewer.

French windows An intruder can easily open these types of door. Fit a mortise lock and mortise bolts, one shooting upwards into the top of the frame on one door and the other to the second door (which overlaps the first), shooting down into the floor.

Metal doors These are normally made of galvanized steel or aluminium and are supplied with good locks. Aluminium replacement doors for domestic use are usually supplied with narrow stile widths which require rim fitting mortise deadlocks or other types of special lock. A locksmith will advise on suitable locks for metal doors and may also be able to fit them for you. A surface-fitting, key-operated bolt can be added to metal doors.

Sliding patio doors Some sliding patio doors are supplied with a lock fitted to the centre stile, which prevents the door being slid open. However, many do not have this facility and rely solely on the locks at the edge of the door, which can be easily overcome if force is used. In this case it is best to fit an additional lock to the top or bottom rail. You can do this yourself, but great care must be taken; if

Fitting mortise lock to timber door
1a Mark out mortise
1b Drill line of holes and chisel out waste
1c With lock inside mortise, mark round forend; chisel out marked area to form recess for forend
1d With face of forend flush with door edge, mark through keyhole to give drilling point; chisel out drilled hole to form keyhole shape
1e With lock fitted, hold escutcheon in place and mark position for fixing screws
1f Throw bolt and mark top and bottom of bolt on jamb; continue lines round to inner jamb and retract bolt

If you are in any doubt about a security problem, go to your local police station and seek the advice of the crime prevention officer. CPOs can be found in virtually every area of Britain and their experience and knowledge of security devices, including details of how to fit them, will prove invaluable. The service is free.

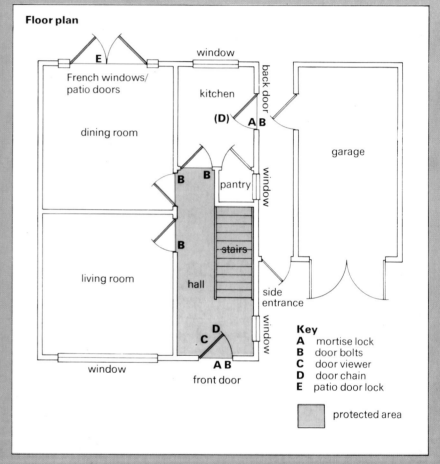

Floor plan

French windows/patio doors

window

dining room

kitchen

back door

(D) A B

garage

B B

pantry

window

B

stairs

living room

hall

side entrance

window

D

C

window

A B

front door

Key
A mortise lock
B door bolts
C door viewer
D door chain
E patio door lock

protected area

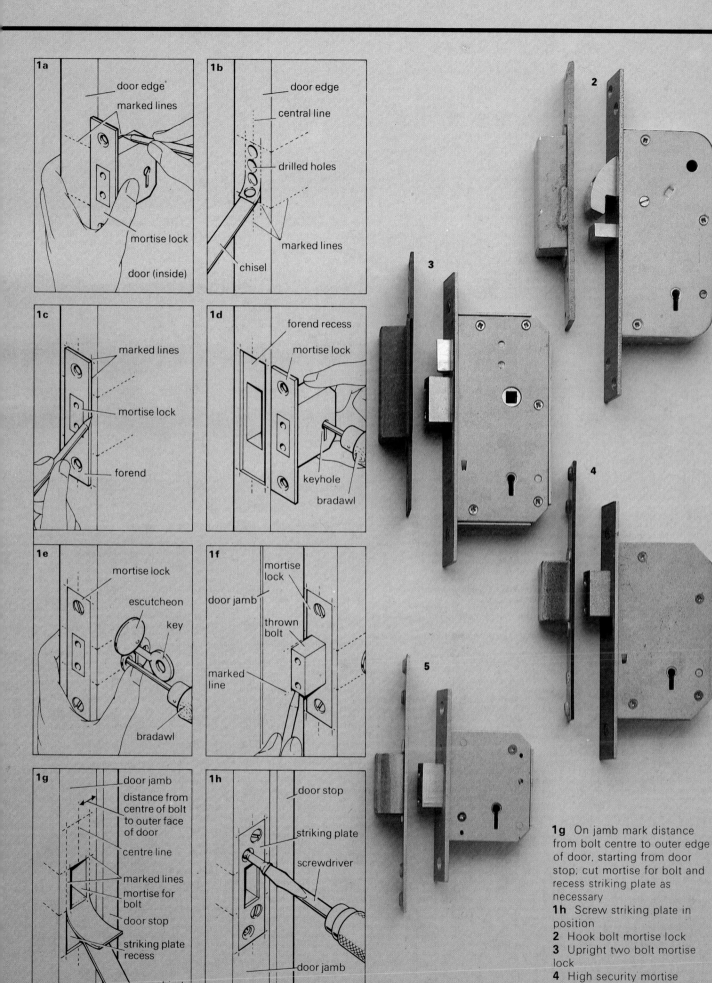

1a
door edge
marked lines
mortise lock
door (inside)

1b
door edge
central line
drilled holes
marked lines
chisel

1c
marked lines
mortise lock
forend

1d
forend recess
mortise lock
keyhole
bradawl

1e
mortise lock
escutcheon
key
bradawl

1f
mortise lock
door jamb
thrown bolt
marked line

1g
door jamb
distance from centre of bolt to outer face of door
centre line
marked lines
mortise for bolt
door stop
striking plate recess
chisel

1h
door stop
striking plate
screwdriver
door jamb

1g On jamb mark distance from bolt centre to outer edge of door, starting from door stop; cut mortise for bolt and recess striking plate as necessary
1h Screw striking plate in position
2 Hook bolt mortise lock
3 Upright two bolt mortise lock
4 High security mortise deadlock
5 Mortise deadlock

you are in any doubt, it is best to have the lock fitted by a professional.

Timber sliding doors There are several types of lock suitable, but these doors are best secured with hook bolt mortise locks which have a deadlocking action. You can use a lock with a claw bolt action which grips a recess in the striking plate, but these are not usually available with deadlocking function.

Interior doors Doors inside the house offer a valuable second line of defence against the would-be intruder, provided the layout is not open plan. In isolated areas or in situations where the house may be left empty for long periods, an intruder could cause considerable damage by smashing down locked interior doors. But since some insurance companies may insist interiors doors are left locked in this kind of situation, it is probably the best course to take. In any case, check your insurance policy before making a decision.

The floor plan shows how locking interior doors can prevent easy access to the hallway and rooms on the ground and first floors. In most cases, the original locks fitted by the housebuilder will offer poor security. Here you can fit mortise bolts at the top and bottom of the door (to operate sideways on single doors), installing them with the keyholes facing the hallway.

Fitting locks

Until the recent advent of magnetic and electronic locking devices, lock mechanisms had involved only two principal methods: a fixed obstruction (or 'ward'), which prevents any but the correct key operating the lock, and a more effective method involving detainers or levers, which are brought together in pre-selected positions by a key. The latter is the principle of the modern range of mortise deadlocks; when properly fitted they are designed to be stronger than a timber door. This means, in the event of a break-in, the wood itself would fail before the lock. The locking bolt is enclosed inside a steel box to prevent the lock being picked; some have up to three anti-picking devices as well. The bolt itself is often enclosed and reinforced with steel rollers which rotate to prevent a thief cutting through the bolt. Once the bolt is locked, it is secured automatically.

When more than one lock is fitted, you can obtain a key which will open all the locks, but you must ask for this when you order the locks. Some manufacturers offer a registration service which ensures replacement keys are only given to the registered lock owners. You should complete the registration document and return it to the manufacturer.

Fitting a mortise lock should offer no problems to the experienced DIY person as long as the manufacturer's instructions are carefully followed. If in any doubt, you should contact a professional since a poorly fitted lock will be inefficient and may reduce overall security. There is a wide range of mortise locks available and many reasonably priced devices provide good security. The British Standard BS 3621 is worth looking for when choosing locks because those with this stamp are resistant to drilling and manipulation from outside, have a minimum of 1000 key variations and comply with a number of other exacting requirements.

Fitting a mortise lock Different manufacturers will suggest different methods of fitting; but as a rule the lock is placed along the central rail (slightly lower than halfway down the door) on a panelled door, or along the outer stile on a hardboard door.

6 Standard rim lock. **7** Rim automatic deadlock; handle can be locked from outside. **8** Rim automatic deadlock; handle can be locked from both sides of door. **9** Door pull. Fitting rim lock: **10a** Hold supplied template on door and mark key cylinder position; drill small holes first then large hole. **10b** Chisel out recess for forend. **10c** Remove fixing plate from deadlock and position plate on door so screw holes coincide with four holes in door. **10d** Fit key cylinder and mark length of protruding bar (should be at least one notch longer than door thickness); remove cylinder, cut bar to required length and fix cylinder with screws (don't overtighten). **10e** Throw bolt on deadlock

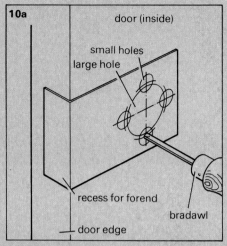

10a
door (inside)
small holes
large hole
recess for forend
bradawl
door edge

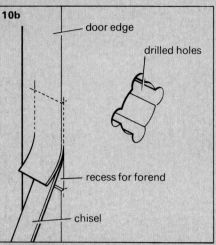

10b
door edge
drilled holes
recess for forend
chisel

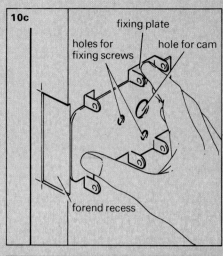

10c
fixing plate
holes for fixing screws
hole for cam
forend recess

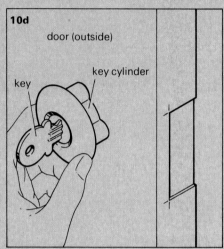

10d
door (outside)
key cylinder
key

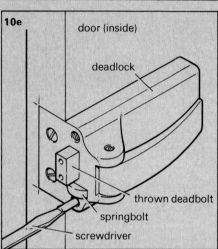

10e
door (inside)
deadlock
thrown deadbolt
springbolt
screwdriver

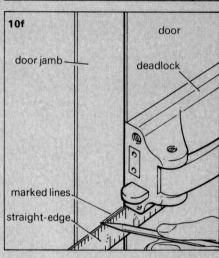

10f
door
door jamb
deadlock
marked lines
straight-edge

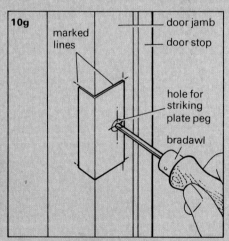

10g
marked lines
door jamb
door stop
hole for striking plate peg
bradawl

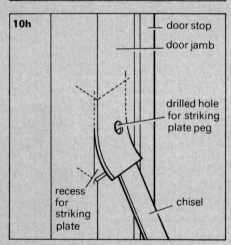

10h
door stop
door jamb
drilled hole for striking plate peg
recess for striking plate
chisel

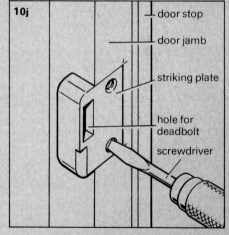

10j
door stop
door jamb
striking plate
hole for deadbolt
screwdriver

and position deadlock over fixing plate so connecting bar is engaged in cam. **10f** Turn key to retract bolt and, with door closed, mark position of striking plate on jamb.
10g Put supplied template on jamb, mark position of striking plate and drill peg hole to required depth (peg is on striking plate).
10h Chisel out recess for striking plate. **10j** Place striking plate in position with peg in hole; secure plate with screws

Position the lock on the inside of the door and draw round it; drill a series of small holes in the area marked and chisel out the mortise. Fit the lock into the mortise so it is flush with the edge of the door; drill out key holes on both sides as recommended by the manufacturer and chisel to key-hole shape. Check you have drilled the key holes correctly and the lock is aligned before fitting the lock and escutcheons. The striking plate is secured to the door frame after you have marked out its correct position in relation to the bolt of the lock. Drill and chisel out a mortise for the striking plate and roughly fit the plate to the frame; any adjustments should be made to the plate and not to the lock position.
Fitting a rim lock This mortise deadlock is not mortised into the edge of the door, but secured

through the door. The deadlocking action varies depending upon construction; most deadlock automatically when the door is closed and some require the key to be turned before they deadlock. The lock is supplied in three parts – a key cylinder, deadlocking portion and striking plate or staple. Again, manufacturers will supply detailed fitting instructions relevant to their particular model; in general terms you will have to drill through the door and some manufacturers will supply a template for this. Insert the key cylinder from the outside of the door and cut the connecting bar to length, according to fitting instructions. Fit the deadlock to the inside of the door and screw the striking plate into the door frame after alignment. You can buy a pull which fits beneath the key cylinder flange.

Additional security devices

A mortise lock fitted to an interior or exterior door will often be all that is needed to upgrade your home security; however there are certain weak areas which may need additional devices to deter the intruder. For example, the porch door is your first line of defence and should be fitted with a good two bolt, five lever mortise lock.

Two bolt mortise lock This is similar to the standard mortise lock but has an extra latch bolt with the deadlocking function. The lock is suitable for exterior doors. The two bolt version is fitted in the same manner as the standard mortise lock.

Hook bolt mortise lock This is widely used to secure timber sliding doors, either flush or single ones, provided there is sufficient space to accommodate the box striking plate in the rim of the door. Installation is similar to the standard mortise lock and the deadlocking function can be triggered either by closing the door or turning the key.

Security mortise bolt This type can be used to secure exterior or interior doors and French windows. They are usually fitted in pairs (to top and bottom of the door) and a standard key opens all the bolts. All that is required for installation is a hole of recommended size drilled into the edge of the door and frame, two shallow rebates cut to accommodate the locking plate and the flange and enable the bolt to be fitted flush into the edge of the door and a hole in the face of the door to take the key. A circular bolt is thrown back by the key, which operates from only one side of the door.

Surface fitting bolts These are the traditional bolts which are usually fitted at the top and bottom of a door. Ensure you use the correct size bolt – for

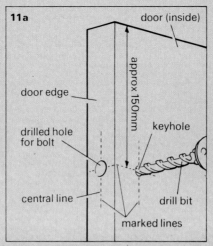

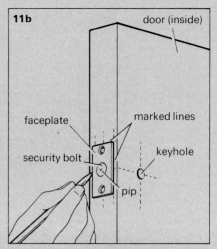

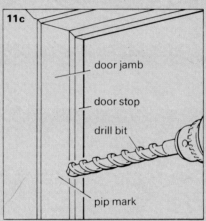

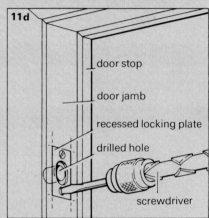

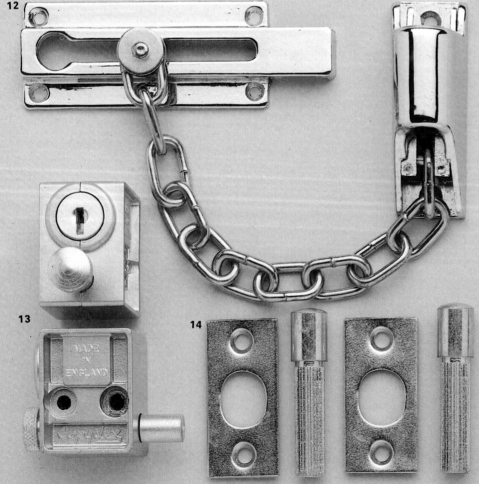

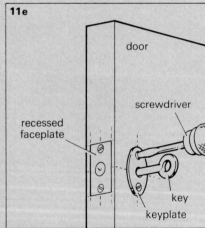

Fitting security bolt: **11a** Mark out and drill bolt hole and keyhole; stop keyhole at bolt hole. **11b** With bolt in hole and faceplate on edge of door, mark and recess faceplate; secure with screws. **11c** With door closed, turn key so pip marks centre point for locking plate on jamb; drill hole to take bolt. **11d** Cut recess and screw locking plate in place. **11e** Fix key plate in position with screws
12 Lockable security chain
13 Lock for sliding doors
14 Hinge bolts
15 Security mortise bolt
16 Surface fitting bolt
17 Door viewer

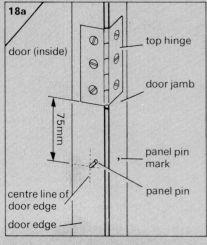

18a
door (inside)
top hinge
door jamb
75mm
panel pin mark
centre line of door edge
panel pin
door edge

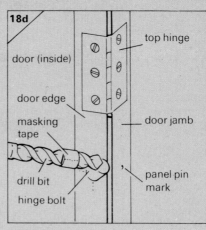

18b
masking tape
drill bit
hinge bolt
area to protrude
area to be recessed

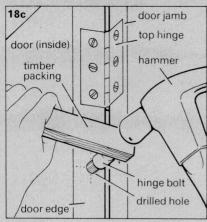

18c
door jamb
top hinge
door (inside)
timber packing
hammer
hinge bolt
drilled hole
door edge

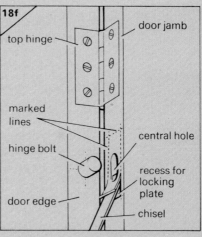

18d
top hinge
door (inside)
door edge
masking tape
door jamb
drill bit
hinge bolt
panel pin mark

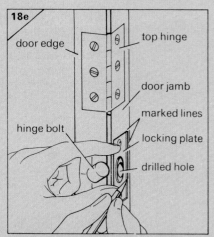

18e
door edge
top hinge
door jamb
marked lines
hinge bolt
locking plate
drilled hole

18f
door jamb
top hinge
marked lines
hinge bolt
central hole
recess for locking plate
door edge
chisel

exterior doors the minimum bolt length should be 200mm (8in) – and the correct size screw; undersized bolts and screws could be forced.

Hinge bolts These are particularly important for outward opening doors where the hinges are exposed. The bolts fit inside the frame, close to the hinges. The keep is rebated into the door frame and the bolt is fitted into the door by drilling a hole for it. Hinge bolts will provide solid protection for a door and frame even if the hinge pin is removed.

Door chains These should be fitted to front and rear exterior doors as a precaution against casual visitors; they allow you to examine visitors' credentials and prevent violent intrusion into the home. Always keep them fixed when the house is occupied. They are easily fitted with screws. Some types incorporate an unlockable plunger which enables the chain to be secured when leaving the house and also prevents a successful intruder locking you out of the house.

Door viewer This is essential when outward vision is hampered by solid door construction or frosted glass; fit a porch light as well for night use. The door viewer comes in two parts, one part screwing into the other through the door. Drill a hole of the required size through the door to fit a door viewer; place a block of wood behind the door when drilling to prevent the drill bit bursting through and damaging the finish of the door.

Anti-jemmy plates These are used where there is a perceptible gap between the edge of the door and the door frame. They are mounted to reduce this gap and to prevent the use of jemmies and other devices of the housebreaker, which might open a non-deadlocking rim lock for example.

Fitting hinge bolt: **18a** Mark position of bolt with pin; close door so pin marks position on jamb. **18b** Use masking tape round drill bit to mark drilling depth; remove pin and drill bolt hole. **18c** Drive in bolt. **18d** Drill hole for bolt in jamb to required depth. **18e** With locking plate over hole, mark round edge and central hole. **18f** Chisel central hole to shape, form recess and fix plate with screws

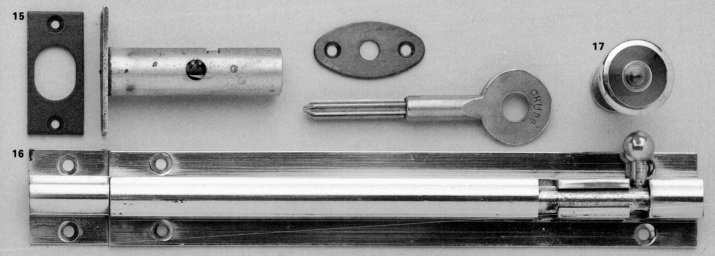

15

16

17

Locks for windows

Over 60 percent of household break-ins occur through windows; intruders choose this route because an unsecured window can be quickly opened from outside. For example, it could take an experienced burglar less than 15 seconds to enter a house through a casement window by breaking or removing a pane.

There is a wide range of window security devices (WSDs) available to secure windows properly, preventing easy access and causing as much obstruction as possible to an intruder. It is worth fitting these to all the windows in your house, even to those which are above the ground floor, since an agile intruder could scale a drainpipe or building projection or climb scaffolding or a ladder which has been carelessly left out. Fanlights should also be protected, as should small permanently shut windows, since once the glass has been removed these can provide access for a slim intruder.

Fitting most WSDs is within the capability of the home handyman; usually, you will find any experience you have gained in installing mortise locks or bolts on doors will be valuable since fitting WSDs often requires similar tools and expertise. Remember too that although an intruder may gain access through a window, he may be unable to retreat through the same opening since the stolen goods may be too large; you should make sure all exterior doors are secured as well.

Preparing for installation

Start by making a plan of window locations and note the size and type of each window and its existing fittings. Check how frequently windows are usually opened since this is a feature you should consider when choosing the WSD you will fit. Examine windows for loose joints and panes and look for rotten sections in timber frames; complete any repair work before fitting security devices.

Window security devices fit to and secure existing fittings or are fitted between moving and fixed window sections. The costs of individual WSDs can vary considerably, but as a general rule those which are fitted to existing fittings semi-permanently are cheaper than key-operated types which are fitted permanently to fixed and moving frames and allow windows to be opened quickly. When selecting WSDs it is best to avoid choosing cheaper semi-permanent types for windows which are regularly opened since they will need to be frequently removed from and replaced on the fitting and may be lost or not used as a result.

Anti-child locks Care should be taken in selecting WSDs for households with young children; in this case the devices will be used to prevent windows being opened easily from inside as well as outside. Devices which lock directly onto handles and stays are suitable since these are difficult to remove.

Warning Where screw heads securing WSDs are visible from outside, it is worth using clutch head screws since these cannot be unscrewed. Alternatively you can file the heads of slot head screws and drill out the heads of cross head screws so they cannot be undone with a screwdriver.

WSDs for timber casements

Timber casement windows are usually fitted with cockspur handles and window stays; securing them can involve replacement of these fittings with more secure types or installing devices which give extra security in addition to the existing fittings.

Replacement units Replacement handles and stays are available in matching sets of various designs and may involve the use of conventional or special keys. With one make, the handle is secured with a conventional key and the lockable window stay can be secured in up to nine positions; so while ventilation is provided, opening the window from outside is extremely difficult. Both the handle and stay are fixed in position using the screws provided.

Window locks There is a variety of window locks available. One type fits flush to the edge of the window and you move a catch to lock a bolt section fitted to the opening frame into a keep recessed into the fixed frame when the window is closed; when you want to open the window undo the lock with the key supplied. There is a version of the same lock for use with metal frame windows and the same key can be used for both versions. Another type of device locks automatically when

1 Casement and fanlight lock
2 Lockable window stay
3 Security bolt for timber casement window
4 Automatic self-lock for timber window (hinged or pivot)
5 Lockable window latch for timber window
6 Fixing of casement lock on timber frame window
7 Fixing of automatic self-lock on timber frame window

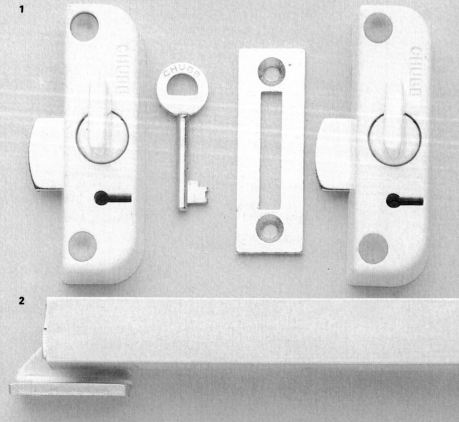

1

2

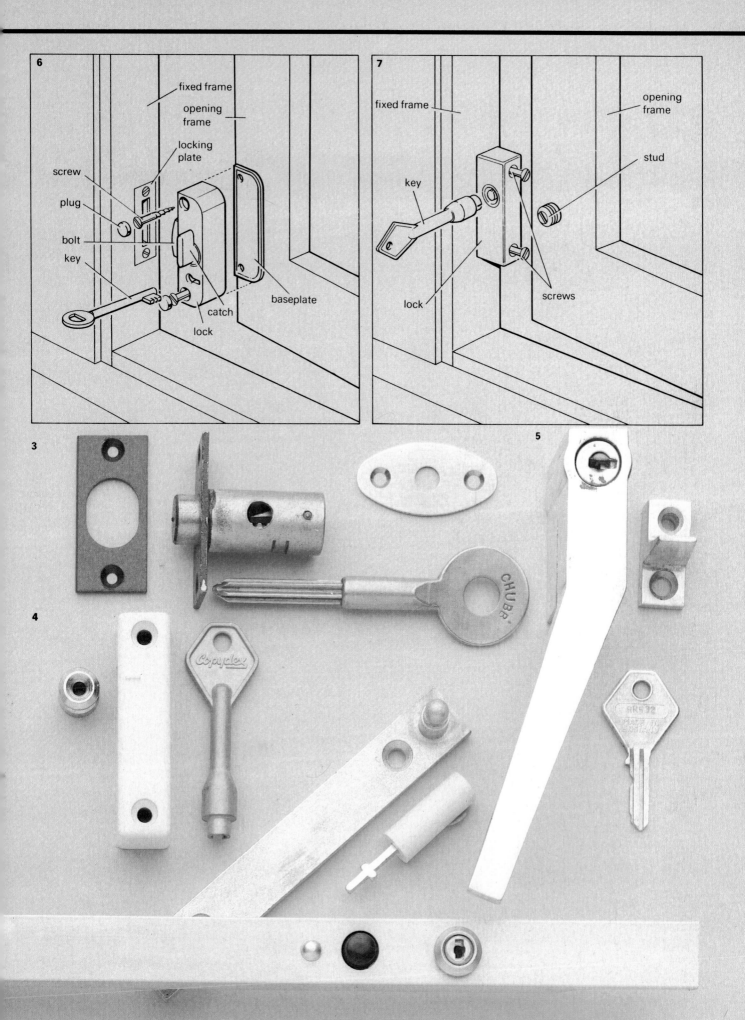

6

fixed frame

opening frame

locking plate

screw

plug

bolt

key

catch

lock

baseplate

7

fixed frame

opening frame

key

stud

lock

screws

3

4

5

the window is closed, in case you forget to lock up. You use a key to open the window.

Warning If you have young children in the house, make sure the keys to locks are not in an easily accessible position since children can quickly learn how they are used.

Window security bolts These are slightly smaller than the security bolts which are used to fit on doors; fitting them involves basically the same process. The bolt section and its casing are mortised into the edge of the opening frame in a central position and, when operated by a splined key, the bolt locks into a plate recessed into the fixed frame; the width of the frame should be 38mm ($1\frac{1}{2}$in) minimum. Security bolts have the advantage of being virtually invisible from outside. On larger casement windows, if the window frame depth will accommodate them, you can use larger door security bolts to give extra bolt depth.

Warning Window security bolts usually require a depth of at least 38mm (or $1\frac{1}{2}$in), plus suitable glazing clearance; so measure your window frame carefully to make sure its depth is sufficient before buying this type of device.

Stay locks These are inexpensive, easily fitted, threaded units which replace the existing stay pins. (If they are in good condition, you can use the screws which secured the old stay pin to secure the new threaded pin; but remember the screws will be accessible when the window is secured in some open positions and treat as described above.) The thread passes through the existing hole in the window stay and is secured from above by a special nut, which is tightened with the key supplied. You can secure a window in a partially open position by fixing through the hole further down the stay; however, since this means removing the locking nut, stay locks are best used on windows which are infrequently opened.

One type of stay lock is available for securing window stays without holes; it is fitted using two screws and is secured with a special locking key.

Other locking devices A number of small locking devices, usually operated with special keys which lock the moving and fixed parts of timber frame windows together, are also available.

WSDs for metal casements

As with timber casement windows, metal ones are usually secured with cockspur handles and window stays and, again, there is a variety of devices you can fit to provide a proper level of security.

Window locks With one typical variety the lock is fixed to the opening part of the window frame and the bolt locks into the fixed frame to secure the window. Special fixing screws are supplied to ensure strong fixing to metal window frames. The keys of this type of lock are interchangeable with those for a version designed for timber windows.

Securing handles There are several other WSDs for securing existing fittings. For example, cockspur handles on metal frame windows can be secured by a device which fits on the fixed frame beneath the handle. When the window is closed, a bolt is locked in an upright position to prevent the cockspur portion of the handle passing; if you want to open

8 Window stay lock
9 Stay lock for timber frame window
10 Stay lock for metal frame window
11 Window latch lock
12 Wedge lock for metal casement window
13 Lock for metal casement window
14 Transom lock
15a Fixing of lock for latch on metal casement window
15b Fixing of lock for latch on metal casement window where window is rarely opened
16 Fixing of wedge lock on metal casement window
17 Dual screw with key
18 Lock for timber sash window
19 Disc tumbler window lock
20 Snap-on lock for sliding windows and doors
21 Lock for sliding windows and doors

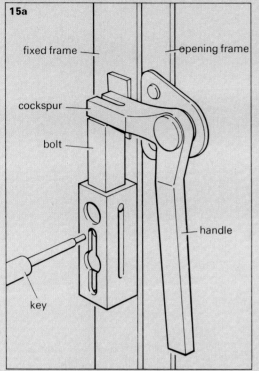

15a

fixed frame · opening frame

cockspur

bolt

handle

key

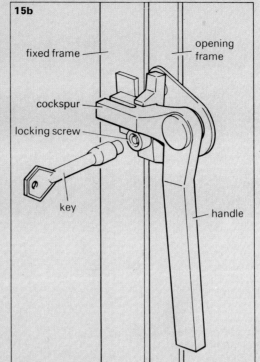

15b

fixed frame · opening frame

cockspur

locking screw

key

handle

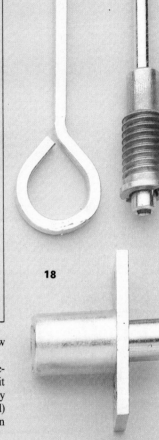

17

18

19

20 WIN-DOR LOCK

21

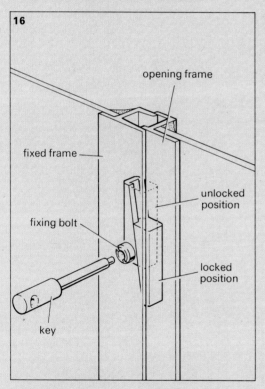

16

opening frame

fixed frame

unlocked position

fixing bolt

locked position

key

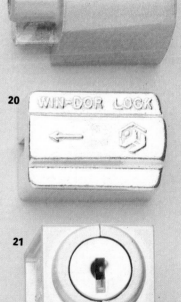

the window, you can release the bolt with a special key. This device is fitted with the self-tapping screws provided; you should drill holes for these according to the manufacturer's instructions. When fitting, make sure the swing of the cockspur misses the bolt body. To secure the handle in the 'shut' position on a window which is infrequently opened, you can fit a device which locks directly onto the cockspur using the special key provided – no tools or screws are necessary.

Securing window stays These fittings can be secured to a metal frame in several ways. They include a device which you can fit to the existing stay without screws or fixing tools; it locks the stay to its retainer to prevent stay movement and the window being opened.

Wedge lock This is fitted in the edge of the casement; when locked with an oval-shaped key, it secures the casement to the frame. It is fitted by drilling one hole (using the template provided) through the casement and securing the lock with an escutcheon screw.

WSDs for other types

For securing other types of window, you can sometimes use the devices available for casement windows; but there are devices which are manufactured specifically for use in these situations.

Transom windows Otherwise known as vents and usually situated above larger casement windows, these are normally fitted with window stays; you can use stay locks to secure them if there is a suitable timber sub-frame. There is a D-shaped clamping device available which is specially designed to prevent stay movement in metal frame transom windows; it is easily fitted with screws.

Timber sash windows These can often be opened from the outside since the centre latch can be undone by a knife or similar tool. If the windows are opened infrequently, you can secure them with strong screws. Otherwise, you can fit a device operated with a special key; a protruding bolt prevents the two sliding panes passing. There are several types available. With one type the bolt is fitted to the upper sash about 100mm (4in) above the striking plate which is fitted to the top of the lower sash. When the key is turned until the bolt is fully extended, the window may be opened a small distance to provide ventilation, but any attempt to force it will be thwarted when the bolt hits the striking plate. Other types have the bolt fixed to the top of the lower sash; the bolt locates in one or more locking plates on the upper sash to coincide with the fully closed and slightly open positions. Again, the bolts are released with a key.

Metal sliding windows These are generally fitted

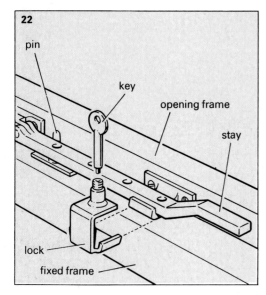

22

- pin
- key
- opening frame
- stay
- lock
- fixed frame

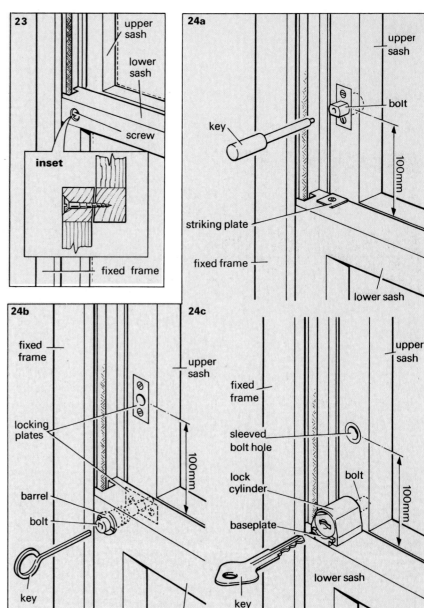

23
- upper sash
- lower sash
- screw
- **inset**
- fixed frame

24a
- upper sash
- bolt
- key
- 100mm
- striking plate
- fixed frame
- lower sash

24b
- fixed frame
- locking plates
- barrel
- bolt
- key
- 100mm
- upper sash
- lower sash

24c
- upper sash
- fixed frame
- sleeved bolt hole
- lock cylinder
- baseplate
- bolt
- 100mm
- key
- lower sash

with special locks which provide good security. For extra protection, you can fit a device which snaps onto the sliding window runner and prevents window movement; another device locks onto the frame. For many types of metal sliding window, you can fit a patio door lock to provide additional security.

Centre pivot windows These are best secured by the window locks available for casement windows. A window lock with versions for both metal and timber frame windows will adequately secure pivot windows with frames of either material.

Fanlight windows For these, the window locks available for casement windows are usually appropriate. Many fanlights have narrow frames and this is a point to consider when buying locks.

Securing fixed pane windows

Most homes have at least one small fixed window; to provide adequate security, this should be glazed with 6mm (¼in) thick wired glass. Check the interior beading is strong and securely fitted so it will withstand any attempts at forcing it.

Where you have a window with a large fixed pane, make sure the frame is in good condition and the pane is properly secured. Where a large fixed window is in a particularly vulnerable position, such as a basement area, it is worth considering the installation of a security grille or iron bars.

Security grilles In some situations, these are the only effective means of providing protection against intrusion. They are supplied in designs to match the existing decor and character of the house. Installation of a grille is best left to the specialist.

Iron bars These should be round iron of not less than 19mm (¾in) diameter or square iron of not less than 19mm .(¾in) section. They should be fixed vertically to the inside of the window at 125mm (5in) intervals; grout them into the brickwork at the top and bottom of the window to a depth of at least 50mm (2in) and recessed at least 50mm (2in) from the wall surface. The bars should pass through flat horizontal iron tie bars, the distance between which should not exceed 450mm (18in), and kept in position by welding or flattening the bars above and below the tie bars. The ends of the tie bars should be cut, splayed and grouted into the brickwork.

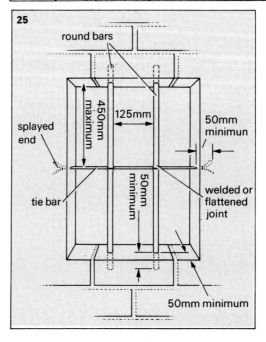

25
- round bars
- 450mm maximum
- 125mm
- 50mm minimun
- splayed end
- tie bar
- 50mm minimum
- welded or flattened joint
- 50mm minimum

22 Fixing of transom lock on metal frame window
23 Securing timber sash window with screws – one at each side
24a Fixing of locking window stop on timber sash; this lock allows window to be locked in slightly open position to provide ventilation
24b Fixing of dual screw on timber sash window; second locking plate fitted to upper sash allows window to be locked in slightly open position
24c Fixing of lock on timber sash window; again upper bolt hole allows window to be locked in slightly open position
25 How to secure fixed pane windows with iron bars

2

DECORATING AND FURNISHING

Paints, brushes, rollers & pads

Until quite recently choosing paint for interior work was fairly straightforward – emulsion for walls and ceilings, gloss for woodwork – and the only real choice you had was on colours.

The real difference today is not in the paint groups themselves – still essentially emulsion and gloss – but in the manufacturing processes constantly being developed which have made it possible to produce several varieties of each type.

This enormous variety can be confusing at first, but once you have sorted out which type of paint is for which job you will find the choice of intermediate finishes they provide invaluable.

Thinning Any proprietary brand of paint is ready for use and should not require thinning. The one exception is with emulsion, where it might be necessary to thin slightly with water when applying the first coat on a porous surface such as raw plaster.

Range of types

Basically, paint is made up of pigment and either an oil or water-based binder. Water-based paint (emulsion, vinyl and latex) dries purely by evaporation, while oil-based paint has a chemical drying agent added. Paints with a water base are not as hard or durable as those with an oil base although they are improving all the time. The greatest advantage of water-based paint is that brushes and rollers can be washed in water; no special cleaning agent is needed.

The proportion of pigment to binder in any paint dictates the amount of gloss the finished product will have. The glossier the finish, the more hard-wearing it will be. There are three main categories of finish: matt, gloss and a range in between the two which varies according to the manufacturer and is designated in many different ways – silk, satin, semi-gloss, suede, eggshell etc.

The following brief description of types, uses and application should help you.

Gloss

This is oil-based and includes resin to give it a hard-wearing quality. The standard gloss that has been available for many years contains alkyd resin, but new manufacturing techniques have produced varying degrees of sheen, such as matt gloss and silk gloss.

Uses For woodwork and metal.

Application Prime and undercoat bare timber and key (rub down well with fine glasspaper) existing gloss finishes before repainting. If you are redecorating with a different colour gloss, obliterate the old colour with one or two layers of the appropriate undercoat.

The smell of the paint will linger for some time after application; allow several hours for drying.

Polyurethane gloss

Polyurethane resin added to oil-based paint makes it tougher, providing a really hard-wearing surface to withstand greater abrasion than standard gloss.

Uses For woodwork and metal.

Application Prime all bare surfaces; although undercoat is not always necessary, you might need to apply two top coats to get a really good finish.

Key existing gloss and then cover with one or two coats, depending on the previous colour.

Silthane

A combination of silicone and polyurethane, this paint is claimed by the manufacturers to be stronger than polyurethane as the silicone gives extra protection, especially during the drying period when paint is most vulnerable. Uses and application are as for polyurethane gloss.

Emulsion

Water-based, but with vinyl or acrylic resins incorporated to make it harder-wearing. This results in varying degrees of sheen in the finish, with a progressively durable surface as the shine increases. The range of finishes available includes matt, silk and satin.

Uses Although normally intended for walls and ceilings, you can use it on woodwork, but be sure to use a water gloss type specially produced for woodwork and don't expect the same hard-wearing qualities as with oil-based paints.

Application Prime bare plaster with a plaster primer or a thinned coat of emulsion (water-diluted) before applying one or two top coats. For previously painted plaster use one or two neat (undiluted) coats of emulsion depending on the colour being covered. Existing gloss surfaces must be keyed with fine glasspaper.

If you have a distempered surface, such as a ceiling in an older house, scrape and wash away with sugar soap all traces of the distemper before attempting to paint. Seal with a special primer sealer and then apply one or two coats of emulsion.

This paint has a less pungent smell which does not linger after application and dries quickly, usually within two hours.

Thixotropic (non-drip)

An alternative type of gloss, this paint is non-drip and of a jelly-like consistency. It is ideal if you find difficulty in painting without drips falling from the brush, as its consistency allows a blob of paint to be picked up by the brush and then applied to the surface where it spreads out normally.

Uses For woodwork, metal and plaster.

Application Take all the normal preparatory precautions according to the surface before applying. Lightly brush out using random strokes and never overbrush as this will cause runs, thus defeating the object of using this particular type of paint.

Remember not to stir the paint before application, however much you are tempted to do so. It may look lumpy and unworkable, but that is the nature of the paint. Stirring will only break down the consistency and possibly ruin your finish. If you do stir the paint through force of habit, leave it for a while until it becomes jelly-like again. If you want to strain a thixotropic paint, stir first to a free-running liquid, strain and then leave to gel again.

Other types of paint

There are occasions when you will want to use a type other than the standard gloss or emulsion, according to the job in hand. These include certain paints with special properties for particular uses.

Primer This may be oil or water-based and is used to seal unpainted surfaces to prevent further coats of paint soaking in. It is vital to use the right type of primer for the surface being painted – wood, metal or plaster – although there is an all-purpose primer available.

Undercoat Usually oil-based, undercoat is applied between primer and top coats to build up the surface and provide the right colour base for the finish paint.

Enamel Term was used by manufacturers as synonymous with gloss; now commonly used to describe an alkyd modified paint.

Anti-condensation For use in steamy conditions, such as in kitchens and bathrooms, this paint is specially formulated to prevent the surface becoming cold to the touch and therefore less conducive to condensation. It is not a cure for condensation, only a way of reducing its effect on painted surfaces. (Normal emulsion paints are satisfactory here, provided the level of steam is not too high.)

Fire-retardant Containing an additive to provide a fire-resistant quality, this type will not resist fire completely, but has a greater resistance than ordinary paint and will reduce the spread of flames. Use it as an added safety measure on expanded polystyrene ceiling tiles or timber, hardboard and chipboard or any combustible surface which can be painted.

Anti-burglar Two types are available, both non-toxic. One remains slippery when dry and is used particularly to prevent people climbing walls. The other dries on the surface, but sticks to the hand when pressure is applied. White spirit will take off the paint, at the same time releasing a dye which cannot be removed.

Bituminous Thick and usually black, this is for areas where high water resistance is needed. Apply it with an old paint brush on the inside of your cast iron gutters and metal cold water tank.

Warning Never apply normal gloss or oil-based types over bituminous paint before applying a coat of aluminium sealer; otherwise the bitumen will bleed through and stain the fresh paint brown.

Paint brushes

Even with all the new additives and manufacturing processes now used to make painting easier, a first-class finish can often be ruined for want of a good paint brush. So don't waste your money on a cheap brush that will have a limited life but buy the best quality you can afford and look after it.

Pure hog's bristle This is the very best quality, with bristles set in rubber mastic which is then vulcanized to hold them firmly. The rough-textured bristles hold paint well and the natural taper at the tips enables you to apply a smooth, even coat.

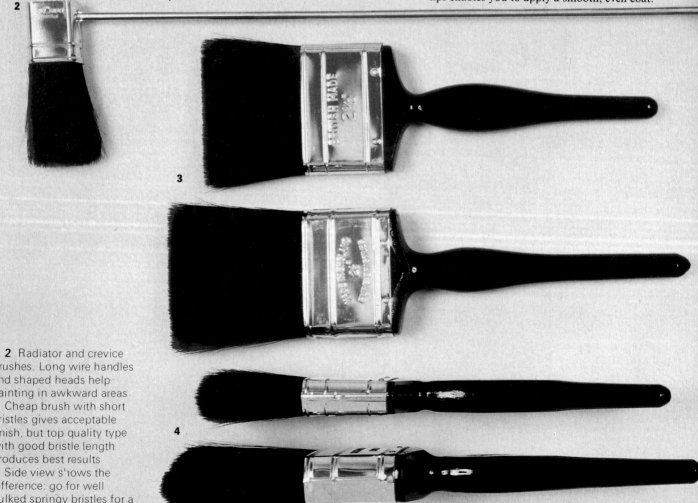

1, 2 Radiator and crevice brushes. Long wire handles and shaped heads help painting in awkward areas
3 Cheap brush with short bristles gives acceptable finish, but top quality type with good bristle length produces best results
4 Side view shows the difference: go for well bulked springy bristles for a smooth finish

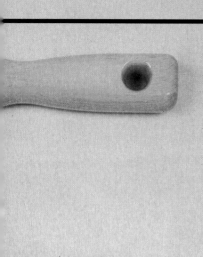

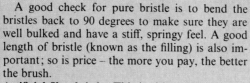

A good check for pure bristle is to bend the bristles back to 90 degrees to make sure they are well bulked and have a stiff, springy feel. A good length of bristle (known as the filling) is also important; so is price – the more you pay, the better the brush.

Artificial fibre bristle This is either cheap animal hair or nylon – the closest synthetic material to pure bristle. Although the bristles may be well bulked they will not have that all-important springy feel. And, being smoother, they will not hold the paint nearly so well or bind sufficiently at the tips. This will result in brush marks on the finished surface.

The worst of the cheap brushes contain the minimum of bristle, causing a 'mouth' through their centre. You can see this if you bend back the bristles and it becomes even more noticeable when dipped in the paint. This type of brush holds very little paint and the bristles are likely to work loose as you are painting. Even worse is when the ferrule (the metal band joined to the handle and covering the bristles) is loose and moves when in use.

Warning All brushes – even the best quality – will shed hairs at first; before you use one for the first time, dip it in clean water and brush it out on a rough surface such as an outside wall of your house. Wash it in soap and water to remove dust and any loose hairs, rinsing out thoroughly in clean, cold water. Finally, dry it out by first squeezing the bristles and then spinning the handle between your palms. Leave to dry.

Before using, ensure the brush is thoroughly dry, as moisture will affect your finish. This is particularly important with oil-based and gloss paint. With water-based and emulsion types, paint will trickle down the handle if the brush is damp, especially when working overhead.

5 Excellent quality, pure bristle brush for minimum effort and maximum coverage
6 Small straight brush for narrow areas
7 Smooth synthetic fibre brush does not hold paint so well as a pure bristle one and tends to leave brush marks on surface
8 Cutting-in brush for painting window frames without smudging onto glass

5

Temporary storage
For short periods between painting you can wrap the bristles tightly in kitchen foil (which is preferable to putting the brush in water) as this will delay the paint from drying on the brush.

A brush to be used with oil-based paint frequently over several weeks is best stored by suspending the bristles in a container with a mixture of three parts white spirit (not paraffin) and one part linseed oil. Before using the brush again, wipe out the bulk of the liquid and brush off any surplus on a clean, dust-free piece of wood or hardboard. You can keep the mixture topped up, but you will need to decant the liquid and remove the solid residue from time to time (**see Cleaning**).

Sizes and types
Brushes are available from 13mm ($\frac{1}{2}$in) bristle width to 150mm (6in). For a useful kit, start with a

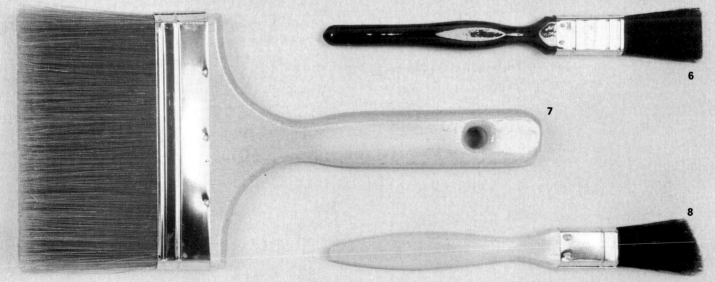

6

7

8

13mm and 25mm (1in) brush for narrow sections and a 50mm (2in) or 75mm (3in) one for larger flat surfaces, such as doors. Use the 75mm size on wet edges that have started to dry before they are joined up, as the larger brush will make for speedier work and eliminate the risk of runs appearing on the finished surface. For walls and ceilings a 100mm (4in) or 125mm (5in) brush will give a good quick finish with the maximum coverage and the minimum of effort, although the smaller size is less tiring to use – especially when there is a lot of overhead work to do.

With this range of brushes you will be able to apply most paints, interior and exterior. Don't throw away your old brushes, even if the bristles are worn down; they are ideal for painting inside gutters or dusting off glasspapered surfaces, so you can still make use of them.

In addition to orthodox brushes there are certain types intended to carry out a specific job. These you can buy as and when you need them.

Cutting-in brush Used for painting window frames, this 13mm ($\frac{1}{2}$in) wide brush has bristles cut at an angle to allow for the normal 3mm ($\frac{1}{8}$in) overlap onto the glass. (With an ordinary brush, even in the steadiest hand, you get smudges on the glass.) You can make one yourself by cutting to an angle the bristles of an old brush.

Crevice and radiator brushes The long wire handle can be bent to any shape and this, with the shaped head, allows you to paint awkward areas, such as behind radiators and pipes.

Paint rollers

These really come into their own on large areas of wall and ceiling. Provided you use the correct type for the job you will get as good a finish as with brushes or pads. Although better suited to emulsion and other water-based paints, rollers can be used to apply oil-based types, but the finish will be slightly stippled. Three basic types are available.

Foam The cheapest type and a good general purpose roller. It gives a reasonable finish and is best suited to the application of water-based paints. Don't overload it, as paint tends to drip easily from foam; if you press too hard paint will ooze out of the ends. If squashed while stored away, a roller will lose its shape. New sleeves can be fitted when necessary.

You can also use this type of roller for applying wallpaper paste – especially with wall coverings, where the paste is applied direct to the wall.

Mohair Here a short, fine pile sleeve is fixed to a rigid cylindrical frame which you can remove for cleaning. Suitable for use with all types of paint, it is ideal for the application of oil-based ones if you want a really smooth gloss finish.

Lamb's wool or nylon Available in a variety of pile lengths and thicknesses which will deal with many different types of surface, this is probably the most popular type of roller for applying water-based paints to walls and ceilings.

For the best results always match a roller to the surface you are painting. Follow the general rule of a smooth surface needing a short pile and a rough surface a longer one and you will not go far wrong. Pile lengths vary from 6mm ($\frac{1}{4}$in) to 31mm (1$\frac{1}{4}$in). Bearing in mind what type is best used where, choose either a foam, short pile mohair, lamb's wool or nylon roller for smooth or lightly textured surfaces. For highly textured surfaces pick

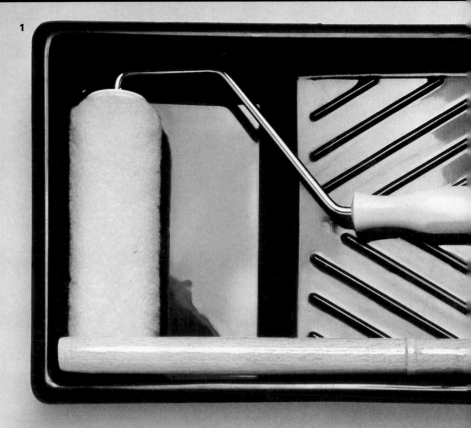

a long shaggy pile lamb's wool or nylon type. For outside walls buy a roller with a tougher pile specially designed for exterior use, as this will be more durable on rough surfaces such as stucco or pebbledash.

Warning Don't use a short pile roller on a heavily textured surface as the pile will not reach right into the indentations and the paint will not cover properly. Conversely a long, shaggy pile used on a smooth surface will coat too heavily.

Small rollers in a variety of pile types are available for reaching behind radiators and small pipes.

Other equipment

To load your roller ready for use you will need a special paint tray (sometimes supplied with it) which is sloped at one end. Pour the paint into the deep end and load the roller by rolling half the pile through the paint and moving up the slope to spread the paint evenly over the pile and remove any surplus.

To save cleaning the tray after use, line it with aluminium foil, which you can throw away when you have finished.

A step ladder with a top platform, on which to place the tray when painting ceilings, is essential unless your tray has special hooks that latch onto one of the top steps.

If you do not have a step ladder you can paint ceilings from ground level with a hollow-handled roller into which you insert a long pole.

For corners and edges you will need a 25mm (1in) paint brush. Paint these areas first, working round the perimeter of the ceiling.

Using a roller

To avoid splashes make sure the roller is not overloaded. Remove any excess while it is still in the tray. Take it carefully to the work surface to avoid 'spinning' and when it needs reloading never pull or push it sharply from the surface.

1 Synthetic pile roller with extension handle and plastic tray supplied
2 Plastic form roller – general purpose, but specially good if using emulsion
3 Medium pile sheepskin – for covering textured surfaces
4 Simulated sheepskin pile – for smooth walls and ceilings
5 Short, fine pile mohair type gives really smooth finish with gloss paint

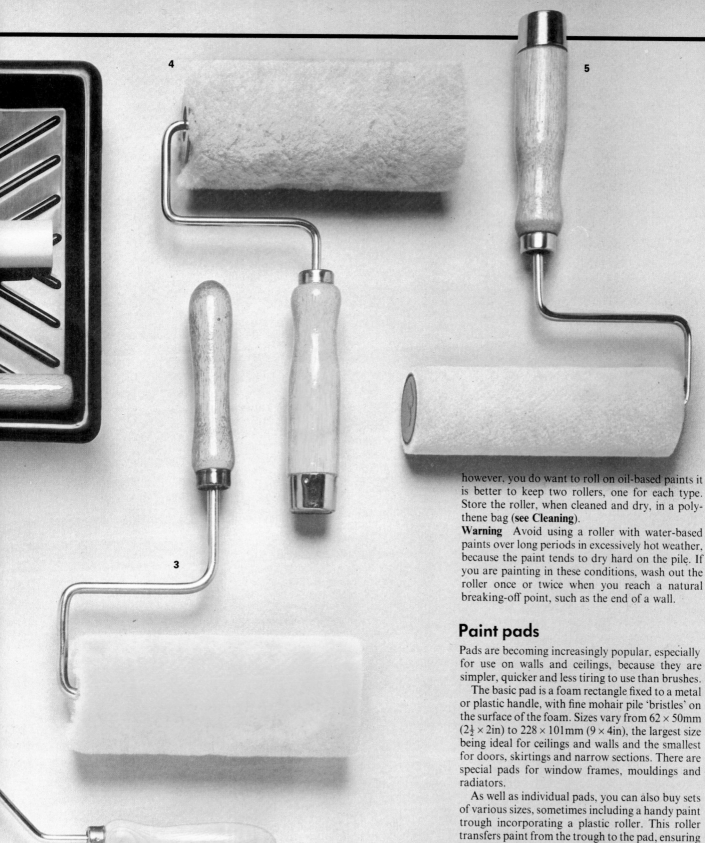

however, you do want to roll on oil-based paints it is better to keep two rollers, one for each type. Store the roller, when cleaned and dry, in a polythene bag (**see Cleaning**).

Warning Avoid using a roller with water-based paints over long periods in excessively hot weather, because the paint tends to dry hard on the pile. If you are painting in these conditions, wash out the roller once or twice when you reach a natural breaking-off point, such as the end of a wall.

Paint pads

Pads are becoming increasingly popular, especially for use on walls and ceilings, because they are simpler, quicker and less tiring to use than brushes.

The basic pad is a foam rectangle fixed to a metal or plastic handle, with fine mohair pile 'bristles' on the surface of the foam. Sizes vary from 62 × 50mm (2½ × 2in) to 228 × 101mm (9 × 4in), the largest size being ideal for ceilings and walls and the smallest for doors, skirtings and narrow sections. There are special pads for window frames, mouldings and radiators.

As well as individual pads, you can also buy sets of various sizes, sometimes including a handy paint trough incorporating a plastic roller. This roller transfers paint from the trough to the pad, ensuring it is not overloaded.

The more usual loading method is direct from the can, paint kettle or an old metal tray. Remember when loading to cover only the mohair and wipe off the excess onto the container before painting. A thin, all-over coating of paint on the pile is all you need for successful application.

Some pads can be detached from the handle, making replacement easy. A hollow-handle type is available to take a broom handle which can act as an extension pole.

Pads will cope quickly with smooth walls and ceilings; they will also give a good covering to

Use the roller in random directions in a crisscross pattern (to ensure even distribution of the paint) and join up all these 'wet' patterns before the paint has started to dry. This will be no problem as rolling paint is far quicker than working with a brush.

Though oil-based paints can be cleaned off, it is a long, messy job and we recommend you keep your roller for use with water-based paints only. If,

lightly textured surfaces. Unfortunately the short pile will not cope with deeper textures without using excessive pressure, causing the paint to ooze out and drip from the foam backing.

Using a pad

You must first rub the pad over your hand to remove any loose pile. Load it carefully, use with random strokes and don't brush out too far before reloading. Clean cutting into corners is a big advantage with a pad, but if you are painting up to wallpaper which is not going to be changed it might be easier to finish off the edges with a 25mm (1in) paint brush. Provided you load and use a pad correctly, you can work quickly with far less danger of splashing than with a brush or roller.

Keep old pads, even when the pile has worn down, as they will be useful for odd jobs such as soaking wallpaper prior to stripping or applying size to walls.

Cleaning

This is always an unpopular job, but if you want to ensure a long life for your painting equipment you must clean it thoroughly after use.

Brushes Wipe off surplus oil-based paint by running the bristles across the back of a knife over the open paint can or newspaper. Then half-fill a container (a jam jar or old bowl will do) with white spirit (turpentine substitute) to clean off what is left. Press the bristles well into the liquid before removing and wiping dry with a rag. Cleaning off the final traces of paint is easier if you rub a little linseed oil well into the bristles before finally washing out with warm water and washing-up liquid or kitchen soap. Then rinse in cold water, shake well and hang up to dry. (If necessary make a hole in the handle to take a piece of wire or string for hanging.)

You can use this cleaning liquid again if you keep it in a screw-top jar, but decant it and leave behind the sediment. Proprietary brush cleaners in liquid form are effective, but costly, and usually have a pungent smell.

Follow the same procedure for water-based paints, but use only warm water and washing-up liquid and then rinse in cold water.

Rollers and pads Clean immediately after use or the pile will stiffen and clog and be ruined. Both rollers and pads are better used with water-based paints as they only require thorough washing under a running tap – hot or cold. If, however, you use them with oil-based paints you must go through the same method of cleaning as for brushes. Use the roller tray for cleaning so you wash the tray at the same time. If you previously kept the tray clean with a layer of kitchen foil, you may prefer to use your old bowl for cleaning off or line the tray with a clean piece of foil and clean the roller in that. Hang up rollers to dry since if you leave them lying around they will develop a flat edge.

Storing

Before storing away brushes, wrap them in newspaper or brown paper, folding carefully so as to keep a square end to the bristles, and secure around the ferrule with an elastic band or string. Don't leave them unwrapped or moths may get at the bristles. Once dry, rollers and pads can be stored flat and unwrapped in a paint tray.

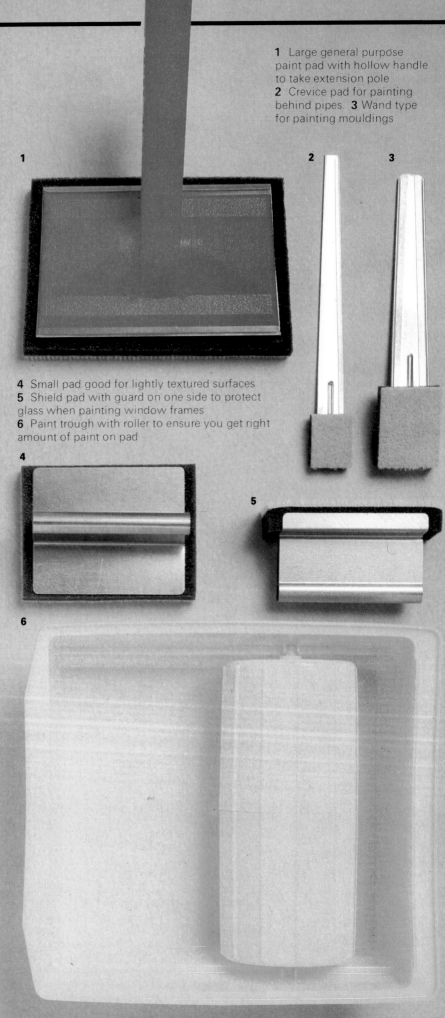

1 Large general purpose paint pad with hollow handle to take extension pole
2 Crevice pad for painting behind pipes. **3** Wand type for painting mouldings

4 Small pad good for lightly textured surfaces
5 Shield pad with guard on one side to protect glass when painting window frames
6 Paint trough with roller to ensure you get right amount of paint on pad

Stripping paint

A new coat of paint can transform a room. But you'll be wasting your time if you don't make sure the surface is properly prepared.

A sound paint film, even if it is several layers thick, is a perfectly suitable base for repainting. Just give it a quick rub down with medium coarse glasspaper wrapped round a wood or cork block, dust well and the surface is keyed ready for its first coat.

A heavy build-up of paint on the closing edges of doors and windows can result in sticking and adding another coat of paint on top of the old layers will only accentuate this problem. There is no need to remove the old paint from the whole surface though; trimming away from the edges themselves is sufficient.

If the paint is peeling, pitted, badly chipped or crazed, however, then the only way you will achieve a satisfactory and long-lasting surface is to strip back to bare wood ready for filling and making smooth before starting to repaint.

There are three ways of stripping: by hand (or mechanical) sanding or applying chemicals or heat.

Hand sanding

This method is suitable only when a very thin film of paint has to be removed. Use a piece of medium coarse wet and dry glasspaper wrapped round a wood or cork block and be prepared to exert plenty of elbow grease when rubbing. Wetting this type of glasspaper reduces the spread of dust.

Left Remove thick paint film evenly with drum sander which does not damage wood
Below Take off heavy coats of bad paintwork rapidly with paint and varnish remover attachment

Above Bad paintwork needs stripping before repainting
Below Remove thin film of paint with medium coarse glasspaper round block

Mechanical sanding

There are various sanding attachments for electric drills, but circular ones are not easy to work with and there is a real danger of scoring the wood if the correct technique is not used. If the wood is scored, you will have to do a great deal of repair work before you can repaint it.

A drum sander is the best attachment to use. This comprises a foam drum onto which an abrasive belt is fixed. The belt action is along the grain so avoiding any circular scuffs to the surface of the wood. The action is efficient and quick, the only drawback being excessive dust.

Various grades of abrasive belts – from coarse to fine – should be used. When dealing with a really thick film start with a coarse grade and switch to a fine grade for the final sweep. After a quick dusting down and a wipe with a cloth dampened with white spirit, you can begin repainting.

You can take off a heavy coat of paint more rapidly with a special power drill accessory known as a paint and varnish remover. This is a chuck-held metal disc with perforations punched through the surface to allow the loosened material to pass through the disc without clogging.

When sanding, take the work outside whenever possible to avoid too much mess indoors and, for personal safety, use a dust mask (or a handkerchief tied to cover up your nose and mouth) and protective spectacles or goggles.

Chemical stripping
Decorating shops stock chemical strippers under various brand names. Use a jelly type as it will adhere to the paint longer and will not run on vertical surfaces.

Chemical stripper can be expensive so it is not really suitable for large areas, nor where a thick film of paint has to be removed as two or even three applications may be needed before bare wood is reached. Pour a little of the stripper into a metal container and, using an old paint brush, apply liberally. After a few seconds the paint will start to shrivel and you can remove it with a flat paint scraper. Keep this as upright as possible to prevent digging into the wood and damaging the surface.

To strip paint from mouldings or other awkward crevices use a shave-hook. The best type is a heart-shaped scraper which has a series of intricate shapes around the workhead for dealing with all types of angles and curves.

When all the old paint has been removed, apply a thin layer of stripper and finish off by rubbing over the surface with medium steel wool. To make the wool last longer, tear off small amounts from the main ball and, as you work, turn the piece inside out until all the edges have been used. This final rub over will remove all small nibs of paint not obvious to the eye.

Chemical stripper will remain in small traces on the surface and must be neutralized before applying fresh paint. So, using a constant supply of clean rags, wipe down the surface thoroughly with white spirit or the solvent recommended by the brand manufacturer.

You must wear an old pair of leather or thick rubber gloves, protective spectacles or goggles and preferably a dust mask as well. And remember to protect the floor covering with newspapers.

Heat stripping
Blowtorches have come a long way since the days when they were filled with paraffin or methylated spirit and needed energetic pumping before igniting. Today they are much easier to use since the simple burner head unit fits onto a throw-away gas cartridge. When ignited you can adjust the power of the flame by turning a ridged screw. Before tackling your surface, it is worth getting the feel of the blowtorch by practising on a scrap piece of painted wood. Hold the blowtorch at a constant distance, about 150–200mm (6–8in) from the paintwork. Play it back and forth across a small area and when the paint starts to wrinkle and melt it is ready for scraping off. If the paint sticks, play the flame over the area again and resume scraping.
Warning Take care not to scorch the wood by concentrating the flame for too long on one spot. Switch to a chemical stripper if the paint is thick in

mouldings and around window frames, where a build-up of heat can easily crack the glass.

If you do scorch the wood, glasspaper or scrape back to bare wood before repainting.

As with chemical stripping, some paint particles will be left and these should be glasspapered down.

Be careful when using the flame under the house eaves as birds often build their nests here and these can be easily set alight. When you are working near open windows, tie back the curtains and place a metal sheet on the floor to catch the hot paint peelings. Wear an old pair of leather or rubber gloves and protective spectacles or goggles.

For hand sanding/finishing off
medium coarse wet and dry glasspaper
wood or cork block

For mechanical sanding
drum sander, abrasive belts, white spirit
protective spectacles or goggles
dust mask

For chemical or heat stripping
chemical stripper or blowtorch
paint scraper, shave-hook
leather or rubber gloves, protective
  spectacles or goggles, metal sheet
metal container, old paint brush, medium
  steel wool, white spirit (for chemical
  stripping)

equipment

Top left Apply chemical stripper liberally with old paint brush
Top right Use shave-hook to remove blistered paint from mouldings and crevices
Centre Make sure paint has shrivelled sufficiently before scraping it off
Above left Keep blowtorch moving at constant distance from paintwork. Scrape off paint as soon as it blisters
Above right Priming paint will not adhere to scorched timber so any charring must be scraped back to sound surface before repainting

Guide to painting faults

Cause	Prevention	Remedy
Pimples Particularly noticeable in shiny, gloss surfaces, these are caused by specks of dust which may have been on the surface, on the brush or in the paint itself. Or a very fine skin on the surface of the paint (especially non-drip gloss) may have got broken and worked into the paint on application.	Make sure the surface is clean and free of dust at each stage of the work: after burning off or rubbing down, and before applying primer, undercoat and top coat. Clean the surface with a tacky (resin-impregnated) rag or a clean, lint-free one dampened with methylated spirit. Pay particular attention to corners since pockets of dust here, though difficult to clean with a rag, will be picked up on the brush and spread across the surface. Use a pointed stick under the rag to ensure every particle of dust is removed from the corners. Paint brushes must be cleaned and even new brushes need rinsing before use as the bristles will contain some dust and loose hairs. Wipe the lid and rim of the paint can before removing the lid otherwise any dust will fall into the tin. It is a good idea to transfer a small amount of paint into a clean paint kettle or other container and work from this. If dust falls into the kettle only a small amount of paint will be affected. Clean the room thoroughly before starting work and allow time for dust to settle before using paint.	Don't try to remove specks while the paint is still wet as you will only add to the problem by smearing the paint. Allow the paint to harden for several days; even though it may seem dry after a few hours, only the surface will have dried. Rub down the affected areas with fine wet and dry glasspaper, wash with clean water, dry thoroughly and apply a new finishing coat. Skin often forms on old paint. If you spot it, carefully lift it away before stirring; if it is extremely thin you can stir it into the paint and then strain the paint through fine muslin or mesh.
Flaking Paint falling away from surface is due to poor preparation or bad use of primer. It can take weeks to show and will usually be confined to small areas on the surface.	Clean and prepare the surface thoroughly. If stripping back to bare wood apply a suitable primer. Emulsion flaking from walls or ceilings normally means you have applied the paint over distemper. Before painting, remove distemper by washing and scraping off the loose material, covering the remainder with a coat of primer sealer.	If flaking occurs in small patches, strip these areas back to the bare surface, fill depressions with fine surface filler and repaint. If flaking is extensive, however, you will have to strip off the whole lot and start again.
Slow drying Sometimes paint (particularly oil-based paint) will take a few weeks to dry or even remain permanently tacky. This indicates you applied the paint over a dirty or greasy surface, used an unsuitable thinner or did not stir the paint before applying.	Clean and prepare your surface thoroughly paying particular attention to skirtings which tend to collect a build-up of polish from the floor. Always stir the paint. You can add a small amount of proprietary dryer to stocks of old paint but never to new paint, which should be returned to the manufacturer for testing.	If the room is badly ventilated, open the windows for a few days to see if this accelerates drying. If not you will have to strip off all the paint with thinners and start again or refer to the manufacturer for advice.
Blisters Mostly affecting exterior woodwork, blisters can vary in size from pin heads to large areas. The cause is moisture in the wood or on the surface, trapped between coats of paint, or there may be resinous knots in the wood. Another less common cause is painting over a soft, thick coat. The action of very strong sunshine when any of these conditions exist is likely to cause blistering.	Try to paint external woodwork towards the end of the summer when, ideally, it should have dried out completely. If this is not possible, try to paint in dry, warm conditions. Don't paint immediately after rainfall or washing down, unless the surfaces are thoroughly dried off. Strip off any thick, soft paint and always apply knotting to all resinous areas after stripping back to bare wood.	Cut off the surface of the blister and with fine wet and dry glasspaper rub back to a sound surface – or bare wood if blistering is extensive. Apply knotting and primer as necessary, fill depressions with fine surface filler and apply undercoat and top coat.
Runs, sags and wrinkles Fine lines or drips on a painted surface result from bad application. Wrinkles are likely to occur on thick, sagging paint.	Do not overload the brush and always brush out each application before adding another. Look at the paint five minutes after application; it may still be possible to brush out any runs.	If you notice runs before the paint has started to dry, brush them out lightly; if paint is drying, you will smear the surface. Or treat as for **Pimples**.
Dull gloss Dull finish occurs if thinners used wrongly, surface not properly primed or undercoated, undercoat not given time to dry or finish over-brushed or painted in damp or frosty conditions.	Prepare thoroughly. Leave the undercoat to dry for the recommended time, avoid using a thinner in gloss paint and do not apply in damp or frosty weather conditions.	Allow the paint to dry, then rub down lightly with fine glasspaper, dust off and apply a new finishing coat.
Grinning The colour of the previous coat shows through the dry paint film indicating another coat is needed. Grinning may also occur if you use the wrong undercoat, do not stir paint sufficiently, thin it too much or overbrush finishing coat.	Use the correct undercoat and the recommended number of finishing coats. Make sure you stir the paint according to the manufacturer's instructions. Never brush out the finishing coat too far.	Apply extra finishing coats as needed.
Brush marks These can be seen in the finished paint. The cause is insufficient rubbing down of the old paint surface, faulty application (applying the paint too thickly and not brushing out correctly) or using poor quality brushes.	Carefully prepare the surface, making sure poor paint is rubbed right back. Apply the paint evenly and finish brushing out in the direction of the grain. Slightly thin excessively thick paint and always use good quality brushes.	As for **Pimples**.

Painting doors, walls & windows

General preparation

For general woodwork wash down the surface with sugar soap, washing soda or a proprietary paint cleaner, rinse off with plenty of clean water and allow to dry thoroughly. Fill in any cracks or holes in the wood with a proprietary wood filler. Make a key for the new paint by lightly rubbing down the old gloss to remove the shine with medium fine wet and dry glasspaper wrapped round a wood or cork block. Lightly wet the glasspaper to reduce the spread of dust and rub with the grain.

With painted walls wash down as for woodwork to remove all grease and dirt. If gloss paint has been used previously, key the surface with wet and dry glasspaper wrapped round a wood or cork block. Fill any cracks in the plaster with proprietary plaster filler, glasspapering smooth when dry. Make good any damaged plaster.

Painting techniques

When you apply free-flowing oil-based paints with a brush, spread and lay off the paint in the following way to avoid runs and sags. Spread a liberal coat using strong pressure on the bristles, finishing with long parallel strokes along the grain. Wiping any surplus paint on the sides of the can or paint kettle, apply lighter strokes across the surface to provide an even spread. Finally lay off with lighter strokes from the tips of the bristles along the original direction.

With emulsion paints, which are water-based and usually heavy bodied, or the gel type non-drip gloss paints (thixotropic), use the minimum of brushing out. Apply with even, random strokes to ensure a full application without paint running.

Keep the brushing of non-drip gloss to a minimum, as too much brushing or over-stirring will only make the paint too thin.

A second coat of gloss can be applied within 12–24 hours. Alternatively leave the paint at least four days to harden, then lightly rub down the surface with fine glasspaper and dust off before applying a second coat.

Always wipe the surface of the paint with a lint-free rag when dusting off before the second coat.

Painting walls

Paint a complete wall without a break to avoid edges showing through. If you have to stop, make sure you break off when you reach a corner, such as on a chimney-breast. Use a 100 or 130mm (4 or 5in) brush, paint pad or roller, working away from the natural light to see where you have painted. With emulsion paint work in 300mm (or 12in) deep horizontal strips across the wall in downward strokes, starting at the top. With oil-based paint work in 600mm (or 24in) squares (see 1a and 1b). If the paint is drying too quickly and the edges cannot be joined up in time to avoid unsightly marks, lower the temperature by turning off any heating to slow down drying. Reverse the procedure when work is complete to accelerate drying.

Painting over wallpaper

Some textured papers provide an ideal surface on which to paint, but thinner types can present problems. Make sure the paper is well stuck down

1a

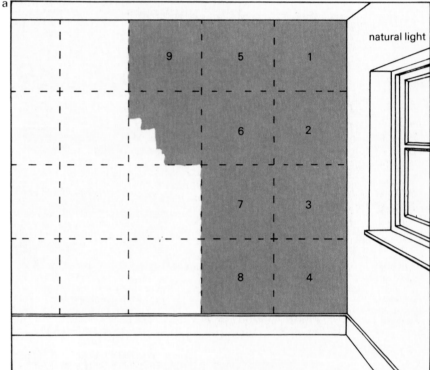

natural light

1b

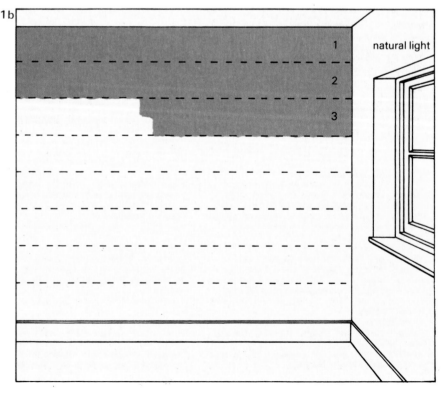

natural light

Below left When applying oil-based paint to walls, work in 600mm (or 24in) squares and start at the top corner nearest the window. Complete the ceiling-to-floor area before starting the next strip and work away from the natural light
Bottom left When applying emulsion, work across the wall, again away from the natural light, with downward strokes in horizontal strips 300mm (or 12in) deep
Below Before painting window frames remove flaking paint and dirt right back to bare wood if necessary, with a paint scraper. Prime exposed wood before applying undercoat and top coat
Bottom centre Use a metal paint shield to prevent getting excess paint on the glass but allow for a 3mm ($\frac{1}{8}$in) strip of paint on the glass to keep moisture off putty
Bottom right Alternatively use masking tape, again allowing for a narrow strip of paint on the glass. Always remove the masking tape while the paint is still tacky

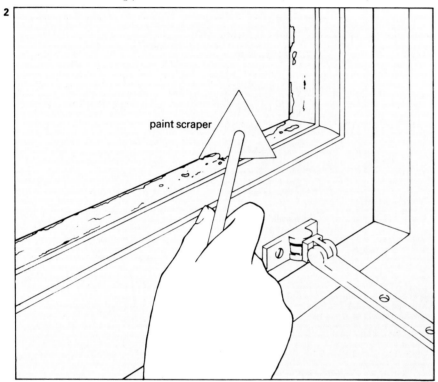

2

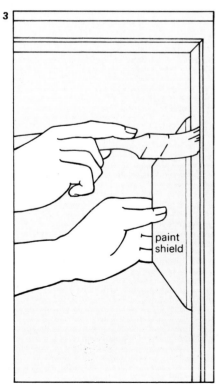

3

paint shield

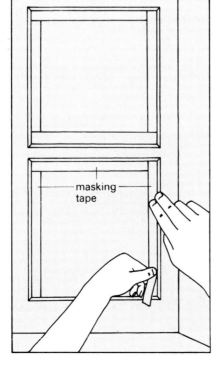

4

masking tape

because the paint can soften the paper and cause it to bubble. The safest way to check the possible results is first to paint a small inconspicuous area, such as behind a piece of furniture permanently placed against the wall. If bubbles result you will either have to make minor repairs to the paper in the same way as for ceiling bubbles or strip off the paper completely.

You may find the texture or pattern of some papers will still show through, even after two or three coats of paint, and seams between lengths that were overlapped when hung will become more evident.

Painting doors
First remove handles, keyhole plates, finger plates and coat hooks to give yourself an uninterrupted surface. If you try to paint round these they will cause a build-up of paint, leading to unsightly runs. Clean out the keyholes to remove dirt and grease, which otherwise will be picked up on the brush and transferred to the rest of the work. It is a good idea to paint the top of the door as well, because although it is not normally visible it will make cleaning that much easier. Open the door and fix it in position with a wedge underneath, leaving both hands free for painting. This will also ensure the door stays where it is until the paint has dried.

Plan to finish painting each area in one session to avoid the edge line showing up where painting is restarted.
Panel doors Preferably use a 50mm (2in) brush, although you can use a 25mm (1in) one to make it easier to cut into mouldings. Don't overload the brush when painting the mouldings, as a build-up of paint will cause runs.
Flush doors A 60mm (2½in) or 75mm (3in) brush is best; if you prefer, a pad or suitable roller can be used. Any of these will enable you to complete the work quickly and join up all the edges before they start to dry.

When painting hinges, clean out the newly painted screw slots with a screwdriver before the paint has started to dry. Wipe the blade immediately after use. Clearing the slots is essential as you may want to remove the door at a later stage or adjust the hinges.

Painting window frames
Pay particular attention to preparing the bottom of the frame to ensure the finished surface is as good as the rest. Clear away all flaking paintwork and dirt, right back to bare wood if necessary (see 2).

Flaking and general deterioration are caused by moisture from condensation running down the glass and mixing with the dust that collects on the frame. Prepare this part of the frame well or it will only deteriorate soon after being repainted. Prime bare wood before using undercoat and gloss.

Always brush about 3mm ($\frac{1}{8}$in) of paint onto the glass to prevent moisture getting into the putty and breaking it up. You may find it easier to use a cutting-in brush, specially angled for this job.

Alternatives are a metal paint shield (see 3), which you rest on the glass at the correct distance from the frame, or masking tape (see 4). If you use tape make sure to remove it while the paint is still tacky. If you leave it until the paint is dry you run the risk of pulling away the paint on the frame.

The general rule for painting frames is to paint any surfaces which show inside the room when the window is open in the interior colour.

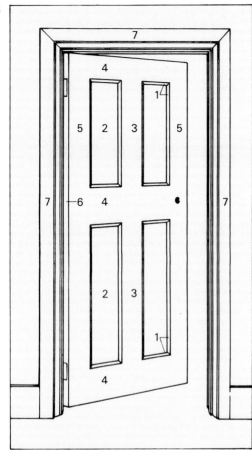

5

7

4

1

5   2   3   5

7   6   4   7

3

2   3

1

4

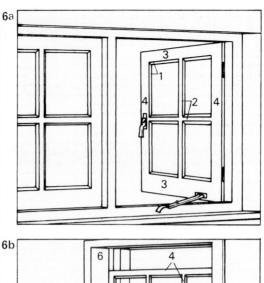

6a

3

1

4   2   4

3

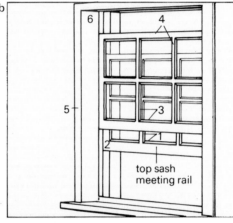

6b

6   4

5   3

2   1

top sash
meeting rail

If you have to shut the door
or window after painting,
work first on the surfaces that
come into contact when
closed, to give them time to
dry thoroughly
Left Always start with the
panel or bead inside edge
sections on panelled door (1)
Far left Follow same
pattern for a casement
window
Below left Paint a sash
window in the same way, but
first pull down the top sash
and lift the bottom one to get
at the top sash meeting rail.
You need only paint those
sections of the runners (5)
that show when the window
is open. Don't get paint on
the cords or you will weaken
them

Order of painting

The order shown for doors **(see 5)** and window
frames **(see 6a and 6b)** is the one used by professionals and is very convenient. Complete the
handle side last to make it easier to open and close
during work, unless doors and windows have to be
closed when painting has finished. In this case surfaces that come into contact when the door or
window is closed must be painted first to allow for
the longest possible drying time.

Warning If you touch a tacky surface with soft
clothing, for example, that leaves bits on the paint
don't rush in with a rag. Wait two or three weeks
for the surface to harden thoroughly before gently
rubbing down with fine wet and dry glasspaper,
lightly wetted. Then dry off the surface and apply
another top coat over the affected area.

Painting faults

Paint itself is rarely to blame for faults in the paint-
work since reputable brands are subjected to
careful quality control by the manufacturers. The
following are the major causes of poor results.
- Poor surface preparation
- Getting dust in the paint
- Poor, incorrect or dirty equipment
- Faulty application technique
- Unsuitable paint for the job
- Adverse weather conditions

Causes of the common faults, their prevention and
remedies are given with each section, but remember
faults may arise through more than one factor.

Use colour to emphasize interior features –
dark tones up to dado rail to contrast with
walls, door and white mouldings (Crown
scheme)

Wallpapering: what you need

As with all jobs around the home, if you have the right equipment you will make your task much easier. Although not all the items shown here are essential, you should use as many of them as you can to ensure the best possible results when papering a wall or ceiling.

1 Working platform Essential to do a good job safely. Hire, buy or borrow two step ladders and a good scaffold board to give easy access to ceilings and top parts of walls

2 Paperhanger's apron Not essential, but has large pockets to carry brush and shears and so saves you time getting up and down step ladder fetching them. Could improvise by hanging plastic carrier bag at top of ladder

3 Paste bucket Must hold reasonable amount of paste. Line inside with polythene to save cleaning out. Tie piece of string across middle of bucket to rest brush on

4 Pasting table Can use kitchen table or board on trestles; but lightweight foldaway pasting table, about 1800 × 600mm (6 × 2ft), is convenient and inexpensive

5 Shears Paperhanger's shears, about 200–300mm (8–12in) long, ensure good, clean cuts

6 Wood seam roller Not essential, but handy for smoothing joins between lengths. Don't use on embossed paper as it will flatten pattern

7 Plumb bob To mark true verticals on walls as guide to hanging paper. You can make your own by tying string to balanced weight.

8 Paste brush Use old 125 or 150mm (5 or 6in) distemper brush

9 Paper-hanging brush For smoothing paper onto wall, Choose pure bristle to avoid scratching paper

10 Pencil and metal straight-edge For marking and measuring

11 Trimming knife For making intricate cuts round fittings and for trimming edges

12 Wallpaper paste Always use adhesive specified by wallpaper manufacturer and follow mixing instructions exactly. If you use wrong paste, paper might not stick properly or mould might develop behind paper. Don't get adhesive on decorative face of paper or paper will discolour

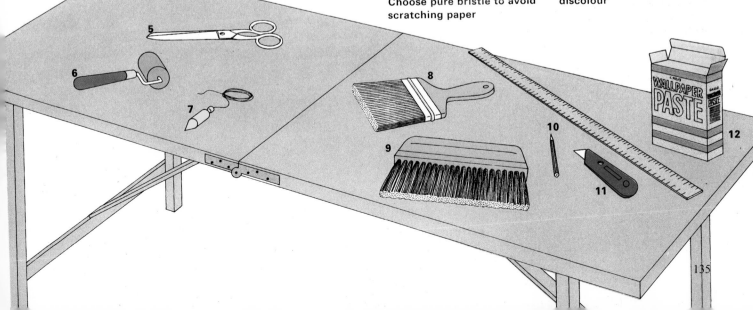

First steps to wallpapering

Once you know the advantages of special types of paper and pattern effects you will be able to choose the right wallpaper for your needs and get on with the surface preparation.

When it comes to choosing wallpaper, go for better quality, medium or heavyweight papers rather than thin, cheap ones which tear and stretch easily when pasted and need very careful handling. Cheaper wallpapers have the design printed directly onto the paper; better quality papers are usually given a protective coating before the pattern is printed. Top quality ones also have a clear coating over the pattern to protect the surface.

Basic types

The following run-down on the various types available will help you to select the right wallpaper for specific areas.

Washable The paper is covered with a clear water-resistant coating of matt or gloss PVA (polyvinyl acetate) making it ideal for use in the kitchen or bathroom.

Vinyl A layer of PVC (polyvinyl chloride) is fused onto a paper backing to produce a really tough vinyl-faced covering that is steam and water-resistant and can even be scrubbed clean.

Ready-pasted Dried fungicidal adhesive on the back does away with the traditional pasting operation. To activate the paste you draw each length of paper through a water-filled trough (usually supplied with the paper) immediately before hanging.

Polyethylene This type, such as Novamura, is lighter than ordinary wallpaper and warm to the touch. It is easier and quicker to hang than other wall coverings because you paste the wall rather than the paper and you do not have to cut the paper into lengths, but use it straight from the roll. Work with the special adhesive recommended for this type of wall covering.

Dry-strip Washable and ready-pasted papers already described are not easily removed using the conventional soak-and-strip method since the water cannot penetrate the water-resistant coating to act on the adhesive. But dry-strip papers and vinyls are available; you peel away the decorative face to leave a paper backing on the wall. If this backing is firmly fixed, use it as a base for re-papering or strip it off in the usual way.

Lining paper Thin paper used under the decorative wall covering to give a high quality finish. It is available in several weights: use light papers on smooth wall surfaces and heavier papers to help conceal uneven surfaces. Hang lining paper horizontally on the walls so the joins between lengths will not coincide with the vertical joins of the decorative wall covering.

Selecting a pattern

If you decide you would like a patterned paper, remember different types of pattern demand varying degrees of skill to apply. Complicated patterns are not easy to match and often mistakes only show when the lengths have been hung.

Free match paper The simplest type to apply since it has random motifs that do not require matching. It is also the most economical as there is no wastage.

Set patterns Demand more skill since you have to match the design horizontally across adjoining lengths. There will be some wastage (especially if the repeat does not fit in with your room height) but this can sometimes be minimized by cutting lengths from two or more rolls at a time.

Drop patterns Can be difficult to match as the design runs diagonally across adjacent lengths – the first length aligns with the third, the second with the fourth, the fifth with the seventh, and so on. Wastage is inevitable, but again this can be minimized by working from more than one roll.

Effects of patterns

Before choosing a design consider the size and shape of your room as the pattern on the wallpaper may appear to alter its dimensions. Vertical lines will seem to increase the room's height, while horizontal stripes will give the opposite effect. However attractive large motifs or bright colours look when you are flicking through a pattern book, remember these can be overbearing in small rooms.

Certain designs will show up faults in the structure of the room. If the ceiling slopes, the motifs in a set or drop pattern will gradually disappear along the ceiling line. This also applies to papering ceilings: if they are not perfect squares or rectangles the pattern will run out of true.

Unfortunately it is not easy to check ceiling line irregularities; they usually become apparent only when the wallpaper is hung. Vertical stripes will emphasize corners that are out of square, so you should always check these before buying this type of pattern. Suspend a plumb bob and string line from a small nail fixed as high up the wall as possible; the string line will hang down at a true vertical and you will be able to see if the corner is square.

Check the condition of your wall surface. If it is undulating or pitted, don't buy a striped paper as this will only emphasize the defects; go for a busy, colourful pattern that will hide the faults.

There is obviously a lot to recommend a free match paper. It is the simplest to hang, there is no wastage and it can disguise many structural defects.

Free match paper

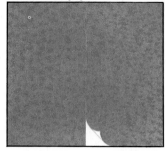

Set patterns

Drop patterns

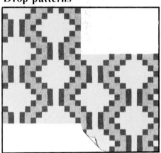

Below Consider the size and shape of your room before buying patterned wallpaper as the design may appear to alter the room's shape; height is increased by vertical stripes, while horizontal lines make the ceiling seem lower

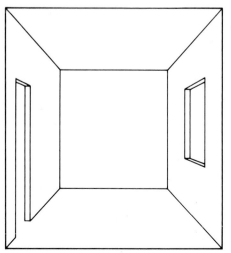

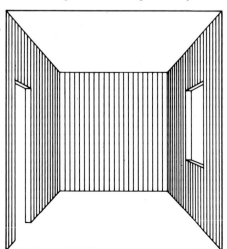

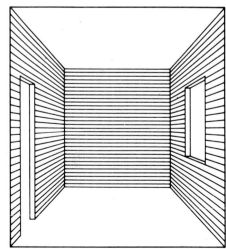

Right With washable papers score the surface with a wire brush to allow water to penetrate to the backing
Below right Remove ordinary paper with a stripping knife, taking care not to dig into the wall
Below left A steam stripper will take off a thick paper rapidly; the steam penetrates the paper and softens the old adhesive

Certain designs will emphasize structural faults in the room, so choose patterned paper carefully. **Above** If your ceiling slopes, don't go for a set pattern as the motifs will gradually disappear along the ceiling line. **Above right** Avoid using vertically striped paper on out-of-square corners

Estimating quantity

Measure the height of the room from the skirting to the picture rail or ceiling and also the distance around the walls, including doors and windows. Check with our calculating chart to see how many rolls of wallpaper you need. If your measurement for the distance around the room falls between two measurements on the chart, use the larger figure.

Basic measurements will be sufficient for plain or free match papers. Where you need to match the pattern you must allow for wastage at the foot of each length according to the depth of the repeat; usually an extra roll for every five is enough, although you may need to allow extra if the repeat pattern is very deep.

Extra paper will also be needed if the room has recesses or projections since the pattern should be centred on these to give a balanced look.

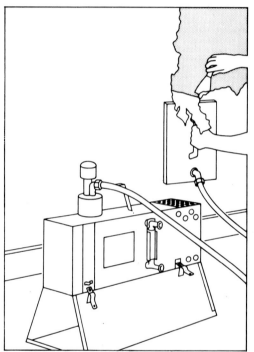

For preparing surface
wallpaper stripper or warm water and washing-up liquid
wallpaper paste (for soaking heavyweight paper)
wire brush or serrated scraper
steam stripper (if needed)
wallpaper stripping knife
medium wet and dry glasspaper
cellulose filler (if needed)
matchsticks (if needed)
glue size or wallpaper paste (for sizing walls)
fungicidal adhesive (for sizing if using vinyl paper)
old brush or paint pad

equipment

NUMBER OF ROLLS REQUIRED – METRIC CHART

Distance in metres round walls incl. doors/ windows	Height in metres from skirting							
	2 – 2.2	2.2 – 2.5	2.5 – 2.7	2.7 – 3	3 – 3.2	3.2 – 3.5	3.5 – 3.7	3.7 – 4
10	5	5	6	6	7	7	8	8
11	5	6	7	7	8	8	9	9
12	6	6	7	8	8	9	9	10
13	6	7	8	8	9	10	10	10
14	7	7	8	9	10	10	11	11
15	7	8	9	9	10	11	12	12
16	8	8	9	10	11	11	12	13
17	8	9	10	10	11	12	13	14
18	9	9	10	11	12	13	14	15
19	9	10	11	12	13	14	15	16
20	9	10	11	12	13	14	15	16
21	10	11	12	13	14	15	16	17
22	10	11	13	14	15	16	17	18
23	11	12	13	14	15	17	18	19
24	11	12	14	15	16	17	18	20
25	12	13	14	15	17	18	19	20
26	12	13	15	16	17	19	20	21
27	13	14	15	17	18	19	21	22
28	13	14	16	17	19	20	21	23
29	13	15	16	18	19	21	22	24
30	14	15	17	18	20	21	23	24

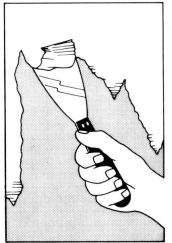

Buying the paper

Most wall coverings are sold in rolls 10m (11yd) long and 520mm (20½in) wide. They are normally supplied ready-trimmed, but if you do select a paper with selvedges (margins) ask your supplier to trim them for you – don't attempt it yourself.

Wallpaper is printed in batches and the colour may vary from batch to batch; make sure every roll you buy bears the same batch number. It is worth buying an extra roll at the outset since you may have trouble obtaining another roll of the same batch later on. Check if you can buy a spare roll on a sale-or-return basis.

If you realize halfway through a job that you will not have sufficient paper and you cannot buy another roll from the same batch, use the odd roll in an area where any colour variation will not be so noticeable, such as on a short wall or in a recess.

Unfortunately even corresponding batch numbers do not always guarantee an exact colour match. Before hanging the paper inspect the rolls in a good light; if you spot any shade differences, decide the best sequence for hanging.

Imperfections in the paper itself can be eliminated when you cut the paper into lengths. But if you find inconsistencies in the pattern take the roll back to your supplier, since you will have a lot of wastage if you try to eliminate 'repeat' defects.

If after hanging the paper you find the pattern on adjoining lengths will not align, it is probably the result of not soaking the rolls with paste for the same length of time or stretching the paper when putting it up.

Storing wallpaper

Always store rolls of wallpaper flat; never stand them on end or you will damage the edges and make it difficult to obtain neat joins between lengths when hanging.

Preparing the surface

To remove the existing paper you will have to soak it with a solution of warm water and washing-up liquid or proprietary wallpaper stripper. Allow extra soaking for heavyweight papers – add a handful of wallpaper paste to the water so the water stays on the wall long enough to soak through to the adhesive.

Stripping off Score the surface of washable wallpapers with a wire brush or serrated scraper to allow the water to soak through to the backing. If the paper is several layers thick or you cannot score it easily, it may be worth hiring a steam stripper to do the job quickly, but use it carefully since it can damage the plaster underneath.

Remove the paper with a wallpaper stripping knife; don't be too vigorous and try not to dig the knife into the plaster, as you will have to fill any holes you make.

Remember you can strip certain types of wall covering just by loosening a corner and pulling off each length, leaving the backing paper on the wall. If this is firmly fixed, use it as a base for repapering or soak and strip as already described.

Rub down the bare walls with wet and dry glasspaper to remove any final nibs of paper. Fill any cracks or holes with cellulose filler and, when hard, rub down any ridges with medium wet and dry glasspaper to form a flush finish.

If you have removed any fixtures, push matchsticks into the screw holes, allowing them to protrude about 6mm (¼in). When you hang the new wall covering ease it over the matchsticks so they poke through the paper and indicate the position for refitting the fixtures later.

Sizing the walls Before papering you will have to size sound, porous walls; this is to improve adhesion and ensure the water from the paste is not absorbed too quickly for you to position the paper correctly. You can buy a proprietary glue size or make your own by diluting wallpaper paste according to the manufacturer's instructions. When using vinyls, size with a diluted fungicidal adhesive since mould may develop on the wall if you use a diluted cellulose adhesive.

Apply the size liberally to all parts of the wall with an old brush or paint pad; take care to wipe off any that gets onto painted woodwork immediately as it will be difficult to remove later. Leave the size to dry thoroughly.

Distance in feet round walls incl. doors/ windows	NUMBER OF ROLLS REQUIRED – IMPERIAL CHART						
	Height in feet from skirting						
	7 – 7½	7½ – 8	8 – 8½	8½ – 9	9 – 9½	9½ – 10	10 – 10½
30	4	5	5	5	6	6	6
34	5	5	5	5	6	6	7
38	5	6	6	6	7	7	8
42	6	6	7	7	7	8	8
46	6	7	7	7	8	8	9
50	7	7	8	8	9	9	10
54	7	8	9	9	9	10	10
58	8	8	9	9	10	10	11
62	8	9	10	10	10	11	12
66	9	9	10	10	11	12	13
70	9	10	11	11	12	12	13
74	10	10	12	12	12	13	14
78	10	11	12	12	13	14	15
82	11	11	13	13	14	14	16
86	12	12	14	14	14	15	16
90	12	13	14	14	15	16	17
94	13	13	15	15	15	16	18
98	13	14	15	15	16	17	19

How to hang wallpaper

Hanging wallpaper the correct way is all important, since the final effect will be ruined if you make awkward turns in the wrong places or don't hang the paper straight. And always remember to prepare the surface properly.

Putting up lining paper

If using lining paper, hang it on the walls horizontally to avoid the joins coinciding with the vertical joins of the decorative paper. Cut the paper into lengths 25mm (1in) longer than the width of the wall to allow for 12mm (½in) turns onto the adjacent walls.

Lay one end of the length on the pasting table, leaving the rest to hang to the floor, and paste this piece carefully. Fold over, with pasted sides together, about 380mm (15in) of paper. Then fold over 760mm (30in) and turn back the first folded piece to make pleats. Continue pasting and concertina pleating in this way until you near the end of the length, then paste this end and fold it over to meet the pleats.

Start hanging the paper from a top corner of the wall, releasing one fold at a time and smoothing out with a roller or brush. Work right round and down the wall with subsequent lengths in the same way, butting adjoining strips together.

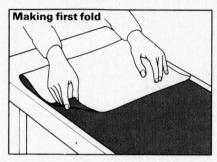
Making first fold

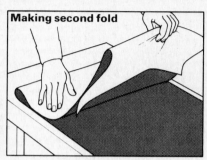
Making second fold

Making final fold

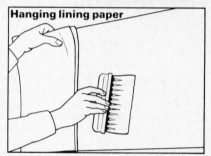
Hanging lining paper

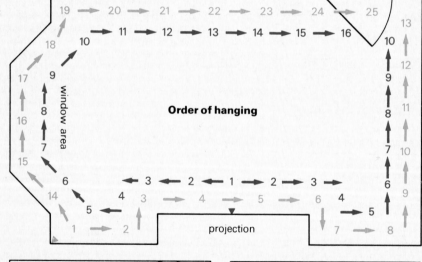
Order of hanging

window area

projection

centre of chimney-breast

Marking the starting point

The usual starting point for vertical hanging is on a wall adjacent to a window so any overlap between adjoining lengths will not cast a shadow. When using paper with a large pattern, centre the pattern on the chimney-breast and on other main features of the room, if desirable, to give an overall balanced look when the room is finished.

On plain wall You must establish a true vertical to align the edge of the first length. Measure out from the corner of the starting wall a distance 12mm (½in) less than the width of the paper (this extra 12mm will be turned onto the window wall). At this point suspend a plumb bob from a small nail as high up the wall as possible. Mark the wall at several points behind the line and use a straight-edge and pencil to join the points together.

On chimney-breast Measure from the pattern centre to the left-hand edge of the paper. Measure this distance to the left of the centre line on the chimney-breast, suspend a plumb bob at this point, mark the vertical line and hang the first length to one side of it. Hang the second length to the other side of the line, butting up to the first length.

Alternatively, you can hang two widths so the motifs at the edges to be butted match up in adjacent lengths at the centre of your chimney-breast or projection. Suspend a plumb bob at the centre of the projection, mark the line as before and hang the first length against this. Hang the second length on the other side of the centre line.

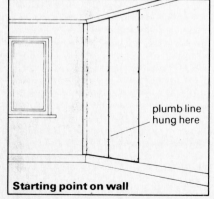
plumb line hung here

Starting point on wall

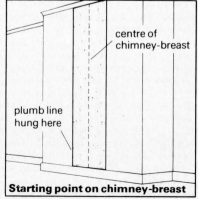
plumb line hung here

Starting point on chimney-breast

Cutting lengths and pasting

Cut the paper into lengths, each about 200mm (8in) longer than the height of the wall to allow for trimming later. If the paper has a set or drop pattern, match the lengths on the pasting table; remember to work from two or even three rolls at once to reduce wastage. As you cut the lengths number them on the back so you can tell at a glance the order in which to hang them. Also indicate which end is to be hung at the top of the wall to avoid hanging the paper upside down.

Lay the lengths, decorative side down, on the pasting table. Line up the end and far edge of the first sheet of paper with the end and far edge of the table, allowing it to overhang by 6mm ($\frac{1}{4}$in). At the other end let the rest of the paper fall onto the floor. Imagine the width of the paper is divided into three strips; paste the centre strip, then paste the section farthest away from you, working towards the edge (never work from the edges towards the centre as the paste will seep under the paper and spoil the decorative face). Pull the paper towards you so the near edge overhangs the table by about 6mm ($\frac{1}{4}$in) and paste this final strip, remembering to work from the centre towards the edge. Fold over the pasted end to the centre of the length, pull the unpasted paper onto the table and paste and fold as before.

You do not need to leave the paste to soak in with thin papers, which you can hang immediately. Heavier papers have to soak for about ten minutes. To save time lay the pasted length (with the ends still folded back onto the centre) on a clean surface and paste the next length. It is a good idea to write the time of pasting on the back of each length to ensure each piece soaks for the same time.

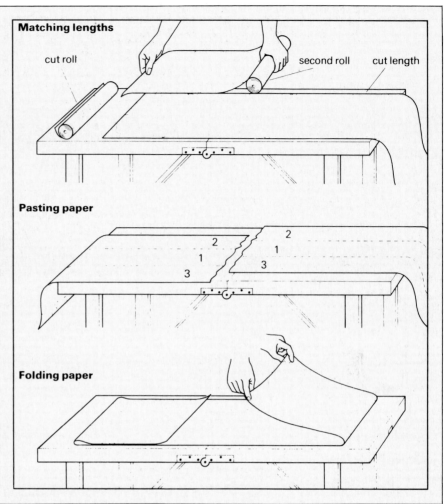

Matching lengths

cut roll   second roll   cut length

Pasting paper

2   2
1   1
3   3

Folding paper

Hanging the paper

Drape the pasted length over your arm, making sure you remember which end is to go at the top of the wall. Unfold the top half of the length, keeping a firm hold on the lower half so it does not stretch. The positioning of the first length is critical. Align the edge of the paper with the line you marked on wall and position the top with the ceiling line, allowing a 75–100mm (3–4in) overlap at the top for trimming and folding. Fold this top edge overlap back onto the pasted side to prevent paste getting on the ceiling; if paste runs onto plaster or woodwork, remove at once with dampened sponge.

Smooth down the centre of the paper with the hanging brush then work towards the edges to expel any air bubbles beneath the paper. Open out the lower half of the paper and repeat the procedure, folding the bottom edge overlap in the same way.

Run the back of your scissors along the edges at the ceiling and skirting board to mark the trimming line. Peel back the paper and cut carefully along the crease before brushing the edges back into place and smoothing down.

Hang subsequent lengths in the same way, matching the pattern (if any) at the top with the length already hung and position the edge of the new length as close as possible to the first. Slide the length along to form a neat butt join. After hanging each length go over the joins with a seam roller, unless the paper is embossed.

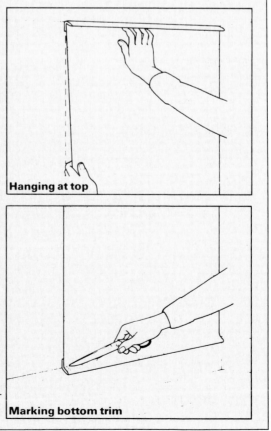

Hanging at top

Marking bottom trim

Vinyl wall covering Always use a latex adhesive when overlapping edges in corners or they will not stick firmly. Use a sharp trimming knife and a straight-edge rather than scissors for the best results and hold the knife at an angle to the wall so you do not dig into the plaster.

Ready-pasted wall covering Roll up each cut length with the pattern facing outwards. Immerse the roll in the trough of water for the time recommended by the manufacturer, usually about a minute. Take hold of the top corners of the paper and gradually pull the roll upwards, leaving the tail of the paper in the trough as long as possible so water will run back into it. Hang as ordinary wallpaper and smooth out each length with a brush or sponge, wiping off any excess adhesive.

Place plenty of newspapers under the trough to avoid splashing the floor covering. The paste at the edges may start to dry before you can brush out the paper so have ready a batch of suitable paste and a small brush to retouch the edges if necessary.

If overlapping edges lift on drying, stick them down with a latex adhesive. If the walls are lined with expanded polystyrene and you wish to use ready-pasted vinyl covering, hang lining paper over the polystyrene first to prevent the vinyl bubbling.

Polyethylene paper For this type of paper, such as Novamura, paste the wall with either the adhesive supplied with the paper or a vinyl adhesive. Since the material is so light to handle there is no need to cut it to length first, so you can hang it straight from the roll. Smooth down with a sponge.

Chimney-breast

Hang your first length of wallpaper in the centre of the projection (as already described when finding the starting point) and hang lengths either side until a gap of less than a full width of paper remains on both sides. Cut a strip wide enough to turn the corner by about 25mm (1in). Paste and hang the top half as usual, leaving the extra 25mm free. This you can brush round the corner after you have fixed the paper round the mantel piece.

Cut off as much surplus paper as possible around

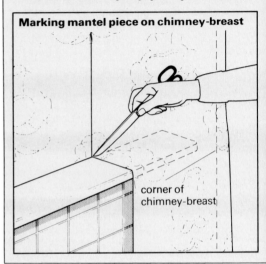

Marking mantel piece on chimney-breast

corner of chimney-breast

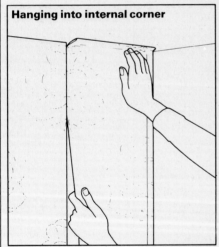

Hanging into internal corner

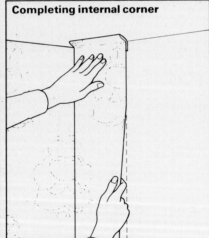

Completing internal corner

Papering external corner

Turning corners

Whenever you have to paper round a corner, use your plumb line on the new wall to establish a true vertical.

Internal corner Never turn more than 12 mm ($\frac{1}{2}$in) of paper round a corner or it will crease. Measure the distance from the edge of the last length to the corner in three places – top, middle and bottom. Add 12mm ($\frac{1}{2}$in) to the largest measurement and cut a strip of paper this width from the next length. Make sure this strip is cut from the correct side of the length or the pattern will not match. Paste and hang this piece with the extra 12mm extending round the corner.

Measure the width of the remaining strip and suspend a plumb bob at this distance from the corner on the new wall, marking pencil lines as before. Hang the strip with its edge aligned with the pencil line. There will be a slight overlap in the corner but this will not be too noticeable.

External corner Follow the same procedure as for internal corners, but when you measure the distance from the last length to the corner add 25mm (1in) to take round. Cut the paper and hang the strip as before. When you hang the remaining piece butt-join the lengths. If the corner is badly out of square, allow for a slight overlap.

Pattern clashes You must decide whether to have any pattern clash nearest to the external or internal corner, according to which would be less noticeable. You may find it easier to check this by using artificial light, when the discrepancy in the pattern is likely to show up more.

the mantle piece, leaving between 25–50mm (1–2in) for final trimming. Starting at the top of the mantel, press the paper into the contours of the fireplace surround and trim off along the crease lines, using small scissors if preferred.

Brush in the paper, including the 25mm turn allowance. Repeat for the other side of the surround, then continue papering on the side wall of the chimney-breast where your original papering was discontinued. There will be a pattern overlap here, but it should not be noticeable in the corner.

Cutting off surplus paper

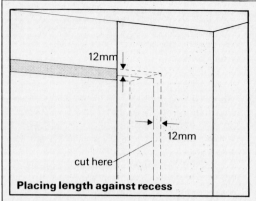
Placing length against recess

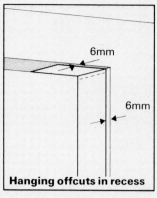
Hanging offcuts in recess

Recessed windows
Place a length of paper against the recess and mark the right-angle, adding 12mm (½in) where the top and side of the recess fall. Cut the length to shape. Measure inside the top and side of the recess, deduct 6mm (½in) from the depth of each and cut pieces of paper to size, matching the pattern as near as possible. Paste and hang these offcuts, butting them up to the back of the recess. Paste and hang the prepared length for the front wall, turning the extra 12mm (½in) into the recess so it overlaps the pieces already hung. If necessary, make a small diagonal snip in the paper where it turns into the corner of the recess for a tidy finish. Repeat for the other side.

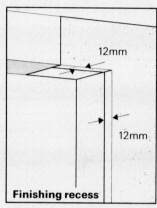
Finishing recess

Doorway
Paste and hang a full length of paper so it overlaps the door. Cut off most of the surplus paper to within 25mm (1in) of the door frame. Make a diagonal cut at the top corner and brush the paper into the angle between the wall and the frame. Turn back the extra paper and trim, then press the paper into place along the top and sides of the frame. Repeat for the other side of the frame. Cut and hang a piece of paper to fit the wall above the door.

Cutting surplus

Cutting angle

Brushing into angle

Light switch
When dealing with a projecting light switch hang the top half of the length then press the paper against the knob of the switch. Make several cuts in the shape of a star from the centre of the knob to about 12mm (½in) past the mounting block. Press the paper over the block and crease it round the base before trimming off and brushing in.

With a flush switch always turn off the electricity at the mains before papering. Remove the fixing screws and pull the cover plate 12mm (½in) away from the wall. Hang the top half of the length and press the paper gently against the switch. Make a square cut in the paper to leave a 6mm (¼in) margin inside the area covered by the plate. Hang and trim the rest of the length and refit the cover plate.

Cutting for projecting switch

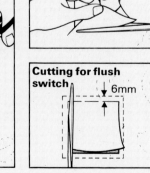
Trimming round block

Cutting for flush switch
6mm

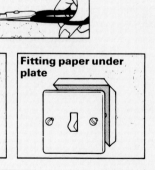
Fitting paper under plate

Stairwell
Paste and fold the paper concertina-fashion or the weight of the paste will stretch the long lengths of paper. Measure the width of the paper and subtract 12mm (½in). Suspend a plumb bob, on the side wall, at this distance from the side and end wall corner and hang the first length of paper to this, turning 12mm (½in) onto the end wall. Continue papering the side wall, butt-joining each length, then paper the end wall.

How to paper a ceiling

If the ceiling is in good condition, size the surface and leave it to dry before papering. If the plaster is uneven, line the ceiling first for the best result. As with walls, always hang lining paper at right-angles to the decorative covering so the joins do not coincide.

Hang ceiling paper parallel to the main window in the room so the joins are not too noticeable (**see 1**).
Measure the width of the paper, deduct 6mm ($\frac{1}{4}$in) for turning onto the end wall and mark this distance in pencil at both sides of the ceiling. Chalk a length of string and fix it at one side with a drawing pin. Stretch the string between the two pencil marks and pluck it so the chalk is transferred to the ceiling (**see 2**).

Cut the number of lengths required, allowing for the pattern to match and for trimming at both ends. Paste and fold each length concertina-fashion as for lining paper hung on walls. Hang the first length flush against the chalk line. Unfold the last pleat and smooth it onto the ceiling. Release the paper one pleat at a time, supporting the rest of the paper with a spare roll. Brush out each section onto the ceiling.

Turn 6mm ($\frac{1}{4}$in) onto the end and side walls then trim and sponge away any surplus paste (**see 3**).
Hang the other lengths in the same way, butt-joining the edges and turning 6mm ($\frac{1}{4}$in) onto both side walls. Remember to allow 6mm in the width of the last length for turning onto the end wall. At a ceiling light, make star-shaped cuts as for projecting light switches. Smooth paper round fitting and trim flaps (**see 4**).

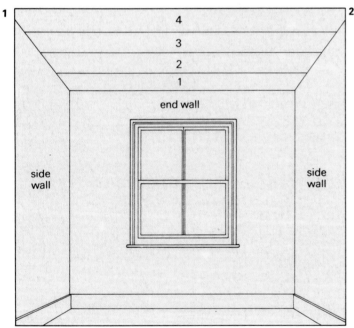

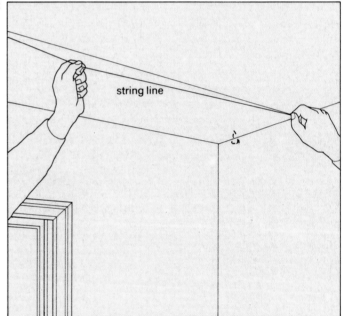

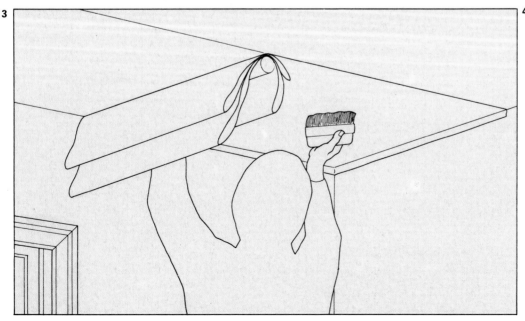

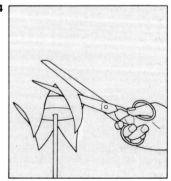

Fixing ceramic tiles

Ceramic tiles provide not only a practical but also a decorative solution to those problem areas in the bathroom and kitchen, where water splashes will ruin the ordinary wall decorations.

Consider first what sort or combination of tiles – plain, patterned or textured, or a mixture of the two – will best suit your colour scheme.

Plain tiles Produced to match the standard colours of bathroom and kitchen ware, this type is the cheapest and plain colours allow greater flexibility when changing other patterns in your rooms.

Patterned tiles Usually based on standard plain tile colours, these feature either a complete pattern or are used in groups of four to form a single motif. They are seen to their best advantage when used as a contrast to plain tiles and can also look attractive when concentrated on small areas.

Textured tiles In similar colours to plain, these are most striking when highlighting one particular area or covering an end wall between two plain walls. There is a limited range of 'feature' tiles with either a special motif or a rural scene. And you can even make up a mural to be hung on the wall like a picture or set into a plain-tiled area.

Heat-resistant tiles For fireplace surrounds and other areas likely to be subjected to extreme heat.

Types of tile

The two basic sizes are 108mm sq × 4mm ($4\frac{1}{4}$in sq × $\frac{5}{32}$in) and 152mm sq × 6mm (6in sq × $\frac{1}{4}$in), but larger sizes are available such as 200mm (8in) sq and 200 × 100mm (8 × 4in). Interesting shapes, some interlocking, are usually more costly and not so easy to work with as rectangular ones.

Certain areas of the room, such as corners and the top edge of a half-tiled wall, need specially shaped tiles to make your job easier and the overall look neater. And you must take these into account when calculating the number of tiles you will need. You should also add 5–10 tiles to your total to allow for breakages

Most tiles nowadays are known as universal tiles, and have all four edges glazed. This means that they can be used for tiling the perimeter of an area to leave a neat edge as well as for filling in the main part. They do not generally have spacer lugs on their edges, so small plastic or card spacers have to be inserted to ensure an even separation between the tiles. Some universal tiles have a slightly bevelled edge, allowing them to be butted together to leave a narrow grouting space.

Old-fashioned round-edged tiles are still sold in a limited number of tile ranges, and are mainly used for restoration work. There are in fact two types. One has one rounded edge (known as RE), and is used at the edge of a tiled area and at external corners. The other has two adjacent rounded edges (known as REX), and is used at external corners in the top row of a half-tiled wall (see overleaf).

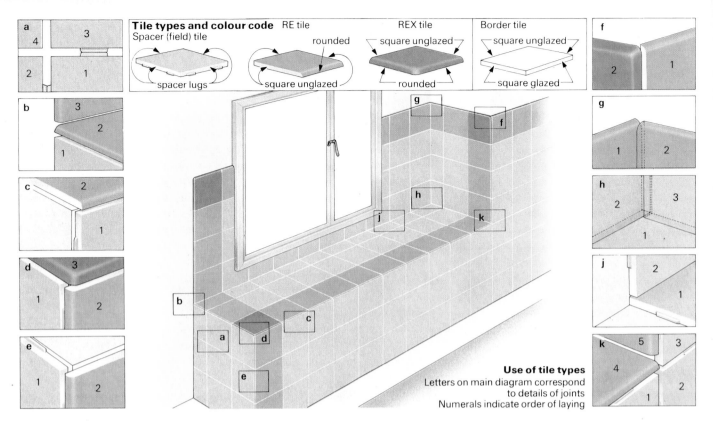

Tile types and colour code

RE tile · REX tile · Border tile

Spacer (field) tile — spacer lugs
RE tile — rounded / square unglazed
REX tile — square unglazed / rounded
Border tile — square unglazed / square glazed

Use of tile types
Letters on main diagram correspond
to details of joints
Numerals indicate order of laying

Preparing the surface

As with nearly all decorative covering jobs it is the preparation that makes or breaks the finish. And this applies particularly with ceramic tiles as, like wallpaper or paint, they have to be fixed to a really smooth, flat surface, which must also be dry and firm.

A good way of finding out just how smooth your walls are is by using a timber straight-edge, about 1m (or 36in) long. Place this at different points across the surface, checking vertically, horizontally and diagonally. If you are getting a noticeable see-saw action a certain amount of levelling will be necessary.

Plaster Where only minor areas are affected, use a proprietary plaster filler. Follow the manufacturer's mixing instructions and then apply with a filling knife to the low areas of the surface. Two or three applications may be necessary to build up to the correct level.

As you become more expert this will not be necessary since you will be able to level shallow depressions accurately when applying the wet mix, using a straight-edge or filling knife.

Bad irregularities over large areas must be completely replastered, a job best left to the professional plasterer. New plaster must be allowed to dry out for at least a month before tiling and, as the surface is porous, sealed with a coat of plaster primer. This sealing is also necessary where a plaster filler has been used.

Wallpaper This must be completely stripped first and the plaster underneath raked out where loose and levelled as above.

Painted Glasspaper down to remove any flaking areas and provide a key for the tile adhesive. Where the paint is direct onto plaster, uneven patches must be levelled as above.

Timber Plane level and give the bare wood a coat of wood primer before tiling.

Ceramic tiles Existing tiles are probably the best base of all, today's thin ceramics being specifically designed to suit tile-on-tile fixing. But as with all other surfaces the base must be sound. So make sure the existing tiles are clean, flat and firmly fixed. Remove any loose ones and refix with tile adhesive so they are level with adjacent tiles.

Half-tiled wall If you intend retiling here and taking the new tiles to ceiling height, you will need to build out the untiled part of the wall level with the existing area to avoid being left with a recess. This levelling up of the wall section can be done with plaster, plasterboard or other suitable building board.

Lining the wall

Where the surface of your wall is so uneven that refilling is impossible and replastering would be too costly, you can create a 'new' wall by lining with plywood, chipboard or plasterboard.

First construct a timber framework on the wall from horizontal and vertical 50 × 25mm (2 × 1in) battens. Drill countersunk holes in the battens at about 400mm (or 16in) spacing. Drill corresponding holes in the wall to take masonry plugs and screw the battens loosely to these using 50mm (2in) long No 8 countersunk screws. Start with the top and bottom horizontal battens. Follow these by the vertical battens spaced at 400mm (or 16in) intervals, working from left to right. Finally fill in with short horizontal battens spaced at 610mm (24in) intervals. Using a straight-edge horizontally, vertically and diagonally, level up the battens using pieces of scrap hardboard, laminate etc. as packing between the battens and 'low' areas of wall before tightening up the screws. Take care with this stage of the job as the final accuracy of the lining could otherwise be affected.

Apply a coat of primer or sealer to all board surfaces and edges, then screw to the battens with 32mm (1¼in) long No 8 countersunk screws through countersunk holes drilled in the boards.

With old-style RE and REX tiles the right type must be used at edges and corners

Opposite page

1 If surface is too uneven to provide suitable base for tiling, screw batten framework to wall. Pack low areas behind battens with pieces of scrap hardboard to ensure framework sits flush against wall. **2** Screw plywood or chipboard panels to battens, butt joining edges

3 To find starting point nail batten to wall, one tile width above floor. Mark off batten in tile widths, leaving equal spaces at each end. At last full tile width nail upright batten to wall at true vertical. Lay first tile at corner formed by two battens. **4** Spread adhesive with small round-ended trowel over one square metre of wall. **5** Comb adhesive horizontally to leave series of ridges. **6** Press tiles into place, butting each squarely against its neighbour with spacer lugs touching. Complete each horizontal row before starting next one

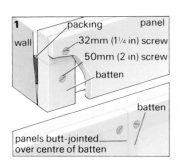

2

407mm (16 in) centres

wall

chipboard
18mm (¾ in)
or plywood panel

**50x50mm
(2x2 in) battens**

610mm (24 in) centres

wall

○ 32mm (1¼ in) No8 countersunk woodscrews
for fixing panels
● 50mm (2 in) No8 countersunk woodscrews
for fixing battens

1

wall

packing   panel

32mm (1¼ in) screw

50mm (2 in) screw

batten

batten

panels butt-jointed
over centre of batten

3

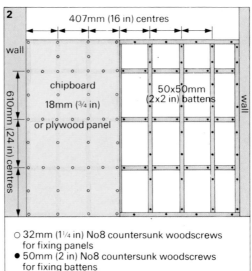

vertical batten

measuring staff

starting point

one tile width

adjoining wall   horizontal batten   floor

4

6

5

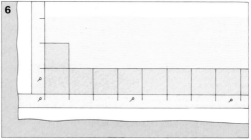

Planning
Very few houses have true vertical and horizontal corners so you must never begin tiling in a corner or at floor level. As you reach the end of each row cut to shape the tiles for these areas.

The first step then is to decide the best starting point by making a measuring staff from a long batten (if your room has several alcoves, you will need a shorter one as well) marked with tile widths. This will enable you to see how many whole tiles

can be accommodated over a particular area. Ideally you should aim for equal size cut tiles at both ends of each wall as this will give the job a balanced look.

Having established the starting point, temporarily fix a horizontal batten to the wall with its top edge one tile width above the floor or skirting board. If the floor line slopes then lower the batten slightly to make the cutting easier later on. It is far easier to trim whole tiles to fit a space than to cut thin pieces to fill tiny gaps. Double-check the batten for correct horizontal before screwing it securely to the wall.

You will now have to establish a vertical line at the starting point near the corner of the wall. To determine this, use a batten and spirit level (or plumb bob and line) and mark the vertical line in pencil on the wall. Follow this horizontal and vertical procedure for every wall.

Fixing with adhesive
The placing of the first few tiles is critical; if they are out of true the entire job will be affected. So temporarily position a few tiles, starting against your vertical line and batten, and check for a perfect right-angle. Only when you are satisfied all is correct should you begin. Starting from this right-angle spread the tile adhesive with a broad knife or small round-edged trowel over about one square metre (or sq yd) of wall area.

Warning Don't use your notched spreader to lift the adhesive from the can as it will come through the notches onto your hands.

Comb this area horizontally to leave a series of ridges. Cover with tiles, pressing them into place with a twisting movement – never slide them across the adhesive as it will squeeze up between the tiles – completing each horizontal row before starting the one above. Make sure each tile is butted squarely against the spacer; the simplest type to use is the small plastic cross type which is pressed into the tile adhesive at the corners of the tiles, but card or matchsticks can be used instead.

As you complete each square metre of tiling be sure to check the tiles are correctly positioned vertically and horizontally by using your spirit level. Complete as many whole tiles as possible before tackling any cutting. When the area above the horizontal batten is complete, allow at least 12 hours' drying time before removing the batten and tiling the bottom course (row). Allow another 24 hours before starting to grout.

There are special water-resistant adhesives for tiled areas likely to be subjected to excessive splashing or heat, such as shower cubicles. You will need a trowel to spread this type in a thin layer and should allow at least 14 days before grouting or allowing the tiles to come into contact with water.

There is a 'fix and grout' product that enables you to stick down your tiles and then grout them in a matter of hours.

Grouting between the tiles
Carefully mix your chosen grouting powder with water to a creamy consistency and rub well into the joints with a dampened sponge. Remove any surplus with a dampened cloth before the grouting is dry. Any remaining traces can be polished off later with a soft dry cloth.

For extra colour you can add a dye solution to a ready-mix grout, or dye powder to a dry grout. Colours available include red, yellow, blue, green, brown and black.

A few of the many shapes, sizes, colours and designs of modern ceramic tiles.
1 Hand-printed all-over pattern, 108mm (4¼in) square. **2, 3** Embossed design and matching mottle, 152mm (6in) square.

4 Pattern with matching plain tile, 108mm (4¼in) square. **5** Combination tile assembled into four-tile pattern, 108mm (4¼in) square. **6** Patterned, 216×108mm (8½×4¼in), **7, 8** Patterned tile, 152mm (6in) square.

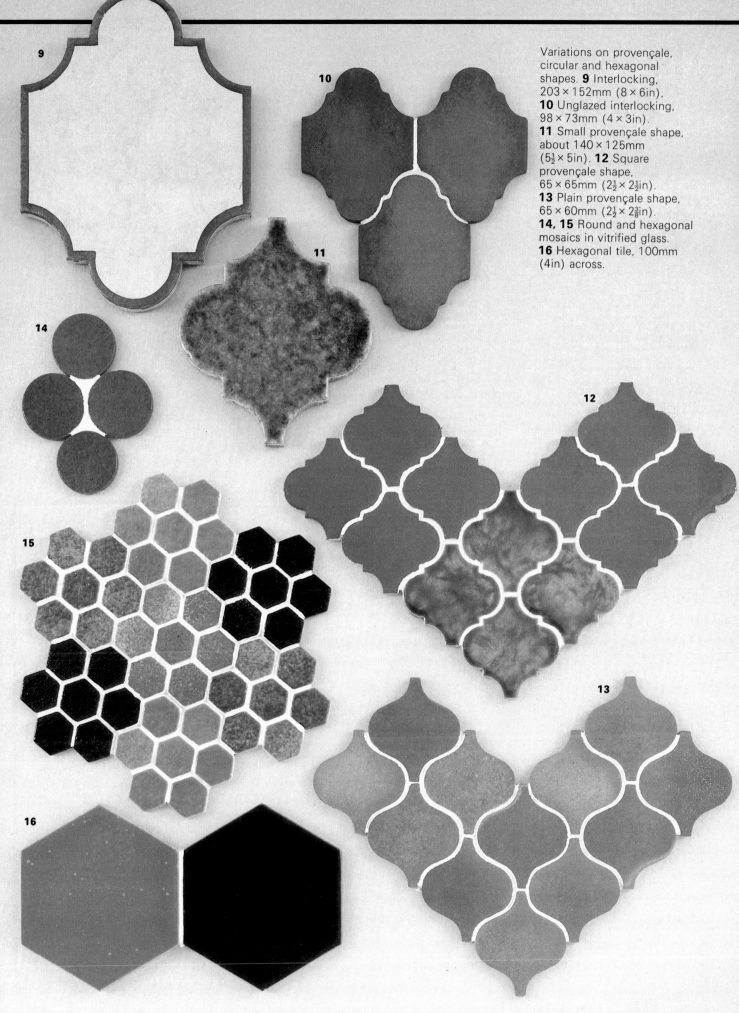

Variations on provençale, circular and hexagonal shapes. **9** Interlocking, 203 × 152mm (8 × 6in). **10** Unglazed interlocking, 98 × 73mm (4 × 3in). **11** Small provençale shape, about 140 × 125mm (5$\frac{1}{2}$ × 5in). **12** Square provençale shape, 65 × 65mm (2$\frac{1}{2}$ × 2$\frac{1}{2}$in). **13** Plain provençale shape, 65 × 60mm (2$\frac{1}{2}$ × 2$\frac{3}{8}$in). **14, 15** Round and hexagonal mosaics in vitrified glass. **16** Hexagonal tile, 100mm (4in) across.

1 Scoring with tile cutter

2 Breaking over matchstick

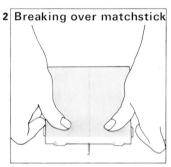

3 Cutting with pincers

4 Tile cutter/pliers

1 To cut tiles to fit, mark required width and score glaze
2 Place tile on flat surface with matchstick under scored line. Press down edges so tile snaps cleanly along line
3 Use pincers to cut thin sections or awkward shapes from tiles
4 With wheeled tile cutter score glaze with cutting wheel and squeeze handles together to cut tile cleanly

Cutting tiles

The most common tile cutter looks like a pencil and has a tungsten carbide tip to score the tile. To snap cleanly, place a matchstick under the scored line and press down evenly on both sides of the tile. A neat break should result. Another type of cutter scores with a cutting wheel. Place the tile in the jaws of the tool and gently squeeze the handles, pincer-fashion, to make a clean break.

To mark an end tile for cutting to size, place it in position (front surface against wall) making sure one edge of the tile butts into the wall. Measure the distance from the end of the wall to the preceding tile in the row. Mark the width required in pencil, first on the reverse, continuing round the edges to the front face when you have turned the tile round. To join up these lines correctly place the tile face up on a firm, flat surface and using a metal straight-edge (your try square is ideal) align the two pencil marks and score through the glaze with your cutter. Use one of the two cutting methods described.

If really thin sections, less than 10mm ($\frac{3}{8}$in) thick, have to be cut, score deeply along the marked line and with pincers nibble away gradually at the waste portion. Never be tempted to take off a huge chunk in this way as the tile will break. Use this method, too, when cutting out L-shaped or curved sections. Make a card template (pattern) of the shape required and transfer it onto the tile.

Projecting pipes are tricky to tile around so use a template again. The safest way to tackle the job is to cut the tile in two, removing from each portion an arc to suit the shape of the pipe. When the two portions are positioned together round the pipe, the joint will not be obvious.

Tiling round fitments

Treat the top edges of sinks, baths and cupboard units as the floor level and nail or screw a horizontal batten above them. This will support the tiles above it while the rest of the wall is being completed. After the adhesive has set, remove the batten and apply the bottom course of tiles, trimming where necessary.

Tiling round windows

The window is very often the focal point of any room so it is important to try to arrange the tiles to achieve a good visual balance, with equal size tiles on either side of the window.

On horizontal sill surfaces fix whole tiles at the front, with any cut ones at the back nearest the window where they are not so obvious.

Above Tiara long tiles add height to small rooms and colours match bathroom equipment ranges, 216×108mm/$8\frac{1}{2}$×$4\frac{1}{4}$in
Below left Florence is a strong design and needs to be used over a large enough area to show off its pattern. It looks well with adjacent walls in matching solid colour tiles

Basic items
hand or electric drill
wood and masonry bits
countersink bit, screwdriver

For surface preparation
timber straight-edge
medium coarse glasspaper
filler, knife, primer (for plaster)
stripping knife (for wallpaper)
block plane, primer, paint brush
    (for wood)

For lining walls
50 × 25mm (2 × 1in) battens
No 8 countersunk screws, 50mm (2in)
    and 32mm (1$\frac{1}{4}$in) long, wall plugs
plywood or chipboard, sealer
hardboard or plywood pieces

For tiling
measuring staff and pencil
batten (for horizontal line)
spirit level, plumb bob and line
tile adhesive and notched spreader
broad knife, small round-ended trowel
grouting powder and water
sponge and two soft cloths

For cutting tiles
tile cutter, matchsticks and pencil
metal straight-edge or try square
pincers (for thin sections)
card and scissors (if template needed)

equipment

Fixing mirrors & mirror tiles

Mirrors play an important part in interior decoration; if they are carefully placed, a small room can be made to look larger and a dark room appear lighter. In every home there is a place where a mirror can be used to great effect – in an alcove, behind display shelving, in a recess or covering a door. But remember a mirrored surface will reflect everything which stands in front of it; so avoid overdoing it by placing mirrors on an adjacent or facing wall since the effect might be confusing and not what you expected.

Mirrors

A wide range of mirrors is available, either drilled for screw fixing or undrilled for other methods of fixing. Your glass merchant will be able to supply you with a mirror of almost any shape or size. Any top quality glass, free of imperfections, is suitable for silvering; 6mm ($\frac{1}{4}$in) float glass is used for most of the larger mirrors. It might be necessary to use a thicker glass for mirror table tops, depending on the size requirements; your glass merchant should be able to advise you.

Decide when placing a special order for a mirror whether you will require a screw fixing. If you do, it is worthwhile getting the supplier to do the drilling for you. Large mirrors are expensive and, since the additional charge for drilling is very reasonable considering the overall cost of the mirror, it is best not to risk drilling the holes yourself.

All mirrors should have polished edges, unless they are to be set into a heavy rebated frame, when a clean cut edge will do. Take care when handling cut mirrors with unpolished edges; wear leather gloves since the edges of the glass are razor sharp.
Screw fixing A drilled mirror can easily be fixed in

Above Large slabs of mirror give an impression of increased light and space to any part of your home, as well as adding a touch of luxury for a relatively low cost

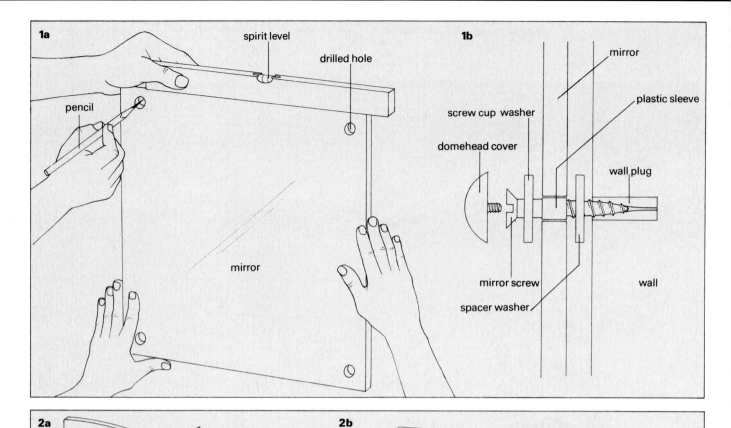

1a spirit level

drilled hole

pencil

mirror

1b mirror

plastic sleeve

screw cup washer

domehead cover

wall plug

mirror screw

wall

spacer washer

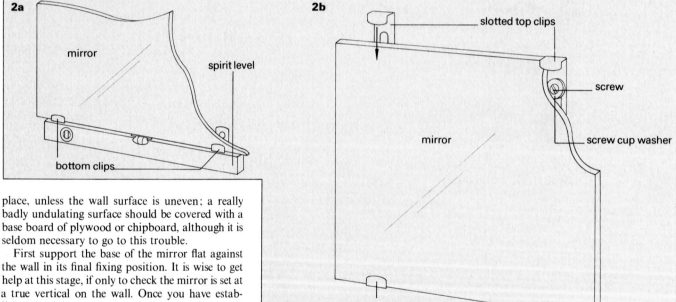

2a

mirror

spirit level

bottom clips

2b slotted top clips

screw

mirror

screw cup washer

bottom clips

place, unless the wall surface is uneven; a really badly undulating surface should be covered with a base board of plywood or chipboard, although it is seldom necessary to go to this trouble.

First support the base of the mirror flat against the wall in its final fixing position. It is wise to get help at this stage, if only to check the mirror is set at a true vertical on the wall. Once you have established the right position, mark with a pencil through the drilled holes onto the wall behind. Remove the mirror and drill the wall at these points, using the correct size masonry bit and wall plugs for the mirror screws.

The screws used have rubber or soft plastic spacers and collars. Various types are available, although the principle is the same with each. The screw passes through a sleeve, which is centred in the hole of the mirror. At the back a spacer washer fits between the mirror and the wall, while a cup washer is placed between the face of the mirror and the countersunk head of the mirror screw. Great care must be taken when tightening the screws; work round them in turn, gradually tightening each one until its head gently squeezes the soft cup washer on the face of the mirror. Check at this stage the mirror is firmly held against the wall. If it is not, don't tighten the screws further since this will cause

the mirror to break. Remove whichever screw is not gripping the mirror firmly, insert packing behind the spacer washer to fill the remaining gap and screw through the packing into the wall. The decorative heads of the screws can then be fitted into the fixing screws to conceal the screw heads and the washers beneath.

Mirror clip fixing Undrilled mirrors can be mounted on a wall using mirror clips. Several types are available, including corner clips, plastic spring clips and hook-on clips. With the hook-on type the bottom clips are screwed to the wall in accurate alignment, so the bottom of the mirror rests on the upward facing jaws. Check your levels carefully before finally fixing these clips.

The upper clips have a long slot in the back plate

1a Hold a drilled mirror in the required position on the wall and mark through the holes; check the mirror is horizontal with a spirit level

1b Secure the mirror with the relevant fixings

2a Make sure the bottom clips are level when fixing an undrilled mirror with clips

2b Fix the top clips, place the mirror in position and slide the top clips down; you can fit additional slotted clips on each side for extra stability

3a Before fixing mirror tiles, remove the protective paper from the tabs on the back
3b To mark the position of the tiles, number each one and write the numbers in order on the board
3c Press the tiles in place, applying light pressure over each tab in turn; don't apply pressure between the tabs since you might break the tile

through which they are screwed to the wall, tightly enough to allow the clip to slide up and down behind the screw head. The mirror is then placed in the bottom clips and pushed flat against the wall, while the downward facing jaws of the upper clips remain in the open position. The upper clips are then slid down so the jaws hold the top edge of the mirror. The mirror can be easily taken down by opening the upper clips and lifting the mirror out of the bottom ones.

Frame fixing Small mirrors can be framed and backed and hung in position using mirror plates or chains. Larger mirrors can be built into wall fitments and held with facing mouldings and beading. A mirror can also be placed in a sliding frame to provide a mirrored door for a unit.

Mirror tiles

The simplest method of providing a large mirrored area is to fix mirror tiles. These are made in two thicknesses – 3mm ($\frac{1}{8}$in) and 4mm ($\frac{3}{16}$in) – and are available in a wide range of sizes. The quality is superior in the thicker 4mm ($\frac{3}{16}$in) tile and it might prove a false economy to buy the thinner version, since the surface of the glass is more inclined to flake. Each tile has self-adhesive tabs stuck to the back; once the protective paper is removed from the tabs, fixing is simple and instant.

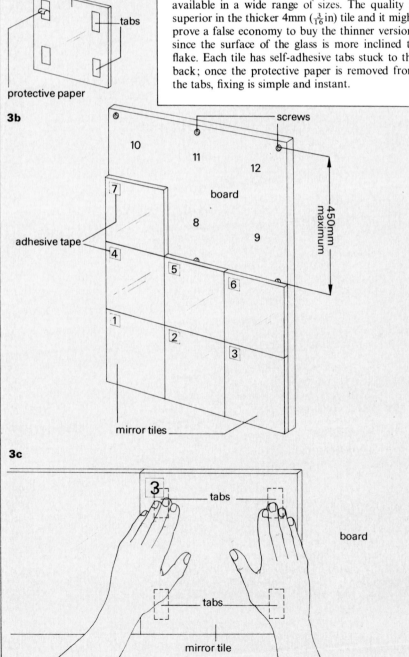

3a
mirror tile
tabs
protective paper

3b
screws
10
11
12
board
450mm maximum
7
8
9
adhesive tape
4
5
6
1
2
3
mirror tiles

3c
3
tabs
tabs
tabs
board
mirror tile

Before you start fixing, you must prepare the surface onto which the tiles are to be stuck. Any surface which is not perfectly flat will cause the tiles to lie in an uneven plane, which will result in a distorted reflection. Plaster surfaces are particularly bad since they are seldom perfectly flat. Although the tabs will stick effectively to painted or untreated plaster – unless the paint is badly flaking – it is advisable not to try it if a perfect surface is required.

Fixing to board Mirror tiles are best stuck down to a suitable board such as plywood or chipboard. The thicker the board the better, since there is more chance of achieving the perfect flatness you require. For a really uneven wall surface use an 18mm ($\frac{3}{4}$in) thick board; don't use board less than 12mm ($\frac{1}{2}$in) thick, even on a wall which looks true.

Screw the board in place using the appropriate wall plugs and countersink the heads of the screws slightly below the surface of the board. The screws should be about 450mm (18in) apart around the edge and across the surface of the board. Don't drive the screws in tight, but stop just as the screw begins to bite into the board; an overtightened screw in a depressed part of the wall will cause the board to follow the depression and lose its flatness. This is more likely to occur with thinner board.

Setting out tiles This is an important stage and should be done with care. Individual tiles are seldom cut with perfect accuracy and can vary slightly. Over a large area this variation can be cumulative and result in a poor finish. Wherever possible set out the tiles loosely on the fixing board before it is screwed to the wall; you will finally fix them into place starting at the bottom and working upwards.

When the tiles are set out squarely to your liking, number each tile, using a small piece of adhesive tape on the face of each, and write these numbers in the same order on the board. Fix the tiles in place so the numbers correspond. Fix them into place in the same order and you will be sure of a perfect run of joints.

Fixing tiles When fixing take care to note the exact position of each tab on the back of the tile. Remove the protective paper and place the tile in position on the board, applying light pressure to each tab in turn. Avoid applying pressure to the tile between the tab positions – especially when using thinner tiles – since this might break them. If you make a mistake and have to remove a tile, use a thin broad bladed knife and try to slide it beneath each pad in turn. Don't try to lever the tile away or you will break it.

New adhesive tabs can be stuck into place on the back of a mirror tile if the original one has to be removed. These tabs have strong adhesive and work effectively the first time on most surfaces. As a safeguard on porous boards, brush away any dust and apply a thin coat of impact adhesive to correspond with the tab positions. Allow this to dry thoroughly before bringing tabs into contact.

Warning Care must be taken in areas where there is excessive moisture; bathrooms are particularly prone to heavy condensation. Never use a porous-type chipboard as a backing for mirrors or mirror tiles in these conditions, since rot will set into the chipboard, causing mould and damaging the silvering of the mirror. Use a resin-bonded plywood and check edges are thoroughly sealed with primer.

An air space of at least 3mm ($\frac{1}{8}$in) should be left between the fixing surface and the back of the mirror; with tiles the tabs determine the space.

Laying ceramic floor tiles

Traditionally ceramic tiles have been used to cover areas around basins, baths and sinks, where splashing is likely to occur. But they are also very practical for covering floors.

Now that central heating has taken the chill from ceramic floor tiles, people are beginning to appreciate their hard-wearing qualities and easy maintenance. Provided it is correctly laid on a properly prepared sub-floor, ceramic flooring has good resistance to impact and general wear and high resistance to crazing. It only needs to be swept regularly and washed from time to time with water and detergent. Stubborn stains can be removed from this type of tile with a household abrasive – or paint brush cleaner.

Types of tiles
It is essential to use only flooring grade tiles – wall tiles are much thinner and would break under pressure. Flooring tiles are available glazed or unglazed. Glazed tiles come in a wide range of colours and patterns and some have a roughened glaze to make them slip-resistant. Unglazed tiles are produced only in plain or mottled colours; but they are the most durable form of tile and are available in a range of anti-slip surfaces and also coving tiles to provide a clean curve from floor to wall. They are more difficult to cut than glazed tiles, but you can hire or buy a special tool for cutting them.

Tiles are made in a variety of shapes, square ones being the easiest to lay. The most common size is 152mm (6in) square, which means you will need 43 tiles to cover 1sq m (36 for 1sq yd). Always buy six or so extra ones for cutting in or in case of breakages.

Mosaic tiles are small squares of glazed or unglazed ceramic covered with peel-off sheets 305mm (12in) square which you remove after laying.

Preparing the surface
It is essential to lay ceramic tiles on a clean, dry, level surface; any distortions may cause the tiles to move and crack under pressure. They can be laid on a solid floor of concrete or existing hard flooring such as terrazzo or quarry tiles or on a suspended timber floor. But in each case the floor needs some preparation before the tiles are laid.
Concrete The concrete must be dry, clean and flat. Tiling will not cure damp, so if the concrete is letting moisture through, lay a damp proof membrane and screed.

Fill any small depressions in the concrete with sand and cement, using a mixture of three parts washed sharp sand and one part cement – and make sure you level off after filling. If there is a slight fall-away in the surface in any direction, correct it with a concrete levelling compound. A badly depressed surface should be levelled with a waterproof screed. Chip away any small nibs of concrete and sweep the surface thoroughly.
Hard flooring Tiled or terrazzo floors should be flat and firmly fixed. Remove any traces of grease

or polish and make sure it is dry before you start tiling. Any loose sections, such as a loose quarry tile, should be securely glued back in place.
Timber floor Make sure there is adequate ventilation below the floorboards to prevent rot forming after tiling. Don't lay tiles directly onto a suspended timber floor made of tongued and grooved boards since the movement of the floor would cause the tiles to shift and crack. Make the floor more stable by covering it with sheets of plywood at least 12mm (½in) thick, fixed at 300mm (or 12in) intervals with countersunk screws. If the floor is likely to be splashed with water, such as in a shower area, use exterior grade plywood.

When all existing floorboards have to be removed, due to rot for example, you can screw flooring grade chipboard directly to the joists and lay tiles on this. Use screws for fixing sheet flooring since nails cannot be relied on to hold the material securely in place once the tiles have been bonded to them. Make sure the panels butt closely together; if any small gaps do appear, pack them tightly with a filler or the floor tiles may crack along the joint lines due to movement on the sub-floor.

Before laying tiles over plywood or chipboard, always brush the surface with a priming coat; most manufacturers recommend a water-based polymer for this purpose. The primer must be properly dry before you begin tiling, so leave it overnight.

Working with adhesive
Manufacturers recommend a cement-based powder adhesive which can be used as a thin or thick-bed adhesive. Use a thin bed of about 3mm (⅛in) for flat-backed tiles; if the tiles have studs on the back or there is a slight unevenness in the floor (test with a straight-edge), use a thick bed of about 6mm (¼in). For thin-bed fixing, you will need about 3.5kg (or 8lb) of adhesive per square metre (or

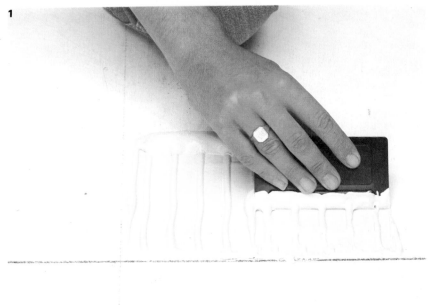

1 Apply adhesive to the floor with a notched spreader; only cover 1sq m (or sq yd) at a time
2 Lay the first tile in the right-angle formed by your marked lines
3 Position the next few tiles with spacer lugs touching, matching any pattern carefully
4 If using studded tiles on a thick bed of adhesive, lightly coat the back of the tiles to ensure they sit firmly on the floor

from the point where the strings cross. If the space remaining at the end of a row is less than half a tile, adjust the string lines half a tile off centre to give a bigger space for the perimeter tiles. This will give a balanced border and avoids having to cut narrow pieces of tile. Check the door will open over the laid tiles; if not, remove the door and trim the bottom edge with a block plane.

Fixing the tiles

Tile one quarter of the room at a time, starting with the section furthest from the door and finishing at the door. Starting from the centre, spread the adhesive evenly over the floor with a notched spreader, which is often supplied with the adhesive. Don't cover more than 1sq m (or 1sq yd) at a time. Place the tiles in position, starting in the angle of the chalked lines. Don't slide them into place or adhesive will build up against the front edge of the tile. When laying studded tiles on thick-bed adhesive, spread a thin layer of adhesive on the back of the tile to ensure a solid bed when it comes into contact with the adhesive on the floor.

Most tiles have spacer lugs to ensure the distance between each one is correct; if yours do not have

3

For laying tiles
chalked string line
nails or pins
tile adhesive
notched spreader
card or matchsticks
   (if needed)
metal straight-edge
tile cutter
pincers or tile nippers
carborundum stone
contour tracer or card and
   scissors (for template)
grouting
clean cloth

For replacing tiles
club hammer
cold chisel
adhesive

equipment

11sq ft); allow double this quantity for a thick bed. There is also a bitumen-based adhesive which can be used for thin-bed fixing.

Cement-based adhesive can be used on concrete or timber floors, but it is not suitable on concrete which has not fully dried out or on ground floors which are affected by damp. In these cases, and for areas subjected to prolonged soaking with water (such as shower floors) use a waterproof adhesive. Always mix the adhesive according to the manufacturer's instructions.

Setting out the tiles

The best way to set out tiles is from the centre of the room so you have an even border all round the edge. To find the centre, mark the halfway point on the two pairs of opposite walls and stretch a piece of string (preferably chalked) between each set of marks. Ensure the strings cross at right-angles and secure the ends with nails or pins. If the strings are chalked, pluck them to leave marks on the floor.

Before fixing down any tiles, try out the layout with dry tiles. Lay one row of tiles in each direction

these, place pieces of card or matchsticks between the tiles to give a space of 3mm ($\frac{1}{8}$in). Remove any adhesive that oozes up between the joints (to leave space for grouting) and clean off any adhesive on the tiles before it sets.

Tile each section of the room in turn, leaving the border until last. If you need to kneel on the tiled area while working, place a board across it to avoid damaging or disturbing the tiles.

Cutting border tiles To cut a tile for the border, lay it face down on top of the last whole tile and slide it forward so the front edge butts against the wall. Mark the back of the tile at each side where the edge of the last tile finishes. Place it on a firm, flat surface and join up the two marks, using a straight-edge as a guide. Score and cut the tile along this line with a tile cutter. The front section of the cut tile will fit neatly in the gap.

Cutting corner tiles Place a new tile face down over the last whole one near the corner. Place a second tile on it, slide it flush to the wall and mark its edge on the tile below. Then move the marked tile to the last whole tile round the corner without turning it. Place the second tile over it, butt it against the wall and mark as before. Score and cut along these lines and nibble the corner away with pincers or tile nippers to give an L-shaped tile which will fit round the corner. Take away only very small pieces at a time; if you try to cut too much at once, you may break the tile. When you have cut the shape you want, smooth the rough edge with a carborundum stone.

Cutting shapes To cut curved shapes, use a contour tracer or make a template and scribe the outline onto the tile. Then nibble away the tile with pincers or tile nippers as before.

To fit a tile round a pipe, cut the tile in two where the pipe falls, cut out a semi-circle from each piece and fit them round the pipe.

When tiling round a WC or wash-basin pedestal, lay full tiles as far as possible round the pedestal. To avoid having to cut very narrow sections, you may have to adjust the layout when setting out the loose tiles. Cut a template for each tile, using a contour tracer to mark the curve – and with this cut the tile; lay it in place before making a template for the adjacent tile. When all the tiles are cut and smoothed, fix them in position. Remember to leave enough space between tiles and pedestal for grouting.

Mosaic tiles Lay mosaic tiles in the same way as ordinary tiles, leaving on the paper. When the adhesive has set, soak the paper with cold water and peel it off. Where possible, use whole mosaic squares, rather than cut ones, to fill in the gaps round the perimeter of the room.

Grouting

When all the tiles have been fixed, leave them for at least 12 hours before grouting. Don't walk on them during this time since any disturbance may affect the bonding of the adhesive. If you used card or matchsticks for spacing, remove them after 24 hours. It is a good idea to wait for 24–48 hours before grouting.

Most tile manufacturers recommend a powder grout which has to be mixed with water to a creamy consistency. Mix only enough to last for about 40 minutes since it becomes unworkable after that time. Cover a small area at a time and rub the grout into the joints with a sponge or the straight side of a notched spreader, making sure all joints are filled. Leave the grout to harden in the joints for about 30 minutes before wiping off the surplus with a dampened cloth. Wipe away all traces of grout from the tiles, rinsing frequently with clean water. You can blend the grout with the tiles by colouring it: mix grout colour mix with the grout powder before adding water.

Warning Try to avoid washing the floor for a week or two, since water may dilute the adhesive and affect the strength of the bond.

Replacing a damaged tile

Chip the damaged tile away with a club hammer and cold chisel, working from the centre, taking care not to damage surrounding tiles. Remove the old adhesive with the chisel and stick down a new tile.

5
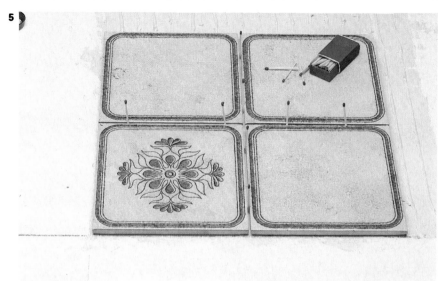

6a

6b
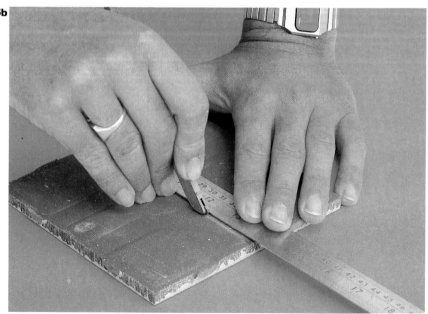

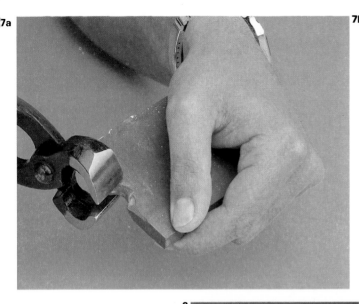

7a

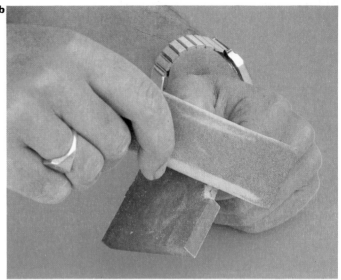

7b

5 If your tiles do not have spacer lugs, use matchsticks to keep a 3mm ($\frac{1}{8}$in) gap

6a To cut border tiles, mark the back of the tile at each side where the last tile finishes

6b Join up the marks and score along the line using a straight-edge as a guide

7a Cut shapes by nibbling small pieces from the tile with pincers

7b Smooth the rough edges with a carborundum stone

8 To fit tiles round piping, cut the tile in two, remove a semi-circle from each piece and position the pieces round the pipe

9a Apply grouting between the tiles with the straight side of a notched spreader

9b Leave the grout to harden and wipe off any excess with a dampened cloth

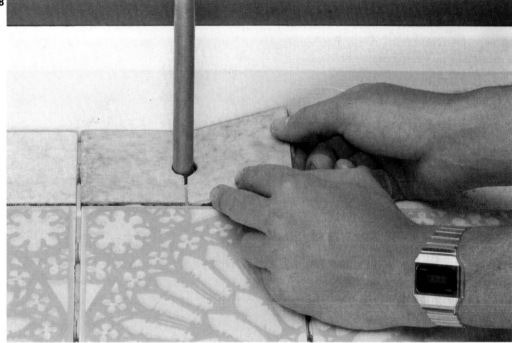

8

9a

9b

Laying cork & vinyl tiles

Cork and vinyl tiles are ideal as floor coverings in different areas of the home and offer a wide range of colours and designs. Using the correct methods, these tiles are quite straightforward to put down, as long as you ensure the surface on which they are laid is dry, firm and level.

Above The pale, smooth colours and textures in this modern kitchen are set off effectively by the warmth of a natural cork floor

One of the real advantages of tiles rather than sheet flooring material is that, when laying, you can deal with awkward shapes one by one and any mistakes in cutting will be confined to individual tiles; you may even be able to reshape those cut in error and put them elsewhere. A mistake in cutting sheet material could involve much greater wastage. Both vinyl and cork flooring come in tile form: vinyl is waterproof, resistant to oil, grease and most domestic chemicals; cork is non-slip, has good thermal insulation and reduces noise.

Vinyl tiles

These offer a wide choice of designs, from alternate rows in two or more colours and chess board effects to more complicated diamond patterns or squares-within-squares using a variety of colours. If you choose a complicated pattern, draw the design on paper to make laying easier – some manufacturers provide blank squared paper for this purpose.

Vinyl tiles are sold in packs sufficient to cover a square metre (or square yard) and the most common size tile is 300mm (or 12in) square. Always buy a few extra tiles since, apart from cutting mistakes, spares can be useful later on when worn tiles need replacing.

Pure vinyl tiles are supple and easy to lay. They have a smooth gloss finish and come in a wide variety of patterns and colours. Vinyl asbestos tiles are cheaper but more rigid and tend to crack if not stuck to a solid, level surface. They are not as easy to lay as the pure vinyl type and the choice of designs is limited, although sculptured and embossed designs are available. Some vinyl tiles are self-adhesive; if wrongly placed, these can be removed immediately and repositioned but, if you move them more than once, the adhesive tends to become less effective. Self-adhesive tiles are protected by a paper backing and you should always cut the tiles to shape before you remove this. If the tiles you choose are not self-adhesive, fix them with special vinyl flooring adhesive.

Cork tiles

Cork tiles come in a range of textures and shades. The choice of finishes is wide, too, and you should consider carefully which is best suited to your needs.

Unsealed Good where a non-slip but not particularly hard-wearing surface is required. This type is supplied with a sanded finish, but you can sand the surface again once the tiles have been laid to conceal any joint irregularities. To make unsealed tiles more durable, you can apply a polyurethane sealer but, before doing this, leave the laid floor for about 12 hours to allow the adhesive to dry thoroughly.

Hard wax These tiles provide a scuff-resistant semi-sheen surface which is particularly suitable for use in the bathroom and living areas, especially where elderly people and children are concerned. After laying the tiles, apply a coat of wax polish to conceal the joins but don't apply a sealer as the wax will prevent a good bond.

Polyurethane Suited to areas likely to be subjected to very heavy wear such as kitchens or playrooms, since the polyurethane coating makes this type particularly tough and long-lasting.

Vinyl-faced Perhaps the most popular cork surface, this consists of a thin layer of cork sandwiched between two layers of vinyl. It is particularly suitable for kitchens where heavy appliances are likely to be moved about, since any indentations recover rapidly and the easily cleaned vinyl surface protects the cork against spilt liquids.

Various adhesives are available for use with cork flooring, but it is important you use the one recommended by the manufacturer for the type of

Above Vinyl tiles make a very practical kitchen floor and are available in a wide range of colours and patterns

making sure the screw heads lie flush with or slightly below the surface.

If the fixing surface is very uneven, cover it with 12 or 18mm (½ or ¾in) chipboard or plywood screwed into position. Use flooring grade chipboard when fixing to timber, and resin-bonded plywood for concrete. On an old, worn, uneven concrete floor you may need to use a levelling compound. When mixed with water the compound finds its own level and provides a smooth, even surface.

Cork Level off any uneven surfaces in the same way as for vinyl tiles. Where timber boards are laid at ground level or on joists or battens on ground level concrete, protect the cork from moisture penetration by fixing bituminous felt paper with bituminous adhesive before overlaying with hardboard or plywood. Ideally you should remove any existing floor covering before laying cork; if this is too difficult, you can lay cork over vinyl tiles and other similar non-porous floor surfaces, provided the existing surface is level. Wash with detergent to remove any grease and use wire wool to remove polish and to provide a key for the adhesive.

It is not advisable to lay cork directly onto asphalt surfaces since these are very non-porous. With natural cork, the solvent in the fixing adhesive is likely to be absorbed into the underside, which may cause the centres of the tiles to sink slightly before the adhesive has fully set. So, before laying cork, use a latex levelling compound on top of the asphalt.

When laying vinyl-faced cork over flagstones and other paved interior finishes laid direct to the earth, first cover the sub-floor with a layer of rock asphalt at least 16mm (or ⅝in) thick, then use a levelling compound. Before laying cork tiles on concrete screeds or solid floors, make sure the floor incorporates an effective damp proof membrane and that it is completely dry. Porous floors such as concrete screed, plywood and chipboard should be primed before the tiles are fixed.

Some kinds of cork tile can be used over underfloor heating although, because of cork's good thermal insulating quality, this could be an unnecessary expense. If you do decide to use cork in this way, make sure the surface heat does not exceed 27°C (80°F). The heating system should have been working for at least two weeks before the cork is laid and should be switched off for at least 48 hours before and after laying. It is better not to use vinyl-faced cork in this situation since the heat will eventually give the tiles a pebbly effect. Also make sure any underfloor hot water pipes are adequately insulated.

Warning Before laying vinyl or cork tiles, make sure timber floors have adequate ventilation underneath. Poor ventilation can cause condensation which could lead to rotting of both floorboards and floor covering.

cork you have chosen. Some tiles are self-adhesive, but if you choose ones which are not, follow the manufacturer's instructions on where to put the adhesive – on both tiles and floor, or floor only.

Preparing the surface
Thorough preparation of the fixing surface is essential for good results. Make sure it is clean, dry and level so the tiles lie perfectly flat.
Vinyl If your fixing surface is slightly uneven, first cover it with plywood or tempered hardboard, smooth side up. You can use hardboard nails if fixing to a timber floor, but with concrete you will have to drill holes, insert suitable plugs and fix the hardboard into position with countersunk screws,

Laying the tiles
Start laying tiles from the centre of the room, which can be located by stretching two lengths of string (preferably chalked) from the mid-point of each pair of opposite walls across the floor so they cross at the centre (**see 1a**). Make sure the pieces of string cross at right-angles and secure the ends with nails or pins.

Position two rows of dry tiles, working from the mid-point to the skirting boards (**see 1b**). This will give you the width of the tiles around the perimeter. If only a very narrow strip is left, the floor will have an unbalanced look, especially if you are using vinyl tiles in a dual colour or chess board design. To prevent this, adjust the string line half a tile width off centre to leave wider perimeter tiles (**see 1c**). If using chalked string, pluck it and the chalk will leave an accurate impression on the floor. Alternatively, use a straight-edge and a pencil to trace the string lines accurately.

Vinyl Lay the tiles in the order shown (**see 2**). Complete each section of the room with as many full tiles as possible, leaving all cutting jobs until later. If using tiles that are not self-adhesive, spread a thin layer of adhesive on the floor (not on the back of the tile) about a square metre (or square yard) at a time. Don't spread more than this because the adhesive sets quickly and the tiles must be laid while it is still tacky. Start laying the tiles, pressing each one firmly into position from the centre of the tile outwards to prevent air being trapped underneath.

Cork Lay cork tiles in the same order as for vinyl tiles, but fit the cut border tiles at the same time as the adjacent full tile. You can ease the tiles slightly for the final positioning, but don't slide them into position. To ensure a good bond, roll the tiles or, using a hammer and a block of wood, bang firmly over the surface. Remove any excess adhesive from the surface of vinyl-faced cork with a clean cloth dampened in white spirit.

Cutting tiles

Use either a strong, sharp pair of scissors or a stiff, sharp knife held against a metal straight-edge to ensure clean cuts.

Edge tiles Place a whole tile A on top of the last tile in the row and another whole tile B over A with its far edge flush to the skirting board. Draw a line across A, using the near edge of tile B as a guide, and cut off and fit the near section of tile A (**see 3**).

Shaped tiles These can be cut by making a card template of the shape required and tracing it on to the tile to be cut. Alternatively, lay tile A on top of the last whole tile in the row nearest the corner and another whole tile B over A with its far edge flush to the skirting board. Draw a line across A, using the near edge of B as a guide (**see 4a**). Slide A on top of the last whole tile in the row around the corner, but don't twist it; the line marked on it must remain parallel with the first skirting marked out. Place tile B over A with its far edge pressed up against the skirting and draw a second line across tile A·using the near edge of B as a guide (**see 4b**). Cut out the L-shaped portion, which will fit neatly around the corner (**see 4c**).

Cutting around pipes The easiest way to cut a tile to fit around a pipe is to make a card template of the required shape and trace the shape on to the tile. Cut a slit directly from the hole made for the pipe to the skirting board (**see 5**). When the tile is fixed and pressed into position this line will hardly be visible – especially with a patterned tile.

Awkward shapes Tiles can be cut using either a card template or a special tool called a shape-tracer or contour gauge (**see 6**). This houses a series of tightly packed wires which, when pressed against a shape, forms its outline. The outline can then be transferred to the tile to be cut.

Doorway Floor coverings get the greatest amount of wear in doorways; if the joins between the coverings are not secure the edges curl up. This

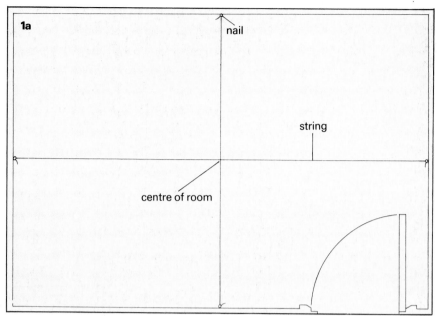

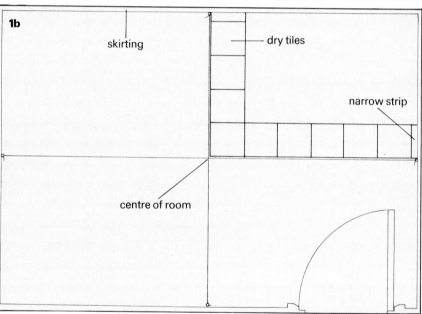

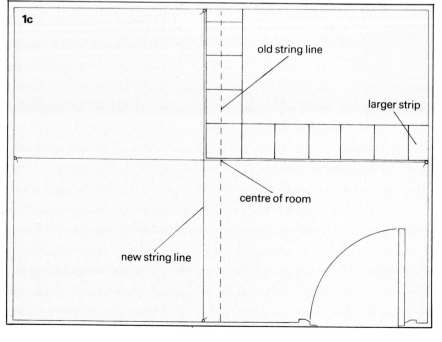

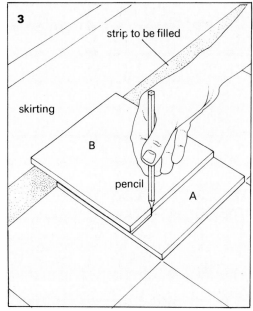

2

		7	
	4	8	
2	5	9	
1	3	6	10

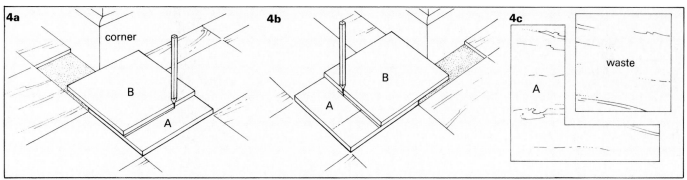

3

strip to be filled

skirting

B

pencil

A

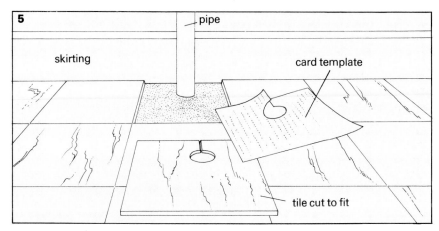

4a

corner

B

A

4b

B

A

4c

A

waste

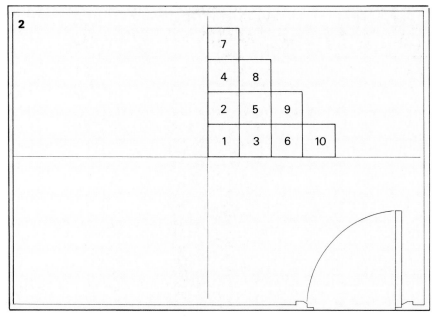

5

pipe

skirting

card template

tile cut to fit

increases wear and tear and can become a hazard. Metal binder bars will solve this problem. Available in various finishes and with different clamping edges that take all kinds of materials, they will join vinyl to vinyl, or vinyl to other floor coverings (see 7).

Door clearance One of the most common mistakes when laying floor coverings is failure to allow for door clearance. The floor level has probably been raised sufficiently to obstruct free movement of the door, especially if using a hardboard base. Vinyl needs a clearance gap or the door's constant rubbing will wear it down very quickly. If the door touches the vinyl, remove the door and trim the bottom edge with a block plane.

Looking after tiles

To maintain the surface of vinyl or vinyl-faced cork tiles, clean them periodically with a mop or sponge and a little mild, liquid detergent. Never use excessive water, strong cleaning agents or abrasives which might damage the finish. Use white spirit to remove stubborn marks from rubber-soled shoes and, should the vinyl become scratched, apply an emulsion wax polish. Prevent spirit-based polishes, rubber compounds and nail varnish remover coming into contact with the surface since these could cause permanent damage to the vinyl.

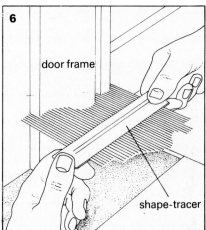

6

door frame

shape-tracer

7

vinyl tile

carpet

metal binder bar

countersunk screw

solid floor

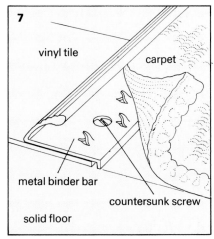

Laying sheet vinyl

Sheet vinyl is a practical, hard-wearing flooring material which only needs to be swept, washed and occasionally polished to keep it in condition. It is therefore suitable for rooms where there are likely to be spills and water splashes.

Buying vinyl
Vinyl is available in a variety of colours, patterns and effects such as ceramic tiles, cork, natural stone and timber and surfaces are both smooth and textured. Cushioned vinyl, which has a layer of foam material between the vinyl and the backing, is quieter, warmer and more comfortable than un-cushioned vinyl and is particularly suitable in the kitchen, where you may spend time standing.

Estimating quantity Most vinyl flooring comes in 2m (or 6ft 7in) widths; it is also available in 4m (or 13ft 1in) widths, which may eliminate the need for joins. If the room is wider than that, you will have to cut the vinyl into suitable lengths and join them. Remember to allow an extra 75mm (3in) for each length. Manufacturers will normally state pattern repeats for the material, so when you are matching patterns you will be able to estimate how much extra is needed. Usually you should allow for an extra pattern repeat on each length except the first. Most suppliers will give you a free estimate on the quantity needed if you submit a floor plan before ordering the material.

Preparing the sub-floor
Vinyl can be laid on almost any floor provided the surface is smooth, level, dry, clean and free from polish or grease – and of sound construction. All types of floor should be covered with flooring grade plywood – at least 4mm ($\frac{5}{32}$in) thick – or tempered hardboard – not less than 3mm ($\frac{1}{8}$in) thick.

Solid floor A solid floor should incorporate a damp proof membrane; if it does not, this is a good opportunity to have one installed and thus save problems later on. Fill any cracks or holes in the floor with a levelling compound which should also be used to level off a slightly sloping floor. To fix sheets of plywood or hardboard you must drill and plug holes and secure with countersunk screws.

Timber floor Check there is adequate ventilation below the floorboards; installation of airbricks will solve problems in this area. Secure any loose boards and punch down protruding nail heads. If the floor is uneven, plane down any projections.

Always lay hardboard sheets rough side up and fix them to the floor with ring shank or serrated nails at 100mm (4in) intervals. The rough surface enables the nail heads to be well bedded in and provides a better key for the adhesive. Hardboard has a low moisture content and if it absorbs any moisture it will expand; when it dries out, it will then shrink. You should wet the hardboard with water, using a dampened sponge, at least 48 hours before laying it. When it dries out, it will grip tightly around the nail heads.

For a very uneven floor, screw down 12 or 18mm ($\frac{1}{2}$ or $\frac{3}{4}$in) flooring grade chipboard at 300mm (12in) intervals, using countersunk screws, to provide a level surface. Alternatively, if the boards are severely warped, rotten or otherwise damaged, it is worth removing them and laying a new floor to avoid trouble later.

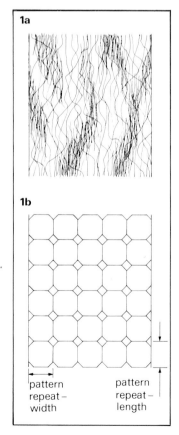

1a

1b

pattern
repeat –
width

pattern
repeat –
length

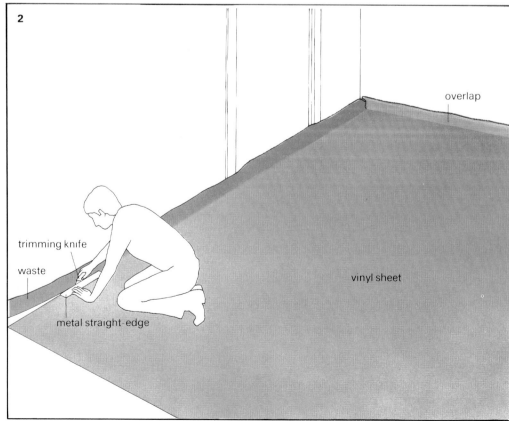

2

overlap

trimming knife

waste

metal straight-edge

vinyl sheet

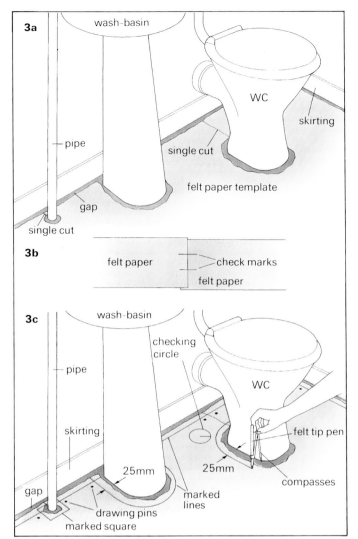

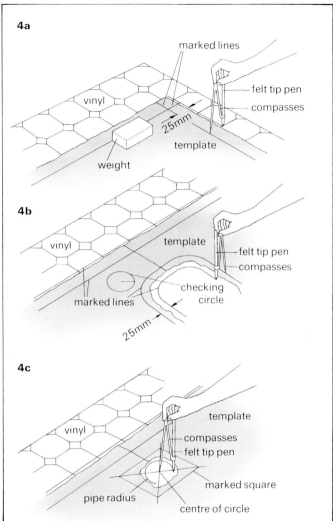

Warning Most manufacturers do not recommend laying vinyl over a timber floor which has been treated with wood preservative, although you can lay Kraft paper with an aluminium facing onto the timber, aluminium side down. If a preservative has been applied, leave it for a month before laying Kraft paper and fixing plywood or hardboard on top. If you have underfloor heating, make sure the temperature does not exceed 27°C (or 80°F).

Preparing vinyl
Before laying vinyl, slacken the roll and leave it in a warm room overnight so it will soften, relax any strain in the sheet and be easier to work. Some manufacturers suggest reverse-rolling the vinyl or laying it flat.

Fitting a single sheet
Since walls are rarely straight, you must cut the vinyl to fit the contour of the walls. If you are working in a small room which can be covered with a single width and the vinyl is very flexible, you can lay it out so it overlaps all round and cut it into the edges of the wall with a trimming knife. Use a metal straight-edge to push the vinyl into the angle between the floor and the wall. If the vinyl is not flexible enough to do this or if you feel more confident having a cutting guide, you should make a template. This is particularly useful when laying vinyl in a bathroom, where you will have to fit the flooring around a wash-basin or WC pedestal. Use

stiff card for the template – or felt paper, which is thick, lies flat and does not slide about; this is the paper used under carpets and you can buy it from a carpet supplier. Make sure any curls are face down.
Making a template Lay a sheet of felt paper – or any stiff card – on the floor to be covered. Rough-trim the paper to fit the required area, leaving a gap of about 16mm ($\frac{5}{8}$in) around the wall and the fittings. When fitting the template – and later the vinyl – on the floor, you will have to make a single cut from the back of the fitting cut-out to the nearest edge; as long as you follow lines on the pattern, this will not show once the vinyl is laid.

If you have to use more than one sheet, overlap the sheets and draw two check marks across the overlap to ensure the sheets can be repositioned accurately later. Once the paper is lying flat and has been roughly fitted, secure it with drawing pins (if working on a timber floor) or heavy weights (on a concrete floor) to prevent any movement.

Use a pair of compasses with a locking device, set at about a 25mm (1in) radius, and with the pointer vertical against the wall or fitting trace the outline of each in turn onto the template with a felt tip pen. Pipes and supports which are true circles can be squared off using a straight-edge on three or four sides. Draw a check circle on the template so you can check the compasses are correctly set when marking the vinyl.
Transferring template to vinyl Lay out the sheet of vinyl to be fitted in a convenient area (face up) and

1a Random pattern with no repeat needs no matching
1b Tile design vinyl has repeat pattern that must be matched when laying lengths
2 When laying single sheet, cut waste with trimming knife held against straight-edge pushed into angle between wall and floor
3a When covering awkward areas, make template to fit roughly around fittings
3b If you need more than one sheet of felt paper, draw check marks on each to help accurate alignment later
3c Secure template to floor; set compasses to 25mm radius and trace fittings outline onto felt paper; for pipes, mark sides of square on paper
4a Hold template on vinyl; with compasses at same radius transfer wall outline
4b Use same procedure to transfer fittings outline
4c Mark diagonals of square to find pipe centre and draw circle of pipe radius on vinyl

163

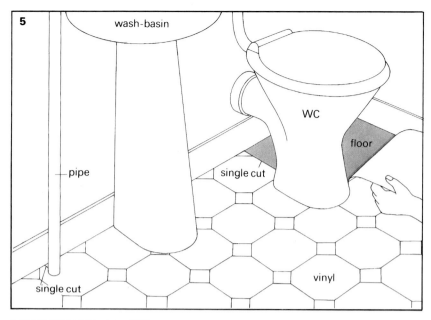

5

wash-basin

WC

floor

pipe

single cut

single cut

vinyl

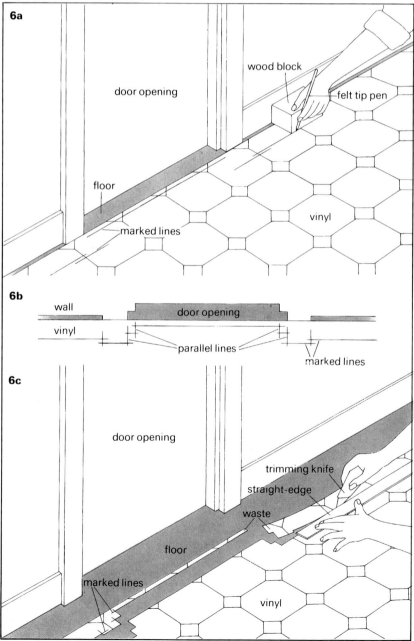

6a

door opening

wood block

felt tip pen

floor

marked lines

vinyl

6b

wall

door opening

vinyl

parallel lines

marked lines

6c

door opening

trimming knife

straight-edge

waste

floor

marked lines

vinyl

position the template accurately on top of it, using pins or heavy weights to prevent any movement. When working with a patterned vinyl, you may have to adjust the template to make sure the pattern runs correctly in relation to the fittings. If using more than one sheet of felt paper, make sure the check marks align.

Check the compasses are still at the same radius and, keeping the point always on and at right-angles to the marked outline, follow the outline so the felt tip pen marks the flooring. Any squared-off pipes can now be traced back, using a straight-edge, the centre of the square located and an accurate circle (the diameter of the pipe) drawn on the vinyl. Before removing the template, check again the compass setting has not altered and that the paper has not moved. Take off the template and cut out or trim the marked areas on the vinyl, which should then fit neatly around the fittings.

Fitting lengths
If the room is too large to be covered by a single sheet, you will have to adopt a different procedure. Measure the width of the room and cut a length of vinyl from the roll, allowing an extra 75mm (3in). Tackle the area by the door first, since this is going to have the most wear and you should always allow a full width of vinyl around it. Lay the vinyl square to the door opening.

Using a square-cut wood block 125 × 75 × 25mm (5 × 3 × 1in), with a felt tip pen on the side furthest from the wall, follow the contour of the wall on either side of the door and across the door opening to mark the outline on the vinyl. Mark on lines parallel to the door opening from the edge of the wall outlines already marked to ensure the vinyl fits snugly in the door opening and the edge is not visible when the door is closed. A shape-tracer is ideal for marking out the outline of an architrave to achieve a really neat finish. You can now cut along the marked lines on each side of the door. Place a straight-edge on the vinyl to be laid and cut along the outline with a trimming knife, with the waste on the outside of the knife. You will find it easier to work if you pull the vinyl away from the wall.

Reposition the first length against the wall with the door and mark a guide line on the floor along the opposite edge. Place your block of wood centrally on this edge and mark lines at either end of the block on both the vinyl and the floor. It is important the length of the block is more than the surplus to be removed from that length of vinyl. Slide the vinyl the length of the block along the edge guide line so the marks transferred from either end of the block coincide. With the block positioned

5 Having cut fittings outline, make single cut from cut-out to nearest edge, following pattern line where necessary, and lay vinyl
6a When laying lengths, trace wall contour and door opening on vinyl with block guide
6b Mark exact position of door opening
6c Cut waste with knife against straight-edge
7a Fit to wall and mark other edge on floor
7b Mark each end of block on vinyl and floor
7c Pull vinyl, length of block, away from wall
7d Trace wall contour on end of vinyl
7e Cut waste with knife against straight-edge
7f Push back to wall; block marks will align
8a Match next length and overlap trim edge
8b Mark pattern repeat on straight-edge
8c Trace wall contour on end of vinyl

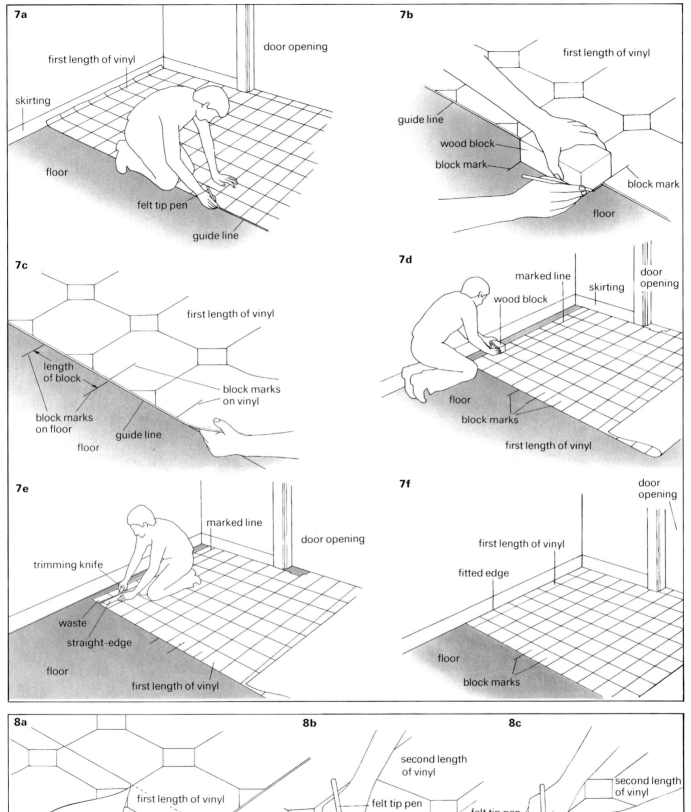

7a

skirting

first length of vinyl

door opening

floor

felt tip pen

guide line

7b

first length of vinyl

guide line

wood block

block mark

block mark

floor

7c

first length of vinyl

length of block

block marks on vinyl

block marks on floor

guide line

floor

7d

marked line

door opening

wood block

skirting

floor

block marks

first length of vinyl

7e

marked line

door opening

trimming knife

waste

straight-edge

floor

first length of vinyl

7f

door opening

first length of vinyl

fitted edge

floor

block marks

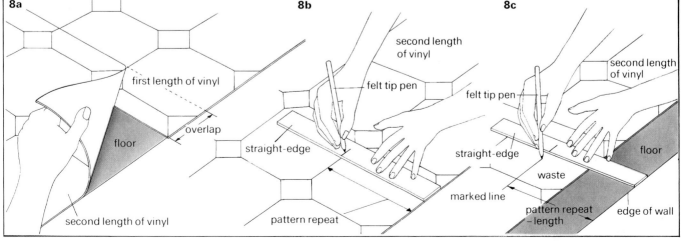

8a

first length of vinyl

overlap

floor

second length of vinyl

8b

second length of vinyl

felt tip pen

straight-edge

marked line

pattern repeat

8c

second length of vinyl

felt tip pen

straight-edge

waste

floor

pattern repeat –length

edge of wall

165

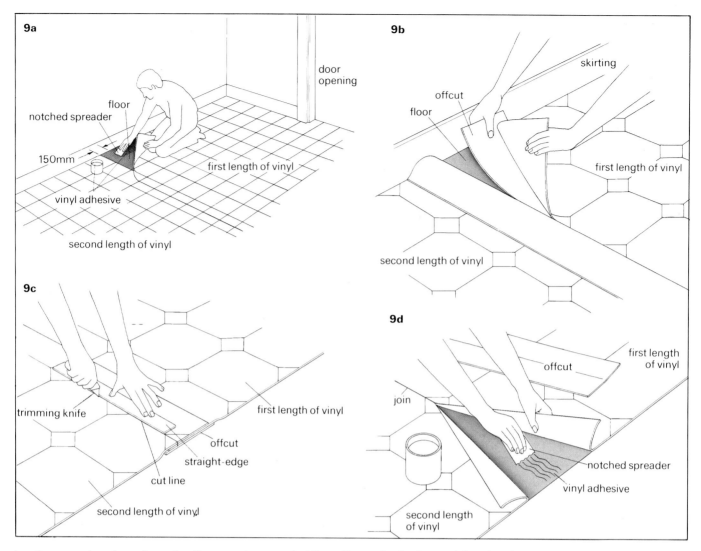

9a Spread adhesive on floor to hold vinyl
9b Lay offcut under overlap of lengths
9c Cut through both overlapping lengths
9d Remove offcut and put adhesive under join

lengthways against the wall, mark a line onto the vinyl as you move the block along the wall. Trim off the surplus with a straight-edge on the marked line. Reposition the vinyl along the guide line and check for fit.

This method ensures a perfect fit, since any irregularities or projections on the wall will be transferred onto the vinyl. Repeat for the opposite wall, sliding the vinyl the length of the block in the opposite direction.

To lay the second length of vinyl, overlap the trimming edges on both lengths and check the pattern aligns and matches exactly. Measure the size of one pattern repeat; the repeat dimension is marked from the wall to the edge of the vinyl to be cut, following the contour of the wall along the width of the vinyl. The surplus, which is never more than the measured dimension of the repeat, can then be trimmed off in the usual way.

Before cutting along the overlapping lengths, spread a 50mm (2in) strip of vinyl adhesive at the ends of the vinyl sheets, stopping within 150mm (6in) of the join, to prevent the lengths of vinyl slipping out of position. Place an offcut of vinyl under the overlapping lengths to protect the blade of the knife as it cuts. Make a vertical cut along the overlap as near to the centre as possible – along the border if you have a tile pattern – through both sheets of vinyl. Remove the surplus vinyl and the lengths will lie neatly together.

When laying the final length of vinyl, position it

against the wall opposite the door and then draw it away until the pattern matches the previous length on the overlap. Measure the width of one pattern repeat and mark a line the same measurement as the pattern width onto the edge of the vinyl, following the contours of the wall; trim off the excess as before. Slide the last length against the wall and trim the overlap as before. Where you cut the overlap will depend on whether you want to save any waste for use elsewhere.

Sticking down vinyl
Vinyl can be loose-laid when just one sheet is used to cover a small area, although you should still stick down the area around a door. When laying more than one length, you should always stick down the vinyl at the ends and along each seam with adhesive or double-sided adhesive tape – as recommended by the manufacturer. Some recommend sticking down the whole floor covering – and certainly the centre sheet if laying more than two sheets of vinyl – particularly when laying cushioned vinyl. Any shrinkage will be in the length of the vinyl. If you make sure you stick down the sheets at each end, you will overcome this problem since each length will be held securely.

When using adhesive, apply it to the floor with a notched spreader. Press the vinyl onto the adhesive and rub with a clean dampened cloth. Always wipe off excess adhesive immediately with a clean, dampened cloth.

Fitting carpets

Carpets are always a major item in any home improvement budget. If you cannot buy them with free fitting, you can fit them yourself following carefully the correct methods; these depend on the type of carpet to be laid and the different ways of fitting available, whether you use carpet grippers attached to the floor or carpet tacks. Properly laid, a good carpet will enhance the room and last for years.

What you need

A good quality carpet is expensive but well worth the outlay since it will withstand wear and tear far better than a cheaper one; it must, however, be laid correctly. This means it must be properly stretched and fitted over a suitable underlay on a sound sub-floor. A well laid carpet will retain its tension, remain flat and not ruck up. An unstretched or poorly stretched carpet will ruck up easily even under normal use and will be disturbed even more if furniture is moved over it; and apart from looking unattractive, it will also wear prematurely and unevenly.

Genuine free-fitting offers do arise occasionally so it is worth taking advantage of them. If there is no free-fitting offer available, you can lay a carpet successfully yourself; but you should make sure the job is within your capabilities since mistakes can be costly.

Well over half the carpets now sold are non-fray tufted types with a foam or hessian backing. Foam-backs need not be stretched during fitting and are therefore quite straightforward to lay. They can be loose-laid, but you will still have to secure edges in doorways. Some hessian-backs may need stretching; check with your supplier before you buy.

Other carpets will have to be stretched, a job you can do yourself if the carpet is plain and the room does not exceed 4.6m (or 15ft) in width or length. Above this size stretching is done at differing angles to suit the installation and you should seek professional advice before tackling this job. In the case of a patterned carpet, incorrect stretching can distort the pattern, so great care is needed.

If you are using body carpet, you will not have to join seams yourself. If you give your supplier the room measurements, the carpet will be delivered to you in a single piece – with an allowance for trimming the edges.

Estimating quantity
Free measuring and estimating is a widespread feature of the carpet trade and it is worth taking advantage of this service, particularly if you have an awkward-shaped room – the supplier will work out the most economical way of carpeting it. If this service is not available, make an accurate scale plan of the room – including doors and windows – and give it to your supplier when ordering.

Types of underlay
All carpets except for felt require an underlay even those with a foam backing; without this, the performance of the carpet – whatever its quality – will suffer. It is therefore false economy to skimp on underlay – and you should never use just old newspaper or old carpet in its place.

Good quality underlay not only improves the feel of a carpet underfoot, but also provides a buffer between the carpet and the floor; this will ensure even wear. Although it is important to lay carpet on a level sub-floor, it is not always possible to achieve perfect smoothness and so a good underlay will help overcome any minor defects. It also protects the carpet from dirt and dust rising through the floorboards and will help reduce noise and heat loss.

Felt Sold in 1.4m (4½ft) widths, various types are available which include jute, animal hair, wool waste and a combination of these materials. In some cases rubber is incorporated in layers into the construction – or a solution of rubber impregnated into the felt.

Polyurethane foam or rubber More springy and resilient than felt, this type gives the carpet a softer feel. When used beneath carpet composed of seamed strips, however, it may not allow the

1 Knee kicker
2 Gripper for ordinary carpet
3 Gripper for foam-backed carpet
4 Felt underlay
5 Bonded felt underlay
6 Polyurethane foam underlay
7 Two kinds of rubber underlay
8 Felt paper
9 Using a knee kicker to stretch carpet taut

4

5

6

7a

7b

8

9

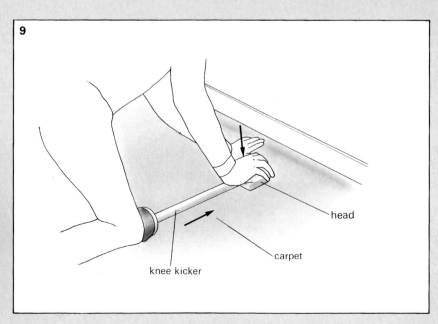

head

carpet

knee kicker

10a

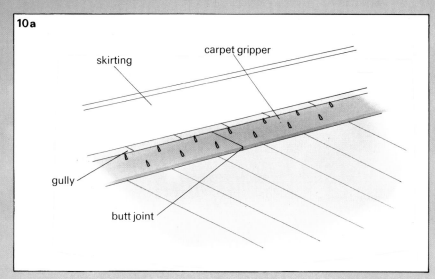

skirting

carpet gripper

gully

butt joint

10b

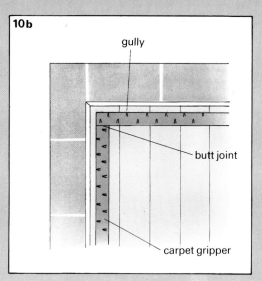

gully

butt joint

carpet gripper

10c

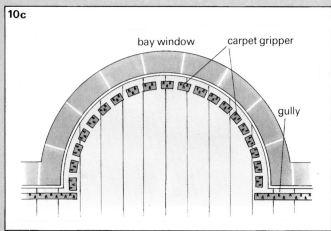

bay window

carpet gripper

gully

10d

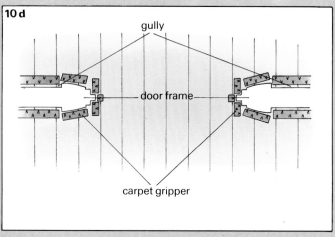

gully

door frame

carpet gripper

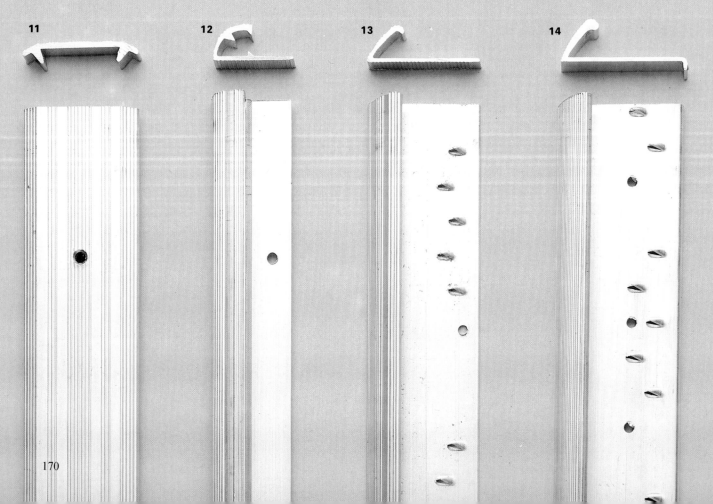

11 **12** **13** **14**

10a Position the carpet gripper about 6mm away from the wall, butt-joining the lengths

10b When you reach a corner, butt lengths together at right-angles

10c For awkward areas such as bay windows, cut the gripper into short lengths and position these on the floor so there is a small gap between each piece

10d At doorways, cut the gripper into short lengths to follow the line of the door frame

Types of binder:

11 Joint cover strip

12 Bar for foam-backed carpet

13 Ordinary binder bar

14 Bar for joining carpet to hard flooring such as vinyl

15 Double-sided bar with fixed central covering strip for joining carpet to carpet

16 Double-sided bar with separate covering strip

seams to bed down as well as they would on felt. Rubber underlay should never be used where there is underfloor heating since the rubber will smell and may eventually disintegrate.

Felt paper This under-carpet covering is used beneath traditional underlay where narrow gaps between the floorboards have not been filled, since it will provide an additional barrier against dirt and dust from underneath the floor. Felt paper is also used underneath foam-backed carpet to prevent the backing sticking to the floor; brown paper can be used instead if there are no gaps between the floorboards. Such protection is essential; if the foam backing sticks to the floor, it is difficult to remove the carpet intact. The backing may also disintegrate under normal use, causing uneven and premature wear to the carpet.

Fitting underlay

To prevent strips of underlay moving, join them at the edges with self-adhesive tape or by tacking or stapling them down; use adhesive on concrete floors. Underlay is never stretched to the same extent as carpet, but it must be pulled taut to eliminate any wrinkles.

Never allow an extra thickness of underlay in areas subjected to excessive wear and tear, such as doorways. Not only is it unnecessary, but the extra thickness will cause a bump in the carpet and result in uneven wear.

Tools and equipment

For successful carpet fitting you must have the right tools and equipment. If you are stretching carpet, for example, a knee kicker is essential; although an expensive item to buy unless you are

going to use it several times, you can hire one. Carpet grippers are the ideal fixings for carpets that have to be stretched, while for those carpets that do not stretch you will have to use the traditional turn-and-tack method. Two basic items needed when fitting carpets are a sharp trimming knife and self-adhesive tape.

Knee kicker

A knee kicker is used to stretch the carpet taut – but not too tight – onto carpet grippers. It is never used on foam-backed carpets, or hessian-backed ones which do not need to be stretched.

In the head of the knee kicker are two sets of pins. The thinner pins are adjustable, so the amount they can project from the head can be increased or reduced. These pins are necessary when stretching shag pile carpets and must be set accurately to grip the carpet backing. If they are set too short, they will snare the pile as the tool is projected forward; if they are too long, they will become embedded into the underlay and pull it out of place or catch the floor underneath. The thicker fixed pins (called nap grips) give the added purchase required for smooth pile carpets.

Using a kicker The knee kicker is literally kicked with the muscle above the knee cap – never with the knee cap itself since this might cause injury. At each point of stretching, only one kick should be used to stretch the carpet onto the carpet gripper; if a succession of kicks is made, the carpet will spring back to its original position between kicks.

The hands play an important part in the technique of using a kicker. The tool is rested on the carpet with the palm of one hand exerting downward pressure on the head of the kicker while the fingers are used to bring the carpet into contact with the gripper pins at the peak of the stretch. The other hand is used to press down on the stretched carpet in front of the head. As the carpet is stretched and pushed over the gripper pins, the natural elasticity will enable it to spring back securely onto the pins.

Generally the better the quality of carpet, the less stretch is needed. But remember the carpet should be taut – never tight.

Carpet gripper

There are two basic types of carpet gripper – one with nails for fixing to timber floors and one with hardened pins for fixing to concrete floors. The gripper consists of a strip of wood about 25mm (1in) wide and 6mm ($\frac{1}{4}$in) thick with two rows of pins protruding from the upper face at an angle. The pins which grip the carpet are positioned every 50mm (2in) along the gripper and strips are available in 750, 1200 and 1500mm (or 30, 48 and 60in) lengths. The carpet is stretched onto the pins, which hold it firmly in place. This is a superior method to tacking since the carpet is held continuously along its edge; carpet tacks normally hold the carpet at 150mm (or 6in) intervals, often producing a scalloped-edge appearance.

A special flat steel strip containing dome-shaped pins has been designed for foam-backed carpets; the pins are made to penetrate cleanly through the foam. This strip is supplied in 2 and 3m (or 6$\frac{1}{2}$ and 10ft) lengths in boxes containing 60 pieces. A normal carpet gripper can be used on foam-backed carpet if preferred.

Fixing a gripper The carpet gripper is fixed to the floor around the edge of the room, except in door-

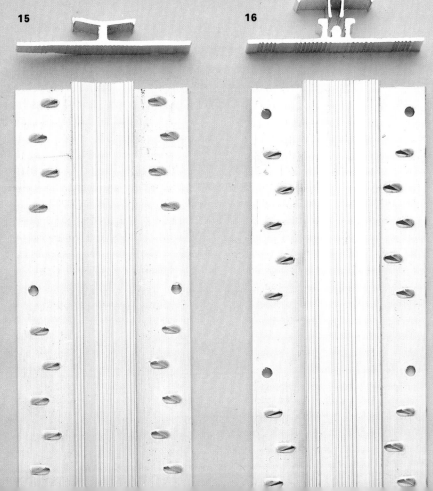

15

16

ways. Lengths should butt up against each other at the edges; where short lengths are needed – at corners, for example – cut the gripper with a saw or tinsnips. There is no need to mitre joins at corners; simply butt together the adjoining pieces at right-angles.

Always allow a space between the back edge of the gripper and the wall. The gully formed should be slightly less than the thickness of the carpet – 6mm ($\frac{1}{4}$in) is usually about the right allowance. Keep a uniform space all round to achieve a smooth, level finish to the carpet edge and make sure the angled pins project towards the wall.

The gripper cannot be bent so in bay windows, for example, cut it into short lengths and fix these to the floor, leaving a small space between each piece. Arrange the gripper to follow the shape of the bay. At doorways, cut short lengths to follow the line of the door frame. If the carpet continues into an adjoining room, fix the gripper around the frame into the next room.

With timber floors the gripper should be nailed down; use a hammer and nail punch to avoid any possible damage to the pins. Where short lengths have been cut off the gripper, insert at least two nails – one at each end.

With concrete floors specially hardened pins are used to secure the gripper, although you can stick it down with PVA adhesive or an adhesive recommended by the manufacturer. Make sure the floor has been cleaned thoroughly or the adhesive will not hold the gripper firmly in place. Spread any surplus adhesive with your thumb onto the edge of the gripper that faces the carpet; by continuing the bond in this way you will ensure a firmer fixing. Allow two days for the adhesive to set.

Even after levelling a concrete floor (if this is necessary), you may still find small uneven patches; in this case, if the longer lengths of gripper will not lie flat, cut them into smaller sections.

Carpet tacks
If you choose to tack down a carpet to a timber floor, you will need two lengths of carpet tacks. To fix the carpet around the edges use 19mm ($\frac{3}{4}$in) tacks; these will go through a double thickness of carpet (where it has been folded under at the edge) and into the floor. In corners, where three thicknesses of carpet result from folding under the edges, use 25mm (1in) tacks.

Use only rustproof tacks or rust marks could form around the fixing points if the tacks ever got wet. Space the tacks at 150mm (6in) intervals around the room; closer spacing will be needed at corners and other awkward areas.

Binder bar
To give a neat, protective finish to the carpet edge, use a binder bar at the doorway. You can tack down the carpet or sew adjoining carpets together, but the edges may eventually work loose. Binders are available in aluminium or brass and in various finishes such as fluted, satin and polished. They are normally supplied in 813mm (2ft 8in) lengths, which is the common distance across the threshold; trim the binder bar with a hacksaw to fit smaller openings. Since the bars contain evenly spaced pre-drilled holes for fixing points, when trimming a bar you may have to take a little off each end to ensure the fixing points remain evenly spaced.

The underside of the bar is usually ribbed to provide a key, if you want to fix it to a concrete

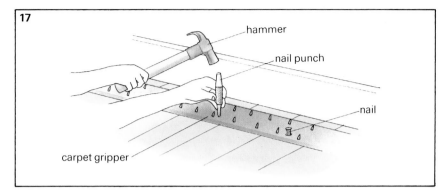

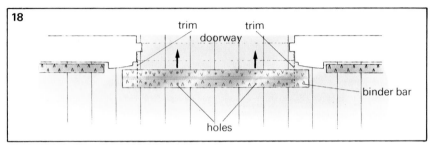

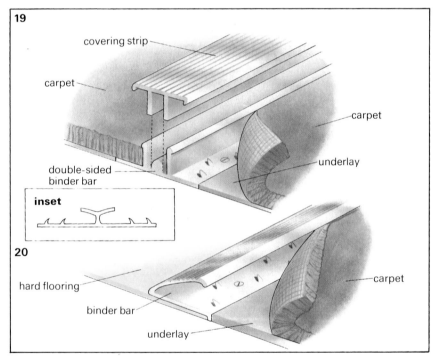

floor with adhesive; but normally it is fitted with screws or nails.

Joining carpet to carpet There is a double-sided bar available which enables you to make a neat join between two carpets at a threshold. Both carpets are stretched onto the angled pins so the respective edges lie close against the centre channel. A central covering strip is then tapped over to conceal the carpet edges and help keep them in place.

Joining carpet to hard flooring For this operation there is a bar with both plain and fitting lips; the plain lip is placed over the edge of the adjoining flooring while the carpet edge is pressed onto the pins projecting from the other side of the bar and tucked under the protective lip. The lip is then hammered down lightly to hold the carpet edge securely. Place a block of wood between the hammer and the binder bar to prevent damage when tapping down the lip.

17 Grippers should be nailed to a timber floor. **18** When trimming a binder bar, cut the same amount off each end; the bar fits under the door stop. **19** Joining carpet to carpet with a double binder bar; the central covering strip may be separate or fixed (**inset**). **20** Joining carpet to hard flooring

Laying carpets

Before laying carpet it is essential to prepare the sub-floor carefully to make sure it is dry, level, flat and clean. Any bumps in the surface will cause the carpet to wear prematurely and unevenly.

Preparing the sub-floor
Clear the room of furniture and inspect the floor thoroughly, walking all over it to check for squeaks, uneven or loose boards and protruding nail heads. If there are any signs of damp or rot, deal with the problem immediately.

Loose and squeaking floorboards Squeaks below a fitted carpet are irritating and not easily remedied once the carpet is laid. They can indicate the nails securing the boards are working loose, causing a floorboard to rise and fall when walked on. Some squeaks may be cured by sprinkling talcum powder or French chalk between the boards. Where squeaking persists, if the boards are loose, secure them with screws. First sink protruding nails below the surface with a nail punch. Drill countersunk clearance holes through the boards for the screws, about 13mm ($\frac{1}{2}$in) from each nail head, drill pilot holes into the joists and tighten the screws firmly,

making sure the heads are below the surface.

Always be careful when hammering nails or inserting screws into floorboards. If you are doubtful about what lies below, lift the board and make sure there are no pipes or wires nearby.

Levelling the surface Check for any sharp edges or uneven boards. Where possible, plane down protruding boards flush with the surround. If, as sometimes happens, a board cannot be levelled off completely, at least round off any sharp edges.

Fill any wide gaps between boards with wedge-shaped wood strips, cut to length and coated on both sides with woodworking adhesive. Tap the strips down firmly and plane down any protruding edges. Fill smaller gaps with mastic.

If the floor is very uneven and cannot be levelled successfully, cover it with hardboard or replace the boards. Level concrete with screeding compound.

Warning Do not lay carpet over thermoplastic tiles unless you have taken measures to eliminate condensation in the room. Otherwise the tiles will 'sweat' and moisture will work through to the carpet, causing mildew stains on the pile. Never use rubber or foam underlays over thermoplastic tiles

Above Fitted carpet not only gives an impression of warmth and cosiness to a room, but it also goes a long way towards improving both heat and sound insulation. Cleaning will be much easier too when there is only one type of surface to look after

– always choose felt. When the sub-floor has been prepared, clean it thoroughly.

Checking doors
Check to see if the new carpet will raise the floor level to a point where the door will not pass easily over it. The door must clear the carpet completely; if it brushes over it as it opens and closes, it wears the pile. The solution is to remove the door and plane off enough from its bottom edge to ensure it clears the carpet. Do this before laying the carpet since it will make the job easier; even if the door does not need modifying, it is easier to lay carpet with the door removed.

Laying the carpet
If you are using carpet grippers to secure the carpet, fix them in position around the edges of the room and fit a binder bar in the doorway (as described).

Take the carpet into the room, open it up fully and position it roughly with excess carpet lapping up the walls. It is usual to lay the carpet with the pile leaning away from the light since this prevents uneven shading in daylight, which may be particularly noticeable in the case of plain carpets. If the carpet has a definite pattern, this should be the right way up as you enter the room.

Fitting the underlay
When the carpet is arranged, roll half of it back to expose half of the floor area. This is to enable you to put down your underlay one half at a time. If you try to put down all the underlay and then the carpet, you will almost certainly disturb the underlay as the heavy carpet is dragged over it.

If you are using felt paper, lay it in strips across the room, butt-joining the edges with self-adhesive tape. Trim the edges of the paper to butt against the carpet grippers. Stick it to the floor with double-sided adhesive tape at the edges of the room and around any projections. An alternative method of fixing felt paper is to use latex adhesive applied from a washing-up liquid bottle.

Put down the underlay in strips across the room, joining the edges with self-adhesive tape. To do this, turn the two lengths of underlay reverse side up and butt the adjoining edges. Remove the protective paper from the tape and press the sticky side down along the joint (**see 1**). Fix the underlay to a timber floor with tacks or staples and with adhesive to a concrete floor. Trim it to butt up against the carpet grippers.

Unroll the carpet to cover the floor and roll up the other half, laying the felt paper and underlay as before. Finally, unroll the carpet again to cover the entire floor.

Fitting a stretched carpet
If possible, start fitting the carpet in a corner where you have a reasonably uninterrupted run of walls – that is, without recesses, radiators or other obstructions. During the initial positioning try to leave only about 10mm ($\frac{3}{8}$in) of carpet lapping up against the starting walls. This will save you having to trim these two edges.

Starting edge technique A special method is used to engage the starting edge of the carpet onto the carpet gripper to ensure the carpet is firmly held during stretching. Using the fingertips with steady downward pressure, press the edge of the carpet

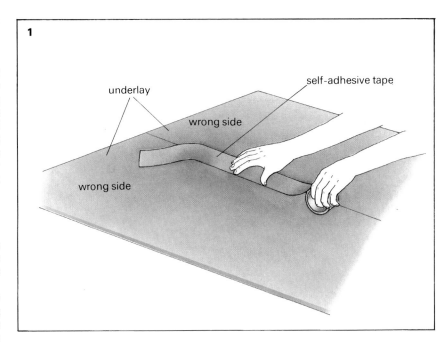

1
underlay
self-adhesive tape
wrong side
wrong side

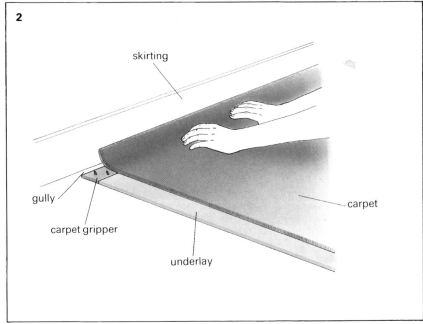

2
skirting
gully
carpet gripper
underlay
carpet

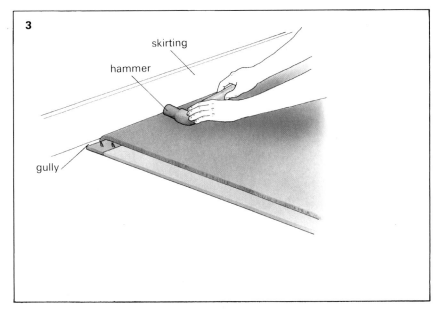

3
skirting
hammer
gully

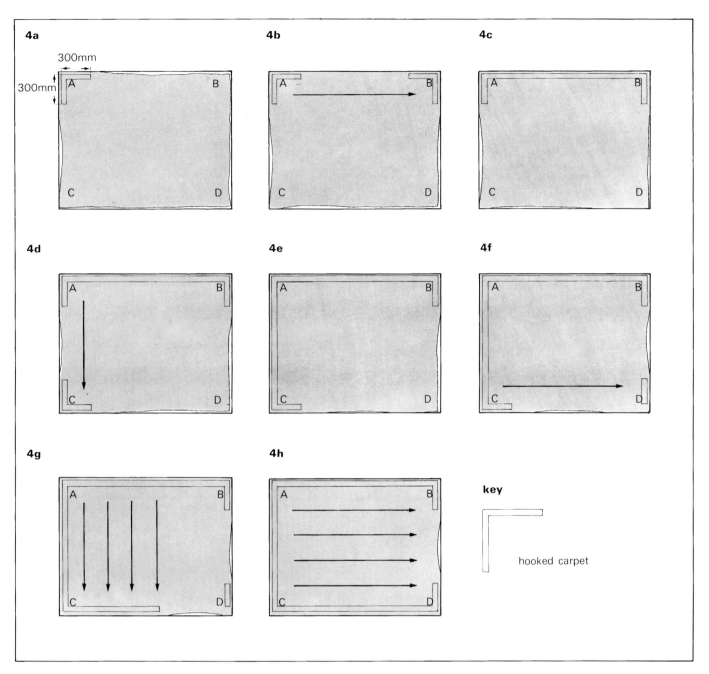

4a

300mm
300mm

A   B

C   D

4b

A   B

C   D

4c

A   B

C   D

4d

A   B

C   D

4e

A   B

C   D

4f

A   B

C   D

4g

A   B

C   D

4h

A   B

C   D

key

hooked carpet

along the wall onto the back row of pins (**see 2**). With a hammer, press the surplus carpet down to form a 'U' shape of carpet between the gripper and the wall (**see 3**). The starting edge technique is used along the first two walls to be fitted; the carpet is hooked along the other two walls by stretching.

Stretching As work progresses, use a knee kicker (as described earlier) if the carpet needs to be stretched. Stretch one part of the carpet and hook it into the pins. Move along a few feet and stretch the next portion, continuing in this way until all the carpet is gripped.

Order of work Using the starting edge technique, begin at corner A and hook about 300mm (12in) of carpet along each wall forming the corner (**see 4a**). Stretch the carpet towards B and hook corner B, using the kicker. Again hook the carpet about 300mm (12in) along each wall (**see 4b**). With the two corners secured, hook the carpet along the length of the wall AB, using the starting edge technique (**see 4c**). Then stretch the carpet from A to C and hook as for corner B (**see 4d**). Hook the

carpet along the wall AC, again using the starting edge technique (**see 4e**).

Stretch the carpet from C to D and hook a section of carpet near D on wall BD (**see 4f**). Then stretch the carpet from wall AB to CD, using the kicker and hooking from C to D (**see 4g**). This will have the effect of securing the carpet along wall AB firmly on the hooks. Three edges of the carpet are now hooked and surplus will be lapping up wall CD.

Finally stretch the carpet from wall AC to wall BD (**see 4h**), working from B to D with surplus carpet lapping up against wall BD. The carpet is now fully stretched and ready to be trimmed and fitted at corners and round any pipes.

Warning Check the carpet carefully to make sure it is evenly stretched. Distorted pattern lines and crooked seams indicate faulty stretching. If the carpet is plain, unseamed faults are not so obvious; look closely to see if the pile is running straight. If there are any distortions, unhook the affected part and restretch it. Do not hook the carpet onto any binder bars at this stage.

Trimming the carpet

Trim the carpet with a sharp trimming knife. At straight edges take off just enough surplus to leave a 10mm (⅜in) overlap to be pressed behind the carpet grippers. Use an awl or spoon handle to turn the trimmed edge into the gulley.

Right-angle projection Press the carpet into the front edge of the projection, using a length of hardboard to hold it firmly in the angle between wall and floor. Trim along the front edge with a knife (**see 5a**), leaving about a 25mm (1in) overlap to avoid overtrimming – you can trim it accurately later. Fold back the carpet towards you. Place a piece of hardboard underneath to protect the carpet below and cut it to fit from the corners of the fireplace, or projection, to the wall (**see 5b**); still leave about a 25mm (1in) overlap.

Corners Cut slits in the carpet at the corners of the room and any right-angle projection so the carpet lies flat around the corner (**see 5c**). Stretch the carpet onto the carpet gripper and trim.

Pipes Lap up the carpet against the front of the pipe, apply latex adhesive to the back of the carpet at roughly the centre of the pipe and cut a slit in the carpet (**see 6a**). Ease the carpet round the pipe and tuck under the edges. For large diameter pipes, it is better to use a card template or a shape-tracer to draw the outline of each half of the pipe on the corresponding sides of the split in the carpet (**see 6b**). Cut out the shapes and ease the carpet round the pipe.

Fitting carpet to binder bar

Tuck the edge of the carpet under the lip and stretch the carpet onto the hooks (**see 7**). Place a piece of hardboard onto the lip to protect it and hammer the lip down.

Fitting foam and hessian-backed carpet

To fit foam and hessian-backed carpets which do not need to be stretched, follow the above instructions but omit stretching. All sides of the carpet should be fitted using the starting edge technique (as described above). Some tufted carpets, however, do stretch through use and this type should be loose laid for a few weeks before fixing. Once it has stretched, you can secure the carpet.

The thickness of foam on a foam-backed carpet may create a slight bump if fitted under an ordinary binder bar; to avoid this, remove some of the backing. Lay the carpet on the top of the metal lip (**see 8a**), then fold it back and with a felt tip pen mark the foam where it meets the edge of the binder bar (**see 8b**). Place a length of hardboard under the folded part and score the foam along the marked line with a trimming knife (**see 8c**); take care not to go right through to the pile. Peel off the section of foam from the edge of the carpet to the scored line (**see 8d**). Tuck the edge under the lip, place a piece of hardboard on top and hammer the lip down.

Warning If the carpet is bonded in foam, it is impossible to trim off the foam.

Joining seams with tape

Although carpet suppliers will seam body widths for you, you may find you have to make a seam to fit carpet into a recess. You may need to make seams if you move house and fit your old carpet into a different shape room. Professionals use stitching or heat-bonding to join seams, but the simplest method for the amateur is to use 50mm (2in) carpet tape and latex adhesive.

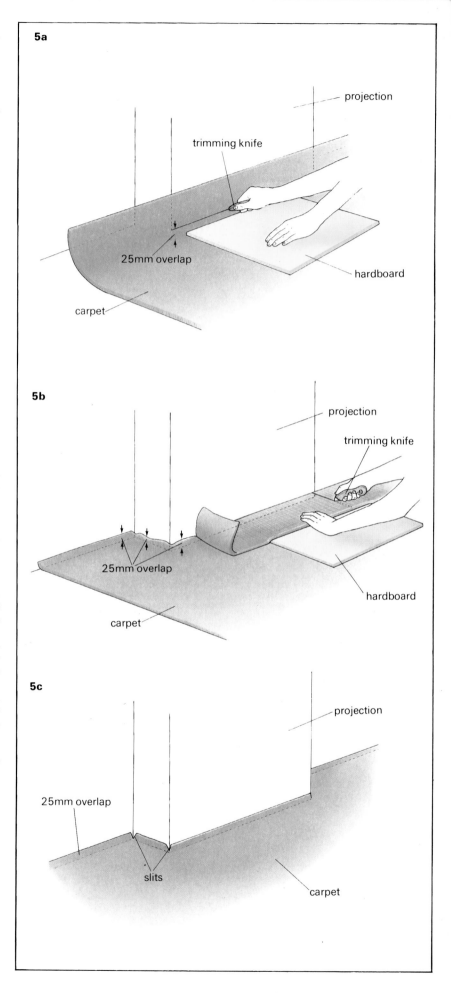

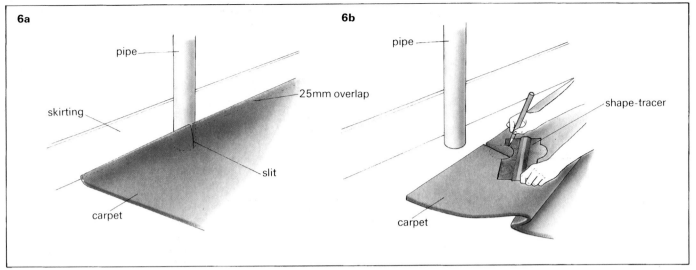

6a

pipe

skirting

carpet

25mm overlap

slit

6b

pipe

shape-tracer

carpet

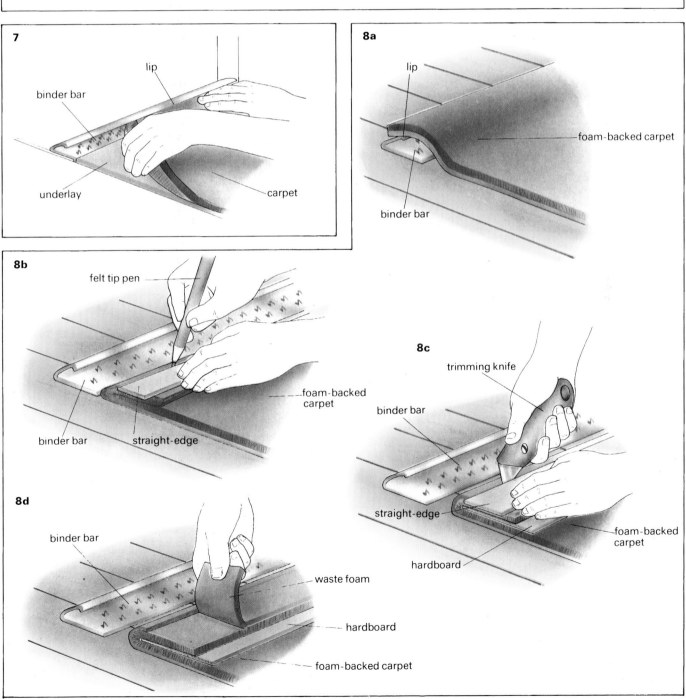

7

lip

binder bar

underlay

carpet

8a

lip

binder bar

foam-backed carpet

8b

felt tip pen

binder bar

straight-edge

foam-backed carpet

8c

trimming knife

binder bar

straight-edge

hardboard

foam-backed carpet

8d

binder bar

waste foam

hardboard

foam-backed carpet

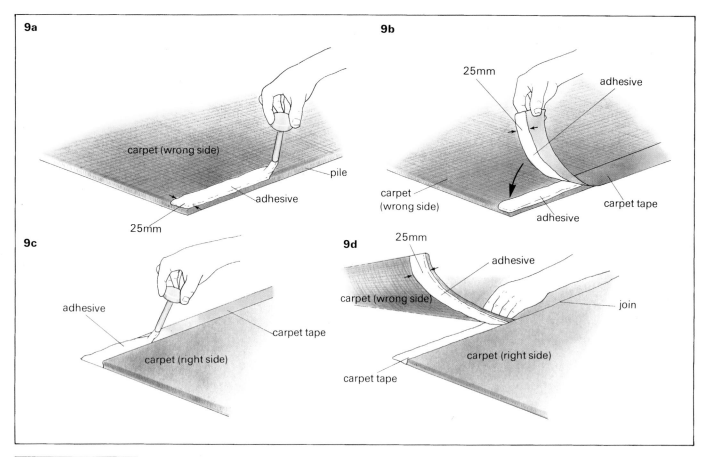

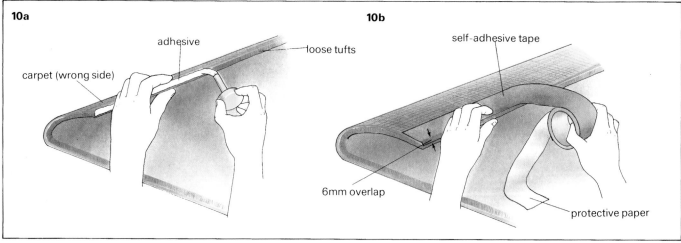

Place one piece of the carpet on the floor with the backing uppermost. Brush a 25mm (1in) band of adhesive along the edge, then halfway down the pile (**see 9a**). Apply a 25mm (1in) band of adhesive to one side of the carpet tape, wait for a few minutes until the adhesive is tacky and then bring into contact the bands of adhesive on the tape and the carpet edge (**see 9b**). Press down firmly along the join. The untreated half of the tape will now be protruding beyond the edge of the carpet.

Turn the carpet over so the pile is facing upwards. Carefully brush adhesive along the protruding half of the tape (**see 9c**). Apply adhesive to the edge of the other piece of carpet as before. When the adhesive is tacky, turn over the second piece of carpet so the pile is uppermost and press the edges of the two pieces of carpet carefully together (**see 9d**), making sure any pattern is aligned. Press down along the seam to ensure a firm join.

Binding edges

If you want to cut a fitted carpet to make a carpet square, you will need to bind the edges – when the carpet does not have an anti-fray backing.

The easiest way to do this is with self-adhesive tape. Turn the carpet edge back to expose the backing and seal any loose tufts with latex adhesive (**see 10a**); apply this with a small brush to make sure it does not come into contact with the surface of the pile. You can take the precaution of brushing adhesive along the whole length, whether loose tufts are evident or not.

Peel the protective paper backing off the tape and press the sticky surface onto the back edge of the carpet, allowing 6mm ($\frac{1}{4}$in) to overlap the edge. Fold the overlap over to adhere tightly against the base of the tufts (**see 10b**). Finish off by pressing the tape firmly down or by tapping it lightly with a hammer.

Laying carpet tiles

The advantage of carpet tiles is they can be loose laid; this means you can move them around from time to time to distribute the wear evenly and replace individual tiles should they become damaged. If you spill something you can simply remove the affected square, wash it clean and leave it to dry flat, away from direct heat, before replacing it.

Carpet tiles are easy to lay and awkward shapes can be dealt with one by one so mistakes in cutting will be confined to individual tiles. They are available in a variety of fibres, surfaces and colours and are usually either mottled or plain; you can achieve a patterned or chequerboard effect by using different colours together or by laying tiles of the same colour so the piles run at right-angles to each other – or you can make a contrasting border. The backing is usually PVC or rubber and some tiles have a self-adhesive backing which is reusable should you want, or need, to move them about.

Warning When buying carpet tiles, check there is a guarantee on the stability of their dimensions so there is no expansion or contraction after they have been laid.

Sizes Carpet tiles are widely available in 500mm (19½in) squares, so four of these will cover one square metre. Some manufacturers have not changed to metric sizes and produce 18in square tiles, four of which will cover one square yard. Another popular size is the 12in square; these tiles are sold in packs of nine to cover a square yard.

Estimating quantity Since there may be a variation in shade between different batches, buy all you need at the same time. Even so, it is a good idea to open

several packets of tiles and mix them up before you lay them so any slight variation in shade is barely noticeable.

The sizes available make it easy to calculate the quantity you need. Make a plan of the room on squared paper and work out the area to be covered. You may have to cut tiles to fit round the edges of the room but, if the border is less than half of one tile, allow only one for every two border tiles.

Preparing the sub-floor

The sub-floor must be clean, dry, level and sound. If it is bumpy, it will cause the carpet to wear in patches; so always remove old or damaged floor coverings. If there is a gap between the skirting and the floor, the tiles may work their way underneath the skirting. Prevent this by closing the gap with hardwood beading (this will also keep out draughts) or by sticking down the border tiles.

Timber floors Make sure there is adequate ventilation below the floor. Fill any gaps between the floorboards with a tough wood filler. Make sure all floorboards are nailed securely down so there is no movement and punch all nail heads well below the surface of the timber with a nail punch.

If the floor is very uneven, cover it with hardboard before laying the tiles. Timber floors treated with wood preservative are unsuitable for most types of carpet tiles, so check first with the tile manufacturer's instructions.

Solid floors Don't lay carpet tiles on a concrete floor which has underfloor heating. If the concrete floor is laid directly onto the ground, bear in mind

Above Carpet tiles will stand up to a great deal of heavy wear and are particularly suitable in a child's room. They are easy to look after since you can clean or replace individual tiles. The best way of equalizing wear on tiles is to move them around at regular intervals

it must have a damp proof membrane. Fill any cracks or holes and smooth off an uneven floor with a levelling compound – you may be able to rub down any bumps or rough spots.

Laying the tiles

If you cannot clear all the furniture out of the room, tile one half at a time. Generally speaking it is better to loose-lay the tiles so they are movable, but you should stick them down in areas where there is likely to be a lot of movement.

You can fix them down permanently with a flooring adhesive (use the one recommended by the manufacturer) or with double-sided adhesive tape so you can move them if necessary. If you place the tape round three sides only, you will find it easier to remove the tile. Always fix the first tile with tape so you have a stable base to work from.

Marking out the room Lay the tiles from the centre of the room so you get an even border round the edges. To find the centre, fix a chalked string line between the centre points of each pair of opposite walls. Snap each string line so it leaves a chalk mark on the floor; the centre point will be where the two lines cross.

Before you stick down the first tile, lay out two lines to the edges of the room to find out how wide the border tiles will be. If only a very narrow space is left on either edge, adjust the string lines to give a wider border; this not only looks better but means you will not have to cut fiddly narrow pieces to fit.

Place the double-sided adhesive tape on three bottom edges of the first tile and press it firmly down in the angle between the two string lines. Loose lay the second tile, butting it up against the first, along the string line; press it down firmly so it lies flat. Lay the tiles along the two string lines in one quarter of the room then fill in so that quarter is complete except for the border tiles.

Some manufacturers suggest laying the tiles in alternate directions and the tiles are arrowed on the back to make this easy.

Stick down tiles where necessary and make sure all are butted firmly against each other so there are no gaps. Lay tiles over the remainder of the room, a quarter at a time, leaving the border uncovered.

Border tiles To get a tight fit at the edge of the wall, mark out and cut each tile individually. To do this, place a border tile on the last complete tile to be laid and butt another tile firmly against the wall on top of this one. Draw a line where the top tile touches the tile below, marking with a ball-point pen on the bottom face of the tile. Cut along this line with a sharp trimming knife held against a metal straight-edge and fix the cut edge of the tile against the wall.

To fit a tile round a corner mark one line as before and slide the tile round the corner, without turning it; draw another line so you have two lines crossing at right-angles. Cut out the rectangular piece, leaving an L-shaped portion which will fit neatly round the corner.

Awkward areas For more awkward shapes, make a card template or use a shape-tracer (or contour gauge) and mark the outline on the tile. When cutting a tile to fit round a pipe, first make a card template of the required shape then trace that shape onto the back of the tile. Cut a slit from the hole made for the pipe directly to the skirting board. When the tile is fixed, this line will be invisible.

Doorways Fit a metal binder bar or threshold strip in every doorway to hold the tiles in position in an area where there is always a lot of wear and tear. Available in a variety of finishes, the bar or strip will also provide a neat join between the carpet tiles and the adjoining floor covering.

1 Start tiling from the centre of the room so you get an even border round the edge
2 To cut an edge tile to fit, place it on the last whole tile, put another tile on top of this so it butts up against the wall and mark where the top tile touches the tile below; you can place a piece of wood between the tiles to prevent scoring right through
3 Cut along the marked line with a trimming knife held against a metal straight-edge
4 Fix the cut edge of the tile against the wall and secure with double-sided adhesive tape
5 To fit a tile round a pipe, make a template of the required shape and trace the shape onto the back of the tile; cut a slit from the hole made for the pipe to the skirting
6 Fit the tile round the pipe and secure with tape for an invisible join

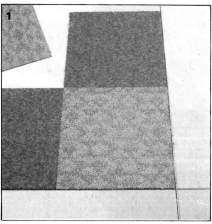

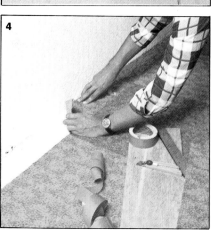

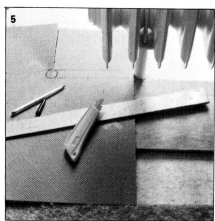

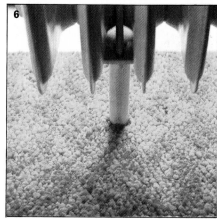

Fitting a stair carpet

Your stair carpet receives more wear than you might expect, so make sure you buy the right type and fit it correctly – for safety and maximum economy.

When selecting a carpet for stairs, bear in mind the heavy wear to which it is going to be subjected. Most people do not realize how many times even a small family use the stairs every day. Wear is not only caused by treading but also by the scraping of heels against the risers and by strong rubbing against the nosing. Long pile carpets (for example shag and semi-shag) are not suitable for staircases and foam-backed carpets are best avoided, if possible, since they are complicated to install.

As in all carpet installations underlay is essential since it provides longer life, increases sound insulation and gives greater comfort. Don't use stair pads, which only cover the tread area. When fitting underlay, make sure there is enough to pass round the nosing of the stair.

To give longer life, a stair carpet should be moved about six months after laying; this enables those parts of the carpet covering the risers to be placed over the treads and vice versa. Subsequently, at longer intervals, the carpet should be slightly moved to equalize the wear. When the carpet is laid, the extra amount is folded against the riser at the bottom of the staircase. Before fitting the carpet, make sure the natural inclination of the pile faces downwards.

Measuring up When buying a carpet, first measure the length you require. Assume the method of installation you are going to use will cause the carpet on the upper landing to overlap the top riser. Begin measuring from the base of the top riser and take the tape lightly over each tread and riser. Add to the total measured length an additional 38mm (1½in) for each step to allow for the space taken by the underlay. Add a further 457mm (18in) to enable the carpet to be moved to increase its life. If the staircase includes a winder, measure along the path taken by the outer edge of the carpet.

Laying the carpet

The two main methods of laying stair carpets are by tacking down and by using tackless strip. Whichever method you use, it is necessary to mark on the stairs the positions of the edges of the carpet and the underlay; the marking for the underlay will also apply to the tackless strips when they are used. The purpose of this marking is to ensure the carpet is laid centrally when it is not wide enough to cover the stair fully. If the steps are 813mm (32in) wide and the carpet is 686mm (27in) wide, a mark should be made on the riser 63mm (2½in) in from each edge. Then make a mark 19mm (¾in) inside the first ones to indicate the width and position of the underlay and of the tackless strip.

Tack-down method

For tacking down a special type of tack is used which is less visible than the normal type. First attach all the underlay, using a separate piece for each step; the width should be 38mm (1½in) less

than the width of the carpet and it must be long enough to cover the tread and lap round the nosing so the lower edge can be secured to the riser below. Align the sides of each pad with the inner pair of marks and position the back edge 25mm (1in) in from the riser. Tack it down at intervals of 150mm (6in) across the back of the tread, stretch it over the nosing and tack it across the riser below.

Starting at the top tread, position the end of the carpet as indicated by the marks so it is properly centred; allow an extra 13mm (½in) for turning under where the material reaches the top riser. Unwrap enough material from the roll to cover the first two or three steps. Before starting to tack, make sure the tuft rows across the carpet are parallel with the nosing. Turn the end of the carpet under so the cut end is not exposed and tack down one corner; stretch the carpet to make it even and

Above By fitting carpet to your stairs you can not only make them safer to use, but you can also draw them into the home's overall design; here the stairs have been covered with the same carpet as that used in the rest of the house, which brings the many different levels together and makes the house seem larger

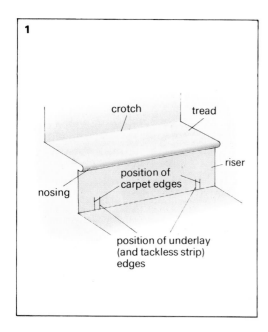

1

crotch

tread

riser

position of carpet edges

nosing

position of underlay (and tackless strip) edges

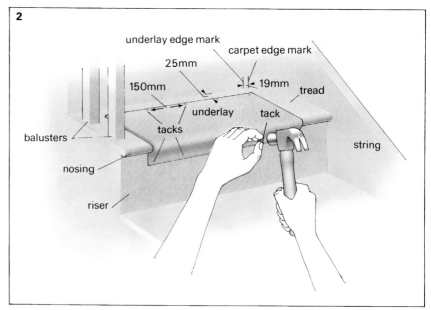

2

underlay edge mark

carpet edge mark

25mm

150mm

19mm

tread

underlay

tack

balusters

tacks

string

nosing

riser

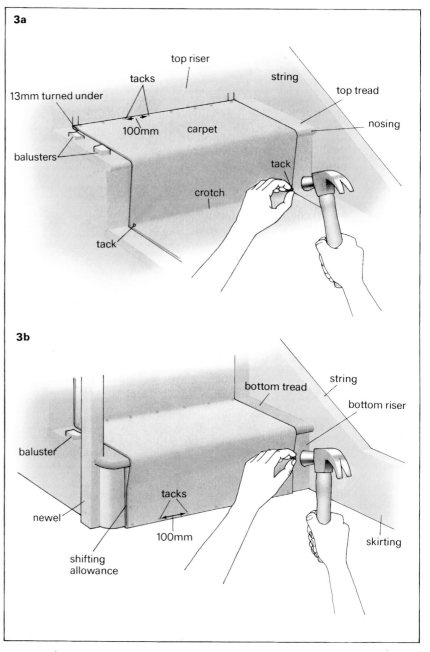

3a

top riser

string

top tread

tacks

13mm turned under

100mm

carpet

nosing

balusters

tack

crotch

tack

3b

string

bottom tread

bottom riser

baluster

tacks

newel

100mm

skirting

shifting allowance

1 To ensure the carpet lies centrally on the stair, mark on the riser the position of the edges of the underlay and the carpet; the marks for the underlay will also apply to tackless strip, if this is used
2 Fitting underlay for tacked carpet
3a Tacking down the carpet, starting at the first tread; the landing carpet should cover the first riser
3b Fitting the carpet at the bottom

tack across the riser at intervals of about 100mm (4in). Continue down the stairs, stretching the carpet over the nosing and tacking the edges in at the crotch. Then insert tacks across the crotch at 100mm (4in) intervals.

Where additional material has been included to allow for shifting, the material is folded in and held against the bottom riser by tacking up the sides. A slight overlap is needed at the bottom end of the carpet so it can be folded back when the carpet is finally tacked at the base of the lowest riser; take this into account also when measuring the shifting allowance. The same is done to the overlap of the landing carpet which covers the top riser.

Tackless strip method
Tackless strip is a flat narrow strip of wood, which is nailed to the floor; it is fitted with pins set at an angle, onto which the carpet is hooked. For laying stair carpets the strip is sold in 762mm (30in) lengths, so to fit a carpet 686mm (27in) wide, cut the lengths down to 648mm (25½in). When installing tackless strips, first mark the stairs as explained above, then fix the strips on the stairs. One strip is nailed across the riser, parallel with and 16mm (⅝in) above the crotch. Another strip is nailed across the tread the same distance from the crotch; this provides a gap into which the carpet is tucked. These distances will have to be increased or decreased according to the thickness of the carpet, since it is important to ensure a tight fit. The pins of both strips should lean towards the crotch.

Next attach the pieces of underlay, which should be longer than those used in the tack-down method. The rear edge of the underlay butts up against the tackless strip on the tread and is tacked down. The front edge is taken over the nosing, stretched down

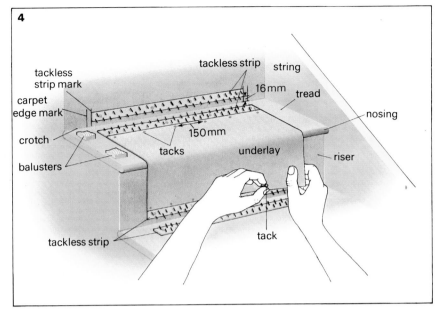

4

- tackless strip mark
- carpet edge mark
- crotch
- balusters
- tackless strip
- tacks
- 150mm
- tack
- tackless strip
- 16mm
- string
- tread
- nosing
- underlay
- riser

the riser and anchored, butting against the top edge of the strip attached to the riser. This prevents heels catching on the edge of the strip.

To lay the carpet, place the end on the top tread with the edge against the riser and one corner tacked down. Use an awl (also known as a bolster, stair tool or cold chisel) to push the edge of the carpet into the gap; keep the carpet stretched and hook it manually onto the pins. Then tack the other corner into the crotch. Draw the carpet tightly over the nosing and down to the crotch of the next step and hook the material onto both strips. Push the carpet

4 Fitting underlay when using the tackless strip method of laying carpet; the underlay should butt up against the strip on the tread
5a Fitting the carpet to the tackless strip on the first tread
5b Using an awl to push the carpet into the crotch of the stair
5c Stretching the carpet before fitting it to the bottom stair

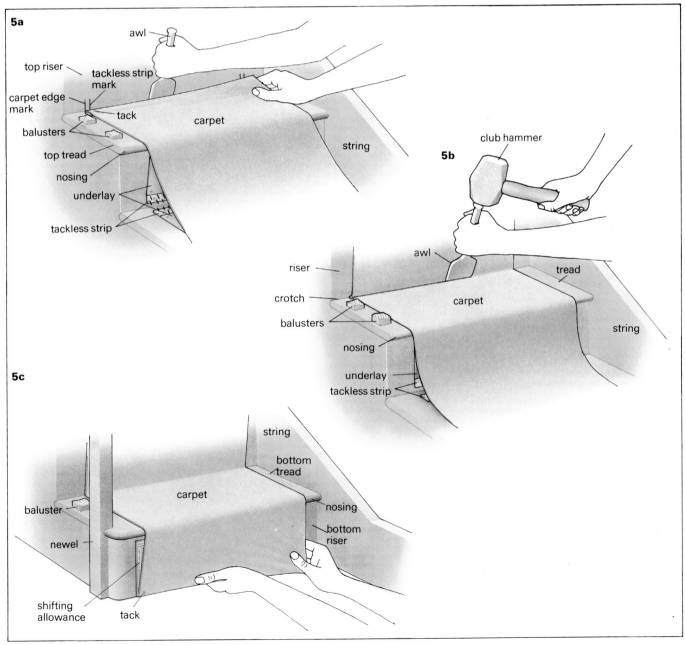

5a

- awl
- top riser
- tackless strip mark
- carpet edge mark
- balusters
- tack
- carpet
- string
- top tread
- nosing
- underlay
- tackless strip

5b

- club hammer
- awl
- tread
- riser
- crotch
- carpet
- balusters
- string
- nosing
- underlay
- tackless strip

5c

- string
- bottom tread
- carpet
- nosing
- baluster
- bottom riser
- newel
- shifting allowance
- tack

into the gap between the strips, using the awl to help tighten the carpet and prevent rucking. Repeat this procedure down the staircase. At the bottom, fold in the end of the carpet and tack across the bottom riser to give a neat finish.

Edge-to-edge fitting
In edge-to-edge fitting, where the steps are covered completely, the tackless strip and underlay have to be wider, although still slightly narrower than the carpet. If the carpet has been cut to width from wider material, latex adhesive should be applied along the edges to prevent the backing fraying and tufts working loose at the edges. Trim those parts that are too wide.

An even simpler method of tackless strip fitting is to use an angled metal strip with bevelled gripper pins along each of the inside faces. The strip fits into the crotch and the carpet is held by the pins. This is similar to the tackless strip although there is no gap into which you can tuck the carpet to tighten it. Another version has two faces to provide extra stretch and is particularly suitable for hessian,

secondary-backed fabric. If you have to use a foam-backed carpet, you can buy pairs of tongued plastic strips. These are fitted close to the crotch of the step, similar to the tackless strip; this enables the foam-backed carpet to be wedged between them. It is essential these components are positioned accurately and conform with the thickness of the material.

Fitting onto winders
Fitting carpets for winding stairs can be difficult. The easiest way is to cut separate pieces for each tread and the riser below, using a paper template to get the right shape. Cut the carpet so the tuft rows are parallel with the nosings and tack the pieces into position. When using tackless strip for edge-to-edge fitting, fit a length of strip along the skirting to hold the carpet along the three sides of the triangle.

By following carefully the methods described either using tacks or tackless strips, you should make a neat job of covering your stairs.

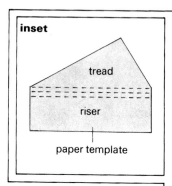

6a Cutting a template of winding stairs to ensure the carpet is cut to the correct shape; make one template for each tread and the riser below it (**inset**)
6b Positioning tackless strip on the winders for edge-to-edge fitting

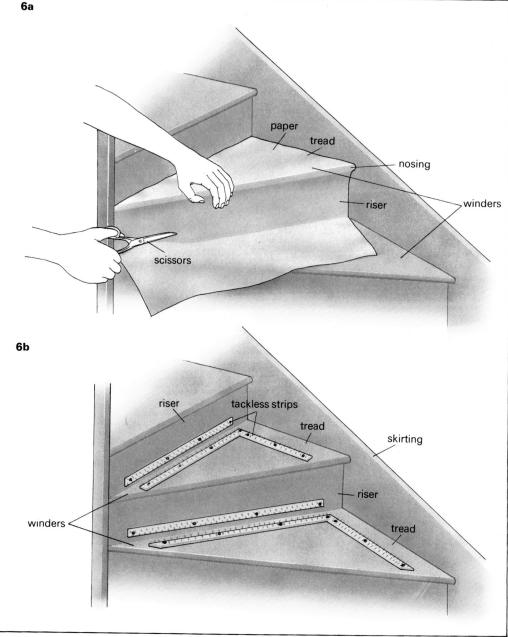

Cleaning & repairing carpets

Carpets will become worn or damaged in the course of everyday use. There is no need to go to the expense of replacing them when you can patch and repair minor damage easily and at a fraction of the cost. You should remember to save remnants and offcuts when carpets are being fitted so you will be able to carry out repairs in the future.

Regular vacuum cleaning, ideally every day, will remove grit which cuts into carpet fibres and backing as it is trodden in. Fluff will form on the surface of new carpets; this consists of short fibres which do not reach the base of the carpet and should be removed for the first few weeks with a hand brush, carpet sweeper or vacuum cleaner. Sometimes, while a carpet is bedding down, short loose fibres may become tangled with stronger fibres, causing small balls or pills of fibre on the surface. These should be trimmed off with scissors; never attempt to pull protruding fibres out of the carpet.

Often the surface of a looped pile carpet may be caught up with a nail, in the base of a piece of furniture for example; this will cause a pulled loop. Look carefully to see if an adjacent loop has been pulled into the base of the carpet; if one has, you may be able to tease it up with a piece of hooked wire and draw the pulled loop back into the surface. If not, you will need to trim the loop level with the surface.

Cleaning carpets

Lightly soiled carpets can be cleaned with carpet shampoo, applied by a manual or electric carpet shampooer following manufacturer's instructions. Treat heavily stained areas separately and test a small area before treating the whole carpet to check for discolouration. The best shampoos produce a dry foam which does not wet the carpet excessively; if the carpet is too wet, this could cause shrinkage and discolouration. After shampooing, leave the pile sloping in one direction and allow the carpet to dry before walking or replacing furniture on it: vacuum it clean when it is dry.

Heavily soiled carpet will have to be treated by professionals – or you can hire a 'steam' carpet cleaner; this is a large vacuum cleaner with a wet shampoo applicator. A hand-held nozzle sprays shampoo and hot water and the carpet is vacuumed so the shampoo, dirt and most of the water is drawn into the waste tank of the cleaner. The carpet is left drier than after ordinary shampooing, so the furniture may be replaced within about an hour.

Removing stains

When treating stains on carpets you should always test an area to discover whether the treatment has any effect on the colour dyes in the carpet. Remember it is much harder to remove all liquids and semi-solids if they are allowed to dry. Stains fall into two basic categories and there are specific treatments for each type of carpet stain.

Water soluble stains These should yield to a carpet

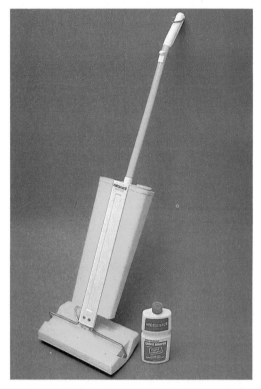

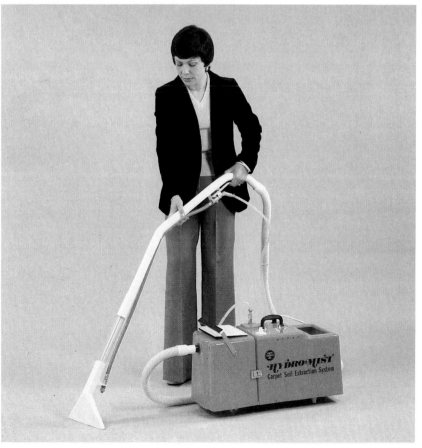

Left Carpet shampooer, suitable for cleaning lightly soiled carpets
Below 'Steam' cleaner, suitable for heavily soiled carpets

Following page
1a When patching woven back carpet, first mark out the damaged area on the back of the carpet and apply adhesive along the marked lines
1b Cut out the damaged area with a sharp knife, placing a piece of hardboard under the carpet for protection
1c Place the damaged piece on a carpet offcut and mark its exact shape with a felt pen
1d Fix strips of carpet tape to overlap the edges of the hole
1e Place the patch over the carpet tape and hammer it down along the edges to ensure a firm bond

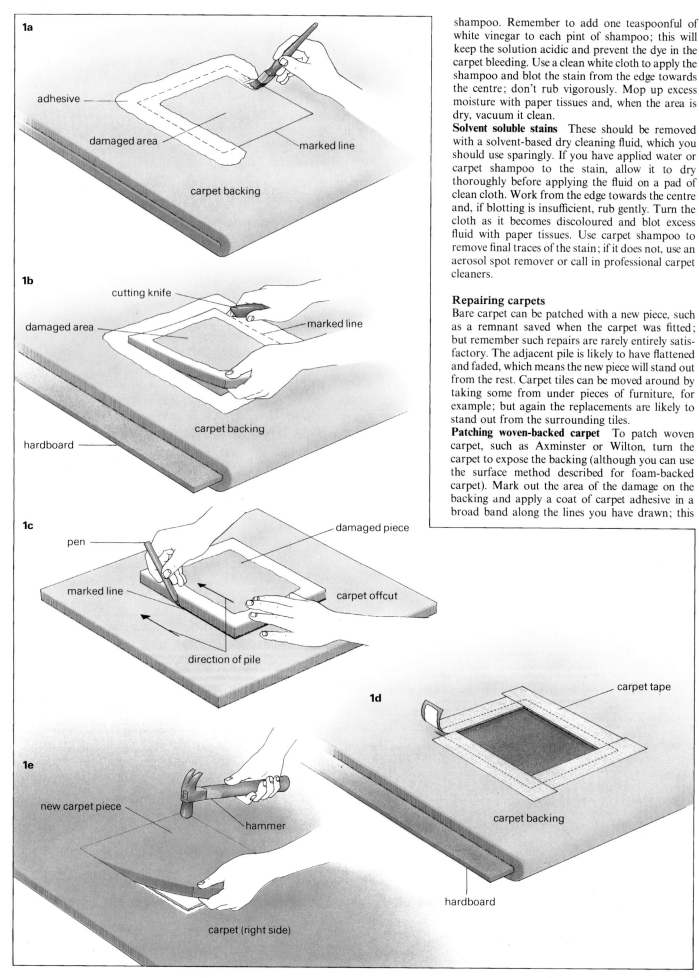

shampoo. Remember to add one teaspoonful of white vinegar to each pint of shampoo; this will keep the solution acidic and prevent the dye in the carpet bleeding. Use a clean white cloth to apply the shampoo and blot the stain from the edge towards the centre; don't rub vigorously. Mop up excess moisture with paper tissues and, when the area is dry, vacuum it clean.

Solvent soluble stains These should be removed with a solvent-based dry cleaning fluid, which you should use sparingly. If you have applied water or carpet shampoo to the stain, allow it to dry thoroughly before applying the fluid on a pad of clean cloth. Work from the edge towards the centre and, if blotting is insufficient, rub gently. Turn the cloth as it becomes discoloured and blot excess fluid with paper tissues. Use carpet shampoo to remove final traces of the stain; if it does not, use an aerosol spot remover or call in professional carpet cleaners.

Repairing carpets

Bare carpet can be patched with a new piece, such as a remnant saved when the carpet was fitted; but remember such repairs are rarely entirely satisfactory. The adjacent pile is likely to have flattened and faded, which means the new piece will stand out from the rest. Carpet tiles can be moved around by taking some from under pieces of furniture, for example; but again the replacements are likely to stand out from the surrounding tiles.

Patching woven-backed carpet To patch woven carpet, such as Axminster or Wilton, turn the carpet to expose the backing (although you can use the surface method described for foam-backed carpet). Mark out the area of the damage on the backing and apply a coat of carpet adhesive in a broad band along the lines you have drawn; this will prevent the carpet fraying when you cut out the damaged area. Place a sheet of hardboard under the carpet and cut along the marked lines with a sharp knife. Put the piece you have cut out upside down on the back of an offcut of the carpet and carefully match the direction of pile and pattern (the pattern will usually show through the back of a woven carpet). Mark out the exact shape of the worn piece onto the new one, coat with adhesive and cut out as before. Lay strips of 50mm (2in) carpet tape around the edge of the hole in the carpet to accept the patch; you can use either self-adhesive tape or woven fabric tape (which requires carpet adhesive). Re-lay the carpet and press the patch into place over the carpet tape; take great care not to push down the surrounding pile as you press the patch into place. Hammer it down along the edges to ensure firm contact with the carpet tape beneath.

Patching foam-backed carpet This is easier because you can patch from above the surface of the carpet. Lay a large offcut over the worn area and match the pile direction and pattern; very carefully cut both layers at the same time with a sharp knife. If it is a large patch, you can tack the pieces down to prevent movement as you cut through. The foam backing will prevent fraying. If you intend to use this method with woven carpet, you will need to apply carpet adhesive along edges of both the hole and the patch roughly halfway up the pile. Cut strips of carpet tape so they will overlap around the hole, raise the edges of the carpet and apply the tape so half its width is exposed (sticky side up). Place the patch in position and hammer down the edges to ensure sound contact with the tape.

Repairing tears Tears in carpet are usually caused by movement of the underfloor; this should be rectified before you make the repair. Tears often occur at the back and front edges of stair treads because of movement between treads and risers. To repair a tear, turn the carpet over and hold the tear closed before sticking 75mm (3in) wide self-adhesive or woven carpet tape along it. If you use woven tape with carpet adhesive, you can make the repair stronger by stitching along the sides of the tear with a curved needle and strong thread.

Repairing frayed edges Frayed edges occur most frequently at doorways and they can be repaired by fitting aluminium binder bars, which are available

in various designs. Use bars with small teeth for woven-backed carpets and bars with small lips to hold foam-backed carpets. Cut the binder bar to length (to fit the doorway) and nail it down; on a concrete floor you can fix the bar with masonry pins or use adhesive. If the carpet has a woven backing, you should seal the edge by working in a 25mm (1in) strip of carpet adhesive and trimming off the loose ends. Make sure the carpet lies flat without rucks or wrinkles before hammering down the lip of the binder bar, using a wood block as protection.

You can also seal frayed edges with carpet tape; this is especially useful for frayed carpet squares. If the carpet has a woven back, cut off a small amount of carpet to give a neat, straight edge. Seal this edge with adhesive, taking care not to get the adhesive higher than the base of the tufts. Stick carpet tape along the edge, allowing 3–6mm ($\frac{1}{8}$–$\frac{1}{4}$in) to overlap; turn the overlap over so it sticks to the base of the tufts all along the edge.

It is more difficult to bind the edges of foam-backed carpet because it crumbles at the edges. The foam may make binding difficult because you need a good key for the adhesive or self-adhesive tape. It may be necessary to experiment with different adhesives to find one which gives the best bond.

Repairing burns You may be able to trim off the tips of burnt fibres to remove a mild cigarette burn; more serious burns on woollen rugs and carpets can be patched with thick knitting wool. Trim off the burnt tufts with a small pair of nail scissors and cut the patching wool into 13mm ($\frac{1}{2}$in) pieces. Hold back the carpet pile around the damaged area and work carpet adhesive into the trimmed tufts with a matchstick. Ease a bunch of wool pieces into the damaged area with a matchstick, filling the hole as tightly as possible. When the adhesive is dry, cut the ends level with the pile and pull out any loose ends. Use a needle to tease the new wool fibres into the fibres of the carpet.

Serious burns in woven, nylon and man-made carpets must be patched using the technique described for worn carpets.

Repairing rush matting This type of floor covering is not easily repaired, but you may be able to stitch loose pieces back into position. Replacement pieces are available for square rush matting, which you can stitch into place to repair worn areas.

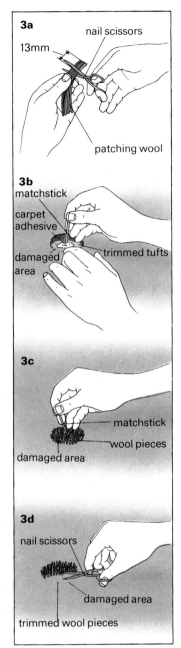

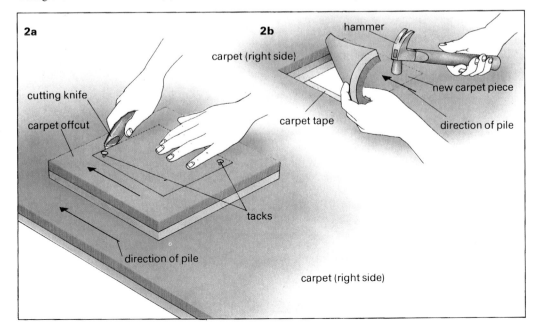

2a When patching foam-backed carpet, place a large offcut on top of the damaged area and cut through both layers at the same time; you can tack down the offcut to stop it moving as you cut through
2b Fix carpet tape to overlap the edges of the hole, place the patch in position and hammer it down firmly
3a To repair a burn, cut strands of patching wool into 13mm lengths
3b Trim off the burnt carpet fibres and work adhesive into the tufts with a matchstick
3c Ease a bunch of wool pieces into the hole, packing them in as tightly as possible
3d When the adhesive is dry, trim the ends of the wool level with the pile

Carpet stains and how to remove them

Stain	Treatment	Method
Animal or baby soiling	Carpet shampoo or biological detergent	Blot or scrape then apply treatment
Beer, wine, spirits	Clean warm water or, if persistent, carpet shampoo	Blot with clean cloth and sponge
Blood	Cold water or, if persistent, carpet shampoo or biological detergent	Sponge with water before stain dries
Burns	Stiff brush or nail scissors then carpet shampoo	Brush or cut away lightly scorched areas then shampoo (serious burns will require retufting or patching)
Chewing gum	Dry cleaning fluid	Scrape off as much as possible then apply treatment
Chocolate, egg, ice cream, soft drinks, vomit	Carpet shampoo or, if persistent, solution of 7ml ($\frac{1}{4}$fl oz) borax with 248ml (10fl oz) water then shampoo	Scrape off then apply treatment
Fruit juice	Carpet shampoo or biological detergent	Blot then apply treatment
Cocoa, coffee, tea, milk	Clean warm water or, if persistent, carpet shampoo or detergent followed by borax solution as for **Chocolate**	Blot with cloth and sponge with water
Adhesive	As for **Chocolate**	Blot or scrape while adhesive is still liquid then apply treatment (old adhesive stains may yield to dry cleaning fluid; if not, seek professional help)
Grass	Methylated spirit then carpet shampoo or biological detergent	Wipe with methylated spirit before applying treatment
Grease, oil, fat, butter, margarine, ointment, perfume, tar, candle wax, shoe polish	Carpet shampoo or solvent-based dry cleaning fluid	Blot or scrape then shampoo; blot excess with tissues, allow to dry and apply treatment with cloth; shampoo again to remove traces
Ink	Carpet shampoo, biological detergent, methylated spirit or dry cleaning fluid	Soak up with tissues then apply treatment; ball pen stains can be removed with methylated spirit (old and indelible ink stains will require professional help)
Paint, varnish	Water for water-based paint such as emulsion, white spirit for oil-based paint such as gloss and varnishes and amyl-acetate (cellulose thinner) for cellulose paints and lacquers; then carpet shampoo	Scrape or wipe off excess, treat with thinner then use carpet shampoo (dried stains may yield to paint stripper applied with care — test a corner first; alternatively seek professional help)
Rust	Carpet shampoo then vacuum cleaner	Blot fresh stains with carpet shampoo on cloth, allow to dry then vacuum (old stains require professional help)
Soot	Carpet shampoo	Blot with treatment on cloth

Renovating ceramic tiles

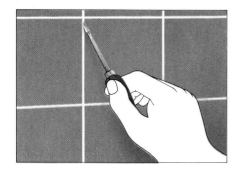

One of the quickest ways to give a face-lift to sound old tiling is to replace grout – filling material round each tile. Rake out old grout with worn screwdriver or old pair of scissors. Take care not to scratch surface of tiles while raking out

Spread new grout over tiles with dampened sponge. Remove any surplus material as you work, leaving just enough to fill gaps between tiles. When grout is almost dry, clean tiles with dampened sponge. Finish off with clean, dry soft cloth

For regrouting
worn screwdriver or old pair of scissors
grout
two sponges, soft cloth

For loose tiles
Small sharp cold chisel
small-toothed notched spreader
impact (contact) adhesive or builders'
    sand and cement mix

For broken tiles
small sharp cold chisel, club hammer
protective spectacles or goggles
flexible filling knife or round-ended
    (gauging) trowel
impact (contact) adhesive

equipment

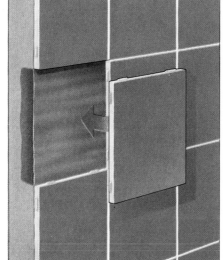

Far left Refix loose tiles before regrouting, chipping away any old cement from tiles with cold chisel. Spread impact (contact) or similar thin-coat adhesive (thicker adhesive will leave replaced tiles proud of surrounding surface) on wall and backs of tiles with small-toothed notched spreader. Refix tiles

Left Mortar may come away with loose tiles. If it does, try to glue back tiles with mortar still in place or chip it away. (If you have replacement tiles, throw away old ones.) Chop away any mortar from wall to form clean surface. Fix tiles with mixture of three parts builders' sand to one part cement. Apply just enough mortar behind each tile to bring its face level with surrounding ones to ensure flush finish over tiled surface

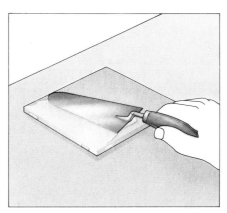

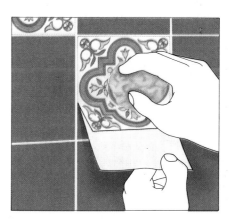

Remove broken tiles and old adhesive with small sharp cold chisel and club hammer. Work from centre outwards and take care as you get near surrounding tiles; protect any fittings from being scratched by broken pieces of tile. Always wear protective spectacles or goggles

Using flexible filling knife or round-ended (gauging) trowel, butter thin layer of adhesive on back of replacement tiles and push them into place. Make sure new surface is flush with old, building up adhesive if necessary. Complete repair by applying new grout

As temporary measure you can easily renovate old crazed tiles with self-adhesive transfers. Decorating entire wall may prove uneconomic so only use them to cover worst of tiles. Remove backing from transfers and smooth them out onto tiles with soft cloth, working from centre outwards

Repairing floor coverings

Over the years most floor coverings – such as sheet vinyl, parquet blocks, cork, ceramic and vinyl tiles – will lose their finish or become damaged. Fortunately you can repair minor damage and renovate floor surfaces without going to any great expense.

Cork tiles

You can renovate the surface of a cork floor with one or two coats of sealer, but you must first remove all traces of polish. Scrub the floor with fine wire wool, dipped in white spirit, and sand with medium abrasive paper before wiping over again with a cloth dipped in white spirit. Allow the floor to dry before applying polyurethane sealer, available in matt, silk or gloss finish.

Damaged tiles Holes or cracks in cork tiles may be filled with plastic wood or wood coloured stopping; when this has dried, rub the surface smooth and treat with sealer so the repair matches the surrounding tiles. If the tiles are worn over a large area, it is advisable to hire a floor sanding machine; but if the tiles are only worn in places, such as around a doorway or in front of a sink, you can replace them with new ones.

Make a clean break between the damaged tile and the surrounding tiles, using a sharp knife held against a metal straight-edge to cut along the join. Use an old chisel to remove the tile; work from the centre to the edge, holding the chisel bevel side down so it cuts between the old tile and the surface without cutting into the sub-floor. Scrape away the old adhesive from the sub-floor so the new tile will lie flush with the old tiles and check the sub-floor is sound and free from movement.

New tiles should be fixed as recommended by the manufacturer. Apply adhesive with a notched spreader to give a good key, press the tile into place from the centre towards the edges and wipe away excess adhesive. Weight the new tile with books until the adhesive has dried, then apply sealer or finish to match the old tiles. If you cannot obtain replacement tiles, you can use different tiles at random intervals or in a pattern to make a feature of the replacement tiles.

Vinyl tiles

You can replace individual vinyl tiles as for cork tiles; thicker tiles will be easier to lay if they are first gently heated with a blowtorch. Some types of tile are self-adhesive and you can lay these after cleaning the sub-floor; otherwise you will have to apply adhesive to the sub-floor. You may be able to patch thick vinyl tiles with glass fibre filler, which can be painted to match the tiles, if the area is small or unlikely to receive heavy wear.

Repairing sheet vinyl This floor covering is prone to curling at the edges and seams, usually a result of failure to stick down the edges sufficiently. Lift up a curled edge and clean the sub-floor by scraping and vacuum cleaning 75–100mm (3–4in) strips. Wash the sub-floor and the back of the vinyl with hot water and detergent, allow it to dry and apply tile adhesive with a notched spreader. When this becomes tacky, press the edge back into place.

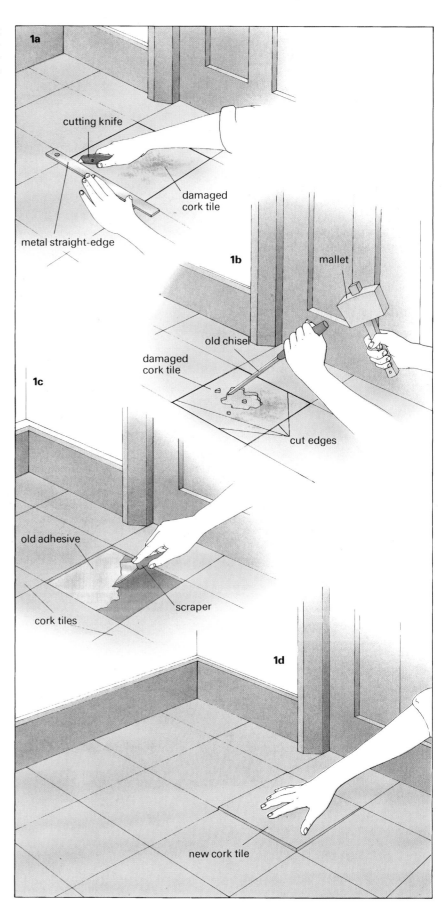

1a cutting knife
damaged cork tile
metal straight-edge

1b mallet
old chisel
damaged cork tile
cut edges

1c old adhesive
scraper
cork tiles

1d new cork tile

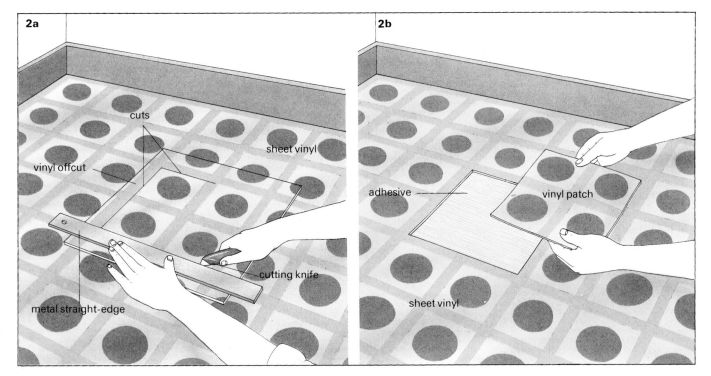

2a

cuts

vinyl offcut

sheet vinyl

cutting knife

metal straight-edge

2b

adhesive

vinyl patch

sheet vinyl

1a To replace damaged cork tile, cut round tile with sharp knife held against metal straight-edge
1b Use old chisel, bevel side down, to remove tile; work from centre outwards
1c Scrape off old adhesive
1d Check fit of new tile and apply adhesive with notched spreader; fit tile, pressing from centre towards edges, and wipe off excess adhesive
2a When repairing damaged sheet vinyl, position offcut slightly larger than area of damage – making sure to match pattern; cut through both pieces, following line in pattern
2b Check fit and pattern match; apply adhesive to floor with notched spreader and fit patch, placing weights on it until adhesive has dried

Splits in sheet vinyl are usually caused by movement of the sub-floor; pull back the vinyl and nail or screw down the floor to prevent further movement. Apply adhesive to the cleaned floor surface and press the vinyl back into place when the adhesive becomes tacky; place weights on the vinyl until the adhesive is dry.

A hole worn into sheet vinyl can be patched with offcuts you have saved or vinyl cut from an area normally hidden under furniture. Cut the patch slightly larger than the damaged area and lay it over the damage to match the pattern. Cut through both pieces with a sharp knife held against a straight-edge; if possible, cut against a line in the pattern so the patch will be less noticeable. Remove the worn area and fit the new piece into position with adhesive; hold it in place with weights until the adhesive is dry.

Ceramic or quarry tiles

If the floor tiles are very uneven, you may decide to replace them or re-cover the floor; a self-smoothing floor screeding compound is applied directly over the tiles to form an ideal sub-floor.

Cracked or crazed tiles cannot be repaired; they must be replaced with new ones. You can, however, make a temporary repair on slightly pitted tiles with cementwork or glass fibre filler. Move a damaged tile carefully so you do not damage adjacent tiles. You should wear protective spectacles when breaking up the tile with a hammer and small cold chisel; start at the centre of the tile and work outwards. When the tile has been removed piece by piece, chip away the bedding mortar so the new tile will lie just below the surface of the existing tiles. Coat the back of the new tile with a thin layer of floor tile adhesive, using a notched spreader. Press the tile into place so it is level with adjacent tiles and move it so there is an equal gap around all its edges. After 24 hours you can fill the joints around the tile with grout or a mortar mix consisting of four parts fine, sharp sand to one part Portland cement.

Timber floors

Ways of repairing damaged timber floors are covered separately in this book; but, if the floor is in good condition, you can improve its appearance – and provide a durable, non-porous surface – by applying a polyurethane sealer. Wash the floor thoroughly with household detergent and water to remove dust and grease, then rinse with clean water and leave the floor to dry. To remove polish and stubborn stains, you can use white spirit; but afterwards always wash with detergent and rinse with clean water to ensure there are no traces of spirit left on the floor. If the floor is painted, you should hire a floor sanding machine and use it to strip the paint back to bare wood; then wash and rinse the floor as before. Apply the sealer, following the manufacturer's instructions, and leave each coat to dry before applying the next (three coats should be sufficient); on the penultimate coat, use abrasive paper or wire wool to give a perfectly smooth surface for the final coat.

Repairing hardwood floors Minor damage to parquet blocks and wood strips, such as deep scratches and cigarette burns, may be repaired by sanding the damaged area or the whole floor if necessary. If the damage is more extensive, you will have to replace the blocks; chop out the first block with a chisel and prise up subsequent blocks with a lever. When chiselling out parquet blocks, you should start from the centre and work towards each end, taking care the chisel does not cut into adjacent blocks. Replacement blocks should be the same thickness as the original ones; slightly thicker ones can be planed down after laying, but do not buy blocks which are too thin. It is quite difficult to place packing pieces to bring them up to the correct height.

Clean and scrape the sub-floor leaving it dust-free. Use a notched spreader to apply adhesive, either to the floor or to the back of the block. Some bitumen-based damp proofing liquids are suitable for fixing wood blocks. The blocks should be tapped into place with a hammer after the adhesive has

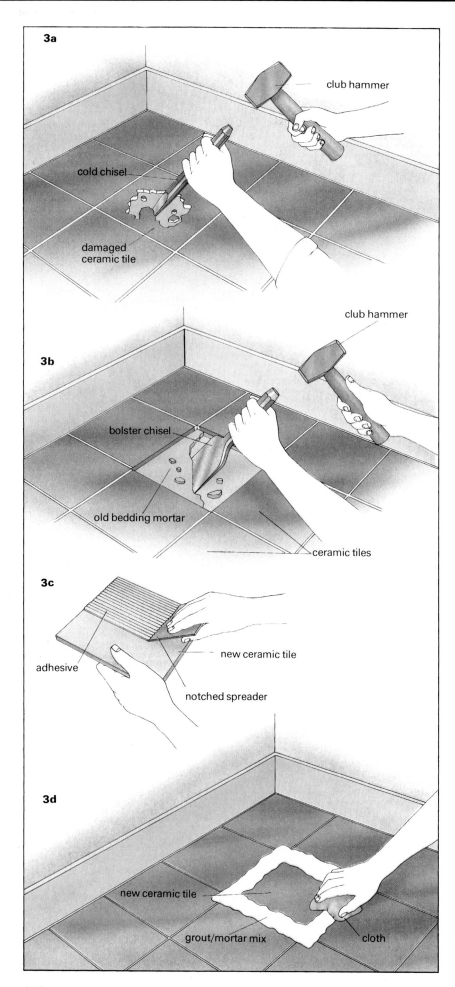

been applied; use a piece of scrap wood to protect the surface of the block.

Wood strips are repaired in the same way as blocks, but lifting them from the sub-floor may prove more difficult. Often the strips are tongued and grooved along their length and they may be fixed with hidden nails (secret nailing), which are inserted at an angle through the tongues as the wood strips are laid. The best lifting method is to free one end of the strip in the manner described to chisel out parquet blocks. It may now be possible to lever up the strip along its length. If this is not so, you can use a circular power saw, set to cut three-quarters of the distance through the strip, running down the centre of the strip. By levering the strip in the middle at the chiselled end you should now be able to split the board into two and pull out each half.

Fitting new strips is similar to fitting blocks; taper the sides of the strip inwards, so when it is hammered down it wedges into place along its length. If the strip is slightly proud of the surface after fixing, you can plane or sand it level.

Concrete floors

Greasy or oily patches on a solid floor in a garage, shed, cellar or kitchen, must be removed before you lay floor coverings. Grease can build up to such a level that it becomes a hazard and you should apply a concrete paint or a proprietary grease removing solution, which you can buy from motor accessory shops. Scrape the floor to remove as much grease and dirt as possible and brush on grease remover solution until the surface appears thoroughly wet. Leave for up to 15 minutes for the grease to soften and agitate it with a stiff brush from time to time. If necessary, apply more solution until the grease stain takes on a soap-like appearance. Wash with water and brush the floor; repeat the treatment if the stain remains after the floor has dried out.

Dusty concrete This can be cured with a concrete hardening and dustproofing liquid. Sweep the floor – or vacuum it clean if possible – and apply the liquid with a brush, according to manufacturer's instructions (two coats may be required). You can use a PVA bonding agent diluted with water, but allow the treatment to dry before subjecting it to normal traffic. According to the wear the floor receives, the treatment may have to be repeated every one or two years. If you need a more durable coloured finish for a garage, store or outside WC, you can apply a brush-on floor sealing compound to give a tough, dustproof coating which is impervious to water and oil.

3a To replace damaged ceramic tile, break up tile from centre outwards
3b Chip away old bedding mortar
3c Apply adhesive to back of new tile
3d Use dampened cloth to apply grout
4a To replace damaged parquet block, chop out first block with chisel and mallet
4b Lever up adjacent damaged blocks
4c Apply adhesive to floor or block
4d Tap new block in place
5a To replace damaged wood strip, chip away end of first strip with chisel
5b If strip will not lift, saw along length
5c Prise up strip with crowbar
5d Remove tongue and taper sides of new strip before tapping it in place

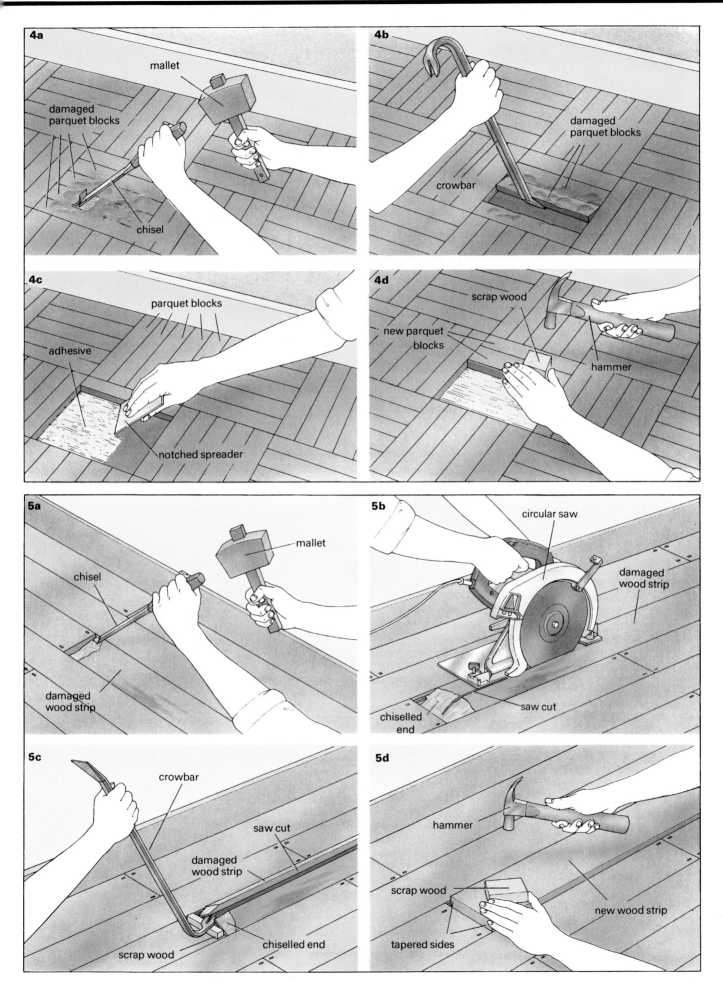

Upholstery: cleaning & general repairs

It is worth getting into the habit of vacuuming your upholstery on a regular basis, since if you spring-clean it once a year, dirt will be ground into the fabric. Most suction cleaners have a special attachment for cleaning upholstery and for removing dust and dirt from awkward places in the backs and sides of chairs.

If possible, you should remove any spillage immediately after it happens. Treatment will depend on the type of fabric, so before you begin always check the manufacturer's instructions to make sure the cleaner you have in mind is suitable. You should check for such things as shrinkage and colour-fastness by making a small test with the cleaner in an inconspicuous place on the upholstery. To avoid overdampening the fabric and the padding beneath, it is best to use a dry cleaner on fabrics to get rid of spots and stains. This type of cleaner only wets the surface and dries very quickly to a powder; when you brush off the powder, it should take the stain with it. At least one make of this type is suitable for cleaning both upholstery and carpet.

Loose covers These can be either dry-cleaned or washed, depending on the composition of the fabric. If you are in doubt, check with the manufacturer's washing instructions or go to a reputable cleaner for advice. Some materials may be liable to shrink or run their colours in the wash and you should check for this before you begin washing.

Fixed covers Very badly soiled areas in fixed fabric covers can be cleaned by using a special upholstery shampoo. Again, to avoid overdampening the fabric, you can use a dry shampoo with an applicator. The shampoo foam is forced through a sponge head in a controlled flow which eventually dries to a powder and is removed with an upholstery attachment on a vacuum cleaner. To make sure the shampoo will not harm the fabric, check on a small, hidden area first.

Alternatively, if you are going to spring-clean your carpets by hiring a hot water soil extraction machine, you can clean your upholstery at the same time. Ask for a special upholstery tool attachment when you are hiring one of these machines, which are available by the day or half-day from specialist hire shops and some carpet retailers. The machines are fairly heavy to manoeuvre; but this should not be a problem when you are cleaning upholstery, since you will probably be able to reach several chairs from one position. A shampoo is mixed with the hot water, 'vacuumed' over the upholstery with one sweep and sucked back with the grime and dirt in the next sweep, which takes out most of the moisture. It is best to treat very dirty areas with a spot remover to loosen the stain before starting to clean with the machine. The upholstery will dry out in a warm room.

Methods of repairing

Burst or frayed machine seams or tears near piping can be repaired by slip-stitching, which if done with care will conceal the damage. Neaten any frayed

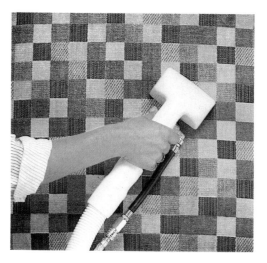

edges by trimming, but don't cut into the fabric itself. If necessary, turn in a tiny piece along either side of the torn edges to make them neat. Use large darning needles fixed down firmly into the padding along the torn edges to hold them together while slip-stitching the tear.

You will need matching strong thread and an upholsterer's half circle 'slipping' needle, which you can buy from the haberdashery department of a large store or possibly an upholsterer's shop. Tie a knot in one end of the thread and insert the needle into one side of the tear a little way in from the end, hiding the knot on the underside of the upholstery. Bring the two edges together by using very tiny stitches on either side, pulling the thread through very firmly each time and keeping the stitches parallel. Remove the darning needles as you go along and finish by fastening off the thread, working the thread end into the seam.

Patches A hole can be successfully repaired by taking replacement fabric from elsewhere (from the underside of the chair or sofa, for example) and patching it in. If this is not possible and you feel it is worth the effort, try locating an extra piece of matching fabric from the manufacturer. Carefully cut away all the damaged fabric, tidying up the edges as you cut. The replacement patch should be slightly larger than the actual hole size and, where necessary, you should carefully match the pattern; if there is a pile make sure it is the right way up. Push the patch down into position onto the padding and underneath the hole edges. Coat round the edges of the patch and the undersides of the fabric edges round the hole with a fabric adhesive, taking care not to let the adhesive touch anywhere else. Wait until the adhesive becomes fairly tacky, press the two surfaces together and leave them to dry. This type of patch will satisfactorily disguise small damaged areas. For anything larger you will need to fit a replacement cover for that particular section: this is covered later in the book.

Leather and vinyl Covers in leather and vinyl cannot be slip-stitched, but provided they are soft

Left A carpet soil extraction machine fitted with a special attachment can be used to clean upholstery
1 When slip-stitching torn fabric, hold the edges together with large darning needles fixed firmly into the padding
2 To patch damaged fabric, position the patch beneath the hole edges, matching any pattern; coat the hole edges and the edges of the patch with adhesive and, when this is tacky, press the two surfaces together

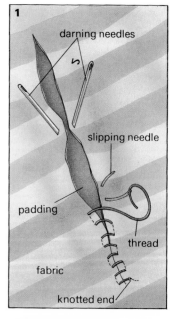

1
darning needles
slipping needle
padding
thread
fabric
knotted end

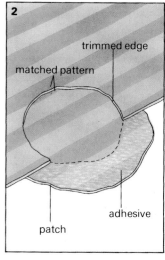

2
trimmed edge
matched pattern
adhesive
patch

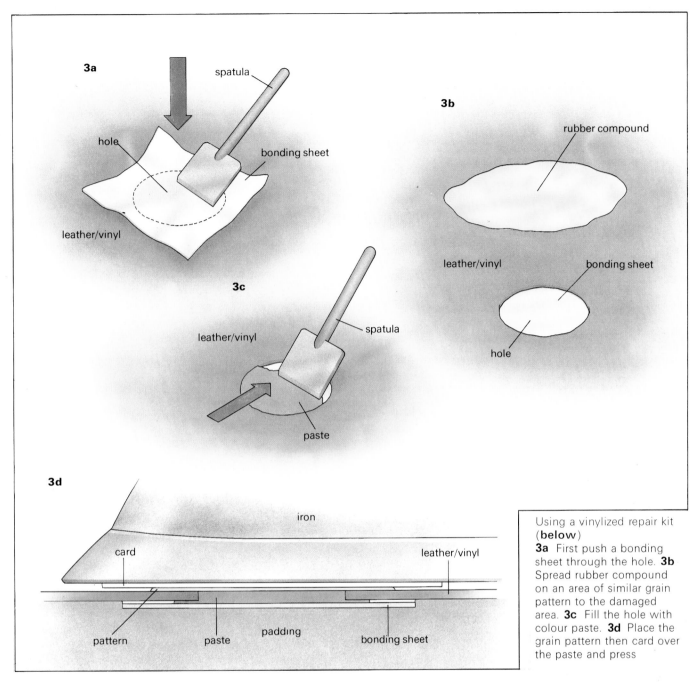

3a

spatula

hole

bonding sheet

leather/vinyl

3b

rubber compound

leather/vinyl

bonding sheet

hole

3c

leather/vinyl

spatula

paste

3d

iron

card

leather/vinyl

pattern

paste

padding

bonding sheet

Using a vinylized repair kit (**below**)
3a First push a bonding sheet through the hole. **3b** Spread rubber compound on an area of similar grain pattern to the damaged area. **3c** Fill the hole with colour paste. **3d** Place the grain pattern then card over the paste and press

and well worn you can repair holes or tears with a special repair kit available from a hardware store or haberdashers. The kit enables you not only to match up the upholstery colour but also the grain, which is particularly important if you want to achieve a good repair.

Clean the surface with white spirit to remove grease and dirt and insert a small piece of bonding sheet (provided with the kit) through the tear to form the base for the repair paste. Mix the paste to the exact colour and use a knife or spatula to spread it into the area. To match the upholstery grain use one of the patterns which come with the kit; alternatively for an unusual grain pattern you can use the rubber compound (which is also supplied) to make a mould of an area identical to that which is damaged to provide a pattern. Place the grain pattern or rubber mould face down over the paste, place a piece of card on top and press down on it for two minutes with a warm iron to imprint the pattern on the paste.

195

Button & foam cushion repairs

Some chairs and sofas have decorative buttons on the seat and back; these often work loose and fall off and can mar the appearance of upholstery which is otherwise in a good state of repair. Fortunately, replacing them is a relatively simple task. If only one or two buttons are missing, you could cover the new ones with pieces of fabric taken from an inconspicuous part of the chair or sofa; if several are missing, you may find it easier to replace all the buttons and cover them in a contrasting fabric.

Metal button trims These, which you cover with fabric yourself, are available in a range of sizes from haberdashery departments of large stores. They are in two sections: the round main part has small claws on the bottom onto which fabric is pressed and the other part is a cap which clamps the fabric down and secures it in position.

If you are using the same fabric, take a piece out of the underside of the chair or sofa or from the tuck-ins of the lower inside arms. You will find it worth experimenting with the fabric and the button trims until you achieve the correct tension across the button face. If the fabric is very thick, which upholstery fabric often is, you may find it very difficult to fit it onto the button trims. You can take the spare fabric to the fabrics department of a large store where you should be able to have the buttons covered at a reasonable cost.

Fixing buttons

When you are fixing a button to the inside back of a chair or settee, it is worth taking the back cover off so you have access to the inside padding. Thread a length of thin stitching twine through the button and then thread the two ends of the length of twine through the eye of a long upholstery stitching needle.

Mark the position of the button with a piece of tailor's chalk on the inside back cover, push the needle through this mark and through the inside padding, making sure the twine comes right through with the needle. Use a slip knot to join the two pieces of twine securely together; but before pulling the knot tight insert a small piece or tuft of felt or cloth between the stuffing and the slip knot to prevent the knot pulling through later and making an unsightly hole.

Tighten the slip knot by pulling one end of the twine. At the same time check the other buttons already in place; if they are deep-buttoned (pulled in very tightly into the upholstery), make sure you match up the depth of the button you are fixing with their depth and pull in accordingly. When the buttons are all the same depth, tie a reef knot to stop the slip knot coming undone later; cut off the twine ends for a neat finish.

Where it is not possible to take off the back cover without a great deal of trouble, you can make a quick repair with the cover on. Thread a long upholstery needle with twine and insert it into the upholstery on the side where you are going to replace the button. Push it through until the eye has

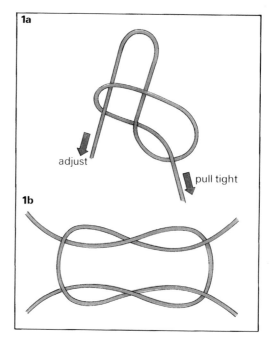

1a Tying a slip knot
1b Tying a reef knot
2a To replace a button, thread a length of twine through the button and then thread both ends through the eye of an upholstery needle
2b Mark the position of the button on the inside back cover; push the needle through the mark and the padding, making sure the twine comes right through with the needle
2c Tie the two pieces of twine with a slip knot; before tightening this insert a small tuft of felt or cloth between the knot and the padding
2d Tighten the slip knot until the button is at the same depth as other buttons on the chair; secure with a reef knot

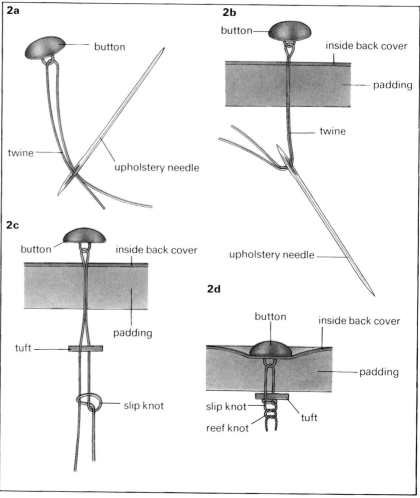

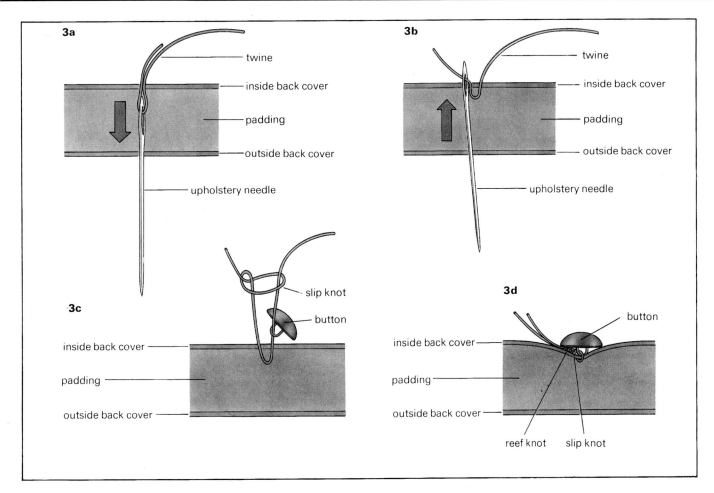

3a

twine
inside back cover
padding
outside back cover
upholstery needle

3b

twine
inside back cover
padding
outside back cover
upholstery needle

slip knot
button

3c

inside back cover
padding
outside back cover

3d

button
inside back cover
padding
outside back cover
reef knot   slip knot

passed through the front fabric and the inside padding, leaving one end of the twine about 100mm (or 4in) long on the side where the button will be replaced. Push the eye back so it emerges close to the insertion point; pull the needle and take off the thread. Pull in both ends of the twine and trim to even them up, leaving enough to allow you to make a slip knot.

Take one end and thread the button on, fixing it with a slip knot and pulling in both ends of the twine to secure it tightly. Check the button is in the correct position and finish off with a reef knot. Cut the ends back as far as possible and tuck them under the button.

Reversible cushions These can be rebuttoned fairly easily but the technique is slightly different. Since you will be working with buttons which have to be sewn in the same position on opposite sides of the cushion, it is best to remove the odd one on the opposite side to the one you are replacing so you can start from scratch. If the stitch holes have enlarged through wear, carefully stitch up this area using a fabric thread pulled out from a place on the cushion which is normally invisible. Fix the buttons slightly away from this point, making sure they are not drastically out of alignment with the rest of the buttons on the cushion.

Where necessary, carefully mark new positions for the buttons on each side of the cushion. Thread a length of twine through a button and thread both ends of the twine through the eye of a long upholstery needle. Push the needle through the marked point on one side, guiding it through the stuffing until it locates the marked point on the other side; pull it out and remove the thread from it.

Thread the other button on one end of the twine

and make a slip knot joining the two twine ends. Pull the slip knot tighter until both buttons are pulled in to the required depth. Secure the twine with a reef knot under the button and cut off the ends as short as possible so they are hidden under the button. Make sure you do not snip the upholstery fabric at the same time.

Repairing foam cushions
When a foam-padded cushion begins to sag at the edges (usually at the front) you will find it a simple matter to strengthen it. If the cushion cover has no zip, find the edge of the cover which has been handsewn and carefully cut along this edge to remove the stitches. Pull out the foam pad; you will need to squash it a little to free it from the cover. Where the cover has a zip, be careful not to catch the foam against the zip edges when you are pulling it out.

Locate the damaged part and, using a sharp knife or pair of scissors, remove it by making a cut across the foam at least 75mm (3in) away from the damaged section. Use the damaged piece as a pattern for cutting a replacement piece from the same kind of foam material, allowing an extra 25mm (1in).

Coat the edges of the replacement part and the places where they will meet the pad with impact adhesive, making sure you do so in a well ventilated room since this material is flammable. Allow the adhesive to become tacky and bring the two surfaces together, pushing them firmly in place. Allow the adhesive to dry completely, fold the foam and push it into the cover. Where necessary, sew the cover edges together using a half circle needle to make slipstitches.

You can make a quick repair with the back cover on:
3a Thread a long upholstery needle with twine and, working from the side on which you are going to replace the button, push the needle into the upholstery until the eye has passed through the inside back cover and into the padding
3b Push the eye back so it emerges close to the insertion point; pull out the needle and take off the thread
3c Pull the twine so both lengths are equal, thread the button onto the twine and tie a slip knot
3d Pull up the slip knot until the button is in the correct position and secure with a reef knot; trim back the ends of the twine and tuck them under the button

Rewebbing a chair

Left The completed webbing
– it should be stretched
taut over the frame
(padding and springs are
removed for clarity)
1 Using a web stretcher;
wrap the webbing around the
stretcher and pull it across
the frame. Hold the stretcher
against the frame edge at a
45 degree angle, press it
down firmly and fix the
webbing in place with tacks;
you can make a web stretcher
by cutting a deep 'V' across
the end of a piece of timber
(**inset**)
2 To fix the springs, tuck
each one under the webbing
where two pieces overlap
and secure with twine; each
spring should be held with
four stitches (**inset**)
3 To replace the hessian
backing, turn in the edges
and tack it to the frame; fold
the hessian round the legs
and fix with tacks

A sagging or lumpy chair seat indicates the springs
or the webbing have come away or the webbing has
simply worn out; it also indicates the seat padding
is in poor condition and needs replacing. Re-
webbing a chair is a fairly straightforward job, but
renewing the padding is slightly more difficult and
is covered separately in the book.

Carrying out repairs
To examine the condition of the springing, turn the
chair upside down and hold it steady by resting it
on another chair or a workbench. Take off the
hessian backing, using a chisel and mallet to remove
the tacks which hold it to the frame; make sure you
work very carefully in the direction of the grain to
avoid damaging the wood. If the hessian is still in
good condition, you will be able to use it again when
you have completed the repair work. If, however,
the backing looks worn or tatty, cut out a new one
using the original as a pattern and allowing at least
25mm (1in) extra all around so you can make a
neat, tucked-in finish.

Removing webbing When you have removed the
hessian, check the condition of the webbing – and
the springs if there are any; some chairs have only a
padded base supported with webbing. Look to see
whether any of the webbing has come away from
the frame or become saggy and slack through wear;
if this is the case, remove it using the chisel and
mallet to knock out the tacks. Try not to enlarge the
holes when you do this; if you do open them up a
little, fill them with a fine wood filler and leave them
to harden. Once the webbing is free from the frame,
use a sharp knife to cut the spring twine which
holds the webbing to the springs, disturbing the
springs as little as possible.

Replacing webbing Turn over the end of the new

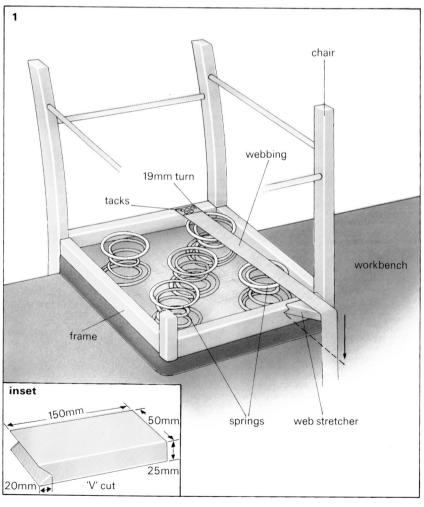

1

chair

webbing

19mm turn

tacks

frame

springs

web stretcher

workbench

inset

150mm

50mm

25mm

20mm

'V' cut

2

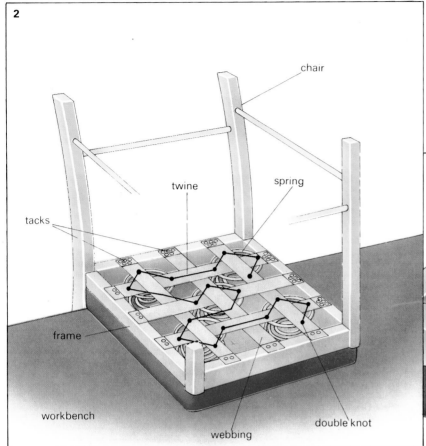

chair

twine

spring

tacks

frame

workbench

webbing

double knot

webbing 19mm (¾in) and, using the original tack holes as a guide, fix the webbing to the front edge of the frame with five tacks, placed in the shape of a 'W', so the wood will not split.

You will need to buy a web stretcher, or make one by cutting a deep 'V' across one end of a piece of 50 × 25mm (2 × 1in) wood. Stretch the webbing across the seat and wrap it around the stretcher from end to end. Pull the webbing across the frame and lay the V-shaped end of the stretcher onto the edge of the frame at about a 45 degree angle. Press

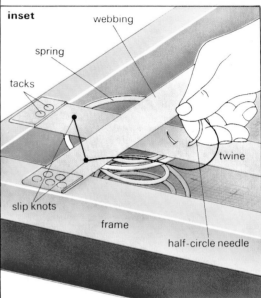

inset

webbing

spring

tacks

slip knots

frame

twine

half-circle needle

3

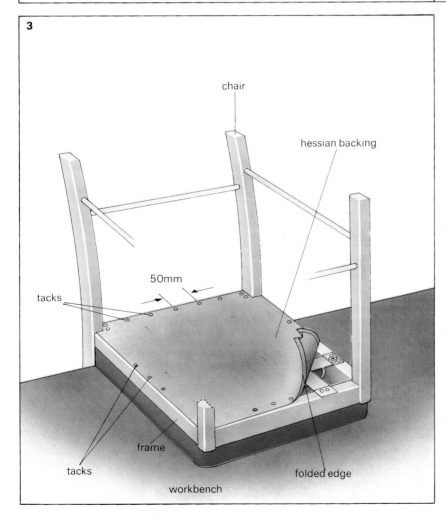

chair

hessian backing

50mm

tacks

tacks

frame

folded edge

workbench

it down firmly until you feel the webbing will not stretch any more. Hold the stretcher in place and fix the webbing with a single row of three tacks. Remove the stretcher and cut off the webbing about 25mm (1in) from the tacks. Turn the end over and secure it with two more tacks.

Again using the old tack holes as a guide, complete the webbing along the length of the frame. Fix strips of webbing across the width of the frame, weaving them through the lengthwise pieces then stretching and tacking as before.

Fixing springs To make sure the springs are secure and will not tear through the hessian, tuck each one under a place where two pieces of webbing overlap. If the springs tend to squeak, put a small piece of felt or some other kind of padding between the two parts of the spring which are rubbing together.

When all the springs are in place, secure them to the webbing using spring twine and a half-circle or springing needle. Each spring should be fixed with four stitches equally spaced around it and caught at the same depth; finish off each stitch with a slip knot. Without breaking the twine, carry one stitch to an adjacent spring and stitch as before. When all the springs have been attached to the webbing in this way, finish off with a double knot and trim the twine.

Replace backing Once you have renewed the seat padding, you can replace the backing. Fold in the edges of the hessian and tack it to the frame with three tacks in the middle of each side. Adjust any creases by taking out the tacks, straightening and retacking. When the hessian is flat, continue fixing it down with tacks every 50mm (2in) along the frame, avoiding previous holes if possible. Fold the hessian into shape around the legs and fix with tacks close together for a neat finish.

Repadding a drop-seat dining chair

A dining chair is subjected to a fair amount of wear and will eventually become flattened and need a new cover. Repadding and recovering this type of chair is a relatively straightforward job.

It is likely the wood frame will have lost all its natural oils through years spent in a heated home and will be liable to split unless handled with care. When you are stripping off the old cover, carefully push an old wide-bladed screwdriver or an upholsterer's ripping chisel under each tack and ease it out with the aid of a mallet; make sure you work with the grain of the wood to avoid knocking out tiny pieces or splitting the frame.

When you have removed all the tacks, clean up the frame with medium fine glasspaper and check for cracks and woodworm. Treat woodworm with a proprietary brand of woodworm killer and fill any cracks with plastic wood. If the chair has been re-upholstered a number of times, there may be a lot of tack holes; it is best to fill the larger ones with plastic wood to give the frame extra strength.

Repadding the seat

A sagging seat usually results from damaged webbing or a broken plywood base; or the padding may have flattened through wear. Loose webbing should be replaced and covered with hessian as described earlier in the book.

Traditional hair and felt padding can be put back into shape if the hair has not become too knotted. Remove the felt layer first, then break up any large lumps of hair with your hands, distributing them evenly, and wash them in warm water. You may need more hair to build up the padding if it is old; this is fairly difficult to obtain and it may be easier to replace this type of padding with polyether foam.
Foam padding Use a medium-to-high density foam for replacing old stuffing; a type which is 25mm

(1in) thick would be most suitable. Carefully measure the frame seat and, using a sharp knife, cut a piece of foam which is slightly larger all round to ensure a good fit. Most dining chairs look better for a slightly raised effect and you can achieve this by sticking a piece of 13mm ($\frac{1}{2}$in) thick foam, about 75mm (3in) smaller all round, on the underside of the main piece in the centre.

Attach the foam directly to the frame by gluing

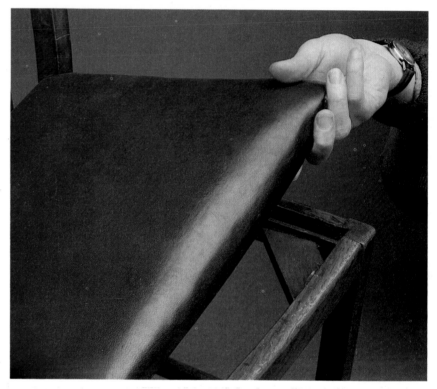

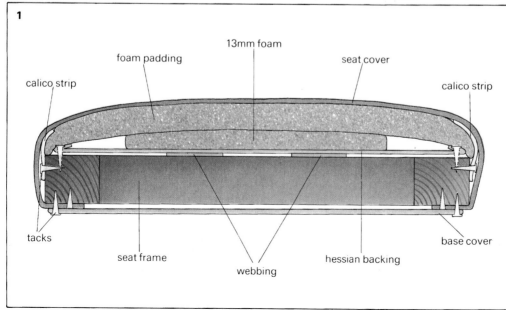

1 Section through a drop-in seat
2 When fitting hessian over the webbing, work from the centre of each side outwards
3 To give a foam padded seat a slightly raised effect, stick another smaller piece of foam onto the underside of the main piece
4 Attach the foam padding directly to the frame with strips of calico
5 Where the new cover is of thinner material than the old one, fix strips of card to the inside of the seat frame; this will pack out the frame and enable the seat to fit snugly
6 Fit the cover over the seat and tack it to the underside of the frame

Figure 1 labels: calico strip · foam padding · 13mm foam · seat cover · calico strip · tacks · seat frame · webbing · hessian backing · base cover

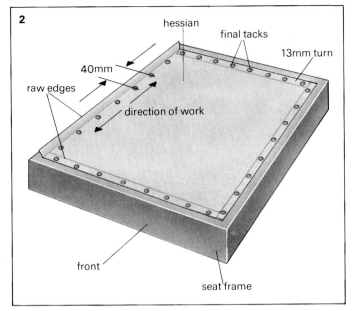

2

hessian

final tacks

13mm turn

40mm

raw edges

direction of work

front

seat frame

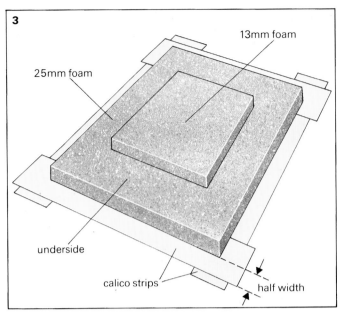

3

13mm foam

25mm foam

underside

calico strips

half width

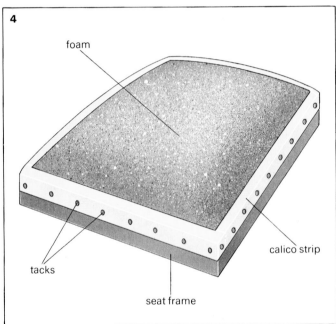

4

foam

calico strip

tacks

seat frame

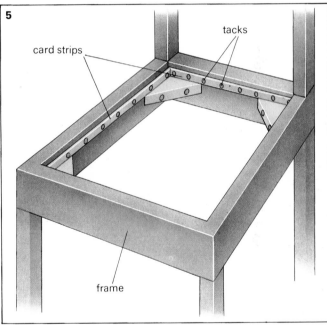

5

tacks

card strips

frame

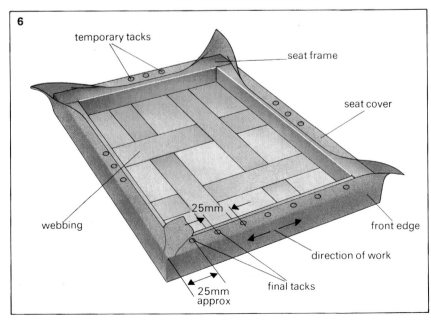

6

temporary tacks

seat frame

seat cover

webbing

25mm

direction of work

front edge

final tacks

25mm approx

it into place around the sides; make sure the adhesive is completely dry before you fit the new cover. Alternatively you can use strips of calico which you stick down onto the foam top and then tack down onto the frame; use strips of calico slightly longer than each side of the foam and stick half the width onto the foam with the other half stretched over onto the frame edge and tacked down. Trim away any excess calico.

Re-covering the seat

You can use the old cover as a pattern for the new one, but allow slightly more material all round; you can trim away any surplus, if necessary. If you are going to use a slightly thicker material, it will be difficult for the seat to fit into the frame and you will need to shave back the inside frame a fraction with a cabinet scraper to allow for this.

If the cover is of a slightly thinner material than before, the seat will not fit snugly. You can remedy this by tacking or gluing strips of card round the insides of the chair frame, but remember to keep them below the top edge to avoid them showing

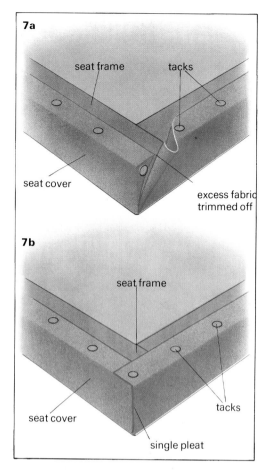

7a

seat frame — tacks

seat cover

excess fabric trimmed off

7b

seat frame

seat cover

tacks

single pleat

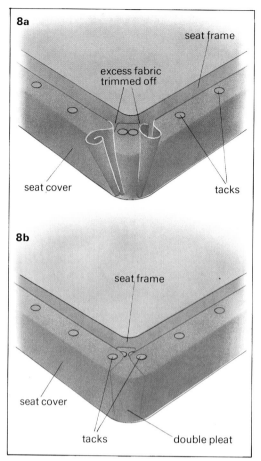

8a

seat frame

excess fabric trimmed off

seat cover

tacks

8b

seat frame

seat cover

tacks

double pleat

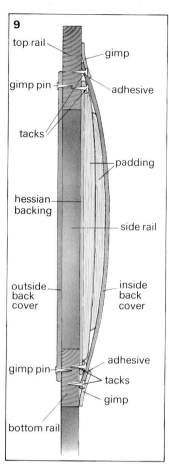

9

top rail — gimp

gimp pin — adhesive

tacks

padding

hessian backing

side rail

outside back cover

inside back cover

adhesive

gimp pin — tacks

gimp

bottom rail

when the seat is in place. If there is a large pattern, make sure when you are cutting that it will be in the centre of the seat to get the best effect. If there is a pile to the fabric, this should brush forward.

Temporary tacking Remember to tack the cover down temporarily before you finish it so you can adjust any puckering or dragging of the fabric which occurs when you are stretching material in several directions. Do all the tacking on the underside of the frame. Fix down the front edge in the middle using three tacks, then fix the back edge and both sides, again using three tacks for each side. Remember to keep the fabric taut across the seat, taking any fullness into the corners. If necessary, adjust the cover by removing the tacks at the front, pulling the fabric tight and retacking.

Securing cover Once you are satisfied with the fit of the fabric, use small upholstery tacks to secure it at 25mm (1in) intervals along the seat frame. Start at the centre front and work to within 25mm (1in) of one corner, driving in the temporary tacks as you go. Then work from the centre front to within 25mm (1in) of the other corner. Repeat this procedure for the back edge, then the sides.

Corners These can be quite awkward to cover neatly, especially if bulky material is used. Where there are rounded edges, finish off the corners with a double pleat; to do this, stretch the material over the frame towards the underside and tack it there securely. Make sure there is an equal amount of fabric left on each side of the tacking point and make pleats with the excess fabric, facing them in towards the corner. Cut away any excess material underneath where it will not show, then pull both pleats taut and secure each with a tack.

Where there is a square corner, it is only necessary to use one pleat. Pull all the fabric round one

corner and fix it there with a tack. Dispose of the extra fabric on the underside by cutting it away; don't cut right to the top of the corner, where it might show. Pull the fabric down from the other side of the corner, taking it over the tacked piece and pleating and tacking it down as you go. Catch-stitch the pleat down, but hide the stitches on the inside.

Finishing off You can now fit the base cover to keep out dust; if the old one is in good condition, you can use this. Alternatively you can replace the base cover with one made from calico or hessian; use the old cover as a pattern for the new one. Turn in all the edges of the new base cover and fix it with tacks, spacing the tacks at equal intervals.

7a At a square corner, pull the fabric round one side of the frame and tack in place
7b Finish off by forming the fabric into a single pleat
8a At a rounded corner, pull the fabric over the frame and secure with tacks
8b Form the fabric into two pleats and tack in place
9 Section of a back pad
10 To retension the hessian backing, undo tacks on two adjacent edges, pull the hessian taut and retack

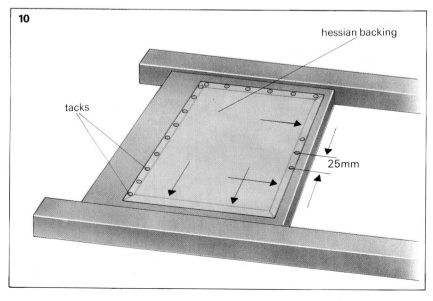

10

hessian backing

tacks

25mm

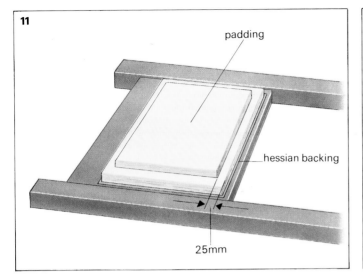

11

padding

hessian backing

25mm

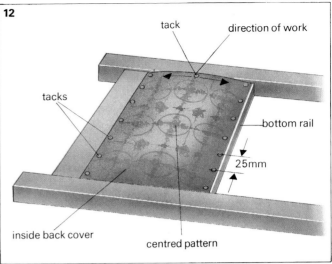

12

tack

direction of work

tacks

bottom rail

25mm

inside back cover

centred pattern

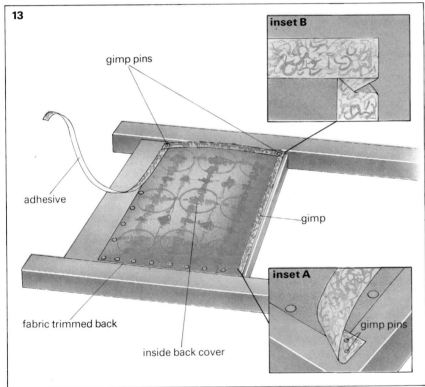

13

inset B

gimp pins

adhesive

gimp

fabric trimmed back

inset A

inside back cover

gimp pins

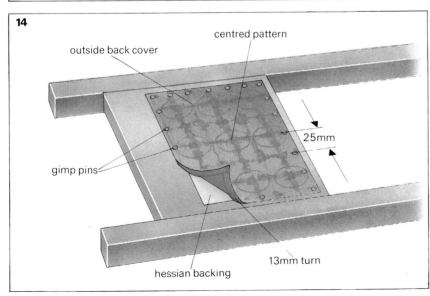

14

centred pattern

outside back cover

25mm

gimp pins

13mm turn

hessian backing

Repairing the backpad

Pull off any trimming on the front of the chair. Use an old chisel and mallet to remove the exposed tacks which hold the upholstery fabric in place, working carefully and in the direction of the grain to avoid damaging the wood.

Renewing padding Remove the covering and take out the old layers of flock or hair which were used as padding. Examine the calico or hessian backing; if it needs tensioning, undo two adjacent edges, pull the backing taut and retack every 25mm (1in). Lay on it a strip of flock or dacron wadding the size of the backing and then another strip 25mm (1in) smaller all around to give a domed appearance to the finished pad.

Replacing cover Cut a piece of covering material 50mm (2in) wider and deeper than the finished pad, making sure any pattern on the fabric is centred. Tack the fabric to the bottom rail at 25mm (1in) intervals, starting at the centre and working outwards. Continue in the same way until the fabric has been tacked down all around and with sharp scissors trim back the material in line with the wood.

Finishing off Fix one end of the gimp (trimming) by pinning it down with two gimp pins at one corner of the pad. Coat the underside of the trimming with latex-based adhesive and press it into position all around, folding it at the corners and pinning it down. When you reach the end, tuck the gimp under 13mm (½in) and pin.

Repairing outside back cover Remove the old cover and cut a new one 25mm (1in) larger all around. Attach it to the rails at 25mm (1in) intervals as before, turning under 13mm (½in) and using gimp pins instead of tacks since the back of this type of chair is not usually trimmed.

11 When fitting the padding, place a smaller piece of wadding on top of the main piece. **12** To fit the cover, centre the pattern and tack the fabric to the frame. **13** Trim the edges with gimp; fix one end with gimp pins (**inset A**) and fold the gimp to shape at corners before pinning (**inset B**). **14** Fix the outside back cover with gimp pins.

Reupholstering an armchair

Reupholstering a padded armchair may seem a daunting task; but as long as you are familiar with the basic reupholstery techniques described earlier in the book and are prepared to take time and effort over the job, you should be able to tackle it successfully. Here we explain how to strip an armchair to its frame and replace each part of the upholstery. It may not be necessary, however, for you to strip the chair completely; if, for example, only the stuffing needs replacing, you can leave the layers underneath intact.

Before you begin any work on the chair, it is important to make copious notes and clear diagrams of how and where each part of the final cover is fixed. Very few chairs are upholstered in exactly the same way and you may find some of our instructions will not apply to your particular chair; your notes and diagrams will ensure you replace everything correctly and retain the shape of the chair.

Stripping the chair

If the frame needs attention, you will have to strip the chair right down. Turn it upside down and place it on trestles or a firm table. Using a mallet and an upholsterer's ripping chisel, remove the tacks which secure the bottom canvas.

Turn the chair right side up and remove the outside back and outside arm covers; on some chairs these will be secured with tacks, but on others they will be slipstitched invisibly. Again, make notes and diagrams to ensure you can replace the covers correctly. Continue by stripping the seat; remove all tacks, including those holding the webbing, from the bottom frame of the chair and lift out the seat intact. Cut the twine holding the springs to the webbing and hessian, count the springs and note their size so you can replace them if necessary. Remove the seat cover and hessian from the stuffing by cutting the stitches; but leave the scrim in place so you do not disturb the shape.

Remove the inside back and inside arm covers which are tacked to the outside of the back and arm frames. Also detach the scrolls, if any; these will be stitched on. If the chair has a calico inner cover, this will be tacked on and should be removed. Take out the tacks securing the scrim which holds the stuffing in place and lift off both the scrim and the stuffing without disturbing the shape. Finally remove the hessian.

Repairing the frame

Check the condition of the frame; you may have to get a carpenter to repair any loose joints and replaced damaged sections of timber. Check the frame has not been attacked by woodworm; treat with woodworm fluid if necessary and allow it to dry before continuing, otherwise the furnishing fabric may be spoiled. Fill any holes left by the original tacks with filler or plastic wood and rub smooth with abrasive paper.

Replacing the webbing

Turn the chair upside down and, using a web stretcher, hammer and 16mm (or $\frac{5}{8}$in) improved (heavy) tacks, fit new webbing over the base of the chair seat in the same way as the original webbing.

Turn the chair right side up and stretch two pieces of webbing vertically on the inside of each arm frame. On the inside back fix three vertical strips of webbing and weave two horizontal ones through them to support the back stuffing.

Replacing springs

Place the seat springs on the webbing in the same position as they were originally fixed. Keep the front ones well forward to take the strain of the front edge; the other springs should be placed slightly towards the centre of the seat to allow clearance at the arms and back for the stuffing.

Working from the inside of the seat and using twine and a springing needle, secure the base of each spring to the webbing; make three oversewing stitches in three places, with a long stitch underneath connecting each set of three. Lash the springs with lay cord or sisal.

Inside back If the chair has back springs, these should be placed at the junctions of the webbing and secured with oversewing stitches in the same way as the seat springs. There is no need to lash these back springs.

Above Although the final cover and stuffing on this chair need replacing, the rest of the upholstery is sound and can be left in place

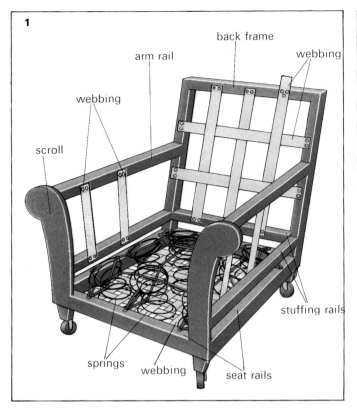

1

- scroll
- webbing
- arm rail
- back frame
- webbing
- webbing
- springs
- webbing
- seat rails
- stuffing rails

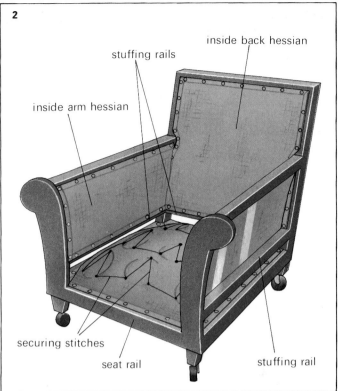

2

- stuffing rails
- inside back hessian
- inside arm hessian
- securing stitches
- seat rail
- stuffing rail

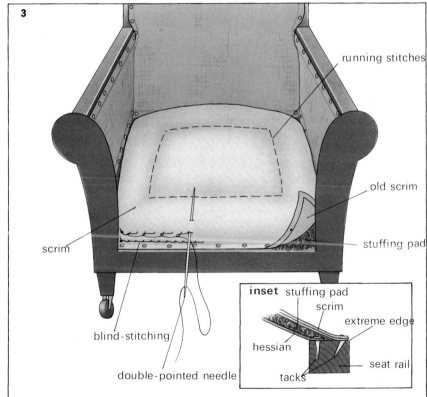

3

- running stitches
- old scrim
- stuffing pad
- scrim
- blind-stitching
- double-pointed needle

inset
- stuffing pad
- scrim
- extreme edge
- hessian
- tacks
- seat rail

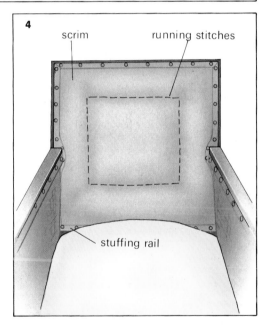

4

- scrim
- running stitches
- stuffing rail

1 With the webbing in place refit the springs and lash them in position; if there are back springs, fix these in the same way – but there is no need to lash them

2 Tack hessian to all inner faces of the frame; on the seat, stitch the springs securely to the hessian

Fixing hessian

Cut a piece of heavy hessian to cover the seat, allowing 25–50mm (1–2in) extra all round. Place the hessian on the springs and temporarily tack it to the top edge of the seat with 13mm ($\frac{1}{2}$in) improved tacks; pull the hessian straight and taut, then drive the tacks home. Turn up the 25–50mm (1–2in) allowance on all sides and tack the hessian to the frame between the original tacks. Secure the springs to the hessian with three oversewing stitches in

three places in the same way as you secured the springs to the webbing.

Inside back Cut a piece of heavy hessian large enough to cover the inside back, again allowing 25–50mm (1–2in) extra all round. If there are back springs, bear in mind you will need extra hessian to cover them. Tack the hessian to the face of the inside back frame in the same way as for the seat, attaching the lower edge to the stuffing rail, but use 13mm ($\frac{1}{2}$in) fine tacks. If there are back springs, stitch them to the hessian as before.

Inside arms Cut two pieces of heavy hessian to cover the inside arms, again allowing 25–50mm (1–2in) extra all round. Fix these pieces to the inside face of the frame as before, attaching the lower edge of each to the stuffing rail; leave the hessian unattached at the back.

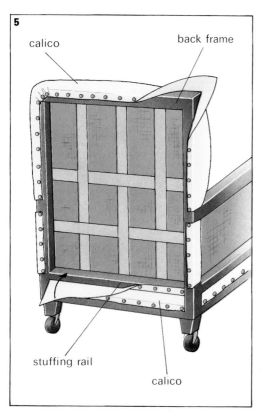

5
calico
back frame
stuffing rail
calico

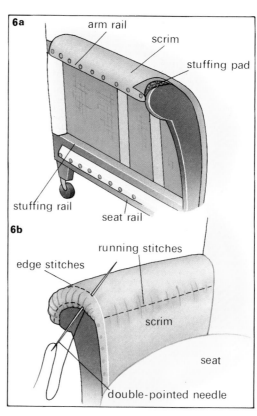

6a
arm rail
scrim
stuffing pad
stuffing rail
seat rail

6b
running stitches
edge stitches
scrim
seat
double-pointed needle

3 Replace the stuffing pad on the seat and cover it with scrim, tacking it to the extreme edge of the rail (**inset**); make running stitches right through the seat centre and form rows of blind stitches at the front to strengthen the edge

4 With the stuffing replaced on the inside back, cover it with scrim secured with running stitches as before

5 Cover the inside back with calico, tacking it to the outside face of the frame

6a On the inside arms replace the stuffing pads and cover with scrim

6b Secure the stuffing with a line of running stitches and form the front of the scroll with edge stitching

7 Cut the final cover pieces to shape using the old cover as a pattern; attach fly pieces to the covers for the inside back, the seat and the inside arms at the same positions as on the original

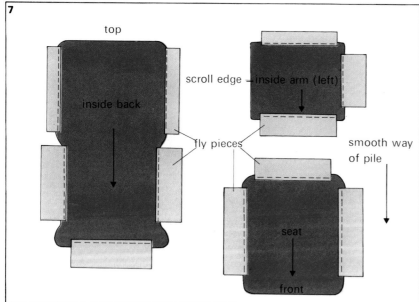

7
top
inside back
scroll edge
inside arm (left)
fly pieces
smooth way of pile
seat
front

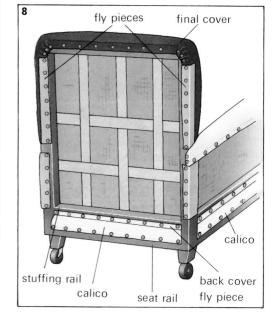

8
fly pieces
final cover
calico
stuffing rail
calico
seat rail
back cover
fly piece

8 When fixing the final cover to the inside back, pull it over the top rail and tack it to the outside face, pleating it at the corners where necessary. Pull the fly pieces round onto the outside back, passing the lower ones through the gaps at the back of the arms, and tack them to the outside faces as before. Tack the bottom fly to the outside face of the stuffing rail and trim all excess fabric from the fly pieces

Replacing stuffing

It is important to disturb the stuffing as little as possible if you are to retain the shape of the chair. To extract the dust from the stuffing, go over each section lightly with a vacuum cleaner attachment.

Seat Replace the stuffing pad on the chair seat and fill in any worn places by adding kerly fibre, coir or horsehair. Cut a piece of scrim to cover the seat, allowing 50–75mm (2–3in) extra all round; turn up the edges and tack the scrim to the top face of the rails all round the seat, using 13mm (½in) improved tacks and driving them in at a slight angle. Secure the scrim to the stuffing with twine and a double-pointed needle, forming a square of stitches right through the centre of the seat.

Using a regulator and a double-pointed needle and twine, strengthen the front edge of the seat by

working the stuffing forwards and making two rows of stitches to hold it securely in position. It is essential the stuffing and stitching are very firm and tight; bear in mind the stuffing will settle and the cover stretch with use.

Place a thin layer of horsehair or fibre over the scrim to cover the indentations made by the stitching; this should be only a skimming layer to even out the surface. Now cover the whole seat with flock, wadding or cotton linters and a layer of calico; turn up the edges of the calico and tack it to the outside face of the seat rails. If there is no front border, tack the calico under the front rail.

Inside back Treat the inside back in the same way as the seat; replace the stuffing pad and cover it with scrim tacked to the inside face of the frame. Secure the scrim with a square of running stitches right

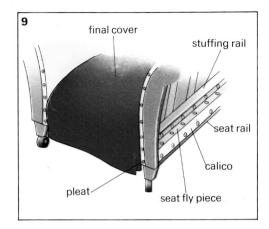

9 final cover
stuffing rail
seat rail
calico
pleat
seat fly piece

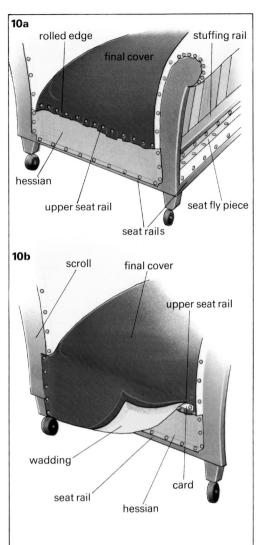

10a rolled edge
final cover
stuffing rail
hessian
upper seat rail
seat fly piece
seat rails

10b scroll
final cover
upper seat rail
wadding
seat rail
card
hessian

through the centre back of the chair. Cover the stitches with a skimming layer of stuffing to even out the surface then top with a layer of wadding, flock or cotton linters. Tack a piece of calico to the outside face of the rails round the top and sides; at the bottom pull the calico through the space between the stuffing rail and the seat frame and tack it to the outside face of the stuffing rail.

Inside arms Replace the stuffing pads on the arms, adding more fibre or hair to form the shape as before. Cover the arms with scrim, fixed with 13mm (½in) improved tacks to the inside face of the stuffing rails and to the outside face of the arm rails; tack the scrim onto the face of the scroll at the front, but leave it unattached at the back.

Using a regulator, work the stuffing forward to form an edge to the scroll at the front of the arms; secure the stuffing with a single line of stitches running across each arm from the scroll to the back. Continue by making rows of edge stitching to form the rolled edge of the scroll. Cover the stitches with a skimming layer of horse hair or fibre, placing a little extra over the edge of the scroll, and top with a layer of wadding or cotton linters to prevent the stuffing coming through.

Fix calico to the inside arms, pulling it through the space at the bottom and tacking it onto the outside face of the stuffing rails at the bottom, onto the outside face of the arm rails at the top and onto the face of the scrolls at the front; leave it unattached at the back.

Fixing final cover
This is where the notes and diagrams you made at the beginning of the job will prove invaluable; follow them closely to ensure you fix the final cover in exactly the right way.

When you look at the old cover you will find fly pieces, usually of strong canvas or hessian, attached at the points where the fabric will be pushed through the frame. These pieces will be invisible when the upholstery is completed and are more economical than using the final cover fabric.

Using the old cover as a pattern and being a little generous in measuring, cut the new cover to size. Make sure any pile on the fabric is running the smooth way down and centre any pattern. Also cut fly pieces to match those on the old cover and machine stitch them in position. When fixing the final cover, always temporarily tack it to the frame and drive the tacks home only when you are sure the fabric is straight and taut.

Inside back Place the cover, which should be large enough to cover the part of the back which will be visible when the chair is finished, on the inside back

9 When fixing the final seat cover on a chair without a front border, pull it down at the front, pleating the fabric at the corners; tack the fabric neatly to the underside of the frame

10a On a chair with a front border there will be two rails at the front of the seat. When replacing the hessian on the seat, also fix hessian to the front border; tack all the various seat layers to the upper seat rail

10b To cover the front border, back tack the fabric and a piece of card to the top edge of the front face of the upper rail, placing soft wadding between the fabric and the hessian; tack the bottom edge underneath the chair and the sides onto the face of the scroll or onto the outside arm frame in the same way as on the original cover

11 When fixing the final cover to each inside arm, take the top fly piece over the arm rail and tack it underneath; the back fly piece is pulled through the gap at the back, round the back frame and tacked to the inside face. Pull the bottom fly under the stuffing rail and tack it up onto the outside face. At the front pleat the fabric and tack it onto the face of the scroll

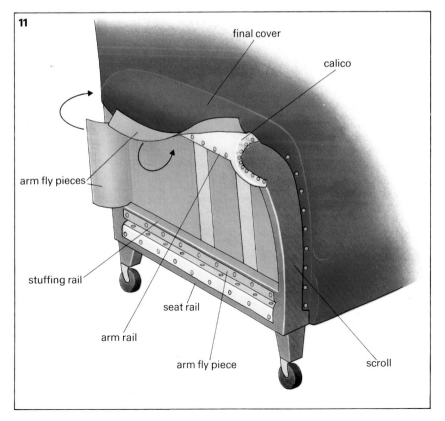

11 final cover
calico
arm fly pieces
stuffing rail
seat rail
arm rail
arm fly piece
scroll

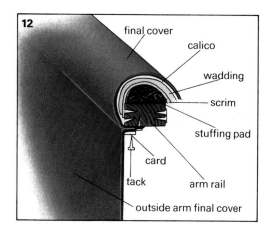

12
- final cover
- calico
- wadding
- scrim
- stuffing pad
- card
- tack
- arm rail
- outside arm final cover

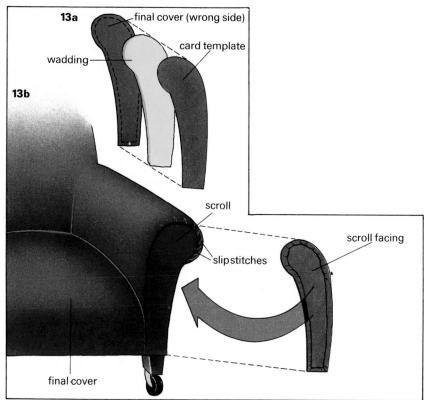

13a
- final cover (wrong side)
- card template
- wadding

13b
- scroll
- slipstitches
- scroll facing
- final cover

and tack the top to the outside face of the top rail. Pull the fly pieces round the sides and tack them onto the outside faces of the side rails; the lower fly pieces should be passed through the gaps between the back and arm frames and tacked as before. Pass the bottom fly under the stuffing rail at the back – not the seat rail – and tack it up onto the outside back.

Seat Place the cover on the seat, tuck the fly pieces under the stuffing rail at the arms and back and tack them onto the top face of the seat rails, then tack the front. If there is a front border, the seat front is tacked under the rolled edge of the seat stuffing; if not, pleat the cover on each front corner as described earlier in the book. Tighten the whole cover and tack the sides and back to the top face of the seat rail.

Inside arms In this case the back fly piece is pulled through the gap and round the side rail, then tacked to the inside face of the back frame; the bottom fly should be tacked up onto the outside face of the stuffing rail. The top fly is pulled over the top of the arm rail and tacked underneath. The front edge should be pleated and tacked onto the

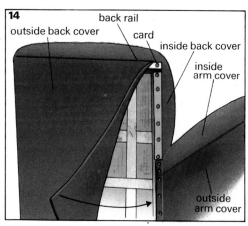

14
- back rail
- outside back cover
- card
- inside back cover
- inside arm cover
- outside arm cover

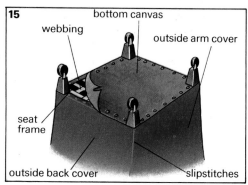

15
- bottom canvas
- webbing
- outside arm cover
- seat frame
- outside back cover
- slipstitches

front of the scroll in the same way as the original.

Outside arms When dealing with the outside arms, you can back tack the final cover in place using a piece of thin card to give a straight edge. Cut a narrow piece of card to the length of the arm and place it on the top edge of the wrong side of the arm cover. Tack both the card and the cover to the outer edge of the bottom face of the arm rail; pull the cover down and tack it underneath the chair to the bottom face of the seat rail. Tack the back edge of this cover to the outside face of the back frame and the front onto the face of the scroll, pleating it as necessary in the same way as with the inside arm. Repeat for the other arm.

Scrolls Make a paper pattern of the front scroll, transfer the outline onto thin card and cut two templates, one for each arm. Place a thin layer of wadding on one side of each piece of card and cover this with a piece of the top cover; cut the cover 25mm (1in) larger all round and with the pile or pattern running the same way as the seat and back. Turn the surplus material to the wrong side of the card pattern – slashing the fabric where necessary so it lies flat – and secure it to the card with a little adhesive. Place the patterns in position on the chair and slipstitch them to the front of the arms.

Outside back Treat the outside back cover in the same way as the outside arms. If the back rail is straight, back tack a card strip and the top edge of the cover to the outside face of the top rail, turn in the side edges and slipstitch them to the outside arm and inside back covers; tack the bottom under the chair. If the back rail is not straight, turn under all edges and slipstitch them in place; tack the bottom edge under the chair as before.   .

Bottom canvas Turn the chair upside down and place a piece of black canvas, cut 25–50mm (1–2in) larger all round, over the bottom of the frame. Turn under the allowance on all sides of the hessian and tack it securely in place with 9mm ($\frac{3}{8}$in) fine tacks, fitting it neatly round the legs.

12 To fix the final cover to the outside arm, back tack it with a piece of card to the underside of the arm rail; pull the cover down and tack it to the underside of the frame. If you wish, you can tack heavy hessian to the outside arm before you fix the final cover

13a To cover the face of each scroll, make a card template of the face and place wadding on top; cut a piece of fabric to shape and glue this with the wadding onto the card

13b Place the facing in position and slipstitch it to the front of the arm

14 If the back rail is straight, you can back tack the final cover in place; otherwise slipstitch it to the inside back and outside arm covers. As with the outside arm, you can tack hessian to the outside back frame before fixing the final cover

15 To finish off, turn the chair upside down and cover the underneath with a piece of black hessian; cut the corners to fit neatly round the legs and tack in place

Gathered

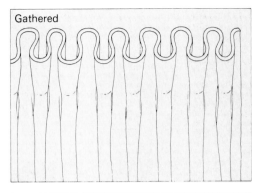

Pencil pleats

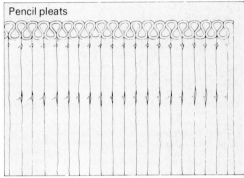

Pinch pleats

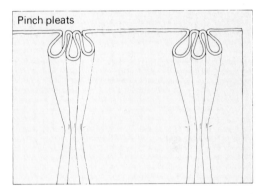

Cartridge pleats

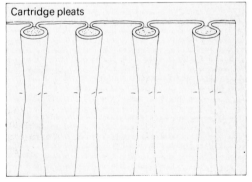

Smocked effect

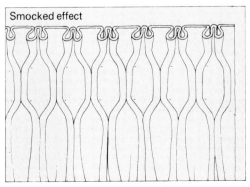

Choosing curtains

1 Cafe curtains have a pleasant country look and are ideal where you want to shut out an unattractive view without sacrificing too much light

2 Types of curtain heading

Curtains are one of the main design factors in any room and, if the windows are large, they can become its most important feature. To get precisely the effect you want, pay attention to the many details which make one pair of curtains look completely different from another. Make a list of these and go through each point, deciding what suits your taste and your window.

Types of heading
A curtain's heading is the way it is gathered before it is attached to the track and the type of heading you choose will dictate the amount of material you need for the curtain.

Gathered This type is the easiest to make and the cheapest since it requires just one and a half times the width of the track in material. Looking very much like the random gathering on a skirt waistband, it is suitable for curtains where the top

3 Make a window look larger by fitting the curtain track well beyond it on each side. This arrangement also allows the curtains to be pulled clear of the frame to let in the most light

4 Try not to conceal the shape of unusual windows. These curtains cannot be drawn; but because the room has a sunny aspect, simple tie-backs let in sufficient light

5 With a wide window you will have to accommodate quite a lot of material when the curtains are drawn back. The problem can be eased by using a lightweight material and lining it. The wall recess in this room also helped to house the curtains when drawn back, since the curtain rail was extended into it

will be hidden behind a pelmet or for simple, short, unlined curtains.

Pencil pleats Also very easy to do, this heading is more even and formal than the gathered type and needs two to three times the track width in material to look effective.

Pinch pleat A very formal triple pleat which alternates with flat sections of material. The finest pinch pleats are gathered and sewn by hand and take two to two and a half widths of the track.

Cartridge pleats This heading consists of single, cylindrical pleats often stuffed with cotton wadding or tissue paper so they keep their plump shape. Like pinch pleats, they alternate with flat sections of fabric and are still done by hand in curtain workshops, taking about double the track width.

Heading tape Although the best pinch and cartridge pleats are still hand-made, you can buy heading tape for all four types. One company now distributes a slightly different kind of heading tape which gives a smocking effect at the top of the curtain. This tape is sewn with four rows of stitching and requires about twice the width of the track in material.

In theory, all you have to do is sew these tapes to the top of the curtain and pull the cords to get the required heading; but in practice some headings are easier to handle than others. To get the best results, follow the manufacturer's instructions carefully and never skimp on material. It is much better to buy a generous quantity of cheap cotton which will always look luxurious because of its fullness, than to use too little of an expensive fabric which will look mean no matter what it costs.

If you are planning to use one of these tapes, ask your retailer for a cord tidy at the same time. When you pull your curtains up to the required width you will have a length of cord left over which you will need when you want to pull them flat for cleaning - this inexpensive accessory keeps this length of cord out of the way.

Deciding on length

Our grandmothers usually had heavy curtains which trailed on the floor to keep out draughts. Nowadays there are two main lengths: to the sill or to the floor – anything in between will give a very awkward 'half-mast' effect. If your curtains will hang to sill level only, keep them just above the sill or 50-75mm (2–3in) below. Floor length curtains should clear the floor by about 13mm (½in) to protect them from dust and dirt. If they are very long and heavy, allow 50mm (2in) clearance since they are bound to drop after a time.

Sill length curtains are best when there is a radiator under the window since long ones will prevent heat getting into the room. If you need light and privacy at the same time, choose cafe curtains which are usually hung to sill length from a pole fitted halfway down the window.

Whichever style you decide on, special weighted tape sewn into the hem will make your curtains hang more neatly.

Lining and interlining

Unless you particularly want the light to filter in through your curtains, it is almost always better to line them, usually with cotton sateen. Besides helping them to hang more attractively, lining protects curtains from dirt and from the sun which will fade and damage any fabric exposed to it over a long period of time. The lining fabric can be hung

6 For net curtains, cotton lace is a practical alternative to synthetic fabric

7 To cover the curtain track above this hall window, a pleated valance has been fitted instead of the more usual straight wood or buckram pelmet

8 separately from your curtains so you can take it down for washing, but you will find the curtains look better if the lining and fabric are treated as one.

To give the outside of your house a co-ordinated appearance use the same colour lining throughout. Cream or ecru is usually best unless most of your curtains are white or have a white background, in which case white lining would be more appropriate. There are several special linings on the market which add more to the effectiveness of your curtains than ordinary ones.

Lightproof Available only in cream, this lining costs more than the normal types but is very useful where you want to block out all the sun's rays, such as in a nursery where children could have difficulty sleeping while it is still light.

Milium This has a special aluminium backing which keeps out more light than ordinary sateen and helps to insulate your home against cold in winter and heat in summer. Although the side which faces the curtain fabric has a metallic look, the other side is quite plain and available in a wide range of colours.

Pyrovatex A flame-resistant material often used in public buildings and office blocks. It consists of plain sateen treated with a fireproof substance.

Interlining Interlined curtains, which are especially thick, soft and heavy, have an additional layer between the curtain fabric and the lining. Usually called bump, this is a thick cotton which has its surface brushed up to make it thicker and help it cling to the other two layers. Interlined curtains offer effective insulation and are particularly good in rooms which are subject to cold and daughts.

Pelmets and valances
A pelmet is a piece of buckram (coarse linen or cloth stiffened with gum or paste) or wood which you place over the top of the curtains to conceal the track and heading. If this covering is gathered or pleated, it is called a valance, while a single piece of draped fabric is called a swag. With the advent of plainer, good looking tracks, these are becoming less common; but if you find your track un-attractive, fix a pelmet or valance yourself or buy one ready made.

Curtain trimmings
The most common curtain decoration is a set of tie backs which give the window a formal look and hold the curtains back so as much light as possible is allowed in. If your window is very narrow, make a single curtain and hold it to one side with a tie.

Link your curtains to other design elements in the room by fixing a border decoration or band in fabric which has been used for upholstery, cushions or lampshades.

One particularly fancy curtain is called a festoon and is lifted up by cords running vertically at intervals across it, rather than pulled to each side. A very old fashioned style of curtain, these were often used in restaurants and public houses.

Choosing fabric
Before you buy your fabric measure carefully, calculating the width and length of material required from the track and not from the window itself. There is no such thing as an average window and you will not know what you need unless you take precise measurements.

If you want linen or cotton, always allow a bit extra for shrinkage since even the best quality, pre-

8 Exotically patterned curtains give a dramatic touch to a plain room
9 If you have a narrow window, hang a single curtain and tie it back to one side only

shrunk ranges will lose a little in the first few washes. Very thick brocades, velvets and wools are hard for the amateur to handle – if you want your curtains to look heavy, it will be cheaper and easier to interline them. Remember, too, that natural fibres are more prone to rot if they are exposed to direct sunlight.

Think about how you will need to care for your curtains. Kitchen windows might be near the cooker and likely to become dirty very quickly, so choose something light, washable and flameproof.

Pattern and colour will be your final problems. Large motifs and heavy fabrics are best left for long curtains. If the curtains play a very prominent part in the look of the room, you might be wise to play safe and choose a natural or plain coloured fabric which will blend in with many different furnishings styles. If you want to redesign the room later, you can do it without a huge cash outlay by changing smaller or less expensive items like pictures, lights, plants and cushions. Big bold patterns give a striking effect, but they will dominate the room, so keep the rest of it simple.

Net curtains

With cane, wood and pinoleum blinds becoming more popular, net curtains are not so widely used, although many people still prefer them. The most commonly available and least expensive fabrics for nets are synthetics like nylon, but these do tend to become grey in a very short time. If you chose this type, wash them before they look dirty – in warm rather than hot water. Treat white nets alone since the smallest amount of dirt or dye from other fabrics will show. If you never wring them out and always hang them up while they are still damp, net curtains will dry crease-free every time.

This curtaining is often sold so the width of the fabric covers the drop of the window and you buy whatever length you need for the width of your window. You will find a slot at the top for hanging and a hem at the bottom already sewn in.

Cotton lace is a good alternative to synthetic nets. Although it is slightly more expensive, it has a crisp, traditional look and is easier to keep looking fresh than the nylon variety. Wool or cotton fabrics are also sold for this purpose; they have a very open weave which lets you see out in the daytime, without allowing your neighbours to peer in.

10

11

10 If you have a slanted window, you can fix narrow tracks or poles at the top and bottom to keep your curtains in place
11 Make sure curtains hung over a working door do not restrict opening

213

Making curtains

There are several advantages in making curtains yourself: not only is it much cheaper than buying them ready-made, but it also allows you greater flexibility in design and choice of fabric – and you can be sure of getting them the right width and length for your windows rather than having to accept the sizes available in the shops. Of course you can have your own fabric made into curtains by a professional, but this is expensive and, since curtains are not at all difficult to make up, it pays to do it yourself.

Measuring for width

To calculate the width of your curtains, measure the curtain track, add any overlap and double this figure. This is only a general guide, however, since gathered or pleated curtains require varying amounts of material depending on the type of curtain tape you use.

Measuring for length

Using a steel measuring tape or rule, measure the distance from the top of the track to the bottom of the window sill or to the floor (since some sills and floors tend to slope, it is best to measure in several places to ensure the curtains will hang in line). To this measurement add 20cm (or 9in) to allow for hems top and bottom; if the curtains will have a stand-up heading, double its depth and add this to your measurement.

Divide the width of the finished curtain by the width of your chosen fabric to give the number of fabric widths and multiply the length of each curtain by the number of widths required.

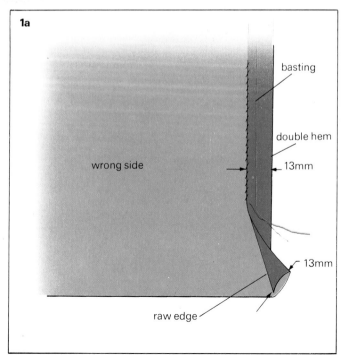

1a

basting

double hem

13mm

wrong side

13mm

raw edge

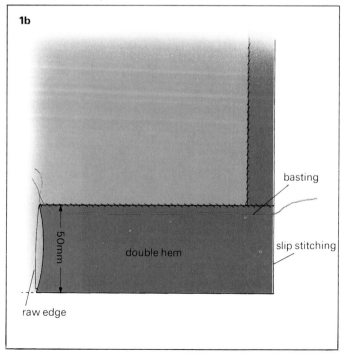

1b

basting

50mm

double hem

slip stitching

raw edge

Left If you want to hang this type of curtain, use a pinch pleat tape and a stand-up heading which will conceal the curtain track

1a Turn double hems down the sides of the curtain to the wrong side of the fabric

1b Make a double hem at the lower edge to enclose the side turnings

2 Position the tape flush with the top of the curtain, turn one end under and machine stitch round three sides; turn under the other end of the tape and stitch

3a For a stand-up heading, turn down its depth plus 13mm and baste 13mm from the raw edge

3b Place the top of the curtain tape on the basting line and stitch in place

3c Gather the curtain by drawing up the cords; knot the ends of the cord to secure the width

For example, suppose you require a finished length of 180cm (or 72in), add 20cm (or 9in) to this figure, giving a total length of 200cm (or 81in). If the track is 240cm (or 96in) wide, including overlap, double this figure to give the finished curtain width: $240 \times 2 = 480$cm (or $96 \times 2 = 192$in). Divide the finished width by the fabric width, for example 120cm (or 48in): $480 \div 120 = 4$ (or $192 \div 48 = 4$); this is the number of widths of fabric required. Multiply the required length by the number of widths: $200 \times 4 = 800$cm/8m (or $81 \times 4 = 324$in/9yd); this is the total length of fabric required.

Patterned material You will need to buy extra fabric in order to match the patterns at the seams on each curtain and to ensure the pattern falls in the same place on both curtains. Divide the length of the curtain by the depth of the pattern repeat and take the nearest whole number above. For example, if your curtains will be 180cm (or 72in) long and the pattern repeat is 25cm (or 10in) deep, you will need to buy a length of fabric with eight pattern repeats.

Unlined curtains

These are obviously the simplest and cheapest to make. If the fabric is not pre-shrunk, either wash it before you cut it to length or allow for a generous temporary hem so you can lengthen the curtains if necessary after the first wash.

Making up Make sure the fabric is square: at one end pull a thread at right-angles to the selvedge or margin of the fabric and cut along this line. Measure the required length, pull a thread at this point and cut along the line as before. If it is not possible to pull threads, fold the material back at right-angles to the selvedge at both ends and use the folds as your cutting lines. Cut the other lengths in the same way, matching the pattern if necessary.

Join the widths for each curtain by placing the right sides of the fabric together, selvedge to selvedge, and machine stitch, using a long stitch and a loose tension. Press the seams open and make several snips at intervals along the selvedge to relieve puckering.

Turn double hems along the sides of the curtain to prevent the edges curling: fold over the edge 13mm ($\frac{1}{2}$in) to the wrong side of the material and fold this over another 13mm ($\frac{1}{2}$in) so the raw edge is no longer visible. Pin and baste this into position, then stitch: you can use a machine but hand sewing the side hems does give a better finish. Press the seams and remove basting stitches.

Making the hem Measure the required finished length and mark this point with a row of pins. Turn up 50mm (2in) double hems and hand stitch; slip stitch the ends and press lightly.

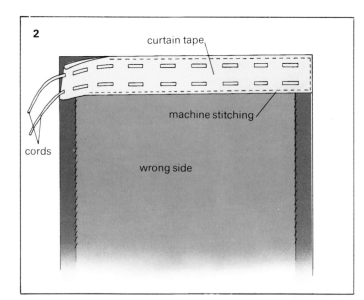

2

curtain tape

machine stitching

cords

wrong side

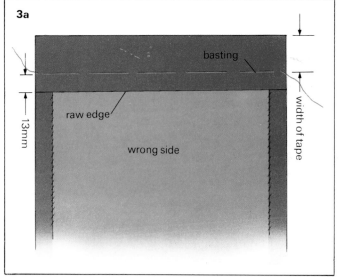

3a

basting

13mm

raw edge

width of tape

wrong side

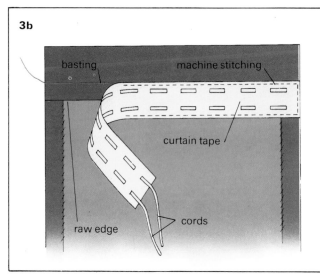

3b

basting

machine stitching

curtain tape

raw edge

cords

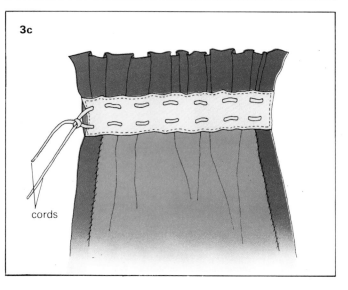

3c

cords

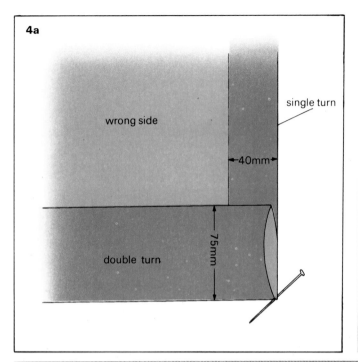

4a

wrong side

single turn

←40mm→

75mm

double turn

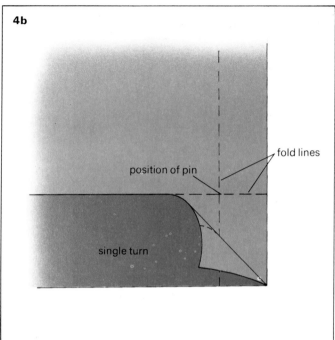

4b

position of pin

fold lines

single turn

Weighting the curtains To help the curtains to hang well insert a length of lead-weighted tape in the bottom hem before stitching down the ends.

Attaching curtain tape At the top of the curtain, turn down the raw edge 13mm (½in) to the wrong side of the fabric and baste. If the curtain will have a stand up heading, turn the top edge down to the depth of the heading, plus 13mm (½in). Baste 13mm (½in) in from the raw edge to act as a guide for positioning the tape. Cut a length of tape to the width of the curtain, plus 50mm (2in) for turnings. Pull out and knot the ends of the cords, then turn the tape under 25mm (1in) at one end, tucking in the knotted ends of the cords. Place the tape on the curtain so it covers the raw edges and baste and machine stitch along the top and bottom edges of the tape and the end you turned under. Pull out the cords at the other end and leave these free. Turn under the tape 25mm (1in) and stitch this to itself, lifting the cords out of the way; remove all basting stitches and press lightly.

Draw up the cord to the required width, adjust the gathers evenly and tie the ends of the cords to secure the width. Push the ends of the cords between the tape and the curtain and slip stitch this end of the tape to the curtain. When the curtain needs laundering you can easily release the gathers by unpicking the stitches and undoing the cords.

Finishing Arrange the curtains in even folds along their length and tie a remnant of fabric loosely round the bottom of the folds; leave the curtains for two to three days so they will hang evenly.

4a To mitre the lower corners of lined curtains, mark each corner with a pin
4b Open out the material and fold back one turn on the lower edge. **4c** Fold up the material diagonally. **4d** Turn in the side and bottom edges and stitch. **5** Place the lining on the curtain and sew the two together with locking stitches
Left Here pinch pleats are used to help full length curtains hang well; the curtains are made without a heading to expose the decorative brass pole

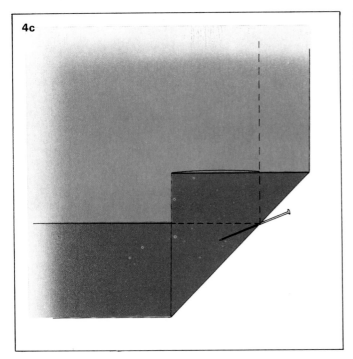

4c

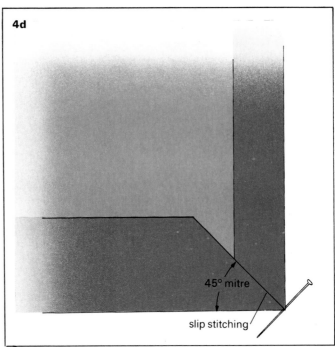

4d

45° mitre

slip stitching

Lined curtains

For the best results you should sew the lining to the fabric; although you can have separate lining, the curtains will not hang so well.

Lining attached Cut the required lengths for the curtains and the lining (the lining should be the same size as the curtains). On both fabrics, join widths and half widths in the same way as for unlined curtains and press seams flat. Press single 40mm (or 1½in) turnings down both sides of the curtain, then press a 75mm (3in) double hem at the bottom. To mitre the corners of the lower edges, mark each corner with a pin, open out the material and fold back one turn on the lower edge. Fold up the material diagonally, then turn in the side and bottom edges to form the mitre. Slip stitch the mitre seam, then stitch the side and bottom hems.

Along the bottom edge of the lining, machine a double hem at the same depth as that on the curtain. Place the lining on top of the curtain, wrong sides together, with the lower edge of the lining 25mm (1in) above the lower edge of the curtain. Pin the two together down the centre and turn back a third width of the lining. Now join the fabrics together with locking stitches, starting about 150mm (6in) from the bottom. Make the stitches about 100mm (4in) apart, keeping the thread fairly loose so as not to pucker the material. Make another row of stitches on the other half of the lining or, if the curtains are very wide, make several rows 450mm (18in) apart.

Smooth the lining flat and turn the side edges under to leave 25mm (1in) of curtain showing. Baste the side and bottom edges of the lining to the curtain and sew the top edges together with a diagonal stitch. Slip stitch the lining to the curtain down the sides and 25mm (1in) along the bottom edge near the corners so the lining hangs free at the lower edge. Attach tape as for unlined curtains.

Detachable lining Make up the curtains and the lining separately as for unlined curtains, but have the lining 25mm (1in) shorter and 50mm (2in) narrower than the curtain. Attach ordinary tape to the curtains, but use special lining tape for the lining. Bring them together with hooks through both tapes.

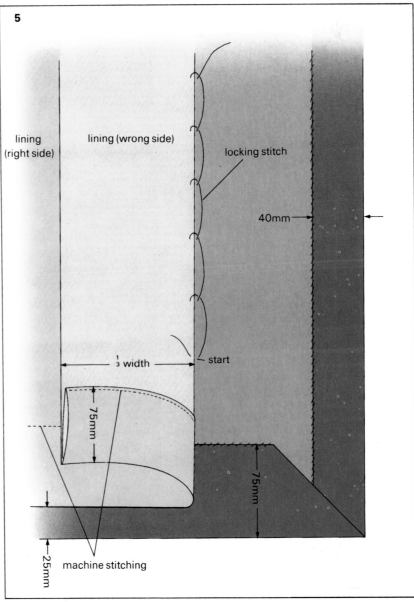

5

lining (right side)

lining (wrong side)

locking stitch

40mm

⅓ width

start

75mm

75mm

25mm

machine stitching

Curtain tracks

The extensive range of curtain tracks enables you to choose the type which best suits your room and the curtains you wish to hang. Make sure the track is strong enough to take the weight of the curtains; some plastic track will not be sufficiently sturdy to hold full length curtains, which may have to be hung on metal track. If the track will be visible when the curtains are hung, choose either a decorative track which blends with the room, or a plain, unobtrusive one which you can paint or leave white. Alternatively hide the rail by fitting a pelmet or valance in front of it.

Pelmet tracks

The traditional and still popular I-section track is not very attractive and therefore is mostly used with a pelmet or valance. It can be made from brass, aluminium, plastic or plastic-covered steel. Brackets, which clip into the top section of the track, hold the rail to the wall, window frame or ceiling. The curtain hooks are attached to double-wheel runners (on metal rails) or to nylon gliders (on plastic tracks). Strong enough to support heavy curtains. I-section rail is sufficiently flexible to be bent into fairly tight curves (useful for fitting square bay windows or for forming overlaps).

You can buy ready-made wood pelmets (finished in dark walnut, other timber or gilt) with the curtain track already fitted and corded on a track board; this is attached by metal clips to the front and side assembly.

Above right Flexible track is useful for taking curtains round corners as well as for fitting in bow and bay windows
Right I-section rail can be bent to enable curtains to overlap or to fit into tight corners
Inset Section of fixing bracket
Below You can conceal unattractive curtain track by fitting a valance rail
Below right You can buy ready-made pelmets which come fitted with curtain track and cording mechanism

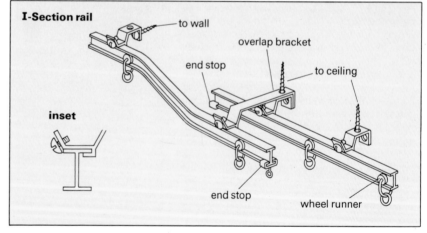

I-Section rail — to wall — overlap bracket — end stop — to ceiling — inset — end stop — wheel runner

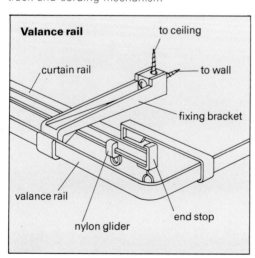

Valance rail — to ceiling — curtain rail — to wall — fixing bracket — valance rail — nylon glider — end stop

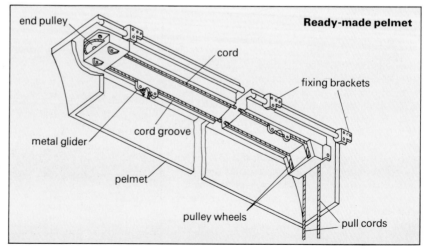

end pulley — cord — Ready-made pelmet — fixing brackets — metal glider — cord groove — pelmet — pulley wheels — pull cords

Non-pelmet tracks

Most modern tracks are designed for use without pelmets or valances. Some of these have the runners concealed in a box section or clipped over a flat rail. Box rails are normally flexible enough to be used in bay windows and recesses and can be bent to a radius as small as 50mm (2in). But if you have to bend the track as tight as this, check with your supplier that the track is suitable.

Tracks for use without pelmets are normally made from plastic or aluminium. Apart from a plain track, various finishes are available such as silver or gold coating, wood grain and carved wood. And you can buy ornamental finials (end pieces) which clip onto the track. You can also buy a fluted trim to clip over straight lengths of track to give the impression of a cornice pole.

Another type of non-pelmet track is the neat, inconspicuous U-shaped channel, in which gliders slide. Ideal in recessed windows, it blends well with the clean lines of modern decor. Made from plastic or coated aluminium, it can be mounted on the wall or ceiling but is only suitable for straight runs. It is often used with a second track for hanging nets behind heavier curtains.

Cording sets Available as optional extras with many tracks, these prevent wear and tear on the curtains caused by hand-pulling; even long curtains can be drawn with ease. Many cording sets have a device included in the kit to assist in the overlapping of curtains. You can fit any good corded curtain track with an electric curtain motor and connect it via a conveniently placed two-way control switch to a socket outlet or fused connection unit.

Curtain poles

For straight runs only, the old style curtain or cornice poles are again popular. The simplest design is a stout pole (of wood, plastic or metal with a brass finish) with plain or ornate turned ends mounted on matching brackets.

Many modern curtain poles are made in the same styles as the old brass ones, but with easy-running false rings which slide in channels hidden behind the poles. Some poles are telescopic, fitting a range of widths, and they are often supplied with integral cording sets.

Hanging nets

Net or café-style half-pane curtains are usually hung on plastic-covered wires pushed through the top hem of the curtains. You can adjust the gathers as required, but it is almost impossible to open the

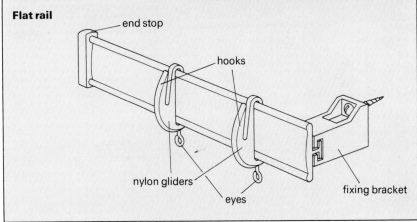

Flat rail

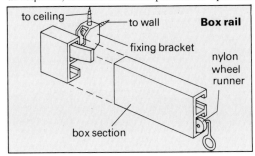

Box rail

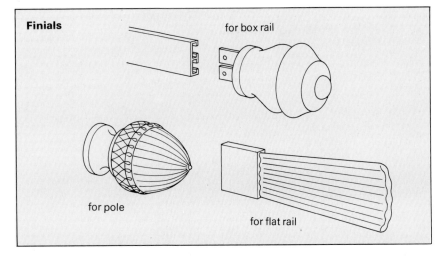

Finials

Above Box rail, designed for use without a pelmet or valance
Top right Aluminium cornice pole giving a traditional brass appearance
Centre right Simple flat rail
Right Types of finial

219

curtains completely; so this method of hanging is really only suitable for curtains which will be left undisturbed.

The neat and simple way of fixing plastic-covered curtain wire is by using rings and hooks. The ring screws into the end of the wire and the hook is screwed into the window frame. This can be done by hand, but if the wood is too hard or you want to put the fixing into the wall (if the window frames are metal) you can use a small round head screw instead. With wall fixing you will have to drill a hole and plug it before inserting the screw. Make sure you leave a 6mm (¼in) clearance between the screw head and the wall to allow for the ring to be hooked over the screw. Trim the curtain wire with pliers so it is slightly shorter than the width required. This ensures the wire is really tight when hung and

the curtain does not sag. Screw the rings into each end of the wire, thread the wire through the top hem of the curtain and stretch the wire across the window, hanging it over the hooks or screws already fixed at each end.

The curtain wire does tend to sag, so hang only lightweight curtains. (If you are hanging floor-to-ceiling nets, use the neat U-channel track.)

An alternative method of hanging fixed net curtains is to use lightweight curtain rods (wood dowels are ideal) although you will not be able to open the curtains completely. The rods are fixed near the top of the window frame using curtain rod brackets; the cranked version is screwed to the window frame and the straight version is fixed to each side of the window recess (useful for metal window frames).

Below left Box rail with fluted trim
Centre left U-shaped rail
Bottom left Double U-shaped rail for hanging two sets of curtains
Below centre Simple wood cornice poles are fairly inexpensive and make a plain window more interesting
Below Plain white track is unobtrusive enough to blend with any style of decoration
Bottom Cording sets make drawing curtains easier; most corded curtain tracks can be fitted with a motor

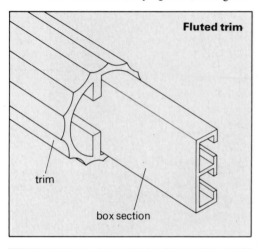

Fluted trim
trim
box section

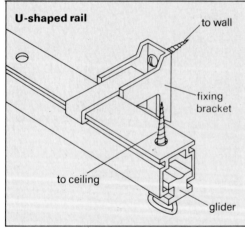

U-shaped rail
to wall
fixing bracket
to ceiling
glider

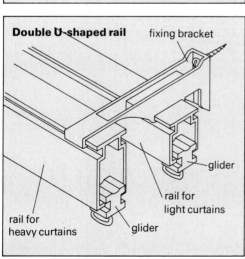

Double U-shaped rail
fixing bracket
glider
rail for light curtains
rail for heavy curtains
glider

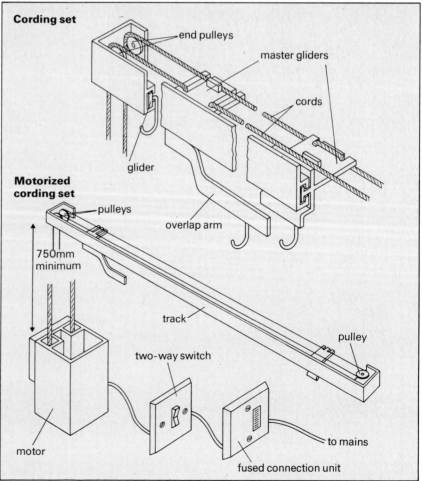

Cording set
end pulleys
master gliders
cords
glider
overlap arm

Motorized cording set
pulleys
750mm minimum
track
two-way switch
pulley
motor
fused connection unit
to mains

Below Some cornice poles are pre-corded and will extend to fit a range of window widths
Below centre Traditional curtain pole
Bottom Curtain pole with false rings
Below right Plastic wire for hanging net curtains
Bottom right You can use lightweight curtain rod instead of wire to hang nets; in this case you will need either cranked brackets for frame fitting or straight ones for recess fitting

Fixing curtain tracks

Unless you are fitting the track in the recess above a window, or you want wall-to-wall curtains, the track should extend either side of the window so the open curtains will hang neatly to the side without cutting out any light. If, however, you have a wide window which you would like to look narrower, you can fit the track just to the end of the window so when the curtains are drawn back they cover the frame and part of the window itself.

The easiest way to put up a track is to screw the fixing brackets to the top of the window frame. Fixing instructions are usually supplied with new track. Always fit the number of brackets recommended by the manufacturer for the length of track used and make sure there is a bracket close to each end to support the weight of the curtains when drawn back. For sill length curtains fit the brackets at equal heights from the sill (or from the floor for floor length curtains) to ensure the bottom hems of the curtains hang in line with the sill (or floor).

Fix the end brackets at each side of the window, then stretch taught a length of string between them and use this to align the other brackets, spacing them at equal intervals. If you have to fix the brackets directly to the wall, make the fixing holes with a masonry drill bit, which has a specially hardened tip for drilling walls. The masonry bit can be used with a hand wheel brace, but it is much easier to use an electric drill set at slow speed.

You can make the holes with a cheap, easy-to-use tool called a jumping bit, which you tap into the wall with a hammer and twist occasionally to clear the dust from the hole.

Many houses have concrete lintels above the windows and you may find it difficult to make the Even with a hammer drill the going can be slow. To reduce the number of fixings in the lintel you can screw the appropriate length of 12mm ($\frac{1}{2}$in) thick timber above the window and fix the track brackets to this. Alternatively, fit a long curtain pole which will extend far enough on each side of the window to avoid the lintel.

When you have made your holes in the wall above the window, it is vital the fixing is secure since the weight of the curtains will otherwise quickly loosen it. A guide to the right fixings to use will be found on pages 12–15. Having inserted a suitable fixing device, secure the brackets with screws.

Curtain pole

ring

fixing bracket

pole

finial

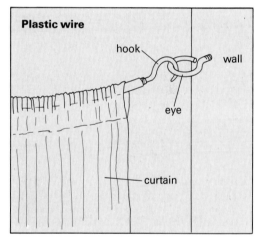

Plastic wire

hook

wall

eye

curtain

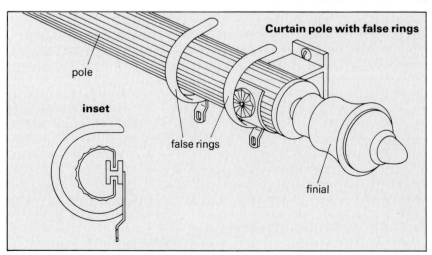

Curtain pole with false rings

pole

inset

false rings

finial

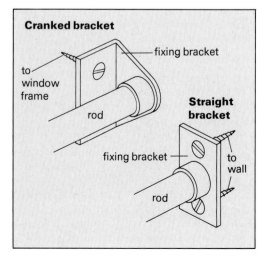

Cranked bracket

fixing bracket

to window frame

rod

Straight bracket

fixing bracket

to wall

rod

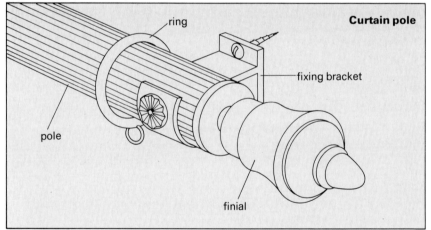

Putting up shelves

Shelves can solve many storage problems in any room in the house and enable you to make use of odd corners and unused space in cupboards and alcoves. Very few tools are needed and the materials are widely available. The methods described here are for permanently fixed shelves, using battens, brackets or angled metal strips.

Shelf loads

The load a shelf can safely carry depends on the thickness of the shelf material, the strength of the supports and the distance between them. If you overload a shelf, it will begin to sag and may eventually loosen the supports. When planning your shelving, take into account the size and weight of the items you want to store and overestimate your needs to allow for future acquisitions. The chart below gives a guide to the maximum span for different shelf materials for medium to heavy loads. If you want to exceed the span given, use intermediate supports. Extra support can be given in a recess by fixing a batten to the back wall.

Recommended maximum distance between supports

Material	Thickness	Maximum span
Blockboard	12mm ($\frac{1}{2}$in)	450mm (1ft 6in)
Chipboard	12mm ($\frac{1}{2}$in)	400mm (1ft 4in)
	18mm ($\frac{3}{4}$in)	600mm (2ft)
	25mm (1in)	750mm (2ft 6in)
Plywood	18mm ($\frac{3}{4}$in)	800mm (2ft 8in)
	25mm (1in)	1000mm (3ft 3in)
Timber	16mm ($\frac{5}{8}$in)	500mm (1ft 8in)
	22mm ($\frac{7}{8}$in)	900mm (3ft)
	28mm ($1\frac{1}{8}$in)	1050mm (3ft 6in)

Shelf material

Natural timber (hardwood or softwood) makes attractive shelves, but you may find the cost prohibitive if you want several shelves. Man-made boards in chipboard, blockboard and plywood are available in a wide range of standard shelf sizes, some of which are wider than the wood normally stocked by timber yards.

Chipboard is popular for shelving since it is light in weight and is available veneered in a wood grain finish or melamine-faced: this is much stronger than unfaced chipboard, which tends to sag under heavy weights.

Shelf supports

Your choice of shelf supports may depend on where you wish to put the shelves. Timber battens and angled metal strips can be used only in recesses since they are fixed to side walls. Metal and timber angle brackets can be used in a recess or on an open wall.

Fixing shelves

The methods of fixing the different types of support vary slightly, but the general principles are the same.

Remember to check, when deciding where to place the shelves, that you will not be drilling into electric cables or water pipes. Cables to socket outlets normally run up from the floor, while those for light switches normally run down from the ceiling; but to be safe, don't drill holes in the wall either vertically above or below these fittings.

Plan the position of the shelves, taking into account the height of objects to be stored and allowing a little extra space above. Also check you will be able to reach the top shelf easily. Lightly mark with a pencil the position of each shelf on the wall. When fixing the shelves in position, use these

1 Timber battens used as shelf supports in recess
2 Angled metal strips used to support shelf in recess

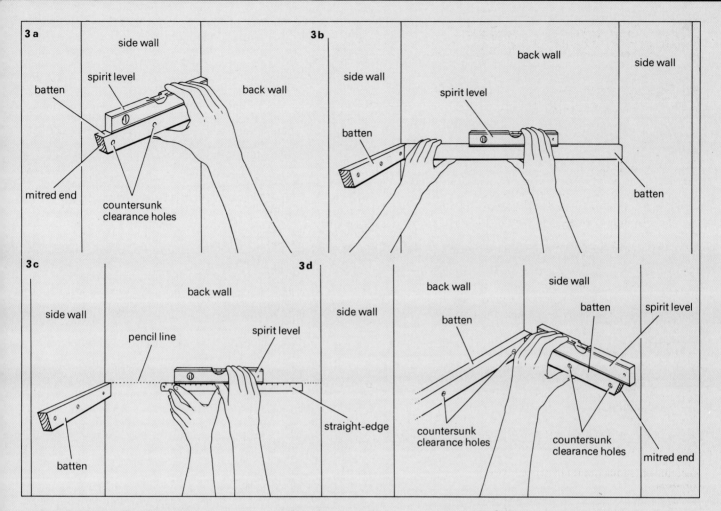

3a batten / spirit level / side wall / back wall / mitred end / countersunk clearance holes

3b side wall / back wall / spirit level / batten / side wall / batten

3c side wall / back wall / pencil line / spirit level / straight-edge / batten

3d back wall / side wall / batten / spirit level / batten / countersunk clearance holes / countersunk clearance holes / mitred end

marks only as a preliminary guide; always check with a spirit level to ensure they are truly horizontal.

Using battens

This traditional system is probably the simplest of all. A timber batten is screwed to each side wall of a recess and the shelf is laid across. For extra support across a long span, fix a batten to the back wall too.

To make the battens you can use softwood or offcuts of the shelf material, such as chipboard. For a lightweight shelf intended to display a few ornaments, you could use $25 \times 12mm$ ($1 \times \frac{1}{2}in$) battens. For large books or heavy kitchen utensils, use $50 \times 25mm$ ($2 \times 1in$) battens. For medium loads, use timber between these two sizes.

Screws Use 50mm (2in) No 6 screws for a lightweight job, 63mm ($2\frac{1}{2}in$) No 8 screws for medium weight shelves and 75mm (3in) No 10 for a sturdy assembly.

Fixing method Cut out both side wall support battens a little shorter than the width of the shelf. Drill a countersunk clearance hole 25–50mm (1–2in) from each end of the batten, depending on the length of the batten and mitre or bevel the front edges of the battens so they will be less noticeable.

If using a back batten, cut it to the width of the recess minus the thickness of one of the side battens; cut the thickness of the back batten off the straight end of the other side batten. Drill holes at not more than 300mm (or 12in) intervals.

Position the first side wall batten at the required height. Rest a spirit level on top to check the batten is horizontal and mark with a bradawl or nail the positions of the holes onto the wall. Remove the batten and drill the holes in the wall to the required

depth. Insert wallplugs or cavity wall fixings, depending on the type of wall involved. Place the batten in position again and partly drive in the fixing screws. Check the horizontal again with the spirit level before finally driving the screws home.

If you are using a back batten, line it up so its top edge is level with the top of the side wall batten already fixed. Place the spirit level on top to check the batten is horizontal. Get someone to hold it in place while you mark the screw positions on the wall as before. Drill the holes, insert plugs (or other wall fixings) and drive in the screws, checking again the batten is horizontal.

If a back batten is not being fixed, use a straight-edge and pencil a line across the back wall level with the top edge of the side batten; use a spirit level to check the straight-edge is horizontal. Line up the second side wall batten with the pencil mark, checking the horizontal with the spirit level. Fix the second side wall batten in the same way as the first, making sure its top edge is aligned with the back batten or pencil line.

Position a squarely cut scrap piece of shelving on the battens in both corners of the recess to check the side walls are square. If there is a gap between the end of the shelving and the side walls, you will have to cut the shelf to fit. The back of the shelf may also need shaping and this must be done first. Pin a length of card or stiff paper onto the back wall batten so it fits exactly into each corner. Using a small block of wood and a pencil trace the outline of the back wall onto the template. Cut along this line carefully, tape the template onto your piece of shelving and transfer the outline. Then use two smaller pieces of card and mark on them the out-

3a To fit battens in recess, position first side batten and check horizontal with spirit level. **3b** Position back batten flush with side batten. **3c** If you are not using back batten, place straight-edge level with top of first side batten and mark across back of alcove to other wall; this will give position for second side batten. **3d** Fit second side batten flush with top edge of back batten.

4a Position card on back batten and use block and pencil to trace outline of back wall onto card; transfer outline onto shelving. **4b** Following same procedure, make templates for side walls. **4c** Measure diagonally from each corner to proposed front edge of shelf on opposite side wall; use string cut to length of diagonals. **4d** Tape string in position on shelving and place side templates on back template; angle of template is found when front corner coincides with diagonal from opposite corner. **4e** Transfer side wall outline onto shelving to give shelf shape

223

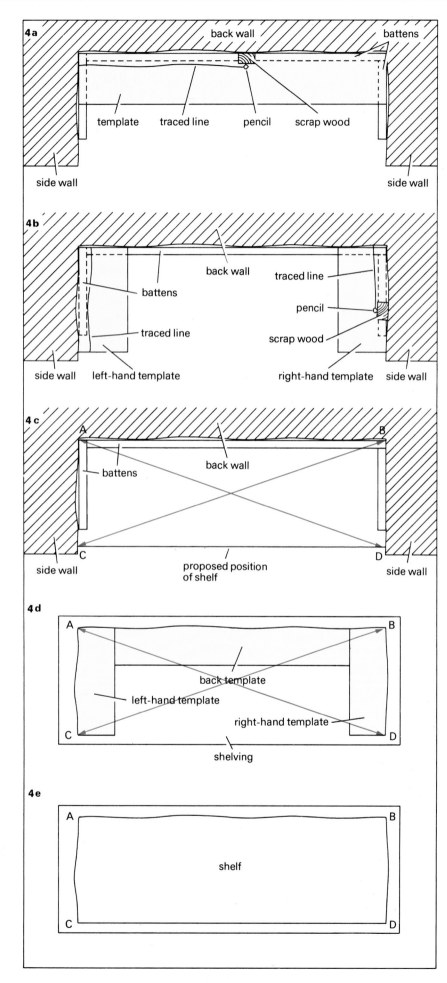

line of each side wall in turn, following the same procedure. Measure from each corner diagonally across to the proposed front edge of the shelf on the opposite side wall, making a small allowance for the trimmed back edge of the shelf before determining the width of the shelf.

Position each side wall template carefully in turn on your piece of shelving. Starting with the left-hand side wall, place the back left-hand corner of the template to coincide with the left-hand end of the already marked shelf. The angle of the template will be determined when the front left-hand corner of the template coincides with the length of the diagonal from the opposite corner.

Tape the template onto the shelf in this position and transfer the side wall outline onto the shelf. Working from the opposite end, repeat this procedure for the right-hand side wall. This will give you the correct outline for your shelf, which can then be cut to shape. Place the shelf on the battens; it can be loose-laid, screwed or glued and pinned in position.

Using angled metal strips
These serve the same purpose as battens, supporting the shelves against the side walls of an alcove. Screw holes are often provided, so you just need to mark the position of the screws on the wall with a pencil. Place a spirit level on the horizontal part of the strip to check the strip is level. Screw in place as for battens, using a screw size to match the pre-drilled holes and ensuring at least 38mm (1½in) of the screw will be in the wall.

If you wish, you can make a recess in the edge of the shelf so the top of the metal strip will be invisible when the shelf is in position. Place a bracket on the shelf side edge and draw round it with a pencil to mark the cutting lines. Chisel out to the required depth with a paring chisel, grooving plane or electric router. Stop the recess just before the front edge of the shelf, so the bracket will be concealed. Recess the other end of the shelf in the same way, fit the angled strips to the side walls of the alcove and slide the shelf on to them.

Using L-shaped metal angle brackets
These can be bought in various sizes; the arm of the bracket should extend almost to the front edge of the shelf to give full support. Some brackets have one arm longer than the other, in which case you must fix the longer arms to the wall.

To fix the brackets, place a straight-edge in the required position, check with a spirit level and draw a line along the lower edge where you want the shelf to be. Measure and mark off the intervals at which you want to place the brackets, putting the end ones a short distance in from the ends of the shelf.

Fix the two end brackets in place first. Hold the first bracket in place on the wall, checking the horizontal and vertical with a spirit level, and mark the screw positions with a pencil. Screw in place as for battens, using screws to match the pre-drilled holes. Before fixing the second bracket, hold it in position and check it is level with the first by placing a straight-edge on top of the two brackets and putting a spirit level on it. Do the same with intermediate brackets.

When all the brackets are in place, lay the shelf in position and mark the screw positions through the holes in the brackets onto the underside of the shelf. Drill pilot holes to take the screws, replace the shelf on the brackets and screw it in place.

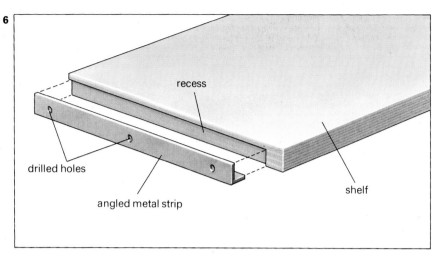

recess

drilled holes

angled metal strip

shelf

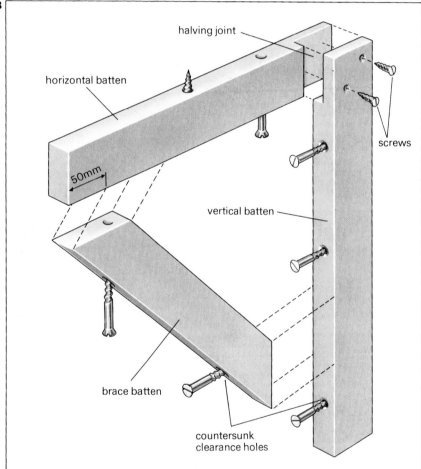

halving joint

horizontal batten

50mm

screws

vertical batten

brace batten

countersunk
clearance holes

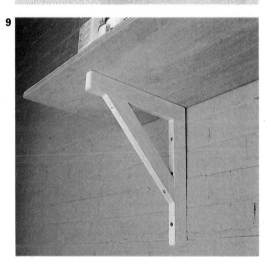

Using timber angle brackets

Strong, home-made brackets are ideal for a garage or workshop where strength is more important than appearance. The brackets are made by fixing two pieces of wood at right-angles and inserting a brace between them to form a triangle.

Use $25 \times 12mm$ ($1 \times \frac{1}{2}in$) softwood for medium loads and $50 \times 25mm$ ($2 \times 1in$) for heavier loads. Cut one length a little shorter than the width of the shelf and another length about 50mm (2in) longer than the first; this will be fixed vertically to the wall. Fit the lengths together at right-angles using a halving joint and glue; screw through the joint. Position another length of wood across the right-angled piece so it forms a triangle, placing it about 50mm (2in) from the end of the horizontal. Mark

where the third piece of wood meets the inside edges of the other two sides of the triangle; mark the two sides and join up these marks across the top and bottom to give you your cutting lines. Cut the brace timber to the exact length, checking the brace fits exactly when you place it inside the right-angle.

Drill three countersunk clearance holes in the vertical batten and two in the horizontal batten; the size of the holes should correspond to the recommended screw sizes. Screw the bracket to the wall and fit the shelf in place, drilling pilot holes for the shelf fixing screws. Finally glue and screw the angled piece in position with countersunk screws.

5 L-shaped metal angle bracket used to support shelf in recess
6 With angled metal strip, you can recess edge of shelf so strip will be invisible when shelf is in position
7 Decorative L-shaped metal angle brackets are available
8 Timber angle bracket; vertical batten should be longer than horizontal one
9 Timber angle bracket on open wall; ideal where strength is more important than appearance

Adjustable shelving systems

You have probably found however much storage space you have, you always fill it. One way to keep up with growing plants, varying book heights, additional equipment and children's changing interests is to install adjustable shelving; this is easy to put up and can just as easily be taken down if you move house. The shelves may be fitted onto brackets which slot into strips or uprights screwed to the wall, so you can move them about and fit additional or wider shelves; alternatively there are free-standing units with adjustable shelves.

Before buying a shelving system decide where you want to put it, what items you need to store and how much flexibility you want; for example, some systems have a variety of special-purpose brackets so you can use a shelf as a desk or work top. Check the length of the brackets available, since some manufacturers do not make brackets for very wide shelves. Some systems have matching shelves you can buy or you can use shelves of your choice.

Wall shelving

Adjustable shelving systems are available in a variety of materials and finishes so you should be able to find one which will fit in with its surroundings. Hardened aluminium is commonly used for uprights and brackets and often for shelves as well; systems manufactured from this material are available in a silver satin finish or a matt anodized finish in gold, silver or black. Units are also made in painted steel. One system, which can be used for commercial or domestic purposes, has matching steel shelves but can also be used with wood or glass shelves. For a living room you may want a wood unit and you can buy teak uprights and brackets with matching teak finished shelves.

Uprights There are two main types of metal upright: those with slots into which the brackets are fitted and those with a continuous channel into which the shelves are slid and clicked or locked into place at the required position. Brackets of the slotted type can be moved at 25mm (1in) intervals; the sliding type is easier to adjust, but more care is needed in lining up the brackets to ensure the shelves are straight. It is easier to fix the sliding-type uprights to the wall since there are no slots to be lined up; with the slotted type you need to line up the slots exactly or the shelves will not be level. Wood uprights have threaded holes into which the brackets are screwed.

Some shelving systems have uprights which will hold hardboard panels, hessian or cork-covered boards or mirrors. For walls which are uneven, there are uprights which hold 3mm (or ⅛in) hardboard panels at a slight distance from the wall.

Uprights are available in two or more lengths, the exact dimensions varying with the make of the system; some are in Imperial and some in metric

measure, but most manufacturers supply supports in the region of 500 and 1000mm (or 20 and 39in). You can butt two lengths together or cut them if necessary for in-between sizes.

Wiring and lighting One system has built-in facilities for an adjustable spotlight, which can be fitted at any height on the upright. Cables for lights or hi-fi equipment can be run inside the uprights and hidden with a cover strip. A switch is available which can be fitted on an upright for connection to a lamp or other appliance.

Brackets These come in 150–600mm (or 6–24in) sizes to fit standard shelf widths, although not all manufacturers make the larger sizes. You should allow for the shelf to overlap the bracket slightly unless the bracket has a lipped edge, in which case it should fit exactly. Wood brackets have rubber grip pads to hold the shelving, while the other type are screw-fixed or have a hooked edge which fits into a groove in the shelf or a lipped end which holds the edge of the shelf. Some systems have special brackets to hold glass shelves.

Some manufacturers make brackets for taking coat hangers for use in a cupboard or alcove wardrobe. To house items which might roll off a

1 Types of upright used in adjustable shelving systems: (**from left**) wood with bookend and screw-in bracket, matt silver and matt black continuous metal channel

2 These brackets, for use with continuous metal channel uprights, come in a range of finishes

3

4

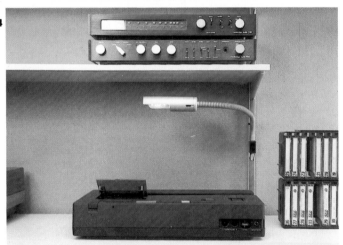

5

6

7

8

9

10

3 Metal shelving system used for simple dining room display
4 Metal shelving system used to house hi-fi equipment
5 Metal shelving system used as work area
6 Metal shelving system used for storage in bathroom
7 Metal shelving system used to take range of kitchen items
8 Free-standing metal shelving system used for central display
9 Metal shelving system with cork panels used for general storage in living room
10 Teak shelving system offering natural finish

straight slope, you can use a shelf supported by brackets which slope slightly towards the wall. This type of bracket is also useful for a worktop shelf since it will not tilt downwards when pressure is put on the front edge of the shelf. Brackets which slope away from the wall can be used for shelves on which magazines can be displayed or used to hold a child's desk or a drawing board; you will, however, need to add raised lipping to the shelf to stop items sliding off and to provide a ledge for pens and pencils. Brackets for fixing pelmets and canopies are also available; these are particularly useful if you want to install concealed strip lighting.

End-pieces For a shelf on an open wall you can fit an end-piece to hold books in place. One system has an end-piece which screws into the shelf to serve as a bracket as well. Some systems include metal shelves and trays with end supports; although intended mainly for commercial use, these could be useful in a kitchen or workshop.

Loads The load a shelf can take depends on the strength of the support and the distance between the supports. Most systems allow for normal domestic loads, but it is advisable to follow the manufacturer's recommendations.

Fixing wall shelving

When fixing the uprights make sure they are vertical and parallel to each other and with slotted supports ensure the slots are correctly lined up; check with a straight-edge and a spirit level. Follow the manufacturer's instructions for spacing between supports, which will be dictated by the load the shelves will carry, and check whether you need to buy

screws; some manufacturers supply screws while others just specify the size of screw required.

Draw a pencil line where the top fixing hole of each upright is to be placed, using a straight-edge and a spirit level to make sure it is horizontal. Make a cross on the line where the top screw of each support is to be placed, making sure the supports are the required distance apart. At each marked point drill a hole of the correct diameter for the wall fixings you are using and insert the fixings. Fix each support at the top with a screw, leaving the screw slightly slack at this stage. Use a plumb line to check the first upright is vertical and mark the positions of the remaining screws. Swivel the support aside while you drill and plug the fixing holes; fix the bottom screw, followed by the intermediate ones, and finally tighten the top screw. Fix the remaining uprights in the same way, checking they are parallel to each other by using a batten cut to the exact distance between the supports.

Place the brackets in position according to the manufacturer's instructions, checking they are level by using a straight-edge and a spirit level. Place the shelves in position and screw them in place or cut grooves as required.

Free-standing shelving

This type of unit provides a storage system which does not need to be fixed to the wall and can be used, if you wish, as a room divider. There is a variety of makes available and you should follow the manufacturer's instructions for assembly. One

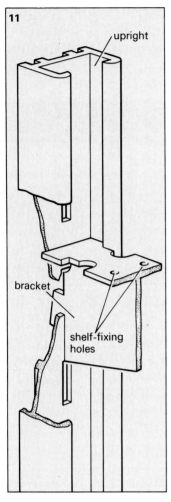

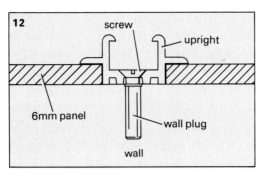

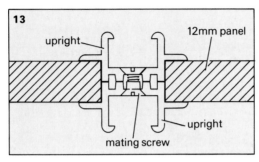

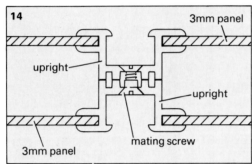

type, which is made of plastic-coated steel, is strong and durable and would be useful in a kitchen or workshop. It has angled uprights from 914 to 2440mm (3–8ft) high and shelves of 864 × 229–610mm (34 × 9–24in). The shelves are adjustable to 50mm (2in) intervals, but changing their position is not as easy as with other systems because the shelves are bolted in place. To assemble the unit, lay two of the angled uprights flat on the ground and loosely bolt the shelves vertically in the required positions. Place the remaining two uprights along the front of the shelves and bolt them loosely in place. Then stand the unit upright, check it is square and tighten all the nuts and bolts.

Stud supports An inexpensive method of providing support for shelves in a free-standing adjustable unit is to use studs screwed into bushes. To take the shelf bush, drill a 10mm (or $\frac{3}{8}$in) diameter hole in the upright to a depth of 10mm (or $\frac{3}{8}$in). Press a bush into the hole and insert the shelf stud; the stud clips into the bush for fast holding. Fit two parallel rows of bushes on the uprights at each side and place studs into the required bushes.

11 Section through continuous metal channel upright. **12** Plan of continuous metal channel with panels, fixed to wall. **13** Plan of free-standing metal channel – with panels – joined with mating screw. **14** Plan of free-standing metal channel with panels, used as room divider. **15** Section through slotted metal upright. **16** Section through T-slotted metal upright. **17** Section through continuous metal channel with squeeze and slide bracket. **18** Section through wood upright and screw-in bracket. **19** Wood upright with bookend

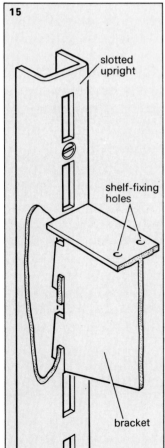

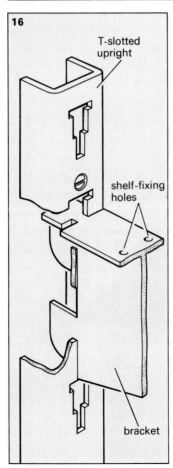

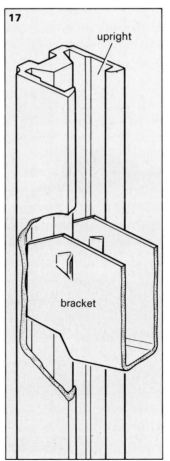

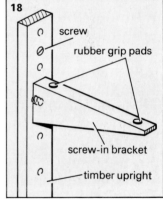

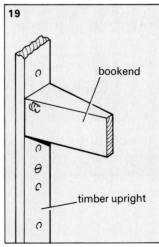

3

ELECTRICITY

ABC of electricity

Electricity is the source of energy for heating, lighting and powering many appliances in your home. In knowing all about it, you can tackle all sorts of repairing and fitting jobs safely.

Rather like the water supply, electricity comes into most homes from some unknown outside source: but how does it arrive and what is it? Pushing down a switch gives immediate light and power to drive fans, cleaners and kitchen equipment; it also provides gradually increasing heat in kettles, cookers, fires, immersion heaters and central heating. But beyond this point electricity is to most people a mystery, and to many something to be feared. Some people even think that electricity leaks out of every power socket without a plug in it, or lamp-holder that does not have a bulb in it. An understanding of the simple principles of how electricity works can help to remove the fear.

Although it may help you to understand electricity by comparing it with the water supply, it is important to remember that this is only an analogy; the electricity supply is in some ways similar to the water supply, but it is quite wrong to suppose it will continue to behave like water in every respect. Electricity will only flow in a conductor; you can compare this to water flowing in a pipe. But while water will keep flowing out of a broken pipe, electricity will not continue flowing out of a broken wire unless there is some other conductor – a screwdriver, a hacksaw blade, some other metal or wet material – to conduct it away. The reason is that electricity does not really 'flow', it is much more like the hydraulic fluid that operates the brakes of a car or the big jacks used in constructional engineering.

Hydraulic fluid transmits pressure along a pipe from one place to another (**see 1**); and if the pipe is cracked, or there is not enough fluid, the system will not work. In the same way, electricity supplied to the home at a certain 'pressure' is used to do the work of driving motors, or making heat and light.

The earth will conduct electricity very easily. The human body will not conduct it so easily, but easily enough. If you touch the bare end of a 'live' wire, or the contacts in a lamp-holder when the switch is on, the electricity will be conducted through your body to the earth. If you are lucky, the electricity will make your arm muscles jerk away as soon as you touch the wire, and you will only suffer an electric 'shock'. If you are unlucky, the electricity will make your finger muscles clamp onto the wire so that you cannot let go. You may die by electrocution or at the least be badly burned and anyone who tries to help you by touching you will suffer the same. In this situation the helper must switch off the electricity or, failing this, try sharply jerking the afflicted person away with a rope, tea towel or scarf, or anything non-conducting (that is, not metal or a wet material) like a broom.

DC or AC

Electricity can be supplied in two ways in domestic circumstances: as direct current (DC) or as alternating current (AC). All batteries – the lead battery

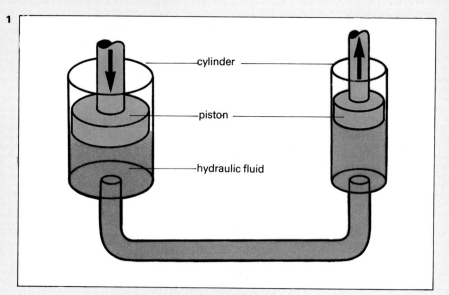

1

of a car, the 'dry cell' of an electric torch or transistor radio, or the rechargeable battery of certain pieces of portable electronic equipment – supply DC. So do many private domestic generators, such as used to be installed in houses and farms far away from public supplies. The national electricity grid now provides AC supply to all but the most remote areas of Great Britain. Light bulbs and simple heaters will work equally well on DC or AC supply, but most modern electrical equipment is made to operate on AC only, and needs special modification for DC supply.

Voltage This term denotes the pressure exerted by the electricity supply. So a torch battery, at 1.5 volts, will give you no more than a tiny tingle if you put your wet tongue across the contacts; but don't try the same thing with your home supply at 240 volts!

It is easy to understand how the electricity from a DC source such as a battery can be imagined as exerting this pressure; but what about AC? In an AC supply the 'direction of flow' of electricity changes backwards and forwards, usually 50 times every second. The 'mains supply' enters your home as two wires: a 'live' wire (L) at a pressure of 240 volts, and a 'neutral' wire (N), which is connected to the earth. The live wire is coloured red and the neutral wire black.

The 'earth' wire

Why, then, is there a separate earth wire inside the home? The reason is that the neutral wire is only conducting to earth while everything is working properly. If a live wire works loose, or its insulation is worn away, it may touch the outside casing of an appliance; this is why any metal part of an appliance that can be touched, switch plates, lamp-holders etc. should be independently connected directly to earth by means of the earth wire.

Current and resistance

To understand a little more about electric current, you have to go back to comparing it with water flowing in a pipe (**see 2**). Suppose there is a pump A, which drives water through the pipe B. The system will only work if there is a complete circuit back to A. The pump A can be thought of as the electricity source, and it will only drive the turbine D if the tap C is open. So C is equivalent to a switch in an electrical circuit, and D is any appliance put into the circuit (see 3).

The flow of the water round the pipe circuit is like the 'flow' of electricity in an electrical circuit. As more water per second flows through D, so it will do more work. In the same way, the greater the quantity of electricity flowing each second in the circuit, the more work it will do. The quantity of electricity per second, called current, is expressed in amperes (or amps for short). But here, once again, you must remember that electricity is not really like water. For instance, if you consider the statement 'more water is flowing per second', you think of it as flowing faster; but electricity always 'flows' at the same speed, and it is the amount of work it is capable of doing that changes. Imagine instead that the water is always flowing at the same pressure and the same speed, but being pumped through pipes of bigger bore.

You can also see that if the pipes were made narrower, it would become more and more difficult to get the water to flow, until eventually the pipe was so narrow that the pressure would not be sufficient to drive the water through at all. The narrow bore of the pipe is therefore exerting resistance. In the same way, part of an electrical circuit can be a resistance. In passing this resistance, the electricity does work. The work may consist of driving a motor or be in the form of heat or light. If there is no resistance to the electric current, electricity will flow through the circuit in such quantity that it is as if a pipe has burst: it can (almost literally) 'drain' the supply. This is why fuses are put into every part of the home electricity supply. If there is a 'short circuit', the large current flowing through the thin wire of the fuse heats it up and causes it to melt – breaking the circuit and stopping the flow.

Volts, amperes, ohms and watts

Resistance is measured in ohms. The relationship between volts, amperes and ohms is very easily expressed: volts = amperes × ohms.
As the domestic AC supply is at about 240 volts, and the safety limit for ordinary appliances is set at 13amps, you can calculate that the minimum resistance a circuit can offer is about 18 ohms.

The work that the electricity does is measured in watts. If you look at the manufacturer's plate on any electric appliance (see 4) you will see that it is rated at so many volts (220–240 volts, AC 50 cycles) and so many watts. The relationship between watts, volts and amperes is: volts × amperes = watts.
The pressure of the electricity supply – its voltage – does not normally change. The working appliance consumes electricity at a fixed rate. If the domestic supply is at 240 volts, and the appliance is rated at 960 watts, it will be consuming current at the rate of 4amps, which is within safe limits. If the total 'load' of appliances on any one domestic circuit adds up to more than 7200 watts, the current will exceed 30amps and the consumer unit fuse may 'blow'.

One thousand watts equal one kilowatt (kW) and electricity consumed over a period of one hour is called a kilowatt-hour (kWh), or one 'unit' of electricity. Electrical consumption is measured and charged for on this basis.

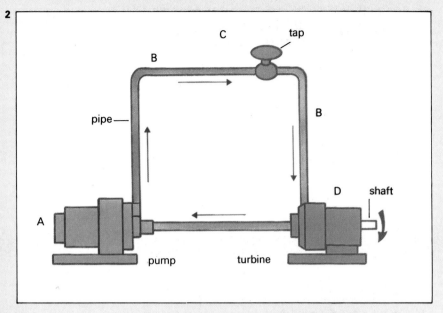

2

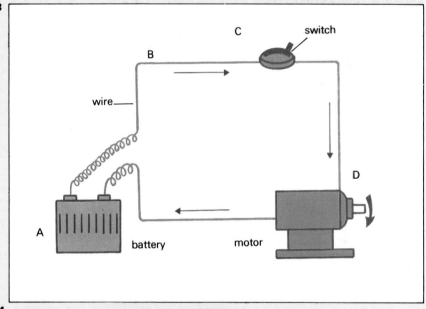

3

4

PHILIPS
TYPE HD 3240
240 V~ 50 Hz
2000W AT 240V
MADE IN GT. BRITAIN

Earthing

When rewiring a plug make absolutely sure the earth wire (yellow/green or green) is properly connected. If it is not you run the risk of an electric shock should the metal casing of an appliance become accidentally live.

The only appliances which do not need earthing are double insulated ones supplied with two core flex and mains operated shavers which are intended for use with special shaver sockets.

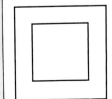

Left symbol for **double insulation**

Source of supply

The main electricity supply enters your home via an underground cable and normally appears at ground level; the system shown here is typical of many homes. On the left is the consumer unit (with a transformer underneath for the front door bell). To the right of the consumer unit is the black meter, which shows the consumption of electricity, and next to that is the sealed unit containing the Electricity Board fuse

When you turn on a switch you naturally expect the light to come on or a particular appliance to work. Circuits feed electricity all round the home, so you can use the power just where and when you want it.

Electricity is generated at a power station and conveyed across country by either underground cables or overhead cables strung between tall pylons. Its voltage is reduced by an enclosed transformer or sub-station in your locality and from there electricity is fed to your home at 240 volts.

Main supply

Cables which conduct electricity from the transformer to the consumer consist of insulated live (red) and neutral (black) conductors protected by an earthed metal sheath. The underground cable terminates in the house at ground level; in districts where there is overhead distribution, the supply is fed into the top of the house through a porcelain tube under the eaves.

In both cases the main supply cable terminates in a sealed unit which holds the service fuse. This fuse is designed to blow if there is a serious fault in the house which has failed to blow the fuse in the consumer unit (or fuse box), thus preventing the supply to neighbouring homes being affected. A 60 or 100amp fuse is connected to the live feed and the neutral conductor is connected to a brass terminal. There is another terminal on the outside of the sealed unit to which the household earth connection is made. The sealed unit containing the fuse belongs to the Electricity Board and must never be opened by the consumer; if the fuse does blow, you should call in the Electricity Board.

Two cables run from the service fuse to the meter, which measures the amount of electricity used. The meter is also the property of the Electricity Board and should never be tampered with by the consumer. The installation from the meter onwards is the consumer's responsibility and includes the two leads from the meter to the consumer unit.

Consumer unit

This contains a main switch and circuit fuses for the whole installation. Most houses have a lighting circuit for each floor so the whole house is not plunged into darkness in the event of a fuse blowing. A high wattage fixed appliance such as a cooker or immersion heater has its own sub-circuit. The cooker is wired directly to its own control switch – into which can be incorporated a power plug for use with other electrical kitchen gadgets. The control switch must be within two metres (or six feet) of the cooker, but separate from it. Make sure you have a long enough lead to the box so you can move the cooker out when cleaning.

Ring circuit

Socket outlets and small fixed appliances such as wall heaters and extractor fans are connected to a ring circuit, formed by a cable comprising a live (red) wire, a neutral (black) wire and a bare earth wire (covered in green/yellow PVC sleeving where it leaves the sheath). The cable used in domestic ring mains is 2.5sq mm twin core and earth, sheathed in PVC. This cable runs from a 30amp fuse in the consumer unit, serves each outlet and returns to the fuse, forming a ring.

The total load for a ring circuit is 30amps (7200 watts). So although it is possible to have an unlimited number of socket outlets on a ring, it is unlikely the number of domestic appliances being used at one time will exceed 30amps. If the circuit were overloaded, the 30amp fuse would blow and therefore maintain the safety requirements. However it is advisable to have a ring circuit for each floor in the house. If the kitchen has a large number of electrical appliances and/or a freezer, you should have a separate ring circuit in the kitchen to prevent overloading and ensure the freezer is not affected by a fault elsewhere.

Plugs used on a ring circuit have square pins and are fitted with 3 or 13amp fuses. The 3amp fuse covers all appliances up to a loading of 720 watts, which includes small appliances such as lamps. A 13amp fuse takes up to 3000 watts.

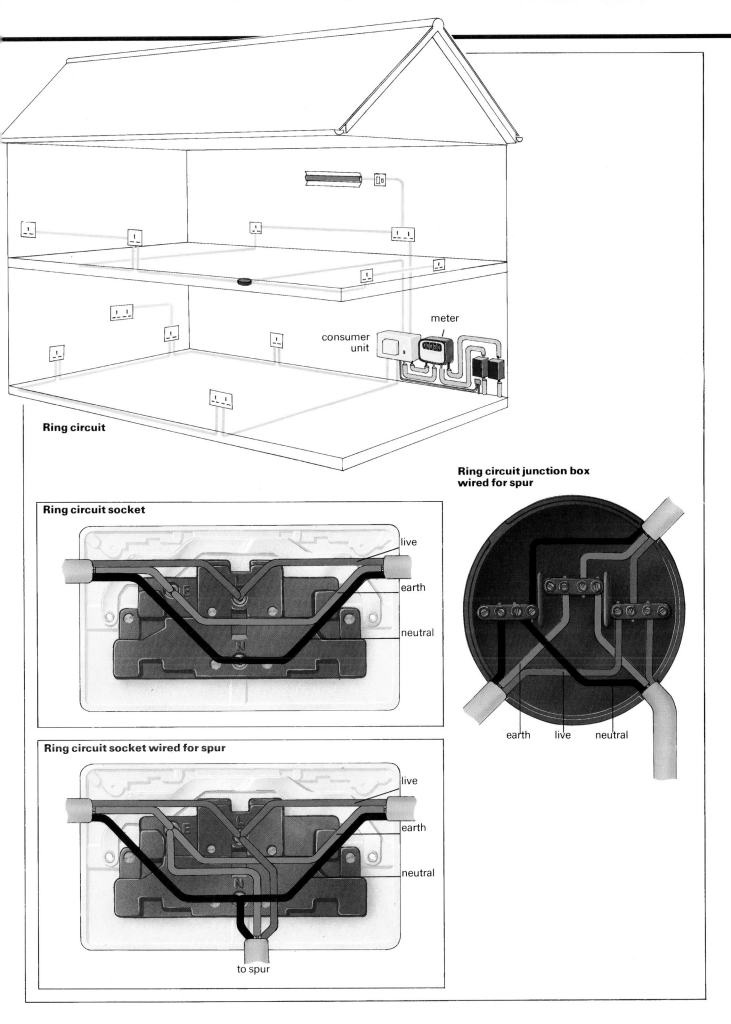

Ring circuit

meter

consumer
unit

Ring circuit socket

live

earth

neutral

Ring circuit socket wired for spur

live

earth

neutral

to spur

**Ring circuit junction box
wired for spur**

earth   live   neutral

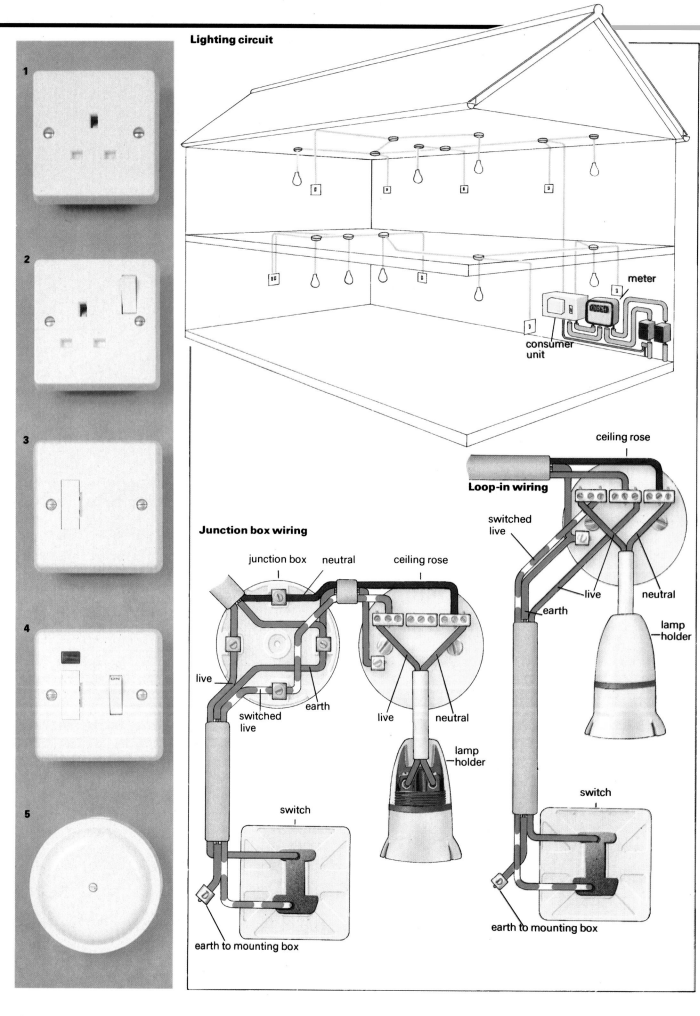

1

2

3

4

5

Lighting circuit

meter

consumer
unit

Loop-in wiring

ceiling rose

switched
live

live

earth

neutral

lamp
holder

Junction box wiring

junction box   neutral

ceiling rose

live

switched
live

earth

live   neutral

lamp
holder

switch

earth to mounting box

switch

earth to mounting box

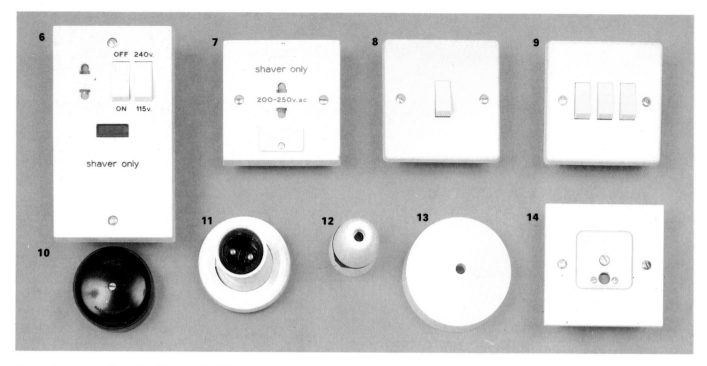

Additional socket outlets may be connected to a ring circuit, but the area served by the circuit should not exceed 100sq m (or 120sq yd).

Non-fused spur extensions

You can connect non-fused spur extensions to the circuit so long as each spur supplies just one single socket outlet, one double outlet or one fixed appliance. The total number of spurs must not exceed the number of socket outlets on the ring main. Only one spur may be connected from each outlet on the ring; for this purpose a junction box wired into the ring is classified as an outlet.

Fused connection units

These outlets, also used on a ring circuit, have the same fuse rating as plugs and are connected to a fixed appliance by a cable or flex. The unit may be switched or unswitched and fitted with an indicator light to show when the supply is connected to the outgoing flex or cable. Like socket outlets, the units can be flush or surface-mounted.

Flex outlets are simply a means of converting from a cable to a flex. A fused, switched connection unit, for example, outside a bathroom may supply a cable leading into the bathroom to feed a wall-mounted heater. Adjacent to the heater would be an outlet to feed the flex into the heater.

The clock connector is a similar type of unit, with a fuse fitted in a special plug into which the flex runs. The plug is retained in the socket by a knurled thumbscrew. Though called a clock connector, this is also suitable for small appliances such as window and wall extractor units.

Lighting circuits

Although lighting circuits are separate from the ring main or power circuit, there is nothing to prevent an individual light being taken from the ring. However, every home should have at least two lighting circuits protected by 5amp fuses. A 5amp fuse will carry up to twelve 100 watt lamps and it is usual, for example in a two-storey house, to plan one circuit for downstairs and another for upstairs. This will provide enough lighting points for decorative effects as well as general illumination.

Shaver units may also be connected to lighting circuits. For use in a bathroom, or room containing a shower, you must buy a unit which incorporates an isolating transformer. Here the socket is isolated from earth to remove the risk of an electric shock.

Lighting cable

Unlike the ring circuit, lighting cable does not return to the consumer unit. The cable now used is a 1sq mm PVC twin core and earth rated for up to 12amps. It is made up of a red insulated core for live, black insulated core for neutral and a bare earth conductor between them. The three conductors are laid side by side, surrounded by a PVC sheath.

The lighting cable travels from the consumer unit to a series of lighting points for ceiling roses or wall light fittings. It also connects to the switch or switches controlling the lamps and must do this in such a way that the individual switch, unless planned otherwise, does not affect other lights.

Two systems

There are two methods of wiring lights – by junction box or the loop-in ceiling rose. With the junction box system, cable is taken to a series of up to ten junction boxes. These are generally sited between ceiling joists or under floorboards close to where the cable is chanelled under the wall plaster to the switch. The loop-in system is more widely used and the ceiling rose incorporates the function of the junction box.

Extra lighting points may be added to an existing system by connecting cable from the junction box or ceiling rose to the new lighting point and switch.

Lamps may be controlled by switches in more than one place in a house – switches on the ground floor and first floor can both control a half-way or landing light. Or two lamps at different places – possibly in a large room – could be controlled by a double switch.

Checking electricity consumption

Increased electricity costs and the need to conserve energy make it even more desirable to keep a check on household consumption. To do this you must read your meter and check it is functioning correctly; you will also need to know how much power different appliances in the home consume; most have the wattage stamped on the body.

Reading your meter

The digital type of meter is similar to a distance meter in a car; you simply read the figures from left to right. The dial type which is probably the most common, requires more attention. It comprises five black dials and one red dial. Since the red dial measures tenths of a unit it can, for this purpose, be ignored.

The black dials show from left to right 10,000, 1000, 100, 10 and single units. Each dial is read in the opposite direction to its neighbour; the 10,000 unit dial is read clockwise, the 1000 dial is read anti-clockwise and so on. When the pointer of a dial is between two figures, always take the lower figure. For example, if the 100s pointer is between 1 and 2, it means that 100-plus units have been recorded. The 10s pointer will show the extra amount in 10s: if it is between 5 and 6, the number of units is 50-plus. The final figure is given by the single units dial which should always be read to the nearest unit.

By subtracting the previous week's reading from the current one, you can see how many units you have used in a week. Multiply this figure by the unit cost (shown on your bill) and you will have the price of the electricity, excluding the standing charge and the fuel cost adjustment.

Checking your meter

On your meter is a rotating disc which revolves a certain number of times for every kWh (kilowatt-hour) or unit of electricity consumed. The number of revolutions per kWh will be marked on the face of your meter. The disc is placed so you can see only the edge on which there is a black mark. You can count the revolutions by noting the number of times the black mark comes into view.

By a simple process you can check if your meter is registering correctly. If, for example, it is marked 500 revs/kWh, a total load of 1kW (for example, a one-bar electric fire or ten 100 watt lamps) will cause the disc to revolve 500 times in one hour. But there is no need for you to watch the disc for a whole hour. Switch off all the electrical equipment in the house and check the disc on the meter is stationary. Then switch on, for example, five 100 watt bulbs so you have a total test load of $\frac{1}{2}$kW. Count the number of times the black mark on the dial comes round in six minutes, using a stop-watch or a watch with a second hand for timing. Work out how many revolutions the disc should make in this time by using the following equation:

500 (revs/kWh) $\times \frac{1}{2}$ (kW) $\times \frac{1}{10}$ (of an hour) = 25.

Compare this figure with the number of revolutions you counted. Allowing for variations in the manufacture of the lamps used, the disc should rotate to within a couple of revolutions of the calculated figure. But before you rush off to tell the Electricity Board that your meter is wrong, double check there is no other equipment switched on. To do this, switch off the test load – the disc should come to a complete standstill.

If you have an hour to spare, you need not count the revolutions. Instead, you can use the sixth (red) dial which measures one tenth of a unit. Since one complete revolution equals one whole unit, just note the position of the pointer at the beginning and end of one hour. If you use a total load of 1kW, the pointer of the dial should make one complete revolution.

Below Two types of electricity meter. The digital type (**top**) can be read in a moment; with the dial meter (**bottom**) read the bottom row – from left to right – first, adding the units indicated on the top right-hand dial. The red dial, showing tenths of units, need not be read

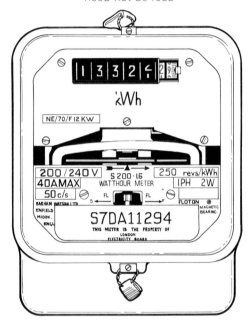

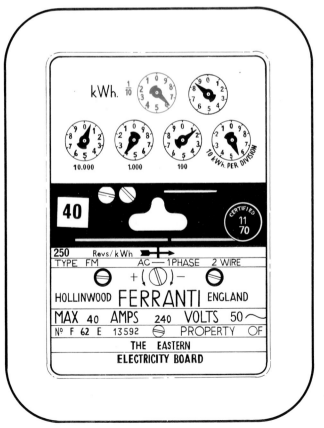

238

Diagnosing electrical faults

Fault	Cause	Remedy
Plug unduly hot	Loose flex terminal Fuse incorrectly fitted Poor quality fuse Fuse of incorrect rating Plug makes poor contact in socket Inferior quality plug Sustained load of 3kW causing reduced conductivity of pins and contacts	Tighten terminal screws Ensure fuse makes contact over whole surface area of metal ends Fit BS 1362 ASTA Cert fuse Fit 13amp fuse if appliance rated at 750 watts or more Renew plug and, if necessary, socket Fit plug of reliable make Renew plug
Sparks at socket outlet	Effect of breaking current in AC circuit If other than when operating switch, loose wire or faulty switch or socket	No action – natural phenomenon Tighten terminals, replace switch or socket
Intermittent power	Loose terminal or fuse or broken conductor Severed flex wire	Tighten terminals and refit plug fuse; if only one appliance affected, check flex terminals in appliance Replace flex
Smell of burning in and around house	Old wiring or frayed flex; loose connection; insulation of wires in heater or other appliance touching hot parts of heater Lamp of too high wattage in enclosed light fitting or shade Electric motor windings of powered appliance burning out, possibly due to blockage	Tighten terminals and replace damaged flexes and damaged exposed cables Fit lamp of lower wattage Check and clear mechanical parts of appliance; otherwise call in electrician
Smell of burning near meter and consumer unit	Cable overheating between consumer unit and Board's service fuse unit. Circuit fuse wire in consumer unit hot and burning plastic before blowing. Loose connection. Fault in Board's terminal box, fuse holder or meter cables	Call Board's emergency service; any fault in this area will almost certainly require withdrawal of Board's service fuse which consumer must not touch
Fuse blows repeatedly without obvious cause	Cable or accessory fault; serious overloading; fuse of incorrect rating; faulty light fitting or appliance; TV suppressor faulty	Reduce load on circuit; fit fuse of correct rating; if circuit fuse, disconnect each appliance in turn to ascertain which causes fuse to blow
Intermittent switch or lamp failure; constant need for lamp replacement	Damaged or worn switch Faulty wiring or loose switch connection Lamp of wrong voltage Lamp burning in cap-down position Mains voltage fluctuation due to nearby substation or mains tester	Replace switch Check wiring and connections Fit long life lamp of correct voltage Replace fitting with one which has lamp burning in cap-up position – could lengthen lamp life Ask Board to fit recording voltmeter
Loose switch	Age and wear	If switch body affected, replace switch; if loose in box, tighten fixing screws
Interference on hi-fi, TV or radio	If recent, faulty suppressor on appliance or new appliance has no suppressor Faulty thermostat Faulty fluorescent tube Faulty dimmer switch	Check each motor driven appliance; replace faulty suppressor Check each thermostat; replace if necessary Replace starter switch Fit new (suppressed) dimmer switch
No light or power	Mains switch accidentally turned off Board's fuse blown; supply failure or power cut	Check mains switch Check power available in neighbouring houses; if so, call Board

Cables and flexes

Cables and flex run all round your home – and it's important to know what each is for to make sure you use the right one for the right job.

Cable and flex are probably two of the most misused words when talking about electricity since, contrary to popular belief, they are not interchangeable. Cable is the main wiring carrying the supply to the many outlets in the home; flex is wiring that, for example, connects a lamp-holder to a ceiling rose or a vacuum cleaner to a socket.

Cables

Cables are not normally handled by the domestic consumer, since they have usually been built into the fabric of the house and make up the permanent wiring. Unlike flexes they are seldom moved during their working life; the expensive fine-wire construction of flex is not needed and many cables have single strand conductors running through them.

Cables connect the household electricity supply to flexes through suitable connection boxes such as ceiling roses or socket outlets. There are regulations to ensure cables are supported by clips at specific intervals depending on whether they run vertically or horizontally. PVC sheathed cable, for instance, can be buried in wall plaster without further protection.

Warning Cable should never be laid in grooves cut into joists because of the danger of floorboard nails penetrating the cable. It should pass through holes drilled at least 50mm (2in) below the tops of the joists.

Colour coding has not changed on cables. Red is live, black is neutral and green is earth, although in some types of domestic cable a bare uninsulated wire is the earth. Interior house cable can be single core (one conductor), twin core, twin core and earth, or three core and earth.

If there is a bare earth when cable is attached to a domestic connection box it should be covered with a short length of green PVC sleeving to insulate and identify it.

In some older houses you could well find the cable made up with a number of strands. This cable usually runs in metal conduit which acts as an earth conductor. In modern homes you will also find cable with conductors made of up to seven strands. This is for circuits which carry heavy current, such as for cookers. All modern cable has an outer covering of PVC which is proof against moisture and most common chemicals and acids so it can be safely buried in walls.

Below A selection of cables and flexes used for different installations in the home
1 Single core double-insulated cable
2 Twin core single-insulated cable
3 Twin core double-insulated cable
4 Twin core and earth double-insulated cable
5 Three core and earth cable
6 Twin core and earth double-insulated cable (conductors made up of seven copper strands)
7 Cooper-sheathed twin core cable insulated with chalk lining

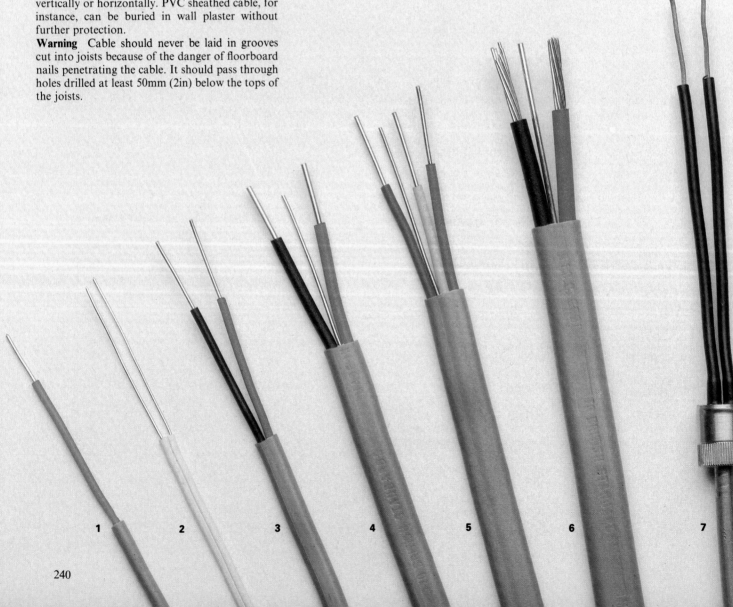

1   2   3   4   5   6   7

Flexes

Flex – or flexible cord – is a conductor of electricity which can be twisted and bent many times without breaking. It comprises metal conductors, each of which is made up of many strands of fine wire (rather than one thick one) encased in plastic or rubber. The finer the strands, the stronger the flex.

Flexes receive a lot of wear and tear, so it is very important they are connected properly and securely. In the case of a plug, the anchorage points must be secure enough to ensure any strain on the flex is taken by the tough outer covering (usually plastic or rubber) and not the metal conductors and the plug terminals. Similarly, connections to appliances must be through equally secure anchorage points to prevent strain at that end of the flex.

If the flex has to be lengthened at any time, it must be connected to another flex of the same type and joined by a proper connector.

Colour coding

Perhaps the most misunderstood aspect of flexes is the international colour code used for the PVC insulating covering. By law the three core flexes – whether sold separately or with an appliance – must have insulation coloured brown for the live wire, blue for the neutral wire and green-and-yellow

bands for the earth. On older appliances you may find the live wire is red, the neutral black and the earth yellow.

There are, surprisingly, no regulations as yet covering two core flexes. You may buy an appliance with, for example, black and white plastic covering and no explanation about which is live and which is neutral. The reason is that here it does not matter which wire is connected to which plug terminal. Table and standard lamps are examples where, in most cases, plain two core flex can be used.

Different ratings

There are many variations in the types of flex and cables, although most have special uses in industry. For the domestic consumer flexes vary little. Cables are more varied; there are, for example, special cables with extra protection for outside lighting and garden use.

Cables and flexes are given a rating based on the area of the conductor's cross-section and are described by this area when ordered from a supplier. A cable for a ring circuit, for example, is described as 2.5sq mm (or 2.5mm²), representing the cross-sectional area of one of the conductors available for carrying the current. The other conductor carries the same current but in the opposite direction. The earth conductor is slightly smaller than the other conductors in the cable and carries current only when there is a fault.

Changing conditions Cable and flex ratings do vary according to installation conditions, but this is unlikely to affect the domestic consumer. In a very hot situation, such as in an industrial process, a cable could be rated much lower than a similar cable in a domestic location because the rating is based on the rise in temperature that occurs when a conductor carries a given amount of current.

8 Cloth-covered and rubber-insulated three core flex with old colour coding
9 Same flex with new coding
10 Rubber-covered and insulated flex with old colour coding
11 Same flex with new colour coding
12 PVC-covered and insulated three core flex with new colour coding
13 Same flex with old colour coding
14 Unearthed P.V.C.-covered and insulated twin core flex with new colour coding

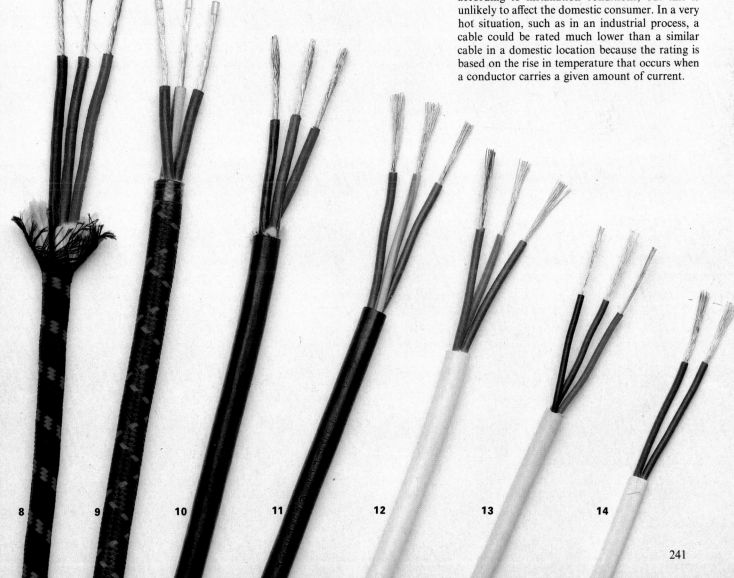

8   9   10   11   12   13   14

Stripping cable & flex

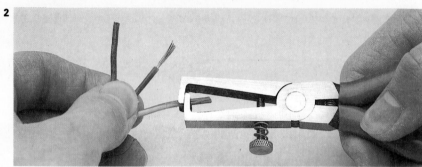

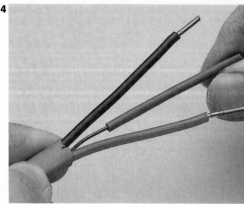

1 Cut carefully along the length of the flex with a sharp knife.
2 Use wire strippers to remove the sheathing and expose the insulated cores
3 Twist the wires together with your fingers
4 After stripping the insulation from cable, slip a length of PVC sleeving over the earth wire
5 On heavy cable, twist the conductors together with pliers

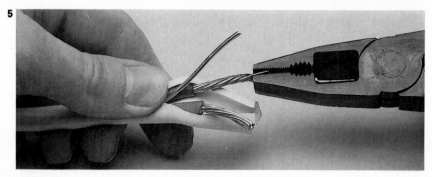

There are certain basic rules you must remember before you start to strip flex or cable for connecting to a plug or appliance or for wiring power or lighting circuits.

● Remove only sufficient insulation to enable the cores to be connected to the terminals; none of the bared wires should be exposed.

● Don't stretch the insulation when stripping or you will weaken the portion remaining on the conductor.

● Take care not to cut through the insulation of conductors, or through a conductor itself, or you will have to shorten the flex or cable and start again. If you damage a conductor the effective current capacity will be lowered and this could cause overheating. Current capacity will also be reduced if you sever any of the fine strands in a length of flex.

Stripping flex
The two most commonly used flexible cords are circular sheathed and braided circular flex. A third, now largely replaced by circular sheathed flex, is twisted twin non-sheath flex.

Circular sheathed Measure the length of sheathing to be removed and carefully run a knife round the sheath, making sure not to damage the core insulation. From this point, make a cut along the length of the flex to the end, cutting through to the inner insulation. Remove the sheathing with pliers, leaving the insulated cores exposed. Measure the length of insulation to be removed from each core and carefully take it off with wire strippers. Always twist the bared ends of each core together to ensure there will be no stray whiskers to cause a short circuit when the conductors are inserted in their terminals.

Circular braided Measure the length of braiding to be removed and cut it off with a sharp knife. Trim off the frayed edges and any textile fillers inside the braid and slip a rubber sleeve over the end to prevent further fraying. Strip the required length of insulation from each core and twist the wires together as before.

Twisted twin Since this type has no sheathing, you only need to strip insulation and twist the cores together.

Stripping cable
The method for stripping cable is basically the same as for stripping flex, but you must take extra care not to damage the conductors since cable is expensive to replace.

Sheathed Measure and strip off the required amount of sheathing using a knife and pliers as previously described. Strip off the insulation from each wire and slip a length of green (or green/yellow) PVC sleeving over the end of the earth wire. With the smallest cables (1.0 and 1.5sq mm), double the bared ends to provide greater contact area in the terminals. Cables of 4sq mm and above have stranded conductors and the ends must be twisted together with pliers.

Non-sheathed single core An example of this is the green/yellow PVC insulated earth cable; simply remove the insulation with wire strippers as described above.

Joining flex

One of the real dangers involving electricity is the joining up of flex, which can be a fire hazard. If you really have to do this job, always use a proper connector and check you have wired it up in the correct way.

Whenever possible avoid joining flex. If you have to, always use a proper connector and never try to join two pieces of flex by twisting the bare wires together and covering them with insulating tape. No matter how careful you are there is always a danger the join may work loose or come apart because it is suddenly stretched. If a join does work loose it can create sparks that may in turn lead to a fire. Among the other hazards, the earth safety lead may become detached in a three core flex join or the essential separation between the live and neutral wires break down, causing a short circuit.

Flex connectors are useful for portable appliances like irons and hairdryers, if you want to use them some distance from a socket. But never use more than one connector on a length of flex and don't trail it under carpets, up the stairs or across a passageway. Apart from the electrical dangers, there is always the risk someone might trip over it. When you require temporary lighting for a Christmas tree, for example, the flex and connector should be tucked against a skirting board and secured with adhesive tape, never by staples.

Before you decide you need to make a connection, consider whether it is easier, possibly cheaper, and certainly safer to buy a longer length of flex and fit it permanently to the lamp or appliance. Alternatively it could be preferable, though more expensive, to have a new power socket fitted, especially if it is for a semi-permanent appliance like a fridge, television or room heater.

Fitting connectors
Proper flex connectors do not only keep the cores separate but the screw terminals keep them securely fixed. Always use the same kind of flexes when making a join; although they need not be the same exterior colour, the amps and number of cores must match – three core must be matched with three core and two core with two core.

Only trim sufficient outer insulating sheath and inner insulation to leave the minimum bare wire to enter the connector terminals. Make sure there are no bare strands of wire exposed by twisting together the strands in each core before connecting. Always connect the brown core with brown, the blue with blue and the green/yellow earth with earth and check the plug at the end of the extension flex is correctly wired and fused.

Types of connectors
Three kinds of connectors are available for use in the home. But check which one is most suitable for the type of appliance involved and where it is to be used.
Connector strips Sometimes called block connectors, they are made of plastic and pairs of screws hold the flex ends. The plastic section can be cut to suit single, two or three core flex, but since the

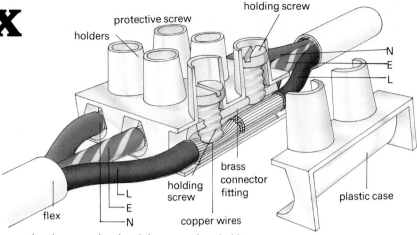

Connector strip

screw heads are not insulated they are only suitable where they can be protected and insulated, such as inside a table lamp or appliance, or in a plastic box with a screw-down cover.
Insulated flex connectors These consist of a screw-down plastic cover with screw terminals inside. You buy them to suit the flex and the appliance: 5amp for small lamps and 13amp for most other uses. They are generally designed to accommodate the live, neutral and earth of three core flex but can be used with two core flex.
Insulated detachable flex connectors Made of rubber or a tough plastic, these are like a self-contained plug and socket and strong enough for outdoor use. They are available in 5 and 13amp sizes. You must always fix the 'male' or plug part of the connector on the flex leading to the appliance and the 'female' or socket half should be connected with the flex end that will be joined to the plug connecting with the mains. If you join them the other way round and they become detached, the part with the pins would be live to the touch – and therefore very dangerous.

Above Plastic connector strip can be cut to suit single, two or three core flex
Below Insulated flex connector suitable for extending portable appliances such as hair dryers
Bottom Insulated detachable flex connector. Plug half must be connected to flex from appliance

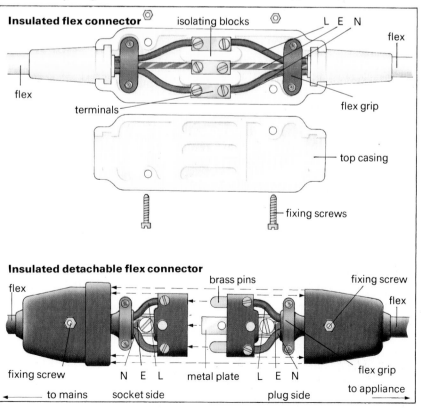

Wiring plugs

Probably the most common electrical job in the home is wiring a plug. It is crucial that the right core is fitted to the right terminal and that all connections are tight.

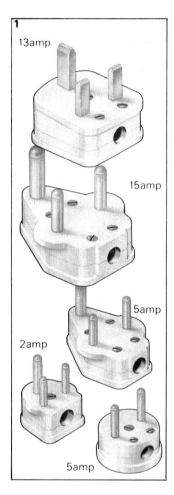

1 Types of plug: 13amp square pin; 15, 5 and 2amp round pin
2 Always check flex colour coding as right core must go to right plug terminal

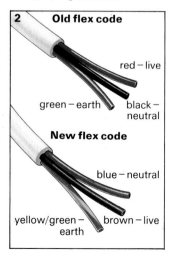

2   **Old flex code**

red – live

green – earth   black – neutral

New flex code

blue – neutral

yellow/green – earth   brown – live

Houses that have been wired or rewired in Britain since 1947 will be fitted with ring main circuits. These are continuous loops of cable linking all wall sockets. The sockets are uniform 13amp outlets with rectangular holes to take the three flat pins of 13amp plugs.

This type of plug is supplied with a 3 or 13amp cartridge fuse (colour coded red and brown respectively). Always fit the fuse recommended by the manufacturer; as a general guide 3amp fuses are used with appliances rated up to 720 watts (for example table lamps) and 13amp fuses are used with larger appliances rated above 720 watts and up to 3000 watts (including kettles, irons and heaters). Some appliances (such as colour televisions, vacuum cleaners and spin dryers) although rated at less than 720 watts require a high starting current and should be used with 13amp fuses. In every case check first with maker's instructions.

Older houses will have radial wiring where separate cables radiate from the fuse board to each socket. These sockets are usually round pin in three sizes. The largest takes a 15amp plug used with larger appliances (such as heaters) while the other sizes take 5 and 2amp plugs used with smaller appliances (drills and table lamps respectively). The outlets may have two or three holes. The two pin sockets are not earthed and should only be used for light fixings with no exposed metal parts or for small double insulated appliances designed to operate without an earth connection and which are supplied only with two core flex.

Where possible it is safer to have radial wiring replaced (by your Electricity Board or a registered electrical contractor) with the properly earthed – and safer – ring main circuit.

Most plugs are made of tough, hard plastic but special rubberized types are available for equipment likely to be subjected to rough treatment, such as electric drills. Always buy a reputable make of plug because on poorer quality types the pins may move and cause a bad connection.

To fit a plug

First familiarize yourself with the colour code of the flex as it is most important the right core goes with the right terminal. With the new code blue is neutral, brown live and yellow/green earth. On older flex black is neutral, red live and green earth.

Remove the cover of the plug by undoing the large screw between the pins. When you look at the plug, with the largest pin (the earth) at the top and the flex outlet at the bottom, the live terminal is on the right (marked L) and the neutral terminal is on the left (marked N).

Prepare the flex by removing about 38mm (1½in) of the outer covering with a knife and fit the flex through the flex grip. This will be either a clamp type secured with two small screws (in which case loosen the screws, thread the flex through the grip and tighten the screws) or a V-shaped grip which

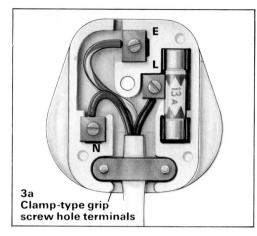

3a
Clamp-type grip screw hole terminals

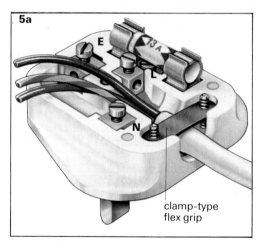

4a

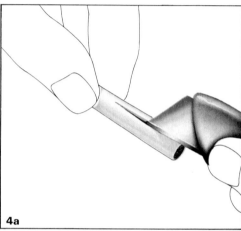

5a

clamp-type flex grip

Earthing

When rewiring a plug make absolutely sure the earth wire (yellow/green or green) is properly connected. If it is not you run the risk of an electric shock should the metal casing of an appliance become accidentally live.

The only appliances which do not need earthing are double insulated ones supplied with two core flex and mains operated shavers which are intended for use with special shaver sockets.

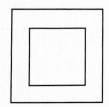

Left symbol for double insulation

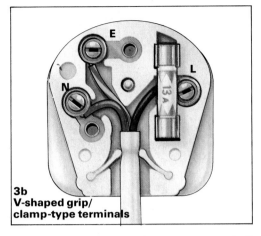

3b
V-shaped grip/
clamp-type terminals

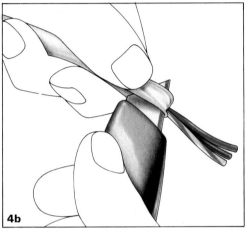

4b

holds about 6mm ($\frac{1}{4}$in) of the flex covering inside the plug. Make sure each core of the flex will reach its terminal, then cut 12mm ($\frac{1}{2}$in) beyond this for joining to the terminals. With wire strippers carefully remove about 12mm ($\frac{1}{2}$in) of the insulation at the end of each core and twist the loose strands neatly together.

Check which type of terminals the plug has. If it has screw holes double back the wires, insert them into the terminal holes and tighten the terminal screws with a small screwdriver to secure the wires. If the terminals are of the clamp type remove the screws, wrap the wires around the terminal posts in a clockwise direction, replace the screws and tighten them. On some plugs the live terminal is under the fuse housing, in which case you will have to remove the fuse before wiring that terminal. Make sure the plug is neatly wired: the insulation must go right up to the terminals and there must not be any straggling wires.

If a fuse is required simply snap the cartridge into the holding clips. Finally double check wires are connected to correct terminals before refitting cover. **Warning** If a plug gets hot the terminal screws may have worked loose and need to be tightened. Always replace a cracked plug immediately; never repair it, even temporarily, with insulating tape since there is a considerable risk the casing will come apart as the plug is put into or removed from the socket and you could get an electric shock.

It is important to check the flex regularly since the point where it joins the plug is particularly susceptible to breaking and fraying (especially on irons and vacuum cleaners). At first sign of wear cut frayed piece to make new end and rewire plug.

3a Screw hole terminals and clamp-type flex grip
3b Clamp-type terminals and V-shaped flex grip
4a Remove outer insulation by cutting along its length with sharp knife
4b Bend insulation away from flex and cut through fold
5a To insert flex in clamp-style grip, undo retaining screws, thread flex through grip and tighten screws
5b With V-shaped grip, simply push flex between two plastic strips
6 Check flex cores will reach terminals, allow 12mm ($\frac{1}{2}$in) extra for joining and cut off excess. Carefully remove insulation with wire strippers or sharp knife
7 Twist strands of each core neatly together

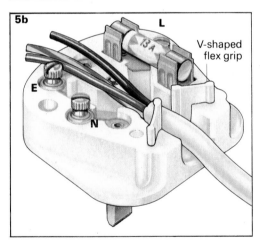

5b

V-shaped
flex grip

E

N

L

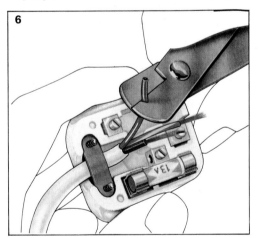

6

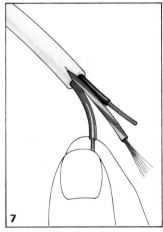

7

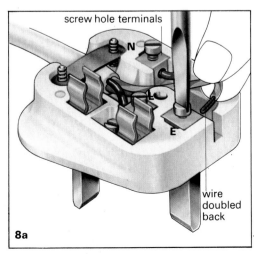

screw hole terminals

N

L

E

wire
doubled
back

8a

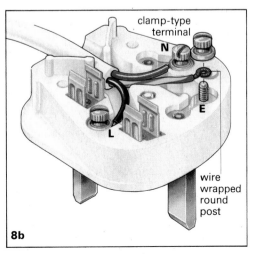

clamp-type
terminal

N

E

L

wire
wrapped
round
post

8b

8a With screw hole terminals, double back wires, loosen terminal screws and insert wires in terminals. Gently tighten screws, taking care not to sever wires
8b With clamp terminals, remove screws and wrap bare wires round terminal posts in clockwise direction. Replace screws and tighten

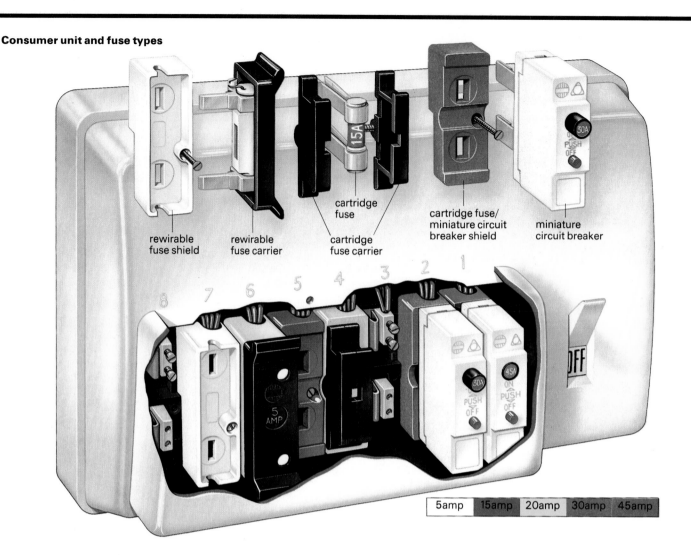

rewirable
fuse shield

rewirable
fuse carrier

cartridge
fuse

cartridge
fuse carrier

cartridge fuse/
miniature circuit
breaker shield

miniature
circuit breaker

5amp	15amp	20amp	30amp	45amp

Repairing fuses

When electric current passes through a wire it causes heating: the thinner the wire the greater the heat. Even the thick wire used in domestic wiring will overheat if too much current passes through it – and may easily set the house on fire. To prevent this, a fuse is built into every circuit. This is a particularly thin piece of wire which will heat up quickly and melt if a more than safe quantity of current passes through it.

Types of fuses
All master fuses – one for each circuit – are mounted on fuse carriers in a fuse box close to the Electricity Board's supply meter. There are two main types, rewirable and cartridge, although miniature circuit breakers are widely used now on new installations.
Rewirable This type has fuse wire stretched between two retaining screws on the porcelain or plastic fuse carrier. The wire is available in three ratings – 5, 15 and 30amp – and you can usually buy a card of wire carrying a supply of all three.
Cartridge This type cannot be rewired since the fuse is sealed inside a tube; once it blows the fuse must be replaced. The advantage of the master cartridge fuse is it is impossible to fit the wrong one

because with the exception of 15- and 20-amp fuses, each of the other cartridges is a different size. The fuses are also colour coded so they can be easily recognized: 5amp is white, 15amp blue, 20amp yellow, 30amp red and 45amp green.
Miniature circuit breakers Used in domestic fuse boxes instead of fuses, these automatically switch themselves off if a circuit is overloaded. When the fault has been corrected the circuit can be reconnected just by resetting the on/off switch.

Why fuses blow
A master fuse will blow if the circuit is overloaded, if the fuse wire is of too low a rating or if a faulty appliance is used with an unfused plug or socket. Before repairing the fuse check you are not using too many appliances on one circuit and make sure you are using the right size fuse for the circuit. If you suspect a faulty appliance, even though it seems to be working adequately, stop using it and call an electrician or contact the manufacturer.

Sometimes a fuse blows simply because it is old; all you need to do is replace it with a new one of the correct rating. If a fuse still blows after being replaced, call an electrician.

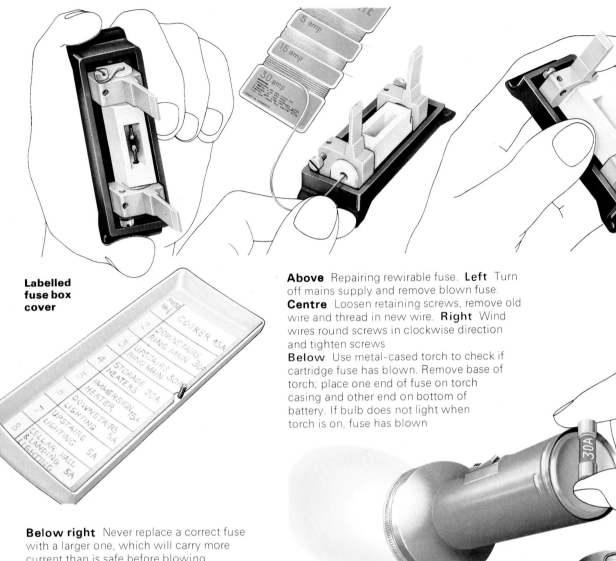

Labelled fuse box cover

Above Repairing rewirable fuse. **Left** Turn off mains supply and remove blown fuse.
Centre Loosen retaining screws, remove old wire and thread in new wire. **Right** Wind wires round screws in clockwise direction and tighten screws
Below Use metal-cased torch to check if cartridge fuse has blown. Remove base of torch; place one end of fuse on torch casing and other end on bottom of battery. If bulb does not light when torch is on, fuse has blown

Below right Never replace a correct fuse with a larger one, which will carry more current than is safe before blowing.
For lighting circuit (up to 1kW) – 5amp
For immersion heater (3–4.8kW) – 15/20amp
For ring main circuit (up to 7.2kW) – 30amp
For cooker (up to 10.8kW) – 45amp

Cartridge fuses

5A	
15A	
20A	
30A	
45A	

Warning Don't try to stop a fuse blowing by putting in a higher rated one.

Tracing faults
If one of your lights goes out see first whether those nearby are still working; if they are it is likely only the lamp bulb has blown. If all your lights are out check whether the street or your neighbours are in darkness too; if they are there is nothing wrong with your fuses – there is a general power failure and you will just have to wait for the power to be restored. If everyone else's lights are working you have an internal power failure, so turn off the relevant switch before investigating.

You will save time and trouble by keeping a small electrical screwdriver, a torch and replacement fuses or fuse wire handy by the fuse box. A supply of candles in the house is also good sense.

Rewiring fuses
Always turn off the mains supply switch before attempting any repairs. If you are really efficient you will have made a numbered plan of the carriers in your fuse box, labelling each one according to the circuit it controls (cooker, downstairs sockets,

upstairs lights etc.). This plan should be taped on the inside of the fuse box door so, when investigating a blown fuse, you can pick out the relevant carrier first time.

If you have not labelled them you must pull out each carrier in turn to find the blown fuse – look for one which has a broken or melted fuse wire. Undo the screws which clamp the fuse wire in place and remove the remains of the old wire. Stretch a new wire of the correct rating loosely between the screws and wind the ends in a clockwise direction round the screws, which must be carefully tightened until the wire is firmly held. Replace the fuse holder and close the fuse box before reconnecting the supply.

Replacing cartridge fuses
The only way of telling which cartridge fuse has blown is to remove one carrier at a time. Turn off the mains switch, remove a carrier, close the fuse box cover and switch on the mains supply. If everything else continues to work you have found the failed fuse. Take out the cartridge and replace it with a new one of the correct rating, refit the fuse carrier, close the box cover and turn on the main switch.

Moving and adding sockets

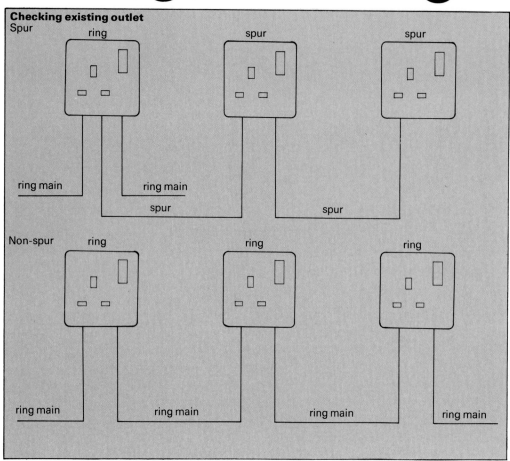

Checking existing outlet

Spur — ring — spur — spur — ring main — ring main — spur — spur

Non-spur — ring — ring — ring — ring main — ring main — ring main — ring main

Before you start work check to make sure the outlet you want to run your spur from is not itself already a spur. Sockets with only one cable are definitely spur sockets, and cannot be used. Sockets with two cables may be on the ring (left, bottom), but may also be on an old two-socket spur (left, top); these are now no longer permitted by the Wiring Regulations. You can test which is which with a continuity tester. Turn off the power at the mains and disconnect the circuit cables; then link the live cores with the test probes. If the socket is on the ring the test light will come on; if it is on a spur, it will not

Electricity is one energy source you can switch on where and when you want it. There is no reason to run a power tool off an extension from the kitchen when you need to work in the garage – or to unplug the bedside lamp when you want to use a portable television in the bedroom. The answer is to provide more socket outlets, a job you can do yourself safely if you follow the correct procedure.

Unless you were lucky enough to have supervised the installation of power points when your house was being built, you may find you have too few sockets and some that are in the wrong place. Moving sockets, adding extra ones or converting a single to a double (or twin) socket are jobs well within the capabilities of the amateur if you follow instructions carefully and make it a golden rule to switch off at the mains whenever you tackle any electrical work. A great part of the work is non-electrical: lifting floorboards to trace cables, drilling holes between joists for new cables or cutting back plastered walls and replastering them after you have buried the new cable and connected the new outlets.

Most homes take their power supply from ring circuits – but it is possible that your home's 13amp socket outlets may be on a radial circuit. This circuit consists of a number of outlets and fixed appliances supplied by one cable, from the consumer unit, which ends at the last outlet. This is quite different from the old radial system of 15amp plugs (with round pins) in which numerous 15amp circuits radiated from a multi-way fuseboard.

These old installations are being phased out; if you still have this system, it could be in a dangerous condition and you should ask your Electricity Board to check the wiring – something the Electricity Council recommends people should have done every five years.

Connecting methods

There are three ways of connecting extra sockets or fixed appliances to the domestic ring circuit, all of which can be handled by the consumer.

Loops By taking a direct loop from the terminals of an existing socket outlet.

Junction box By inserting a junction box in the ring cable – generally under the floor – and taking one or two sockets from that.

Consumer unit By running a separate cable from the consumer unit.

Sockets connected by way of loops or junction boxes are called spurs; you can take only one new socket on a spur from any existing socket or from a newly installed junction box. Spurs not only supply extra socket outlets but can also be used to supply a fixed appliance, such as a wall heater.

Flush-fitted box

wall   knock-out holes

Surface mounted box

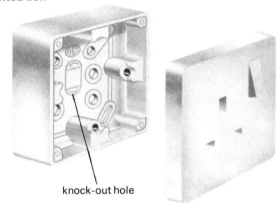

knock-out hole

Here a fused switch connection – placed close to the appliance – replaces a socket outlet. Some fixed connections incorporate a pilot light to show when the appliance is on. Each spur may feed one single socket outlet, one double socket outlet or one fixed appliance.

Generally there is one ring circuit for each floor in a house. You should run your loop or junction box from the nearest existing socket outlet or nearest accessible part of the ring circuit to the new outlet. If you want to run the spur from a socket, make sure the outlet is not itself a spur. Undo the screws on the front plate and gently pull the outlet from the wall box and examine the wiring. If there are two red, two black and two earth (possibly green-sleeved or bare) conductors in the box, the outlet is probably not a spur. To make quite sure examine the nearest socket outlets each side of it. If there is only one set of conductors on these, your original choice is already a spur and should not be used. If neither outlet is a spur, then you know you can loop out of the first one you examined. Replace the frontplates and switch the mains back on until you are ready to begin work.

Planning outlets

While you are planning for extra outlets, you must decide what type of fitting you want. The choice is between flush-fitted sockets or sockets on wall-mounted boxes. More work is involved in installing the flush type, but the wall-mounted

socket can be an obstruction to furniture and vacuum cleaners at ground level and can rob you of space when fitted above a work surface.

If you are in the habit of using an adaptor plug on some of your existing outlets, it may be worth investing in a double (or twin) socket and changing that for the single while you are working on the terminals behind it.

Socket height Socket outlets should not be less than 150mm (6in) above the floor or above a working surface in the kitchen or elsewhere. In rooms being used by elderly people or active invalids, outlets should be 1m (or 3ft) from the floor to eliminate bending.

Cable The cable used in a ring circuit is 2.5sq mm and the usual type for domestic installations is polyvinyl chloride (pvc) sheathed twin and earth, or may be tough rubber sheathed (trs) cable. Older ring circuits are wired in the Imperial-sized cable (called 7/029), which has seven strands. But it is quite all right to use the metric-size cable when adding to a ring circuit wired with 7/029 cable.

Decide carefully where your new cable will run. There will be problems, for example, if you have a modern house or flat in which underfloor wiring on the ground floor was installed before a solid floor was laid. The costly solution to this, in terms of cable, may be that you will have to run cable from the consumer unit up to the first floor, under the floorboards and then trail it down the cavity of the wall to the position of your intended outlet. Alternatively you could bury the cable in the plasterwork (the cable does not need any additional insulation) or run it on the surface of the wall – in which case you must clad it in a plastic conduit. Surface cables look unsightly in living rooms and create a further problem when decorating.

Another method is to remove your existing skirting and replace it with ducting, in metal or plastic, designed to house cables. Never consider cutting sockets into existing skirting boards. It is dangerous, illegal and may invalidate any insurance claim in the event of a fire.

If you do have a solid floor and need only one or two extra socket outlets, you will find it simpler to loop out of an existing outlet and bury the new cable in the wall.

Cutting plaster

There are two methods of making a channel in plaster. You can do it with a club hammer and brick bolster after first scoring with a sharp knife two straight lines in the plaster along the intended cable route, chipping out the depth you require. Or you can use a specially designed router, which works off an electric drill at a slow speed. Before you start routing you must drill a series of guide holes along the intended cable route. It is unlikely your plaster will not be deep enough to take a cable, but if you are unlucky you will just have to get to work again with the chisel.

Before you start laying cable, prepare the recesses or mountings for new sockets or position the junction boxes – preferably out of sight beneath floorboards. Where you run cables across joists you should run them through holes drilled at least 50mm (2in) below the top of the joists. Never lay cable in the grooves cut in the tops of joists because of the danger from nails that may be driven through and penetrate the cables.

When replacing floorboards, use screws instead of nails, which will enable you to identify the cable

Wiring new outlet in solid floor room
Cable in cavity wall

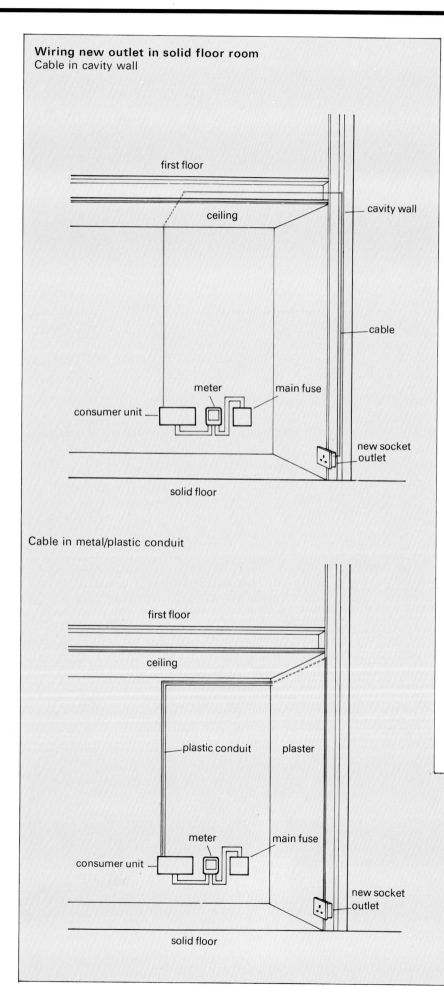

first floor

ceiling

cavity wall

cable

meter

main fuse

consumer unit

new socket outlet

solid floor

Cable in metal/plastic conduit

first floor

ceiling

plastic conduit

plaster

meter

main fuse

consumer unit

new socket outlet

solid floor

run and to reach it more quickly on future occasions. Before replacing the boards you should cut out a small section of the board at the skirting board end to protect cable running up or down the wall, behind skirting and then under the boards.

Warning Care must be taken not to damage any existing cables or pipes. Make sure current is turned off at the main; gas and water should also be turned off.

Wall sockets

Cutting out the recess for a flush socket box is quite simple. Mark on the wall in pencil an outline of the knock-out box, score the lines with a sharp knife and, using a brick bolster and club hammer, chip away until you reach the brickwork. Drill a series of close-spaced holes all round and then chip away another layer until you reach the required depth. Test the knock-out box fits, knock out the required access holes in it (sharp taps with a cold chisel are usually enough) and fix a grommet in each hole. This is a rubber or plastic ring, with an exterior slot which fits neatly in the hole, to protect the cable. Drill the mounting holes, plug them and screw the knock-out box into the recess, making good the edges with plaster.

Fixing a wall-mounted box is much easier. You only need to channel out enough plaster to accommodate the cable run from the floorboards and behind the skirting (unless it is being channelled into a wall from another socket) and into the box, which is plugged and screwed to the wall.

Moving existing sockets

If you intend to line your rooms with plasterboard or panel boards fixed to battens, you must plan how you are going to reposition your existing outlets. If you already have wall-mounted sockets, you can cut a snug opening into your lining where each socket is situated, turning the outlets into flush fittings. If your existing outlets are flush fitting, with a knock-out box recessed into the original wall, you have several alternatives.

You can check, by easing the knock-out box from the wall, whether there is enough slack cable on the ring to allow you to move the entire outlet forward to the new surface. If there is plenty of slack, you can fit a new wall-mounted box and reconnect to the socket terminals. If there is not enough cable, check whether the cable is fed from above or below. In each instance you will probably be able to find enough cable to enable you to reposition the outlet either higher or lower than it was on the old wall. But remember, the socket

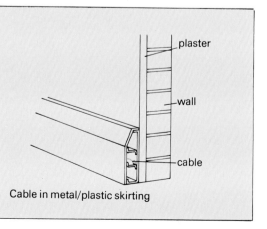

plaster

wall

cable

Cable in metal/plastic skirting

Marking box position

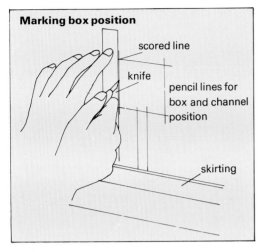

scored line

knife

pencil lines for box and channel position

skirting

Cutting out box recess
Removing plaster

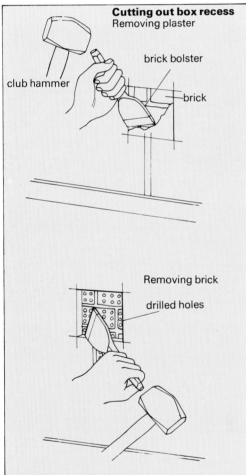

club hammer

brick bolster

brick

Removing brick

drilled holes

Cutting out channel with router

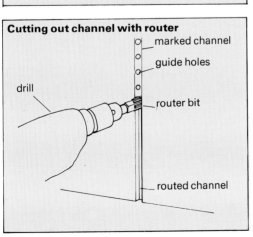

marked channel

guide holes

drill

router bit

routed channel

Running cable under floorboards

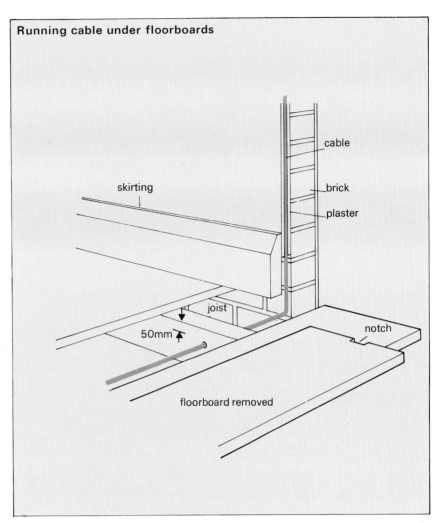

skirting

cable

brick

plaster

joist

50mm

notch

floorboard removed

Knocking out holes in flush-fitted box

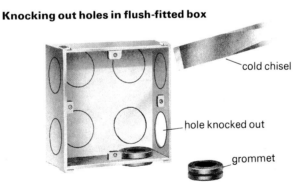

cold chisel

hole knocked out

grommet

should be at least 150mm (6in) above the floor and never be installed in a skirting board.

If this is also impossible, you will have to fit a three-way terminal block into the existing knock-out box, which converts it into a junction box. You must run cable from a knock-out hole (not forgetting to use a grommet) at the top or bottom of the box and use this to feed one single or one double wall-mounted socket outlet positioned nearby on your new wall. You must also cover the modified knock-out box with a blank plate.

Wiring up sockets

Electricity can be supplied where you want it, as long as you have enough outlets. You can install new power points or move existing ones yourself.

Having done all the non-electrical work such as lifting boards, chanelling plaster to take cables, or cutting recesses for the new knock-out boxes and installing them, it is time to start wiring with 2.5sq mm twin core and earth PVC sheathed cable. This is quite simple and safe if you turn off the mains before you start work.

Changes to the Regulations
The latest (15th) edition of the IEE Wiring Regulations contains a significant change as far as adding spurs to existing circuits is concerned. It was permitted to extend ring circuits by adding spurs feeding *two* single sockets, one double socket or one fixed appliance; now a spur may feed only *one* outlet of any type, whether it is a socket outlet or a fused connection unit.

The new Regulations allow spurs to be connected to modern radial circuits too, with the same restrictions applying.

Since many homes will already contain spurs feeding two sockets, it is therefore extremely important to check whether any socket to which a spur is being attached is actually on the main circuit.

A socket with two cables connected to it could be one on a ring circuit, an intermediate socket on a modern radial circuit or the first socket on an old two-socket spur. You can tell the first and third possibilities apart using a continuity tester (see page 248). To identify the second, check which circuit supplies it at the main consumer unit; radial power circuits have only one circuit cable connected to the circuit fuseway, while ring circuits have two.

Loops
If you are running a loop from the back of an existing socket to connect to a new spur socket outlet or a fixed appliance, you must start by cutting your cable to length. Since you will need to feed about 125mm (5in) of cable into the recessed knock-out box, surface-mounted box or junction box from which the new spur will receive its power, remove about 100mm (4in) from the outer sheath and then strip about 15mm ($\frac{5}{8}$in) of the insulation material from the red and black conductors. The earth conductor will be bare and you should slip on a short length of green/yellow PVC sleeving (generally available where you buy twin core and earth cable), leaving just 15mm ($\frac{5}{8}$in) bare at the end.

You are now ready to run the cable into its channelling or under the floor, depending on the route you have chosen. Cable under floors should be run in holes drilled at least 50mm (2in) below the top of joists and secured only by cable fixing clips. If you are running cable in plaster, you should wedge it in position while you are connecting up. The cable sometimes wriggles free and if this

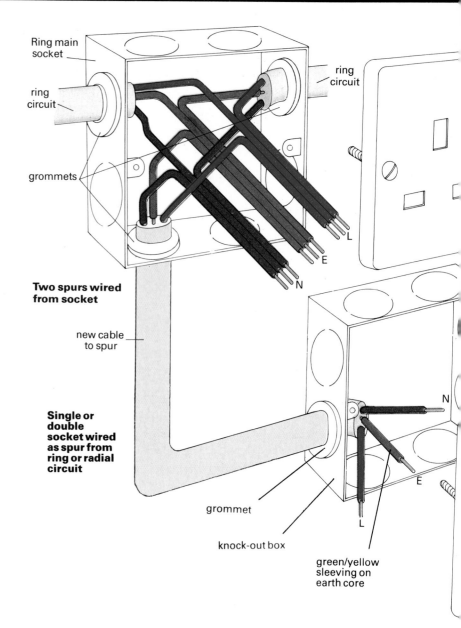

Two spurs wired from socket

new cable to spur

Single or double socket wired as spur from ring or radial circuit

grommet

knock-out box

green/yellow sleeving on earth core

happens you should secure it with a couple of dabs of contact adhesive – but make sure the cable is in the right place.

Socket to socket
Thread the 125mm (5in) of unsheathed conductors into the knock-out hole you have prepared (into which you must always place a rubber or plastic grommet as protection for the cable) and loosen the wires on the terminals on the back of the socket plate. Arrange the new conductors alongside the entwined pairs already there; red with reds, black with blacks and earth (or green) with earths. Put each set of three wires in their respective terminals. Reds go to the live terminal, blacks to the neutral terminal and greens to the earth terminal. All terminals are clearly marked on the back of the socket plate. Tighten the terminal screws, check the conductors are secure and replace the front of the socket outlet.

You can now connect the spur to the new outlet. Simply enter the spur knock-out box in the way described and connect each of the three conductors

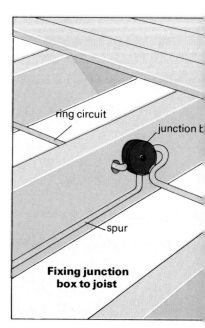

Fixing junction box to joist

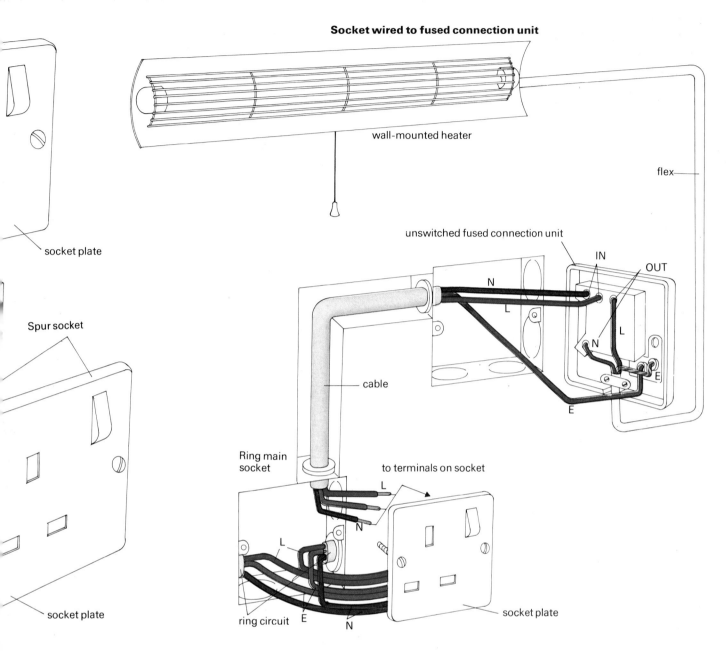

Socket wired to fused connection unit

wall-mounted heater

flex

unswitched fused connection unit

IN

OUT

N

L

L

N

E

E

cable

Ring main
socket

to terminals on socket

L

N

L

E   N

ring circuit

socket plate

socket plate

Spur socket

socket plate

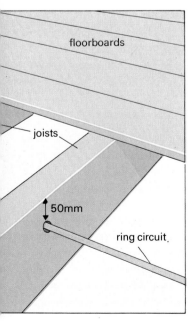

floorboards

joists

50mm

ring circuit

to its relevant terminal. Screw the socket plate on, plug in an appliance that you know is working, turn on the mains and switch on at the new outlet. If the appliance works, your wiring is correct. Only then – and again with the mains switched off – should you plaster the cable into the wall or replace the floorboards.

Sockets on stud partition walls
Mounting socket outlets on plasterboard-covered stud partition walls used to involve either cutting away part of the stud to get a secure fixing or using fiddly retaining clips. It is now possible to buy a flush mounting box which has spring-loaded lugs at each side; this is simply pushed into place in the prepared cut-out, ready to receive the spur cable and socket outlet faceplate.

Fused connection unit
Follow the same wiring procedure if you are running a loop from a socket outlet (or a junction box) to a fused (switched or unswitched) connection unit for connecting with a fixed appliance, such as

a wall-mounted heater. At the connection unit there are six terminals – two live, two neutral and two earth. The live and neutral conductors from the loop cable must be connected to the terminals marked IN. The other terminals are marked OUT and to these you connect the live and neutral leads in the appliance's flex, feeding the flex in through a knock-out hole at the bottom of the unit. The earth leads can connect to either of the two earth terminals. When this is done, check the wiring.

Warning Check there is a 3 or 13amp cartridge fuse in the pull-out holder at the front of the unit (manufacturers sometimes forget to include one) and do not be too violent in clearing the knock-out hole or you may shatter the plastic casing. Never connect to an appliance rated at more than 13amp (or 3kW), because it will need a separate circuit from the consumer unit.

Junction boxes
If you are supplying your extra sockets or fused connection unit through a junction box, you will already have sited this within reach of the ring

circuit cable and secured it to a joist, a short length of timber between joists or another suitable timber fixture. Knock out three holes: for the ring cable to enter and leave the junction box and a third for the spur cable, which should be prepared as already explained. There are three terminals in the box: live, neutral and earth. It does not matter which you use as long as you are consistent – but it is bad practice not to connect to the properly designated terminals. Try to avoid cutting the ring cable. You should be able to strip away the outer sheath and cut away enough insulation at a suitable point so there is sufficient bare wire to lay in the terminal (with the corresponding conductors from the spur cable) under the terminal screws. Connect the other end of the new cable as already described, either to a new socket outlet or to a fixed connection unit.

Terminal block conversion

If you are turning an existing outlet into a junction box by using a three-way terminal block inside an existing recessed knock-out box or surface-mounted backplate, you must first remove a knock-out hole

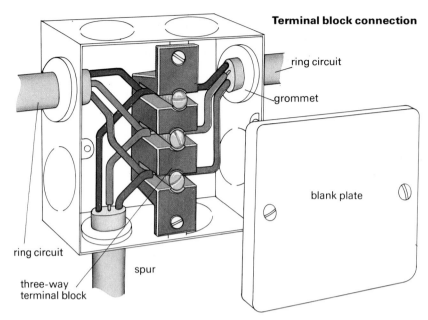

Terminal block connection

ring circuit

grommet

blank plate

ring circuit

spur

three-way
terminal block

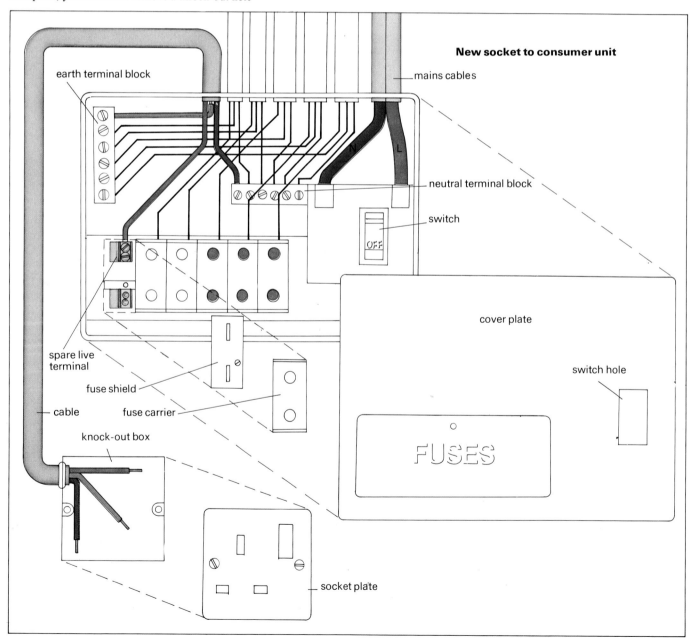

New socket to consumer unit

earth terminal block

mains cables

neutral terminal block

switch

cover plate

spare live
terminal

switch hole

fuse shield

cable

fuse carrier

knock-out box

FUSES

socket plate

to get the new spur cable into the box. Connect the three sets of conductors and earths: the cable going into the existing socket and the cable leaving one single outlet, one double one or one fused connew spur cable, which can be used to connect either one or two spur outlets or one fused connection unit. Before connecting the spur, cover the knock-out box or backplate with a blank plate.

Consumer unit connection

If you are running an extra single socket outlet or a fused connection unit (up to 13amps) direct from the consumer unit, you wire the socket or unit in the normal way – but with only one set of conductors. The other end of the cable is fed directly into the consumer unit and great care must be taken here because a wrong connection could cause a lot of expensive damage.

The consumer unit is clearly marked inside: the red (live) wire from your cable must be connected to a spare live terminal block, the black conductor must be connected to a spare terminal on the neutral terminal block and the earth must be connected to its corresponding place on the earth

terminal block. Use 2.5sq mm cable for the circuit, and fit a 20-amp fuse in the consumer unit.

Double socket

When you are replastering a single socket outlet or removing it to run off a spur, you should consider whether it is worthwhile replacing the outlet with a double (or twin) socket outlet. The terminal connections on double sockets match those on single outlets; all you have to do is exchange them.

The easiest method is to place a slim surface-mounted box over the recessed knock-out box (if you have one and provided you have enough cable). Smooth the edges of the entry hole with a file to ensure the stripped insulation does not chafe. You will probably have to secure the box to the wall with plugs each side of the old box, so take care not to drill into the ring circuit cable. If you have an existing surface-mounted box, you must remove this and replace both the backplate box and the socket outlet.

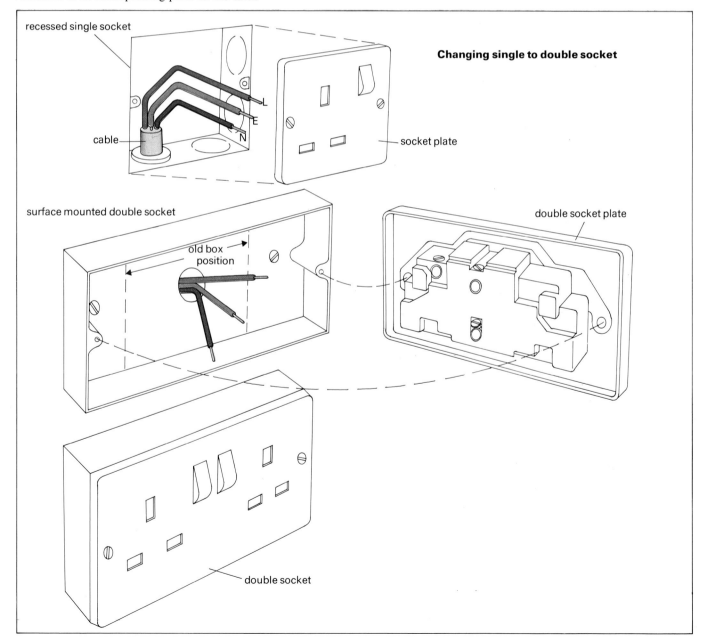

recessed single socket
cable
L
E
N
Changing single to double socket
socket plate
surface mounted double socket
old box position
double socket plate
double socket

Adding lights and switches

It is a simple operation to add an extra ceiling light, controlled by its own switch, to an existing lighting circuit. If as in most modern homes the wiring is flat twin PVC-sheathed cable, it is likely the loop-in system is used, which means an extension can be taken direct from an existing ceiling rose.

In recently wired installations the circuit cable also contains an earth continuity conductor (ecc), which is looped in and out of an earth terminal in the ceiling rose. If your lighting circuits are wired on the junction box system – common until the mid-1960s – there should normally be one junction box for every light and its switch.

Loop-in extension

Drill a 13mm (½in) diameter hole in the ceiling at the new light position and another hole in the ceiling immediately above the new switch position. Any floorboards above will have to be raised, as will some along the new cable route to gain access above the ceiling. Switch off at the mains and remove the ceiling rose and pendant flex at the connecting light. Take care not to separate joined wires; if necessary use insulation tape to keep them together temporarily.

Take your coil of 1sq mm two core and earth PVC-sheathed cable and mark 'mains' on the end of the sheath; push the end through the hole in the ceiling at the connecting light, leaving the existing wires protruding from the ceiling. Then pull through sufficient cable from the floor above (or in

the roof space) to reach the position above the new light. Thread the cable through holes drilled in the joists, at least 50mm (2in) below the top of the joists, and pass the end of the cable through the hole in the ceiling, leaving about 300mm (12in) for connections at the new rose. Cut the cable at the old ceiling rose position, leaving about the same amount for connections.

Take the cable coil to the switch position and push the end through the hole in the ceiling. From above, run it to the new light and pass the end down alongside the first cable marked 'mains'.

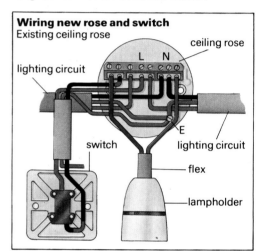

Wiring new rose and switch
Existing ceiling rose

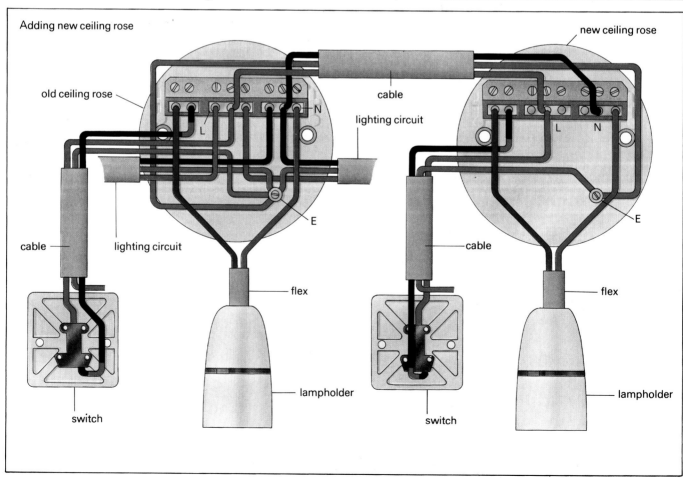

Adding new ceiling rose

Mounting a new ceiling rose

If there is no suitable mounting for the new light, fix a piece of 100 × 25mm (4 × 1in) timber between the joists just above the ceiling, having first drilled a hole in the timber to take the two sheathed cables. Cut the cable at the switch position about 1.37m (4ft 6in) above floor level, leaving about 300mm (12in) for connections.

Knock out the thin plastic in the base of the ceiling rose, thread in the two cables and fix the rose to the ceiling with screws 25mm (1in) long. Strip about 50mm (2in) of sheathing from the end of the cable marked 'mains' and about 6mm (¼in) of insulation from the end of the red and the black wire. Insert the bared end of the red conductor into one of the terminal holes in the live (centre) terminal and tighten the screw. Connect the black wire to the neutral terminal, using the middle hole. Push the cable slack back into the ceiling, making sure the end of the sheath will be within the rose.

Prepare the end of the other cable in the same way and connect the red wire into one of the other two holes in the live terminal. Slip a short piece of red PVC sleeving or insulation tape over the end of the black wire and insert this into the inner terminal hole of the two-hole (switch wire) terminal bank. Slip green/yellow PVC sleeving over the bare earth wires and connect them to the earth terminal.

Now connect the pendant flex. Strip about 75mm (3in) of sheath from the end of a length of two core flex. Bare the ends and connect the brown to the outer hole of the switch wire terminal and the blue to the outer hole of the neutral terminal. Tighten all terminal screws and hook the flex wires over the anchor pieces: thread on the rose cover and screw it to its base. Connect the lampholder to the other

end of the flex, using the same method as for the ceiling rose; if the unsheathed wires protrude from the cap, the flex wires must be shortened.

Connecting a switch

If the switch is to be surface-mounted, take the plastic surface box and knock out a thin section for the cable. Hold the box in position against the wall and mark the fixing holes. Drill and plug them to take No 8 screws. If the switch is to be flush-mounted you must use a metal knock-out box. The cable from the ceiling to the box can be fixed to the surface, using plastic cable clips spaced no more than 400mm (16in) apart or buried in the plaster.

The end of the cable is stripped and the conductors prepared as for a ceiling rose. The red wire, which is the live feed, is connected to the common terminal. The black wire, the switch wire, is enclosed in a short piece of red PVC sleeving or PVC insulation tape and connected to the L2 terminal. The earth should be enclosed in green/yellow PVC sleeving and connected to the earth terminal in the mounting box. The switch is secured to its box by two screws supplied.

Replacing the existing rose

Replace the existing wires as before; if you had an old type ceiling rose, replace with a modern one with in-line shrouded terminals. Strip and prepare the end of the new cable as for the first ceiling rose. Connect the red wire to the centre terminal (alongside another red wire if there is no spare terminal hole), the black wire to the neutral terminal and the earth wire in green/yellow PVC sleeving to the earth terminal. Any existing unsleeved earth wires in the rose should be sleeved before reconnecting.

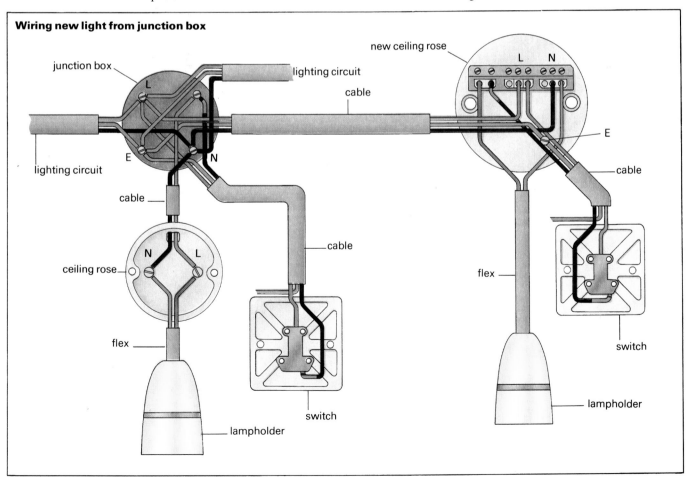

Wiring new light from junction box

junction box

lighting circuit

lighting circuit

cable

ceiling rose

flex

lampholder

switch

cable

new ceiling rose

L   N

cable

E

cable

flex

switch

lampholder

Junction box extension

After switching off the power, locate an existing, suitably placed junction box by lifting boards or checking in the roof space, unscrew the cover and examine the wires and terminals. The red live wire of the new cable is connected to the terminal having two or more red wires, the black neutral wire is connected to the terminal containing two or more black wires and the earth wire with its green/yellow sleeving goes to the terminal containing the earth wires. The remainder of the work is the same as when looping out of a ceiling rose to another rose.

Moving a light

When a ceiling light is to be moved, take down the existing pendant (having, of course, switched off the power) and pull back the cables into the ceiling space – taking care not to separate wires connected to any one terminal. Mark which of the two wires or sets of jointed wires were connected to the flex terminals, for it is from these the extension is made. Nail a piece of 100×25mm (4×1in) timber between the joists, about halfway down, and fix a four-terminal 5amp junction box to it. Drill a hole in the ceiling at the new position and lift boards and drill holes in the joists as necessary for the route of the new cable from the junction box to the light. Run a length of cable from the junction box to the light and pass the end through the hole in the ceiling. Connect the live wire to the switched live rose terminal, and the neutral and earth wires as before.

At the junction box, connect the existing wires to the box terminals. If the existing light was a loop-in ceiling rose, all four terminals in the box will be used. Otherwise only two, plus earth, will be needed. Prepare the end of the cable as already described and connect the red to the single wire which was connected to flex. If this is a black wire, enclose the end in red sleeving or PVC-insulated tape before connecting it to the junction box terminal. Connect the black wire to the terminal now containing one, two or more black wires and connect the earth with its green/yellow sleeving to the one containing the earth wires. If the circuit has no earth, connect it to a spare terminal. Replace the box cover.

Fitting an extra light

When you need an extra light that is to be controlled by an existing switch, follow the instructions given for moving a light, except that instead of using a junction box you leave the original light in position, install a new ceiling rose and connect the new cable to the existing ceiling rose terminals carrying the flex wires.

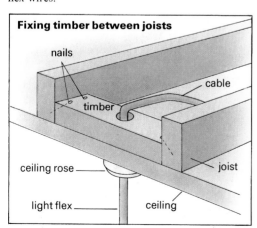

Fixing timber between joists

nails — timber — cable — ceiling rose — light flex — ceiling — joist

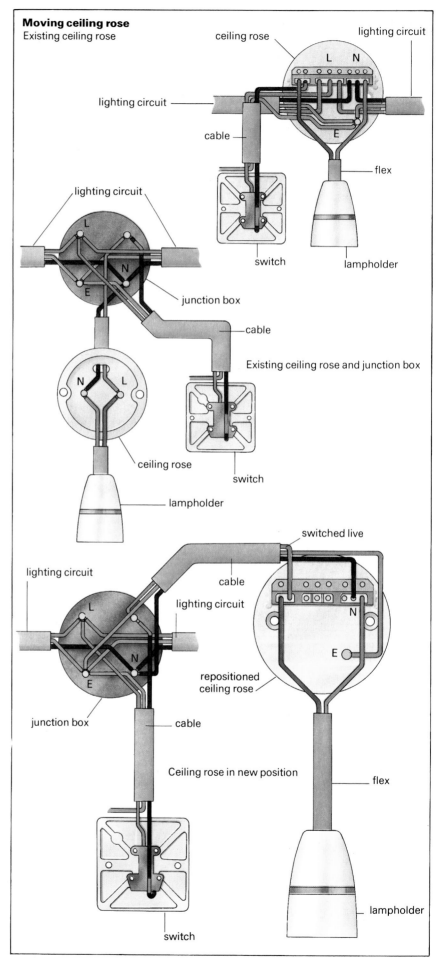

Moving ceiling rose
Existing ceiling rose

ceiling rose — lighting circuit — lighting circuit — cable — flex — switch — lampholder

Existing ceiling rose and junction box

lighting circuit — junction box — cable — ceiling rose — lampholder — switch

Ceiling rose in new position

lighting circuit — lighting circuit — junction box — cable — switch — switched live — repositioned ceiling rose — flex — lampholder

258

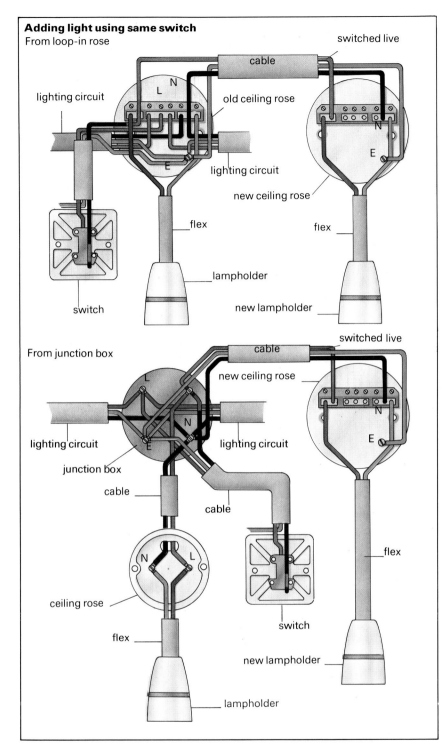

Adding light using same switch
From loop-in rose

lighting circuit

switched live

cable

L N

old ceiling rose

new ceiling rose

lighting circuit

E

N

E

flex

flex

lampholder

switch

new lampholder

From junction box

switched live

cable

new ceiling rose

L

N

lighting circuit

lighting circuit

E

junction box

N

E

cable

cable

flex

N L

ceiling rose

switch

flex

new lampholder

lampholder

Fitting an extra switch
Adding a second switch to a lighting point, such as at the end of a hall or at the back door to provide another switch in a kitchen, not only adds to your convenience but probably helps you to save electricity. Replace the existing one-way switch with a two-way switch, install a two-way switch in the second position and link the two switches together by fitting a 1sq mm three core and earth PVC-sheathed cable.

If the existing switch is the modern square plate mounted on either a plastic surface box or a metal flush-mounted box, remove the existing switch, push the end of the new cable into the box through the existing grommet, run the cable up the wall through the ceiling, under the floorboards (or roof space) and down through the ceiling to the second switch position, where you fit either a surface or flush-mounted recess box.

Three terminals A two-way switch has three terminals – Common, L1 and L2. The two existing wires disconnected from the one-way switch are connected to terminals L1 and L2, although it does not matter which goes to which terminal. The three core and earth sheathed cable has three insulated wires: red, yellow and blue. The red wire goes to the Common terminal, the yellow wire to terminal L1 and the blue to L2. The earth in its green/yellow sleeving is connected to the earth terminal of the box. At the second switch there are only three new wires plus the earth. The red wire is connected to the Common terminal, the yellow to L1 and the blue to L2 and the green/yellow-sleeved earth to the box's earth terminal. Arrange the wires neatly in each box and secure the switches with the screws provided with the fitting.

Fitting a cord switch
Cord-operated ceiling switches are made in one and two-way versions; so in a bedroom, for example, you can fit a switch on the ceiling above the bed-head as well as the normal switch by the door. The three core cable is passed down through a hole in the ceiling instead of down the wall and the switch fixed to the ceiling. If necessary mount the switch on a piece of timber fixed between the joists, as already described. The connections are the same as for a wall switch.

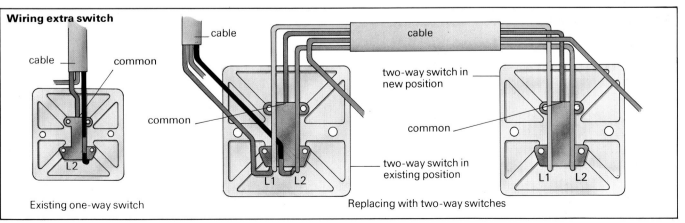

Wiring extra switch

cable

cable

cable

common

common

two-way switch in new position

common

two-way switch in existing position

cable

L2

L1 L2

L1 L2

Existing one-way switch

Replacing with two-way switches

Dimmers and time switches

The dimmer is an electronic device which contains a semi-conductor, associated components and a TV suppressor. But unlike the old resistor dimmer, which consumed unwanted wattage and became very hot, the modern version does not use a significant amount of electricity and can be regarded as an energy saver.

These switches have been designed to replace any one-way lighting switch of the square-plate pattern, simply by removing the existing switch and fitting the dimmer in its place; this is connected to the same wiring and does not require any modification to the circuit.

If you are replacing the old round (tumbler) switch mounted on a wood block or plastic plate (pattress), it is necessary to replace the block or pattress with a standard flush-mounting box.

Warning In all cases follow the manufacturer's instructions for fitting and always turn off the electricity at the mains before you start work.

Types of dimmer

The low-priced dimmer consists of a rotary action knob which reduces lighting from full brilliance down to off. This is adequate for most purposes, its one disadvantage being that the control has to be set each time the dimmer is switched on, since it has to be rotated through the full dimming operation to switch off the light.

There are many situations where it is more convenient to switch a dimmed light off and on without having to adjust the control; this can be achieved by fitting a combined dimmer and on-off switch. One type has a slide control for dimming; another has a milled-edge dial and a third a single push-on/pull-off control for switching.

Two-way switch A dimmer can be inserted in a two-way switching circuit to allow, for example, a landing light operated from both landing and hall to be dimmed as required. The dimmer switch can be fixed in any position, but for ease of wiring it is best installed near one of the two-way switches and preferably mounted on the same box, which would replace the existing one gang box (which takes a single switch).

To do this, remove the two-way switch and its box and fit a dual box, which in the case of a flush-mounted fitting will mean enlarging the recess in the plaster. A dual box is slightly larger than the ordinary two gang box (which takes two switches) used for double socket outlets and has two fixing lugs in the centre to take a fixing screw for each switch.

If the existing switch, in which a dimmer is to be incorporated, is a two gang unit controlling the hall and landing light, the two gang unit is retained. The dimmer, which is a one gang unit, must only be wired to control one of the lights.

Dimming two lights Dimmer switches with a single knob incorporating push-on/pull-off action are made in two gang versions to control two different lights.

Dimming part lighting A special combined dimmer/

1 Wiring for dimmer switch and for ordinary switch
2 Wiring two-way dimmer with ordinary two-way switch
3 Portable plug-in dimmer incorporating on/off switch
4 One or two-way dimmer with separate on/off switch
5 One or two-way dimmer with separate on/off switch
6 One or two-way combined dimmer and on/off switch
7 Light sensitive dimmer (on at dusk, off at dawn)
8 One or two-way combined dimmer and on/off switch with chrome finish
9 Master/slave touch dimmer
10 One or two-way sliding dimmer and separate on/off switch
11 Milled-edge drum dimmer and separate on/off switch
12 Combined dimmer and on/off switch which has facility to provide both dimmed and fixed lighting
13 One or two-way combined dimmer and on/off switch
14 Combined dimmer and on/off switch with chrome finish
15 Time lag dimmer

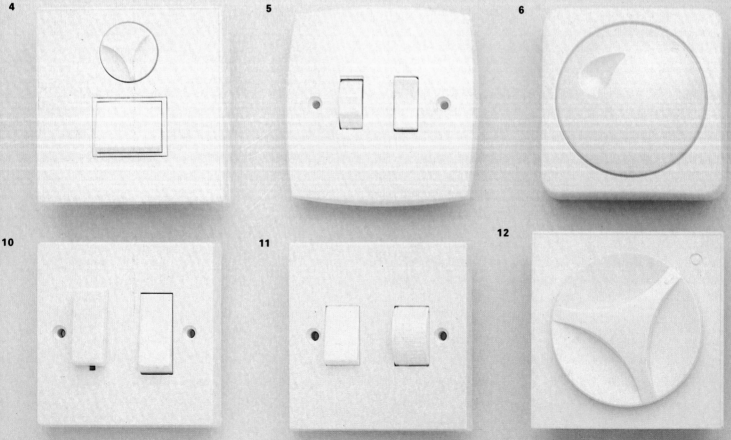

4

5

6

10

11

12

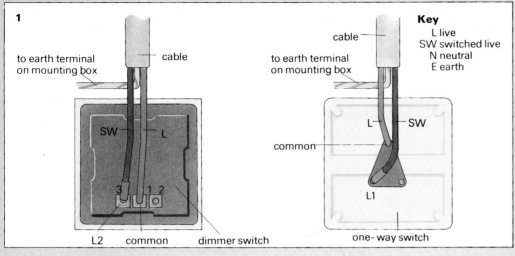

1

to earth terminal
on mounting box — cable

SW — L

3 — 1 2

L2 — common — dimmer switch

cable

to earth terminal
on mounting box

Key
L live
SW switched live
N neutral
E earth

L — SW

common

L1

one-way switch

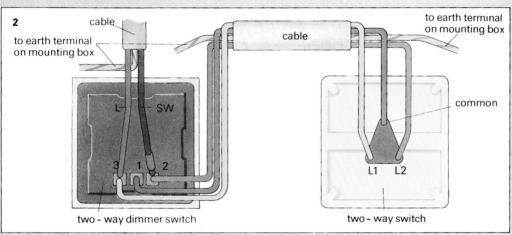

2

to earth terminal
on mounting box — cable

L — SW

3 1 2

two-way dimmer switch

cable

to earth terminal
on mounting box

common

L1 L2

two-way switch

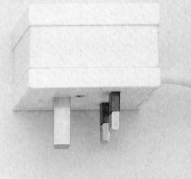

3

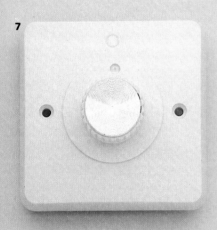

7

8

9

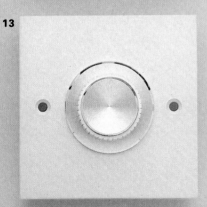

13

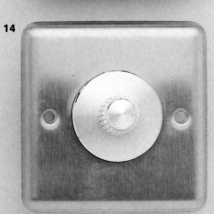

14

15

on-off switch can be used to replace any existing two-gang switch unit to provide the facility for dimming some lighting in a room, while using the rest of the lighting at a fixed intensity. In a dining/living room, for example, you can have a rise-and-fall pendant over the dining table under dimmer control, while the centre light, wall lights or spotlights may be at fixed intensity, or vice versa.

There is a more expensive unit available which provides dimming facilities on two different sets of lighting and, like all the other dimmers, requires no alteration to the wiring when replacing a conventional switch, in this case a two gang switch.

Table lamp dimmer

Table or standard lamps may be put under dimmer control by fitting a lampholder adaptor. You simply remove the lamp, fit the dimmer in its place and insert the lamp in the dimmer lampholder. Intensity is controlled by a knob on the side of the dimmer.

Another version is available in the form of a plug adaptor. This is either connected to the flex of the portable lamp or has its own pins to connect with a socket outlet and has a socket of its own into which the lamp is connected.

Armchair or bedside dimming is possible with a portable dimmer switch, which is sold in either white or orange and has a black weighted base. The dimmer is controlled by rotating the top and slight downward pressure switches the light on or off. The control unit is connected by a flexible cord to a socket adaptor, into which the portable lamp is plugged.

Touch dimmer

The most recent type available is the touch dimmer, which is operated when a gentle touch on a small touch pad, fitted flush into the switch plate, operates the dimming and/or switching. These dimmers all fit standard square flush-mounted metal boxes.

One touch on the pad dims the light; repeated tapping varies the dimming until the desired level is reached. There are separate touch pads for changing the light level up and down and the unit has a memory which restores the light level after a power cut. These dimmers, which contain a fuse to protect the circuitry, must not be fitted into a two-way circuit.

Master touch dimmer

Another version of the touch dimmer enables dimming to be controlled from more than one switching position. For two-way switching, a master touch dimmer is fitted in place of a switch at one position and a slave dimmer at the second point or each point on an intermediate switching circuit. The master has a neon indicator.

Dimmer switch failure

Dimmers should be chosen and treated carefully because they contain delicate components. Never exceed the watts rating. Low-priced equipment with ratings of only 200 watts are satisfactory for simple light fittings; but if you are likely to install a multi-light fitting at a later date, it is better to fit a dimmer in the 400–500 watts range. This also applies to wall lights when there is a chance that more powerful replacement bulbs will be fitted later on.

If a dimmer is overloaded it will almost certainly fail. Dimmer failure is sometimes caused by failure

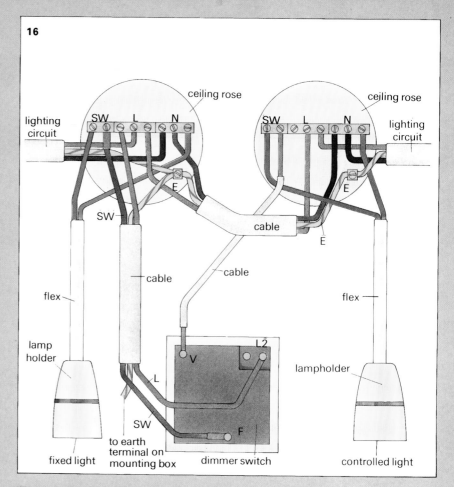

16

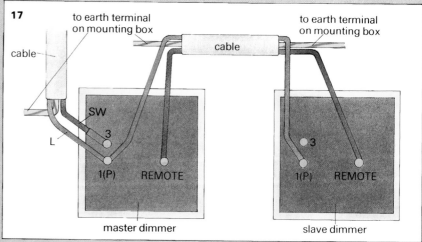

17
master dimmer   slave dimmer

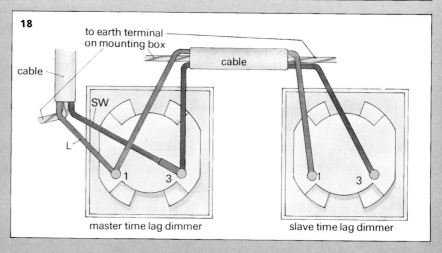

18
master time lag dimmer   slave time lag dimmer

of a light bulb when a surge of heavy current flows in the circuit and through the dimmer: this short circuit can exist long enough to destroy the semiconductor. To eliminate these risks, manufacturers are beginning to introduce small sand-filled cartridge fuses – similar to, but smaller than, a 13amp plug fuse – into their dimmer switches.

Types of time switch

The conventional vacuum-operated time lag switch – used with stair and corridor lighting to save electricity – will operate for up to five minutes, but can be dangerous to stair users because it gives no warning before cutting out. The control, which can also be fitted in place of any square-plate switch, comes in a touch pad version.

However the most up-to-date version is a device which incorporates a time lag control with the touch pad facility but maintains a degree of light; the light does not cut out, but fades and then holds indefinitely at a safety level. A slight touch will then turn off the light electronically. This is also a standard square-plate switch and can replace any one-way switch without wiring modifications.

Also available is a master time lag dimmer of the touch pad type which can be used in a two-way or intermediate switching circuit. It is fitted in place of one of the two-way switches (or intermediate switches in a multi-switching circuit) and the other remains as an ordinary switch; but it also operates the light or lights and begins the time lag sequence.

Burglar deterrent switches
Leaving lights on in a house may deter a casual would-be intruder, but it is unlikely to fool a professional house-breaker. Deterrent lighting should be switched on and off at the proper time and solar-operated devices, which go on at sundown and off at sunrise, are available.

One of the most useful for the home is a dimmer switch fitted with a photo cell which enables the light to be left on at a low level and therefore is not expensive to run. This can be used to replace any modern square-plate one-way or two-way switch without modification to the wiring.

Another type of burglar deterrent is the combined on-off time switch which operates as an ordinary switch and can be set to turn lights on or off automatically at frequent intervals to give the impression the house is being used. Bear in mind, house-breakers know which rooms are used when.

16 Wiring dimmer switch to provide both fixed and controlled light in same room
17 Wiring master dimmer to slave
18 Wiring master time lag dimmer to slave
19 Slimline time switch with socket outlet, override switch and facility for two on/off switchings in 24 hours
20 Time switch with socket outlet, override switch and facility for one or two on/off switchings in 24 hours
21 Time switch with socket outlet, override switch and facility for hourly on/off switching

Installing spot and wall lights

Wall-mounted lights and spotlights offer wide scope for lighting arrangements since they can be installed in any room as the main lighting or to supplement existing lighting, which is usually supplied by a conventional ceiling rose. If you have individual lighting, such as a rise and fall pendant over the dining table, wall lights can be used to provide general illumination.

Spotlights are particularly versatile since they can be fitted on the wall or the ceiling and can be used to highlight particular features of the room such as pictures, displays or even curtains. Spotlights are particularly useful for providing local lighting for reading, sewing and other similar activities since they are available with swivel brackets which allow the light to be directed as required. Wall lights or spotlights are also very useful in a double bedroom since light can be localized, causing the minimum disturbance to the other occupant.

Types of lamp Spotlights use two principal kinds of lamps: a reflector lamp of 75 watts is available in clear (white), blue, green, red and yellow; the PAR 38 sealed beam spotlight and floodlight (100 and 150 watts) is available in the same range of colours. The latter is suitable for both indoor and outdoor use, the floodlight version giving a wider beam of light suitable for illuminating outdoor areas. When buying fittings for spotlights, check which size and type of lamp it will accept; on some models the wattage is stamped inside the holder.

Fittings These are usually made of either polished or matt aluminium or finished in enamel in a variety of colours including white and pastel shades of green, yellow and mauve. Lighting track is particularly useful for holding spotlights. Available in various lengths, this can be fixed to the ceiling or wall and will take a number of spotlights which can be locked in position on the track.

Wiring wall lights

New wall lights may well need wiring extensions from the existing circuit, unless you are fortunate enough to move into a new home where wall lights have already been installed by previous owners or decide to fit wall lights with a flexible cord from a plug and socket outlet. In the case of new circuit wiring, the power may be run from three sources – from an existing lighting circuit, from a ring circuit via a fused connection unit or from a new lighting circuit in the consumer unit.

The lights are usually added to the circuit supplying the same floor, although there is much to be said for using a different circuit – from another floor, if it is a two-storey house, or from a circuit supplying other rooms, if a bungalow. A different circuit will mean the lights in the room will be supplied from more than one circuit, preventing a blackout should a fuse blow. This will also ease pressure on the ground floor or main living area lighting circuit, which tends to become overloaded if extra lights are added. There are regulations covering the maximum number of lights on one circuit – 12 lamps not more than 100 watts each on one circuit and fewer when one or more 150 watt lamps are fitted. Where added wall lights – especially those having two lamps, even if they are only 40 or 60 watts – will exceed the regulation number, use another circuit or install a new circuit, which can be a fused spur from a ring main.

Wiring from existing circuits Although wall lights are more conveniently controlled independently from the other lighting, wiring can be simplified by connecting to the existing fittings and using the existing light switch by the door. In this case the wall lights should have their own switches so they may be turned off if you want just a main light.

1 Screw cap crown-silvered spotlamp
2 Bayonet cap reflector spotlamp
3 Screw cap reflector spotlamp
4 Dual box
5 Bayonet cap reflector spot lamp
6 Screw cap sealed beam PAR 38 lamp
7 BESA box with brass bush
8 Architrave box

9

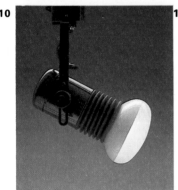

10

11

12

13

14

15

The problem with this arrangement is that to have the wall lights on you must also have the main light on. This can be overcome either by fixing a cord-operated ceiling switch or by replacing the lampholder in the ceiling with a switched version, if it has an open shade. A more satisfactory solution is to connect to the neutral terminal on the existing light and replace the existing one gang switch with a two gang switch; the second switch will be for the wall lights. Mount the new switch on the same box and use the existing unswitched live to supply both switches. This technique has been covered earlier in the book.

Where, however, the existing circuit is wired on the loop-in ceiling rose system, as most modern circuits are, there will be a live terminal as well as a neutral one at the rose; this is the ideal source of electricity for the wall light circuit. If not wired on the loop-in system and if the ceiling light switch is located in the wrong part of the room, it will be necessary either to locate a junction box on the lighting circuit to allow access to a live terminal or to run a cable from the lighting circuit fuseway in the consumer unit.

Whichever method you use to obtain the source of electricity, you will need a four terminal 15/20amp plastic junction box – the basic accessory for the wiring – and flat 1.0sq mm twin core and earth, PVC sheathed cable.

The junction box is fixed under the floor to a piece of timber between the joists, roughly equidistant from the wall lights and the wall switch position. A convenient position for the box is above the existing ceiling light, if the light is used for looping. Run a length of cable from the junction box to each wall light, preferably a separate cable to each. This will save you having to run two cables down the wall to all but the last wall light, and having to house two cables and the connectors in the confined space behind the backplate.

Run a cable from the junction box to the switch position; if this is the same as the existing switch, a two gang unit replaces the one gang switch. Run a final cable from the junction box to the source of supply – the ceiling lighting point, a junction box or the consumer unit. When making the connections at the junction box, ensure the ends of the sheathing terminate within the box and all earth conductors are enclosed in green/yellow PVC sheathing.

Wiring from ring circuit In this case it is necessary to insert a fused connection unit into the 30amp ring main and fit a 3amp fuse in the unit to protect the lighting wiring, which has a lower current rating. The simplest method is to loop out of a convenient 13amp socket outlet connected to the ring cable and not fed from a spur cable.

The socket outlet you choose should be on the first floor, if in a two-storey house, so cable may be run under the floorboards; this will save having cable running up walls and will also normally mean the lights are on a different circuit than, for example, table lamps, which will be on the ring circuit in the ground floor rooms.

Turn the power off and remove a socket outlet to check it is not a spur, as described earlier in the book. A single socket box can be replaced by a dual box which is slightly longer than a two gang box and has two extra screw-fixing lugs for mounting two single accessories side by side (in this instance one will be the fused connection unit). If connecting the fused connection unit to a double socket, you will need a separate single box for the unit alongside the socket box. The fused connection unit must be connected to the socket outlet terminals by 2.5sq mm twin core and earth PVC-sheathed cable.

From the fused connection unit run a length of 1.0sq mm twin core and earth PVC-sheathed cable to the junction box feeding the wall lights and switch. Connect the 2.5sq mm cable to the mains terminals of the fused connection unit and the 1.0sq mm cable to the load terminals.

9 Track-mounted spotlights. **10** Track-mounted spot with reflector lamp. **11** Track-mounted spots. **12** Spotlight for wall or ceiling mounting. **13** Clamp-on fitting. **14** Sealed beam spot for wall or ceiling mounting. **15** Outdoor sealed beam spot. **16** Wiring a cord-operated switch to a ceiling light. **17a** The wiring system for the existing junction box and ceiling rose. **17b** Wiring a two gang switch from the junction box system. **17c** Wiring a separate switch from the junction box system

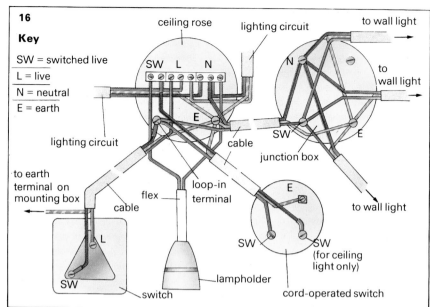

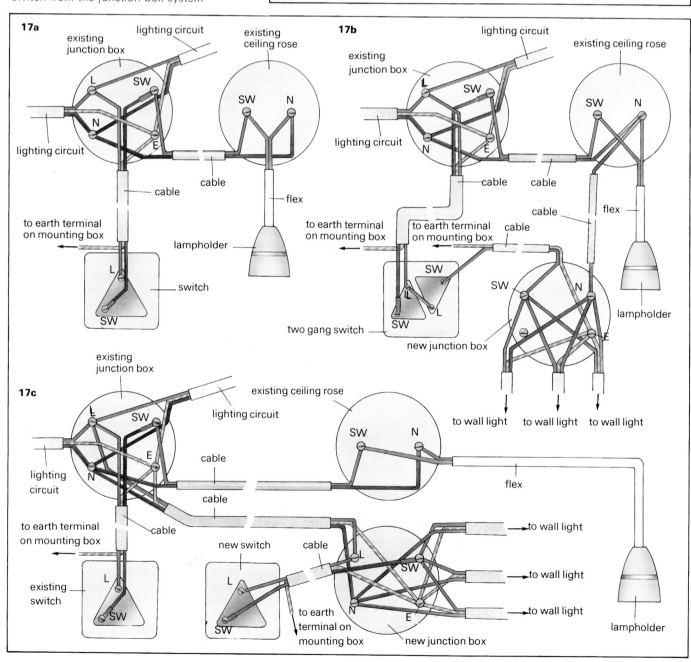

266

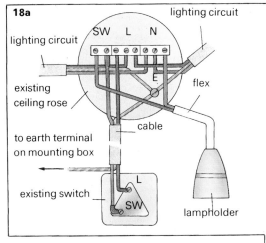

18a

lighting circuit

lighting circuit

SW L N

E

existing ceiling rose

flex

cable

to earth terminal on mounting box

existing switch

L

SW

lampholder

18b

lighting circuit

existing ceiling rose

SW L N

E

lighting circuit

cable   cable

new junction box

flex

to earth terminal on mounting box

to earth terminal on mounting box

N

E

SW

cable

SW

E

L

SW

two gang switch

to wall lights

lampholder

18c

lighting circuit

SW L N

existing ceiling rose

E

lighting circuit

new junction box

cable   cable

flex

to earth terminal on mounting box

to earth terminal on mounting box

N

E

L

SW

cable

L

SW

L

SW

existing switch   new switch

to wall lights

lampholder

Mounting wall lights

Most wall light fittings are situated at the traditional height of 1.8m (6ft) above floor level; they can be fitted at any preferred height, depending upon the height of the ceiling and the style of the fitting.

Usually they have a backplate or base which has an open back. Regulations require the ends of cables, cable connectors and fitting flex to be totally enclosed in non-combustible material; a plastic or metal box is usually sunk into the wall and covered by the backplate of the fitting. Often the wall lights will have a circular backplate with two fixing holes drilled at 50mm (2in) fixing centres which match the standard 'BS' circular conduit box (termed BESA).

A plastic box can be used for all but very heavy fittings. If a metal box is used, fit a male brass bush into the threaded conduit entry in the edge to prevent the cable chafing as it enters the box. The metal version is also used for lights having a rectangular backplate with drilled fixings, made of wood, metal or plastic. Many wall lights, however, have no BESA plate and some are very narrow and of shapes unsuited to the BESA box. These require a narrow metal knock-out box (half the width of a socket outlet box) called an architrave box and designed for use with an architrave plateswitch. Remove the knock-out disc from the box and fit a PVC grommet to protect the cable.

The box is sunk into a chase cut into the wall, fixed with screws in plugged holes. Thread in the circuit cable, dropping it down from the ceiling; the cable may be clipped to the wall or buried in the plaster as desired. Trim and prepare the end of the cable in each box by stripping off the sheathing down to about 19mm ($\frac{3}{4}$in) and remove about 9mm ($\frac{3}{8}$in) of insulation from the two insulated conductors; slip green/yellow PVC sleeving over the bare end of the earth conductor. Using a two way insulated cable connector (already connected to the fitting wires in some wall light fittings), connect the red circuit wire to the brown wire of the fitting, the black to the blue and the earth wire of each to the earth terminal in the box. If there is no earth terminal, as in a plastic box, terminate the earth with a one way cable connector.

With a BESA box, secure the fitting to the box lugs with M.4 metric (2BA) screws (usually supplied). With an architrave box, the fitting can be fixed directly to the wall using screws in plugged holes. Should one of the fixing holes coincide with the box, it will be necessary to fix a drilled metal cover to the box using M3.5 metric (4BA) screws; drill another hole in the cover for a self-tapping

screw to hold the fitting. Run cable down to the switch and fit as described earlier in the book. Check the power is still turned off and connect the cable to the existing ceiling fitting, junction box or fuseway as relevant.

Mounting spotlights

Spotlights can be mounted at any height on a wall or in any position on a ceiling. Wiring is the same as for wall lights, except when the spotlights are to be ceiling-mounted; here a cable is passed through a hole pierced in the ceiling as for a conventional ceiling rose.

Most spotlight fittings have a circular base drilled for 50mm (2in) fixings and are therefore suitable for mounting on a BESA box. Many are sold ready wired with a short length of three core

18a Existing loop-in ceiling rose system. **18b** Wiring a two gang switch from the loop-in system. **18c** Wiring a separate switch from the loop-in system. **19a** Wiring a new circuit from the consumer unit. **19b** Wiring a new circuit from a ring circuit. **20a** Mounting a wall light on a BESA box. **20b** Mounting a wall light on an architrave box; where it cannot be screwed both sides of the box, fit a metal cover and hold the fitting with a self-tapping screw

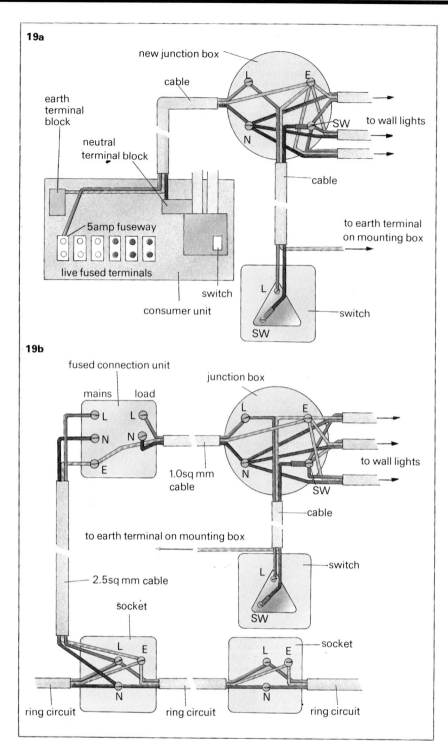

19a

new junction box

cable

earth terminal block

neutral terminal block

L E

SW → to wall lights

N

cable

to earth terminal on mounting box

5amp fuseway

live fused terminals

switch

consumer unit

L

switch

SW

19b

fused connection unit

mains   load

L   L

N   N

E   E

junction box

L   E

N

SW → to wall lights

1.0sq mm cable

cable

to earth terminal on mounting box

2.5sq mm cable

socket

L   E

N

ring circuit

L   E

N

ring circuit

L   E

N

ring circuit

switch

L

SW

socket

circular sheathed flex passing out through a small hole in the baseplate edge. This means instead of being mounted over a BESA box, the base can be fixed directly to the wall and the flex connected to a plug and socket outlet, ceiling rose or switched fused connection unit.

Lighting tracks enable one or more spotlights to be mounted in line on a ceiling or wall. Lighting pendants and the occasional small appliance may also be plugged into a lighting track. Domestic tracks come in standard lengths and couplers enable you to extend the track to any length. The tracks have a current rating of 16amps, although in practice the load is limited to the current rating of the circuit feeding the track. From a 5amp circuit the limit is 1200 watts; from a 3amp fused spur it is 720 watts; from a 13amp fused spur up to 3120 watts may be run off. The last is necessary if a large number of high-powered spotlights are to be connected to the track.

A lighting track is basically a PVC extrusion containing two bare conductors (live and neutral) with an earth strip, enclosed in an anodized aluminium track. Spotlights fitted with track adaptors clip into the track and will slide along until locked into position. Flexible cord adaptors may be fitted to the track to operate a lighting pendant or an appliance fitted with the adaptor in place of a conventional plug. A cord-operated 2amp switch to control up to 480 watts is available, which may be clipped into the track if required. A track can be connected directly to fixed wiring either at a wall lighting point or at a ceiling point in place of a ceiling rose and operated by conventional wall switches. Alternatively flexible cord can be connected to the track terminals, which in turn are connected to a ceiling rose, cord outlet or to a plug and socket outlet.

Warning Every spotlight and wall light must be under the control of an isolating switch, such as a conventional wall switch, even when the fittings have their own integral switches. This is to ensure the lampholder and other live parts are dead whenever you attend to the fitting. A cord-operated, or push-button, integral switch does not indicate whether the fitting is on or off. Spotlights are made in the 100–150 watt range, so check the lighting circuit will not be overloaded; if the circuit would be overloaded, a ring circuit spur should be used to supply the power.

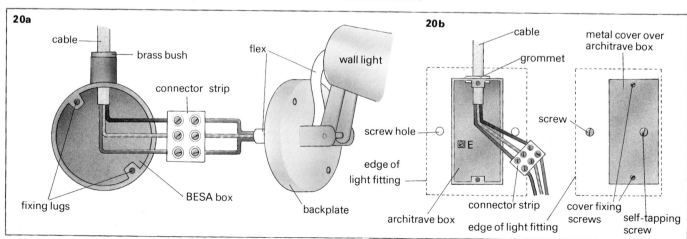

20a

cable

brass bush

connector strip

flex

wall light

fixing lugs

BESA box

backplate

20b

cable

grommet

metal cover over architrave box

screw hole

E

edge of light fitting

screw

connector strip

architrave box

edge of light fitting

cover fixing screws

self-tapping screw

Wiring a converted loft

Extending existing electrical wiring into the roof space to allow extra lighting points and socket outlets is generally similar to wiring extensions in other parts of the house. Adding lights to an existing lighting circuit and sockets to an existing ring circuit have been covered earlier in the book.

Switches, ceiling roses, socket outlets and other wiring accessories can be similar to those used in other parts of the house. They will usually be made of moulded plastic and you can locate them in positions of your own choice. There are no special regulations for loft conversion schemes in IEE Wiring Regulations, but the whole conversion must conform to them as in other parts of the house. Where the scheme includes a bathroom, special electrical precautions must be taken; these are the same as for a conventionally situated bathroom.

Lighting wiring restrictions

It is usually a simple job to connect new wiring to the lighting circuit supplying the upper floor of a two-storey house, but you must consider the restrictions in terms of the electrical load. Before running new cables, check how many lights are already supplied from the circuit. The normal 5amp lighting circuit has a maximum load of 1200 watts; this figure is obtained by multiplying the current rating (5amps) by its voltage (240 volts). The figure does not mean 1200 watts of lighting is actually connected to the circuit at any one time; in practice it is somewhat less.

Assessing load The regulations stipulate you treat each lampholder, containing a lamp of 100 watts or smaller, as 100 watts for the assessment. Lampholders containing lamps larger than 100 watts are assessed at their actual wattage; most lamps used on a domestic lighting circuit are 100 watts or less, including common fluorescent tubes (fluorescent tubes are rated above the stated wattage, so check on this when buying them). A 150 watt lamp is equivalent to one-and-a-half lampholders and a 200 watt lamp is equivalent to two. Count the number of lampholders on the circuit, add the number

you wish to include in the loft conversion and adjust your figures for any 150 or 200 watt lamps. If the final figure is no more than 1200, you can add the chosen number of new lights as described earlier in the book.

If there are two lighting circuits, use the most convenient; in a bungalow for example, the cables will already be in the roof space, running across and between the joists.

Socket wiring restrictions

You can normally add extra sockets to a ring circuit, subject to the area restrictions in the Wiring Regulations (see overleaf). The cables forming the ring circuit on the floor below the loft conversion will normally be under the floorboards. It is rare to find a ring circuit cable which has already been run into the roof space, except possibly to supply a heat/light unit mounted on a bathroom ceiling. Such a cable is most likely to be a spur; as such, you should not use it to supply any other

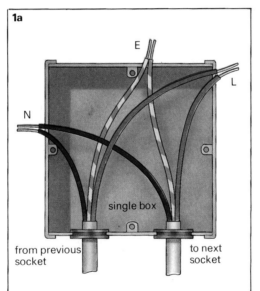

1a

E

L

N

single box

from previous socket

to next socket

Extending ring main from socket outlet:
1a Existing socket wiring
1b Extended wiring with single box replaced by dual box; if extending from double socket outlet, replace double box by dual box and connect two single socket plates in place of original double plate
2a Circuit at original ring socket outlet (overleaf)
2b Extended ring circuit. Fused connection unit, protected by 3amp fuse, can be installed to supply lighting in converted loft area; cable for lighting circuit should be connected to load terminals on fused connection unit (**inset**)

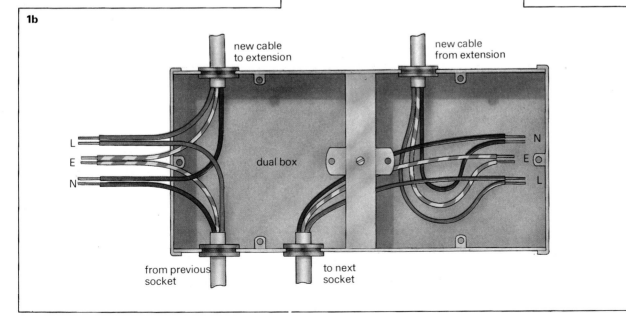

1b

new cable to extension

new cable from extension

L
E
N

dual box

N
E
L

from previous socket

to next socket

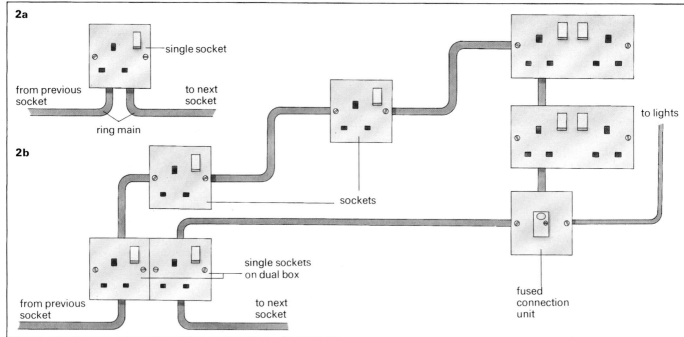

2a

single socket

from previous socket

to next socket

ring main

2b

sockets

single sockets on dual box

from previous socket

to next socket

to lights

fused connection unit

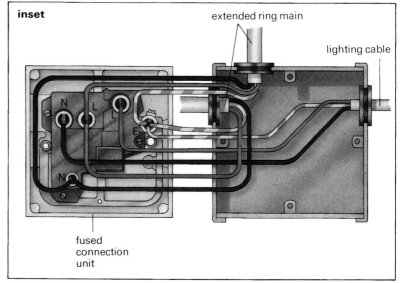

inset

extended ring main

lighting cable

N L L E

N

fused connection unit

outlets apart from the one appliance it serves.

Assessing load Before you run new cables from an existing ring circuit you will have to check on the location of existing socket outlets to ascertain the floor area already served. A domestic ring circuit can supply an unlimited number of 13amp socket outlets and fixed appliances supplied from fused connection units; the latter should have an individual rating of not more than 3000 watts, but an immersion heater or water heater should preferably be wired on a separate radial circuit. Any one ring circuit, however, is limited to supply an area of not more than 100sq m (or 1000sq ft). Before you extend the ring circuit, measure the area of the rooms which have socket outlets run from the circuit and add the area of the proposed loft conversion; if the total is below 100sq m, you can extend this circuit into the loft conversion.

Most three or four-bedroomed houses have two ring circuits; one supplies outlets on the ground floor and the other supplies those on the upper floor. In this case it is a simple matter to measure the area of each; in most cases it will be no more than about 50sq m (or 500sq ft) so you can add the loft space and still not exceed 100sq m (or 1000sq ft). If there is only one ring circuit, you will almost certainly need a new circuit for the loft conversion; this has been covered earlier in the book.

Check which sockets are on which circuit; if you have two ring circuits, remove each of the relevant 30amp circuit fuses in turn and test each socket by plugging in a table lamp. Any fixed appliances, supplied from fused connection units, have to be checked individually as the circuit fuses are removed.

Extending a ring circuit

Use 2.5sq mm twin core and earth flat PVC-sheathed house wiring cable when extending a circuit. The type of extension will depend upon how many outlets you require. If you only need one single socket outlets or one double socket outlet, with no lighting or fixed appliances included in the power circuit, you only need a single length of cable

forming a spur. This is connected to the ring circuit at an existing ring socket outlet or at a junction box inserted into the ring cable; this technique has been described earlier in the book.

Extending cable If the loft space is being converted into a living and/or sleeping area, you will need more than one single or double outlet; you may also need one or more fixed lights as recommended and possibly one or more fixed appliances.

When extending the ring circuit for a full-scale conversion such as this, you will need to extend the ring cable itself. This is done either by opening it up at a socket outlet on the floor below or by cutting cable under the floorboards and running two cables from the break; choose the most convenient method. The two cables resulting from this operation will be the outward and return legs of your ring cable extension. One cable goes to the first new outlet and the other to the last; the remaining outlets are linked together by cable in the form of a ring between these two cables, which are connected into your existing ring circuit at the break in the cable on the floor below. Use two single sockets mounted on a dual box to restore the final ring if connecting in at a socket outlet or two 30amp junction boxes if cutting into the cable.

Running cable The two cables of a ring circuit extension (or the single spur cable if you are using this method) have to be run up the wall from the floor to the loft space via the ceiling. You could run the cables up through a cupboard, but not against a hot water cylinder since the cable will only withstand a maximum temperature of 65°C (150°F). Since structural work will be necessary during the conversion, you should be able to cut a chase into the wall to bury the cables. Make sure you fit all your circuits before decorating.

Different methods

If the existing ring circuit cannot be extended into the loft space because of the area calculation, there are three other possible methods of providing a power circuit for the conversion; you can provide a new ring circuit, a 30amp radial power circuit or install a new one or two-way consumer unit in the loft space. The last method is particularly suitable if the conversion is to be a self-contained flat.

New ring circuit You can fit any number of socket outlets and fixed appliances on a ring circuit. To install it, run two 2.5sq mm twin core and earth PVC-sheathed cables up into the roof space and connect them to a spare 30amp fuseway in the consumer unit. If there is no spare fuseway then you will have to fit a one-way consumer unit or switched fuse unit beside the main consumer unit; this should be connected to the meter by the Electricity Board. Run the ring cables from this unit, using 2.5sq mm twin core and earth PVC-sheathed cable, and protect the circuit with a 30amp fuse. You should provide two lengths of 16sq mm single core PVC-sheathed cable to connect the switched fuse unit to the meter.

Radial power circuits The Wiring Regulations permit two sorts of radial power circuits, either of which could be ideal for providing power in a loft conversion. Which is chosen depends on the actual floor area being served. If this area does not exceed 20sq m (215sq ft), then the circuit is wired up in 2.5sq mm twin core and earth cable and is protected by a 20-amp fuse or miniature circuit breaker (MCB) in the main consumer unit. If the area is more than 20sq m but does not exceed 50 sq m (540 sq ft), then 4.0 sq mm cable is used and a 30-amp cartridge fuse or MCB (but *not* a rewirable fuse) is fitted in the consumer unit. Either circuit can feed an unlimited number of socket outlets.

If there is no spare fuseway in the consumer unit, you will have to fit a switched fuse unit as before; buy an MCB or cartridge fuse type and use 4.0sq mm cable as previously described.

Separate consumer unit Install a two-way consumer unit in the loft space and connect it with 4.0sq mm twin core and earth PVC-sheathed cable to an MCB or cartridge type switched fuse unit next to

Extending ring main between socket outlets:
3a Existing ring cable. **3b** Ring main extended using two 30amp junction boxes.
4a Original ring circuit. **4b** Extended ring circuit
Installing new ring main: **5a** Ring cables run from spare 30amp fuseway in consumer unit; detail of consumer unit wiring (**inset**).
5b Ring cables run from switch fuse; detail of switch fuse wiring (**inset**)

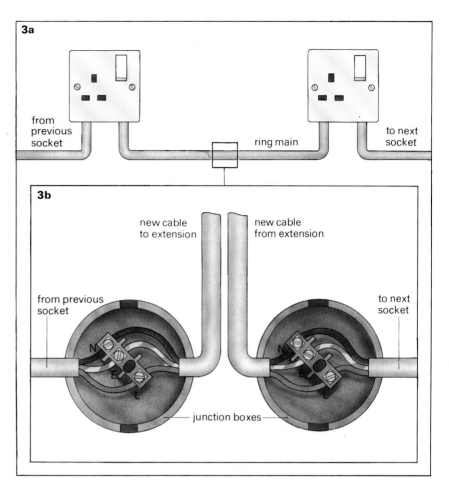

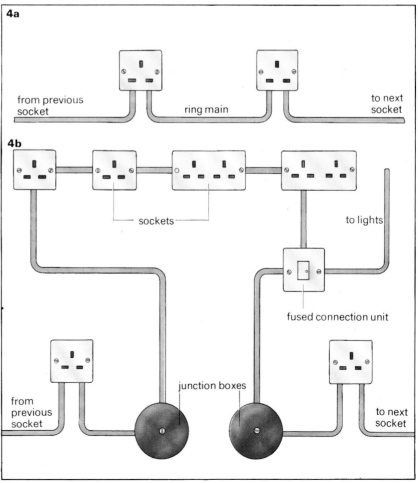

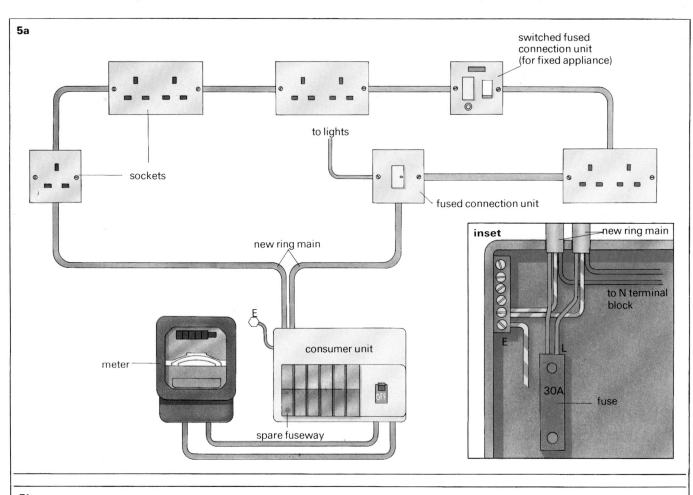

switched fused
connection unit
(for fixed appliance)

to lights

sockets

fused connection unit

new ring main

inset

new ring main

to N terminal
block

E

L

30A

fuse

meter

consumer unit

spare fuseway

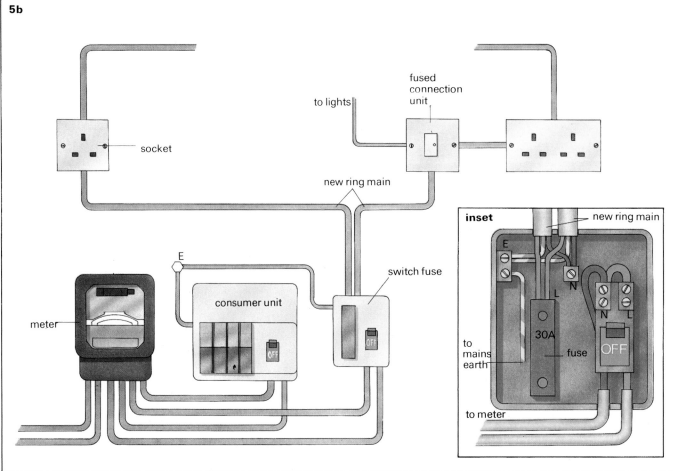

fused
connection
unit

to lights

socket

new ring main

inset

new ring main

E

N

L

N   L

30A

fuse

OFF

to
mains
earth

to meter

meter

consumer unit

switch fuse

OFF

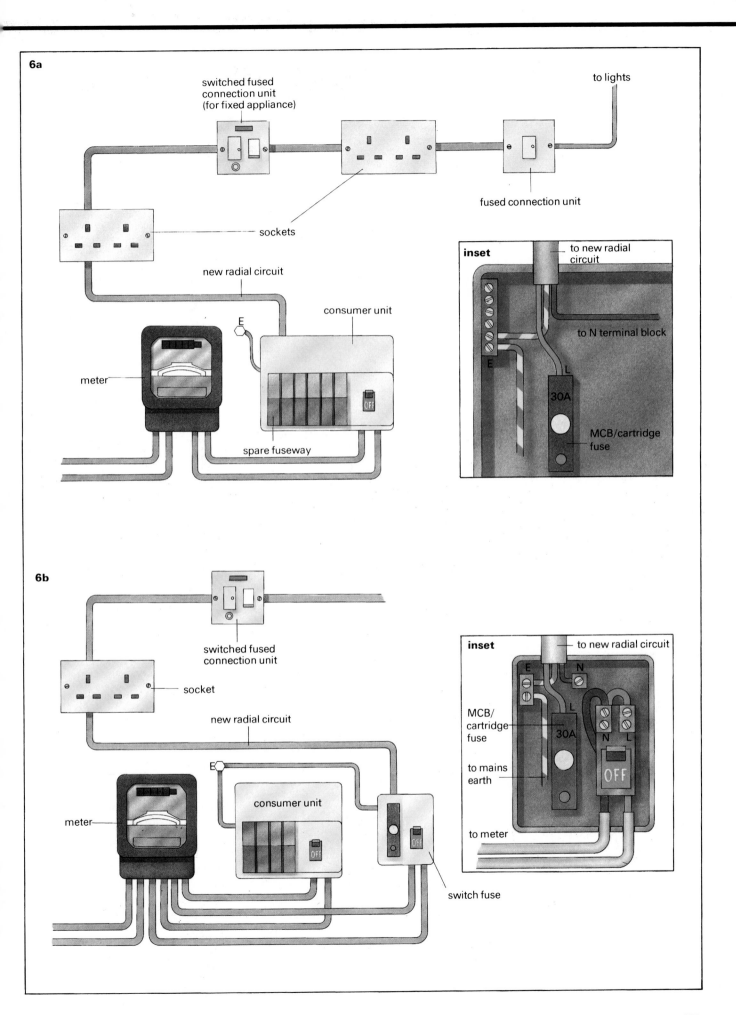

6a

switched fused connection unit (for fixed appliance)

to lights

sockets

fused connection unit

new radial circuit

consumer unit

meter

E

spare fuseway

inset

to new radial circuit

to N terminal block

E

L

30A

MCB/cartridge fuse

6b

switched fused connection unit

socket

new radial circuit

meter

E

consumer unit

OFF

switch fuse

inset

to new radial circuit

E

N

MCB/ cartridge fuse

L

30A

N

L

OFF

to mains earth

to meter

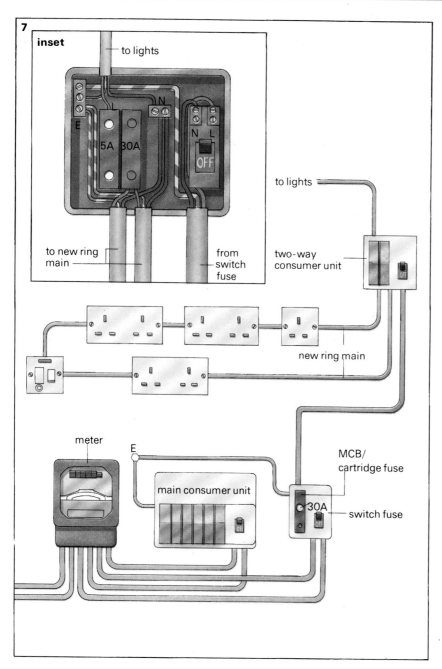

7 inset

to lights

E
5A 30A
N
N L
OFF

to lights

two-way
consumer unit

to new ring
main

from
switch
fuse

new ring main

meter

E

main consumer unit

MCB/
cartridge fuse

30A

switch fuse

Installing new radial circuit:
6a Circuit run from consumer unit; MCB or cartridge fuse must be used at consumer unit (**inset**)
6b Circuit run from switch fuse; again MCB or cartridge fuse must be used at switch fuse (**inset**)
Installing new two-way consumer unit in loft area:
7 Circuit fed from 30amp switch fuse at meter; detail of new consumer unit wiring (**inset**)

the main consumer unit. The switched fuse unit should be fitted with a 30amp fuse; the two-way unit should have a 5amp fuseway for the lighting circuit and a 30amp fuseway for the ring main in the loft. Use 1.0sq mm twin core and earth PVC-sheathed cable for the lighting circuit and 2.5sq mm cable of the same type for the ring main.

Extending a lighting circuit

Use 1.0sq mm twin core and earth PVC-sheathed cable. It is normally only necessary to insert a junction box into the cable running between the joists in the roof space. Alternatively you could connect the new cable to a loop-in ceiling rose mounted on the ceiling immediately below the roof space; pass the cable through the existing hole in the ceiling after you have moved the ceiling rose.

However, since the construction of the loft conversion will probably require re-routing of existing lighting cables and possible partial rewiring (as described below), make provision to connect the

roof space lighting wiring at the appropriate stage.
Using power circuit Although technically correct, it is not always the best installation practice to have all the new lights on the same lighting circuit. If the lights immediately below, including those serving the landing or hall, are on the same circuit and the fuse blows, the exit route and the loft conversion itself will be in darkness. Check whether the hall and landing lights are on the same circuit as the bedroom lights by withdrawing the bedroom lighting circuit fuse and trying the landing and hall lights. If these are on a different circuit to the bedrooms, connect into the bedroom circuit; if they are on the same circuit, it is a good idea to supply one or more of the fixed lighting points from the power circuit in the loft conversion.

Connect these lights to the power circuit via a fused connection unit containing a 3amp fuse. If you supply only one light in this way, its location will depend upon the nature and layout of your loft conversion scheme; the light should be near the entrance. You could fit another light on the stairway outside the entrance to the loft area. This should be controlled by two-way switching, with one of the two switches fitted at the bottom of the stairs. If your conversion warrants only one light of this kind, the fused connection unit can be a switched version so you can use it to control the light. If you require two-way switching in this case, fit a special switched fused connection unit which has a two-way switch instead of the usual one-way switch.

The above considerations are obviously unnecessary if you are installing a separate two-way consumer unit in the loft since the lighting circuit will be independent of those below.

Wiring alterations
Existing wiring in the loft space will usually be lighting circuit wiring; although it is unlikely to be associated with your new wiring, it is almost sure to be disturbed as the structural alterations are made. This will probably mean all cables are re-routed; where they cross joists they should be threaded through holes drilled in the joists at the regulation (minimum) depth of 50mm (2in) below the tops of the joists.

If all the existing wiring is in metal conduit, it can be difficult and often impossible to move the conduit; in some cases you may be able to let the conduit into notches cut into the tops of the joists. Such conduit installations in the home are generally old and will require rewiring and the fitting of outlet boxes at lighting points. The better and less costly alternative is to replace the conduit with a new PVC-sheathed cable installation. This is still more desirable since earthing is often ineffective or non-existent in an old conduit installation. If conduit drops to switches are buried in plaster, you can leave them and run the new cables down the conduits to the switches.

If your wiring is old, the sheathing will be tough rubber or lead; in either case the insulation is likely to have perished and you should renew the installation. It is therefore important to have the present wiring surveyed before you start the conversion, even if rewiring or re-routing is not required. Make sure you make any wiring additions or changes needed in the bedrooms below your conversion before the conversion is finished; once it is completed, the changes will become difficult and costly.

Fitting a new consumer unit

There is nothing more aggravating than wanting to add new electrical equipment in the home and not being able to include a new circuit to supply it. You may find you need to install a larger consumer unit than the one already fitted in order to cope with this, which is a job you can do yourself.

The final stage of wiring up a new consumer unit **Inset** Check whether your unit has miniature circuit breakers **(left)** or fuse carriers **(right)**

Downstairs lighting

Upstairs lighting

Immersion heater

Downstairs ring main

Downstairs ring main

Upstairs ring main

Upstairs ring main

Cooker

1a

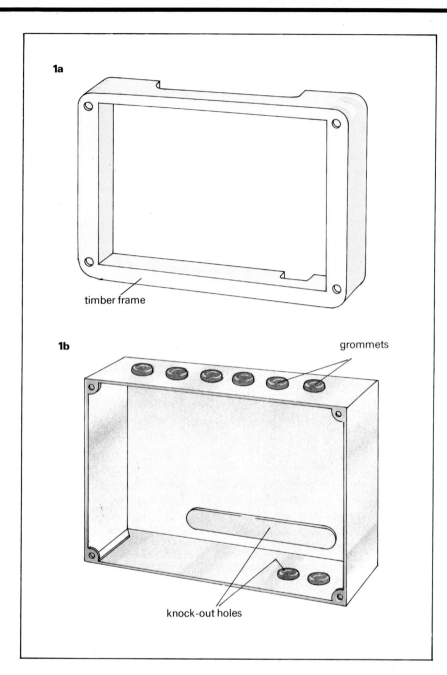

timber frame

1b

grommets

knock-out holes

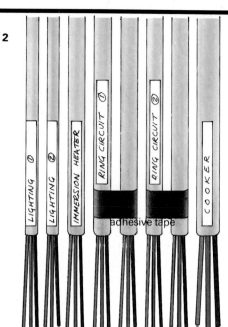

LIGHTING ①

LIGHTING ②

IMMERSION HEATER

RING CIRCUIT ①

RING CIRCUIT ②

COOKER

adhesive tape

wiring regulations do not permit any fuse to supply more than one circuit, you have two alternatives: either fit a main switch and fuse unit next to the consumer unit or replace the unit with a larger one with more fuses. A separate switch and fuse unit needs a separate mains connection and since Electricity Boards will not allow more than one pair of leads connected to their meter, a special terminal box has to be fitted on the consumer's side of the installation. Such a unit can provide one, two or four extra circuits. It is more satisfactory to replace the consumer unit and normally it is a waste of time and money to fit one smaller than an eight-way; this will, for example, supply two lighting circuits, two ring circuits, a cooker, an immersion heater and leave two spare fuseways for future expansion.

Choosing unit

There are three principal types: one with fuses that can be rewired or fitted with cartridge fuses, another fitted with miniature circuit breakers (mcb) and a third which accepts either fuses or mcbs. The circuit breakers give the best protection, while cartridge fuses are next best; most units have wire fuses because they are cheapest. New consumer units now often incorporate mcbs and an RCD (residual current device) – see page 279.

The current required to blow a wire fuse is twice the rating of the fuse, which means a 10amp current is required to blow a 5amp fuse. A cartridge blows at one and a half times its rated current and an mcb operates when only one and a quarter times its rated current flows in the circuit. An mcb also operates much quicker than a fuse and reduces the risk of fire or damage to the circuit or appliance. If price is a consideration, it is worth remembering an mcb costs about three times as much as a fused unit. You do not repair an mcb; you simply press a button or turn on a switch to reactivate it – as long as you have dealt with the problem that caused it to break the circuit. Fuse wires and cartridges must be replaced and it is vital to keep spares.

Five ratings Circuit fuses and mcbs are made in five ratings, each with a different colour code, for domestic use: 5 (white), 15 (blue), 20 (yellow), 30 (red) and 45 (green). Consumer units do not usually have provision for a 45amp fuseway, which occu-

A consumer unit is a comparatively modern piece of electrical equipment which combines the necessary double pole main switch with a single pole fuseboard in one casing. It should be situated as close as possible to the Electricity Board meter, to which it is connected by the meter tails which provide the supply. The switch is double pole so both the live and the neutral supplies are cut off simultaneously when the main switch is turned off. The fuses in the consumer unit, which protect individual circuits and equipment from excess current caused by a fault or overloading, interrupt the current in the live circuit.

Deciding number of circuits

The size of consumer units varies from two-way, for an installation with only two-circuits, to 12-way; the most common unit installed in a home is eight-way. Generally the size is determined by the number of circuits involved when the house is built. So when an additional circuit is required, perhaps for a shower heater or power point in your garage, there is no spare fuseway. As the

276

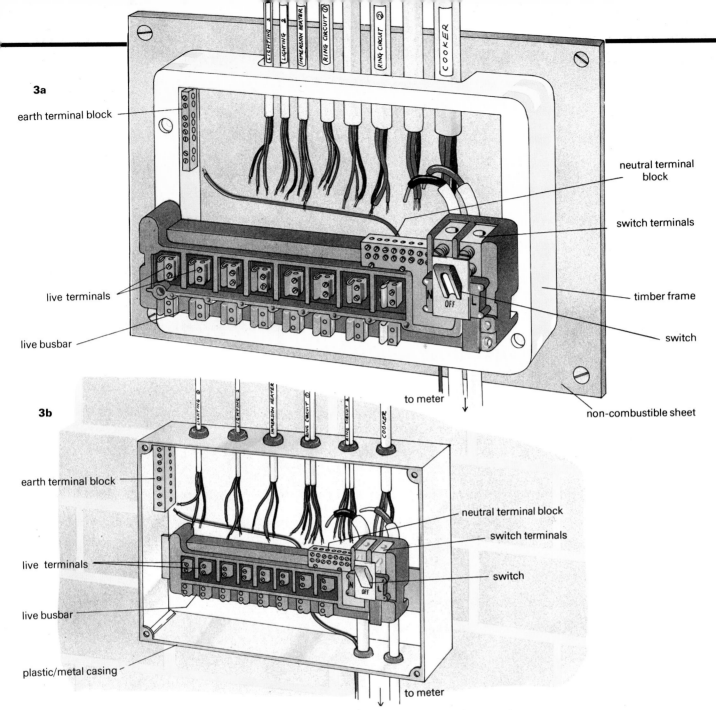

3a

earth terminal block

neutral terminal block

switch terminals

live terminals

timber frame

live busbar

switch

to meter

non-combustible sheet

3b

earth terminal block

neutral terminal block

switch terminals

live terminals

switch

live busbar

plastic/metal casing

to meter

1a Recesses for meter leads in timber frame of plastic consumer unit
1b Knock-out holes for circuit cables in all-metal – or plastic – units. (Terminals are omitted in these diagrams)
2 Labelling cables and taping ring circuit cables together
3a Feeding cables into plastic/timber frame unit
3b Feeding cables into all-metal – or plastic – unit

pies the space of two standard fuseways in some units and is needed only for a circuit supplying, for example, a large cooker with a loading of 17kW or more. If you are changing your existing unit for a larger installation, you will probably find your present fuses or mcbs will be suitable for your new unit and will save you some expense.

Disconnecting mains
Before you remove your existing consumer unit or fuseboard, the power must be disconnected at the mains by the withdrawal of the service fuse and you must give your Electricity Board at least 48 hours' notice, in writing, that you require a temporary disconnection.

Electricity Boards are obliged by law to isolate a consumer's installation from the mains on request during normal working hours.

You can usually make the change in one day and if electricity is disconnected at 9am you can have the supply restored at 5pm. If by midday you realize you cannot complete the job in time, you can always ask for reconnection to be postponed.

Preparing for installation
Some preparatory work can be done a day or so before you have the electricity cut off. Check you have all the materials and equipment you require. Remove the cover from the new unit and the fuses or mcbs, if they are bought already fitted. This leaves only the main switch, terminal banks and the copper busbar to which the fuse units are screwed. Consumer units are made entirely in metal, or plastic, or a plastic casing with a timber frame. The metal and all-plastic units have knock-out holes at the top and bottom and at the back. If it is a plastic case on a timber frame, you should either drill holes or cut recesses for the cables in the timber frame (at the top or bottom or both, depending on whether your circuit cables run up from ground level or down from ceiling height); if the cables are channelled into the plaster, they can be brought into the unit through the back of the timber frame. If the unit is to be mounted on a combustible material a sheet of non-combustible material should be fixed between the unit and the wall.
Strip cable Strip about 50mm (2in) of sheathing

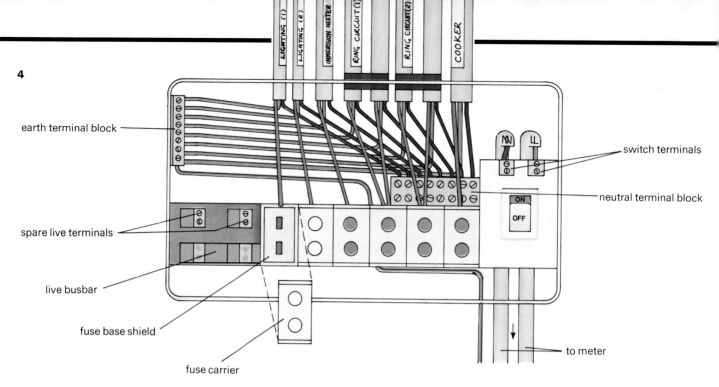

earth terminal block

switch terminals

neutral terminal block

spare live terminals

live busbar

fuse base shield

fuse carrier

ON

OFF

to meter

LIGHTING (1) LIGHTING (2) IMMERSION HEATER RING CIRCUIT(1) RING CIRCUIT(2) COOKER

NN LL

from the 16sq mm cable and take about 13mm (½in) of insulation off each conductor. Connect the red (live) conductor to the L terminal and the black (neutral) conductor to the N terminal. Tighten the screws and replace the insulated sleeves, where fitted. Make sure you have enough cable for the Electricity Board official to connect up. Your existing earthing lead should be connected to the earthing terminal on your new unit after the supply has been disconnected. If you are fitting a new earthing lead, you can fit it to the earthing terminal but don't connect it to earth; the Electricity Board official will do that.

Check all the circuits are labelled on the existing consumer unit. If not, by switching on all lights and appliances and then withdrawing fuses one by one, turning off the mains switch before pulling out each fuse, you can identify the circuits. Label them by attaching self-adhesive stickers on the cover of the consumer unit and then prepare a second set of labels which will go on the cables.

Changing over
When the electricity has been cut off, take off the cover from the existing consumer unit and remove the fuses. Loosen the terminal screws on each fuse holder in turn and disconnect the live circuit wires, which should all be red. As you disconnect, wrap the appropriate identification label round each circuit cable. Where two cables were connected to one fuseway in a ring circuit, use a piece of adhesive tape to bind them together until you reconnect to the new unit. Release the wires from the neutral and earthing terminals. Remove the frame or casing of the unit, replaster any holes and make good any decoration as required.

Fixing unit Take the frame, or casing, of the new unit, hold it in position on the wall and mark the fixing holes. Drill and plug the holes and screw the unit into position. Don't forget to fix a non-combustible sheet between the unit and the wall if you are mounting on a combustible material. Feed the circuit cables into the casing and connect them to the fuseways (an mcb unit may require the mcbs to be positioned first). Starting at the main switch end of the unit, connect your cooker circuit (if you have one) or the first of your

ring main circuits. Connect the red conductor to the first live terminal, the black to the first terminal on the neutral bank and, after fitting some green/yellow PVC sleeving if none is present, connect the bare earth conductor to the first earthing terminal. The end of the cable sheathing must be within the case or the frame. Continue to connect up in descending order of rating: 30, 20, 15 and 5. Any spare fuseways must be fitted with blanking plates until required. The circuits should, ideally, be rearranged where necessary when the current rating of any new circuit is known.

Fitting fuse bases
Screw the fuse bases – they are sometimes called shields – into their correct position according to their rating on the live busbar. This is important because it would be dangerous, for instance, to fit a 30amp base and fuse carrier to a 5amp circuit. The fuse bases and carriers are sold together, so when you buy your new equipment you must know exactly what your circuit ratings will be. The bases are manufactured to accept only a carrier of their own rating (or sometimes smaller) – you can never fit a 15amp fuse carrier into a 5amp base and so on. The colour coding of bases and carriers helps to eliminate mistakes and aids quick identification when you are changing a fuse wire or a cartridge if a circuit blows. When the bases are installed, replace the terminal cover if there is one and insert the fuse carriers. Finally replace the fuse cover (having taken care to identify the circuits with adhesive labels inside the cover) and wait for the electricity man to call to reconnect you. It is unlikely he will test your work unless new circuits have been added at the same time as you installed the new consumer unit: but the decision is his and you must be prepared for him to check out the work.

Earth sleeving Until recently sleeving on earth wires was always green in colour; this has now been standardized to green/yellow, although you are still likely to come across the old sleeving, particularly in older houses.

4 Circuit cables wired up correctly into new consumer unit

Residual current devices

A residual current device (known as an RCD) is a double pole mains switch which automatically trips (switches off) when there is sufficient leakage of current from a live wire or earth terminal to earth. It does not normally operate, however, when a circuit is overloaded or if it develops a short circuit (when the live and neutral wires are in contact with each other. RCDs used to be known as earth leakage circuit breakers (ELCBs); the term is retained here because it is more familiar.

The ELCB is used as an alternative or back-up device for earthing; in other words it is used where earthing is likely to be poor or ineffective. It is fitted with a tripping coil which is energized by current leaking to earth through it or in some part of the installation, producing an out-of-balance current in the circuit breaker. When the tripping coil is energized, an electro-magnet lifts a latch and releases the switch mechanism which is operated by a powerful spring. On release, the switch contacts open and the circuits and/or faulty apparatus are isolated from the mains electricity.

The current required to energize the trip coil is a tiny portion of the current flowing through the circuit breakers under normal conditions. By cutting off the current to a circuit when there is an earth leakage, the ELCB does the work of a fuse – but with much less current and with greater speed. For example, a 30amp rewireable fuse (the largest in most homes) requires 60amps to blow it; a 30amp cartridge fuse requires 45amps and a 30amp miniature circuit breaker (MCB) requires 37amps. The large currents required to cut off the supply when there is an earth leakage put great strain on the circuit wiring and a very good earthing system is needed if the fuse is to blow or the MCB is to operate. But a modern ELCB needs less than 1 amp to operate, so the fuses and any MCBs remain intact since the ELCB trips off instead.

How it works

An earth leakage current returns to the electricity supply system, usually at the substation which might be some distance from the house. But instead of returning through the neutral conductor, as current does in its normal state, it has to follow an alternative path. Originally the faulty current left the house through the mains water pipe, through the mains water network and onto the substation. Because water authorities are now using insulated pipes, the mains water system may no longer be used as the sole means of earthing in new or existing installations. Now the metallic sheathing of the Electricity Board's cable provides a continuous metallic path for the earth leakage current back to the substation. In some areas the Electricity Board also offers another system known as protective multiple earthing (PME). This takes advantage of the fact that the neutral pole of the mains electricity is solidly connected to earth at the substation and gives a first class earthing system.

Earthing terminal The Electricity Board sometimes provides a terminal in the house for earth connection, for which it may make a small charge. Where the Board is unable to provide an earth terminal – either because the metallic sheathing is not continuous or because PME has not been adopted in the area – the consumer must find an alternative, since he is responsible for earthing.

For direct connection of an earthing circuit to earth, the impedance (AC equivalent of DC resistance) of the earth connection must not exceed 4 ohms to enable it to carry the 60amp or more current which may result from a leakage. Earth terminals provided by the Electricity Board meet these requirements; but alternative systems provided by the consumer are unlikely to do so. For example, simply installing an electrode in the ground to provide an earth terminal would result in fuses failing to blow should an earth leakage fault occur; the installation would be dangerous with a high fire and electrocution risk. The solution here would be to install an earth leakage circuit breaker in conjunction with an earth electrode.

Installing earth electrode The copper or copper-sheathed electrode must be a minimum of 1200mm (or 48in) long and it should be driven vertically into firm soil so the clamp terminal is just above ground level. Firm soil is essential to provide good electrical conductivity between the electrode rod and earth; the moisture content of the subsoil will further improve conductivity. When deciding on a suitable position for the electrode, bear in mind the concrete foundations of a house wall are probably not more than 300mm (or 12in) below ground level and they protrude between 75 and 100mm (3 and 4in) beyond the faces of the wall. If your consumer unit is situated in a cellar, you can drill a hole – larger than the electrode – in the wall, drive the electrode horizontally through this into the subsoil and seal around it with mastic; or drill a hole in the floor and insert the rod, but in either case beware of the presence of a damp proof membrane which would be punctured by this process and

Above Voltage-operated ELCB
Left Current-operated high sensitivity ELCB
Below Earth electrode

> **WARNING**
> You should consult the Electricity Board before undertaking any protective installation since there are now new regulations on earthing circuits.

ON
CRABTREE
TYPE PS60 ELCB
40A
415V 3Ph 50Hz
30mA RATED TRIP
Test often using Button T
OFF
CMC-SWISS MADE

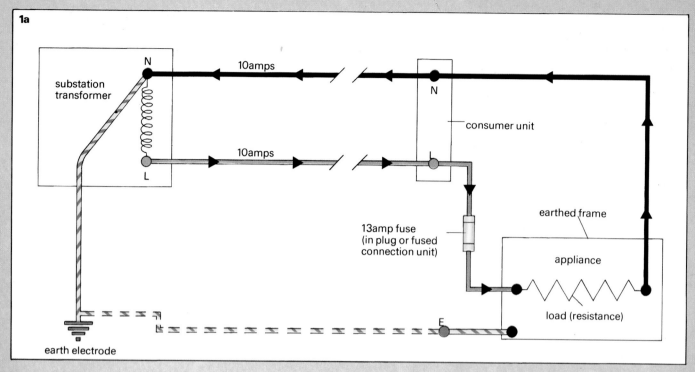

1a

substation transformer

N

10amps

consumer unit

N

10amps

L

L

13amp fuse
(in plug or fused
connection unit)

earthed frame

appliance

load (resistance)

E

earth electrode

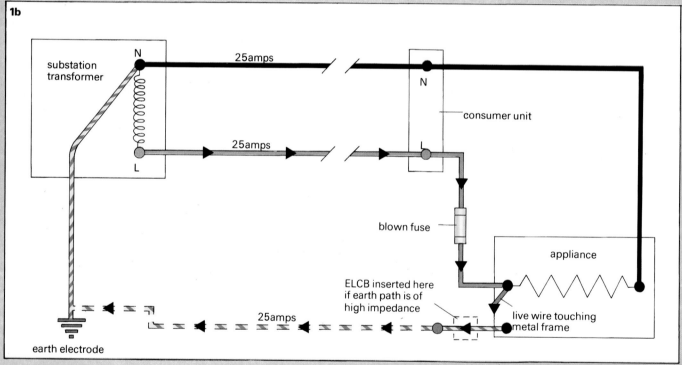

1b

substation transformer

N

25amps

consumer unit

N

25amps

L

L

blown fuse

appliance

ELCB inserted here
if earth path is of
high impedance

25amps

live wire touching
metal frame

earth electrode

allow damp to penetrate. Connection to the terminal clamp should be with 6 or 10sq mm single core green/yellow PVC-insulated cable; at the connection point fix an indelible label stating: 'Safety Electrical Earth – Do Not Remove'.

Types of ELCB
There are two main types of ELCB installed in the home: one is voltage-operated and the other current-operated. The current-operated ELCB

should be your first choice, but if the product of the operating current and the impedance of the earth loop (as measured on an impedance tester by the Electricity Board or an electrical contractor) exceeds 50, you must use the voltage-operated type.
Voltage-operated This is the cheapest ELCB and is simply a double pole circuit breaker with trip coil and tripping mechanism. The circuit breaker section has four main terminals – a conventional double pole mains switch and two subsidiary

1a The normal current path from the substation to an appliance via the consumer unit
1b The current path where current from a short circuit, caused by the live wire in an appliance touching an earthed frame, returns to the substation via earth

280

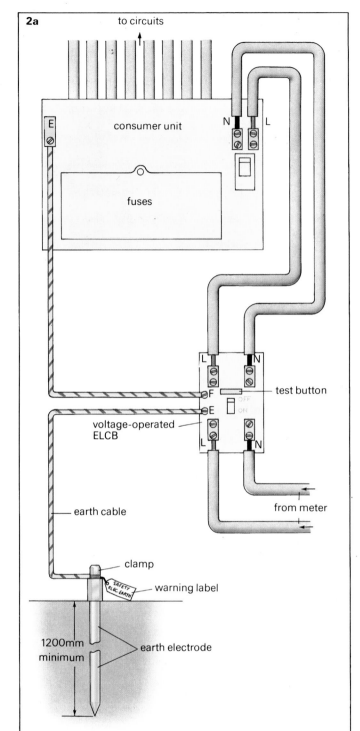

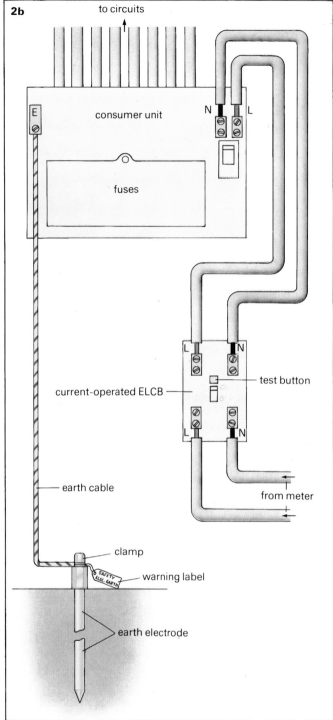

2a The wiring of a voltage-operated ELCB to the consumer unit and an earth electrode

2b The wiring of a current-operated ELCB to the consumer unit; the earth lead from the consumer unit goes directly to the earth electrode

terminals. The mains leads from the meter are connected to one pair of live (L) and neutral (N) terminals; the other pair are load terminals which feed the installation and are normally connected by two leads to the mains terminals of the consumer unit. The subsidiary terminals are marked 'F' and 'E'. The F terminal is connected to the earth terminal on the consumer unit; the E terminal is connected to the earth clamp terminal of the earth electrode in the soil. Any leakage of current to the earth conductor in the main circuit passes through the tripping coil of the ELCB, energizing the electro-magnet which trips the circuit breaker. About 40 volts is needed to operate the tripping device and the current required to produce this voltage is very small.

Since the leakage current in the earth conductor must flow through the tripping coil to operate the release mechanism, this type of ELCB is not wholly reliable. For example, if fault current flows to earth via another path, such as a gas or water pipe (called a parallel earth path), it bypasses the ELCB and the ELCB does not trip. If this parallel earth path is satisfactory, sufficient current will flow to blow the fuse. If not, the gas or water pipework indoors will remain live and be dangerous.

Warning It is not a good idea to install two or more voltage-operated ELCBs to protect different sections of the installation, unless the respective earthing rods are at least 2.5m (or 8ft) apart and are 2.5m (or 8ft) away from buried water or gas pipes.

Current-operated This has been developed to over-

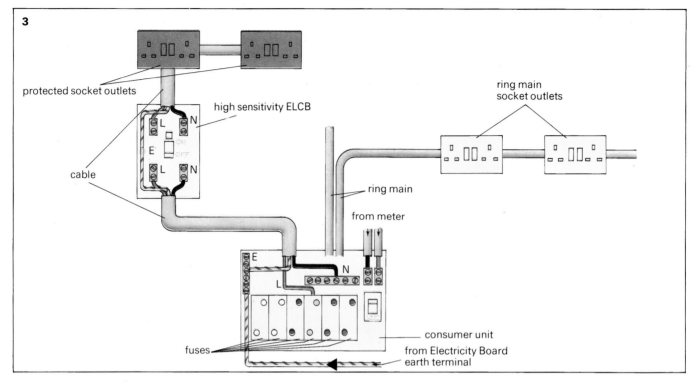

protected socket outlets

high sensitivity ELCB

ring main
socket outlets

cable

ring main

from meter

E

N

L

consumer unit

from Electricity Board
earth terminal

fuses

come the disadvantage of the voltage-operated ELCB. Although similar in style to the voltage type, its tripping coil is not energized directly by earth leakage current and has no earth conductors connected to it. There are four terminals – L and N mains terminals and L and N load terminals. The earthing lead from the consumer unit in this case goes direct to the earth electrode.

This type of ELCB works on the current balance principle – that current flowing into a circuit is equal to the current flowing out. For example, if 10amps flow into a circuit through the positive or live wire, you can expect 10amps to return via the negative or neutral wire. However, if a live wire touches earthed metal, some of the return current is diverted from the main circuit into the earth circuit; this causes an out-of-balance current in the main conductor. At the instant of the fault, the live pole of the mains switch will be carrying a lot of current and the neutral pole less, since some will be leaking to earth. By having an out-of-balance current sensing device and by connecting this to a tripping coil, you have a current-operated ELCB. No matter which path the earth leakage current takes, the sensing device will detect the out-of-balance in the mains lead and operate the tripping coil. The normal current-operated ELCB of 60–100-amps rating needs less than ½-amp of out-of-balance current to operate, which means the earthing system needs to carry only that amount of current for the ELCB to work.

High sensitivity ELCB An ordinary ELCB gives no protection from direct electric shock, which is generally caused by touching a live wire or contact when also touching earthed metal or standing on the ground. With a normal current-operated circuit breaker this is because the amount of current required for it to operate is more than that required to electrocute someone; with a voltage-operated type it is because the current flowing to earth via another path (through the human body) does not flow through the ELCB trip coil. There is, however, a current-operated high sensitivity ELCB

which will protect you against electrocution if you touch a live wire while in contact with the ground either directly or via earthed metal.

It must be emphasized, however, that neither this ELCB nor any other device installed in the home will prevent you being electrocuted if you come into contact with both live and neutral poles of the 240V supply, even if you are standing on an insulated surface or wearing rubber boots in the garden. But if you are in contact with the ground at the same time, there is just a chance the high sensitivity ELCB will trip before you are electrocuted.

The high sensitivity ELCB, which trips at 30 milliamps in a fraction of a second, is especially useful for selective circuits such as those used for power tools, hedgecutters, mowers and other appliances where shock risk is fairly high. It should not be inserted in the main house circuits because, if condensation or some other small earth leakage current causes it to trip, it will cut off the power to the whole house. This is called nuisance tripping and is not only inconvenient, but it could also cause a serious accident.

A consumer unit is now available in which an ELCB protects some socket outlets and a conventional mains switch controls other circuits including lighting. Where a circuit is installed to supply a few socket outlets, it is best to use fittings of a different colour for the protected ones, so only these are used with high shock risk appliances.

A high sensitivity ELCB is available for plugging into a 13amp socket, from which you can run high risk power tools. Similar to an adaptor but larger, it is a useful safety device for the home.

It is also possible to fit a special socket outlet containing an ELCB in place of an existing double socket outlet, or as an addition to the circuit in the form of a spur.

The current Wiring Regulations require ELCB protection for any socket being used to power electrical equipment used out of doors; this can be provided by a special socket, as mentioned above, or by a separate ELCB protecting the circuit.

3 The wiring of a high sensitivity ELCB to the consumer unit, using 4.0 or 2.5sq mm cable, and to the socket outlets; use different coloured fittings to distinguish protected sockets from ring main sockets. There are now consumer units that incorporate an ELCB (current operated)

Wiring in an electric cooker

The average domestic electric cooker consists of an oven, a hob containing three or four rings and a grill. The conventional position for the grill is below the hob and usually built into it, although with some models it is positioned at eye level. Some models have a double oven.

The majority of cookers are compact, self-contained, free-standing units positioned against the wall and connected to a wall-mounted control switch by means of a trailing cable to allow the cooker to be moved forward when you want to clean behind it; a lockable bogie placed under the cooker will make it easier to move. Other models are built into the kitchen units; these usually have separate hob and oven sections and are termed split-level cookers, the oven being raised to a more practical height for cooking.

Circuit rating

Electric cookers are heavy current-consuming appliances, having loadings of up to 12kW (12,000 watts) for medium size cookers and even higher loadings for large, family size cookers including the double oven models. Cookers with loadings up to 12kW are usually supplied from circuits of 30amp current rating, while those in excess of 12kW are usually supplied from circuits of 45amp rating.

Although the maximum current demand of a 12kW cooker on a 240v supply is 50amps with everything switched on, allowance in rating the circuit has been made bearing in mind that rarely in the average home are all the rings, the grill and the oven in use at any one time. This means the circuit rating need only be 30amps. Even if everything is in use at one time, the current demand on the circuit at any one moment is still probably less than 50amps. This is because the rings, the grill and the oven are thermostatically controlled or include a simmering device which reduces the total current demand. In rating the circuit, allowance has also been made for an electric kettle plugged into the socket outlet of the cooker control unit and therefore taking current from the cooker circuit. Although a high-speed electric kettle takes up to 13amps from the circuit, kettles are assessed at only 5amps.

There is an official formula for arriving at the circuit requirements of an electric cooker, based on the average use when cooking for a family. The first 10amps is estimated at 100 percent and the remaining current at 30 percent; 5amps is allowed for an electric kettle plugged in the cooker control unit. If the current demand of a 12kW cooker is 50amps, the first 10amps is included, the remaining 40amps is estimated at 12amps and there is a 5amp allowance for a kettle. The total assessed load is 27amps and the circuit required is therefore 30amps.

Although the regulations permit a 12kW cooker to be supplied from a 30amp circuit, it is always worthwhile considering installing a 45amp circuit, provided the consumer unit will accept a 45amp fuse unit; some cannot. If there is no spare fuseway for an electric cooker circuit in the existing consumer unit and a separate switch fuse unit has to be installed, it is worth fitting one with a 45amp rating. A 45amp circuit means a larger size cable, but the extra cost is comparatively small and the work involved is the same as for a 30amp circuit.

Cooker circuit

A circuit for an electric cooker consists of a two core and earth flat PVC-sheathed cable starting at a fuseway and terminating at a 45amp cooker control unit or cooker switch. From the control unit or switch the same size cable runs through a cable entry into a terminal block in the cooker. Where the oven and hob are separate, one cooker control unit and switch can be used for both provided neither is more than 2m (6½ft) from it.

Top A free-standing electric cooker needs a 30 or 45amp circuit, depending on its loading; a microwave cooker, however, simply runs off a 13amp fused plug and socket outlet

Above A split level cooker requires the same circuit rating as an ordinary cooker

Cooker control unit This is a double pole switch and a switched 13amp socket outlet mounted on one panel. It is made with or without neon indicators and is available in either surface or flush-mounted versions.

Cooker switch This is simply a 45amp double pole plate switch without a kettle socket outlet, with or without a neon indicator and available in surface or flush-mounted versions. The cooker switch is cheaper than a control unit since it has no socket outlet; it can be fitted when you do not want to operate the kettle from the control unit, which can often be a disadvantage and also potentially dangerous. If the control unit is fixed in the traditional position above the cooker, the kettle flex could trail over the rings; if these are switched on, the flex will burn and could start a fire or give an electric shock before the fuse blows.

With the introduction of the ring circuit, the traditional single utility plug and socket in the kitchen has largely been replaced by numerous socket outlets; this means a socket on the control unit is unnecessary, since the kettle can be used from one of these extra socket outlets.

Cable sizes

For a 30amp cooker circuit, you should use 6sq mm cable and 10sq mm cable for a 45amp circuit. Cable is available in grey or white sheathing; white is usually preferred, especially if part of the cable is fixed to the surface and if the trailing section between the control unit or switch and the cooker is visible.

Cable route

Having decided on the position for the control unit or switch, which must be within 2m (or 6ft) of the cooker so it can quickly be reached by someone using the cooker, choose the route for the cable. Where the consumer unit is on the same floor as the control unit in the kitchen (as in the conventional house), the simplest route is under the ground floor – assuming this is of timber construction. Run a cable down the wall below the consumer unit and pass it behind the skirting (if any) and into the void of the suspended floor. Feed it under the joists, where it can lay unfixed on the sub-floor, and up through a hole drilled in the flooring immediately below the position of the control unit or switch.

If you have a solid ground floor (as in many modern houses), you will have to find an alternative route. This usually means running the cable up the wall above the consumer unit and into the void above the ceiling, under the upstairs floorboards and down through a hole in the ceiling above the control unit or switch. If you adopt this route, you will have to lift floorboards and probably drill through joists.

Where the bathroom – and particularly a combined bathroom/WC – is above the kitchen, you may have problems raising floorboards and the

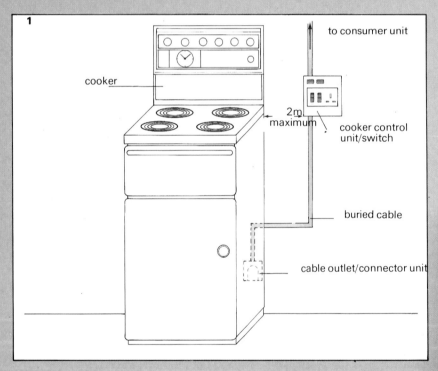

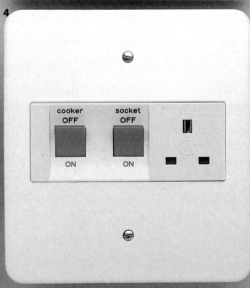

1 The wiring layout for a free-standing cooker. The cable outlet or connector unit is hidden when the cooker is in position against the wall; make sure there is sufficient cable between the cable outlet or connector unit and the cooker to allow the cooker to be pulled forward
2 & 3 Cooker control units (45amp double pole switch and 13amp switched socket outlet) with neon indicators
4 Cooker control unit

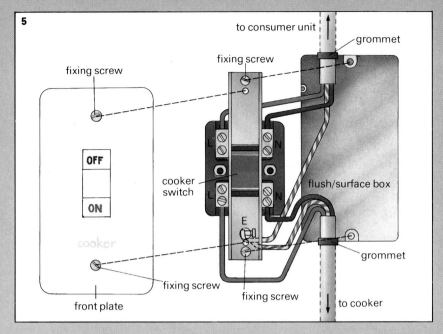

5 Wiring a cooker switch; with the type shown you must remove the front plate from the switch before connecting the cables
6 Cooker control unit
7 45amp double pole cooker switch
8 Cooker control unit (30/50amp)
9 Connector unit

cable route will have to be diverted. Under these conditions it is best to prepare the route before buying the cable, so you can measure 'the exact length required and save buying too much of this relatively expensive material.

For a single-storey building with a solid floor, the cable can readily be run in the roof space. In a flat which has solid floors and where there is no access to the ceiling above, surface wiring will be necessary. Here the cable can be enclosed in conduits which can be in the form of hollow skirting.

Fitting control unit

Surface-mounted control units are available in two versions. One is all-plastic, with an enclosed back and thin plastic sections which are knocked out to provide entry holes for the cable; it is fixed to the wall with a couple of screws. The second type consists of a square plate, usually metal, which is mounted on a metal box; both are finished in white and the box is fixed to the wall with screws. The box has a selection of knock-out holes fitted with blanks, two of which are knocked out for the cables and fitted with PVC grommets to protect the cable sheathing. A range of smaller, oblong plastic control units is also available; these are mounted on plastic surface boxes or metal flush boxes.

The standard flush-mounted control unit is also of square plate design, mounted on a matching metal box sunk into the wall so it sits flush with the plaster. This box also has knock-out holes for the cable and these must be fitted with PVC grommets. This type is suitable where the cable is buried in the wall; where it is not possible to bury all the cable – such as with a tiled wall – you will have to cut short channels above and below the box to feed in the cable.

A cable trailing down a wall from the control unit to the cooker is not only unsightly, but can also be an obstruction. It can be fixed to the wall with cable clips for most of its length provided the final loop is left free in case you want to pull out the cooker from the wall. However undue strain is likely to occur on the bottom clip and to overcome this you can fit a connector unit.

Connector unit This consists of a terminal block fitted into a metal flush box and a moulded plastic cover plate with an entry hole for the cable. The connector unit is fitted about 1200mm (or 2½ft) above the floor – or lower if necessary; the cable running down from the control unit is connected to the terminals, the cable preferably being buried in the wall. The trailing length of cable running from the cooker is also connected to the terminals on the connector unit and the sheathing is clamped to prevent any strain being exerted on the terminals when the cooker is moved out from the wall. If the cooker is changed or temporarily removed, you can disconnect it easily by releasing the cooker cable from these terminals.

Cable outlet unit An alternative arrangement is a cable outlet unit. Here the cable between the control unit and the cooker is not cut, but merely passes through, and is clamped in, the outlet box, which should be positioned behind the cooker.

Connecting control unit

Having fixed the box to the wall with about 200mm (or 8in) of each cable within the box, strip the sheathing off the end of each cable, leaving about 25mm (1in) within the box; strip about 8mm (⅜in) of insulation from the ends of the four current carrying conductors. Slip green/yellow PVC sleeving over the bare earth wires, leaving about 8mm (⅜in) exposed. Connect the red circuit conductor to the mains terminal marked L and the black to the mains terminal marked N. Connect the red conductor of the cooker cable to the load terminal marked L and the black to the load terminal marked N. Connect the two earth conductors to the earth terminal of the control unit. Arrange the wires neatly in the box, fix the switch to the box and screw the cover and

285

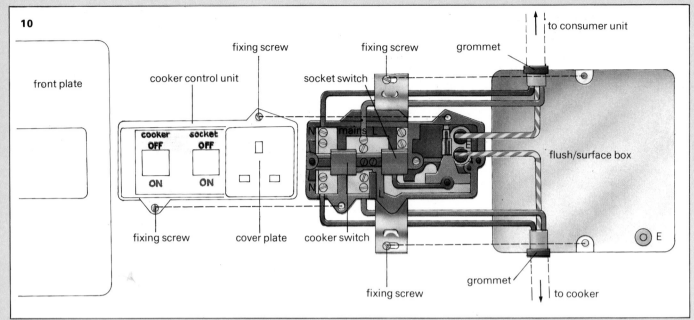

10

front plate

cooker control unit

fixing screw

fixing screw

socket switch

grommet

to consumer unit

cooker OFF

socket OFF

ON

ON

N mains L

N

L

flush/surface box

fixing screw

cover plate

cooker switch

fixing screw

grommet

to cooker

E

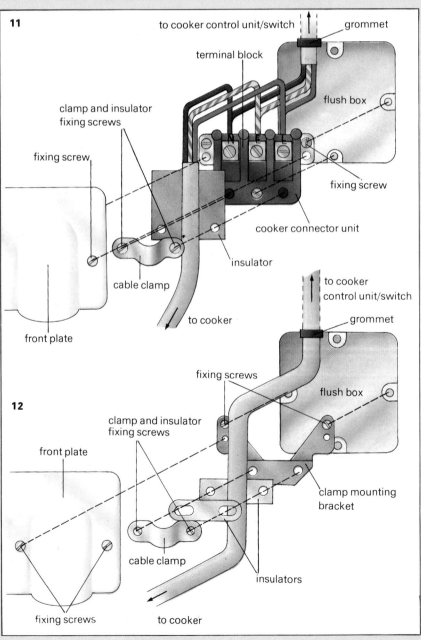

11

to cooker control unit/switch

grommet

terminal block

clamp and insulator
fixing screws

fixing screw

flush box

N E

fixing screw

cooker connector unit

insulator

cable clamp

to cooker

front plate

12

to cooker
control unit/switch

grommet

fixing screws

flush box

clamp and insulator
fixing screws

front plate

clamp mounting
bracket

cable clamp

insulators

fixing screws

to cooker

front plates to the switch assembly. Separate cables are not required for the socket outlet since this is connected internally to the cooker terminals.

The method of connection is the same for a cooker switch. With a unit made entirely of plastic, the cables are threaded into the unit with the cover removed and the unit fixed to the wall. The cable connections are then made and the cover replaced.

Connecting to consumer unit

With the mains switched to OFF, remove the consumer unit cover, run the cable into the unit and prepare the end of the conductors as before. The red wire is connected to the fuseway terminal, the black to the neutral terminal bank and the green/yellow PVC-sleeved earth wire to the earth terminal bank. Insert and fix the fuse unit, replace the cover and put the main switch back to ON.

Switch fuse unit Where there is no spare fuseway, you will have to install a separate switch fuse unit consisting of a double pole 60amp mains switch and a fuse unit of 30 or 45amp current rating. Fit the unit near the consumer unit and connect two 3m (or 10ft) lengths of 10sq mm PVC-sheathed cable – a red insulation cable to the L terminal and a black insulation cable to the N terminal. Also connect 6sq mm green/yellow insulated earth cable to the E terminal. The cooker circuit cable is wired to load or circuit terminals as for the consumer unit.

The mains leads are connected to the mains by the Electricity Board. You may also have to fit a two-way service connector box for the two pairs of meter leads you will now have.

Connecting split-level cooker

The same circuit cable from the 30 or 45amp fuseway to the cooker control unit or switch is required for a split-level cooker; the one control will serve both sections provided each is within 2m (or 6ft) of the control unit. If the control unit is fixed midway between the two units, they can be spaced up to 4m (or 12ft) apart, which is adequate for most kitchen layouts. Otherwise a second control unit is required, one being linked to the other using the same size

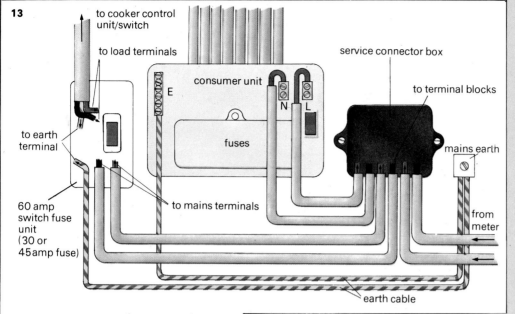

13

to cooker control unit/switch

to load terminals

consumer unit

E

service connector box

N L

to terminal blocks

fuses

to earth terminal

to mains terminals

mains earth

60 amp switch fuse unit (30 or 45amp fuse)

from meter

earth cable

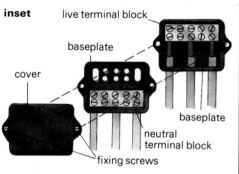

inset

live terminal block

baseplate

cover

baseplate

neutral terminal block

fixing screws

10 Wiring a control unit; remove the front and cover plates before connecting the cables. **11** Wiring a connector unit; use a box with four mounting lugs. **12** Connecting a cable outlet unit. **13** Connecting to the mains if there is no spare fuseway in the consumer unit; the wiring at the service connector box (**inset**) **14** The wiring for a split level cooker supplied from one control unit or switch between the two sections. **15** The wiring for a split level cooker supplied from one control unit or switch at one side of the two sections. **16** The wiring for a split level cooker supplied from two control units or switches looped together by the circuit cable

cable as for the circuit.

Where, as in most cases, the one control unit is to serve both sections of a split-level cooker, you can either run two cables from the load side of the control unit – one to each section – or, depending on the relative positions, you can run one cable to the nearer of the two sections and then run a cable from the terminals of the nearer one to the other section.

Every cable must be of the same size as the main circuit cable, even though one or both may carry less than the total current. The reason for this is that, with no intervening fuse, the cable rating is determined by the rating of the circuit fuse.

The cables being run direct to the sections of a split-level cooker can be fixed to the surface or buried in the wall to suit individual requirements.

Connecting small cookers

Microwave cookers, which are becoming increasingly popular in the home, have loadings around 500 watts and are fitted with flex to be run off a 13amp fused plug and socket outlet. These, therefore, need no special circuit. The same applies to baby cookers, which have a maximum loading of 3kW.

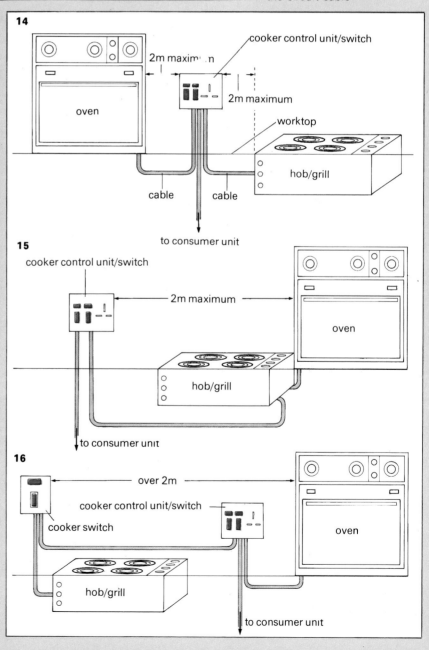

14

cooker control unit/switch

2m maximum

2m maximum

worktop

oven

hob/grill

cable

cable

to consumer unit

15

cooker control unit/switch

2m maximum

oven

hob/grill

to consumer unit

16

over 2m

cooker control unit/switch

cooker switch

oven

hob/grill

to consumer unit

Choosing and fitting cooker hoods

There are basically two types of cooker hood – recirculating and ducted. There are also models which are suitable for either recirculation or for direct extraction from the rear or top via ducting to the outside air. With one make of this type there is a wall grille as an optional extra. Each hood is fitted with a fire shield which is kept open during normal use by a fusible cord; this 'fuses' in the event of a cooking fat fire and releases the shield.

Apart from a filter to catch dust and grease and, in the case of a recirculating hood, a charcoal filter to catch smells, cooker hoods contain one or more fans and most models incorporate one or more electric lamps to illuminate the hob during cooking. Fans can be either two-speed or three-speed where there is an extra boost speed besides low and normal. Switches, together with a neon indicator, are positioned in front of the hood for easy access and operation.

Buying cooker hoods

The position of the cooker hood and the amount of trouble to which you are prepared to go in installing it are among the factors which you should consider when buying a hood. A recirculating hood is simply screwed to the wall or underside of a kitchen cabinet; since no outlet to the outside air is required the hood can be fitted to any wall providing a suitable fixing, giving scope for planning. Where smells and steam are particularly troublesome, a ducted hood is preferable; but ideally this type of hood should be positioned against an outside wall using a short length of ducting which passes through a hole cut into the wall behind or just above the hood. An inside wall, however, should not be completely ruled out; although the ducting should be as short as possible, lengths up to 6m (or 20ft) can be installed with the ducting fixed to a vertical exhaust in the hood and run up and over to a hole cut in the outside wall. In this case bear in mind you will have to conceal the ducting.

Cooker hoods must be positioned at the correct height for efficient and safe operation. It is generally recommended the hood is positioned 600–900mm (or 24–36in) above a hob or 400–600mm (or 16–24in) above an eye-level grill or top oven; but always follow manufacturer's instructions on this. The hood should be positioned as near as possible to the minimum height for maximum efficiency in operation.

When fixing a cooker hood above an eye-level grill if a special mounting bracket is not provided, it is an advantage to use a mounting block 100–125mm (4–5in) thick to site the hood further away from the wall and prevent the airflow being obstructed by the grill.

Warning Remember, where your cooker has an eye-level grill, the cooker hood should be operated at all times when the grill is used; otherwise the heat from the grill could damage the hood.

Size of hoods Cooker hoods are made in a number of sizes and your choice will depend upon the width of the cooker, since the hood must give adequate cover of the hob. A size which covers most British made standard cookers is 600mm (or 24in); for wider cookers there is a 900mm (or 36in) hood.

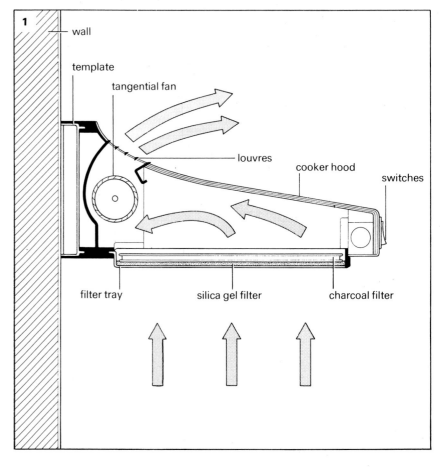

Besides these two sizes, at least one make of cooker hood is available in smaller and intermediate sizes of 550mm (or 22in) and 700mm (or 28in) as well.

Fan and lights Two-speed models have a single tangential fan located at the rear of the hood to give maximum stability and are powered by a two-speed motor; three-speed models have two tangential motors which provide three-speed facilities. Lighting may be with a single lamp which is sometimes fluorescent; some models have two lamps. The fans and lights are switched independently with the fans having multi-switch controls.

Hood finishes White and brushed aluminium are the most popular finishes, but hoods are also available in a variety of other finishes including stainless steel, teak veneer and oak veneer.

Installing cooker hoods

The type of installation work required will depend on the model you have chosen. General guidance for fitting typical models is given below, but you should always check with the manufacturer's instructions.

Fitting recirculating models

A template with relevant fixing instructions is usually provided with each hood. A hood can be screwed directly to the wall or fitted to the underside of a kitchen cabinet. It is sometimes necessary to reinforce the cabinet fixings; so if you decide to fix the hood to a cabinet, first check these fixings. Also make sure the wall construction will provide proper support for the hood fixing screws.

Fitting ducted models

These can also be fixed directly to the wall and some models can be fixed to the underside of a suitable cabinet using the template where provided. Check the cabinet fixings before fitting the hood.

You will need a ducting kit and a length of ducting. One typical kit contains a rectangular-to-round adaptor to connect the rectangular outlet in the hood to the round ducting, a louvre flap for the outside and duct sealing tape. The items in this kit are designed for attaching to 125mm (5in) diameter flexible ducting, although the size of ducting required varies; for example, another type of hood requires 100mm (4in) ducting. When ordering ducting from your supplier, buy it slightly longer than required.

The duct is fitted to the rearwards exhaust in the hood or to the vertical exhaust, depending on the location of the outlet hole cut in the outside wall and the route of the duct. To fit a duct to the rearwards exhaust of a hood which is either wall or cabinet-mounted using the ducting kit described above, first make a hole in the wall on the centre line of the hood outlet to take the 125mm (5in) diameter ducting. Open up the hood, remove the back blanking plate and fit the outlet in position. Connect one end of the ducting to the circular side of the adaptor and tape the joint to ensure an airtight seal. Push the ducting into the hole in the wall so the fixing plate on the adaptor is flush with the inside wall surface. Make good the plaster and cement round the ducting on the outside wall surface. Fit the foam seal onto the adaptor, locate the cooker hood outlet on the adaptor and fix it to the wall or cabinet. Fit the louvre onto the outside end of the ducting and seal round the joint with mastic or putty. Fit the louvre flaps where relevant.

To fit a duct to the vertical exhaust of a hood which is either cabinet or wall-mounted, using the same type of kit, first make a hole suitable for the ducting on the centre line of the vertical outlet. The

Left Ducted cooker hood; this model can be adapted to recirculate
1 Section through a recirculating cooker hood, showing the tangential fan, different filters and the direction of air flow
Below Recirculating cooker hood

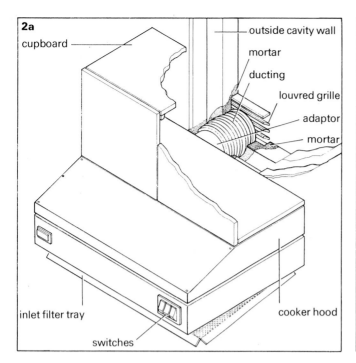

2a
cupboard
outside cavity wall
mortar
ducting
louvred grille
adaptor
mortar
inlet filter tray
cooker hood
switches

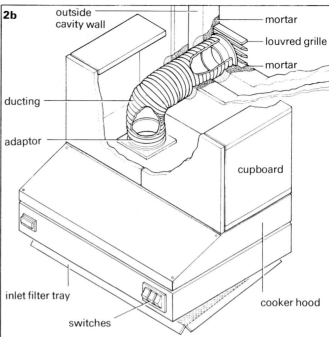

2b
outside cavity wall
mortar
louvred grille
mortar
ducting
adaptor
cupboard
inlet filter tray
cooker hood
switches

hole should be at least 200mm (8in) above the top of the hood so the bend in the ducting will not be too tight. When mounting on a cabinet, cut a hole in the cabinet base using the hood or template (if supplied) as a guide. Remove the top blanking plate and fit the outlet in place. Connect the adaptor to the outlet and fix the hood to the wall or cabinet base. Push one end of the ducting through the hole in the wall and bend the other end down onto the adaptor, making sure the bend has a minimum inside radius of 125mm (5in). Tape the joint, make good the wall and fit the louvre in place as before.

Warning Make sure you do not kink flexible ducting since this will restrict the air flow and could fracture the walls of the ducting; keep the number of bends to a minimum and make them with as large a radius as possible. Take care to seal all joints well and keep the length of ducting to a minimum – in any case below 6m (or 20ft). Whenever possible don't exhaust into a prevailing wind or into existing flues if there is any danger of fumes re-entering the house at another point.

Assembling the hood
To assemble the hood and fit the filters on a typical model, you should first remove the filter tray according to the manufacturer's instructions. Make sure the grease filter completely covers the holes in the grille, remove all internal packing pieces and refit the filter tray. Detach the outlet grille and remove any packing pieces and the plastic bags from the charcoal filter(s). Shake the filter(s) to remove any loose dust generated during transit. When refitting the filter(s) and grille, make sure the filter completely covers the holes in the grille and the charcoal is evenly distributed within the filter(s).

Wiring up the hood
The electrical loading of a cooker hood ranges from about 80 to 220 watts depending on the size and number of fans and lights; but the loading is never more than 250 watts for a domestic model, which means a hood can be supplied from a 5amp circuit or a spur from a ring main with a 3amp fused outlet.

A suitable outlet is a 13amp switched fused connection unit, fused at 3amps, fixed close by the cooker hood and connected to it by 0.75sq mm three core PVC circular sheathed flexible cord. The fused connection unit can be supplied from a spur cable looped out of the ring main at the terminals of a nearby 13amp socket outlet using 2.5sq mm twin core and earth PVC-sheathed cable. Replace the 13amp cartridge fuse in the connection unit by one of 3amp rating. You could supply the cooker hood from a lighting circuit, providing an earth connection is available, but this is not recommended since it can cause an overload.

Cooker hoods have neon indicators to show when they are switched on, so an indicator on the connection unit is not necessary. A 13amp fused plug and socket outlet may be fitted in place of the connection unit.

Warning On no account put articles on a cooker hood and don't leave the cooker rings on when not covered by pans, since this may impair the efficiency of the filters and the cooker hood.

Maintaining cooker hoods
Make sure the cooker hood is switched off before cleaning it with warm water containing a mild detergent such as washing-up liquid; don't use too much water. Activated charcoal filters are effective for 12–18 months depending on use and replacements are available from the hood manufacturer. When renewing them, take the opportunity to wipe clean the inside of the cooker hood. The grease and foam filters should be washed about once a month; allow them to dry before replacing in the hood. Use a soft, short-haired brush to clean the impeller and the outlet grille, together with the circular motor cooling vent.

Before replacing any parts on a cooker hood, disconnect it from the electricity supply by removing the circuit fuse. To replace a lamp, follow the manufacturer's instructions and use the same type and size of lamp or tube as the original. Faults occurring in a cooker hood should be repaired by a qualified electrician or the hood returned to the manufacturer for repair.

2a Fitting the duct to the rear exhaust of a cabinet-mounted cooker hood
2b Fitting the duct to the vertical exhaust

Installing night storage heaters

Storage heaters are a relatively efficient method of supplying heat in the home; because heat is stored, you do not have to provide a continuous supply of energy. After the initial supply needed to provide the heat for storage, the electricity can be switched off and heat will still be emitted. There are various makes of storage heater available and these are of two types: storage radiators and storage fan heaters.

Storage radiators

The storage radiator is simply blocks of heat storage material into which is inserted a spiral element; the blocks are enclosed in a metal casing which comes in various finishes. Traditionally, concrete bricks have been used for the heat storage material, but now other lighter, more efficient materials are used. There are layers of insulation material between the storage blocks and the metal casing to control the amount of radiant heat emitted from the casing; this ensures the output is extended over many hours instead of being expelled in a short time.

During the day the rate of heat output gradually drops, although many models of storage radiator have a mechanical boost device which when opened (manually or automatically) in the evening lets out more heat until most of the heat has been transferred from the storage blocks into the room. Once the storage blocks have received their full charge of heat, there are no means by which you can control the output. You can, however, vary the quantity of heat charged overnight by adjusting an

1 Cut-away of a night storage radiator, showing the relevant component parts

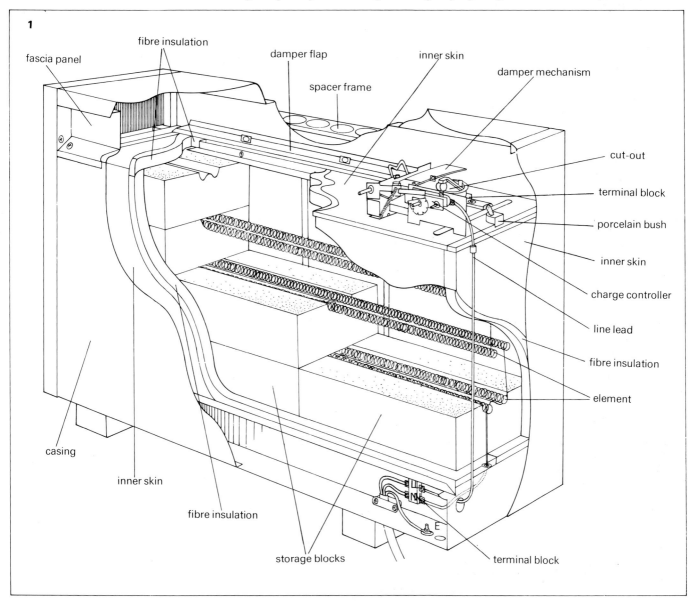

1

fascia panel
fibre insulation
damper flap
spacer frame
inner skin
damper mechanism
cut-out
terminal block
porcelain bush
inner skin
charge controller
line lead
fibre insulation
element
casing
inner skin
fibre insulation
storage blocks
terminal block

input control. In colder weather the input control can be left at its maximum setting, while in milder weather the input control can be turned down to reduce the heat output and save electricity.

Storage radiators are made with a number of electrical loadings ranging from 1.2kW to 3.3kW. The loading represents the amount of heat stored and therefore the number or size of storage blocks and the overall dimensions of the casing; but it is not the rate of heat output. Stored heat is conveniently quoted in kWh (kilowatt hours). A heater of 1.2kW loading can store up to a maximum of 9.6kWh in eight hours (1.2 × 8) and a 3.3kW heater can store up to 26.4kWh in an eight hour switch-on period. Smaller size heaters are suitable for the hall or small rooms and the larger sizes for larger rooms; for an average size room a 2kW storage radiator which can store up to 16kWh is suitable. The heat output rate is about half the charge rate; this is because the heater is off-charge for 16 hours.

Radiator circuit wiring

Because all the storage radiators in the house are generally switched on at the same time with no diversity of use, they are not supplied from plugs and sockets like direct acting heaters. Instead they are supplied from separate circuits switched by the Board's time switch. These are run from a separate consumer unit from that which supplies general services such as lighting, socket outlets, cooking and water heating. A separate unit is necessary because it has to be time-controlled so the circuits to the heaters are energized only during the overnight off-peak period.

The size, or number of fuseways, of the consumer unit depends upon the number of storage heaters installed, the number of radial circuits and, in some cases, the number of heaters connected to one radial. It should be at least a four way unit and preferably a six way unit, since even if you are starting with two storage radiators you may wish to add more later. Also, if you have an immersion heater, it is usually financially worthwhile to connect this to one fuseway in the time-controlled consumer unit to take advantage of the cheaper rate of electricity overnight. You should, however, make arrangements for an optional daytime boost, which normally means you will need a second immersion heater or a dual immersion heater with one element connected to the 24-hour supply.

Each single storage heater circuit is wired in twin core and earth PVC-sheathed cable, fused and rated according to the heater loading, and terminating at a 20amp double pole switch fixed about 300mm (or 1ft) above floor level near the radiator controls. It is common practice to use 2.5sq mm size conductors protected by a 15amp fuse and taking a load of up to 3kW. The radiator is connected to the switch by three core flex passing through a cord outlet. The switch is of the same dimensions as a one gang socket and needs the same depth of box. It can be either surface-mounted, using a plastic surface box, or flush-mounted on a one gang box sunk into the wall flush with the plaster.

Connecting the box and switch Remove a cable knock-out blank; if it is a metal flush box, you will need to fit a PVC grommet to protect the cable from rubbing against the metal. Run the cable into the box and fix the box – if it is flush-mounted, you will have to cut out the wall to sink the box flush.

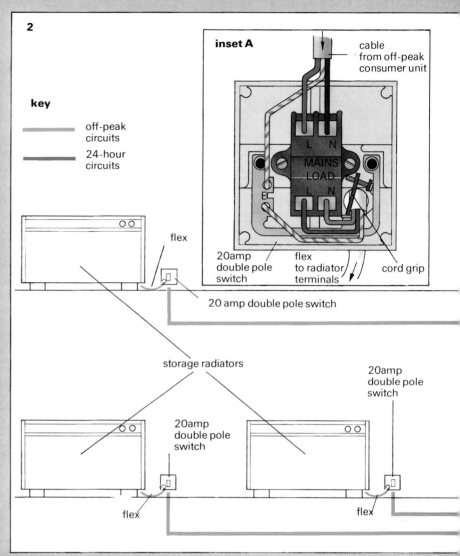

2

key

off-peak circuits

24-hour circuits

inset A

cable from off-peak consumer unit

20amp double pole switch

flex to radiator terminals

cord grip

flex

20 amp double pole switch

storage radiators

20amp double pole switch

20amp double pole switch

flex

flex

HEATER   FAN

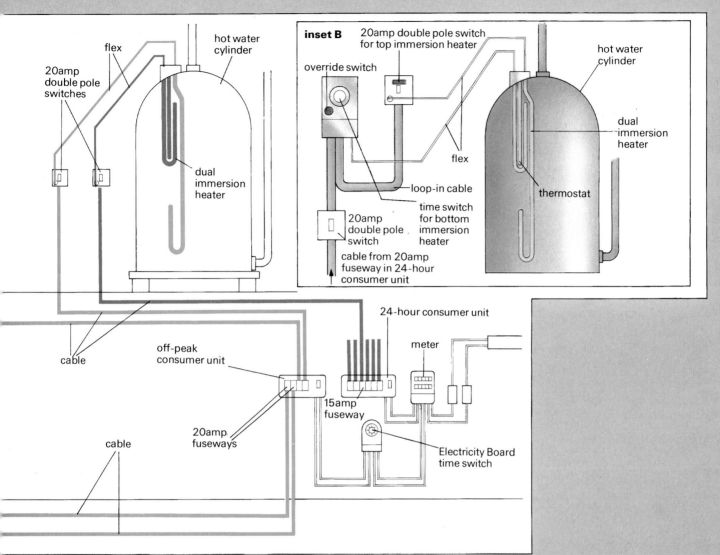

inset B

20amp double pole switch for top immersion heater

override switch

hot water cylinder

flex

dual immersion heater

loop-in cable

thermostat

time switch for bottom immersion heater

20amp double pole switch

cable from 20amp fuseway in 24-hour consumer unit

20amp double pole switches

flex

hot water cylinder

dual immersion heater

cable

off-peak consumer unit

20amp fuseways

cable

24-hour consumer unit

meter

15amp fuseway

Electricity Board time switch

2 Circuit diagram for storage radiators and an immersion heater; the immersion heater switches are wired in the same way as the radiator switch (**inset A**). The bottom immersion heater is connected to the off-peak circuit and the top one to the 24-hour circuit. Alternatively, for large quantities of hot water during the day, the time switch can be set to the off-peak period and connected to the bottom immersion heater. The override switch can be used to heat up the entire contents of the cylinder during the day. The 20amp double pole switch is wired to the top immersion heater and can be used as a daytime booster for small amounts of hot water (**inset B**).
Above left 25amp twin double pole switch. **Far left** 20amp double pole switch with flex outlet.
Left White meter

Prepare the ends of the cable by stripping off the sheathing and about 9mm (or ⅜in) of insulation from the two current carrying conductors and slipping green/yellow PVC sleeving over the bare earth wire. Connect the red insulated conductor to the mains terminal L, the black to the mains terminal N and the green/yellow sleeved earth wire to the earth terminal E in the box. If at this stage the storage radiator is in position, you can also connect its flexible cord to the switch; if not, fix the switch to the box using the screws supplied.

When you connect the flexible cord to the double pole switch, thread it into the flex outlet hole with the switch removed from its box and strip about 100mm (4in) of sheathing from its end, exposing the three cores coloured brown, blue and green/yellow. Strip off about 9mm (or ⅜in) of insulation from the exposed end of the conductors. Connect the brown wire to the load terminal L, the blue to the load terminal N and the earth to the terminal E alongside the existing earth terminal. Then fix the switch to the box using the screws supplied.

Connecting the consumer unit Install the consumer unit as already described earlier in the book. Remove the cover of the unit and dismantle as much of it as necessary. Fix the frame or casing to the wall fairly close to the existing 24-hour consumer unit and meter, using a backing sheet of non-combustible material if the unit is open-backed. Run the circuit cables into the unit and prepare the

ends for connection by removing the necessary amount of sheathing and insulation. Connect the red insulated wires to the fuseway terminals, the black insulated wires to the neutral terminal bank and the green/yellow sleeved earth wires to the earth terminal bank. Connect a 1m (or 3ft) length of 10sq mm red PVC-insulated single core cable to the mains terminal L, a 1m (or 3ft) length of 10sq mm black insulated cable to the mains terminal N and a 1m (or 3ft) length of green/yellow insulated 6sq mm cable to the earth terminal bank. The Electricity Board will connect the two mains leads to a white meter and time switch and you should connect the earthing lead to the mains earth terminal.

Installing a single storage radiator Ideally, even one heater should be connected to the Board's time switch, but it can be operated from any ring circuit 13amp socket. You will, however, need a time switch to limit the charge period to eight hours. This can be a plug-in time switch, which has a socket outlet into which you plug the storage heater. You can use the white meter tariff and set the time switch to coincide with the cheap rate period. The time switch has an over-ride switch which enables the heater to be given a boost charge in the evening when needed, but at a higher rate for the electricity used. This is more satisfactory than using a direct acting heater for a short period since any heat not used goes towards the night charge.

293

Storage fan heaters

A storage fan heater resembles in appearance a storage radiator, but it is generally larger and has an inlet and outlet grille. The fan heater is normally of a higher loading and contains a tangential fan. This draws in cold air which passes through ducting in the storage casing and over the storage blocks, where it is heated and expelled as controlled temperature warm air into the room.

These heaters have more thermal insulation than storage radiators, so only a small proportion of heat is emitted as radiant heat via the casing. This often combats condensation without wasting a lot of heat. The heater section is energized only during the eight-hour overnight period when the cheaper rate for electricity applies. Heat is emitted only when the fan is running; to enable the fan to be switched on at any time, the fan circuit is connected to the 24-hour electricity supply. This means the supply will be at a more expensive rate (except at night); but since the fan consumes less current than the average electric lamp, this is usually not significant in terms of cost.

Fan heater circuit wiring

As with storage radiators, the heater section of this type of appliance is supplied from a time-controlled consumer unit. The circuit is wired in twin core and earth PVC-sheathed cable with each cable starting at a separate fuseway in the consumer unit; the usual cable size is 4sq mm with fusing of 20 or 25 amps. However, instead of terminating at a 20amp double pole switch, the cable terminates in a 25amp twin switch fixed close to the storage heater.

The circuit to the fan is run in 1.5 or 1.0sq mm twin core and earth PVC-sheathed cable. Where more than one storage fan heater is being installed, all fans can be supplied from one 5amp circuit. This circuit can be run separately from a 5amp fuseway in the general services consumer unit on the 24-hour supply or it can be supplied from a spur on the ring circuit via a fused connection unit connected to the ring cable and fitted with a 3amp fuse. This circuit cable also runs into the 25amp twin switch and, when supplying other fans of storage fan heaters, is looped in and out of the twin switch. For a maximum of two fans, you can run the circuit cable from an existing 5amp fuseway supplying a lighting circuit; but it is usually more convenient to run it off the ring circuit. If you decide to do this, you should locate a 13amp socket outlet fairly close to one heater. ′

The fused connection unit is linked to the socket outlet by a short length of 2.5sq mm twin core and earth cable and may be mounted on a one gang box

3 Cut-away of a storage fan radiator, showing the relevant component parts.
4 Circuit diagram for storage fan heaters and the connections for the 25amp twin double pole switch (**inset**)

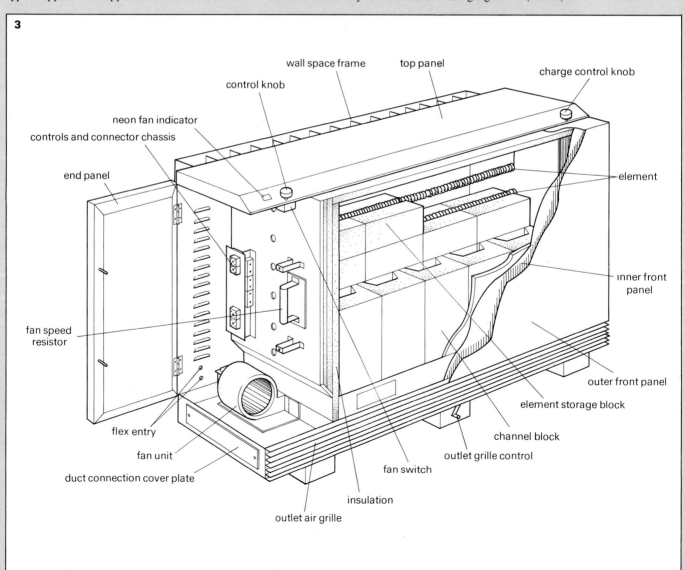

3

- wall space frame
- top panel
- charge control knob
- control knob
- neon fan indicator
- controls and connector chassis
- end panel
- element
- inner front panel
- fan speed resistor
- outer front panel
- element storage block
- channel block
- outlet grille control
- flex entry
- fan unit
- duct connection cover plate
- fan switch
- insulation
- outlet air grille

fixed adjacent to the socket outlet. Alternatively you can mount a one gang socket and fused connection unit on a dual box, which is slightly wider than a two gang outlet box and has two extra fixing lugs at the centre for the fixing screws of both accessories. If the existing socket is flush-mounted, you should remove the existing one gang box and cut out a larger chase for the dual box in the wall. If the existing socket outlet is surface-mounted, you will find replacing a plastic box presents little difficulty. If there is a two gang socket, you will have to mount the fused connection unit separately.

Installing the switch After you have run the circuit cables under the floorboards – and with two cables at each storage heater switch position – you can fix the 25amp twin switch. The unit has two separate switches both operated by a single rocker; this is so it meets safety regulation requirements that all poles of circuits at a heater must be capable of being isolated from the mains by the operation of a single switch. The switchplate has two cord outlets; one is for the heater flex which is connected to the switch marked 'heater' and the other is for the fan circuit flex which is connected to the switch marked 'fan'. There is a choice of surface or flush-mounting and the switch is available with or without neon indicators. A special flush-mounted box is required to take the switch, so buy this at the same time.

Remove two knock-out blanks for the cables; if using a flush metal box, fit the necessary PVC grommets. Thread in the two cables and fix the box to the wall using screws in plugged holes. If you are using a flush box, you will have to cut a chase into the wall so, when it is fixed, the box is flush with the plaster. Prepare the ends of the cable by removing the sheath but leave about 25mm (1in) within the box. Strip about 9mm (or ⅜in) of insulation from the four insulated wires, connect the red and black wires of the heater circuit cable to the mains terminals L and N respectively of the heater switch and the red and black wires of the fan circuit cable to the mains terminals L and N respectively of the fan switch.

Thread in the two flexible cords from the heater and strip about 150mm (6in) of sheathing from the end of each and about 9mm (or ⅜in) of insulation from the six wires. Connect the brown and blue wires of the heater flex to the load terminals L and N of the heater switch and the brown and blue wires of the fan flex to the load terminals L and N respectively of the fan switch. Connect the two green/yellow sleeved earth circuit wires and the two green/yellow insulated flex wires to the four earthing terminals. Neatly arrange all the wires in the box and fix the switch to the box using the screws supplied with the switch.

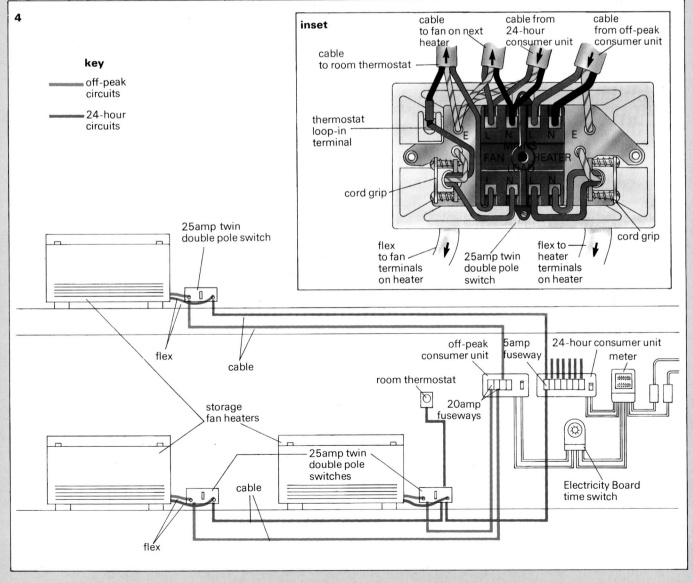

Immersion heaters

One great advantage of an immersion heater fitted to your hot water cylinder is that it can be used to supply as much or as little hot water around the home as you need at any particular time. It can also supplement other heating systems such as gas, oil or solid fuel. With care, you can fit it yourself.

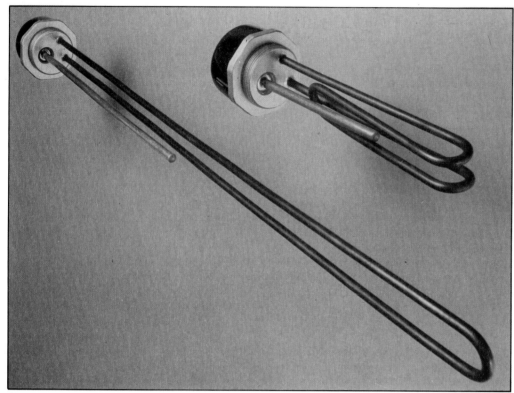

Left Immersion heaters are available in different lengths. You can buy a dual-element model, which heats either the top or all of the cylinder, or a single element one. If you decide on the single heater, you will find it is more economical to fit two, one at the top of the cylinder and the other lower down near the bottom
1 Types of immersion heater shown fitted into the hot water cylinder
1a Single element in varying lengths to suit different size cylinders
1b Separate heaters can be fitted so the top of the cylinder is heated for small amounts of water and all the cylinder heated when larger amounts are needed
1c The dual-element heater does the same job, but has the advantage of being a single fitting

1 Types of immersion heater

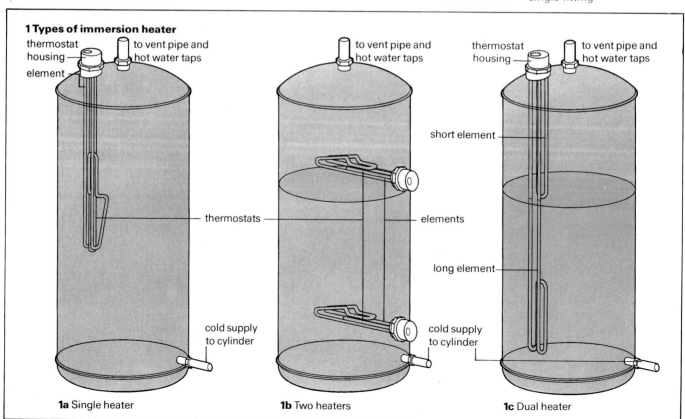

thermostat housing — element — to vent pipe and hot water taps

to vent pipe and hot water taps

thermostat housing — to vent pipe and hot water taps

short element

thermostats — elements

long element

cold supply to cylinder

cold supply to cylinder

1a Single heater   **1b** Two heaters   **1c** Dual heater

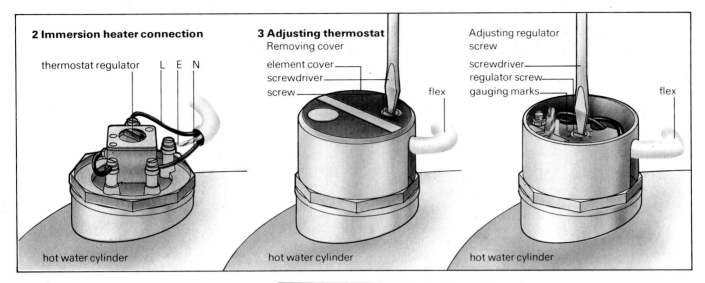

2 Immersion heater connection

thermostat regulator L E N

hot water cylinder

3 Adjusting thermostat
Removing cover

element cover
screwdriver
screw

flex

hot water cylinder

Adjusting regulator
screw

screwdriver
regulator screw
gauging marks

flex

hot water cylinder

One of the most convenient methods of supplying hot water in the home is by installing an immersion heater in your hot water cylinder, although it is a fairly expensive form of heating to run if used constantly. Heaters are made in a range of lengths and loadings to suit the different types of cylinder and to give varying quantities of hot water. On some the heating element is coated with a titanium sheath; this is specially for use in hard water areas where corrosive substances in the water would adversely affect an ordinary element without a special coating.

The length of the heater can range from 245–914mm (10–36in). The type most commonly fitted is the single-element one which will heat the whole cylinder. It is, however, more economical to have two elements, one fitted near the top and the other about 50mm (2in) from the bottom of the cylinder. The top element heats enough water for hand or dish washing and the bottom one heats the whole cylinder, when for example you want a bath. There is also a dual heater, with a short and long element, which operates on the same principle. Both systems are independently switched so you can have either or both elements on at any time to suit your needs.

Special long heaters are needed for indirect and self-priming cylinders and for rectangular tanks. Hot water cylinders designed to work on the Electricity Board's White Meter tariff have either two heaters or a dual-element one to heat part or all of the water.

Wiring heaters
Common ratings for the heater are 1, 2 and 3kW, but because the immersion heater is considered to be a continuous load, whether you keep it switched on all the time or not, it must be supplied by its own circuit direct from the consumer unit using 2.5sq mm cable from a separate 20amp fuseway. The cable runs to a 20amp double pole switch (usually with a pilot light) which should be sited near the heater and close enough for anyone to operate if they are adjusting the thermostat. The wiring from the switch to the heater should be a 20amp rubber heat-resistant flex.

If you are installing two heaters in one cylinder, your double pole switch should incorporate a second switch which allows you to have either one or both heaters working. In this case a separate flex must run to each heater from the switch.

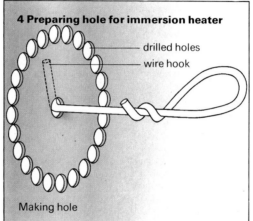

4 Preparing hole for immersion heater

drilled holes
wire hook

Making hole

2 Wiring up the heater after removing the element cover
3 Adjusting the thermostat via the regulator screw
4 Making a hole in the cylinder to fit a heater; the wire hook is used to prevent the cut-out section falling into the cylinder

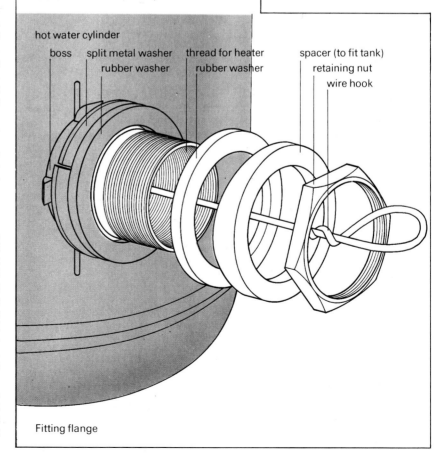

hot water cylinder

boss split metal washer thread for heater spacer (to fit tank)
rubber washer rubber washer retaining nut
wire hook

Fitting flange

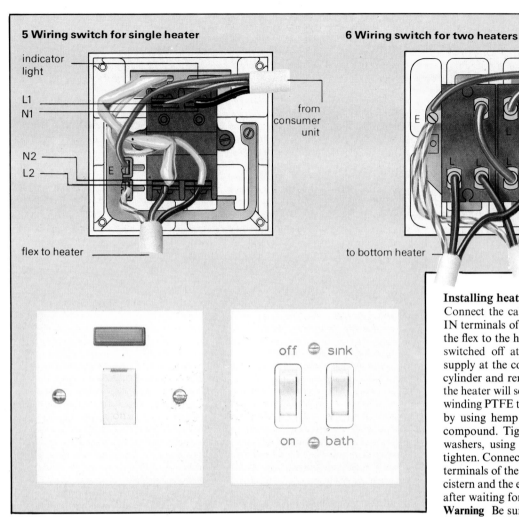

5 Wiring switch for single heater

indicator light

L1
N1

N2
L2

E

from consumer unit

flex to heater

6 Wiring switch for two heaters

E

L N

from consumer unit

L L L N

to bottom heater —— to top heater

off ⊖ sink

on ⊖ bath

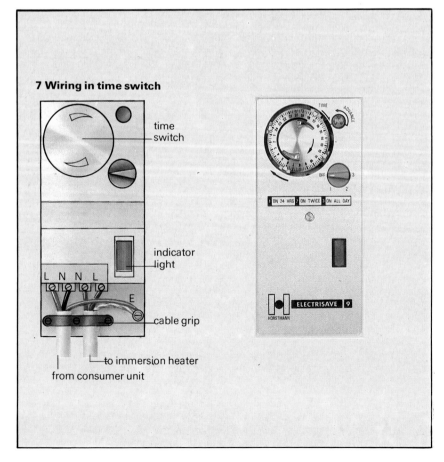

7 Wiring in time switch

time switch

indicator light

L N N L

E

cable grip

to immersion heater

from consumer unit

TIME ADVANCE

OFF 3
1 2

1 ON 24 HRS 2 ON TWICE 3 ON ALL DAY

ELECTRISAVE 9
HORSTMANN

Installing heater

Connect the cable from the consumer unit to the IN terminals of the switch and connect one end of the flex to the heater, making sure the electricity is switched off at the mains. Turn off your water supply at the cold water storage cistern, drain the cylinder and remove the relevant boss, into which the heater will screw. The threads are sealed first by winding PTFE tape against the direction of turn, or by using hemp string and a non-toxic plumbing compound. Tighten the heater against its sealing washers, using a large wrench – but never over-tighten. Connect the free end of the flex to the OUT terminals of the switch, turn on the stopcock at the cistern and the electricity at the consumer unit and, after waiting for the cylinder to refill, switch on.

Warning Be sure to clamp the flex at both ends in the cord grips fitted to the heater and switch, and use the correct flex grips to secure it to the walls. Otherwise the flex might become entangled in linen (if in an airing cupboard) and be pulled away.

Cutting boss Most cylinders are now made with at least one boss fitting. However, if you have a direct copper cylinder, without a boss, in good condition you can cut a hole to take the heater. Mark out the required diameter hole and cut it with a hole saw fitted to an electric drill. Alternatively, drill a series of holes around the edge of the circle, knock out the centre and file the edge smooth. You can buy a patent fitting that includes the boss, a thread to take the heater thread, washers and a retaining nut. Don't try to cut a boss in an indirect self-priming cylinder.

Adjusting thermostat You must turn off the heater before attempting to adjust the thermostat setting. You reach it by unscrewing any screws holding the cap in place. Use a screwdriver to obtain the required setting, generally 60°, 71° or 82°C (140°, 160° or 180°F). In hard water areas scale tends to build up in cylinders at temperatures above 60°C (140°F) which is the lowest acceptable temperature for normal domestic purposes. The thermostat automatically turns off the power supply when the required temperature is reached.

Using time switch An immersion heater can be controlled by a special time switch, which offers two on and off periods in each 24 hours.

5 Wiring up switch when fitting single heater
6 Wiring up switch when fitting two heaters
7 Wiring up time switch to heater

Bathroom fittings

The bathroom can be one of the most dangerous places in the home if you don't follow the rules for electrical safety. But it can also be one of the most comfortable with the introduction of electrical fittings. As long as you install them correctly they will not only work at maximum efficiency, but need never be a cause for anxiety to you or your family.

There is nothing worse than a bleak, chilly bathroom to greet you on a cold morning. Yet even the largest bathroom can be greatly improved with the addition of a wall-mounted infra-red heater for instant warmth, a small oil-fitted electric radiator, a heated towel rail (to warm towels when you have a bath and to dry them afterwards), a combined heater/light unit or a shaver socket combined with a mirror light.

Two important factors, however, must be remembered: these installations must be correctly wired and appliances must be fixed so securely that they can be removed only by using proper tools. Correct wiring means no socket outlets – except for the shaver – are permitted inside a bathroom (or washroom) and only cord-operated switches are allowed inside the room if they are within reach of the bath or shower; this is taken to be a distance of 2m (6ft 6in).

Heated towel rail

A good selection of these is available, so choose the largest one that will fit in your bathroom. It is a good idea to buy one that incorporates a pilot light because this means you are less likely to forget to turn it off. Towel rails must be connected to the ring circuit through a switched fused connection unit that is sited outside the bathroom.

Decide where you are going to install the appliance, first making sure the plaster or plasterboard wall is strong enough to make a secure fixing. Use a spirit level to check the appliance is being fixed horizontally and mark with a pencil the fixing holes for the screws. Drill and plug the holes.

Prepare the route for your cable (2.5sq mm twin core and earth PVC-sheathed) from the ring circuit to the switched fuse connection unit; install the unit as close to the appliance as possible – but outside the bathroom. Decide on the route for the appliance flex to reach the connection unit. If this entails a long run you may have to install a flexible cord outlet box – linked to the connection unit with 2.5sq mm twin core and earth cable. The wires from the appliance are then connected to their corresponding terminals on the cord outlet box.

When you have completed the installation, check all terminal and fixing screws, turn on the mains and switch on the appliance to check it is working.
Oil-filled radiator The installation method for oil-filled radiators is similar to that for fitting a heated towel rail.

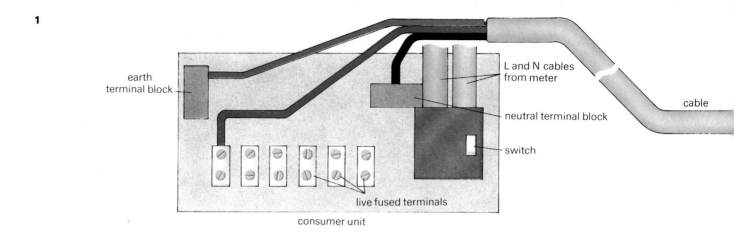

1

earth
terminal block

L and N cables
from meter

neutral terminal block

switch

cable

live fused terminals

consumer unit

2

socket

ring circuit

cable

L
L

N

E
N

cable

terminal block

L
E

N

ring circuit

fused connection unit

flexible cord out

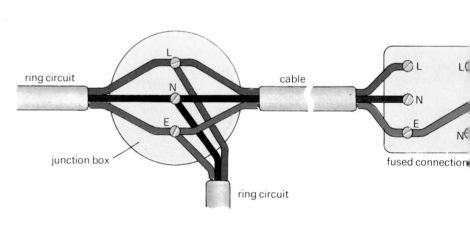

3

ring circuit

L

N

E

cable

L
L

N

E
N

junction box

ring circuit

fused connection

fused connection unit

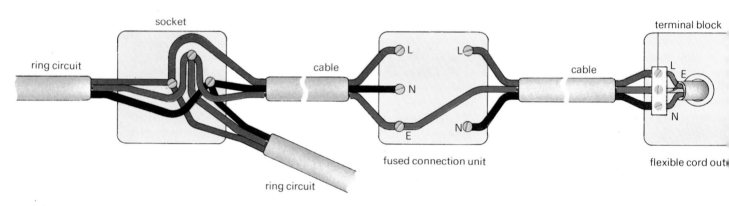

4

from fused connection
unit or direct from
consumer unit

E L L

N N

pull switch

Wall heater

This must also be fed from the ring circuit, using a switched fused connection unit and a flexible cord outlet as described for a towel rail. The heater should be fixed as high on the wall as possible and preferably not above a bath or a shower. Alternatively you may connect the appliance to a cord-operated isolating switch (incorporating a pilot light) and connect the switch to the ring circuit via a connection unit as before.

The appliance is fixed to the wall with plugs and screws; always ensure it is properly secured before connecting up and switching on.

Light/heater units

The ultimate in space-saving, this unit incorporates a lamp in the centre of a ceiling fitting with a heating element around the outside. A cord-operated switch within the unit operates the heater. The master switch should be a cord-operated ceiling switch. It should not be connected to a lighting circuit because many units have a total loading of 850 watts and if used simultaneously with a number of other lights on the circuit it could overload the maximum 1200 watts capacity and cause a fuse to blow in the consumer unit – not a happy thought if you are in the bath at the time.

There are two ways of supplying such a unit. One is through a switched fused connection unit, the other by running a separate circuit from a spare fuseway in the consumer unit, using either 1 or 1.5sq mm twin core and earth cable. You must take great care in connecting up at the consumer unit; the circuit should be controlled by a 5amp fuse.

The appliance should be securely mounted to a timber batten screwed between joists in the ceiling

1 Wiring appliance direct to consumer unit. **2** Wiring appliance to ring circuit socket outlet via fused connection unit. **3** Wiring appliance to junction box via fused connection unit. **4** Wiring appliance to fused connection unit or consumer unit and including pull switch. **5** Wiring shaver socket to ceiling rose.

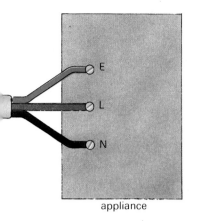

appliance

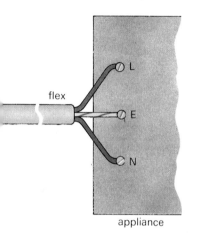

flex

appliance

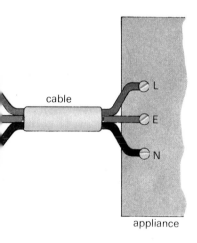

cable

appliance

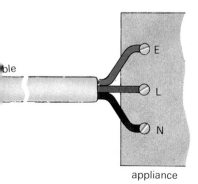

ble

appliance

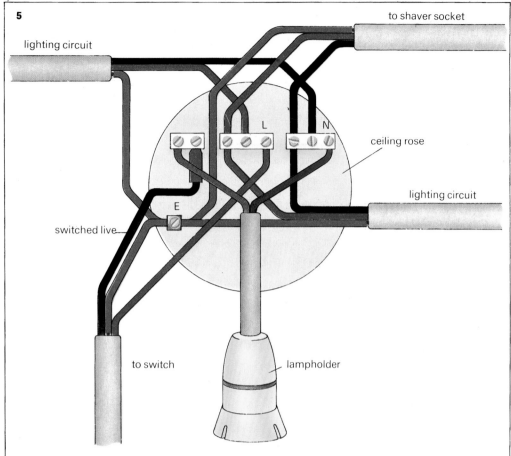

5

lighting circuit

to shaver socket

L   N

ceiling rose

switched live

E

lighting circuit

to switch

lampholder

or roof space. Connect the ceiling cord-operated switch between the appliance and the connection unit; if you are running the appliance from the consumer unit, fit an isolating ceiling cord-operated switch within reach of the appliance.

Ceiling rose If by installing a heat/light unit you are making the existing ceiling rose redundant, you must remove the pendant flex, rose, switch wires and switch. Having disconnected the switch wire at the rose, disconnect at the switch or switches; pull the cable through from the ceiling space and discard it, replastering any recess where the switch was fixed.

You must install a junction box between the joists above the rose and use this to seal off (or terminate) the cables that run to the rose. You will have to take great care doing this, ensuring the conductors fitted to the rose are connected to their corresponding terminals in the junction box. With an older installation, earthing was probably not used; if earthing is used, connect the earth to its proper terminal in the box. With an older installation you may have difficulty identifying all the cables. If you have any doubts, always seek expert advice – don't trust your own judgement.

Shaver sockets
The specially designed shaver socket for use in the bathroom is available in several types: some come complete with a mirror light. The shaver supply unit can be connected directly to the lighting circuit without using a fuse in the spur, because it contains an isolating transformer. The unit has a two-pin socket that accepts British, Continental and American standard round and flat-pin plugs. It is possible to buy a dual voltage socket outlet for 240 or 115

volts in cases where the shaver does not adapt. Shaver sockets are also made without isolating transformers for use in other rooms.

It is impossible to run other appliances off a shaver socket because a thermal unit will cause them to cut out.

Remember when installing a shaver socket that anyone who is short-sighted needs to get quite close to a mirror with their spectacles off. So avoid placing it over a deep sink or cupboard that forces them to stand and peer. If you have a rechargeable electric razor, make sure there is a shelf near the socket where you can leave the shaver to recharge.
Mirror light This is a boon when you are making-up, or shaving with an electric or wet razor. Units are available which combine a striplight and a shaver socket at the end.

Having decided the position of the shaver and/or mirror light unit, trace a pencil outline round the box (available flush, semi-flush or surface-mounted) or mark the securing screw holes. Thread your cable through a hole drilled in the wall through the back of your surface-mounted box or through knock-out holes. Secure the box. Trim the cable sheath, strip the insulation material and connect up in the normal way to the correct terminals. The earth terminal is generally riveted in the base of the box; the live and neutral conductors go to terminals on the reverse side of the socket unit. Then secure the unit to the box with the screws provided, turn on the mains and test the light.
Warning If you have any doubts about the safety or suitability of a product, don't buy it. The yellow and blue label of the British Electrotechnical Approvals Board attached to a product proves it has been tested to the British Standard for electrical safety.

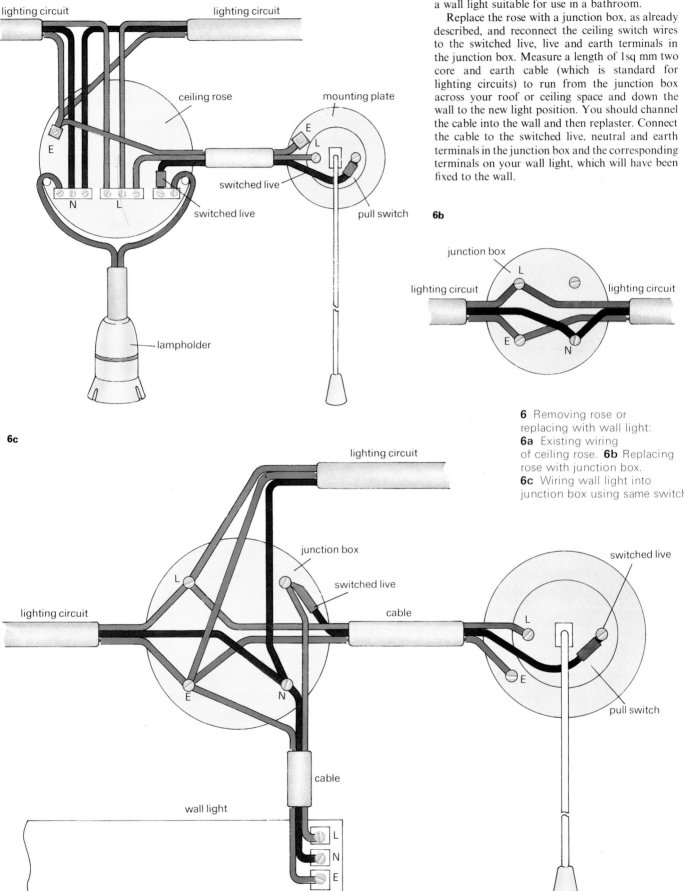

6a

lighting circuit

lighting circuit

ceiling rose

mounting plate

E

L

E

N

L

switched live

switched live

pull switch

lampholder

As an alternative to making the existing wiring and ceiling switch redundant, you may decide to alter your lighting by converting them to operate a wall light suitable for use in a bathroom.

Replace the rose with a junction box, as already described, and reconnect the ceiling switch wires to the switched live, live and earth terminals in the junction box. Measure a length of 1sq mm two core and earth cable (which is standard for lighting circuits) to run from the junction box across your roof or ceiling space and down the wall to the new light position. You should channel the cable into the wall and then replaster. Connect the cable to the switched live, neutral and earth terminals in the junction box and the corresponding terminals on your wall light, which will have been fixed to the wall.

6b

junction box

lighting circuit

lighting circuit

L

E

N

6 Removing rose or replacing with wall light:
6a Existing wiring of ceiling rose. **6b** Replacing rose with junction box.
6c Wiring wall light into junction box using same switch

6c

lighting circuit

junction box

switched live

cable

lighting circuit

L

E

N

cable

wall light

L

N

E

switched live

L

E

pull switch

Safety in the bathroom

You can make your bathroom among the most comfortable rooms in the home if you choose the right materials and equipment – taking full advantage of all the electrical appliances that make life so much easier. But if you fail to follow the safety rules, you could be walking into danger whenever you use it.

Electrical appliances such as mirror lights, instant shower units, shaver sockets, heated towel rails, radiators and radiant heaters can add a touch of luxury as well as efficiency to any bathroom. But electricity can also make the bathroom potentially the most dangerous room in the house.

Socket outlets

It is against wiring regulations to install a socket outlet in a bathroom (or washroom), with the exception of purpose-made shaver units fitted with an isolating transformer which makes the units safe. Many striplights are available with combined shaver sockets, but unless these clearly state they have an isolating transformer they must not be installed in bathrooms.

Never use a mains voltage appliance in the bathroom by feeding it from a socket outlet from the landing or another room. However tempting it may be to trail a mains portable television in at bathtime, NEVER do it. Settle for a transistor radio if you are going to have a long soak. And never let other members of the family persuade you to let them use a hairdrier on the end of an extended lead.

Lights and switches

You must not have lights with open lampholders because this makes it possible to remove the lamp and use the lampholder as a socket for an appliance. All lights and appliances must be cord-operated if within reach (2m) of the bath or shower. Flexible cord should not be used to hang lampholders, which must always be fixed to the ceiling. Lampholders must also be beyond the reach of anyone showering or taking a bath and must be shrouded with an insulating material; or totally enclosed light fittings should be used. Mirror lights are specially designed, whether or not they have shaver units, to be safe in the bathroom.

Heaters

If you want an open reflector-type wall-mounted heater it must be installed out of reach of anyone using the bath or shower. It is also a good idea to have it operated by a switch outside the bathroom as well as by a cord inside the room; in the case of real emergency this means the appliance can be switched off even if the door is locked and quick access is difficult. This also applies to electrically heated towel rails and radiators. When installing a towel rail or radiator it is worth fixing a cord-operated ceiling switch that incorporates a pilot light to show when the appliance is on. All electrical equipment of this sort sited within the bathroom must be securely cross-bonded to earth by means of special earthing clamps.

Secure fittings

Make sure all fixtures are securely fitted and can only be removed by using the appropriate tools. This may sound fundamental but it is sometimes difficult to achieve in modern houses where plasterboard internal walls are used and do not always offer a strong anchorage point.

Warning There is always a danger of inheriting potential electrical hazards when you buy an older house. You must be especially careful where a scullery or bedroom has been converted to a bathroom without proper regard to safety. Always remove all socket outlets or old power points, move wall switches to outside the room and replace flex pendants with ceiling fittings.

UNSAFE

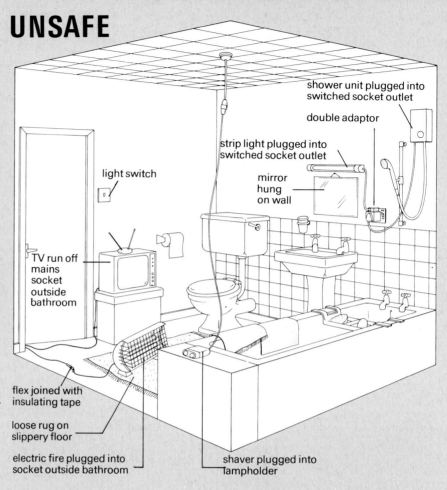

light switch

TV run off mains socket outside bathroom

flex joined with insulating tape

loose rug on slippery floor

electric fire plugged into socket outside bathroom

shower unit plugged into switched socket outlet

double adaptor

strip light plugged into switched socket outlet

mirror hung on wall

shaver plugged into lampholder

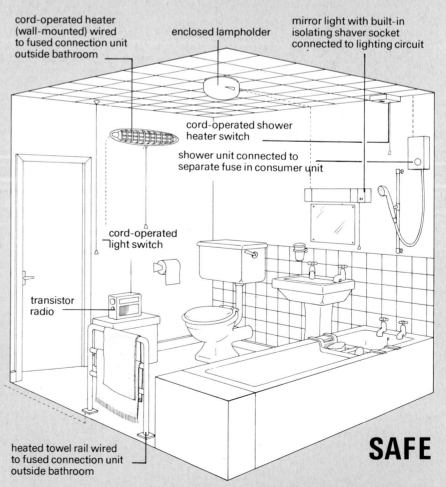

cord-operated heater (wall-mounted) wired to fused connection unit outside bathroom

enclosed lampholder

mirror light with built-in isolating shaver socket connected to lighting circuit

cord-operated shower heater switch

shower unit connected to separate fuse in consumer unit

cord-operated light switch

transistor radio

heated towel rail wired to fused connection unit outside bathroom

SAFE

Outside wiring

Wiring to sockets or lighting points attached to the outside walls of a house can be part of the domestic circuit. Wiring to a point in the garden, greenhouse or separate garage, however, has to be treated as a different installation, with its own main switch and fuse unit. Sockets supplying outdoor appliances must now have ELCB protection (see page 282).

Because wind and rough weather will cause wear and tear, sockets, switches and cables must be tough, weatherproof and protected from the possibility of accidental damage. Professional help with outside wiring is essential because electricity used outside is potentially more dangerous than inside.

Surface wiring

Wiring a porch light, socket or switch onto the outside wall of a house is not difficult as long as you use weatherproof equipment. Sockets are usually in galvanized steel with covers and the switches are plastic. It is best to keep wiring on an outside wall to a minimum; it should be protected in plastic tubing or conduit and the connections, where the cable joins the switch or socket or light fitting, have to be water- and weatherproof. The wiring can be taken as a spur from the ring main, although a porch or outside light can be taken from a lighting point, as described earlier in the book; in this case the cable goes through the wall as close to the light as possible. Study the wiring layout of the house to plan the shortest route from the new position to the existing wiring; this will give a neater installation.

To take a cable from the inside of a house to the outside, drill a hole through the wall using a masonry bit of up to 300mm (1ft) long if it is a cavity wall. Insert a short length of plastic tube or conduit; this must be angled so the outside end is lower than the inside (to keep out rainwater) and cemented in place. Fit an elbow to the outside end.

Overhead wiring

With the overhead method of wiring, the PVC twin core and earth cable is supported by a galvanized steel cable called a catenary wire. The power cable is relieved of any stress or strain by being clipped and taped to the catenary wire which is itself suspended from permanent supports not less than 3.5m (11ft 6in) above ground or 5.2m (17ft) if above a drive. To get the right height you may have to attach a weather-treated post to the greenhouse or garage and brace it to withstand strong winds. You must fit supporting vine eyes, one into a heavy duty plug on the house wall and the other into the side of the post near the top. The ends of the catenary wire are threaded through the eyes and twisted firmly round the main length of wire.

Since the catenary wire will be under strain for many years, it is vital to have a strong joint at each end. It is also a good idea to have an adjustable eye bolt fitting or a turnbuckle at one end of the catenary wire so it can be stretched tight. The catenary wire must be earthed using single core 6sq mm PVC-insulated earth wire connected to it by a corrosion-resistant screw-type connector and connected to the mains earth point in the house. Cable from the switch fuse should come through the wall using a tube or conduit as already described. The mains cable should be 2.5sq mm or 4sq mm and in one continuous length from the switch fuse to the new switch or socket.

A downward rainwater 'drip loop' of slack is usually left at each end and the supply cable is attached to the catenary wire by using slings or bitumen-impregnated insulating tape; this is turned two or three times between the cable and wire. Non-corrosive buckle-type cable clips are wrapped round the tape for strength.

Underground wiring

You can run ordinary PVC-sheathed cable underground so long as it is protected by impact-resistant PVC conduit. However, except for very long runs it is probably simpler to use special cable, armoured PVC-insulated cable being recommended. It has two cores – red and black insulated – and an extruded covering of black PVC over the galvanized wire armour; the wire armour usually serves as the

1 Outdoor plug, socket and cover
2 Components of outdoor gland used for connecting armoured cable to metal box
3 Twin core armoured cable, stripped back to show various layers, connected to metal box with indoor gland; separate earth wire connects to earth terminal on metal box
4 Exploded indoor gland
5 Weatherproofed switch
6 Twin core armoured cable connected to metal box with outdoor gland
7 Three core armoured cable stripped back to show various layers; yellow core is used as earth wire

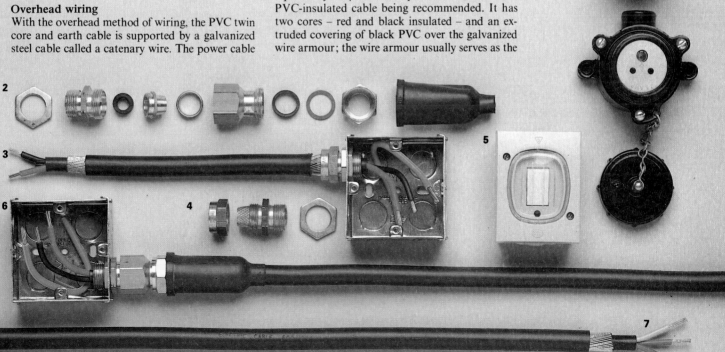

earth conductor. It is necessary to fit a metal screwed compression gland, secured by a lock nut and bush, over the wire armour at each end of the cable; this gland fits the conduit entry hole of a flush metal box, fixed inside the building or house, which is used as a junction box if the entry point of the armoured cable is some distance from the main switch or switch fuse. A terminal block inside the box is used to connect the armoured cable to ordinary twin core and earth PVC-sheathed cable. Alternatively the cable can be run to the switch mounting box. In both cases a short length of 4.0sq mm single core green/yellow PVC-insulated cable is used to connect the switch or terminal block earth terminal to the earth terminal on the box.

Some Electricity Boards may insist on the use of three core armoured cable, the yellow core being used for the earth and enclosed in green/yellow sleeving for identification.

A more expensive cable is the mineral-insulated, copper-clad type (MICC); this has two wires inside a protective copper tube which also serves as an earth connection. With mineral-insulated cable it is necessary to fit a seal at each end; if the cable runs directly into the switch and fuse unit, choose a seal which has an earth wire termination. A screwed gland can also be fitted with each seal if required. The cable runs from the main switch and fuse unit in the house to the control panel in the building outside, taking as direct a route as possible but avoiding all places likely to be disturbed in the future. The trench must be dug about 500mm (20in) deep and care taken not to damage any water or drainpipes and other cables you encounter. If there is a space below the ground floor of your house, it is easy to have a hole knocked through the wall; but be careful not to interfere with the damp proof course. The cable needs to be protected at points where it is exposed and securely fixed to the wall using special clips designed for the purpose. Additional protection can be given by galvanized steel channelling screwed to the brick or woodwork.

Below Layout showing wiring from house to outbuildings — over or underground — with details of connections to consumer unit inside house (**inset A**), taking cable through wall inside conduit pipe and connecting to catenary wire (**inset B**), fixing catenary wire to post (**inset C**) and outbuilding control panel (**inset D**); when wiring up use cable for lights and flex for other appliances

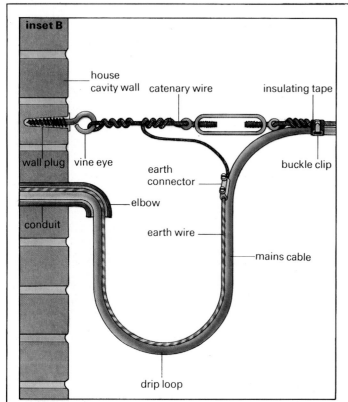

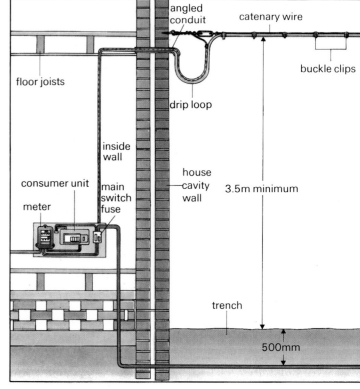

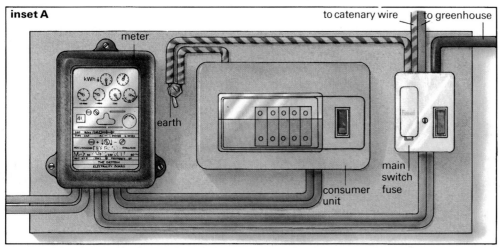

Control panels

In an integral or attached garage the cable can run direct to sockets and light fittings; but ideally the cable should terminate in a control panel with a main switch. In the damper atmosphere of a greenhouse or garden shed, a control panel is strongly advisable for safety; switched points and socket outlets can then be connected to the switch. Permanent switches and fused connection units with red neon indicators are preferable, since most of the equipment will be permanently connected. With a plug and socket there is always a risk of damp working its way between the face of the plug and the socket surface, resulting in a current leakage. Providing ELCB protection for all socket outlets on the panel is required by the Wiring Regulations.

Fused connection units, switches and sockets should be installed 1200mm (4ft) from the floor and wired with twin core and earth PVC-sheathed 2.5sq mm cable. The cable is taken from each in turn back to the outlet on the main switch. Fused connection units and sockets should be mounted on metal mounting boxes inset into a timber board, or on moulded plastic surface-mounted boxes, with cable holes drilled through the board.

In a greenhouse fit a strong frame to the back of the board to protect the cable and leave access for the mains cable. Once the wiring is complete, fit a back cover of weatherproof plywood and mount the board at chest level on a strong support. The wiring to the electrical equipment and heaters can be by PVC-sheathed three core flex secured at intervals to the greenhouse; there should be no trailing or loose cable or flex. With aluminium greenhouses you may have to drill small holes in the appropriate positions to allow buckle clips to be fixed with screws and nuts. In this case the PVC-sheathed cable will be in contact with metal and the greenhouse must be earthed by bolting an earth clamp to the frame and connecting a 6sq mm green/yellow PVC-insulated earth cable to this and to the earthing terminal of the main switch.

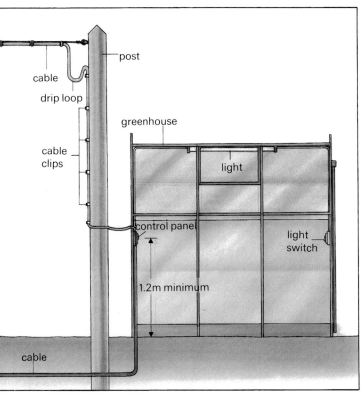

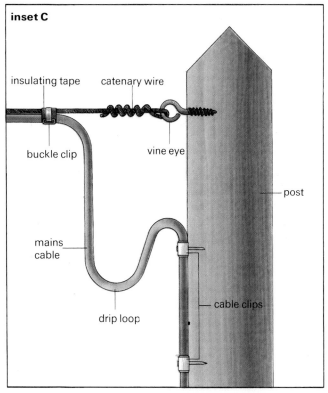

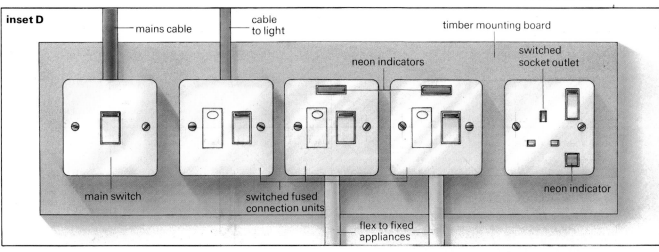

Garden lighting

Garden lighting is practical, attractive and not expensive to run; two units of electricity will light the average garden from dusk to midnight. The lighting of walls, patios and possible danger points such as steps helps prevent accidents and discourages intruders. Effective outside lighting also lengthens the time you can enjoy the garden and can reveal an unexpected attraction in familiar surroundings. This can be achieved by using fittings attached to the outside of the house or with the more mobile low-voltage lighting set. But whichever you use, it must be safe.

Mains voltage lighting
There are complications in using mains electricity outdoors. Many lighting fittings can be fixed to the wall of the house and connected through the bricks to the house wiring; but garden spotlights, pool lights and lights in herbaceous borders will need an outdoor connection. Weatherproof 13amp sockets mounted on the outside wall of the house are an inexpensive way of providing temporary lighting for the patio; remember that they must be protected by an ELCB (see page 282).

Types of light Spotlights are the most effective way of lighting a garden. Mains voltage 100 and 150 watt spotlamps screw into waterproof holders and are tough enough to withstand most outdoor conditions; the holders can be supplied with an earth spike or a mounting bracket. Spotlights can also be mounted on trees or walls to light a path or section of the garden. When lighting trees, the spotlights should be placed at ground level or low down on the trunk and directed so their light goes up into the branches.

Tungsten-halogen miniature floodlamps give 300–500 watts of brilliant light from a small finger-size glass phial mounted on a fitting about 150×75mm (6×3in). They are powerful for their size and have a life of about 2000 hours. To light the garden, they should be placed high on a wall and must be fixed in a horizontal position.

The simplest method of lighting paths, patios and porches is to use the 'light brick' or 'bulkhead' fitting; this is a square or oval of opal or moulded glass which clips over a weatherproof holder. The fitting is commonly available in sizes from $200 \times 125 \times 114$mm ($8 \times 5 \times 4\frac{1}{2}$in) and is suitable for a 60 or 100 watt lamp.

Post lanterns wired with buried armoured cable can be mounted on a low wall or on anti-tamper bollards and used to light entrances and drives.

Low voltage lighting
There are several low voltage lighting sets available; these can be safely installed even at ground level, where children are likely to touch them. They operate at 12 volts through a portable mains transformer (the output of the transformer is described in volt-amps rather than watts); you simply plug the transformer into any convenient socket outlet and trail the cable down the garden, connecting in spotlamps at any point in the length of the cable. The lamps are easily attached and can be pushed into the earth on spikes or fixed to trees.

Types of lighting set The 'ropelight' is a recent innovation and operates from a 12 volt DC supply, which can either be a special mains transformer/rectifier or a car battery. It consists of a line of coloured lights within a hose-like flexible plastic tube. The lights come in 10m (or 33ft) lengths which can be draped around the garden. Fixed flashing lights are available or you could use chaser lights, which appear to move along the rope.

There are also specially mounted lighting units which can be used under water or floating on the surface. If these lights are used with a 12 volt submersible pump, special water jet rings can be clipped around the lights to give illuminated fountains. Both fountains and lights can be controlled on one cable from an indoor switch or a waterproof junction box and transformer can be concealed close to the water in a simple rockery stone or brick housing to protect it from the weather.

A waterfall can look particularly effective when lit. Small lights can be concealed among the plants and stones on the edge of the stream and low

Equipment for garden lighting (Elsworthy Electronics):
1 Transformer
2 Pool lights, available with different colour lenses, which can be used under water or floating on the surface
3 Spotlights, also available with different colour lenses, which can be bracket-mounted or fixed to spikes and driven into the ground

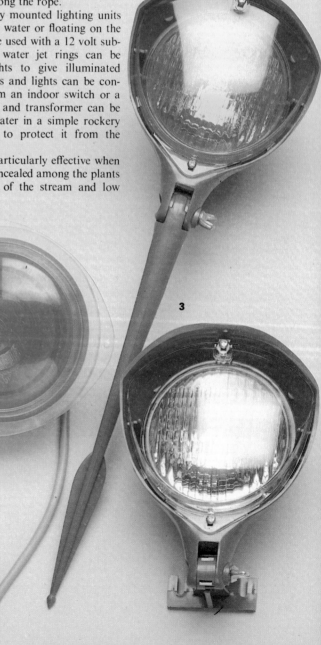

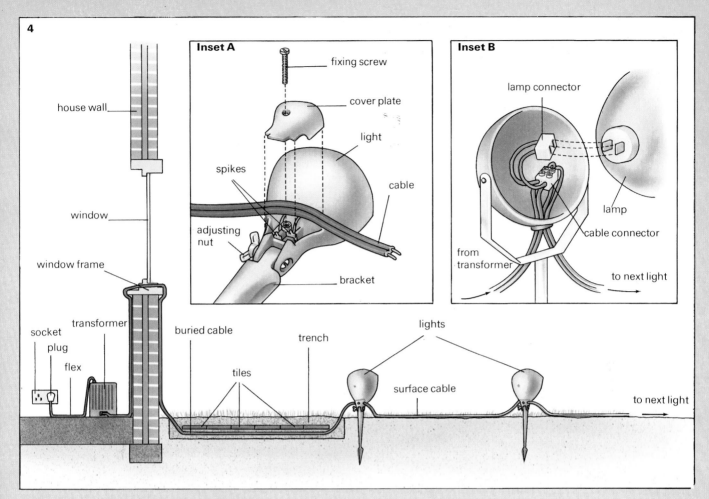

4

Inset A
fixing screw
cover plate
light
cable
spikes
adjusting nut
bracket

Inset B
lamp connector
lamp
cable connector
from transformer
to next light

house wall
window
window frame
socket
plug
flex
transformer
buried cable
trench
tiles
lights
surface cable
to next light

voltage lamps are purpose-made to be concealed in simulated rocky stones.

Connecting up lighting sets Position the transformer under cover in the house, garage or shed close to a 240 volt mains socket outlet. The rating of the transformer will limit the number of lamps you can have. A transformer with a 36 volt-amps output can serve up to two lamps; a 72 volt-amps rating is suitable for up to four lamps and 108 volt-amps rating is for a maximum of six lamps.

Connect special low voltage, twin core cable to the transformer output connector block. One end of the cable is sealed for weatherproofing, so be sure to connect the unsealed end to the transformer. Run the cable to where the lights are required; it can be taken outside through a small hole drilled in the fixed part of a window frame. It is safe to allow the cable to trail on the surface of the ground so the positions of the lights can be easily changed; or you can bury it in a trench, which you should then cover with tiles to prevent accidental damage from garden tools.

When the lights are roughly positioned, connect them to the low voltage cable. With one low voltage system you should take the back cover plate off each light, drape the cable in its channel and press the cable down with your thumb so the projecting metal spikes make an electrical connection. Replace the cover and adjust the light to the desired angle. Fit the transformer mains lead with a plug to suit the socket outlet; the plug should be fitted with a 3amp fuse. You can now plug the transformer in and switch it on. To ensure a satisfactory electrical connection after each season's use, you should move each light along the cable by about 25mm

(1in) and then reconnect it; wrap insulating tape round the previous connection area.

Another system uses conventional connector strips and a car-type lamp connector; in this case you must bare the cable and connect it in the screw connectors at each fitting.

Planning lighting
Colour is important when lighting outdoors and most spotlamps are sold with colour filters. The thing to remember when lighting a garden is to concentrate on what is being lit and not on the lights themselves. White is most effective since it brings out colour; red turns foliage brown, while yellow turns it grey. Green highlights grass and foliage, while blue has a mysterious quality especially on birch trees; it also attracts insects, so place it away from a terrace or patio. Lights should be hidden from view or placed behind large plants; where concealment is difficult, you should mount them above the normal lines of vision.

Concentrate on trees and larger shrubs. Trees such as elm, which have a high canopy, should be lit from below so the spotlight shines upwards into the leaves. Silver birches should be lit so the beam just touches the main limbs and conifers should catch the light along the edges of their branches. One or two spotlights placed in herbaceous borders can give a dramatic effect, casting a warm glow over the flowers.

When experimenting, choose a dry night and use an ordinary 150 watt lamp in a simple bowl reflector. Seen from a distance, this will give you an idea of the effect you will get when you eventually install the proper equipment.

4 With a low voltage wiring system the transformer is connected to a socket outlet inside the house; the cable to the lights is taken through the wall or window frame and over or underground (protected by tiles) to the outside lights and looped in from light to light. The cable is fixed to each light by removing the cable cover and pressing the cable onto the projecting prongs; the cover is screwed back on to make the electrical connection (**inset A**). A car-type lamp showing the lamp connector and the cable looped into the terminal strips (**inset B**)

Bells, buzzers and chimes

Fitting a bell, buzzer or door chime is a simple job, since many are sold in kit form specifically for DIY installation. All work off a low voltage supplied by dry batteries or a small safety transformer which is permanently connected to the mains and reduces your 240 volt household supply to 3, 5, 8 or 12 volts. You will need a transformer system for a bell push with a light; if you just want a bell or chime without illumination, a system operated on dry batteries is easier and cheaper to install. Batteries normally last for about 12 months, depending on the amount of use. Prices vary considerably according to the signal which is produced and the kind of external fitting used.

Trembler bells An electro-magnet causes a hammer to vibrate against a metal gong (or dome) and produces the familiar clear ringing tone.

Buzzers An electro-magnet causes a diaphragm to vibrate. Pitch and volume can be varied and some produce a tone similar to a fog horn.

Chimes These have a double-ended plunger, mounted on a spring drawn through an electro-magnet, which strikes the metal chime bars and produces a double note. Some can be wired to a second bell push on another door, which will produce a single note so you will know which door to answer.

Sonic musical signals Produced in a variety of pre-programmed tunes, this type gives an individual touch to surprise any caller.

How they work

Bells, buzzers, chimes and sonics may be operated by battery or transformer (in some cases either), but check first with the manufacturer's installation instructions. Some are specially made so they do not cause interference on a television set or radio. The bell push is a spring-loaded switch; as it is pressed two contacts join to complete the circuit.

Usually manufacturers supply installation instructions and wiring diagrams with their kits, but the basic principle is a simple circuit which is completed when the bell push is operated.

Batteries are often fitted inside the case of the bell or chime and connection to the push is by twin core flex usually called bell wire. This is often sold in white or cream; you can paint over it to match your existing wall colour. Since domestic fittings are operated off a low voltage, there is no danger of getting a shock or of causing a fire with this wire. It can be left exposed along the edge of skirting, round

Top A DIY battery-operated bell kit
1 Basic wiring for a bell and bell push powered by a battery
2a Installing a bell push in a door jamb; connect the two terminals before securing the bell push
2b Installing a bell push in the centre of a door; secure the bell wire with insulated clips and leave a coil of slack wire on the hinge side to reduce bending when opening

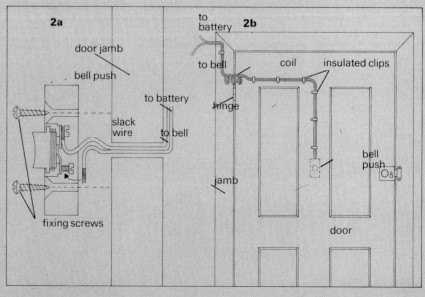

Above A small buzzer unit; this can be battery-operated or connected to the mains via a transformer
You can connect two bells to one bell push; use the parallel system (**3a**) for two bells with the same resistance and the series system (**3b**) for bells with a different resistance – here you must increase the voltage to get an effective signal
4 To operate a bell from the mains, connect it to the consumer unit via a transformer or to the ring main via a transformer and fused connection unit (**inset**)

door frames or even along the edge of coving. Small insulated fitting clips secure the wire to the surface, but take care not to sever the wire when nailing. Bell wire should be clipped to the surface at about 300mm (or 12in) intervals.

How they are installed
The hall is the best site for the sounding unit, but this will obviously depend on what sort of accommodation you have. Many people have them in the kitchen, but there is a risk of steam corroding both batteries and sounding unit.

If the distance between bell and push is more than about 9m (30ft) you may need to increase the voltage of the battery or the thickness of the wire because the resistance of the wire reduces the effective voltage. The loss of about $\frac{1}{2}$ volt for every 9m (30ft) of wire may not be noticeable when the batteries are new, but after a while the bell or chime

signal will weaken and then stop altogether.
It is a simple matter to install a bell push at the front and back doors to operate one sounding unit; you can also fit a second sounding unit to work from the same push – this is useful in a large house or where the occupant has hearing difficulties. Two methods can be used to wire a second bell or set of chimes.
Parallel This method is for bells or chimes which have the same resistance.
Series This system is for bells or chimes which do not match. Here increased voltage is necessary, otherwise either only one bell will work or neither will give a loud enough sound. The series system cannot be used for trembler bells.

If you fit a transformer, you must connect it to the mains using 1sq mm twin core and earth cable. It can be connected as a spur from a ring circuit, but most consumer units have a 5amp fuseway designed for this connection. If you take a spur from the ring circuit, use a fused connection unit with a 3amp fuse.

Transformers usually have three connections on the output side. If you take the bell wire to the outer connections, this gives an 8 volt supply; taken to the middle and one of the outer connections, it gives a 5 volt supply; and taken to the middle and the other outer connection a 3 volt supply. Transformers are also available which give a 12 volt supply for use when two fittings are run in series or for long wiring runs. All this is clearly marked on the transformer case, so you should have no difficulty selecting the right connections.

To fix the unit you have chosen, drill a hole through your door jamb to run the bell wire from the bell push to the battery and sounding unit. The bell push must be wired to its two terminals before it is screwed into the jamb. You should leave a loop of wire inside the push so it can be removed for

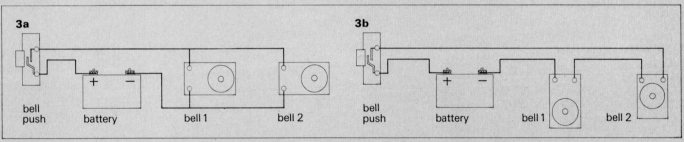

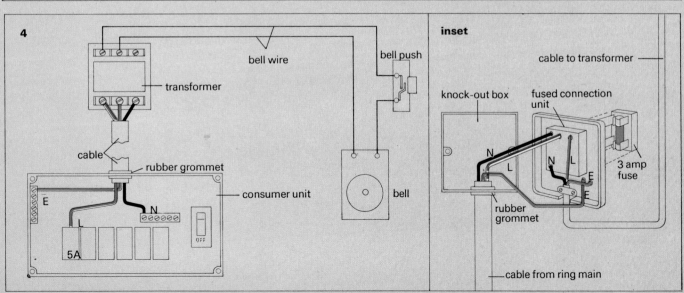

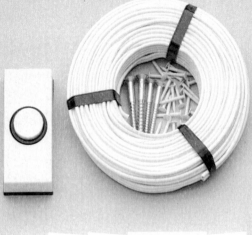

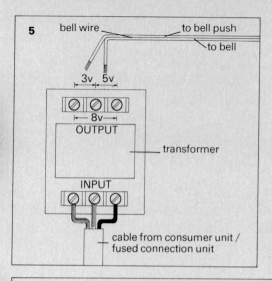

5
bell wire   to bell push
to bell

3v   5v
8v
OUTPUT
— transformer

INPUT

cable from consumer unit /
fused connection unit

Far left A DIY chimes kit operated by battery and containing a chime, push button, bell wire, fixing screws and enamelled wiring nails

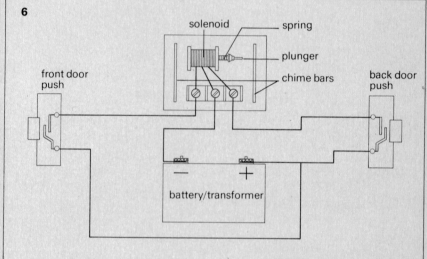

6
solenoid   spring
plunger
front door push   chime bars   back door push

battery/transformer

inspection. Alternatively fix the bell push to the door and run the wire from the push through a hole in the door to the hinged side and onto the jamb, leaving some slack wire between the door and the jamb to prevent excessive bending when the door is opened and closed; otherwise the bell wire will very quickly break. Ideally, form the slack wire into a small coil by wrapping a few turns round a pencil before attaching the wire to the jamb. Continuous conductor hinges are available which overcome the need for slack wire, but these are expensive.

Attach the housing of the sounding unit to the wall with plugs and screws, and clip or screw the cover over it. Usually the cover is made of plastic or wood, but some manufacturers make more decorative ones in such materials as ceramic. Make the electrical connections according to one of the circuits illustrated.

How to correct faults
If your bell stops working, it may be due to a flat or damaged battery, a loose connection, faulty bell push or dirt in the sounding mechanism.

Any contact in a bell or buzzer can be cleaned by rubbing a piece of card between the contact and screw, but don't use abrasive material. You need a soft brush, dipped in lighter fuel, to clean the solenoid spring and plungers on a chime to ensure the plunger can move freely.

Warning Always disconnect the fitting before servicing any unit.

5 By varying the wiring to the connections you can get an output of 3, 5 or 8 volts from your transformer; the connections are clearly marked to make selection easy
6 Chimes wired into two push buttons — one at the front and one at the back door — via a battery; alternatively you can wire them through a transformer connected to the mains circuit

Fitting TV aerials and sockets

The television set is now a standard fixture in many homes, providing hours of entertainment. But a poor picture can spoil this fun. Depending on the area in which you live, there is a range of aerials to cope with the quality of reception – and various devices that enable you to enjoy your favourite programmes anywhere in the home.

There are three normal positions for a television aerial: on the roof, in the loft or placed on top of the set or elsewhere in the room. A roof fitting, sited as high as possible, is the most satisfactory method, although this job is probably best left to a professional. You can keep down the bill by laying the special coaxial cable yourself and getting the rigger to connect up after he has completed the installation on the roof. An aerial on top of the set is only really satisfactory where there is outstanding reception, whereas an aerial in the loft can provide excellent viewing, if you are not too far away from one of the broadcasting authorities' transmitters.

If you move into a new area and notice few rooftop installations, you can usually assume the area has good reception. It may mean there is no

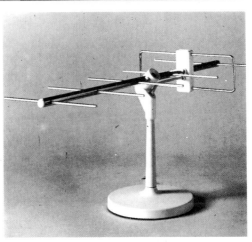

Top When you move into a new area it is worth checking to see how good the television reception is, If the signal is poor, you will have to fit a roof aerial
Centre An indoor aerial which sits on top of the set: this type is only suitable for use where the reception is outstanding
Bottom left A rooftop aerial gives the best results in any area
Bottom right An aerial fitted beneath the eaves of the house can provide good reception and is not as conspicuous as a rooftop installation

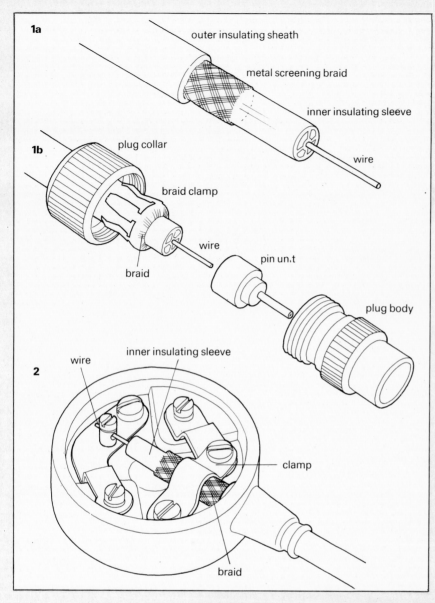

1a outer insulating sheath

metal screening braid

inner insulating sleeve

wire

1b plug collar

braid clamp

wire

pin unit

braid

plug body

2 inner insulating sleeve

wire

clamp

braid

1a When connecting the aerial to the set make sure you use the right cable – a low-loss coaxial type
1b Using the correct plug – a coaxial type with special braid clamp – is vital for a sound connection
2 Wiring the coaxial cable to the set from a junction box on the aerial

reception, so check with the BBC and IBA engineering information services and see a local dealer. He usually will not mind you doing the job yourself because, like some television rental companies, he probably contracts his aerial work out to someone else anyway.

Television aerial installations are becoming more sophisticated and, by using a combination of the most sensitive roof aerial and masthead amplifiers, you can pick up distant TV stations.

Connecting cable
Use low-loss coaxial cable to connect the aerial to the set. This is expensive to buy and you should take the shortest possible route when you lay it, not only for economy's sake but because a short run helps to maintain the signal's strength. The cable consists of an outer insulating sheath, a metal screening braid (which stops unwanted signals being picked up), an inner insulating sleeve and a final inner wire which actually carries the signal. Avoid bending it sharply as this can seriously affect reception.

You can run the cable in plastic conduit, bury it in plaster or fix it to your walls with cable clips. In some modern homes you may be able to run it from the roof or loft, through the roof space and down

the cavity in your walls to an aerial socket outlet (which can be either flush or surface-mounted) or direct to the plug which connects at the back of the television set.

If you run the cable externally, either from a roof aerial or through the eaves in the case of a loft aerial, you must check it periodically to see whether it is being chafed by the wind rubbing it against roof tiles or brickwork. If you bury it, you cannot take the aerial with you when you move; this need not be particularly inconvenient, since when moving from one area of the country to another, you may well need a different aerial because different channels are used in different areas and signal strengths vary considerably. So it is as well to include the aerial in the fixtures and fittings when you sell.

Wiring up
When wiring the cable either to the plug or in the weatherproof junction box on the aerial, remove 38mm (1½in) of outer insulation and loosen and fold back the braid to leave about 20mm (¾in) of inner insulation clear; then remove 6–13mm (¼–½in) of the inner insulation from the braid.

The cable is fed through an access hole (and protected by a grommet) at the junction box, the inner wire connected to the terminal and the braid clamped down with a metal clamp. The junction box is generally covered with a clip-on PVC cover.

When wiring up the plug, slip on the plug collar and the braid clamp, tighten the screw on the clamp, thread the inner wire into the pin unit and screw the collar onto the plug body. Unless the screening braid is properly clamped it will not do its job effectively.

Fixing the aerial
The aerial should now be screwed into the highest possible point in your loft and as far away from galvanized steel water tanks as possible, since the metal may deflect the signal. When you have done this, point the aerial so the shortest element or cross piece is nearest to the transmitter and, by trial and error, establish the best position (by going down to the set to check the pictures on the different channels or getting someone else to look for you) before bolting the aerial into its optimum position. Your dealer should have sold you the appropriate UHF aerial for your district and this may have from five to up to 21 elements (or cross pieces).
Amplifier If your signal is particularly weak and needs boosting, you will have to install an amplifier close to the aerial. A number of manufacturers produce these and in the case of a roof aerial the fitting should be left to the rigger. If you are fitting one to your loft aerial, you will need an amplifier and accompanying power unit. The amplifier is bolted to the aerial masthead and the coaxial cable enters and leaves this (the method of connection depending on the type of amplifier), runs into and out of the power unit and then into the set in the normal way. The power unit, which should be connected to a fused connection unit with 2.5sq mm twin core and earth cable, contains a transformer which sends 18 or 24 volts output into the amplifier along the coaxial down cable.

An amplifier will not alter the quality of the signal, only its strength, and may exaggerate any faults caused by an inadequate aerial.
Aerial sockets The neatest way of connecting your aerial to the set is via a specially designed aerial

socket, which eliminates trailing cable across the floor. These are connected in the way described for the aerial junction box. You will, of course, need another length of cable and two plugs to connect from the socket to the set. Sockets are available which also provide a connection for your FM radio (from a separate VHF aerial).

Fitting an extra outlet
If you wish to run a second set off the same aerial but in another room, you will need a splitter unit; this can be fixed to a skirting board with countersunk screws. Generally this has a socket outlet for the set in the same room and the usual terminal and braid clamp for the cable from the aerial and for the cable that carries the signal to a second set

elsewhere in the house. Adding an extra socket may reduce picture quality in areas where the reception is already below par.

Another method is to use a combined splitter-amplifier which contains its own power unit and is connected to the mains, via a fused connection unit, using 2.5sq mm twin core and earth cable. This has an input coaxial socket to take the cable from the aerial and up to four output sockets for sets in different parts of the house.

Extending cable   The cable connector is a simple device that enables you to extend existing cable. It has female sockets at both ends and these take the standard coaxial plug. Again it will further diminish the quality of the picture if you are already suffering from a poor signal.

3 A combined splitter/amplifier strengthens the signal and provides outlet sockets for sets in different parts of the house
4a Wiring up an aerial socket to provide for both television and FM radio
4b The front plate of a TV/FM radio aerial socket
5 A splitter unit enables you to run two sets off the same aerial
6 If you need to extend cable, always use a proper cable connector

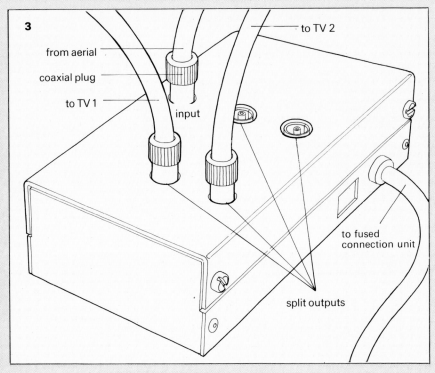

3 from aerial / coaxial plug / to TV 1 / input / to TV 2 / split outputs

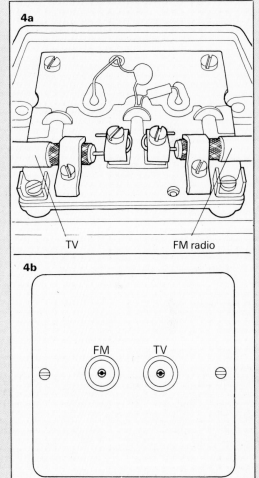

4a   TV   FM radio

4b   FM   TV

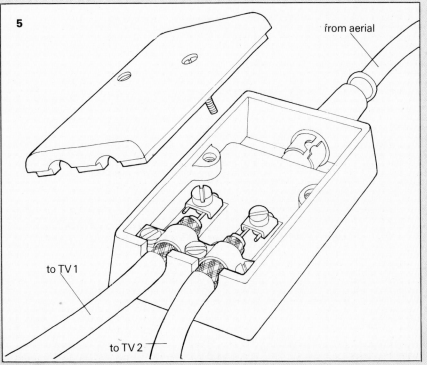

5 from aerial / to TV 1 / to TV 2

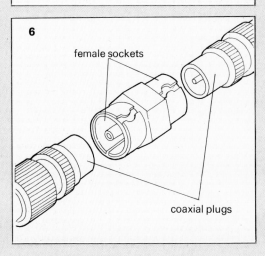

6 female sockets / coaxial plugs

4

PLUMBING

Cold water:
from mains to storage cistern

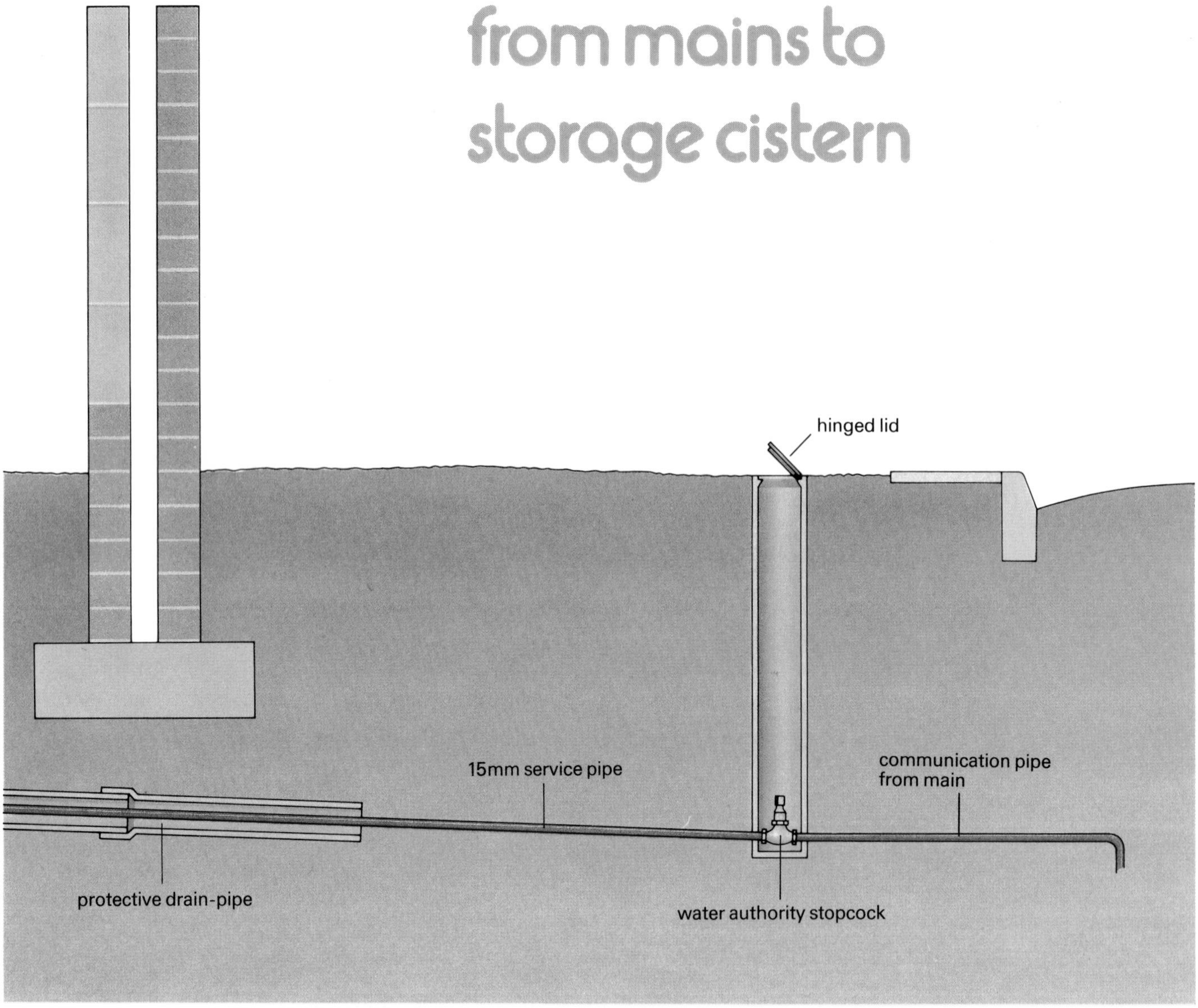

hinged lid

15mm service pipe

communication pipe from main

protective drain-pipe

water authority stopcock

An unlimited supply of water 'on tap' is assumed by most of us to be a basic service and, apart from exceptional circumstances such as a drought, we barely give a thought to its source and distribution.

Cast iron mains, buried deep below the surface, take water from the area authority's reservoirs through the consumer area. A communication pipe links the main to the boundary of each property and it is at this point that the responsibility of the householder for his own water supply begins.

Main supply
Outside each house – possibly set into the footpath – is a hinged metal plate. This covers a purpose-made pit, 1m (3ft) or more deep, which houses the main stopcock connecting the water authority's communication pipe to the service pipe. This stop-cock, unlike those inside the house, may have a specially shaped shank that can be turned only with one of the authority's turn-keys.

Pipe/tubing dimensions Before metrication, water supply pipes were designated by their internal diameters. The sizes most commonly used in domestic plumbing were $\frac{1}{2}$, $\frac{3}{4}$ and 1in. Since then thin-walled tubing, such as copper and stainless steel, has been designated by its external diameter. The equivalent sizes of tubing are 15, 22 and 28mm respectively. Thick-walled tubing, such as lead or iron, is still designated by its internal diameter (12, 19 and 25mm/$\frac{1}{2}$, $\frac{3}{4}$ and 1in sizes).

Copper is now the material most commonly used in plumbing and, except where otherwise stated, pipe sizes relate to thin-walled copper or stainless steel tubing.

Service pipe Properties built in Britain before 1939 will probably have a lead or iron service pipe. In a more recent house, however, this pipe is likely to be of 15mm copper tubing, though a pipe of larger diameter may be used in areas where water pressure is low.

The service pipe should slope slightly upwards to the house to allow air bubbles to escape. But it is extremely important, as a precaution against frost, that it should be at least 750mm (30in) below the surface of the soil throughout its length. You should remember this if, at any time, you want to

Domestic water comes from a main buried deep beneath the highway, through a communication pipe, and is connected just inside your boundary with a stopcock, which is reached via a hinged lid at ground level and should only be turned on and off with a special water board key. A service pipe takes the water (protected from risk of subsidence by being threaded through old or cracked drain-pipes) under your garden and foundations through to the kitchen

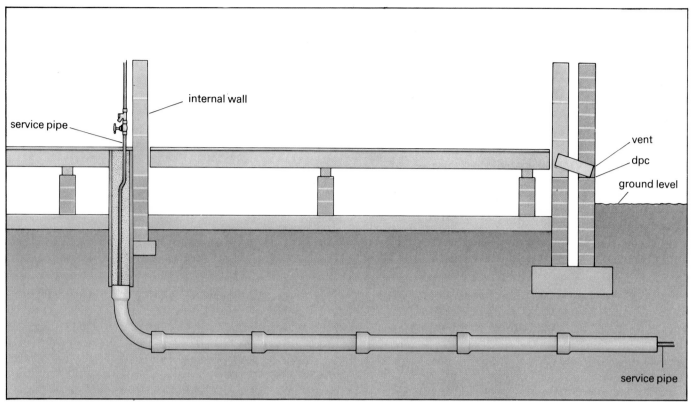

internal wall

service pipe

vent

dpc

ground level

service pipe

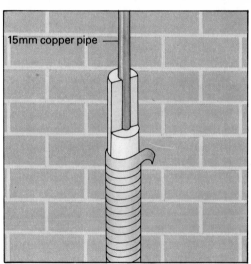

15mm copper pipe

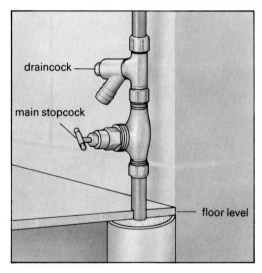

draincock

main stopcock

floor level

landscape the front garden. A sunken garden, constructed over the service pipe, could reduce the depth of soil insulation below the required minimum, which might be disastrous during a period of severe and prolonged frost.

Protection Where the service pipe passes under the foundations of the walls of the house it should be threaded through lengths of drain-pipe to protect it from possible damage resulting from settlement.

In most cases the service pipe enters the house through the solid floor of a kitchen. If the kitchen has a hollow, boarded floor special precautions must be taken against the risk of frost damage. There is little point in protecting the pipe throughout its journey to the house, only to expose it to icy draughts that may whistle through the underfloor space.

The best means of protection is to thread the pipe, at the time of installation, through the centre of a 152mm (6in) drain-pipe and to fill the space between the service pipe and the walls of the drain-

pipe with vermiculite chips. An existing pipe can be protected – without having to dismantle it – by snapping over it two sections of expanded polystyrene pipe-lagging and binding these with several thickness of glass fibre pipe wrap.

Internal supply

The main stopcock is fitted into the service pipe just above ground floor level and immediately above it is the draincock. These two fittings enable the water supply to the house to be cut off and the internal system to be drained whenever required.

Stopcock This is probably the most important piece of plumbing equipment in the home. The first step in virtually any plumbing emergency – burst pipe, leaking cold water storage cistern or leaking boiler – should be to turn off this stopcock to cut off the water supply.

Make sure every member of the household knows where it is and how to operate it. Turn it on and off two or three times at least twice a year to ensure it

Above Diagram showing where the service pipe or rising main (as it is often called) sometimes enters the house through a boarded floor – which means special precautions should be taken to protect it from icy underground draughts. After leaving the protection of the old drain-pipes beneath the house the service pipe should be threaded through stone pipe packed with vermiculite chips
Far left Alternatively you should lag it by snapping round it two sections of expanded polystyrene lagging and binding them with glass fibre wrap
Left The internal water supply can be cut off in any emergency by closing the main stopcock – usually found under the kitchen sink. The draincock immediately above makes it easy to empty the internal water system

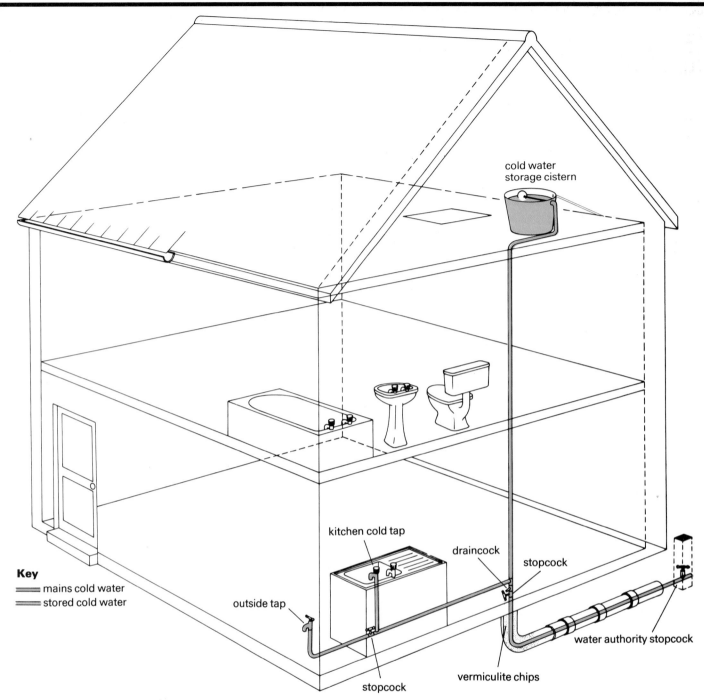

cold water
storage cistern

kitchen cold tap

draincock

stopcock

outside tap

Key
mains cold water
stored cold water

stopcock

vermiculite chips

water authority stopcock

will move easily. A neglected stopcock can jam and therefore prove troublesome in an emergency.

Main connections There will be at least one branch 'teed off' from the service pipe – often referred to as the rising main – about 600mm (24in) above floor level. This is the 15mm supply pipe to the cold tap over the kitchen sink. Since this tap supplies water for drinking and cooking it is important it is connected direct to the main.

In some places the cold water supply to the bathroom and WC flushing cisterns is also taken direct from the main. Hot water supply may be provided by a multi-point instantaneous water heater and the need for a main cold water storage cistern eliminated altogether.

Most water authorities, however, allow only the cold tap over the kitchen sink – and perhaps a garden water supply – to be connected directly to the main. Bathroom cold water services are supplied from a storage cistern usually situated in the roof space.

Roof space The rising main travels to the roof space by the most direct route, preferably against an internal wall. However with cavity wall infilling and efficient thermal insulation this is less important than it used to be.

The roof space through which the rising main passes to connect to the ball valve serving the main cold water storage cistern is vulnerable to frost. This is particularly so where the ceilings have been lagged to conserve warmth in the rooms below. The bedrooms will be warmer, but the roof space will be that much colder. If the floor of your roof is insulated, you should remove the covering from the area directly under the storage tank to allow warm air to rise from the rooms below to the tank.

The rising main in the roof area should be as short as possible, thoroughly lagged and kept well away from the eaves. Particularly where the cold water storage cistern is made of modern plastic material, the rising main should be securely fixed to the roof timbers to reduce noise from vibration.

The equipment we describe is shown in colour – kitchen sink, outside tap and stopcock, bath, wash-basin, WC, cold water storage tank, rising main, internal stopcock, draincock, service pipe and water board stopcock. Mains cold water is shown in blue, stored cold water in green, domestic hot water in red and central heating water in purple

Cold water:
storage cistern and distribution pipes

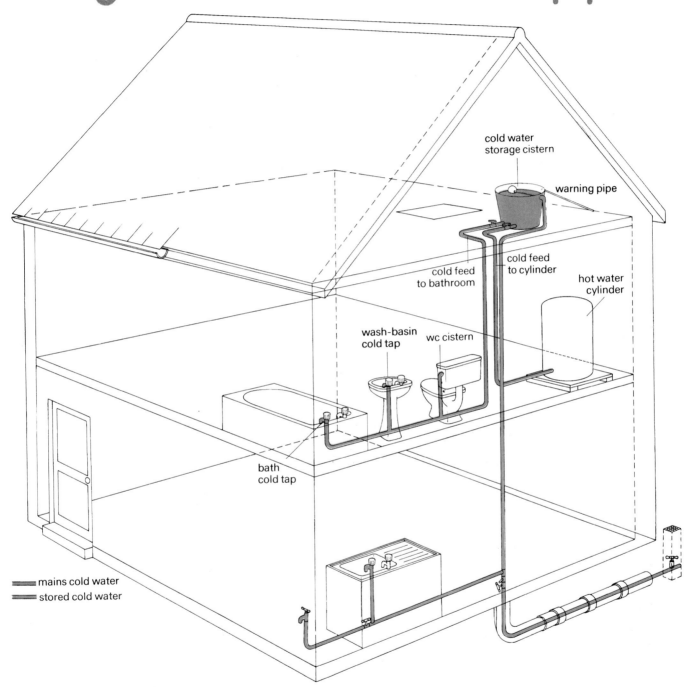

cold water
storage cistern

warning pipe

cold feed
to cylinder

cold feed
to bathroom

hot water
cylinder

wash-basin
cold tap

wc cistern

bath
cold tap

mains cold water
stored cold water

The water supply is pumped through the mains to your home – but the story doesn't end there. You must have a storage tank in order to keep an amount of water in reserve, and distribution pipes to feed it around the home.

The cold water storage cistern eases immediate demand on the mains during peak periods, such as first thing in the morning when large quantities of water are used for baths and WC flushing. The cistern will refill slowly, then more quickly as

demand on the mains drops. The storage cistern also provides a reserve of water against possible shut-down of the mains. When water is cut off for a few hours for mains repairs, you need only draw off in advance sufficient water for drinking and cooking; the cistern will keep the hot water system, bath taps and WC operating. It will also provide a supply of water under constant, relatively low pressure for a cylinder storage hot water system.

Although available in various capacities, most water authorities stipulate a maximum of 225 litre (50 gal) for storage cisterns. They are now usually

Above Our standard house plan shows the flow of cold water from the mains in blue and the stored cold water in green

321

made of plastic materials, although galvanized steel and asbestos cement types are still found. The cistern is normally situated in the loft and sometimes in the upper part of an airing cupboard. The loft is the best place, since it allows the maximum amount of fall from the cistern; water is supplied under greater pressure, ensuring a strong flow at the outlets. Since the full cistern will be heavy (the water in a 225 litre/50 gal cistern will weigh over 200kg/4cwt), it is usually placed over a dividing wall and if possible, as a frost precaution, against a flue in constant use.

The supply of water to the cistern from the rising main is controlled by a ball valve which shuts off the water when the cistern is full. A warning pipe extending outside the house and acting as an overflow is connected near the top of the cistern to indicate when the ball valve is faulty. This pipe must be of at least 22mm diameter and should be set at a slight fall to ensure a continuous flow of water.

There are also two distribution pipes, usually fitted near the bottom of the cistern: one serves the bathroom cold taps and the WC cistern, the other supplies the hot water storage cylinder. A vent pipe from the top of the hot water cylinder is positioned over the cistern. This allows air to escape when the cylinder is filling up. It should never enter the water as this would cause hot water to be siphoned into the cold cistern.

Replacing storage cistern

If you have a galvanized steel storage cistern that is badly corroded (rust patches around the tappings and on the inside walls) it will be cheaper and quicker in the long run to replace the cistern rather than to repair it, since the rust spots are likely to reappear in a few years.

The modern tendency is to install a cylindrical

replace the cistern, so plan your work for the least inconvenience.

Removing old cistern Cut off the water supply to the inlet pipe and turn on the bathroom taps to empty the cistern. Some water will be left in the bottom of the cistern below the distribution pipes and you will have to bale this out. Disconnect all fittings with an adjustable spanner and lower the cistern through the access hatch.

Fitting new cistern Do as much preparatory work as possible on the cistern before taking it up to the loft where space is likely to be restricted. The best way to cut the holes for the pipe connections is with a hand or electric drill and a hole saw attachment. The attachment, which has a circular cutter with a twist drill centre, should be the same diameter as that of the pipe connection thread which will pass through the wall of the cistern. Mark the centre of the hole to be made in the cistern, position the twist drill on the mark and drill a pilot hole; the circular cutter will then come into contact with the cistern wall and complete the hole.

Holes can be made in a plastic cistern by heating the end of the correct size metal pipe with a blowtorch and burning a hole of the exact diameter through the plastic wall with the hot end of the pipe.

First cut the hole for the water inlet pipe. If your cistern has a back plate to support the ball valve, the position of the hole will be dictated by the position of the ready-drilled hole in the plate. If the cistern does not have a back plate cut the hole about 40mm (or 1½in) from the rim.

Fit the stem of the ball valve into the hole using two large washers, one metal and one plastic, on each side of the cistern wall. The plastic washer should be next to the cistern with the metal one supporting it. Screw a nut onto the outside stem with an adjustable spanner. Now attach a com-

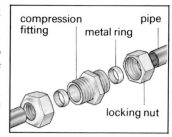

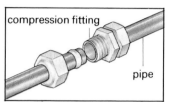

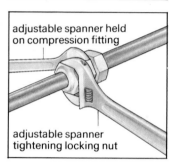

Above When fitting a compression joint, use one adjustable spanner on the locking nut and another to pull the other way on the compression fitting

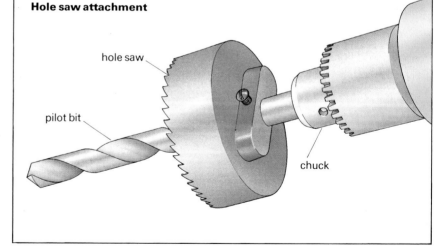

Hole saw attachment

hole saw

pilot bit

chuck

plastic cistern since this is light, easily fitted and will not corrode. It is also flexible enough to be squeezed through small trapdoors into lofts.

If your new cistern is smaller than the old one you will have to extend the pipework; make sure your extra pipe is of the same diameter. You will also need compression joints to connect the pipes: each joint has two locking nuts and two metal rings which fit over the ends of the pipes being joined. When the nuts are tightened the rings grip the pipes to give a watertight seal.

You will have to shut off the water supply to

pression tap connector to the protruding stem; the other end of the connector will be joined to the rising main inlet.

Make the hole for the overflow pipe opposite the ball valve and at least 19mm (¾in) below it. Cut the holes for the distribution pipes about 50mm (2in) from the base of the cistern to prevent grit and debris being drawn into the plumbing system. Using metal and plastic washers as before, fit compression joint tank connectors to the holes and attach nuts outside.

When all the connections have been made take

Above left A typical polythene storage cistern in position – on a platform for extra pressure – with distribution pipes connected **Above** This saw hole attachment can be fitted to either an electric or hand drill to cut holes for the pipe connections when installing a new metal cold water storage cistern

cold water storage cistern

stored cold water

warning pipe

gate valves

cold feed to bathroom

cold feed to cylinder

mains cold water

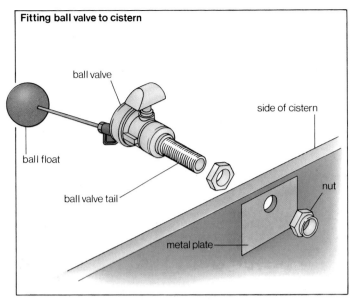

Fitting ball valve to cistern

ball valve

ball float

ball valve tail

side of cistern

nut

metal plate

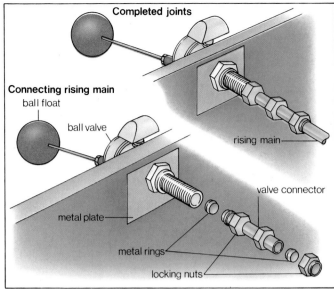

Completed joints

Connecting rising main

ball float

ball valve

rising main

valve connector

metal plate

metal rings

locking nuts

the cistern up into the loft. Stand it on a firm, level platform – stout planks or a piece of chipboard nailed to the joists – so its entire base is supported. Connect all the pipework squarely to the cistern walls to avoid straining the plastic when the nuts are tightened. Turn on the water and watch for any leaks as the cistern fills. If leaks do occur shut off the water supply, drain the cistern and tighten any loose joints. Never try to tighten joints with water in the cistern as you may split the plastic and cause a flood.

When the cistern is nearly full the ball valve must be set so the water level is at least 25mm (1in) below the warning pipe. Carefully bend the float arm to the correct angle (on some valves you merely adjust an alignment screw). To check the valve is working properly draw off a small amount of water and watch that the cistern refills to the correct level.

Repairing steel storage cistern
If you have a galvanized steel storage cistern that is showing signs of corrosion on the inside, you can recondition it.

Cut off the water supply and drain the cistern as already described. Dry the cistern thoroughly and remove every trace of rust with abrasive paper or a wire brush (always wear protective spectacles when using the latter). Fill any deep pit marks in the metal with an epoxy resin filler and, when set, apply

two coats of a taste and odour-free bituminous paint, leaving it to dry between coats. Make sure the paint is completely dry before refilling the cistern. This treatment will protect the cistern from rust for at least two years and can be repeated when necessary.

You can treat a new galvanized steel cistern with bituminous paint to protect it from corrosion, but first rub down the interior with abrasive paper to provide a key for the paint.

> **To replace cistern**
> adjustable spanners
> electric or hand drill
> saw hole drill attachment
> compression joints
> extra matching pipework
>   (if extending pipes)
> metal and plastic washers
> stout planks or chipboard (for platform)
>
> **To repair steel cistern**
> abrasive paper or wire brush
> protective spectacles
> epoxy resin filler
> bituminous paint (taste and odour-free)
>
> **equipment**

Above left Make sure when you are fitting a new valve stem to the cold water storage cistern that the plastic washer sits inside the metal one
Above The compression tap connector is joined to the protruding stem. Join the rising main to the unattached end of the connector
Below left When repairing a galvanized cistern, clean off all rust with a wire brush
Below centre Make good all pit marks with an epoxy resin filler
Below Give the tank a protective covering with a coat of taste and odour-free bituminous paint

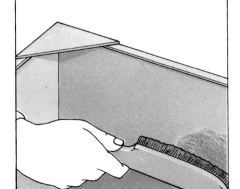

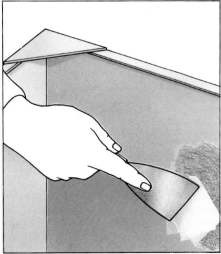

Hot water:
simple cylinder systems

Running hot water used to be regarded as a luxury in many homes. Today we would probably consider life unbearable without it—and even the Government accepts this fact by making grants available to help install this facility in older properties. Whether you use electricity, gas, oil or solid fuel as a means of heating, there is a system available to suit your needs—and your pocket. But do make sure you decide first what your own requirements are, since this will ultimately affect what system you choose as the most suitable for your home.

There are a number of ways to provide a 'whole house' hot water supply, but one of the most popular is undoubtedly the simple, direct cylinder storage hot water system. Simple cylinder systems are heated either by electricity or by solid fuel, gas or oil-fired boilers, sometimes supplemented by an electric immersion heater for use during the summer months.

Copper cylinders are the most common, with capacities from 115–160 litre (25–35gal). The cylinder is supplied with water from the cold water storage cistern by means of a 22 or 28mm ($\frac{3}{4}$ or 1in) distribution pipe, which enters the cylinder near its base.

A 22mm ($\frac{3}{4}$in) vent pipe rises from the dome of the cylinder to terminate open-ended over the cold water storage cistern. This vent pipe branches off to supply the hot water taps in the bathroom and over the kitchen sink.

The cylinder is connected to the boiler by 28mm

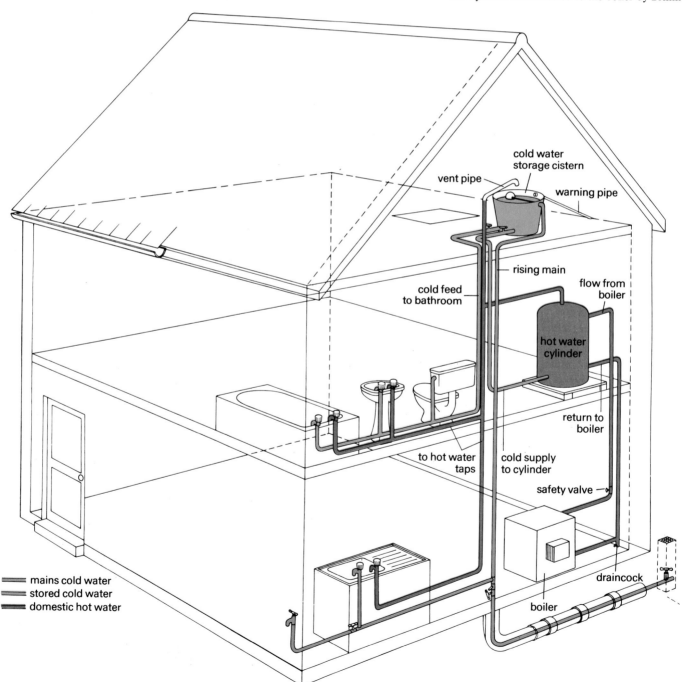

cold water storage cistern

vent pipe

warning pipe

rising main

cold feed to bathroom

flow from boiler

hot water cylinder

return to boiler

to hot water taps

cold supply to cylinder

safety valve

draincock

boiler

mains cold water
stored cold water
domestic hot water

(1in) pipes. The flow and return pipes of the boiler connect to the cylinder's upper and lower tappings respectively. If the cylinder is to be heated by an immersion heater only, the cylinder flow and return tappings are blanked off.

A boss, or fitting, is usually provided in the dome of the cylinder to enable a vertical immersion heater to be inserted. Alternatively there may be one or more bosses in the cylinder walls for shorter horizontal immersion heaters. A vertical immersion heater should extend to within 75mm (3in) of the base of the cylinder as only the water above the level of the heating element will be heated.

How the system works

When the boiler is first lit the water in it heats up, expands and becomes lighter. It is pushed up the flow pipe into the upper part of the cylinder by the colder, heavier water flowing down the return pipe from the lower part of the cylinder to the boiler.

This circulation continues for as long as the boiler fire is alight. Hot water is stored in the upper part of the cylinder ready to be drawn off from the taps and gradually spreads downwards until the cylinder is filled with hot water. The hot water draw-off points are taken from above the dome of the cylinder so if the water supply to the house is cut off the cylinder will still be full of water after the hot taps have stopped running.

Provision must be made, therefore, for the cylinder to be drained when necessary. Where the system has a boiler, a draincock with a hose connector is fitted on the return pipe close to the boiler. If the cylinder is heated by an immersion heater only, a draincock is fitted on the cold water distribution pipe to the cylinder, close to its connection to the cylinder. A spring-loaded safety valve is usually fitted close to the boiler on either the flow or return pipe to eliminate any risk of a dangerous buildup of pressure within the system.

Many homes built in Britain before 1939 have a rectangular hot water storage tank instead of a cylinder. These tanks are fitted with a circular hand hole with a bolt-down cover to give access for cleaning. If you have a tank of this kind remember it cannot be drained from the hot taps. Never attempt to unscrew the bolts and remove the cover without first emptying the tank by the draincock provided.

Packaged plumbing systems

Demands for the provision of hot water on tap in older homes and the conversion of large old houses into self-contained flats have resulted in the development of packaged plumbing systems in which the cold water storage cistern and the hot water storage cylinder form one unit.

Early forms of packaged plumbing consist of a 115 litre (25gal) capacity cylinder underneath a relatively low capacity circular copper storage cistern. These cisterns are large enough to supply the hot water system, but not the bathroom cold taps or the WC cistern, which have to be connected directly to the rising main. These units can only be

Below Comparison between modern and old direct cylinder systems
Below right Essential features of an early packaged plumbing unit; the oval shape makes the unit easy to fit in confined spaces

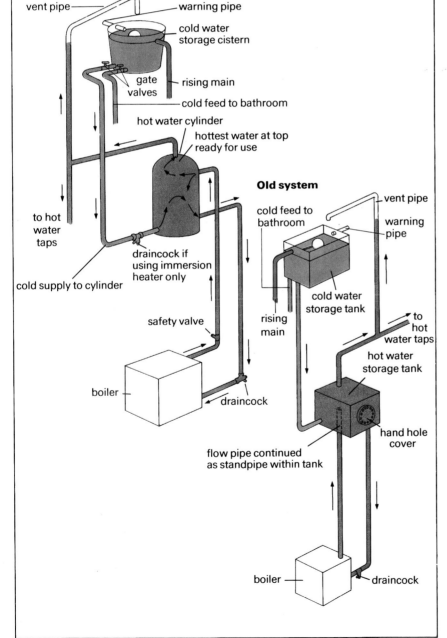

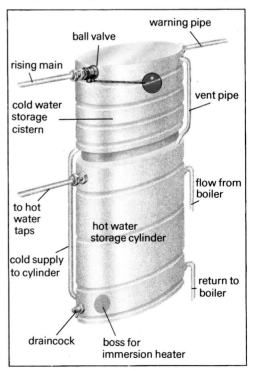

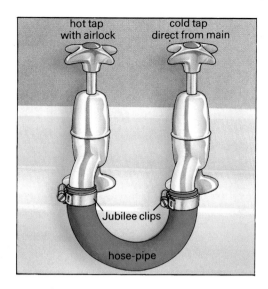

hot tap with airlock

cold tap direct from main

Jubilee clips

hose-pipe

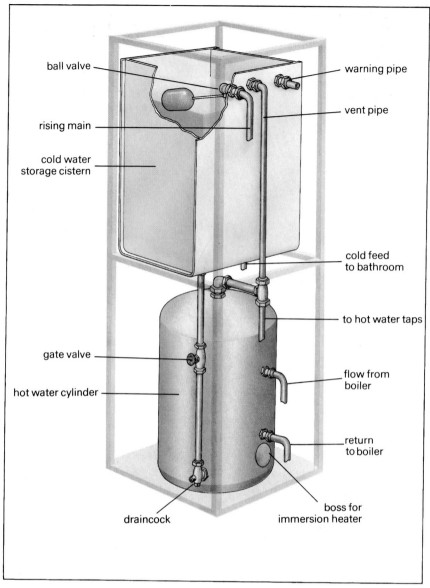

ball valve

rising main

cold water storage cistern

gate valve

hot water cylinder

draincock

warning pipe

vent pipe

cold feed to bathroom

to hot water taps

flow from boiler

return to boiler

boss for immersion heater

fitted where this arrangement is permitted by the local water authority.

More recently larger packaged units have been developed with hot water cylinders of up to 160 litre (35gal) capacity and cold water storage cisterns with the standard capacity of 225 litre (50gal). These may be regarded as 'whole house' packaged plumbing systems. They need only be connected to a cold water supply and provided with a heat source to supply all hot and cold water demands.

Airlocks
A poor or intermittent flow of water from a hot tap, sometimes accompanied by hissing, spitting or bubbling, indicates an airlock is obstructing the supply pipe. Airlocks can usually be cleared by connecting one end of a length of hose-pipe to the tap giving trouble and the other end to the cold tap over the kitchen sink which is usually supplied direct from the rising main. When both taps are turned full on the mains pressure should blow the air bubble out of the system.

Airlocks recur when the cold water supply pipe to the hot water storage cylinder is too small. If this pipe is only 15mm ($\frac{1}{2}$in) in diameter it will be unable to replenish water drawn off from the 22mm ($\frac{3}{4}$in) pipe to the hot tap over the bath. The water level in the system's vent pipe – normally the same level as that in the cold water storage cistern – will fall, allowing air to enter a horizontal length of pipe. If a gate valve is fitted into the cold water supply pipe to the cylinder, it must be the correct size – at least 22mm ($\frac{3}{4}$in) – and must be kept fully open.

Other possible causes of persistent airlocks are too small a cold water storage cistern (it should be the standard 225 litre/50gal) or a partially jammed or sluggish ball valve serving the cistern.

Scale and corrosion
Direct cylinder hot water storage systems are prone to scale formation and corrosion.

Scale formation When hard water – and most water supplied in central, southern and eastern England is hard – is heated to 71°C (160°F) and above, calcium bicarbonate dissolved in the water is changed to insoluble calcium carbonate. This is deposited in solid form as scale or fur on immersion heaters and the inside of boilers.

When scale forms inside a boiler it insulates the water from the heat of the fire and the water in the

cylinder takes longer to heat. As the scale accumulates hot water is forced through ever narrowing channels, resulting in gurgling, hissing and banging. Scale also insulates the metal of the boiler from the cooling effect of the circulating water – the metal becomes thinner and eventually a leak develops.

Corrosion A flow of rusty red water from the hot tap is a sure indication corrosion exists somewhere in your water supply system. It may be in the cold water storage cistern, so empty the cistern and treat the inside with taste and odour-free bituminous paint. However, if the cistern is free from rust, corrosion must be taking place within the boiler and you should take early action to avoid a leaking boiler.

Remedy There are many products available which remove boiler scale but it is better to prevent it forming in the first place by using chemical additives in the cold water storage cistern.

A corroded boiler must be replaced or the metal will wear through and a leak will occur. To protect a new boiler use a chemical scale inhibitor which also helps avoid corrosion.

Chemical additives, however, do need continual renewal and a more positive, permanent remedy is to install an indirect hot water system.

Above A whole house packaged plumbing system which will cope with all hot and cold water demands **Above left** Clearing an airlock in the supply pipe to a hot tap

Storing hot water is one area of plumbing that might well be a mystery to many householders. But it is important to understand the basic principles of the systems available and how they operate, particularly if you want to use hot water as a form of heating in the home.

Hot water:
indirect cylinder systems

If you decide to install central heating an indirect storage hot water system is essential. But even if this is not among your immediate plans, an indirect system is a good investment if you live in an area where water is hard or corrosive, since this system is more resistant to scale formation and corrosion.

The system has two circuits. A primary circuit is heated by the boiler, flows to a closed coil, or calorifier, in the hot water cylinder and returns to the boiler to be reheated. The secondary circuit flows from the outer part of the hot water cylinder, where it is heated indirectly by the hot water passing through the calorifier, to the taps.

The water in the primary circuit is never drawn off and any losses from evaporation are made up from a small, usually 25 litre (5gal) tank – this is why indirect systems are relatively free of the problems of scale and corrosion. When the water in the primary circuit is first heated, dissolved air – a prerequisite of corrosion – is driven off. At the same time calcium bicarbonate dissolved in the water is converted into a small amount of calcium carbonate which is deposited on the inside of the boiler. Since any given volume of water contains only a certain quantity of scale-forming chemicals, no more scale will form in the boiler. Deposits that may form in the outer part of the storage cylinder will be minimal as the stored water will rarely reach the temperature at which scale forms.

An indirect system does not, however, mean absolute freedom from corrosion since air will dissolve in the water in the tank supplying the primary circuit and may also enter the circuit via cracks too small to allow water to escape.

The tank supplying the primary circuit also copes with the expansion of heated water, so the ball valve in the tank should be adjusted to provide for only 25 or 50mm (1 or 2in) of water when the primary circuit is cold. Hot water will flow back into the tank, rising to a level above the ball float.

The cold supply should connect to the primary circuit at its coldest point, normally close to the boiler on the return pipe from the cylinder. The cold supply used to be connected to the vent pipe of the primary circuit at high level, but water in the feed and expansion tank tended to overheat, leading to heat loss and condensation problems in the roof – and sometimes even to the plastic ball float melting in the heat. So this practice was discontinued.

Indirect systems and central heating
If you plan to combine your hot water system with central heating, the two must connect at the primary circuit. The flow pipe to a small, gravity-activated, central heating circuit is usually taken at high level from the boiler to cylinder flow pipe. It is then dropped to the radiators it will supply; the return pipe is taken to the return pipe from cylinder to boiler. A larger, pumped, central heating system will probably be connected to flow and return tappings on the opposite side of the boiler to those serving the hot water cylinder.

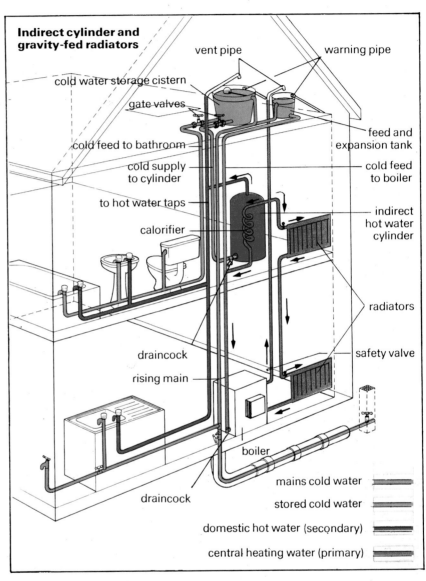

Indirect cylinder and gravity-fed radiators

- vent pipe
- warning pipe
- cold water storage cistern
- gate valves
- cold feed to bathroom
- feed and expansion tank
- cold supply to cylinder
- cold feed to boiler
- to hot water taps
- indirect hot water cylinder
- calorifier
- radiators
- draincock
- safety valve
- rising main
- boiler
- draincock

mains cold water
stored cold water
domestic hot water (secondary)
central heating water (primary)

Above Indirect cylinder system with two gravity-fed radiators
Left Ball valve in tank supplying primary circuit should be adjusted to prevent water overflowing when it expands on heating

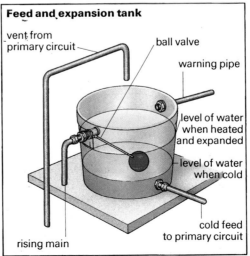

Feed and expansion tank

- vent from primary circuit
- ball valve
- warning pipe
- level of water when heated and expanded
- level of water when cold
- cold feed to primary circuit
- rising main

Indirect cylinder and pumped central heating

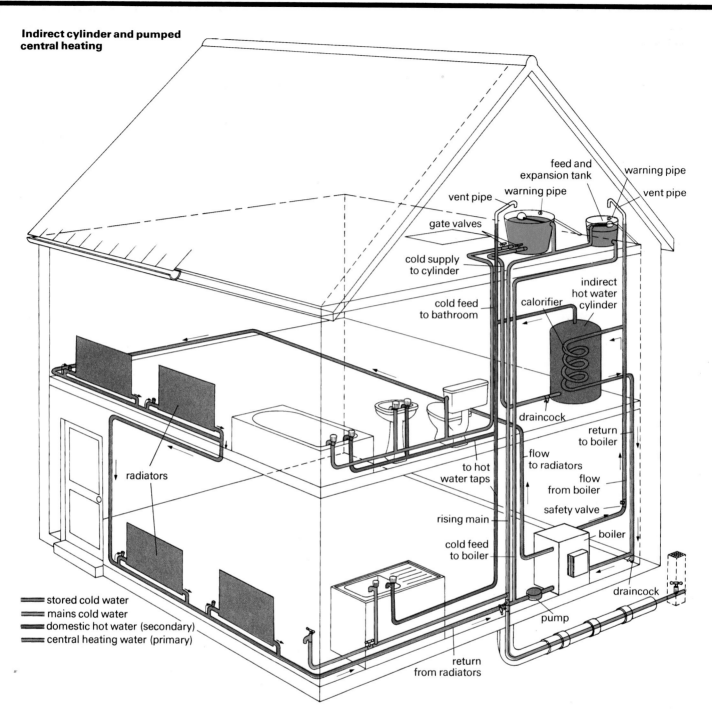

feed and expansion tank

warning pipe

warning pipe

vent pipe

vent pipe

gate valves

cold supply to cylinder

indirect hot water cylinder

cold feed to bathroom

calorifier

draincock

return to boiler

flow to radiators

flow from boiler

to hot water taps

radiators

safety valve

rising main

boiler

cold feed to boiler

draincock

pump

return from radiators

stored cold water
mains cold water
domestic hot water (secondary)
central heating water (primary)

Above Indirect cylinder system with pumped central heating
Right With self-priming cylinder, water flows through secondary cylinder and up vertical pipe into primary cylinder. When system is full, air trapped in primary cylinder prevents return of primary water to secondary cylinder. When water is heated, air in primary cylinder is displaced back to secondary cylinder, thus maintaining airlock between systems

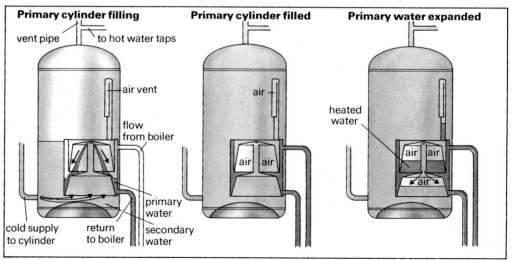

Primary cylinder filling

vent pipe

to hot water taps

air vent

flow from boiler

cold supply to cylinder

return to boiler

primary water

secondary water

Primary cylinder filled

air

air   air

Primary water expanded

heated water

air   air

air

Indirect packaged unit

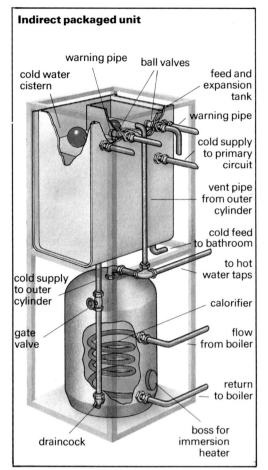

- warning pipe
- cold water cistern
- ball valves
- feed and expansion tank
- warning pipe
- cold supply to primary circuit
- vent pipe from outer cylinder
- cold feed to bathroom
- to hot water taps
- cold supply to outer cylinder
- calorifier
- gate valve
- flow from boiler
- return to boiler
- draincock
- boss for immersion heater

Self-priming indirect cylinder and pumped central heating

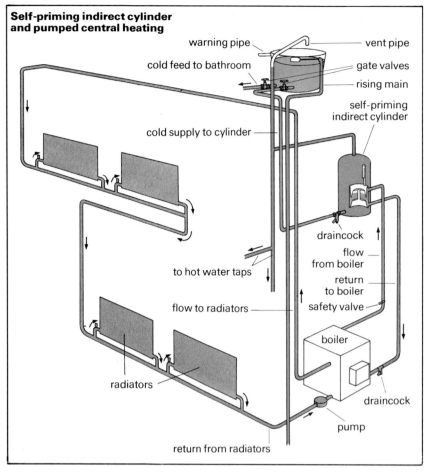

- warning pipe
- cold feed to bathroom
- vent pipe
- gate valves
- rising main
- self-priming indirect cylinder
- cold supply to cylinder
- draincock
- flow from boiler
- to hot water taps
- return to boiler
- flow to radiators
- safety valve
- boiler
- radiators
- draincock
- pump
- return from radiators

Above Self-priming indirect cylinder used with small central heating unit
Above right Conventional indirect packaged plumbing unit with small feed and expansion tank within cold water cistern
Right Packaged plumbing unit with self-priming indirect cylinder

Self-priming packaged unit

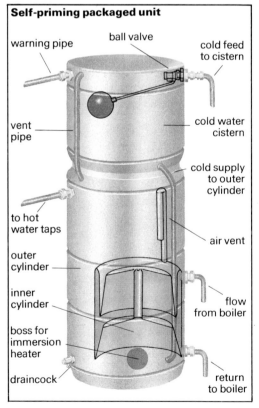

- warning pipe
- ball valve
- cold feed to cistern
- vent pipe
- cold water cistern
- cold supply to outer cylinder
- to hot water taps
- air vent
- outer cylinder
- inner cylinder
- flow from boiler
- boss for immersion heater
- draincock
- return to boiler

Warning If the central heating system has copper circulating pipes and thin-walled pressed steel radiators, use a reliable corrosion inhibitor in the feed and expansion tank to prevent any possible electrolytic corrosion.

Self-priming cylinders

Supplied direct from the cold water storage cistern, self-priming indirect cylinders do not need a separate feed and expansion tank and can, therefore, provide a simple and relatively cheap means of converting a hot water system from direct to indirect operation.

When a hot water system incorporating a self-priming cylinder is first filled with water, this overflows into the primary circuit through an inner cylinder which also serves as a heat exchanger. Once the circuit is full a large air bubble forms in the inner cylinder to prevent the return of the primary water. The inner cylinder also provides for the increased volume of the primary water as it expands upon heating.

The water in the primary circuit must never be allowed to boil as this would displace the air bubble in the inner cylinder and allow the primary and domestic hot water to mix.

When buying a self-priming cylinder make sure the particular model is large enough to cope with the expansion of the primary – and any central heating – circuit.

Packaged plumbing

There are packaged plumbing indirect systems as well as direct ones. Some of these combination units have a self-priming cylinder while other conventional units have an ordinary indirect cylinder and a small 14 litre (3gal) feed and expansion tank within the cold water storage cistern.

Hot water: gas and electric systems

As long as hot water is available at the turn of a tap most of us are happy. But have you thought whether your heating system is really suitable for your needs? Your heater may be providing water that you don't use and therefore is wasting money. Gas and electric heaters offer a choice to give you the hot water you want.

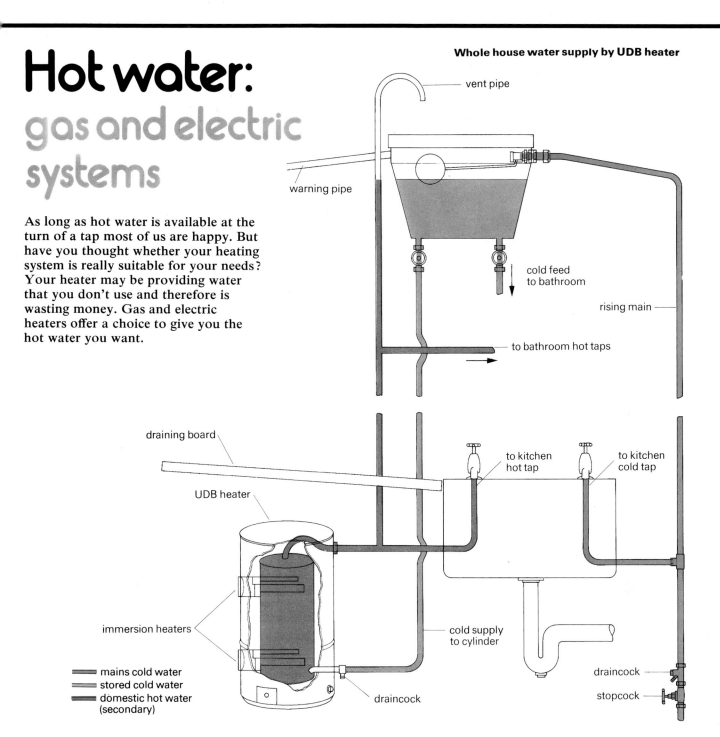

vent pipe

warning pipe

cold feed to bathroom

rising main

to bathroom hot taps

draining board

to kitchen hot tap

to kitchen cold tap

UDB heater

immersion heaters

cold supply to cylinder

draincock

draincock

stopcock

■ mains cold water
■ stored cold water
■ domestic hot water (secondary)

There are two main types of gas or electric heaters – storage cylinder and instantaneous – to provide running hot water in the home. Your choice will depend on how much hot water you use: if you require a constant supply in large quantities, a storage cylinder heater is probably the best, although large multi-point instantaneous gas heaters can also be used. If you need small quantities of hot water for relatively short periods at a time, instantaneous heaters are the answer since they will provide an adequate supply.

Storage water heaters

Available to run off either gas or day (or off-peak) electricity, storage heaters will give an ample supply of hot water. These are available to provide the whole house with hot water or to supply one particular area.

UDB heaters

If you intend to use one or more electric immersion heaters as the sole heat source for a simple, direct cylinder hot water system, it is best to install an Under Draining Board water heater instead of a conventional cylinder.

UDB heaters are specially designed to heat water economically by electricity. They have a 115 litre (25gal) capacity, are very heavily insulated and, as the name suggests, fit under the draining board of the kitchen sink, close to the hot water draw-off point in most frequent use.

They usually have two horizontal immersion heaters, one about a third of the distance from the top of the cylinder and the other near the base. The upper heater is switched on all the time to provide an immediate source of hot water for hand basins and sinks. The lower heater should be switched on about an hour before larger volumes of water are

Off-peak water heater

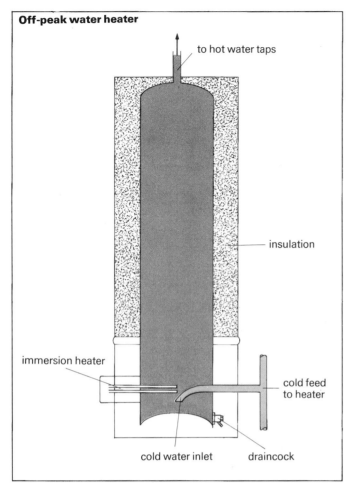

to hot water taps

insulation

immersion heater

cold feed to heater

cold water inlet

draincock

Open outlet heater

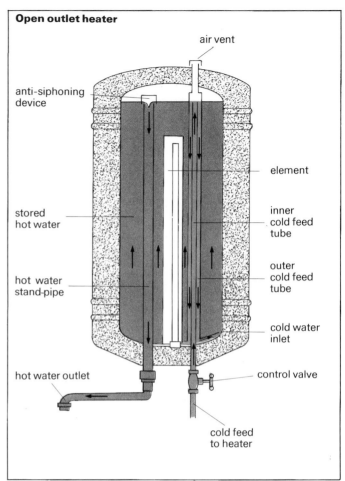

air vent

anti-siphoning device

stored hot water

element

inner cold feed tube

outer cold feed tube

hot water stand-pipe

cold water inlet

hot water outlet

control valve

cold feed to heater

Instantaneous gas water heater

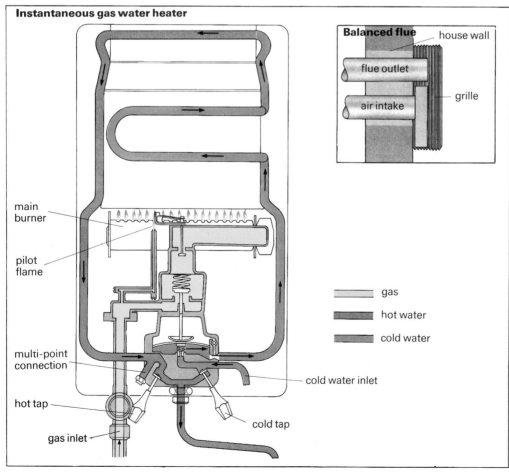

main burner

pilot flame

multi-point connection

hot tap

gas inlet

cold water inlet

cold tap

Balanced flue

house wall

flue outlet

air intake

grille

gas

hot water

cold water

required, such as for baths or household washing.

UDB heaters must be supplied from the main cold water storage cistern and must have a vent pipe, as with other cylinder hot water systems.

Off-peak heaters

These are a development of the UDB heater, designed to take advantage of the cheaper electricity rates available during the night. Storage heaters of this kind are tall, slim, heavily insulated cylinders with a 225 litre (50gal) capacity – estimated as sufficient to meet the daily demand of the average family. The immersion heater, situated near the base, switches on at night and off in the morning, leaving the cylinder full of hot water.

The shape of these heaters encourages the separation of hot water stored in the upper part of the cylinder from cold water flowing in near the base to replace the water drawn off. The cold water inlet usually has a special spreader which distributes water evenly over the base to prevent it mixing with hot water at a higher level.

Open outlet heaters

Designed for use with gas or electricity, open outlet heaters are usually of 5 or 10 litre (1 or ·2gal) capacity and are installed immediately above the area they serve. This type of heater may, if the local water authority permits, be connected direct to the rising main (in which case a cold water storage cistern would be unnecessary) or be supplied from the cold water cistern.

When hot water is required, a control valve on the inlet side of the appliance is opened. Cold water flows into the base and hot water overflows down a stand-pipe, through an open outlet and into the sink. The stand-pipe lip is fitted with an anti-siphoning device which, when water has been drawn off, ensures the level within the heater is about 12mm ($\frac{1}{2}$in) below the lip to allow for the increased volume of heated water.

Instantaneous water heaters

The great advantage of this type of heater is that you heat only the water you are going to use immediately; there is no reserve of stored water which, however thoroughly the cylinder is lagged, slowly loses its heat.

There are drawbacks to this method of water heating: the rate of hot water delivery is lower than that of a storage system and, in hard water areas, there is a tendency for scale to form. Also these heaters do not raise water to one particular temperature: they raise it through a range of temperatures as it passes through the heater. In cold weather you may find the temperature of the water at the outlet too low or the rate of flow markedly reduced.

Like the open outlet type, instantaneous heaters may be connected direct to the rising main. Incoming cold water flows through a system of small bore copper tubing within the appliance and is heated either by a gas flame or by a powerful electric element as it flows.

Multi-point gas heaters

Large multi-point instantaneous gas heaters can provide the whole house with hot water. The development of the balanced flue means gas appliances can be used, with complete safety, in any room having an outside wall. A balanced flue gas appliance has its combustion chamber sealed

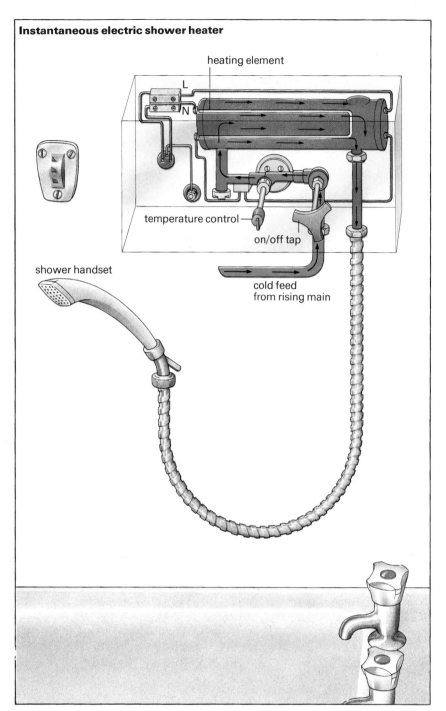

Instantaneous electric shower heater

heating element

L

N

temperature control

on/off tap

shower handset

cold feed from rising main

off from the room in which it is situated. The air intake and flue outlet are positioned close together on the outside wall; however strongly the wind may be blowing against the flue outlet, it will be blowing equally strongly against the fresh air inlet and the appliance will continue to operate.

The use of the balanced flue is not, of course, limited to instantaneous water heaters. Gas space heaters and gas boilers for use with central heating systems may also have balanced flues.

Electric heaters

A hot water supply for the whole house cannot be provided with electric instantaneous heaters, but this type is particularly valuable for use with showers where there would not otherwise be enough pressure for the shower to operate efficiently, and for providing hot water in outside WCs not connected to the main sources of hot water.

Single stack above-ground drainage

Building regulations introduced in Britain in the mid-1960s required all main drainage stacks to be confined within the fabric of the building as a frost precaution. This provided drainage installers with a strong incentive to keep the number of pipes to a minimum and encouraged the use of the single stack system; but there was opposition to its adoption, since it is possible for waste seals to be sucked out by the force of waste matter passing from more than one fitting at the same time, allowing drain gases to enter the house. There is also the possibility of a blockage at the foot of the stack, resulting in sewage backing up into the kitchen sink. These problems should not arise, however, if the system is properly designed and installed.

Layout and design
Compact planning of rooms with sanitary fittings is essential for a successful single stack plumbing design. In a two-storey house the bathroom should be immediately above the kitchen and, in multi-storey blocks of flats, kitchens and bathrooms should be one above the other throughout the building.

Preventing loss of seal Branch waste pipes from baths, showers, basins, bidets and sinks should be kept short and have minimal falls to the main stack. Pay particular attention to the waste pipe from any wash-basin, since this pipe will be of small diameter – about 30mm (or 1¼in), and is very likely to run full when the basin is emptied. This can result in the seal being sucked or siphoned out. To prevent siphonage this pipe should be no longer than 1.68m (or 66in). If this is impossible, take a 15mm (or ½in) diameter vent pipe from immediately behind the trap to join the main stack at least 1m (or 3ft) above the highest connection to it.

As a further precaution, it is essential all waste fittings have a deep seal trap of 75mm (or 3in) instead of the shallow seal traps commonly used with a two-pipe drainage system.

Avoiding contamination To prevent the outlets from baths, sinks and basins being fouled by discharges from the WC, the branch pipes from these fittings should be connected to the main drainage stack either well above or well below the point where the stack is joined to the pipe from the WC. This is usually not a problem with sink and basin waste pipes, but there may be difficulties in the case of pipes from baths, showers or bidets. You can deal with this by offsetting the waste pipe and taking it through the bathroom floor to discharge into the stack well below the WC pipe connection. An easier solution is to use a patent collar boss, a fitting which allows bath, basin and shower wastes to discharge into the stack at the same level as the pipe from the WC but with no risk of blockage or contamination.

The main stack Soil pipes used in older two pipe drainage systems are often only 75mm (or 3in) or 87mm (or 3½in) in internal diameter; in one-pipe systems the main stack must have an internal diameter of at least 100mm (or 4in). It should connect to the underground drain by an easy bend to prevent blockages or foaming back of detergent filled water.

Ground floor wastes
Where single stack drainage is installed, ground floor sanitary appliances may be connected to the main stack. Alternatively, their wastes may be disposed of in the same way as in a two pipe drainage system: WC wastes are taken directly to the underground drain by a short branch drain; bath, sink and basin wastes are taken to discharge over a yard gully. This system has the advantage of eliminating the risk of blockage at the foot of the stack which, while unlikely in a properly designed single stack system, is not entirely non-existent. Where ground floor appliances are connected to the stack, the first sign of such a blockage is sewage flowing back into the bath or kitchen sink.

If branch waste pipes discharge over a yard gully, make sure the discharge takes place above the level of the water in the gully but below the grid. This stops the grid becoming foul from waste discharges, prevents the risk of flooding if the grid becomes choked with fallen leaves and ensures the full force of the discharge is available to cleanse and flush the gully. Providing a back or side inlet gully will serve this purpose best. There are also gully grids manufactured with slots through which waste pipes can be passed and which are useful where a new waste pipe is to be taken to an existing gully.

Making connections
Modern single-stack drainage systems are almost universally constructed of PVC tubing. Small diameter branch waste pipes are joined by solvent welding; ring seal jointing (which allows for thermal expansion and contraction) is used to join sections of large diameter main stack pipe. These processes can be carried out by the home handyman, but if you intend making a connection to the drainage system of your house – for a new shower or wash-basin for example – you must obtain the approval of your local authority. The building inspector will give you advice on how to carry out the work so you do not create a health risk or impair the functioning of the system.

Above In the single stack drainage system, developed in the 1960s, all appliances discharge into one main pipe which connects to the underground drain; there is no separation of soil and waste discharges as in older systems. The narrower pipes on the houses above are rainwater downpipes and not connected to the internal drainage system

Right How the single stack system works. To prevent all risk of outlets from waste appliances being contaminated by discharges from the WC, you can fit a collar boss to the main stack (**Inset A**); alternatively you can offset the waste pipe and connect it to the main stack well below the point at which the stack meets the WC soil pipe (**Inset B**); ground floor sinks can be connected to the main stack or be taken to discharge over a yard gully (**Inset C**)

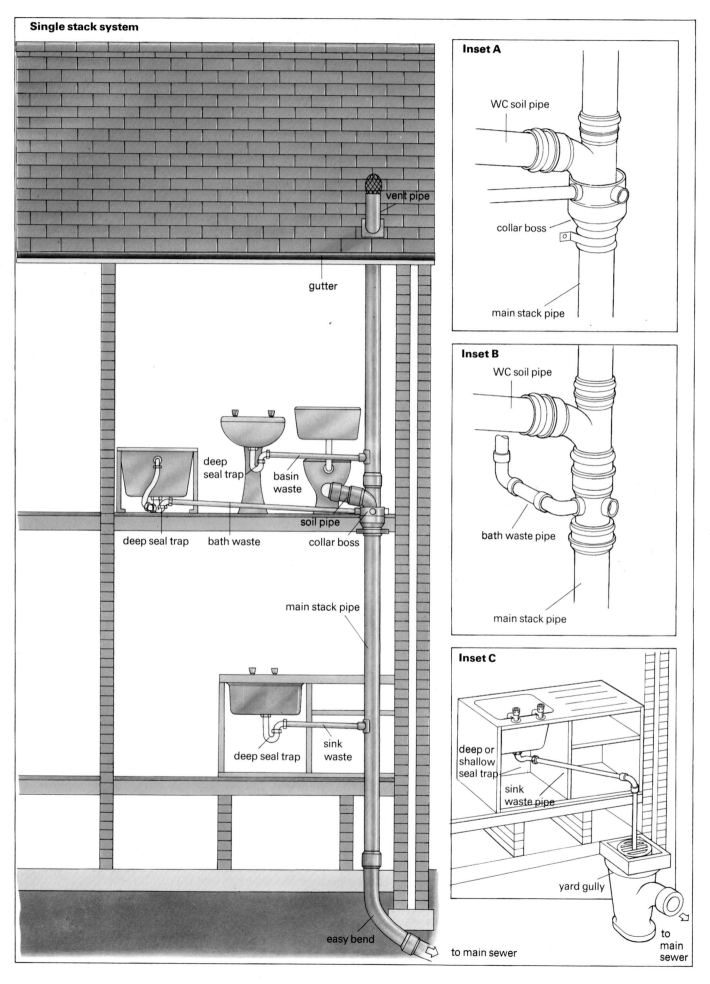

Single stack system

vent pipe

gutter

deep seal trap

basin waste

deep seal trap

bath waste

soil pipe

collar boss

main stack pipe

deep seal trap

sink waste

easy bend

to main sewer

Inset A

WC soil pipe

collar boss

main stack pipe

Inset B

WC soil pipe

bath waste pipe

main stack pipe

Inset C

deep or shallow seal trap

sink waste pipe

yard gully

to main sewer

Two pipe above-ground drainage

The two pipe system of above-ground drainage was developed in the 19th century when, for health reasons, it was felt that soil pipes disposing of waste from WCs and slop-sinks should be kept separate from waste pipes from sinks, basins, bidets and baths. This system was used until the 1960s, which means the rear elevation of many homes in Britain is marred by two iron pipes, at least one of which rises to above the level of the eaves. Buildings of more than two storeys, in which there are a number of soil and waste fittings, might well have more than two pipes on the external elevation.

Soil pipes
If soil appliances such as WCs are situated on the ground floor, they are connected by a short branch to the main underground drain at the nearest inspection chamber or manhole. The outlets from upper floor soil appliances are connected by a short branch soil pipe to a main soil pipe (usually made of heavy cast iron) running vertically down an external wall and joined at its base to the underground drain. This extends above the level of the eaves and acts as a vent pipe to allow sewer gases to escape. A cage is fitted on the upper end to protect it from rubbish and birds' nests.

Waste pipes
Sinks, basins, bidets and baths are not directly connected to the underground drain. The outlet pipes from ground-floor appliances discharge over the grid of a yard gully joined by a branch drain to the nearest inspection chamber.

Arrangements for the disposal of wastes from upper floors depend on the local drainage by-laws in force at the time the system was installed. Sometimes the wastes discharge over a rainwater hopper head set into the upper end of a rainwater downpipe,

Above An old fashioned drainage system, with at least two iron pipes running down the outside wall
1 The two pipe system where waste and soil appliances discharge into separate pipes
Inset Hooper head set in a rainwater downpipe

Following page
2 The range of traps: plastic 'P' (**a**) plastic 'S' (**b**) plastic 'P' bottle (**c**) plastic 'S' bottle (**d**) metal 'P' (**e**) metal 'S' (**f**)
3 The depth of seal on 'P' 'S' and 'P' bottle traps

which in turn discharges over a yard gully. This is **1** not very satisfactory since rainwater hopper heads are not self-cleansing and soapy water decomposing on their internal surfaces can be a source of unpleasant smells. Draughts up the rainwater downpipe can carry even more unpleasant smells from the yard gully. To prevent this, the drainage bylaws of some local authorities require upstairs wastes to flow into a main waste pipe, discharging over a yard gully but, like the main soil pipe, taken upwards to terminate open-ended above the level of the eaves.

Waste traps

Bends in pipes at the outlets of sanitary fittings are filled with water which provides a seal to prevent gases from the drain or waste pipes passing back through the fittings. These are known as traps and in the case of yard gullies and WCs are an integral part of the appliance. Separate traps, made of brass, gunmetal or PVC, must be fitted immediately below the waste outlet of all other appliances. Where outlets from more than one appliance are connected to the same branch soil or waste pipe, the traps of these appliances must be ventilated to prevent the water seal being sucked out by the force of waste matter passing through. The vent pipes either end above the level of the eaves or are taken back to join the main soil or waste pipe at least 1m (or 3ft) above the highest connection to it.

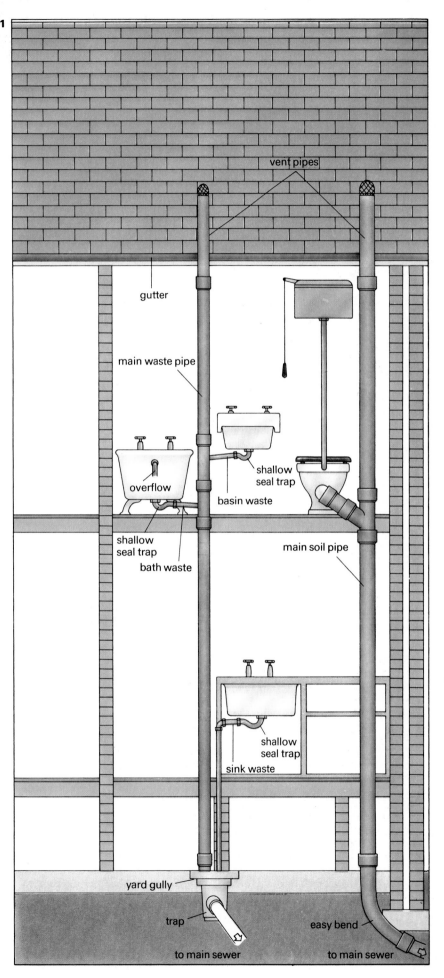

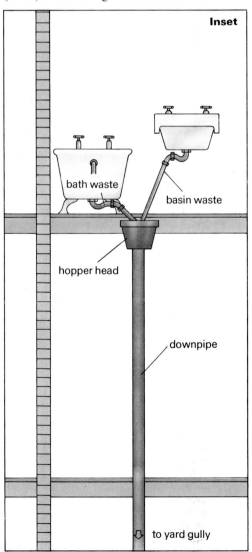

Inset

2 Types of trap

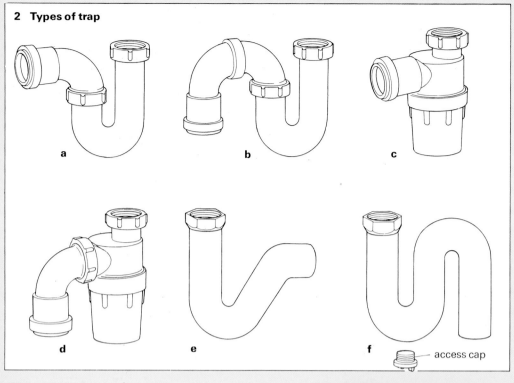

a   b   c

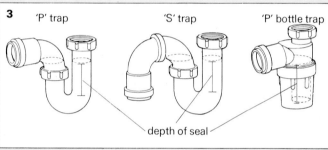

d   e   f

access cap

3

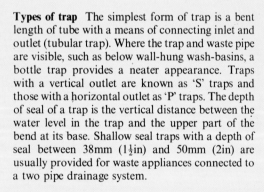
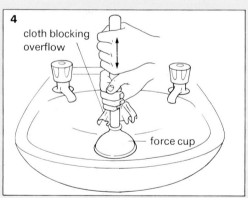

'P' trap   'S' trap   'P' bottle trap

depth of seal

4 Using force cup to clear blockage. **5a** To clear blocked 'U' trap, remove drain plug with rod. **5b** Push wire into trap. **5c** Probe round bend with curtain wire. **5d** Replace drain plug **6a** To clear bottle trap, unscrew bottom. **6b** Push curtain wire into pipe to remove blockage

Types of trap The simplest form of trap is a bent length of tube with a means of connecting inlet and outlet (tubular trap). Where the trap and waste pipe are visible, such as below wall-hung wash-basins, a bottle trap provides a neater appearance. Traps with a vertical outlet are known as 'S' traps and those with a horizontal outlet as 'P' traps. The depth of seal of a trap is the vertical distance between the water level in the trap and the upper part of the bend at its base. Shallow seal traps with a depth of seal between 38mm (1½in) and 50mm (2in) are usually provided for waste appliances connected to a two pipe drainage system.

Clearing blockages

Since traps retard the flow of waste water they are the most common site of blockage in the outlet of any soil or waste appliance. If water fails to flow away when you remove the outlet plug from a sink, wash-basin or bath, try clearing the blockage by plunging. For this you will need a force cup or sink waste plunger which you can obtain from any hardware store. Place the cup over the waste outlet of the appliance. Hold a dampened cloth firmly against the overflow outlet to prevent the force of the plunger being dissipated up the outlet and plunge down sharply three or four times. This should move the blockage and allow waste water to run away.

If plunging fails to clear the trap, it is likely a solid object is lodged in it. All traps are provided with some means of access to enable you to remove

4

cloth blocking overflow

force cup

such objects. The entire lower part of a bottle trap can be unscrewed and other traps have a screwed-in access cap at or near their base. Remember to place a large bucket under the waste pipe before unscrewing a cap or removing the lower part of a bottle trap. To clear the blockage, probe into the trap with a piece of flexible wire, such as expanding curtain wire.

A very slow discharge from the appliance indicates a partial blockage, usually caused by a build-up of grease. To deal with this, pour a proprietary chemical drain cleaner into the waste outlet.
Warning Chemical cleaners are usually based on caustic soda; so they should be kept away from children and used with extreme care, strictly according to the manufacturer's instructions.

5a
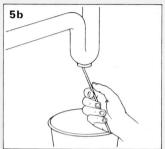

5b

5c
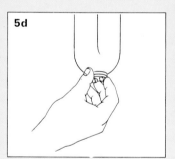

5d
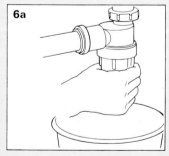

6a

6b
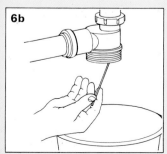

Underground drainage

There are two principal systems for disposing of wastes after they have been discharged from above-ground pipes; your home will have one of them. Here we describe the construction and layout of the two systems, where blockages are likely to occur and how to detect and clear them.

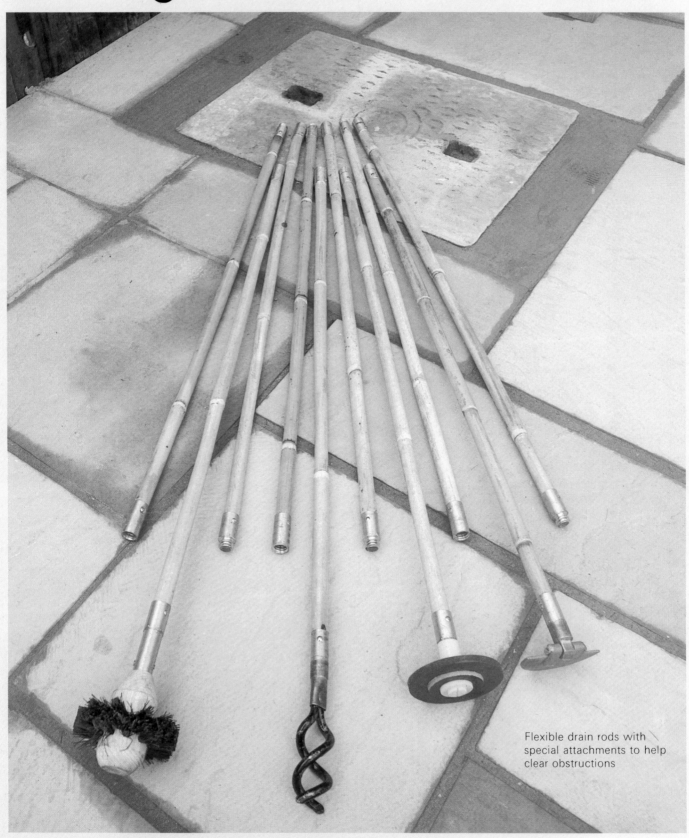

Flexible drain rods with special attachments to help clear obstructions

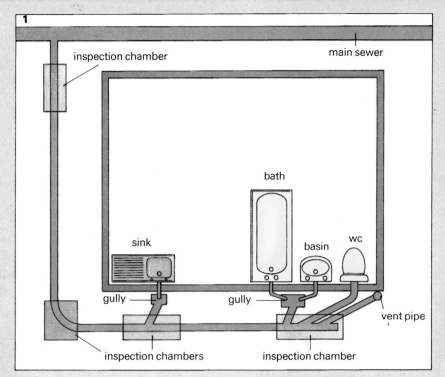

1

inspection chamber

main sewer

bath

sink

basin

wc

gully

gully

vent pipe

inspection chambers

inspection chamber

Domestic underground drainage systems, which take the wastes from pipes above ground to the public sewer, are laid out according to certain general principles. For example, drains must be laid in straight lines and sloping downwards so they are self-cleansing. They should be adequately ventilated and protected from damage which might arise from subsoil settlement. There must also be an inspection chamber or similar means of access at junctions of branch drains and changes of direction in the system to enable blockages to be cleared.

Older systems

Many older houses have systems constructed of glazed stoneware pipe 610mm (2ft) long with an internal diameter of 100mm (or 4in), laid on a 150mm (or 6in) deep concrete bed to give protection against settlement. Pipes are joined either with neat cement or a strong cement/sand mix and are laid at a gradient of 1 in 40 – or 75mm in 3m (3in in 10ft). Inspection chambers are made of brick, usually rendered internally with cement and sand. Drains pass through these chambers in stoneware half-channels with a concrete ledge or benching built up on each side.

There is an intercepting or disconnecting trap in the final inspection chamber before connection to

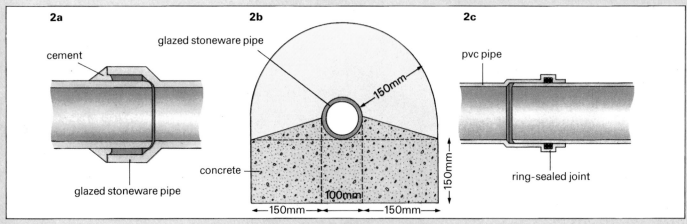

2a

cement

glazed stoneware pipe

2b

glazed stoneware pipe

150mm

concrete

100mm

150mm

150mm

150mm

2c

pvc pipe

ring-sealed joint

the public sewer. This is designed to prevent sewer gases, and possibly rats, entering the house drains. To allow fresh air along the drains to carry gases out through the above-ground soil and vent pipes, a low level ventilator or fresh air inlet is usually connected to the final inspection chamber. It ends above ground in a metal box with a hinged mica flap resting against a grille inlet.

Modern systems

Modern houses have systems constructed from 100mm (or 4in) pipes, but these are more likely to be made of PVC or pitch fibre than glazed stoneware; ring-sealed joints are used to connect them. Drains of this kind will move or give slightly to accommodate any ground settlement and do not need to be laid on a concrete bed. Smoother internal surfaces and a reduction in the number of joints means gradients shallower than in older systems can be safely used. Falls of 1 in 60 – or 75mm in 4.5m (3in in 15ft) – and 1 in 70 – or 75mm in 5.25m (3in in 17ft 6in) – are common.

Inspection chambers may still be made of brick, but they are not rendered internally since cement rendering is likely to flake off and cause a blockage. Any rendering necessary is applied to the outside of the chamber before earth is filled in. Some pre-

3

fresh air inlet

manhole cover

rodding eye

rodding arm

stoneware stopper

drainpipe

stoneware half-channel

to main sewer

intercepting trap

4

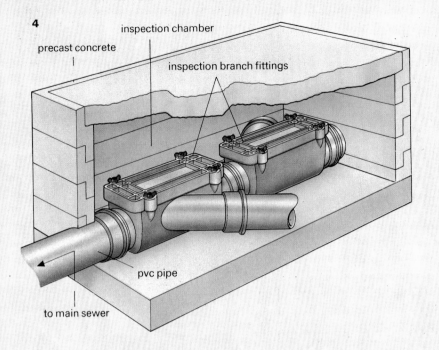

precast concrete

inspection chamber

inspection branch fittings

pvc pipe

to main sewer

Clearing blockages Before you can clear a blocked drain, you need to know where the blockage is. Raise the covers of the inspection chambers. If the chamber nearest to the house is flooded but the one nearest to the boundary is clear, the blockage must be situated between these two points. You can remove the blockage by a process known as rodding, for which you need a set of flexible drain rods. Screw two or three rods together, lower one end into the flooded manhole or chamber and feel for the entrance to the drain. When you have found it, push the rods towards the blockage, screwing more on as needed. Twist in a clockwise direction to help the rods move along the pipe. You must never twist them anti-clockwise or the rods will unscrew and you could end up with several lengths left in the drain. When you reach the blockage, give one or two sharp prods which will usually clear it. There are special tools available which you can screw onto the ends of rods to help clear difficult obstructions.

If all the inspection chambers are flooded and your drainage system has an intercepting trap, it is likely the trap is the site of the blockage. To clear it, screw two drain rods together and a 100mm (or 4in) rubber disc or drain plunger onto the end. Lower the plunger into the chamber, feel for the half-channel at the base and move the plunger along it

5

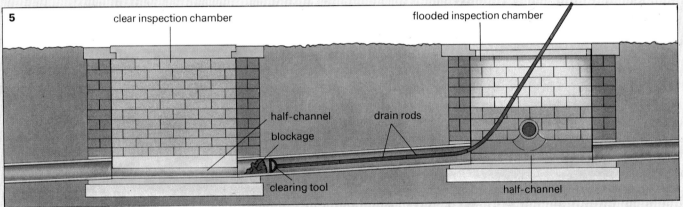

clear inspection chamber

flooded inspection chamber

half-channel

blockage

drain rods

clearing tool

half-channel

1 A typical domestic underground drainage system
2a Section through the joint of stoneware pipes
2b Foundations for a stoneware pipe
2c Section through the joint of PVC pipes
3 An early inspection chamber with intercepting trap and fresh air inlet
4 A precast concrete inspection chamber
5 Clearing a blocked drain: lower drain rods into the flooded chamber and push them into the drain until you reach the blockage. A few sharp prods should clear the system

fabricated chambers are made of concrete sections or plastic reinforced by glass fibre.

The intercepting trap has been abolished as it is the commonest area of blockage in older systems. There is no need for it where there is a properly designed and ventilated sewer which should contain neither offensive smells nor rats. There is no fresh air inlet which, being situated at ground level, is likely to be subjected to accidental damage and is a common source of drain smells. In modern systems where drains are connected without interception directly to the sewer, all domestic drains and the sewer are adequately ventilated by their above-ground drainage stacks.

Drain blockages
Trace the course of your drainage system so you will be able to take appropriate action when a blockage occurs and inspection chambers are flooded. Make sure the covers of the chambers can be easily raised and note where branch drains enter and if there is an intercepting trap in the final chamber. Learn to recognize the signs of blockage, such as a flooding gully and sewage leaking from the cover of an inspection chamber. Another indication is when you flush your WC and water rises to the flushing rim and subsides very slowly.

until it reaches the point at which the half-channel descends into the intercepting trap. Plunge down sharply three or four times to remove the blockage.

After clearing a blocked drain remember to run the household taps to flush water through the drain and to wash down the sides and benching of the chambers with hot water and washing soda.

Rodding eye stopper blockage The length of drain from the intercepting trap to the public sewer is the responsibility of the householder, even though it may lie wholly or partly under the public highway. Intercepting traps are provided with a device known as a rodding eye, connected to a rodding arm and sealed with a stoneware stopper, through which this section of the drain can be rodded. Sometimes, as a result of back pressure from the sewer, the stopper falls out into the trap to cause a partial blockage. Regularly check the stopper is in place. If its loss and a subsequent blockage remain undetected, the level of sewage rises in the inspection chamber until it reaches the rodding arm and then flows down this arm to the sewer; meanwhile the sewage in the base of the chamber decomposes and becomes more and more foul. Discovery of the blockage usually follows investigation of a complaint about an offensive smell near the front gate.

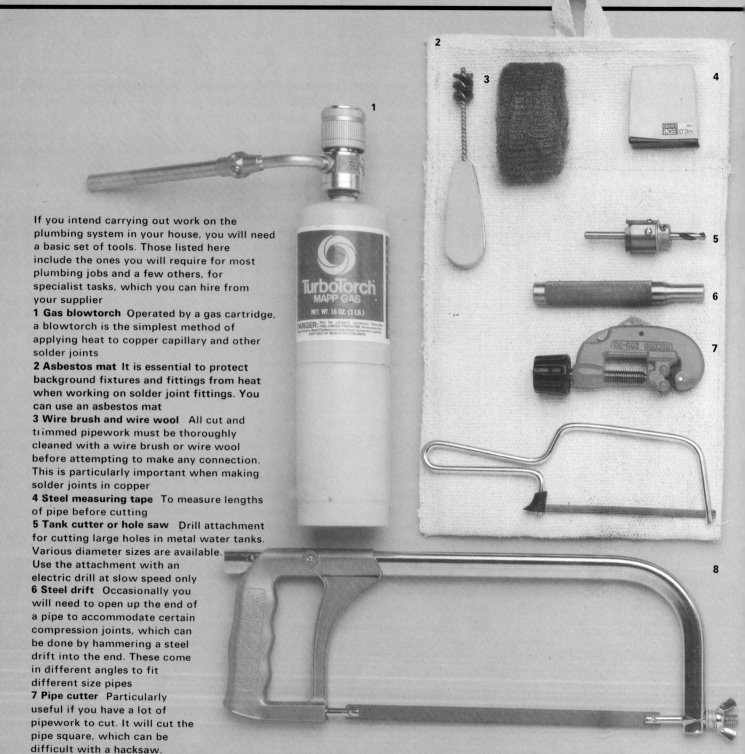

If you intend carrying out work on the plumbing system in your house, you will need a basic set of tools. Those listed here include the ones you will require for most plumbing jobs and a few others, for specialist tasks, which you can hire from your supplier

1 Gas blowtorch Operated by a gas cartridge, a blowtorch is the simplest method of applying heat to copper capillary and other solder joints

2 Asbestos mat It is essential to protect background fixtures and fittings from heat when working on solder joint fittings. You can use an asbestos mat

3 Wire brush and wire wool All cut and trimmed pipework must be thoroughly cleaned with a wire brush or wire wool before attempting to make any connection. This is particularly important when making solder joints in copper

4 Steel measuring tape To measure lengths of pipe before cutting

5 Tank cutter or hole saw Drill attachment for cutting large holes in metal water tanks. Various diameter sizes are available. Use the attachment with an electric drill at slow speed only

6 Steel drift Occasionally you will need to open up the end of a pipe to accommodate certain compression joints, which can be done by hammering a steel drift into the end. These come in different angles to fit different size pipes

7 Pipe cutter Particularly useful if you have a lot of pipework to cut. It will cut the pipe square, which can be difficult with a hacksaw.

Clamp the cutter to the pipe and rotate it round the pipe, gradually increasing the pressure screw so the cutting wheel scores through the pipe to make a clean, accurate break. Remove the internal burr on the cut pipe by using the reaming part at the end of the tool

8 Hacksaw or junior hacksaw Both are useful for any type of metalwork and will cut all pipe used in domestic plumbing

9 Bending machine On pipes or tubes of 22mm (or ¾in) diameter and over, bends can be formed more easily with a bending machine; although expensive, it can be hired readily. It is designed to produce a curve without distorting the circular hole running though the bend. Be sure to use

the right size former or guide around which you push the pipe for the bend you require. Hand benders are available for pipe up to 22mm (or ¾in) diameter

10 Bending spring To make bends in the small diameter metal pipes used in domestic plumbing. Make sure you use the right size spring for the tube being bent.

11 Files For trimming and smoothing flat and round surfaces in plumbing work use a flat file and a round rat's-tail file

12 Pipe wrench The coarse serrated teeth of a pipe wrench grip iron pipework firmly for turning. Never use a pipe wrench with copper pipe since the thin walls may collapse under the pressure. (Protect the surface of the pipe with cloth to prevent the teeth scoring it.) You can achieve extra leverage by sliding a length of pipe over the handle of the wrench; this is usually necessary when tightening or unscrewing old, stubborn joints that will not loosen easily

13 Gland nut pliers This tool has adjustable jaws and is good for undoing thin nuts in awkward places; but it is not strong enough for heavy work

14–16 Wrenches Three types are useful: the Stillson pattern (**14**), the mole (**15**) and the adjustable **(16)**. The mole wrench, although not a substitute for spanners, can be used on a variety of plumbing fittings for tightening or loosening joints. Like pipe wrenches, the teeth of a mole wrench may score the surface of metal if not protected. The other wrenches have the advantage of fitting several nut sizes, which would each require an individual fixed spanner. The adjustment enables the jaws to close tightly round a nut without marking the surface of the metal. They are available in a range of sizes, but for plumbing work the minimum practical size is 254mm (10in)

17 Basin and bath wrenches Special types of plumbing wrenches with right-angle jaws which can be used vertically and horizontally. They are ideal for reaching the coupling nuts recessed under fittings which are inaccessible to ordinary wrenches

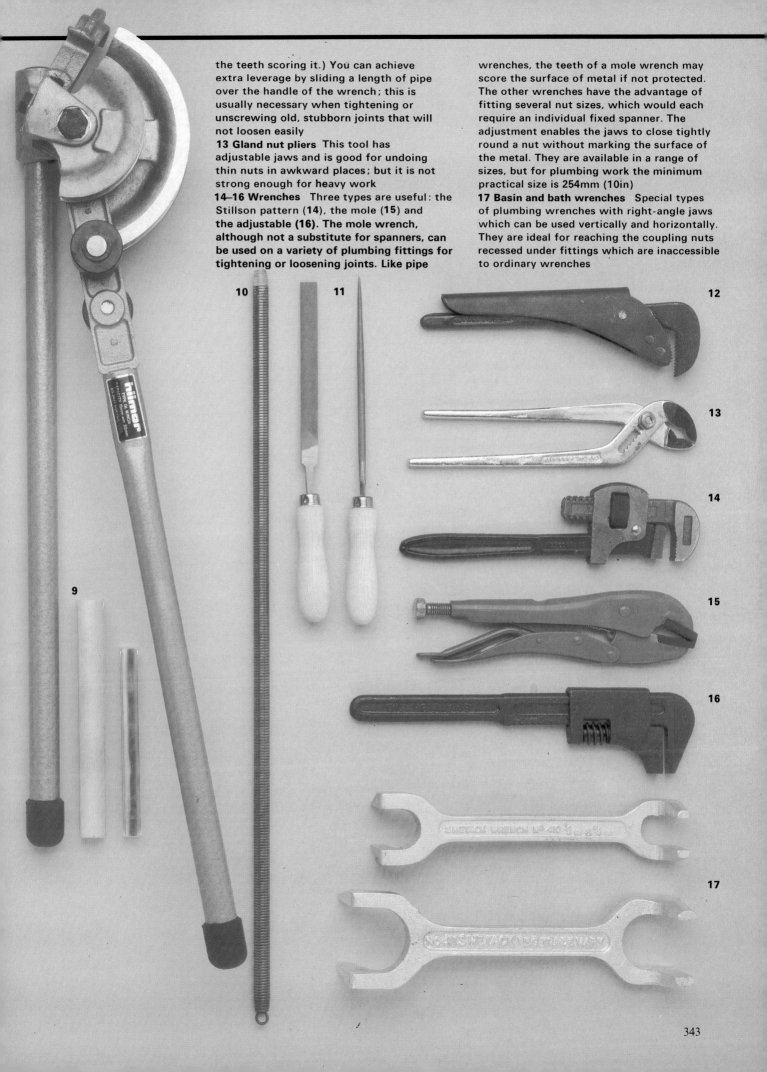

9

10

11

12

13

14

15

16

17

Bending and joining tubes

You can bend most of the light gauge tubing used in domestic plumbing systems quite easily and you will need to do this when running lengths of tube round corners or when installing tubing in awkward situations.

Incidentally, bending tube is always preferable to incorporating angled fittings into the tube run, since any fitting of this sort will tend to restrict the flow of water through the tubes.

Types of tubing
Steel, aluminium, brass and copper tubing will be held in stock by most metal suppliers, in a wide range of diameters and thicknesses; you can also buy rectangular section. Stock size diameters are 3–150mm (0.118–6in), each being available in a range of wall (metal) thicknesses. It is sometimes possible to obtain shaped tubing, such as fluted or spirally twisted, but these types are not easily bent and joined.

Square section in various metals and finishes, with patent fittings to make right-angle joints, is available for a variety of structures. With this type of section you require little more than a mallet and hacksaw to make items such as a frame for a coffee table of a hi-fi rack. You can also use plumbing fittings to make structures, but you may need pipe-threading tools to thread the ends of the pipes before assembly and the end product may not be very elegant. Copper tubing can be used with soldered capillary joints and fittings to make a towel rail, which you could connect to your hot water system.

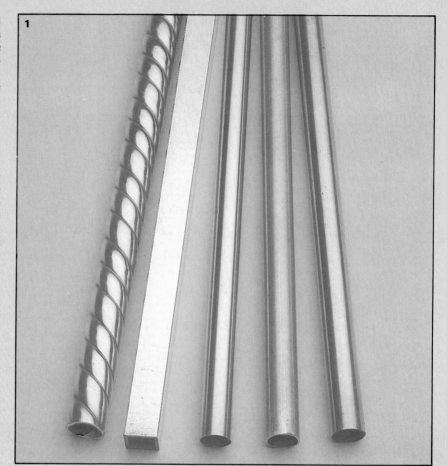

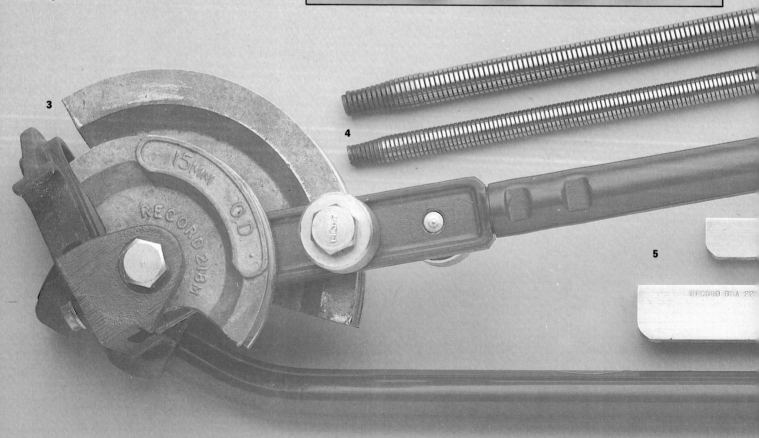

1 Types of tube: (from left) fluted brass, rectangular section, standard brass, aluminium and copper
2a Unless bend radius is at least four times diameter of tube, wrinkling may occur at throat and thinning on heel of tube
2b To determine bend allowance (heating length), you will need to know bend angle and radius
3 Bending machine
4 Bending springs
5 Formers for bending machine
6 Pipe cutter

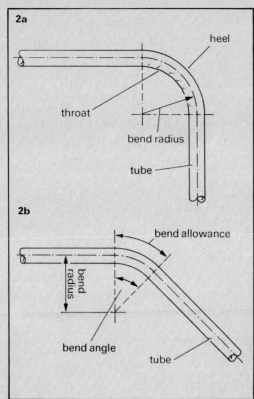

2a

heel

throat

bend radius

tube

2b

bend allowance

bend radius

bend angle

tube

Large radius bends are easier to form, but tight bends will cause some thinning of the metal on the heel (or outside) of the bend; they will also increase resistance to flow.

Cutting tubes
Use a pipe cutter to cut copper tubing; other types of tube may be cut with a fine-tooth hacksaw. After cutting tubing, remove any burr from the inside of the tube with a rat's-tail file and clean the outside of the cut with emery cloth.
Using filler Filler can be used in light gauge tubing to prevent it thinning while being bent. Pack the tube firmly with dry silver sand or resin and plug the ends to prevent losing the filler during bending.

Annealing metal
The copper tube used in domestic plumbing systems is normally sold in a 'half hard' condition, which ensures that it does not sag when clipped in straight, horizontal runs. However, it is still soft enough to be bent as required.

Copper gradually gets harder with age and old tube may therefore not bend that easily. In this case you will need to soften the tube around the section to be bent and to do this you have to use the annealing process.

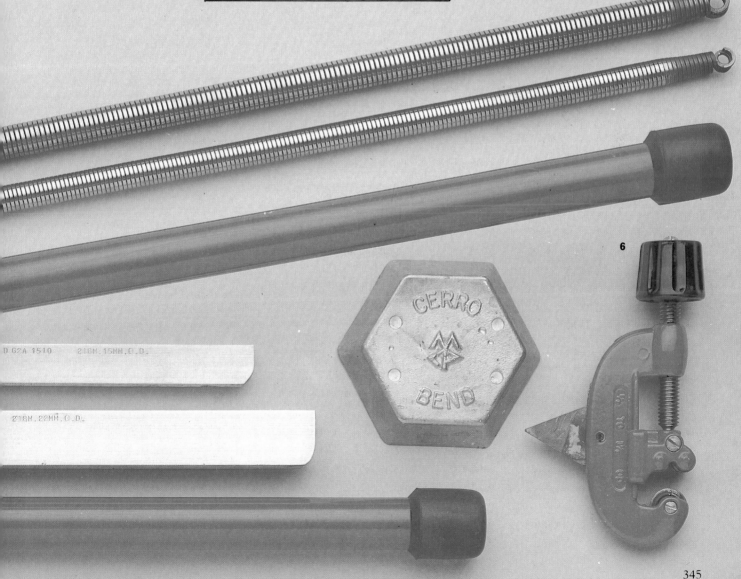

6

Heat the area around the section of tube to be bent, working an extra 50mm (2in) or so at either end. Use a propane blowtorch and heat the tube carefully and evenly along the length of the bend.

It will help if you have any firebricks handy to place these behind the heated section of tube, since these will reflect back any wasted heat.

Continue heating the tube until it glows an even red colour; then immediately quench the heated section in cold water. The water should be in a suitable, heat-resistant container. Take care when you immerse the tube where the open end points, since hot water may shoot out of it if the other end of the tube is immersed in the water.

If you get any discoloration on the outside of the tube, you can clean this off with wire wool.

Bear in mind that you cannot anneal stainless steel in this way.

Bending methods

Depending on the gauge of tube you are working with and the number of bends you have to make, there are two ways of bending tube – over the knee, with the help of a bending spring to prevent the tube from kinking, or with a bending machine.

Bending over the knee This is suitable where you only have to make a few simple bends in 15mm (or ½in) copper tubing. You can bend 22mm (or ¾in) tube using this method, but you will need more strength and skill to ensure an accurate bend. One point to remember is that copper tube made to BS 2871 may kink if you are using this method to make tight bends.

If you use the knee method, the bend in the tube must be at least 150mm (6in) from the end of the tube to allow you sufficient leverage on the tube.

First insert inside the tube a greased bending spring of the same diameter as the tube you are bending. Sit or kneel with one knee bent at right angles to the body and hold the work so that the centre of the proposed bend is directly over the vertical plane of the knee. It will help if you place a folded duster on your knee underneath the tube.

Make sure the bending spring is positioned centrally through the section to be bent and then pull each end of the tube back towards you evenly to form the bend at the knee. Before you complete the bend, move the tube about 25mm (1in) to either side and then finish the bend. This will ensure that the bend does not have too tight a radius.

To remove the bending spring, twist it clockwise to reduce its diameter so that you can slide it out of the tube. One way to ensure the spring comes out easily is to overbend the tube slightly and then bring it back to the required angle.

If the bend is a long way from the end of the tube, attach a piece of strong cord to the loop at the end of the spring. Then measure the distance from the centre of the proposed bend to the end of the tube and mark this length from the middle of the spring onto the length of cord with a strip of tape. This is to ensure that when you feed the spring into the tube you will position it in the right place.

Having bent the tube, you can twist and pull on the cord to release the spring. If you want greater purchase, tie the cord onto a piece of wood or rod to provide a handle.

If the spring does jam inside the tube, you can try releasing it by lightly tapping the tube around the spring with a wooden mallet. The normal cause of a jammed spring is bending the tube at too tight an angle.

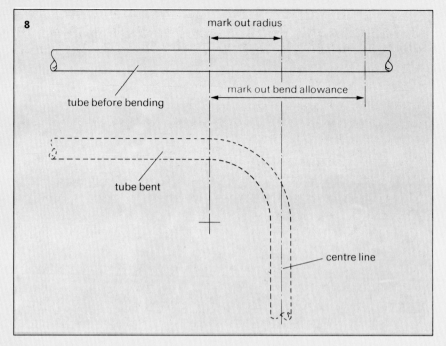

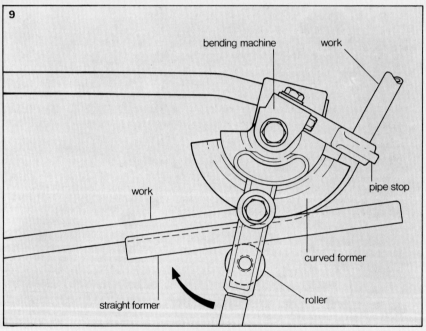

Using a bending machine You can hire a standard bending machine for tubing of 15mm (or ½in) and over. The machine consists of a former mounted on a bar and is held in a vice. A pivoted arm forces a roller over the tube, which is placed in the groove of the former. The machine is suitable for light gauge copper and aluminium tubing and should produce a curve without distorting the tube.

There are different types of machine available, but they mostly use the same techniques. Some are mounted on an integral stand, whereas others are operated freehand. Check first that the correct former has been fitted and that the roller is positioned properly.

Position the tube under the tube stop so that the marked spot for the start of the bend is at the leading edge of the curved former. Fit the straight former in position under the roller and along the section of tube to be bent.

You should still insert a bending spring into the tube; make sure this is in the correct position.

8 Marking out bend allowance
9 Using bending machine

Working with plastic tubing

Plastic tubing, now available for hot and cold water supplies and drainage, has been welcomed by both amateur and professional plumbers since it is light, easy to handle, long-lasting and cheaper than copper tubing. There are four main types of plastic tubing that can be used in domestic plumbing systems – polyethylene, polypropylene, polybutylene and PVC.

Polyethylene tubing
The advantages of black polyethylene tubing are the ease with which it can be cut and joined, the long lengths obtainable – which eliminate expensive couplings – and its built-in resistance to frost. It is, however, rather clumsy and ugly and does have a tendency to sag, so horizontal lengths need continuous support. It is particularly useful for taking a water supply to a stand-pipe at a distance from the main house supply; when used underground, where appearance is unimportant, it does not need support and its frost-resistance eliminates risk of bursts. This makes it valuable if you want to run a water supply to the bottom of the garden.
Joining polyethylene tubing Non-manipulative (type A) compression joints, such as those used with copper tubing, may be used to join polyethylene tubes. Because the polyethylene is thicker than metal, you will generally need a fitting one size larger than the nominal size of the tube. A metal insert is provided to support the walls of the tube when the cap nut is tightened.

Polypropylene tubing
This type of tubing and its respective fittings have been produced mainly for the DIY market since they are so easy to work with. The polypropylene is coloured white and has a naturally greasy feel to it.

Because polypropylene cannot be solvent-welded, all fittings are provided with ring seals. These have several advantages over solvent-welded fittings. They are much easier to make joints with, they allow for the natural expansion of plastic tubing when subjected to heat, and they can be taken apart quite easily when necessary for maintenance work.

Polybutylene tubing
Available in 15 and 22mm (or $\frac{1}{2}$ and $\frac{3}{4}$in) sizes, this type of tubing is suitable for both hot and cold water supplies. It is flexible and can be bent in a similar way to polyethylene tubing.

The fittings used with this type of tubing are very simple to make. You only have to slide a short

1 Joining polyethylene tubing with a non-manipulative compression joint
2a–e Making a solvent-welded joint on PVC tubing
2a Cut the end of the tube with a hacksaw
2b Remove any burr with a half-round file
2c Roughen the external surface of the tube and the internal surface of the socket with abrasive paper
2d Brush solvent cement evenly over the interior of the socket and over the end of the tube where it will fit into the socket
2e Section through the completed joint

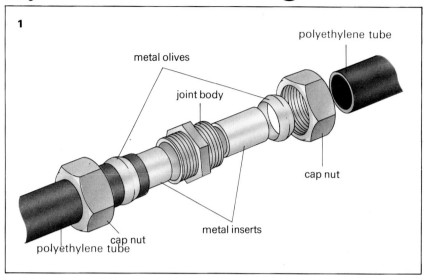

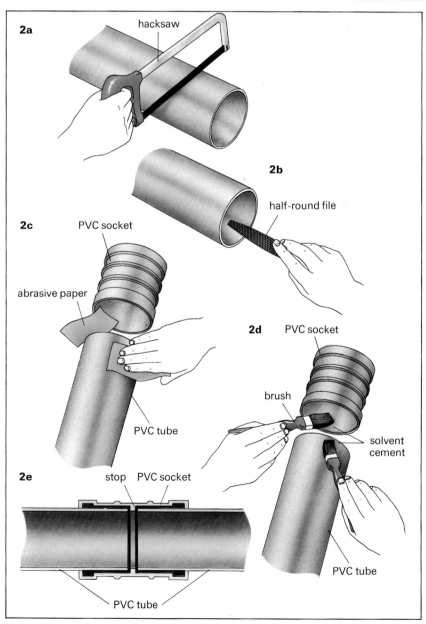

metal liner into the cut end of the tube and then push this end into the plastic fitting. The seal is made by a rubber 'O' ring and the tubing is held in place with a spring grab ring.

PVC tubing
PVC tubing is semi-rigid and therefore not normally bent. You can get a range of fittings for this type of tubing and these are either solvent-welded or compression. Normally coloured grey, PVC tubing is suitable for cold water services.

A modified version – known as muPVC – is becoming more widely available. Coloured white, it is suitable for carrying hot water and is being accepted in some areas by the local water authorities. Large diameter tubing – 36, 42 and 110mm (or $1\frac{1}{4}$, $1\frac{1}{2}$ and 4in) – is used for waste services and has either solvent-welded or ring-seal fittings.

Here we give general instructions for making solvent-welded and ring-seal joints. Manufacturers of PVC tubing and fittings do supply detailed instructions, which vary slightly from one make to another, so check carefully those of the manufacturer who supplied your materials.
Solvent-welded joint Cut the tube end squarely

with a hacksaw or other fine tooth saw and remove all swarf or burr with a half-round file. Roughen the exterior surface of the tube and the internal surface of the solvent-weld socket with medium glasspaper and wipe with a clean cloth to remove any particles. Don't use steel wool since this will polish the surfaces. Check the length and alignment, then apply a coat of approved spirit cleaner and degreaser to the inside of the socket and to the tube end for at least the distance it will fit into the socket.

Using a spatula or brush, apply solvent cement evenly to the tube end and the interior of the socket. Push the tube end hard into the socket with a slight twisting motion, hold it in position for about 15 seconds and then remove any surplus cement with a clean dry cloth. The joint may be handled after two or three minutes, but it should not be put into use for 24 hours.
Fittings As with compression and soldered capillary fittings used with copper tubing, there is a variety of fittings available for connection to tap and ball-valve tails and other screwed connections.
Warning There are two nominally cold water supply pipes for which uPVC tubing with solvent-welded joints should not be used. These are the supply pipe from the cold water storage cistern to the hot water storage cylinder and the supply pipe to the primary circuit of an indirect hot water system. The water in these two pipes can become very hot at times.

If you wish to use plastic tubing for these and other hot water runs, you must work with muPVC or polybutylene tubing and fittings.
Ring-seal joint One advantage of ring-seal jointing is it allows for the expansion of a waste-pipe resulting from the drainage of warm wastes from sinks, baths and basins. A 4m (or 13ft) length of PVC or polypropylene pipe will expand by over 13mm ($\frac{1}{2}$in) when subjected to an increased heat of 39°C (70°F).

To make a ring-seal joint, cut the tube end square with a fine tooth saw. Chamfer the end with a file. Insert the tube into the ring-seal socket as far as the pipe stop and mark round the tube with a pencil to show the insertion depth. Withdraw the tube and make another pencilled mark 10mm (or $\frac{3}{8}$in) nearer to the tube end than the original one: it is to this mark the tube must finally be inserted to form the joint.

Clean the recess within the ring-seal socket and insert the sealing ring. Lubricate the tube end with a little petroleum jelly and push it firmly home past the joint ring, then withdraw it until the second mark you have made is level with the edge of the socket. This will allow a 10mm (or $\frac{3}{8}$in) space for expansion at each joint.

Bending plastic tubing
Because polyethylene and polybutylene tubing are both flexible, lengths of either can be bent to the desired angle.

If you bend these types of tubing cold, you will have to clip the bent section into position. Try to ensure that the bend is as gradual as possible – preferably not less than 150mm (or 6in) for 15mm (or $\frac{1}{2}$in) tubing.

You can bend the tubing to a tighter angle if it is heated. The usual method is to immerse the section to be bent in boiling water.

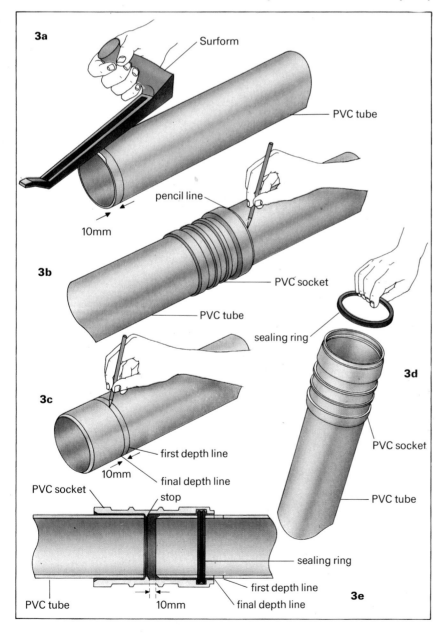

3a — Surform — PVC tube
pencil line
10mm
3b — PVC socket — PVC tube
sealing ring
3d — PVC socket — PVC tube
3c — first depth line — 10mm — final depth line
PVC socket — stop
sealing ring
PVC tube — 10mm — first depth line — final depth line
3e

Fitting compression joints

Plumbing jobs will invariably involve fitting together pipes. Compression joints will link any type of pipe normally found in the home and, apart from their versatility, they ensure a watertight result if fitted properly.

You will find the compression joints and fittings now available make extending or replacing your existing pipework a relatively easy task. There are two main types: non-manipulative (type A) and manipulative (type B).

Non-manipulative The type A compression joints and fittings have many purposes and the range includes straight couplings, bends, reducing couplings, 'T' junctions to enable branches to be connected to existing pipe lines, 'cap and lining'

connectors for joining copper tubing to the threaded tails of taps and ball valves, and fittings with threaded ends for connecting to screwed iron or brass sockets.

They are manufactured in metric sizes, the ones you are most likely to require being 15, 22 and 28mm. Some of them can be fitted without adaptation to the Imperial-sized pipework found in houses more than two or three years old. For example, 15 and 28mm compression joints can be fitted direct

There is a wide range of compression joints and fittings available
1 Straight swivel coupling (copper to iron)
2 Elbow coupling (copper to copper)
3 'T' junction
4 Bent swivel coupling (copper to iron)
5 Wall plate elbow fitting
6 Straight coupling
7 Tank connector
8 Straight coupling (lead to copper)

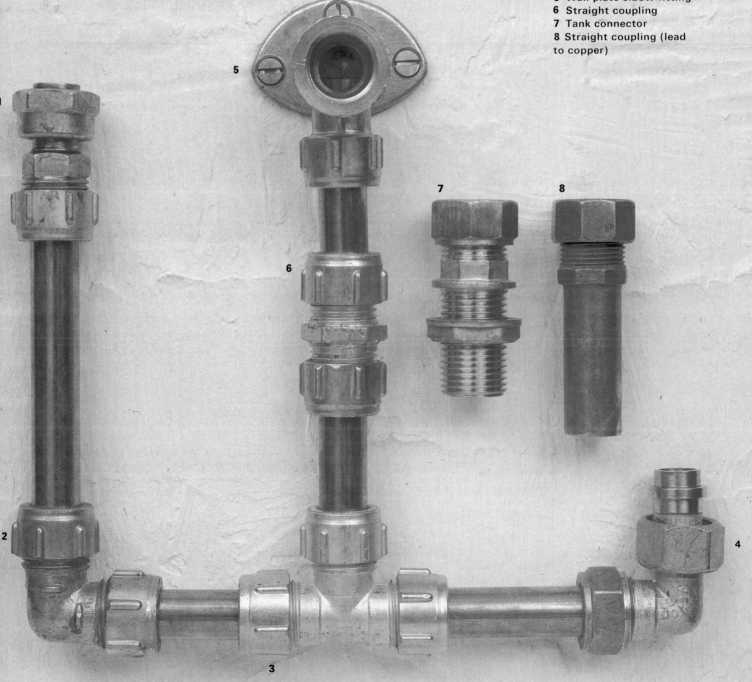

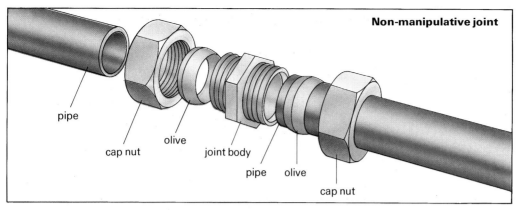

Non-manipulative joint

pipe
cap nut
olive
joint body
pipe
olive
cap nut

Left Components of non-manipulative joint
Below Before fitting joint, smooth down cut tube
Bottom Stages of fixing joint to pipes
Right Components of manipulative joint
Far right Open up pipe with steel drift
Below right Fitting and tightening joint
Bottom right Spring used to support wall of tube while bending

to $\frac{1}{2}$ and 1in tubing respectively, and 12 and 54mm fittings to $\frac{3}{8}$ and 2in tubing. For other fittings you will need an adaptor which you can obtain from your supplier. Adaptors are required to connect a 22mm compression joint to $\frac{3}{4}$in tubing and 35 and 42mm joints to $1\frac{1}{4}$ and $1\frac{1}{2}$in tubing.

Manipulative This type of fitting is less likely to be needed by the householder although water authorities usually insist upon its use for underground pipe work. Manipulative compression joints cannot readily be dismantled nor will they pull apart as a result of ice formation or ground settlement.

Making a non-manipulative compression joint

For work with this type of joint you need only a hacksaw (although for a major project it is probably worth having a wheel tube cutter), file, two open-ended spanners of the appropriate size and joint paste (such as boss white). Before fitting a type A compression joint to a length of copper tubing or pipe, cut the tube end square or square it off with a file after cutting. Remove all internal and external burrs or rough edges with a file or penknife. If you use a tube cutter, this can be fitted with a reamer which will remove internal burrs easily.

Dismantle the joint into its three components: joint body, cap nut and soft copper ring or 'olive'. Slip the cap nut over the end of the tube and follow this with the olive. Smear the outside of the tube and the olive liberally with a joint paste (to give an extra safeguard against leakage) and insert the tube end into the joint body as far as the tube stop. Use your fingers to screw the nut as tight as you can then, holding the joint body with a spanner, give the cap nut a complete turn with another spanner – don't use a wrench here or you may overtighten the nut. One turn should ensure the cap nut compresses the olive against the tube wall to make a watertight joint.

When you have had sufficient practice at making joints you will not need to dismantle the compression joint before fitting it onto the tube end. Simply loosen the cap nut and push the tube end through the cap nut and olive into the joint body as far as the tube stop.

Making a manipulative compression joint

Type B joints do not have an olive. Fitting is begun by slipping the cap nut and joint body over the pipe ends which you then 'manipulate'. This is usually done by hammering an instrument known as a steel drift into the pipe end to open it up. Smear the pipes with a generous amount of joint

Making non-manipulative joint

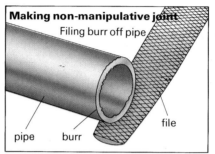

Filing burr off pipe
pipe
burr
file

Removing burr from inside pipe with reamer

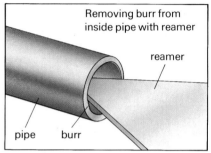

reamer
pipe
burr

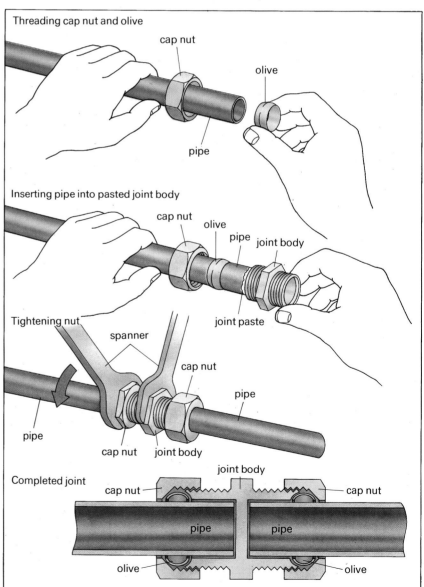

Threading cap nut and olive
cap nut
olive
pipe

Inserting pipe into pasted joint body
cap nut
olive
pipe
joint body
joint paste

Tightening nut
spanner
pipe
cap nut
joint body
cap nut
pipe

Completed joint
joint body
cap nut
cap nut
pipe
pipe
olive
olive

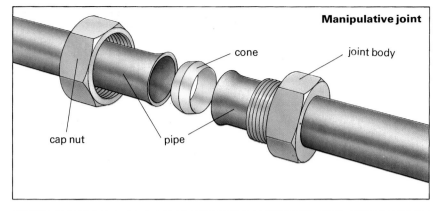

Manipulative joint

cone
joint body
cap nut
pipe

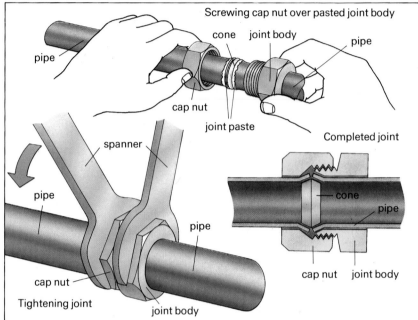

Screwing cap nut over pasted joint body

pipe
cone
joint body
pipe
cap nut
joint paste

Completed joint

spanner
pipe
pipe
cap nut
joint body
Tightening joint

cone
pipe
cap nut
joint body

Making bend in pipe

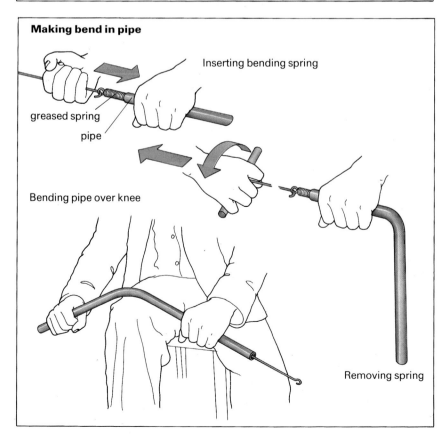

Inserting bending spring

greased spring
pipe

Bending pipe over knee

Removing spring

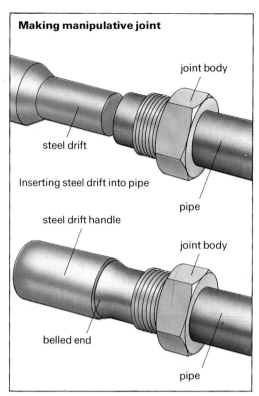

Making manipulative joint

joint body
steel drift
Inserting steel drift into pipe
pipe

steel drift handle
joint body
belled end
pipe

paste, place a cone insert in the belled end of the pipes and tightly screw the cap nut onto the joint body. This secures the pipe ends so they become an integral part of the joint.

Stainless steel tubing
Although light gauge copper tubing is most widely used in modern domestic plumbing systems, you may find some stainless steel tubing. Type A and type B compression joints can be fitted to this material and there is a range of chromium plated fittings for this purpose. The methods for fitting them are the same as for copper tubing but, to prevent the tube end splitting, always cut stainless steel with a hacksaw rather than a tube cutter. You will probably have to use more force when tightening the cap nut to obtain a watertight joint, since stainless steel is a harder material than copper.

Spring bending
There is a variety of bend joints and fittings available but, if you have a major plumbing project in mind, it is worth mastering the technique of spring bending. By this method you can make bends in 15 and 22mm copper tubing and 15mm stainless steel tubing with the aid of a bending spring. This supports the wall of the tube as it is bent and prevents it splitting or the shape of the section distorting.

Grease the spring and insert it in the tube to span the point at which you wish to make the bend. The tube can be bent by hand over your knee. For the best results, overbend slightly at first then bring the tube back to the required angle. To withdraw the spring insert a bar into the loop at the end, twist clockwise to reduce the spring's diameter and pull.
Warning If the tubing kinks at the bend, never attempt to hammer it smooth until the spring has been withdrawn. If you do, you may well find the spring has become locked in the tube and is impossible to remove.

351

Fitting soldered capillary joints

Soldered capillary joints and fittings are neater, less obtrusive and cheaper than compression joints. Their effectiveness depends on capillary action by which any liquid, including molten solder, flows and fills a confined space between two smooth surfaces. Capillary action can be demonstrated by dipping the end of a small bore transparent tube into a bowl of water. The water rises up the tube to a level above that of the water in the bowl; the smaller the bore of the tube, the higher the water will rise.

To ensure effective capillary action, soldered capillary joints and fittings are manufactured to fit very closely with the lengths of copper tubing for which they are designed.

There are two kinds of capillary joint: integral ring fittings (also known as Yorkshire joints after the name of a well-known make) which incorporate sufficient solder to make the joint, and end-feed fittings, into which solder wire has to be fed.

The equipment you need for making soldered capillary joints is a blow torch (a butane gas cartridge one will do), a hacksaw or tube cutter, a

file, wire wool, a tin of suitable flux (obtainable from the supplier of the joints) and a small sheet of asbestos or pad of glass fibre (to protect flammable surfaces behind the joints being made). If you are using end-feed fittings, solder wire will also be needed for joining up.

Warning When using a blow torch don't forget the fire risk involved. It is all too easy to become so engrossed in making a perfect joint that you do not notice blistering paintwork and smouldering timber. Always use a sheet of asbestos or pad of glass fibre behind every joint as you make it. Take special care when working in confined areas and among the bone dry timbers in the roof space. Plastic materials will be irrevocably damaged if subjected, even briefly, to the extreme heat of a blow torch flame, so be careful when working near an acrylic bath or a plastic WC cistern.

Making a soldered capillary joint
Meticulous cleanliness is the secret of success in making soldered capillary joints. First cut the end of the copper tube square with a hacksaw or tube

Above Soldered capillary joints come in a wide range of shapes and sizes to cope with the plumbing jobs in the home – and include many useful fittings as well. The joints are available either with solder (known as integral ring joints) or without (end-feed), to which you will have to apply your own solder to fit them

cutter and remove any external or internal burr with a file – or with a reamer fitted to the tube cutter. Clean the end of the tube and the bore of the fitting with wire wool or fine abrasive paper and apply chloride based flux to the cleaned surfaces of the tube ends and the fitting. Insert the tube ends into the fitting as far as the tube stop, making sure the pipes align and the ends fit in securely for a watertight joint.

Integral ring fitting If using this type of fitting, you now need only apply sufficient heat to melt the solder, which will then flow to fill the confined space between the tube wall and the inner surface of the fitting. Place a small sheet of asbestos or a pad of glass fibre behind the joint and apply the flame of the blow torch first to the tube either side of the fitting (except in the case of stainless steel tubing – see below) then to the fitting itself. When you see a bright ring of solder all round the mouth of the fitting the joint is completed. Brush off any excess solder while it is still hot, leaving a fillet around the joint.

End-feed fitting Follow the same procedure as for integral ring fitting but, after heating the tube

and the fitting, apply solder wire to the mouth of the fitting only. For a 15mm fitting you will need about 13mm ($\frac{1}{2}$in) of solder wire; for a 22mm fitting, 19mm ($\frac{3}{4}$in); for a 28mm fitting, 25mm (1in). Bend the solder wire to mark the appropriate length and feed it into the joint. When the indicated length has been fed in, the joint will be nearing completion. As with an integral ring fitting, the joint is completed when a bright ring of solder appears all round the mouth of the fitting. Brush off excess solder.

Once you have made the joint, leave it undisturbed until the tube and fitting are cool enough to touch. In most circumstances the use of a soldered capillary fitting will involve making more than one joint. There will, for example, be the two ends of a straight coupling, or three ends where a 'T' junction is being inserted in a run of pipe. If possible, make all the joints on one fitting at the same time. If something prevents you doing this, wrap a damp cloth round the joints already made to prevent the solder melting when the next joint is made.

1 The integral ring joint: all you have to do is heat the end to soften the solder already applied before joining up
2 The end-feed joint: to join up you heat the fitting and the tube, but you must apply your own solder
3 The easiest way to cut tube is with a tube cutter: clamp the tube and score round it until it breaks away cleanly
4 Having removed the burr with a file or reamer fitted to the tube cutter, clean the end of the tube and the bore of the fitting with wire wool (or abrasive paper)
5 Before joining up, apply chloride-based flux to the cleaned areas on both the tube and fitting (overleaf)
6 With the integral joint, heat the tube either side of the fitting and then the fitting itself by using a blow torch
7 Make sure you remove any excess solder, while it is still hot, with a brush
8 With an end-feed joint, after heating the tube and fitting, apply solder wire to the mouth of the fitting only. Check the length of wire needed and bend it at the appropriate point. When you have fed that amount into the fitting, you know it is ready to be joined up to the tube

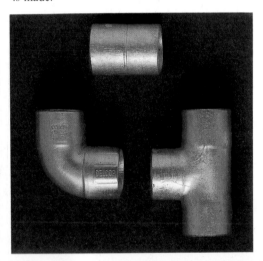

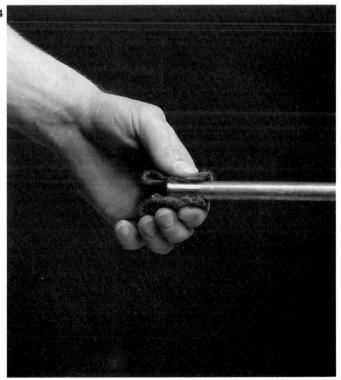

Stainless steel tubing

Soldered capillary joints can be used with thin-walled stainless steel tubing as well as with copper, but here you must use a phosphoric acid based flux – not a chloride based one, since this damages stainless steel. If you have difficulty in obtaining the right flux, don't be tempted to use any other kind: use compression fittings instead of soldered capillary ones. Handle phosphoric acid flux with care or you may burn your fingers: use a small brush to apply it to the tube end and the bore of the fitting. Finally, make sure you direct the flame of the blow torch only at the fitting, not at the tube: besides being a poor conductor of heat, stainless steel marks easily.

Metric fittings

In the case of compression joints and fittings 12, 15, 28 and 54mm metric fittings can be used, without adaptation, with $\frac{3}{8}$, $\frac{1}{2}$, 1 and 2in Imperial-sized tubing respectively. However, this does not apply to soldered capillary fittings, where an exact fit is much more important. If you want to add a metric extension to existing Imperial-sized plumbing by means of soldered capillary fittings, use a specially manufactured adaptor. Where the above sizes are concerned, however, it is simpler to use a compression coupling or 'T' for the actual connection to the Imperial-sized tubing and then, once the first length of metric tubing has been fitted, to carry on using soldered capillary joints.

5
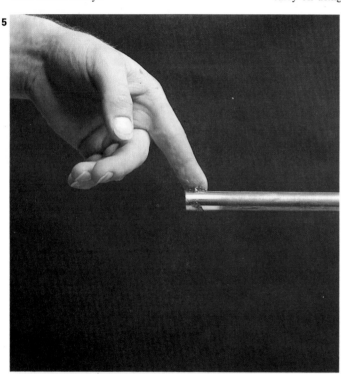

6
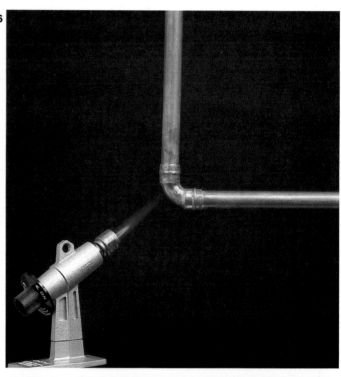

7

8

Taps, mixers and draincocks

Taps, which provide the practical outlet for your water system throughout the home, come in a variety of shapes and mechanisms – and include mixers, which enable you to control the temperature of water whether in a basin, bath or sink. One type of tap often overlooked is the draincock, which serves a more functional purpose in plumbing repair work.

Taps
The four most common types of tap are the pillar, bib, shrouded head and Supatap, all of which are also referred to on pages 357–360 in the section dealing with repairing leaks.

Pillar tap This vertical inlet tap is generally used

One difference in this type of tap is the method of connecting hoses – for example when filling a washing machine. Because the nozzle turns as the tap is operated, a special connector is necessary. It is secured in position by means of clips fitted over the ears of the tap; the body of the connector turns with the tap, while the swivel outlet designed for a hose connection remains stationary.

Mixers
These are simply two taps with a common spout and are often fitted to basins, baths or sinks, enabling you to use exactly the temperature of water you want.

Bath mixers These are now often supplied with a

1 Bib tap with hose union outlet
2 Supatap and hose connector
3 Section through basin mixer with pop-up waste
4 Sink mixer
5 Section through bath/shower mixer
6 Draincocks in the home; draincock in closed position (**inset**)

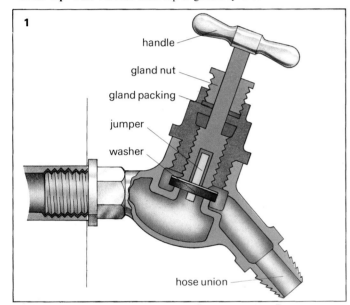

1

handle
gland nut
gland packing
jumper
washer
hose union

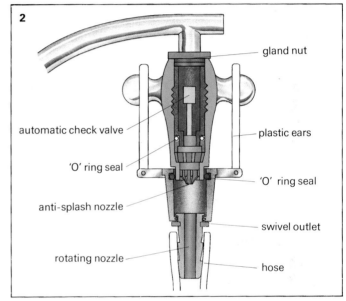

2

gland nut
automatic check valve
plastic ears
'O' ring seal
'O' ring seal
anti-splash nozzle
swivel outlet
rotating nozzle
hose

inside the home. A 15mm (or $\frac{1}{2}$in) tap is normally fitted to sinks and wash-basins and a 22mm (or $\frac{3}{4}$in) tap to baths. The metric sizes relate to the copper tubing to which they are fitted – not to the taps themselves. These taps fit into holes already provided in the appliances they are to serve.

Bib tap This type has a horizontal inlet and in modern homes is most commonly used to provide an outlet for the garden or garage water supply. A bib tap used for this purpose should ideally have a threaded nozzle onto which a hose connector can be screwed. It is also important to have the tap angled away from the wall or post to which it is fitted to prevent knuckles being grazed or knocked when turning the handle.

Shrouded-head tap This type has a handle specially designed to cover the headgear and was originally developed to prevent gland failure through detergent dripping from the handle of the tap into the mechanism. It has since become popular because of its neat and attractive appearance.

Supatap This tap works on a totally different principle from other taps, since it is controlled by turning the nozzle of the tap. Earlier models had the disadvantage of being too hot to touch, since the heat from the water transferred to the metal ears comprising the handle. Recent models are made with special plastic ears which do not conduct heat.

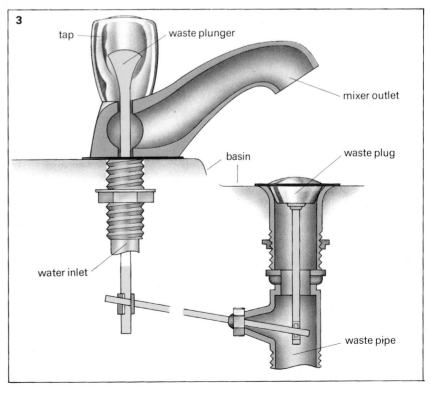

3

tap
waste plunger
mixer outlet
basin
waste plug
water inlet
waste pipe

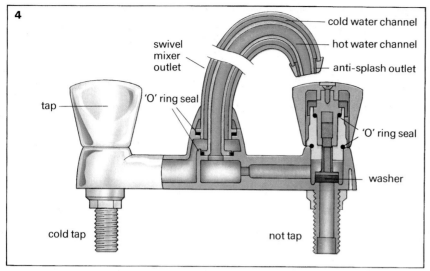

4

- cold water channel
- hot water channel
- swivel mixer outlet
- anti-splash outlet
- tap
- 'O' ring seal
- 'O' ring seal
- washer
- cold tap
- not tap

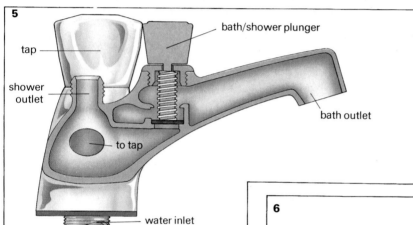

5

- tap
- bath/shower plunger
- shower outlet
- bath outlet
- to tap
- water inlet

water could be contaminated by coming into contact with the stored water.

To get over this problem, a special sink mixer has been developed which, although resembling bath and basin mixers in appearance, has in fact separate channels for the hot and cold water within its body. The two streams of water mix in the air after they leave the nozzle. Sink mixers frequently have a swivel nozzle, which enables you to direct the required temperature of water to any part of the sink – or, where there are twin sinks, to either sink. To make sure the nozzle is cool to the touch, cold water flows through the outer of the two channels within the mixer.

Draincocks

The simplest tap of all is the draincock, which should be fitted wherever any section of a hot or cold water or central heating system cannot be drained from an ordinary tap. Draincocks are closed by means of a washered plug which can be turned with a spanner or, in emergency, with a wrench or pair of pliers. A hose connector outlet is provided to enable easy drainage of the system. Draincocks should be fitted in the following places:
- ● Immediately above the main stopcock to enable the rising main to be drained.
- ● On the return pipe and close to any hot water cylinder storage system heated by an electric immersion heater only – and on any indirect hot water cylinder system.
- ● At the lowest point of any part of a central heating system which cannot be drained from the draincock beside the boiler.

flexible shower hose and sprinkler; the water, which can be mixed to the required temperature, is diverted from the spout to the shower sprinkler at the flick of a switch.

Basin mixers Some of these incorporate a pop-up waste, which eliminates the rather unsightly, traditional basin plug and chain. Pressure on a knob situated between the handles of the mixer activates the waste plug, which pops up to allow the basin to empty.

Sink mixers These are rather different in design, since water authorities prohibit the mixing of water from the rising main and water from a storage cistern within any plumbing system. This affects the sink since the hot water is supplied via the hot water storage cylinder (which in turn is supplied from the cold water storage cistern), while the cold water is supplied directly from the rising main. This means the hot and cold supplies are under unequal pressure and therefore mixing would be difficult. Apart from this, there is a possibility the mains

6

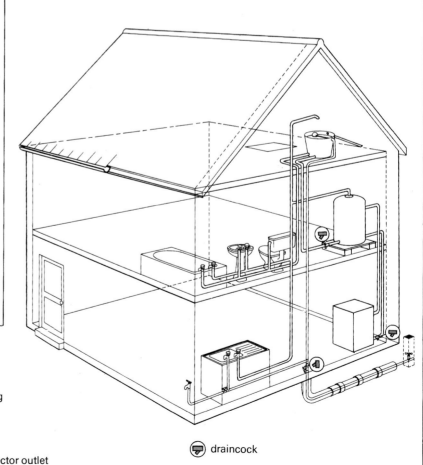

Inset

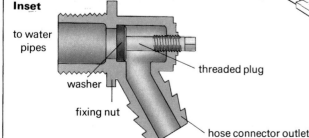

- to water pipes
- threaded plug
- washer
- fixing nut
- hose connector outlet

⊖ draincock

A basic item of plumbing equipment, the tap is constantly used by all the family and must periodically be serviced or adjusted. So the sooner you learn to do this for yourself the better. One of the commonest faults is washer failure, identified by a dripping tap.

Repairing taps and washers

The types of tap most common in the home
Right Shrouded-head tap
Far right Supatap
Below right Bib tap
Below Washer failure is causing this pillar tap to leak and drip water – a fault that can be easily put right

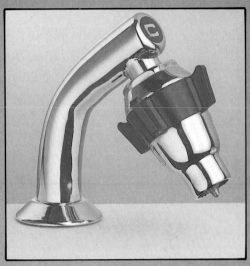

Plastic taps
Although all the taps included here are made of metal, plastic types are now available. These have some important advantages over metal ones. They remain cold to the touch even when controlling very hot water. They also have a non-rising spindle and an 'O' ring seal, which can be replaced if it wears. If you are connecting this type of tap to copper pipe, take care not to overtighten the female brass connection coupling or you may damage the plastic fitting.

Pillar taps

To rewasher the conventional pillar tap (**see 1**), you must cut off the water supply to the tap. If the fault is in the cold water tap over the kitchen sink (which should be supplied direct from the mains) you will need to turn off the main stopcock. Other taps may have a stopcock or gate valve on the distribution pipe serving them; if so, turn off this valve. If there is no such valve, tie up the arm of the ball valve serving the main cold water storage cistern and open all bathroom taps and the kitchen hot tap to drain the cistern and distribution pipes.

Unscrew the protective cover of the tap (**see 2a**). You should be able to do this by hand, but if not you can use a pipe wrench (**see below**), although you must pad the jaws to avoid damaging the chromium plating on the tap.

Insert an adjustable spanner (**see below**) under the base of the cover (**see 2b**), unscrew the head-gear nut and remove the headgear. The jumper (or valve) of the cold water tap over the kitchen sink will usually be resting on the valve seating in the body of the tap (**see 2c**). Remove it, unscrew the small retaining nut (**see 2d**) and replace the washer. If the nut proves difficult to unscrew you can replace the jumper and washer complete.

Some taps may have the jumper pegged into the headgear. Although it will turn, it may not be easy to remove. You may have to unscrew the retaining nut with the help of a little penetrating oil. If the retaining nut will not move, insert the blade of a screwdriver between the plate of the jumper and the base of the headgear and break the pegging. Replace the jumper and washer complete, but burr the stem of the jumper with a coarse file to ensure a tight fit. Reassemble the tap and turn on water.

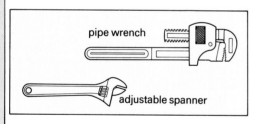

pipe wrench

adjustable spanner

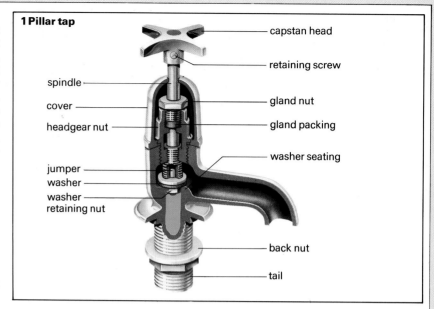

1 Pillar tap

capstan head
retaining screw
spindle
gland nut
cover
headgear nut
gland packing
washer seating
jumper
washer
washer retaining nut
back nut
tail

2a

2b

headgear nut

2c

jumper
washer

2d

washer retaining nut

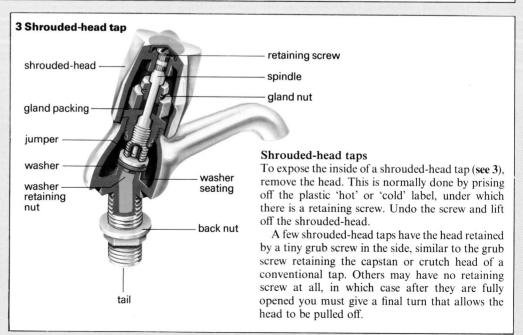

3 Shrouded-head tap

shrouded-head
retaining screw
spindle
gland nut
gland packing
jumper
washer
washer retaining nut
washer seating
back nut
tail

Shrouded-head taps

To expose the inside of a shrouded-head tap (**see 3**), remove the head. This is normally done by prising off the plastic 'hot' or 'cold' label, under which there is a retaining screw. Undo the screw and lift off the shrouded-head.

A few shrouded-head taps have the head retained by a tiny grub screw in the side, similar to the grub screw retaining the capstan or crutch head of a conventional tap. Others may have no retaining screw at all, in which case after they are fully opened you must give a final turn that allows the head to be pulled off.

Supataps

Rewashering a Supatap is a quick job that avoids cutting off the water supply. Open the tap slightly and with a spanner unscrew and release the retaining nut at the top of the nozzle (**see 4a**). Start turning the tap; there will be an increasing flow of water, but this will cease as the check valve falls into position. The nozzle will then come off in your hand (**see 4b**).

Tap the nozzle on a hard surface (not one that will chip) to loosen the anti-splash device in which the washer and jumper are fixed. Turn the nozzle upside down and the anti-splash will drop out. (**see 4c**). Remove the washer and jumper by inserting a blade between the plate and the anti-splash (**see 4d**) and insert a new set. Replace the anti-splash in the nozzle (**see 4e**) and reassemble the tap, remembering the nozzle screws back on with a left-hand thread (**see 4f**).

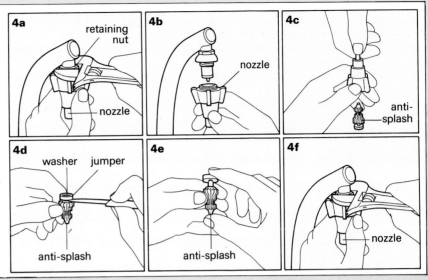

Continued dripping

Occasionally a tap will continue to drip even after being fitted with a new washer. This indicates the valve seating has been scratched and scored by grit in the water supply and no longer gives a watertight connection.

There are reseating tools available, but the simplest way to deal with this problem when it affects a conventional tap is to use a new nylon washer and seating kit (**see 5**). The nylon seating is placed squarely on the brass seating of the tap. Put the new washer and jumper in the headgear of the tap and screw them down hard into the tap body, forcing the nylon valve seating into position. This method cannot be used on Supataps, but the manufacturers of these taps make and supply a reseating tool for the purpose.

5 Washer and seating kit

6 Removing tap head

7 Shrouded-head tap with 'O' ring

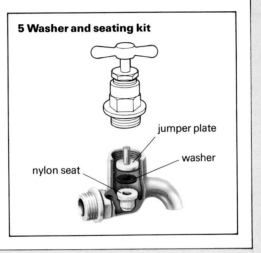

ing and removing the tiny retaining grub screw. If taking off the head proves difficult, open up the tap and unscrew and raise the protective cover as high as possible. Insert two pieces of wood (at back and front) between the base of the raised cover and the body of the tap. Then close the tap down again and the upward pressure of the cover will force off the head or handle (**see 6**).

The gland-adjusting nut is the first nut through which the spindle of the tap passes. To tighten, turn in a clockwise direction. Eventually all the allowance for adjustment will be taken up and the gland packing will have to be renewed. To do this, unscrew and remove the gland packing nut. Existing gland packing material can be removed with the point of a penknife. Repack with strands of wool steeped in vaseline, press down hard and reassemble the tap.

Some modern taps have a rubber 'O' ring seal instead of a conventional gland (**see 7**). These are less likely to give trouble, but if they do simply renew the ring.

Gland failure

Another common fault in taps, gland failure, is indicated by water escaping up the spindle when the tap is turned on. The tap can also be turned on and off very easily, with just a spin of the fingers, which often causes water hammer (the effect of shock waves in the pipes produced by the sudden cessation of flowing water). Causes of gland failure may be back pressure resulting from the connection of a hose or detergent-charged water running down the spindle and washing grease from the gland packing.

To adjust or renew the gland of a conventional tap, remove the capstan or crutch head by unscrew-

Fitting new taps

Before you renew a tap the existing one has to be taken out and this can be the most difficult part of the job. The back nut, which secures the tap underneath, is likely to be inaccessible and may well be firmly fixed by scale and corrosion.

Cut off the water supply to the tap and then unscrew the 'cap and lining' nut that connects the tail of the tap to the water supply pipe. With a basin or sink it may be necessary to disconnect the waste pipe, take the appliance off its mounting and turn it upside down on the floor in order to get a better purchase on the back nut. A cranked 'basin spanner' will help do this.

Removal of old bath taps can be particularly difficult because of the cramped and badly lit space in which you will have to work. It may prove better to disconnect the water supply and waste pipes and pull the bath forward to give yourself more room to work.

8 Fitting pillar tap
8a Into thin appliance

8b Into thick appliance

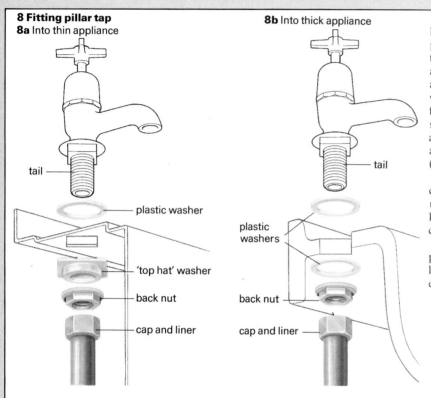

tail

plastic washer

'top hat' washer

back nut

cap and liner

tail

plastic washers

back nut

cap and liner

Pillar taps When fitting new pillar taps slip a plastic washer over the tail of the tap and insert the tail into the hole provided for it in the top of the appliance. Slip another plastic washer over the tail as it protrudes through the appliance and follow it with the retaining back nut. Where the tap is being fitted into an appliance of thin material, such as a stainless steel sink or an enamelled steel fitted basin, a 'top hat' or spacer washer must be used under the appliance to take the protruding shank of the tap (**see 8a**).

With an appliance of thick material, such as a ceramic wash-basin, a flat plastic washer can be used (**see 8b**). When fitting a tap into a basin of this kind do not overtighten the back nut, since the ceramic is very easily damaged by rough handling.

Pillar taps are connected to their water supply pipes by means of a 'tap connector' or 'cap and lining' joint. This incorporates a fibre washer that ensures a watertight connection.

9 Bib tap

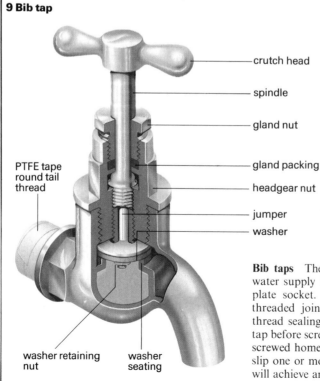

crutch head

spindle

gland nut

gland packing

headgear nut

jumper

washer

PTFE tape round tail thread

washer retaining nut

washer seating

Bib taps The type used for a garden or garage water supply is usually fitted into a screwed wall-plate socket. To ensure a watertight fit with a threaded joint of this kind, bind PTFE plastic thread sealing tape round the threaded tail of the tap before screwing into the socket (**see 9**). If, when screwed home, the tap is not upright unscrew and slip one or more metal washers over the tail. You will achieve an upright fit by trial and error.

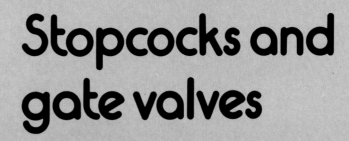

Stopcocks and gate valves

Stopcocks and gate valves enable you to control and stop the flow of water through the pipes in your house. You should know where they go in your water supply system if you intend to carry out plumbing repairs and which ones to turn off in the event of an emergency.

Stopcocks

Every household water supply system has one stopcock provided by the water authority. This is installed in a pit with a hinged metal lid, usually under the pavement outside the house, but sometimes just within the boundary of the property.

Types of stopcock and gate valve found in domestic water supply systems
Left Water authority stopcock. This may have a specially shaped shank that can be turned only with the authority's key
Below Mini stopcock or regulating valve
Bottom left Screw-down stopcock
Bottom right Gate valve

Modern houses also have one or more screw-down stopcocks inside. These are manufactured with a variety of inlets and outlets so they can be fitted to plastic, copper, iron or lead pipe. The main internal stopcock is located just above the point at which the rising main enters the house, often under the kitchen sink. It is set into the rising main and usually has a crutch or capstan head like an ordinary tap. The stopcock is normally kept fully open; to close it to stop the flow of water, you turn the handle or head in a clockwise direction – this pushes a washered valve or jumper firmly onto the valve seating.

Renewing washers Since stopcocks are rarely turned off, their washers have a long working life and only occasionally have to be renewed. When this is necessary, turn off the water supply to the stopcock (you may have to get the help of the water authority to arrange this) and unscrew and remove the headgear to gain access to the jumper and washer. Unscrew the small retaining nut, pull off the old washer and fit a new one. If you have trouble unscrewing the retaining nut, fit a new jumper and washer set; these are available from DIY shops.

Gland packing failure A more common fault in screw-down stopcocks, this is indicated by water dripping from the stopcock spindle. It should be dealt with immediately since constant dripping of water onto a timber floor in the usually confined and ill-ventilated position in which a stopcock is situated can result in dry rot. To prevent the drip you may find it sufficient to tighten the first nut through which the stopcock spindle passes; this is known as the gland adjusting nut. If this does not work, you must repack the gland. You need not cut off the water supply to the stopcock to do this; simply turn the stopcock off. Unscrew and remove the small grub screw which retains the head or handle and pull the handle off. Then unscrew and remove the gland adjusting nut to gain access to the gland. Using the point of a penknife, pick out all existing gland packing material and replace it with wool soaked in petroleum jelly. Pack this down tightly and reassemble the stopcock.

Jammed stopcocks The most common fault in stopcocks is jamming through disuse. If you cannot move the handle, apply penetrating oil to the spindle; usually after about a week of applying oil and trying to turn the handle, the stopcock will operate normally. It is, of course, best to prevent jamming by opening and closing the stopcock a few times at least twice a year.

Fitting new stopcocks Make sure the new stopcock is the same size as the pipe into which it is to be fitted. If, for example, you fit a 15mm (or $\frac{1}{2}$in) stopcock into a 22mm (or $\frac{3}{4}$in) pipe you are effectively reducing the diameter of the pipe to 15mm (or $\frac{1}{2}$in). Also check the stopcock is fitted the right way round: screw-down stopcocks have an arrow engraved in the body which must point in the direction of the flow of water. If the stopcock is fitted the wrong way round, water pressure will force the jumper onto the valve seating and prevent water flowing even when the stopcock is fully open.

Mini stopcocks

These are fitted at the point where a water supply pipe connects with a ball valve or the tail of a tap. They are opened and closed with a screwdriver and enable you to renew tap or ball valve washers or replace taps and ball valves without affecting the rest of the plumbing.

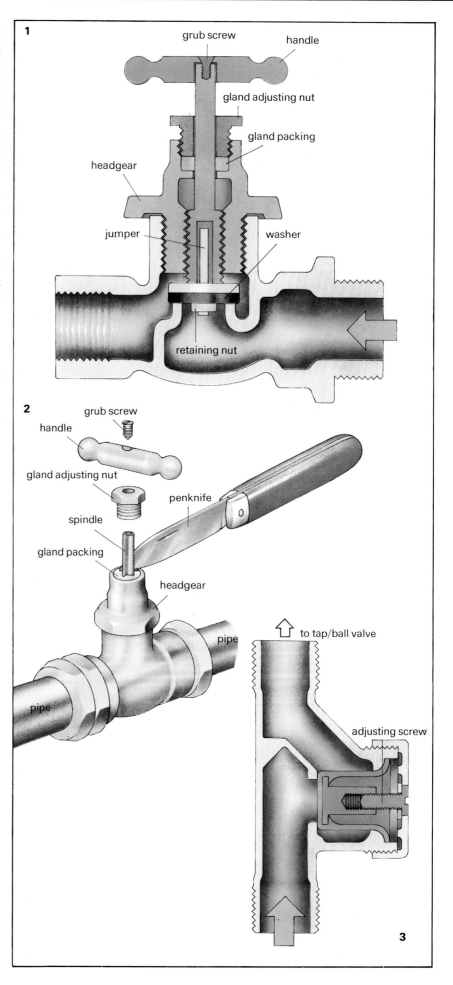

1 grub screw · handle · gland adjusting nut · gland packing · headgear · jumper · washer · retaining nut

2 grub screw · handle · gland adjusting nut · penknife · spindle · gland packing · headgear · pipe · pipe

3 to tap/ball valve · adjusting screw

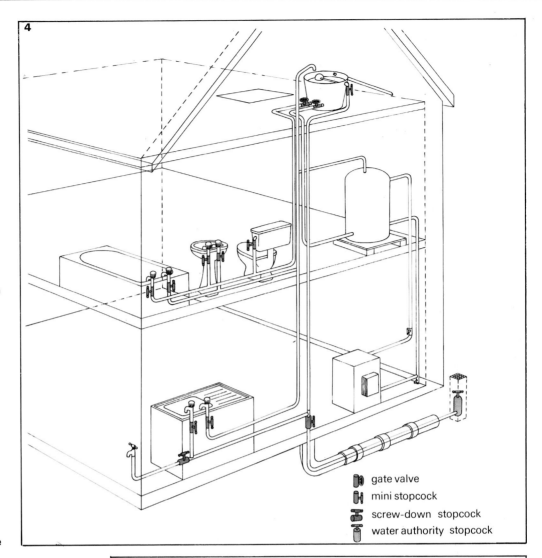

1 Features of a screw-down stopcock; the water flows from right to left
2 If water drips from the spindle of a screw-down stopcock, remove the gland packing and replace it with wool soaked in petroleum jelly
3 Features of a Markfram regulating valve (or mini stopcock); the water flows up through the valve
4 Refer to our standard house layout to locate the stopcocks and gate valves in your own home
5 Features of a gate valve; the water is cut off by screwing down a metal gate

	gate valve
	mini stopcock
	screw-down stopcock
	water authority stopcock

Gate valves

Gate valves are used where water pressure is low and where it is important there is an unrestricted flow of water. They are normally fitted into the supply pipe from the storage cistern to the bathroom cold water taps and are often placed immediately below the storage cistern; this allows part of the plumbing system to be isolated for repair or maintenance without affecting the rest of the system.

A gate valve has a larger body than a screw-down stopcock and usually a wheel, rather than a crutch or capstan, head. When you close the valve a metal plate, or gate, screws down to block the pipe; when the valve is open the plate is withdrawn to allow water to flow freely. Because this type of valve has a metal-to-metal seal it does not give as complete a cut-off of water as a screw-down stopcock, although this is not important in the situations in which gate valves are used. You can fit them either way round but, like stopcocks, they must be the same size as the pipe into which they are fitted.

Warning In normal use gate valves must be kept fully open. A partially closed valve on the supply pipe from the cold water cistern to the hot water cylinder is a common cause of recurring airlocks.

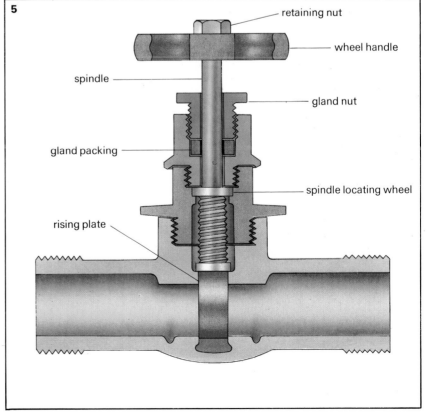

363

Ball valves

Ball valves are vital parts of the plumbing system in the home, since they control the amount of water in your cold water storage and WC cisterns. They must operate efficiently, otherwise the cisterns will overflow – or not fill up correctly.

The purpose of the ball, or float, valve is to maintain water at a constant level in cold water storage and WC flushing cisterns. All ball valves have a metal or plastic arm terminating in a float (not necessarily a ball) that rises or falls with the level of the water in the cistern. As the water level falls the movement of the float arm opens the valve to allow water to flow through it; as the level rises the arm closes the valve.

The older types of ball valve – the Croydon and the Portsmouth – control the flow of water by a washered metal plug. The main disadvantage of these is that failure of the washer or dirt or corrosion on the parts can cause leaks. Modern ball valves, which have a rubber diaphragm instead of a washered plug, are designed to overcome these problems.

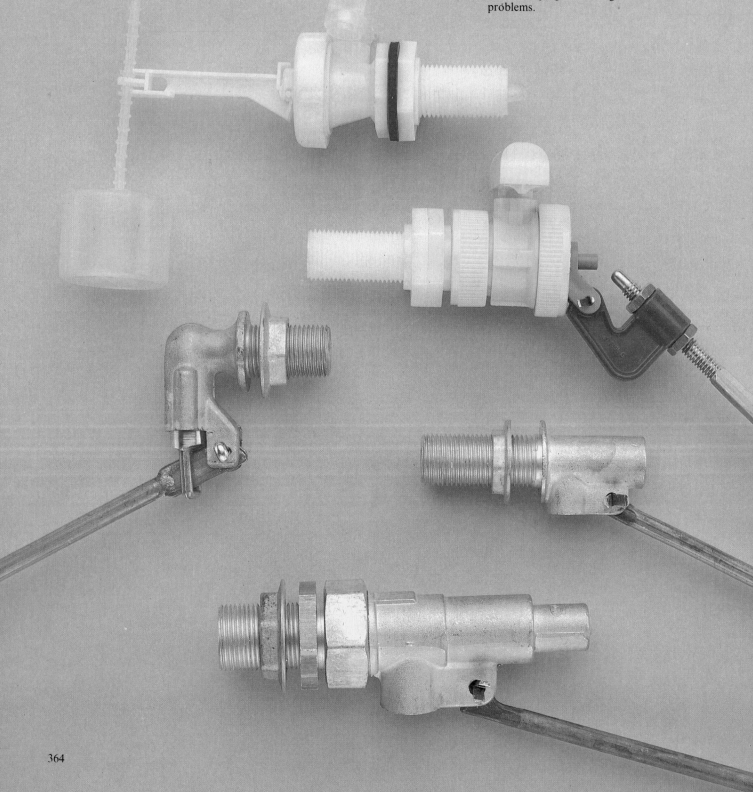

Croydon and Portsmouth valves

On both these valves a washered metal plug is forced tightly against the valve seating to prevent a flow of water when the cistern is full. The plug of a Croydon moves vertically within the valve body. When the valve is open, water splashes into the cistern via two channels built into either side of the body of the valve. Croydon valves are always noisy in action and, for this reason, are now rarely, if ever, installed in homes.

The Portsmouth valve is the one now most likely to be found in installations, particularly new ones. Its plug moves horizontally within the valve body and the end of the float arm is bent over to fit within a slot built into the plug. The noise of these valves used to be reduced by fitting a silencer tube into the valve outlet. This is a plastic or metal tube that delivers incoming water below the level of the water already in the cistern; it eliminates splashing and reduces the ripple formation that is a common cause of noise and vibration in ball valves. Unfortunately water authorities no longer permit the use of these silencer tubes, since in the event of water pressure failure they could cause water from storage and flushing cisterns to siphon back into the main.

Dealing with leaks A steady drip from the cistern's warning pipe indicates a worn washer – a common fault on the Croydon and Portsmouth valves. It may be possible to cure the leak, at least temporarily, without changing the washer simply by lowering the level of the water in the cistern. There is no need to cut off the water supply to do this: remove the cover from the cistern, unscrew and remove the float from the end of the float arm. Take the arm firmly in both hands and bend the float end downwards, then reassemble. This will keep the water below the normal level, which is about 25mm (1in) below the warning pipe in a cold water storage cistern and 13mm ($\frac{1}{2}$in) below the warning pipe in a flushing cistern. (If you need to raise the water level in a cistern, bend up the float end of the arm.)

Changing the washer If lowering the level of the water does not cure the leak, you will need to change the ball valve washer. First cut off the water supply at the nearest stopcock. Some Portsmouth valves have a screw-on cap at the end of the valve body: this must be removed.

Straighten and pull out the split pin on which the float arm pivots and remove the float arm; insert the blade of a screwdriver in the slot in the base of the valve body from which the float arm has been removed and push out the plug.

The plug has two parts: a body and a cap retaining the washer, but it may be difficult to see the division between these parts in a plug that has been in use for some time. To replace the washer you will need to remove the retaining plug: insert the blade of a screwdriver through the slot in the body and turn the cap with a pair of pliers. This can be very difficult, so don't risk damaging the plug. If the cap will not unscrew easily, pick out the old washer with the point of a penknife and force a new washer under the flange of the cap, making sure the washer lies flat on its seating.

Cleaning It is important to remove any dirt or scaling on the metal parts as this can also cause leaks. Before reassembling the plug, clean it with fine abrasive paper and smear with petroleum jelly.

When to replace the valve Continued leaking after renewal of the washer may indicate the valve seating of the plug has been scored by grit from the main or

a low pressure valve has been fitted where a high pressure one is required. In either case, a new valve will be needed.

Ball valves are classified as high pressure (HP) or low pressure (LP) depending on the diameter of the valve seating and are usually stamped accordingly on the valve body. High pressure valves are usually installed where the water supply is direct from the main and low pressure valves where the water supply is from another storage cistern, as is usually the case with WC flushing cisterns.

Using the wrong kind of valve will result in either constant leaks or a long delay in the refilling of the cistern. Where a WC flushing cistern is supplied from a cold water storage cistern only a metre (or 3ft) above the level of the WC suite, it may be necessary to fit a full-way valve – which has a wider orifice – to ensure the cistern refills rapidly after it has been flushed.

Equilibrium valve

In some areas water pressure may fluctuate considerably throughout a 24-hour period. In such cases, the provision of an equilibrium valve is

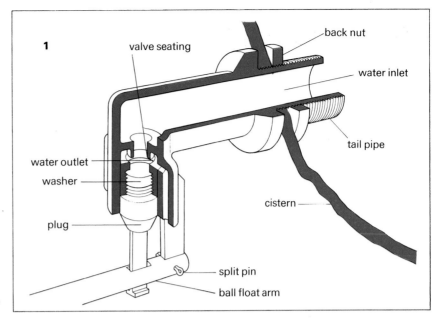

1 valve seating / back nut / water inlet / water outlet / washer / tail pipe / cistern / plug / split pin / ball float arm

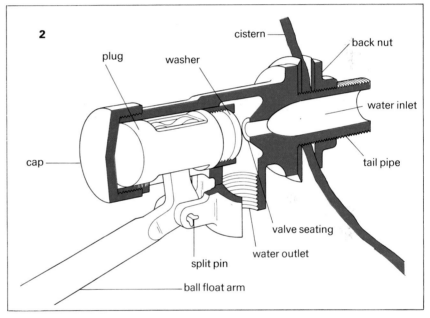

2 cistern / back nut / plug / washer / water inlet / cap / tail pipe / valve seating / water outlet / split pin / ball float arm

Opposite page Types of ball valve: Torbeck **(top left)**, diaphragm **(top right)**, Croydon **(centre left)**, Portsmouth **(centre right)** and equilibrium **(bottom)**.

1 The Croydon ball valve: the plug moves vertically in the valve body and water enters through channels on either side
2 The Portsmouth ball valve: the plug moves horizontally and water enters through a single channel

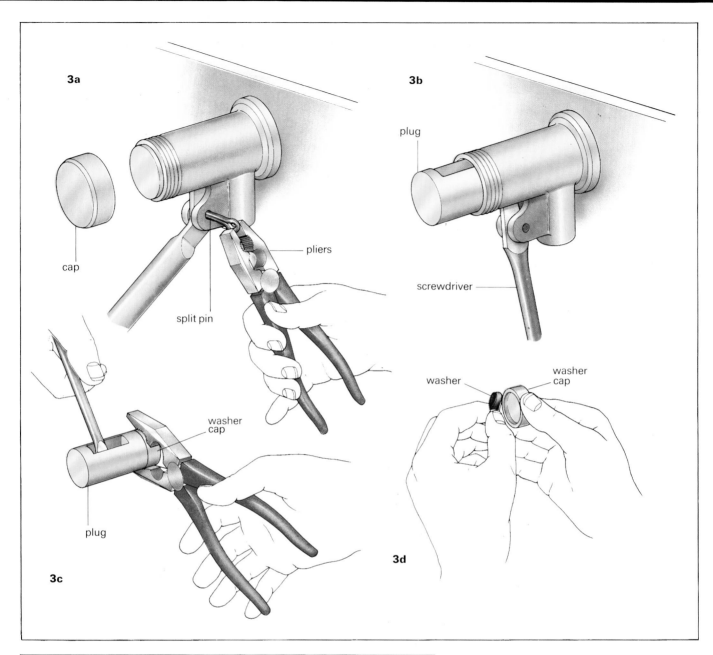

3a

cap

pliers

split pin

3b

plug

screwdriver

washer
cap

washer

3c

plug

washer
cap

3d

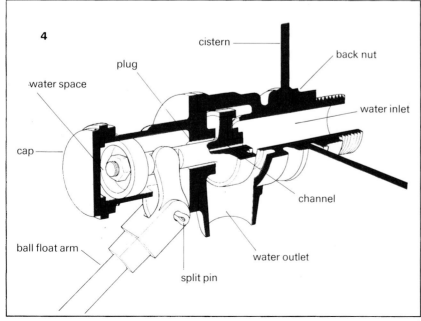

4

cistern

back nut

plug

water space

water inlet

cap

channel

ball float arm

split pin

water outlet

recommended. This valve has a wide nozzle orifice but is closed by a special plug with a channel bored through its centre: this allows water to pass through to a sealed chamber behind the valve. The plug is therefore in a state of equilibrium: water pressure is equal on each side of the plug and the valve opens only at the prompting of the float arm – not partly as a result of the pressure of water in the rising main trying to force the valve open.

An equilibrium valve is also useful in preventing water hammer – shock waves produced when the conflict between water pressure in the rising main and the buoyancy of the float result in the valve bouncing on its seating.

Diaphragm valves

A new type of ball valve – the diaphragm valve (also known as the Garston or BRS as it was developed at the Government's Building Research Station at Garston) – has been designed to reduce noise and eliminate other common ball valve problems. It may be made of brass or plastic and has a tough, score-resistant nylon nozzle that is closed, when the cistern is full, by a large rubber or plastic dia-

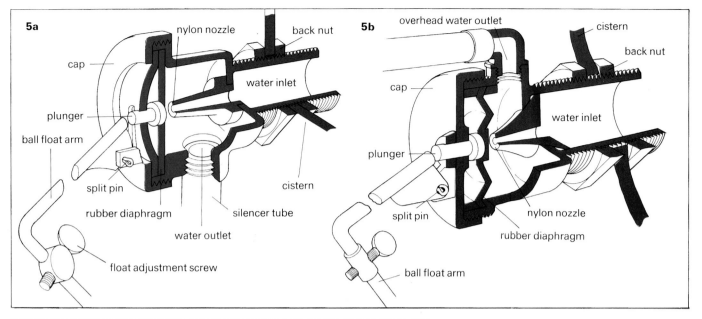

5a
cap
nylon nozzle
back nut
water inlet
plunger
ball float arm
split pin
rubber diaphragm
cistern
silencer tube
water outlet
float adjustment screw

5b
overhead water outlet
cistern
back nut
cap
water inlet
plunger
split pin
nylon nozzle
rubber diaphragm
ball float arm

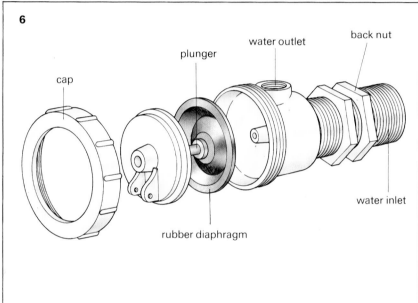

6
cap
plunger
water outlet
back nut
rubber diaphragm
water inlet

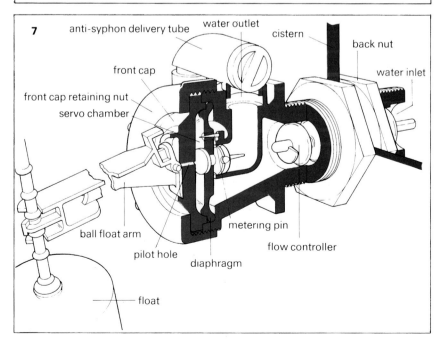

7
anti-syphon delivery tube
water outlet
cistern
back nut
front cap
water inlet
front cap retaining nut
servo chamber
ball float arm
metering pin
pilot hole
flow controller
diaphragm
float

phragm. This diaphragm is pushed against the nozzle by a small plunger actuated by the float arm. All diaphragm pattern valves have some means of adjusting water level without having to bend the float arm.

An important feature of this kind of valve is that it has few moving parts. These are anyway protected from the water by the rubber diaphragm, so the valves cannot jam as a result of scale or corrosion.

Early models of diaphragm valves were fitted with silencer tubes, but since these have fallen out of favour, manufacturers have developed overhead outlets with a distributing device that can be directed at the side of the cistern to ensure silent action. Modern diaphragm valves also have a detachable nozzle which allows them to be changed quickly from high pressure to low pressure.

Poor flow from a diaphragm valve is usually due to the diaphragm jamming against the nozzle or, more likely, to debris from the rising main accumulating between nozzle and diaphragm. The valve can be easily dismantled for cleaning and servicing: to release the nozzle simply turn by hand the large knurled retaining cap – but remember to cut off the water supply first.

Torbeck A more recent development is the Torbeck valve, which has some of the features of the diaphragm valve and some of the conventional equilibrium valve. It operates solely by water pressure acting on both sides of the diaphragm and has been found to be very efficient. It is also silent in action, unlike the other types of valve.

3a To change washer on Portsmouth or Croydon valve, pull out split pin holding ball arm (having cut off water supply). **3b** Push out plug with screwdriver. **3c** Insert screwdriver through slot in plug body and turn washer cap with pliers. **3d** Remove washer and fit new one. **4** Equilibrium ball valve. **5a** Early diaphragm valve fitted with silencer. **5b** Modern diaphragm valve with overhead outlet; spray delivery ensures silent action. **6** To dismantle diaphragm valve, unscrew cap and remove components. **7** Torbeck valve includes features from diaphragm and equilibrium ones

Plumbing in a washing machine or dishwasher

Plumbing in a washing machine or dishwasher involves tapping an existing water supply pipe and taking a branch from it. This can be done using a conventional compression tee; but if you are plumbing into hot and cold water, as is necessary with many machines, you will have to bend a pipe. An alternative and easier method is to use a thru-flow valve which connects directly to the flexible hose of the machine. Or you can fit a control valve, which is even easier since it does not involve cutting a section out of the supply pipe.

Whichever method you choose, you must first turn off the main stopcock and drain the water from the supply pipes you are going to use.

Using a compression tee

Cut out a 19mm (¾in) section from the drained supply pipe and insert a 15mm (½in) compression tee. From the outlet of the tee take a short length of 15mm (½in) pipe to terminate in a stopcock to which the outlet of the flexible hose of the machine is connected. Special washing machine stopcocks with a back plate for fixing to the kitchen wall are available for this purpose.

If you are connecting to the hot and cold water supply pipes of the kitchen sink, you will probably find these run down the kitchen wall parallel to each other and about 100mm (4in) apart. This means the branch pipe from the further supply pipe will need to be bent to pass the nearer one. Make two bends within a short distance of each other so the pipe bypasses the other supply pipe.

Fitting a thru-flow valve

Proprietary through-flow valves provide a simple means of tapping a 15mm (½in) copper water supply pipe for connection to a washing machine, dishwasher or garden hose. The valve incorporates its own 15mm (½in) tee junction and one end of the tee has no tube stop.

Before fitting, cut off the water supply and drain the pipe to which the valve is to be connected. Decide on the level at which you want the connection to be made and, with a hacksaw, cut out a section of pipe 28mm (or 1⅛in) long. Cut squarely and file away any burr.

Unscrew the cap nuts and remove the olives from the two compression couplings of the tee: slip the cap nuts, followed by the olives, over the two cut ends of the pipe. You can clip sprung clothes pegs onto the pipes to prevent them slipping down. Apply boss white to the pipe ends and olives.

Pull out the upper length of pipe enough to allow the end of the tee without the tube stop to be pushed over it. Then push back the pipe and allow the valve to slip over the lower section of pipe until

1 Plumbing in the machine to a single stack system using compression tees. The outlet can discharge over a yard gully or (**inset**) into the main stack pipe. With a two pipe drainage system, the outlet discharges into the main waste pipe (or over a yard gully)
2a To fit a thru-flow valve, a section of existing pipe has to be removed
2b Push the end of the valve without the tube stop over the upper length of pipe; slip the valve over the lower pipe and tighten the coupling nuts
2c Section through the fitted thru-flow valve
3a Marking the hole for a control valve
3b Fitting the back plate
3c The pipe inlet fits into the drilled hole
3d Section through the fitted plumbing-in kit

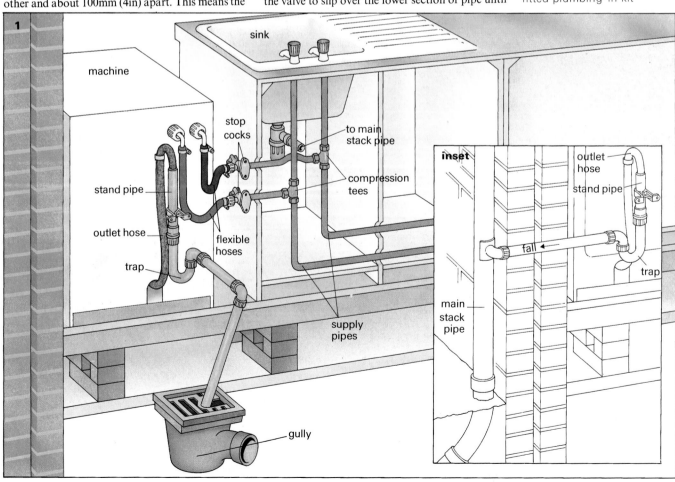

1

sink

machine

stop cocks

to main stack pipe

compression tees

stand pipe

outlet hose

flexible hoses

trap

supply pipes

gully

inset

outlet hose

stand pipe

fall

trap

main stack pipe

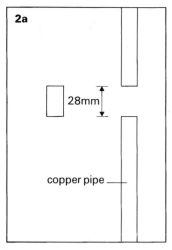

2a

28mm

copper pipe

held by the tube stop. Tighten up the two compression coupling nuts with a spanner. Make sure the plastic control knob is turned to the 'off' position and turn on the main stopcock.

Fitting a control valve

A proprietary washing machine control valve is an alternative method of connecting a washing machine or dishwasher to a 15mm ($\frac{1}{2}$in) copper supply. It is a relatively easy method since it does not involve cutting the supply pipe – you simply drill a hole in it.

First cut off the water supply and drain the pipes to which the machine is to be connected. Decide on the point at which the hose connection is to be made and remove any paint from the pipe at this point, then clean with fine emery cloth.

Mark the centre of the hole on the front of the

pipe with a centre punch, tapping the punch lightly with a hammer to avoid kinking the pipe. Carefully drill an 8mm ($\frac{5}{16}$in) hole at this point, making sure the hole is central, and do not allow the drill bit to pass through the pipe to damage the back. Place the back plate of the fitting behind the hole in the pipe, checking it is correctly positioned by inserting the pipe inlet in the front plate in the hole and ensuring the screw holes align. Check the rubber seal round the pipe inlet is in position; tighten the fixing screws and fix the back plate to the wall, using the screws and wall plugs provided. To complete the operation, screw the tap body into the front plate. You can adjust the position of the outlet if necessary by removing one or more of the washers on the tail of the tap.

This simple method does to some extent restrict the flow of water through the hose. If you wish to

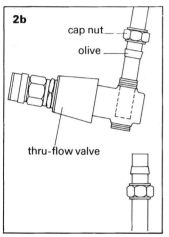

2b

cap nut

olive

thru-flow valve

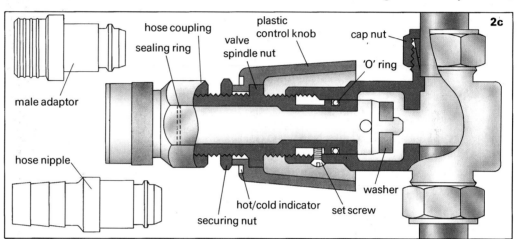

2c

hose coupling

sealing ring

plastic control knob

valve spindle nut

cap nut

'O' ring

male adaptor

hose nipple

securing nut

hot/cold indicator

set screw

washer

use this type of fitting but want a more conventional connection to the water supply pipe, you can cut the pipe and insert a 15×15mm ($\frac{1}{2} \times \frac{1}{2}$in) compression tee with a 15mm ($\frac{1}{2}$in) female iron threaded outlet into which the tap body can be screwed. Wrap PTFE thread sealing tape round the threads of the tap tail to make a watertight joint.

Fitting a self-drilling valve

The great advantage of this type of valve is that you can fit it to the existing system without having to turn off and drain the water supply. First fit the backplate to the wall behind the point on the pipe at which you want to fit the valve. You may have to pack this out to ensure the pipe fits in the groove of the backplate. Then fit the saddle over the pipe onto the backplate and finally screw the valve into the saddle to make the connection into the pipe. Full instructions are supplied with the valve.

Providing drainage

You can dispose of the water from a washing machine or dishwasher by hooking the outlet hose over the kitchen sink. If the machine is not near a sink, however, install a stand pipe outlet and hook the outlet hose of the machine permanently into it. Make the stand pipe with 38mm ($1\frac{1}{2}$in) PVC tubing at least 600mm (or 2ft) long. A trap should be provided at the base and the outlet taken either to an external gully or, where the kitchen is on an upper floor, to the main stack pipe of a single stack drainage system. Remember to consult the building control officer of your local council before making any connection to a single stack drainage system.

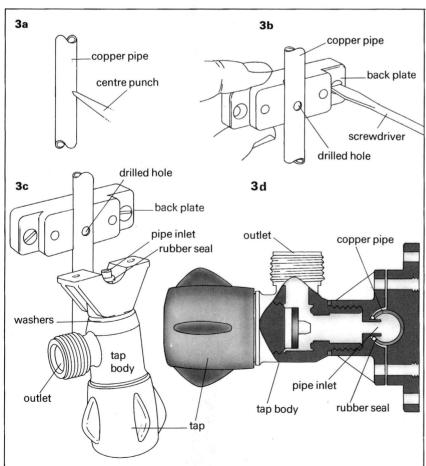

3a

copper pipe

centre punch

3b

copper pipe

back plate

screwdriver

drilled hole

3c

drilled hole

back plate

pipe inlet
rubber seal

washers

tap body

outlet

tap

3d

outlet

copper pipe

pipe inlet

tap body

rubber seal

Fitting an outside tap

An outside tap, with a hose connector, is virtually essential for the gardener or car owner. It saves connecting a hose to the tap over the kitchen sink, which can involve an inconvenient suspension of other kitchen activities and, by creating back pressure within the tap, may lead to early gland failure – indicated by water round the spindle.

Fitting an outside tap is a job you can easily do yourself, particularly if you use a proprietary garden tap kit – you should be able to obtain one of these from your local builders' merchant or DIY stockist. Before you begin work you should get in touch with your local water authority to find out whether, and under what conditions, they will permit the connection of an outside tap to the rising main. Normally this will be allowed, but the authority will probably make an extra charge on the water rate for the use of the tap.

Preparing for installation

Drill a 25mm (1in) diameter hole through the external wall to within 350mm (or 14in) of the rising main and about 75mm (3in) above the level at which the tap will be fitted. You can use a cold chisel and club hammer to make the hole, but an electric drill with a 25mm (1in) bit will, of course, make the job easier – particularly if the drill has a hammer action.

Turn off the main stopcock and drain the rising main from the tap over the kitchen sink – if there is a draincock immediately above the stopcock, drain from this as well. Use a hacksaw to cut a 19mm ($\frac{3}{4}$in) piece out of the rising main at the same distance from the floor as the hole which you have cut through the wall. Make sure your cuts are made squarely and remove any burr from the pipe ends with a file.

An outside tap is a useful addition to the home's plumbing system since it will ease the demand on the kitchen tap when watering the garden or washing the car. You will also be saved the inconvenience of wet feet messing up the floor, buckets slopping water or hose pipe trailing over the kitchen sink

Carrying out installation

Unscrew the cap nuts and olives from the two ends of the crosspiece or run of the tee junction supplied with the kit. Smear the pipe ends with boss white and slip first a cap nut and then an olive over one of the cut ends of the pipe. Smear the olive with boss white. To make fitting easier the tee junction has no pipe stop at one end; pull out the pipe end and slip this end of the tee over it. Push the olive up to the tee and loosely screw on the cap nut – don't tighten it. Fit the cap nut and olive over the other pipe and apply boss white as before, then push the tee up over this pipe end until the pipe end is firmly against the pipe stop. Move the olive up to the tee and screw on the cap nut. Make sure the outlet of the tee is directed, parallel to the wall, towards the hole you have cut in the wall. Hold the body of the tee with an adjustable wrench and tighten the cap nuts with a spanner – this will help prevent overtightening.

Screw-down stopcock Although not included in the garden tap kit, you should fit a screw-down stopcock into the length of pipe inside the kitchen.

During winter this can be turned off and the outside tap opened to preclude any risk of frost damage. Fitting this stopcock will also reduce the time the rest of the plumbing system is not in action; once it is in position – and turned off – the main stopcock can be opened so water flows through the rising main and all the domestic plumbing fittings can be brought back into use. This means you can take your time over fitting the outside tap and avoid possible mistakes from trying to get the job done too quickly.

Cut a 200mm (or 8in) length from the 330mm (13in) pipe without elbow; fit one end of this into the tee in the rising main using a compression joint (cap nut, olive and boss white) in the same way as for fitting the tee. Attach the free end of the pipe to the inlet side of the stopcock, again using a compression joint. Take the 330mm (13in) length of 15mm ($\frac{1}{2}$in) copper tube with elbow attached and push it through the hole in the wall, from the inside, so the fixed connection of the elbow is inside the wall. Carefully measure the distance between the outlet of the screw-down stopcock and

Making the tee junction:
1a Fit the cap nut and olive over the pipe end;
1b Push the body of the tee junction over the end of the pipe coated with boss white;
1c Fit the bottom pipe into the other end of the tee;
1d Tighten the cap nuts with a spanner, holding the body of the tee with an adjustable spanner

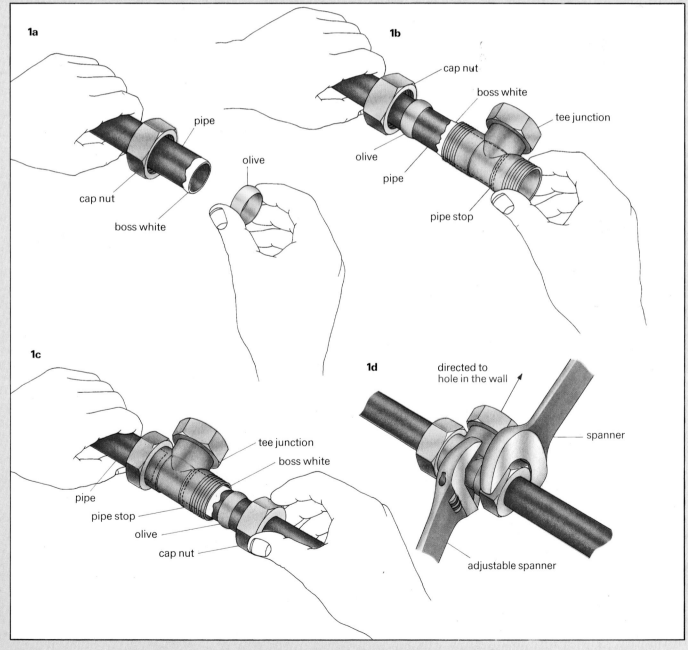

1a
pipe
cap nut
boss white
olive

1b
cap nut
boss white
tee junction
olive
pipe
pipe stop

1c
tee junction
boss white
pipe
pipe stop
olive
cap nut

1d
directed to hole in the wall
spanner
adjustable spanner

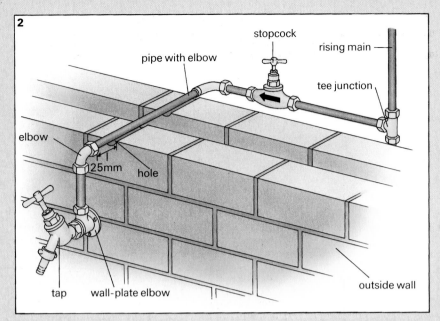

2

stopcock
pipe with elbow
rising main
tee junction
elbow
25mm
hole
tap
wall-plate elbow
outside wall

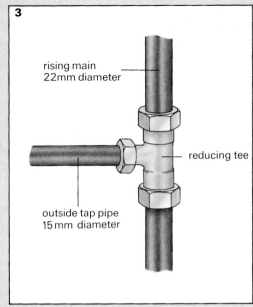

3

rising main
22mm diameter
reducing tee
outside tap pipe
15mm diameter

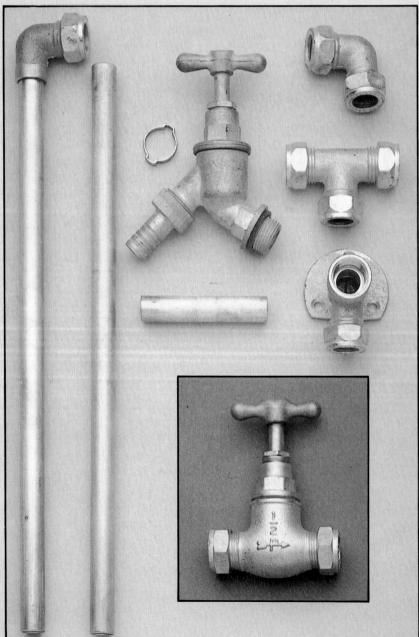

the outside end of this elbow and allow extra length for the pipe which will be within the fittings. Using a hacksaw, cut the remaining piece of copper tube without elbow to the required length and connect the two ends to the elbow and the outlet of the stopcock with compression joints as before.

Finishing off Outside the house, cut the pipe end so 25mm (1in) is projecting from the hole in the wall. Connect the elbow joint to this pipe end so the outlet of the elbow points downwards to the position at which you want to fix the outside tap. Place the wall-plate elbow against the wall, mark the screw positions and drill and plug the wall. Cut the short piece of copper tube to length, if necessary, and connect the outlet of the elbow projecting from the wall to the inlet of the wall-plate. Then screw the wall-plate to the wall. To ensure a watertight joint, bind PTFE thread-sealing tape round the tail of the tap and screw the tap into the wall-plate elbow. If, when it is first screwed home, the tap is not upright, add washers to the tail until it comes to the right position. The tap handle will be angled away from the wall so you can turn it without grazing your fingers. Use an exterior grade filler to repair the hole in the wall.

Warning These instructions for fitting an outside tap apply only to houses with a 15mm ($\frac{1}{2}$in) copper or stainless steel rising main. Some houses, where water pressure is low, may have a 22mm ($\frac{3}{4}$in) rising main and a reducing tee will be needed; this is fitted in the same way as an ordinary tee. Also, in older houses there may be a lead or heavy galvanized steel rising main. To connect an outside tap to a main of this kind, you should seek professional help – at least for fitting the tee junction to the rising main.

2 Section through wall showing connections at the rising main, the stopcock inside and the outside tap fittings
3 Reducing tee connection in rising main
Left A garden plumbing kit and optional screw-down stopcock (**inset**)

Fitting sinks, basins and bidets

Installing a new sink, wash-basin or bidet may appear a daunting task, but it should be a job well within most people's capabilities as long as the correct procedures are followed. The general principles of fitting taps have been covered earlier but there are specific areas of fitting certain units which need explanation.

Fitting sinks

Whatever type of sink you choose, there is one general principle you should follow when fitting it: carry out as much work as possible before you place it in position. If your new sink has a sink mixer tap arrangement, you should fit flat plastic washers over the tails of the mixer before inserting them into the holes provided in the sink top. When you have inserted the tails, fit top-hat or spacer washers over them under the sink to accommodate the protruding shanks of the mixer before you screw home the back nuts.

A special sink waste facility incorporating a flexible overflow pipe is manufactured for modern sinks. Bed this into the outlet hole of the sink onto a layer of non-setting mastic and connect the open end of the flexible pipe to the overflow outlet on the sink, inserting a rubber washer between the frontpiece and the sink. Screw the trap, which has a 50mm (or 2in) seal for a two pipe drainage system or a 75mm (or 3in) seal for a single stack system, onto the slotted waste outlet. For a double sink, only the outlet from the section nearer to the drain is separately trapped and you should take the outlet from the other section to connect to this above the trap, using a 'banjo' fitting, or double sink set, to make this connection.

An electrically operated sink waste disposal unit provides a convenient means of disposing of soft household wastes such as vegetable peelings and dead flowers. If you are fitting one of these, check the size of the sink outlet: it should be 87.5mm (3½in) instead of the usual 38mm (1½in).

Fitting wash-basins

The three basic types of wash-basin – pedestal, wall-hung or countertop – each have their advantages. The water supply and waste pipes can be concealed within the pedestal basin, but a wall-hung type may be preferred where floor space is limited; the latter also gives you choice of fitting level. Usually these are installed with the rim about 812mm (or 32in) from floor level, but you can vary this by moving the hanging brackets. The waste outlet from the basin usually passes through a hole in the hanging bracket. To fix the basin to the bracket, bed the waste outlet into the basin outlet hole on non-hardening mastic, pass the waste outlet through the hole in the bracket and place a plastic washer over the waste outlet before screwing on the back nut. Countertop units take up more space, but conceal plumbing and provide room for storage. They should be sealed into the countertop (following the manufacturer's instructions) and plumbed in in exactly the same way as a sink unit, except the cold water supply is normally taken from the cold water storage cistern, not direct from the main.

Wash-basins are usually made of ceramic, but

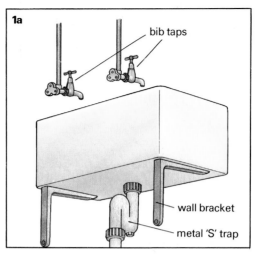

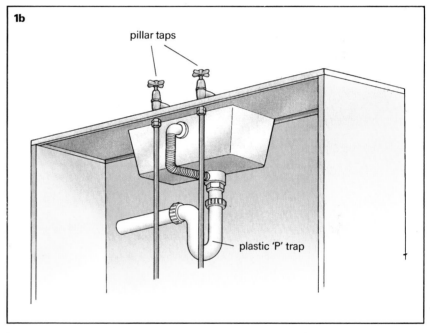

1a Typical old-fashioned ceramic sink
1b Modern sink unit with double drainer
1c Double sink unit with swivel mixer outlet

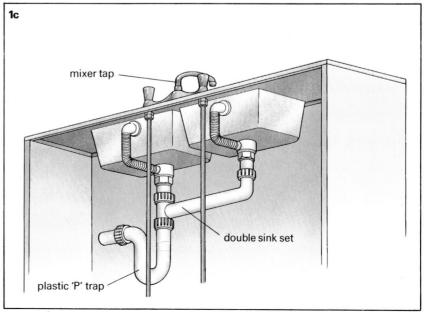

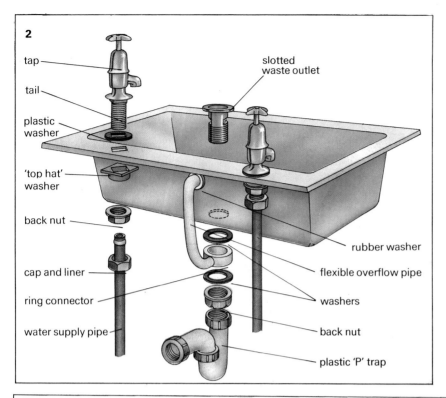

2

- tap
- tail
- plastic washer
- slotted waste outlet
- 'top hat' washer
- back nut
- cap and liner
- ring connector
- water supply pipe
- rubber washer
- flexible overflow pipe
- washers
- back nut
- plastic 'P' trap

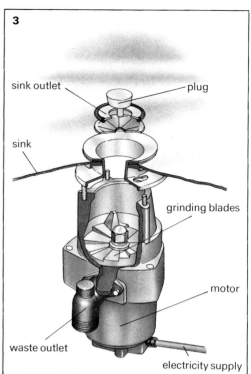

3

- sink outlet
- plug
- sink
- grinding blades
- motor
- waste outlet
- electricity supply

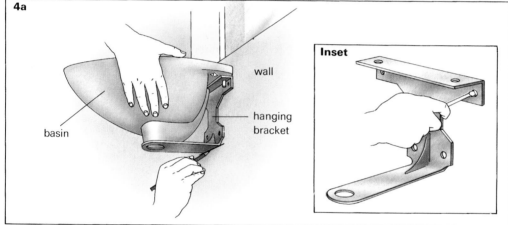

4a

- wall
- hanging bracket
- basin

Inset

2 Installing metal sink with slotted waste outlet
3 Electrically operated sink waste disposal unit
4a Marking fixing positions of concealed hanger for wall-hung basin and (**inset**) screwing hanger in place
4b Plumbing in wall-hung basin
5 Plumbing in ceramic basin
6 Plumbing in bidet with through-rim supply, ascending spray and pop-up waste
7 Installing bidet with rim supply and ascending spray

other materials such as plastic, stainless steel and enamelled pressed steel are also used. Since ceramic basins are made of relatively thick material you should not find it necessary to fit a top-hat or spacer washer under each tap. Use flat plastic washers between the back nuts and the basin and tighten the nuts sufficiently to hold the tap firmly, taking care not to overtighten. The overflow of the basin usually consists of a channel built into the appliance and a slotted basin waste outlet is bedded into the basin outlet hole on non-setting mastic. Make sure the slot in the waste fitting coincides with the outlet of the built-in channel. A conventional 'U' trap or a bottle trap may be provided between the basin waste outlet and the waste pipe. It is better to use either a chromium plated or plastic bottle trap for a wall-hung basin.

Warning Take care when carrying out work on ceramic basins since they are easily damaged.

Fitting bidets

The simplest and cheapest form of bidet – an 'over rim supply' type – resembles a ceramic wash-basin apart from the shape and the level at which it is fitted. It is supplied with water from a hot and

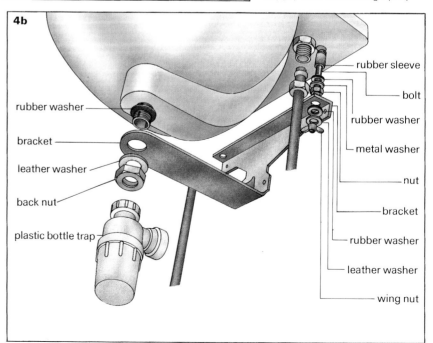

4b

- rubber washer
- bracket
- leather washer
- back nut
- plastic bottle trap
- rubber sleeve
- bolt
- rubber washer
- metal washer
- nut
- bracket
- rubber washer
- leather washer
- wing nut

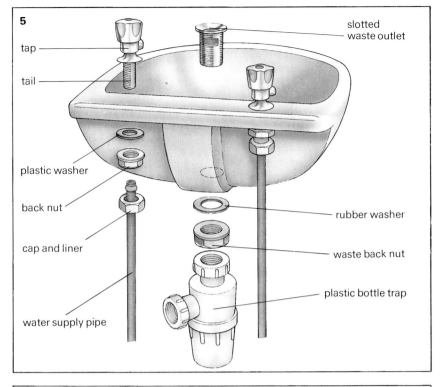

5

- tap
- tail
- plastic washer
- back nut
- cap and liner
- water supply pipe
- slotted waste outlet
- rubber washer
- waste back nut
- plastic bottle trap

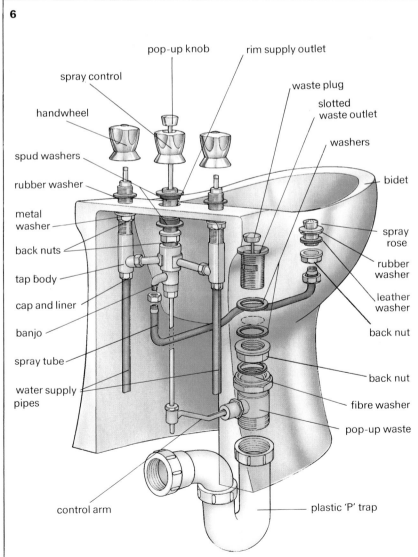

6

- spray control
- handwheel
- pop-up knob
- rim supply outlet
- waste plug
- slotted waste outlet
- washers
- bidet
- spray rose
- rubber washer
- leather washer
- back nut
- back nut
- fibre washer
- pop-up waste
- plastic 'P' trap
- control arm
- water supply pipes
- spray tube
- banjo
- cap and liner
- tap body
- back nuts
- metal washer
- rubber washer
- spud washers

cold tap or, more probably, a basin mixer and the waste is dealt with in exactly the same way as that of a wash-basin. You can provide the water supply by connecting 15mm ($\frac{1}{2}$in) pipes to the existing bathroom hot and cold water supply pipes using a 'T' joint.

The more complex and expensive 'rim supply with ascending spray' bidet presents special problems. In this type of bidet, mixed hot and cold water flows in via a rim similar to the flushing rim of a WC pan and this warms the rim and makes it comfortable for use. By pressing a knob you can divert the inflowing water into an ascending spray directed towards those parts of the body to be cleansed.

You must take special care with a submerged water inlet of this kind to prevent any possible contamination of the rest of the household water supplies. Using a 15mm ($\frac{1}{2}$in) distribution pipe, take the cold water supply directly from the cold water storage cistern and take a 15mm ($\frac{1}{2}$in) hot water supply pipe directly from the vent pipe above the hot water storage cylinder. Never connect the hot or cold water supply as a branch from a distribution pipe supplying any other fitting. As a final precaution, make sure the water inlet to the bidet is at least 2.75m (or 9ft) below the level of the base of the cold water storage cistern.

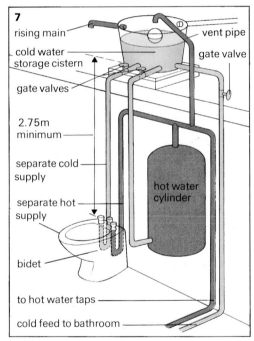

7

- rising main
- vent pipe
- cold water storage cistern
- gate valve
- gate valves
- 2.75m minimum
- separate cold supply
- separate hot supply
- hot water cylinder
- bidet
- to hot water taps
- cold feed to bathroom

Warning Don't make the mistake of assuming that, because of the use to which it is put, a bidet should be regarded as a soil fitting and connected directly to the drain or soil pipe in a two pipe system of above-ground drainage. A bidet is an ablution fitting and its waste should be dealt with in the same way as that of a bath or wash-basin.

Installing a bath

If you want to replace an old bath with a modern pressed steel or plastic one you can do the job yourself, provided you have help to move the old bath out. Modern baths are much lighter than the traditional cast-iron ones and an acrylic plastic bath is particularly suitable for DIY installation, since one strong person can easily carry it upstairs and plumb it in. Pressed steel baths are liable to accidental damage in storage and installation, so care is needed in handling them. This drawback, however, has been largely overcome by the introduction of the 'super-steel' bath, made from material 50 percent thicker – and so much tougher – than ordinary pressed steel baths.

If you choose a bath with taps in the same position as those in the old one, fitting will present few problems.

Removing the old bath

As with many plumbing projects, removing the old fitting is more difficult than installing the new one. Your bath is likely to have been installed many years ago and the plumbing fittings – connected in the cramped, ill-lit space between the end of the bath and the wall – may be difficult to undo. You will almost certainly need a bath tap spanner which can be used in a vertical position in the limited space behind the bath.

Cut off the water supply to the bath taps by closing the stopcock on the cold water storage cylinder or, if there is no stopcock, by tying up the ball valve serving the cistern and running the taps until water ceases to flow. Remove the bath panels (where they exist) and apply penetrating oil to the nuts securing the water supply pipes to the taps and the waste pipe to the bath trap. (An aerosol of penetrating oil is easier to use and more effective than rubbing on oil.) Use the bath tap spanner to undo the nuts connecting the tails of the taps to the water supply and the nut connecting the trap to the waste pipe. If it is impossible to undo these nuts in this way, you can cut through the tap tails and the trap with a hacksaw and the nuts can be turned once the bath has been moved.

The overflow pipe may be connected directly to the bath trap; but in an old installation, it is more likely to be taken straight through the wall to discharge into the open. In this case cut through the pipe and block the hole to prevent draughts.

If the bath has adjustable feet, you can lower them before moving the bath and probably avoid damaging glazed wall tiles around the bath. Either get someone to help you remove the bath or cover it with a blanket (to prevent metal flying) and go to work on it with a sledge-hammer, so you can take it out piece by piece.

Plumbing in the new bath

Do as much of the plumbing as possible before moving the bath into place. Fit the taps or bath mixer into the holes, using a flat plastic washer between the base of the tap and the surface of the bath. Underneath you will probably need to fit a top-hat washer before screwing on and tightening the back nut. Make sure your 22mm ($\frac{3}{4}$in) hot and cold water supply pipes are the right length to

connect to the tap tails and that they are fitted with tap connectors or 'cap and lining' joints.

Bed the 38mm ($1\frac{1}{2}$in) bath waste outlet down, in non-hardening mastic, into the hole provided at the bottom of the bath. Fit a plastic washer over the protruding threaded end of the waste outlet and secure with the waste fixing nut. Fit the bath trap (which will almost certainly have a flexible overflow pipe fitted) to the waste, using a non-hardening mastic and hand-tighten the coupling nut. If you choose a trap without a built-in overflow pipe, you should

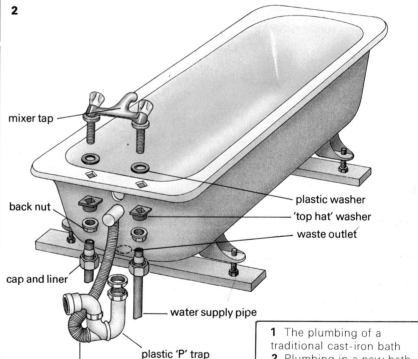

1 The plumbing of a traditional cast-iron bath
2 Plumbing in a new bath with a flexible overflow pipe built into the trap
3 Two types of bath wrench; the adjustable one (**top**) is particularly useful for reaching into tight corners
4 Before plumbing in an acrylic bath, turn it upside down and assemble the frame and cradle
5 The tile-on-tile method is one way to close the gap between an existing tiled area and the bath rim

(labels on figure 1:) adjustable feet; spreader batten; water supply pipes; metal 'P' trap; overflow pipe

(labels on figure 2:) mixer tap; back nut; cap and liner; flexible overflow pipe; plastic washer; 'top hat' washer; waste outlet; water supply pipe; plastic 'P' trap with built-in overflow

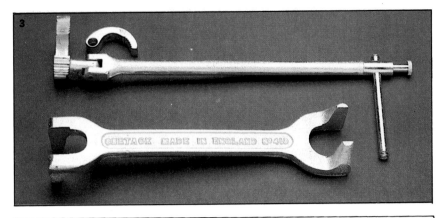

3

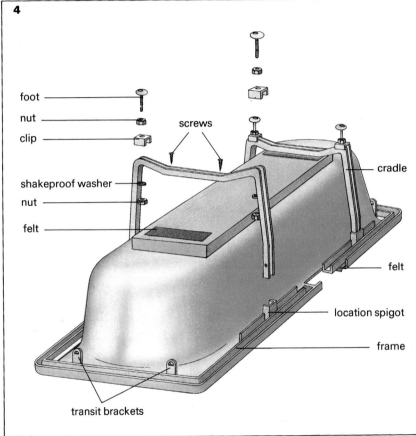

4

foot

nut

clip

screws

shakeproof washer

nut

felt

cradle

felt

location spigot

frame

transit brackets

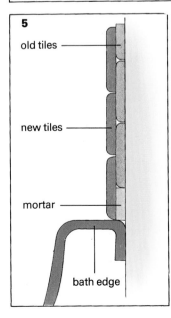

5

old tiles

new tiles

mortar

bath edge

connecting the trap to the waste pipe; but if you are doubtful about fixing, say, plastic to lead, change the waste pipe (and connections) to a material which is compatible with your bath plumbing. This is quite straightforward, especially if, in the case of an older house, you are discharging into a hopper head set in a rainwater downpipe.

Acrylic baths These are fitted in felt-lined frames and cradles to prevent them moving in use. Begin by assembling and fixing the frame and cradle according to the manufacturer's instructions.

If you are using soldered capillary joints for the bathroom water supply pipes, keep the blowtorch well away from the bath and shield it with a piece of asbestos as you work. Use a PVC rather than a metal trap and waste pipe because the thermal expansion which takes place when the bath is filled with hot water could result in the acrylic being damaged.

Coping with settlement

The type of floor in your bathroom is important because baths often take months – and frequent use – before they settle and find a permanent level. Settlement is more noticeable when a bath is placed on a timber floor and sinks into the softwood; it is often accentuated when softwood pieces are used as spreader battens to distribute the load on the feet over a larger area of floor, or as a means of adjusting the height of the bath (this applies even on a concrete floor). Settlement is rarely more than about 3mm ($\frac{1}{8}$in), but may be greater than this if the floor gives under its increased load. Some settlement of the feet into the floor (or battens) does have the advantage of anchoring the bath if it is otherwise unfixed. Alternatively you can use hardwood battens or quarry tiles as packing to avoid settlement. Drill holes in the feet of the bath and screw through these and the packing into the floor.

If the bath area is tiled, any settlement will leave a small gap between the bath rim and the bottom course of tiles; this is not only unsightly, but also provides an entry point for insects and moisture (which can build up and cause rot in the fabric of the building).

Sealing the gaps

If you are tiling above the bath and have not taken precautions against settlement, wait until the bath has settled then lay the bottom course of tiles as close to the bath rim as possible to allow the minimum grouting line. You may want to retile the whole area, particularly if your new bath is lower than the old one; this you can do with the tile-on-tile technique. First fill the gap flush to the existing tiles with a mortar mix of three parts sand to one part cement, then lay the first course of new tiles close to the bath rim, again allowing a small gap for grouting. If you do not want to retile the bath area, you can close any gap below the existing tiles by raising the bath with packing or by adjusting the feet (as described above). Alternatively bridge the gap using quadrant tiles or fill the cavity with a non-hardening mastic.

Quadrant tiles These are available in sets consisting of straight lengths, mitred internal corners and rounded external ends, together with the appropriate adhesive.

Lay out the tiles without adhesive to see whether any have to be cut. If so, always cut the centre tile in each row. Cut them by scoring across the glazed convex surface in the required cutting place, bend-

ht a slotted waste outlet and the overflow pipe must be fitted with the appropriate ring connector. This is slipped over the waste, using a plastic washer between it and the bath, and secured with the waste fixing nut.

Before you move the bath into position, make sure the branch waste pipe that is to connect to the trap is the right length. When you are satisfied all the plumbing will connect properly, move the bath into place and ensure it is level by placing a straight-edge across the rim (widthways and lengthways) and checking with a spirit level. Adjust any fall by screwing or unscrewing both feet on one side or end respectively. The fall of the bottom of the bath towards the waste outlet is built in and need not be taken into account. Make the connections, starting with the supply pipe to the furthest tap, then the flexible overflow pipe (which may be connected with a jubilee clip or a nut and bolt through the overflow outlet), then the near tap and finally the waste pipe to the bath trap.

A number of permutations exist when it comes to

6a If you need to cut a quadrant tile, score across the glazed surface and tap the waste piece with the end of a cold chisel
6b Alternatively score the cutting line and snap the tile with a pair of pincers
6c You can also use a hacksaw to cut halfway through the tile; then snap the tile by hand
6d Always start laying tiles at an internal corner
7a When using non-hardening mastic, apply an even pressure to the tube while pushing it forwards slowly
7b Trim and lift off any surplus mastic with a knife

ing a piece of stiff card around the curve as a guide; tap the waste section with the flat end of a cold chisel to form a clean break. Alternatively, use a pair of pincers to snap the tile. Another method is to saw part way through the back surface with a hacksaw and snap the tile from the front, using glasspaper to clean the broken edge.

Start tiling with an internal mitred corner and continue until you reach nearly midway on that edge. Lay the corner tiles at the other end and again work towards the middle. If necessary the last tile can be cut to fill the gap. Keep your joints uniform for an overall balanced look. Before you stick the tiles down, make sure the top edges of the bath are clean and dry; apply adhesive to the flat back edges of the tiles and press them into position. Don't slide the tiles into place and keep adhesive off the glaze.

Trim any surplus adhesive away with a sharp knife and wipe over the glaze with a rag dipped in white spirit. When the adhesive is dry, grout between the tiles in the usual way.

Mastic sealant This remains firm but pliable so it can expand or contract in the cavity and, unlike a cellulose filler, it will not shrink and fall away. It is available in a range of colours to match popular sanitary ware and is easily applied from tubes. One large tube is usually sufficient to fill a gap up to 3mm ($\frac{1}{8}$in) wide, providing the depth of the cavity is not too great. If the cavity is deep, pack it with sand and cement mortar if you can do so without it falling to the floor behind the bath. This will save a considerable amount of mastic.

Your tube may have a tapering nozzle, which can be cut at marked positions to correspond with the width of the gap. To master the technique of applying it, remember the tube must be pushed forward slowly during application and you should squeeze it out at an even pressure to produce a clean concave line. Ideally the depth of the mastic should be 6mm ($\frac{1}{4}$in). Any surplus mastic left on the bath or tiles can be trimmed off with a knife. Make sure the blade is not too sharp, otherwise it will score the surface of the bath or the tiles.

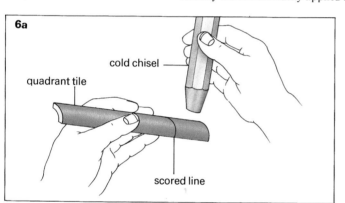

6a
cold chisel
quadrant tile
scored line

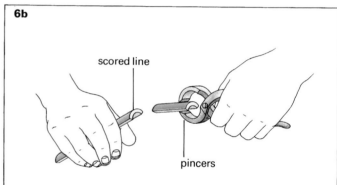

6b
scored line
pincers

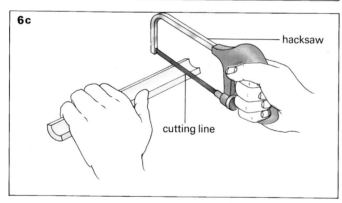

6c
hacksaw
cutting line

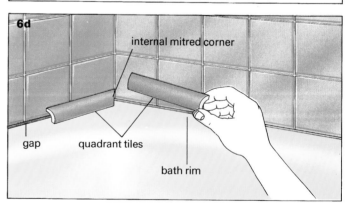

6d
internal mitred corner
gap
quadrant tiles
bath rim

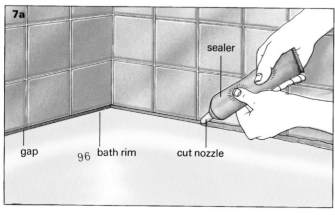

7a
sealer
gap
bath rim
cut nozzle

7b
knife
sealer

Fitting showers

Showers are a useful addition to your washing facilities, particularly since they are so economical with water. Whether you want a unit over the bath or a cubicle, you can fit it yourself.

A shower cubicle can be installed practically anywhere in the home: squeezed into a corner of a bedroom, onto a landing or even into the cupboard under the stairs. You will require a space about 2m (or 6ft) high and 1m (or 3ft) square. Shower units can, of course, be fitted above a bath using a fixed wall attachment or a flexible arm which connects to a mixer tap set and can also be hung on a wall; in this case the plumbing is simplified since the drainage is already installed.

Plumbing requirements

Most types of shower can be installed in conjunction with a hot water cylinder storage system, but there are a number of plumbing requirements necessary to ensure a safe and successful system.

Water pressure There must be enough water pressure to provide sufficient spray and this depends on the height between the shower sprinkler and the base of the cold water storage cistern. The best results will be obtained if the vertical distance between these points is at least 1.5m (or 5ft). It may be possible to reduce this 'head' to an absolute minimum of 1m (39in) where pipe runs are short and there are few bends.

Where this amount of head is not available, the cheapest and simplest solution is to raise the cold water storage cistern onto a platform in the roof space (if there is room) and lengthen the rising main and the distribution pipes by means of compression fittings.

If you live in a flat or ground floor maisonette, it may not be possible to raise the cistern; but you can boost pressure by installing an electrically operated pump: this does, however, substantially increase the cost of providing a shower.

Hot and cold supply You must have hot and cold water supplies which are mixed manually or thermostatically to give a comfortable temperature – and the supplies to the mixer must be under equal pressure. The hot water will be under constant pressure from the main cold water storage cistern and the cold must be taken from the same cistern and never directly from the main supply.

It is not only illegal to mix water from the mains with water from a storage cistern, it is also impractical and dangerous. If you try to do this, the shower will run cold until the cold supply is turned

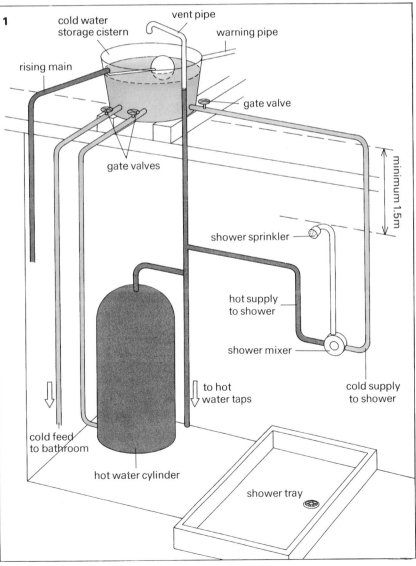

Top right Pre-fabricated cubicles enable you to install showers easily in virtually any room in the home. They can stand in a corner or, as here, fit unobtrusively into a suitable cupboard
1 The plumbing requirements for a shower

Figure labels:
1
cold water storage cistern
vent pipe
warning pipe
rising main
gate valve
gate valves
minimum 1.5m
shower sprinkler
hot supply to shower
shower mixer
cold supply to shower
to hot water taps
cold feed to bathroom
hot water cylinder
shower tray

off, then it will run scalding hot. For safety reasons, the cold supply must be taken to a mixer in its own separate distribution pipe from the cistern and must not be a branch from a pipe supplying other fittings; otherwise flushing a WC or running the cold tap of a wash-basin, for example, could reduce the pressure on the cold side of the shower and seriously scald someone using it.

Bath/shower fittings

When fitting a shower over a bath, the simplest method is to use a rubber tube taken from an over-head sprinkler and connected to the two bath taps by push-on rubber connectors. Such cheap and simple fittings can work satisfactorily if you do not mind adjusting the taps until you get the required temperature.

Alternatively you can use a bath/shower mixer which you buy as a set and fit it in place of the ordinary hot and cold taps. Water flows into the bath while you adjust the taps to the required temperature; you divert the flow upwards to the shower sprinkler by operating a lever or switch.

Showers fitted over baths need either a plastic shower curtain or panels of rigid glass or translucent plastic to prevent water splashing onto the floor. Shower curtains are cheaper, but rigid panels are more effective and give a more professional appearance.

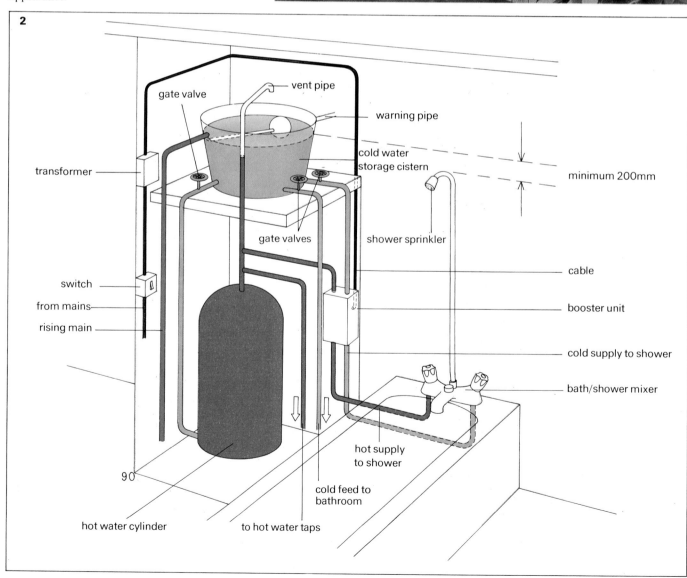

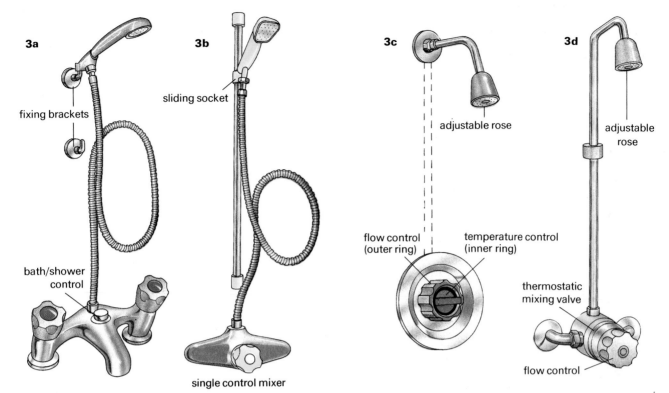

3a fixing brackets
bath/shower control

3b sliding socket
single control mixer

3c adjustable rose
flow control (outer ring)
temperature control (inner ring)

3d adjustable rose
thermostatic mixing valve
flow control

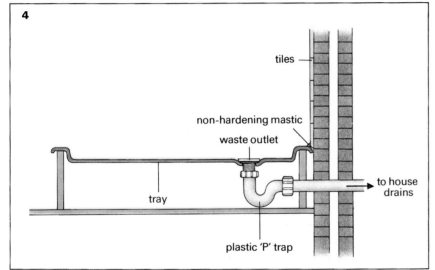

4
tiles
non-hardening mastic
waste outlet
tray
to house drains
plastic 'P' trap

Top left This shower unit fits snugly over one corner of the bath; a plastic shower curtain prevents water splashing into the room when the shower is in use
2 If the necessary amount of pressure is not available, fit an electric booster pump on the hot and cold supply pipes to the shower mixer
3a Bath/shower mixer with flexible hose
3b Single control shower mixer with adjustable height
3c Dual control mixer with concealed plumbing
3d Thermostatic mixer with fixed riser
4 A shower tray and its plumbing connections

Instantaneous shower heaters
Lack of cylinder-stored hot water, or the presence of other plumbing problems, need not rob you of a shower, since you can install an instantaneous gas or electric shower heater. There are a number of models available and they need only be connected to the rising main by means of a 'T' joint and to the electric or gas supply. Instantaneous heaters are reliable, but do increase the cost of a shower. The flow rate is lower than that of a shower run off a storage cylinder and hard water scale can present problems in some areas.

Installing a shower

You can buy a prefabricated cubicle which includes a shower tray or fit a tray enclosed by curtains. You can also fit the shower in a corner and use the existing walls for two sides; angled tube can then be fitted to the walls to carry the curtains. In any case, the walls and floor of the shower area should

be made of waterproof materials such as ceramic tiles or plastic or stainless steel. If using tiles, make sure the fixing adhesive and grouting is water-resistant, otherwise water will seep behind the tiles and cause them to lift from the surface.

Most independent cubicles are fitted with manual mixing valves which mix water to the temperature required by turning a single knurled knob; some also incorporate a flow control. Thermostatic mixing valves are also available; these are designed to maintain the temperature despite fluctuations in either hot or cold water pressure, but will not accommodate the difference in pressure between a mains cold water supply and a hot supply under pressure from a storage cistern.

First cut off the water supply by closing the stopcock serving the cold water storage cistern or by tying up the ball valve serving the cistern and running the taps until water stops flowing. Connect the water supply to the shower mixer using 15mm ($\frac{1}{2}$in) copper tubing. Make sure the joints are watertight by wrapping PTFE plastic thread-sealing tape round the fittings before tightening them. From an appearance point of view you should conceal the pipes in channels cut into the wall plaster or box the pipes in with panels.

To fit the waste outlet to the shower tray, bed it in non-hardening mastic and secure it with a back nut over a plastic washer. For connection to a two-pipe drainage system use a shallow seal trap of 50mm (2in); with a single stack drainage system, use a deep seal trap of 75mm (3in).

Warning With the exception of the bath mixer type of shower, all shower installations require the approval of the local water authority, who may impose certain conditions, such as increasing the size of the cold water storage cistern to cope with the extra demand on the water supply. Make sure you check this out first, before you make a start on the work.

The WC suite

Whichever type of WC you are dealing with, you can carry out installation and repair work yourself. As well as ensuring efficient operation, you may have to mend leaking joints or replace damaged pans.

WC suites can be designated by the basic kinds of flushing action into two main types: wash-down and syphonic. The former, where the bowl is cleansed after use by the weight and momentum of a 9 litre (2gal) flush delivered from a high or low level, is more commonly in use in British homes. Where efficient, discreet and silent operation is more important than initial cost, it is likely a syphonic WC suite will have been installed. This depends upon siphonic action where falling water creates a partial vacuum so atmospheric pressure pushes more water through the system. This gives a larger water area and permits the use of a close coupled suite in which the flush pipe is not visible and where the flushing cistern and pan are combined in one unit.
Wash-down When this type of suite is working correctly, flushing water should flow with equal force round each side of the pan with the two streams meeting at the front; there should be no whirlpool effect as the pan empties. If flushing fails to cleanse the pan effectively, there are a number of faults you should look out for. Check the cistern is filling to its full capacity, a point about 13mm ($\frac{1}{2}$in) below the level of the overflow pipe usually indicated by a mark on the inside wall of the cistern. Also, for a low level cistern, see if the diameter and length of the flush pipe are those recommended by the manufacturer and if it connects squarely to the flushing inlet of the WC pan.

Another case of ineffective flushing is blockage of the flushing inlet and the flushing rim of the pan by jointing material, hard water scale, flaking, rust or other debris. Also check with a spirit level to make sure the pan is set dead level and see if the outlet of the pan connects squarely to the socket of the branch drain or soil pipe. If not, you will have to remove the pan and reposition it (see below).
Siphonic There are two types of siphonic suite:

single trap and double trap, the former being the simplest. It has an outlet which is at first restricted and then enlarged. When flushed the overflow from the pan fills the restricted section of the outlet completely and, passing on to the wider section, carries air with it to produce the partial vacuum on which siphonic action depends.

Double trap siphonic suites have a pressure-reducing device connecting the space between the two traps with a channel through which flushing water passes. The flow of water over this device draws air from the space between the two traps to produce an instant partial vacuum. When the system is working properly you can see the water level in the pan fall before the flushing water reaches the pan. If it is not working properly, the most likely cause is blockage of the pressure-reducing device by scale or other debris and you will have to remove the cistern to get access to the pressure-reducing device and clear the obstruction.
Warning Remember to tie up the ball valve arm and empty the cistern before starting any work.

Pipe joint problems
It is now common practice to use a flexible joint to connect both upstairs and downstairs WCs to the branch drain or soil pipe. The joint may be made with a plastic push-on drain connector or by filling the space between the pan outlet and the soil or drain-pipe socket with a non-setting mastic filler. In older systems downstairs WC pans are connected to the branch drain with a joint made either of cement or two parts cement to one part sand. If this kind of joint were used for the outlet of a WC in a compartment with a timber floor, it would tend to crack and fail due to the movement of the floor-boards; upstairs WCs are therefore connected with a putty joint to the socket of the branch soil pipe. The putty may harden and crack over time, result-

1a Low level wash-down WC suite
1b If the flush pipe or flushing rim becomes blocked, the WC will not operate efficiently
1c Use a spirit level to check the pan is level
2a Single trap close-coupled siphonic WC suite
2b Double trap close-coupled siphonic WC suite
3a Standard push-on drain connector
3b Offset connector where the top pipe is set slightly to one side of the lower pipe
3c Conversion bend; the top pipe is at an angle of about 100 degrees to the lower one
4a You can bring a pan forward by using an extension piece between the conversion bend and the flexible connector
4b Where there is a shortage of space, fit a modern, slimline cistern

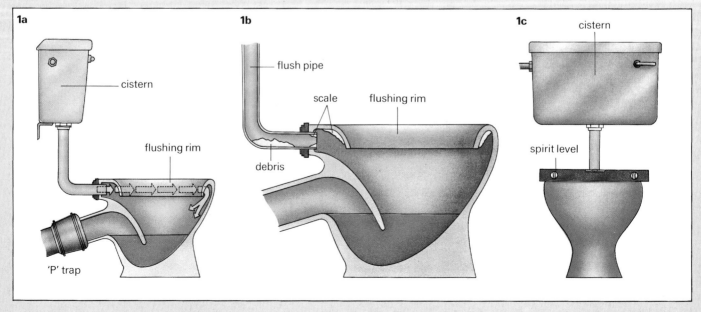

1a cistern / flushing rim / 'P' trap
1b flush pipe / scale / flushing rim / debris
1c cistern / spirit level

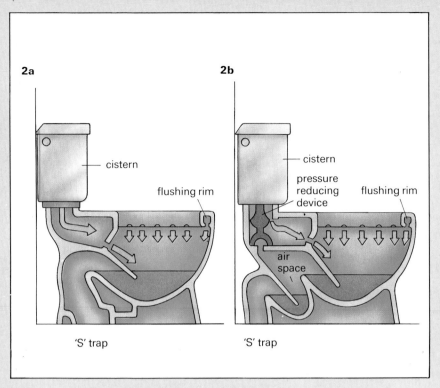

2a

cistern

flushing rim

'S' trap

2b

cistern

pressure
reducing
device

flushing rim

air
space

'S' trap

ing in a leak between the pan outlet and the soil pipe socket; you should deal with this as soon as you notice it.

Generally it is possible to stop the leak without removing the pan. Rake out the existing jointing material and bind waterproof building tape two or three times round the pan outlet, caulking it down hard into the soil pipe socket. Fill the space between the outlet and the socket with a non-setting mastic filler – making sure there are no unfilled areas – and bind waterproof tape twice around the joint. Alternatively you can disconnect the flush pipe, unscrew the pan from the floor, pull it forward and, after raking out the jointing material, replace the existing joint with a push-on drain connector.

Conversions and improvements

You may have to repair your WC system or modernize it for more efficient operation. In doing so you may run into difficulties, but these can be overcome if you take the right action.

Changing level The pan of a low level suite should be 50–75mm (2–3in) further from the wall behind it than the pan of a high level one. If you are converting a high level suite to low level operation, you may find you have fitted the new cistern with its short flush pipe in such a way that the projection of

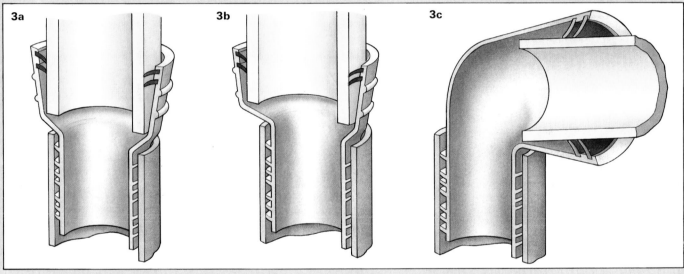

3a

3b

3c

4a

conversion bend

extension piece

flexible connector

WC pan

drain
outlet

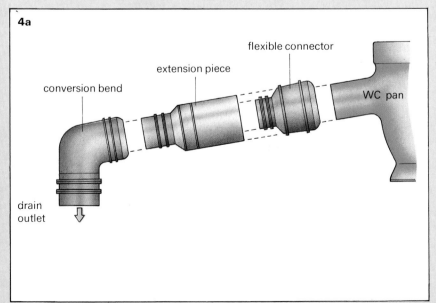
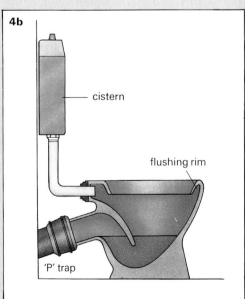

4b

cistern

flushing rim

'P' trap

the cistern makes it impossible to raise the WC seat. To correct this you can bring the pan forward about 50mm (or 2in) using elongated connectors to join it to the drain. This may cause space problems in small bathrooms or WC compartments; as an alternative and simpler solution you can fit a modern slimline flushing cistern or flush panel instead of a conventional low level cistern.

Removing and replacing pans If your toilet pan is cracked or has a crazed surface, you will have to replace it since there is no safe or effective way of renovating it; you should carry this out as soon as the problem becomes apparent. Removing a WC pan in order to replace it where there is a mastic or putty-jointed outlet can be a simple task: undo and remove the fixing screws, disconnect the flush pipe and pull the pan forward. In older systems, however, downstairs WC pans are set into a bed of cement and sand and, if this has been done with yours, you will need a cold chisel and club hammer to prise the pan from the floor.

When you are removing a pan with a cement-jointed outlet, you will have to disconnect the flush pipe, unscrew and remove the fixing screws and break the pan outlet just behind the trap. Pull the pan forward, leaving the jagged remains of the pan outlet protruding from the drain socket. Stuff a wad of newspaper into the drain to prevent pieces of outlet and cement falling in and causing a blockage. Carefully break away the remains of the pan outlet with a cold chisel and hammer, keeping the blade of the chisel pointing towards the centre of the pipe. Aim to break the outlet down to the shoulder of the socket at one point and the rest of the outlet should come out fairly easily. Remove the jointing material in the same way. Try not to damage the drain socket; if you accidentally do so, you can use push-on drain connectors directly into the drain. Carefully remove the wad of newspaper with the cement and pieces of stoneware it has trapped, so none of the debris falls into the drain.

Before installing a new pan, remove all cement from the floor to give a level surface. Don't set the new pan in a bed of cement; fix it down with brass screws, drilling and plugging the floor beforehand if necessary. You should slip lead washers over the screws before inserting them to avoid damaging the ceramic surface of the pan and should use a mastic joint or push-on connector to join the outlet of the new pan to the branch drain or soil pipe. If you find the pan is not set level, unscrew it slightly, lift it up and place pieces of scrap wood or linoleum underneath it.

Warning If you have to leave the pan unconnected for any length of time, cover the drain socket with a board held in place by a heavy weight to prevent rats from the sewer entering the home.

5a To remove a pan with a cement-jointed outlet, break the outlet just below the trap. **5b** Lift the pan clear. **5c** Chip away the edges of the outlet. **5d** Remove the old bedding cement. **5e** If necessary, use packing beneath the new pan

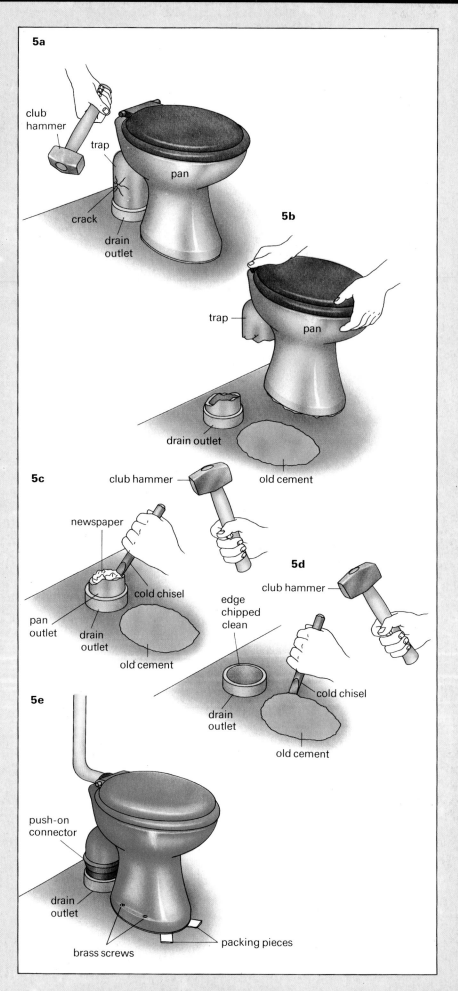

The WC cistern

The fittings plumbed in to any home are in constant use and it is therefore important they are not only installed correctly but also properly maintained. You should know how each works to be able to tackle any jobs yourself.

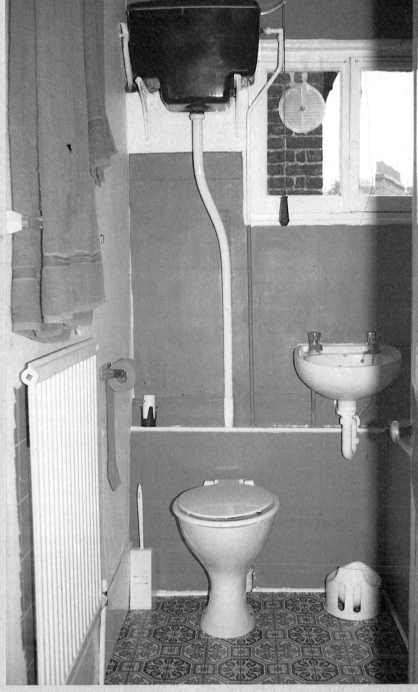

The direct action, low-level cistern (**above**) has now largely replaced the bell flushing type (**above right**) because it is quieter and more efficient in action, as well as looking neater

There are two kinds of WC flushing cistern in common use in Britain: the bell flushing cistern and the direct action cistern. Both are designed to prevent water wastage by delivering a measured 9 litre (2gal) flush, induced by siphonic action, and are therefore sometimes referred to as water waste preventers – or WWPs.

Bell flushing cisterns

This type of cistern is no longer installed when a house is built; but there are still many of them in use in older houses, particularly when the WC is outside. It is made of heavy hard-wearing cast iron and has a well in its base through which the flush pipe is continued open-ended to a point about 25mm (1in) above full water level. A heavy iron bell, with three or more lugs built into its rim, stands on the base of

the cistern, covering the flush pipe extension.

The flush is operated by raising the bell by means of a lever and chain and then releasing it suddenly. As the bell falls, its wedge shape forces water trapped within it over the open end of the flush pipe and in falling it takes air with it, creating a partial vacuum. In this way a siphon effect is produced and the pressure of the atmosphere pushes the contents of the cistern under the rim of the bell and down the flush pipe. The siphon effect is broken and the cistern refills when it has emptied sufficiently to allow air to pass under the rim.

Faults Bell flushing cisterns are prone to noise, corrosion by condensation, and continuous siphonage where, after flushing, the cistern fails to refill and there is a continuous flow of water down the flush pipe until the chain is pulled for a second time.

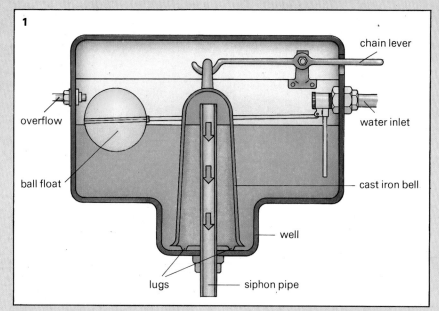

has a flat base and may be made of plastic or ceramic material. A stand-pipe, which serves as a continuation of the flush pipe, rises to above water level and is then turned over and extended to form a dome with an open base about 25mm (or 1in) above the base of the cistern. A circular metal plate is raised within the dome when the flushing lever is operated and this throws water over the inverted 'U' bend into the flush pipe to start the siphonic action. This plate has a number of holes in it to allow water to pass through freely when the flush is operating. When the plate is raised these holes are closed by a valve – usually a plastic disc known as a siphon diaphragm, a siphon washer or a flap valve.

Faults   Failure of the diaphragm is the most common fault in direct action cisterns. It is usually indicated by increasing difficulty in operating the flushing mechanism – two or three sharp jerks on the flushing lever may be required. If your cistern is displaying this symptom, remove the lid and check the cistern is filling to the correct level. There may be a mark to indicate this level inside the cistern wall; if not, adjust the ball valve by bending the

1 An old-fashioned bell flushing cistern – noisy and prone to corrosion and continuous siphonage
2 A modern direct action flushing cistern – the most common fault is failure of the diaphragm

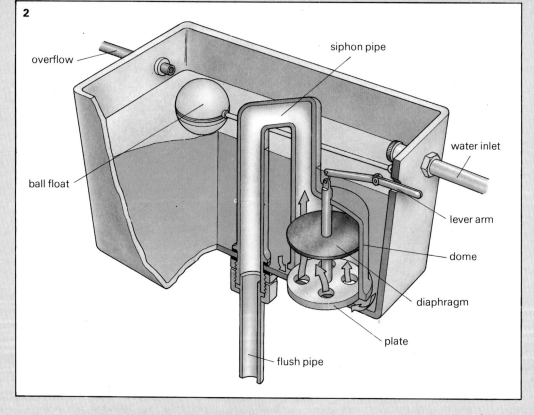

Continuous siphoning results from debris accumulating in the well of the cistern, often coupled with a too rapid refill of water through the ball valve, and the lugs on the rim of the bell wearing away. To solve the problem, clear out the debris, reduce the flow by partially turning off a stopcock control and build up the lugs with an epoxy resin filler. You cannot, however, eliminate the problem of noise.

The ideal solution is to replace the old cistern with a modern direct action one.

Direct action cisterns
For new and replacement work in modern homes direct action cisterns, sometimes called low level cisterns despite the fact they may be installed at high level, are most often used. This type of cistern

float arm upwards to give a full level about 13mm ($\frac{1}{2}$in) below the overflow outlet.

If the water level is correct, it is almost certainly the diaphragm which is at fault. Cisterns vary in construction but the following is the usual way of replacing the diaphragm. Tie up the ball valve arm to prevent more water flowing in and flush to empty the cistern. Unscrew the nut connecting the threaded tail of the siphon to the flush pipe and disconnect the flush pipe. Unscrew the large nut immediately beneath the cistern. Hold a bowl under the cistern as you do this since it will still contain about $\frac{1}{2}$ litre (or 1pt) of water. Withdraw the siphoning mechanism to reach the diaphragm.

When you buy a replacement diaphragm it is unlikely you will know the right size, so buy the largest available and you can easily cut it to the

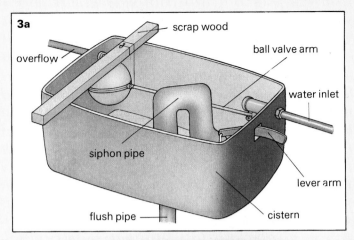

3a
overflow
scrap wood
ball valve arm
water inlet
siphon pipe
lever arm
flush pipe
cistern

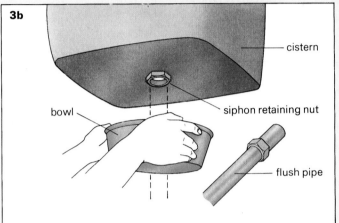

3b
cistern
bowl
siphon retaining nut
flush pipe

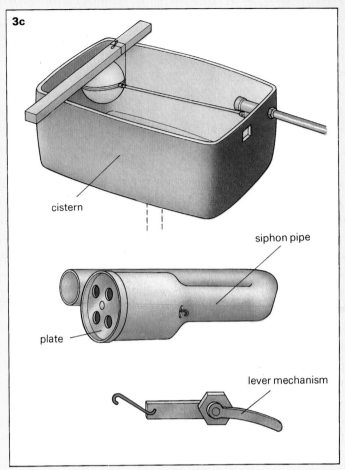

3c
cistern
siphon pipe
plate
lever mechanism

correct size and shape with a pair of scissors. Remove the old diaphragm and place the new one so it covers the circular metal plate completely and touches, but does not drag on, the walls of the siphon dome. Reassemble the cistern and reconnect the flush pipe. After flushing, the cistern should refill and be ready for use within two minutes. Slow refilling may be due to a sticking ball valve, an accumulation of debris behind the rubber diaphragm of a BRS pattern valve or the use of a high pressure valve where water is supplied under low pressure from a storage cistern.

Condensation can also be a problem in direct action cisterns as well as in the bell flushing type. Ceramic cisterns, cisterns of toilet suites situated in bathrooms and cisterns supplied direct from the main are particularly likely to be affected. Beads of moisture appear on the outside of the cistern below the water level and may give the impression the cistern has become porous.

Where a cistern is in the bathroom you should avoid drip-drying clothes over the bath and always fill the bath with cold water about 25mm (1in) deep before turning on the hot tap. Another way of combating the problem of condensation is to provide a radiant heat source and improved ventilation, for example by installing an electric extractor fan. In extreme cases, you can line a ceramic cistern with strips of expanded polystyrene sheet of the kind used under wallpaper. Before you do this, empty the cistern and make sure it is completely dry. Use an epoxy resin adhesive to fix the polystyrene sheeting and leave the cistern empty until the adhesive has set thoroughly.

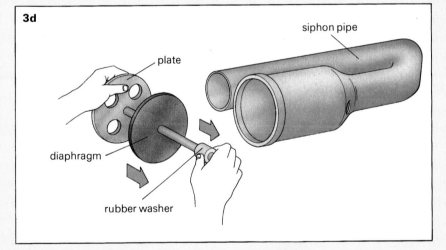

3d
plate
siphon pipe
diaphragm
rubber washer

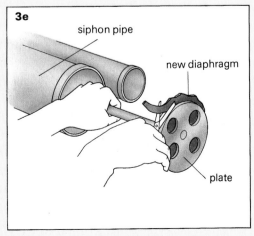

3e
siphon pipe
new diaphragm
plate

3a To replace the diaphragm in a direct action cistern, first tie up the ball valve arm and flush the cistern to empty it
3b Disconnect the flush pipe and catch any remaining water in a bowl
3c Remove the siphon mechanism and detach the operating lever
3d Withdraw the plate from the siphon and take off the diaphragm
3e Slide a new diaphragm onto the plate, trim it to fit if necessary and reassemble the cistern

Fitting a waste disposal unit

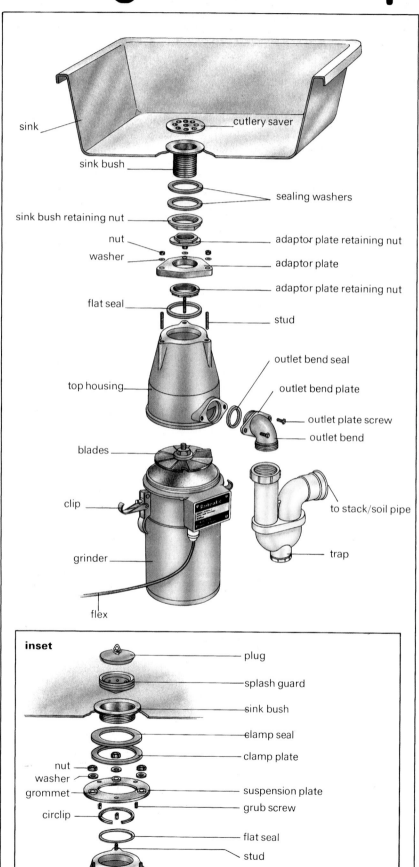

sink

cutlery saver

sink bush

sealing washers

sink bush retaining nut

nut

adaptor plate retaining nut

washer

adaptor plate

adaptor plate retaining nut

flat seal

stud

outlet bend seal

top housing

outlet bend plate

outlet plate screw

outlet bend

blades

clip

to stack/soil pipe

grinder

trap

flex

inset

plug

splash guard

sink bush

clamp seal

clamp plate

nut

washer

suspension plate

grommet

grub screw

circlip

flat seal

stud

top housing

A waste disposal unit fits under the sink and is plumbed permanently into the sink outlet and the waste pipe. Installation of the unit is relatively simple, provided you are fitting it to a stainless steel sink. Models generally fit an 89mm (3½in) diameter outlet hole, although one model is now made to fit the standard 38mm (1½in) outlet – and in another case a modification kit is available. Waste disposal units can be fitted to vitreous enamel sinks, but great care must be taken since the enamel will craze very easily.

Methods of installation vary according to the type of waste disposal unit you buy; detailed instructions are included with each model. It is, however, worth bearing in mind several general points. When fitting the unit, plan the plumbing carefully; never fit pipes where they will hinder access to the unit or any of its controls and avoid tight bends, kinks, tee junctions and stopped ends wherever possible. The waste pipe should not be shared with any other appliance and the waste outlet should be below the gully grating. Bottle traps should never be used with this unit. Make sure the bore of the trap and the waste pipe are readily accessible and check the fall on the waste pipe is at least eight degrees to the horizontal.

Motor Most models have a 420 watt (½hp) capacitor-start induction motor. This type of electric motor, with no carbon brushes or commutator, has a solid rotor (armature); it is characteristically robust and, being a brushless machine, needs no periodic attention and is unlikely to fail in service. The motor should last at least 20 years.

Being a capacitor-start motor, it will start immediately on full load. Some waste disposal units have motors of lower power, but these are adequate for the specific duties they are to perform. Some have both forward and reverse facilities; reverse is normally used to release a jammed disposal unit, although one type operates alternately in forward and reverse – to prolong the life of the disposer's cutting blades, it is claimed.

A self-reversing actuator is available with one model; this can be surface-mounted or flush-fitted to the wall or other suitable surface near the disposal unit itself. The actuator is pneumatically operated and has no electrical connections; the sheath containing the fibre-optic light-guide and pneumatic tube will have to be recessed in a channel if the actuator is flush-fitted to the wall.

Power supply The electrical supply to a disposal unit can be taken from a 13amp outlet – either through a fused plug and socket or a switched fused connection unit. The fused connection unit is preferable, since it makes a permanent connection for the disposal unit and avoids flex and a plug lying loose under the sink when the socket is used for another appliance.

Making connections

Whether you connect the disposal unit through a switched fused connection unit or a socket outlet, the circuit can be a spur branching out from the ring circuit. The connection to the ring circuit can be made at one of the existing socket outlets in the kitchen. To save cable and work, choose the socket outlet nearest to the waste disposal unit provided it offers an easy run for the new cable. Before starting work, switch off the power at the mains and check the chosen socket is not itself a spur.

Run the new cable from this socket outlet to the position of the outlet for the waste disposal unit – which should be on the wall fairly close to the disposal unit, but conveniently placed for switching on and off. Use 2.5sq mm twin core and earth flat PVC-sheathed cable. If the cable is to be surface-mounted, choose white sheathing and knock out a thin section from a one gang plastic mounting box to make an entry hole for it; thread in the circuit cable and screw the box to the wall, using the appropriate wall or cavity fixings. For flush mounting, remove one of the knock-outs in a one gang steel box, fit a PVC grommet in the hole and thread the cable through this; sink the box into the wall flush with the plaster.

Strip about 125mm (5in) of sheathing from the end of the cable, leaving about 13mm ($\frac{1}{2}$in) of sheathing within the box. Slip a length of green/yellow PVC sleeving over the bare earth conductor and strip about 8mm ($\frac{5}{16}$in) from the end of the two insulated wires.

Socket outlet If you are wiring up a socket outlet, connect the red wire to the terminal marked L, the black wire to terminal N and the PVC-sleeved earth wire to terminal E. Lay the wires neatly in the box and fix the socket in place with the two screws supplied with it. All you need to do now is wire a 13amp fused plug onto the flex from the unit.

Fused connection unit If you are wiring up a switched fused connection unit, prepare the ends of the cable as for the socket, but connect the red wire to the mains terminal L, the black wire to the mains terminal N and the earth wire to an E terminal in the unit (some have two E terminals). Thread in one end of the three core sheathed flex and strip off about 100mm (4in) of sheathing. Fix the end of the sheathing under the flex grip and strip off about 8mm ($\frac{5}{16}$in) of insulation from the end of each of the three cores. Connect the brown wire to the load terminal L, the blue wire to the load terminal N and the green/yellow wire to an E terminal. Lay the six wires in the box and fix the connection unit onto the mounting box with the screws supplied.

Remove the terminal cover of the waste disposal unit and thread the other end of the flex through the cable entry grommet. Check the length of the flex; if necessary, cut it to length but allow sufficient slack to lower the motor housing if ever necessary and about 150mm (6in) within the terminal box. Strip off about 150mm (6in) of the sheathing and secure the end of the sheathing under the flex grip. Strip off about 8mm ($\frac{5}{16}$in) of insulation from the end of each of the three cores. Connect the brown wire to terminal L, the blue wire to terminal N and the green/yellow wire to terminal E. Place the wires neatly in the box and replace the cover.

Loop-in socket Turn off the power at the mains, release the socket from its box and knock out another cable entry hole in the box. If this is metal, you will have to knock out a metal blank and fit a PVC grommet. With the circuit cable from the disposal unit outlet neatly laid and fixed, push the end of the cable through the knock-out hole into the mounting box; cut the cable, leaving about 125mm (5in) in the box. Strip off the sheathing, leaving about 13mm ($\frac{1}{2}$in) within the box. Bare the ends of the two insulated wires and enclose the earth wire in PVC sleeving. Loosen terminal L of the existing socket and insert the end of the red wire into the terminal alongside the other two red wires; tighten the terminal screw. Connect in a similar way the black wire to the N terminal and the earth wire to the E terminal. Lay the nine wires in the box and refix the socket to its box.

Releasing jammed unit

The most likely trouble to be experienced with the waste disposal unit is when waste jams up in it. With a reversible action model you simply flick the reversing switch and restart the motor. Since the jamming stalls the motor, however, this will run hot and operate a thermal cut-out. Wait about five minutes for the motor to cool and the cut-out to reset. With a non-reversible action disposal unit a key is used for releasing the jammed unit. Switch off the connection unit or pull the plug out of the socket; by the time the release has been accomplished, the motor will have cooled and the cut-out reset. Switch on and restart the machine.

Left Exploded view of a waste disposal unit which fits into a standard 38mm sink outlet; units normally fit sink outlets of 89mm diameter (**inset**).
Below Waste disposal unit adapted to fit a standard sink outlet
Below right Unit requiring 89mm sink outlet
Bottom right Unit with pneumatically operated self-reversing actuator; the sheath containing the fibre-optic light-guide and pneumatic tube connects the actuator to the unit
Bottom Cutaway of a self-reversing disposal unit showing the component parts

Protection
from hard water

Scale formation is all too common in hard water areas and its effect on the plumbing system can be as dramatic as the damage shown in the photograph opposite. Protective measures should therefore be given serious consideration, such as the installation of a fully automatic domestic water softener, one example of which is shown in the illustration below.

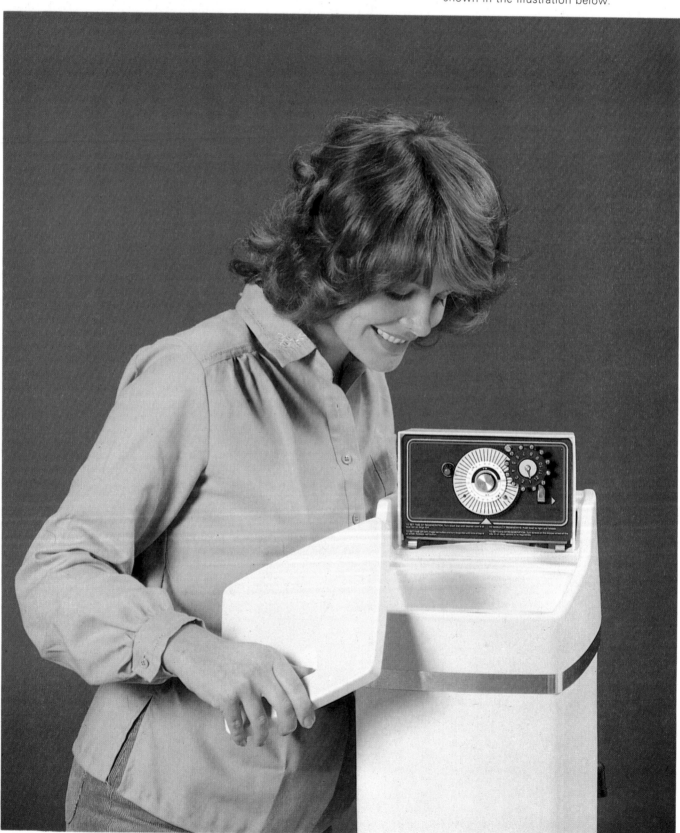

A hot water cylinder choked by scale formation; it became ineffective after only five years' service

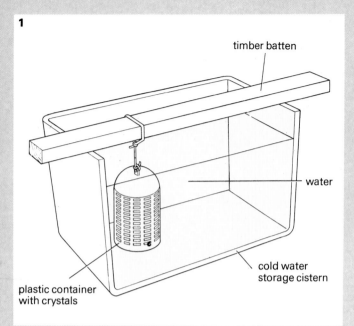

timber batten

water

cold water
storage cistern

plastic container
with crystals

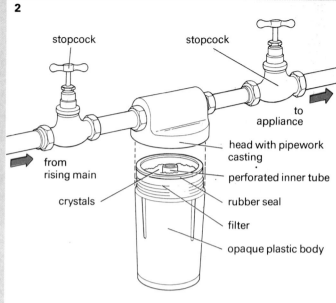

stopcock

stopcock

to
appliance

from
rising main

head with pipework
casting

perforated inner tube

crystals

rubber seal

filter

opaque plastic body

You can tell whether you have hard or soft water by the effect it has on soap. Soft water dissolves soap readily, producing a rich lather; hard water tends to produce a sticky, insoluble curd that matts woollens, produces poor lather from shampoo and leaves a dirty tide mark round baths and wash basins. Another obvious sign is the amount of scale in a kettle; if the kettle regularly 'furs up', there is a need to protect your plumbing system from the action of hard water scale.

Hardness is caused by dissolved bicarbonates, sulphates and chlorides of calcium and magnesium, which are present in the geological structure of much of Britain in the form of chalk and limestone. The natural water table dissolves these mineral salts in varying proportions, so the hardness varies from area to area depending on the source of supply. Water hardness can be expressed in various ways. The most common measurement is parts per million of carbonate hardness in water; for example water of 200ppm contains 200g of carbonate hardness per cubic metre of water. It is generally accepted that water containing between 100 and 200 ppm is 'medium hard' and above that it is 'hard' to 'very hard'.

Excluding the South West and a few small districts, the whole area south of a line drawn from the Wash to the Bristol Channel has hard water. Above this line, the East Midland counties and the North East are predominantly hard water areas.

How hard water affects plumbing
When water is heated to temperatures in the region of 71°C (160°F), the dissolved bicarbonates of calcium and magnesium are changed into insoluble carbonates which are deposited as scale on immersion heaters and the internal surfaces of boilers, hot water cylinders and pipework.

Because scale is a poor conductor of heat, it insulates the water in the boiler from the heat source and, as scale accumulates, more fuel is needed to heat the same volume of water, pipes become blocked and circulation is impeded. Each time the water is heated more scale builds up, insulating the metal of the heater from the cooling effect of the water and leading to burnt out immersion heaters and leaking boilers.

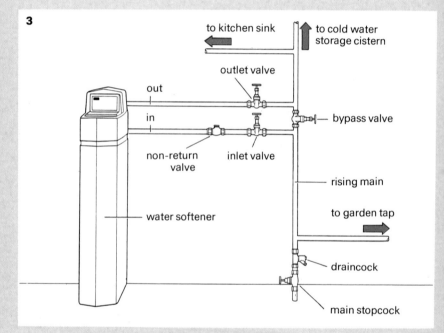

to kitchen sink

to cold water
storage cistern

outlet valve

out

in

bypass valve

non-return
valve

inlet valve

rising main

water softener

to garden tap

draincock

main stopcock

There are two ways of dealing with the problem. You can reduce or prevent the formation of scale by various means, without softening the water, or you can use a water softener.

Reducing scale
You can reduce the formation of scale by various mechanical means or by using a chemical scale inhibitor. Since scale forms at temperatures around 71°C (160°F), you can help prevent it by keeping the thermostat of your electric immersion heater set at 60°C (140°F). If you have a gas or oil-fired boiler, you should be able to keep the temperature of that at 60°C (140°F) too, but a solid fuel appliance may be less controllable. If you have a direct hot water system, you can convert it to an indirect system, which is less susceptible to scale on radiator circuits.

Chemical scale inhibitor Scale formation can be reduced or prevented in many cases, by introducing into the water supply minute quantities of a proprietary non-toxic chemical. It stabilizes the

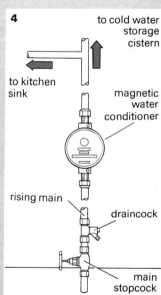

to cold water
storage
cistern

to kitchen
sink

magnetic
water
conditioner

rising main

draincock

main
stopcock

1 A container of scale inhibiting crystals suspended in the cold water storage cistern will stabilize bicarbonates in the water supply so they do not produce insoluble scale when the water is heated
2 Hot water supply appliances fed directly from the rising main, such as an instantaneous water heater, can be protected against scale formation by plumbing a special dispenser, containing crystals, into the rising main
3 An automatic water softener, again plumbed into the rising main, will give complete protection to the central heating and hot water systems
4 A magnetic water conditioner will prevent scale forming in the system as long as water is in motion.

Above You can easily check whether you have hard water by noting the scale formation in a kettle. If it 'furs up' regularly, your water is hard and you should protect the plumbing system
Above right Joints and bends in pipework are very susceptible to heavy scaling, if the scale is allowed to build up, it will impede circulation

bicarbonates in the water supply to prevent an insoluble scale when heated. But it does not soften the water and the effect on soap will be unchanged.

The chemical crystals come in an open-work plastic container which you suspend in the water of the cold water storage cistern. They dissolve very slowly in the water and are effective for six months, when the container should be refilled. There is a special grade of crystals for a combination tank since the water in the cold water feed tank becomes warm because of its proximity to the hot water storage cylinder.

Some scale inhibitors have a dual role. In naturally soft water areas the crystals can protect the system against corrosion caused by the acidic nature of the water. Other crystals can be used to protect hot water supply appliances fed directly from the rising main. In this case a special dispenser is plumbed into the supply pipe leading to the appliance. Fit it on the outlet side of the stopcock in the cold water pipe but as far away as possible from the hot water storage vessel. It can be fitted to a horizontal or vertical pipe. In both cases you need to leave clearance to allow for refilling with new crystals. If you fit a stopcock each side of the container, you will not need to turn off the water at the mains when you renew the crystals. Use the same type of metal for the connections between the stopcocks, scale reducer and storage vessel.

Magnetic water conditioner This conditioner, recently developed for domestic use, precipitates the hardness salts in the water into microscopic crystals by passing the incoming mains water supply through a magnetic field.

The self-powered permanent magnet prevents the normal conglomerates of interlinked crystals forming insoluble scale as long as the water is in motion. The magnetic unit does not affect water pressure and, as long as the individual hardness salts are held in suspension by water flowing, existing scale will dissolve.

The small compact magnetic unit is easily plumbed into the rising main as it enters the house. It can be mounted vertically or horizontally as long as it is easily accessible. Since there is an integral strainer which requires occasional cleaning, it is advisable to fit a stopcock on each side of the unit.

If continuous water flow is required while any servicing work is being carried out, a bypass with its own stopcock may be introduced round the unit.

Softening water
The installation of an automatic (mains) water softener will convert even the hardest water supply to total softness and give complete protection to the hot water and central heating systems.

A mains water softener operates on the principle of 'base exchange' or, as it is commonly called, 'ion exchange'. A container, plumbed into the rising main, holds a specially manufactured synthetic resin through which incoming hard water flows. The resin is not a chemical and no chemicals are used in the softening process. The resin absorbs the unwanted calcium and magnesium ions and releases sodium ions in their place.

After a period of use, the resin becomes saturated. When this happens the softener automatically washes, rinses and flushes the hardness salts from the resin with a salt solution, leaving the resin 'regenerated' so the softening process may continue. All you have to do is put fresh supplies of common salt in granular form into the appliance at frequent intervals to keep the salt topped up.

When buying a mains water softener, make sure you get the size suited to the needs of your household; the supplier will be able to advise you on this. It is possible to install a water softener yourself, but since installation may vary slightly from one model to another it is important to follow the manufacturer's instructions.

The total removal of the hardness salts from water means soap no longer produces sticky insoluble curds. This gives rise to other benefits not possible with the alternative methods of scale prevention. Not only will softened water slowly dissolve existing scale deposits, but it will also make savings on soaps, shampoos and similar items as well as prevent washing machines clogging and dishwashers breaking down.

Recent medical evidence does suggest that the risk of heart attacks is increased in soft water areas. For this reason, therefore, you would be advised not to soften the drinking water supplied through the kitchen-sink cold tap.

Softening water

Most people in Britain take the quality of their water for granted; but the water which comes out of the taps is often far from perfect. Depending on the location it is soft, moderately soft, slightly hard, moderately hard, hard or very hard – and it is these classifications which affect the home to a much greater extent than is often realized.

Types of water

Pure water does not exist in nature. The nearest approach to purity is rainwater, although even this picks up gases, dirt, soot and other impurities as it falls through the air. When it reaches the ground it collects even more impurities, depending on the type of soil and rock with which it comes in contact.

Surface water Scotland, parts of Northern England, Wales and the West Country have a high rainfall and a rocky terrain giving rise to surface water, which tends to pick up organic matter in the form of such things as decaying vegetation and animal matter. This water is relatively soft.

Ground water The rest of Britain, including parts of the North, East Anglia, most of the Midlands, the South and South East, has a sedimentary geological structure; so water drains down to a water table. This ground water dissolves calcium and magnesium, iron, silica and other mineral salts from the porous chalk and limestone through which it flows. This water, with its high dissolved mineral content, is relatively hard.

Hard and soft water

The classifications of water are part of a system of measurement from which you can tell to a greater or lesser extent the degree of calcium and magnesium carbonate hardness in water. This is expressed in parts per million of carbonate hardness or degrees of hardness, as indicated in the following table.

Classification	Degree	PPM
soft	0–3	0–50
moderately soft	3–7	50–100
slightly hard	7–11	100–150
moderately hard	11–14	150–200
hard	14–21	200–300
very hard	over 21	over 300

The effects of hard water can be quite dramatic and it is in the kitchen and bathroom that hard water can be seen to be most damaging – furring up kettles, scumming and discolouring baths and wash-basins, blocking shower roses, leaving stainless steel surfaces greasy and spotty, clogging washing machines and hindering the operation of dishwashers.

But plumbing is probably the greatest sufferer, since scale deposits accumulate on immersion heaters and other heat transfer surfaces; more fuel is therefore needed to heat the same quantity of water. Tests have shown 15 percent more fuel is used when scale is 1.5mm ($\frac{1}{16}$in) thick, 20 percent with 3mm ($\frac{1}{8}$in) scale, 39 percent with 6mm ($\frac{1}{4}$in) scale and 70 percent with 13mm ($\frac{1}{2}$in) scale. This is not only a waste of energy while the scale is forming, but also expensive when it comes to replacement, especially when a breakdown due to scale deposits

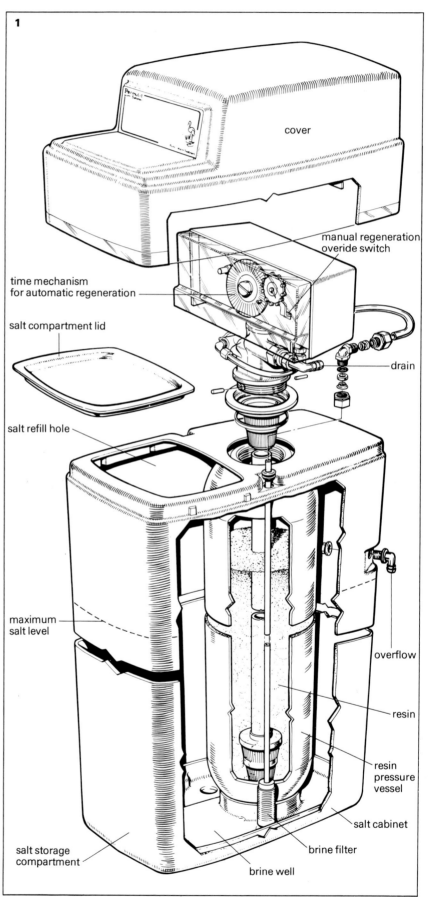

1

cover

manual regeneration overide switch

time mechanism for automatic regeneration

salt compartment lid

drain

salt refill hole

maximum salt level

overflow

resin

resin pressure vessel

salt cabinet

salt storage compartment

brine filter

brine well

can occur within four years in an area of 28 degrees (400ppm) hardness.

It is generally accepted hard water problems become most apparent in areas of over 16 degrees (229ppm) hardness. Most of the heavily populated areas of Southern England are affected; London, for example, has 20 degrees (286ppm) hardness. If you want to check on the hardness in your area, the local water authority will be able to give you the information.

Living in a soft water area is, therefore, of considerable advantage. There is none of the scaling of hot water pipes or tanks which can lead to water pressure problems or inefficient heating systems and soft water will mean lower housekeeping bills, especially those related to soap powder.

Corrosion Naturally soft water can be slightly acidic in some areas and this aggressive characteristic can set up a corrosive action in plumbing systems. The problem can be overcome by adding a proprietary non-toxic corrosion inhibitor to the water system, as described earlier. In any event, the advantages of living in a soft water area far outweigh any of the minor disadvantages. It should be noted hard water is rarely aggressive and water softening does not cause acidity to develop.

Scaling This can be cured in the same way as corrosion; scale inhibitors can be introduced into the water system, as explained earlier. But they

will not, of course, soften water. The installation of a water softening appliance will not only prevent all the problems of hard water already outlined, but will also slowly remove existing scale deposits.

Water softeners
The water softener has existed in various forms since the early 1900s, but it was not until quite recently that automatic machines became available. Modern automatic domestic softeners are designed to blend into most kitchen or bathroom settings and are manufactured in a range of sizes to meet the varying requirements of the house and family.

If installing a softener outside Britain, it will be necessary to check with the relevant local authority since different factors affect water in different parts of the world and the mineral content will vary.

As with most appliances, the bigger the unit the greater the capacity it has for producing softened water. The choice will, therefore, depend on the size of the home and family in relation to the hardness of the water; it is important you ask the manufacturer or your local supplier for advice on exactly the right model to suit your needs, bearing in mind the area in which you live.

It has been estimated the benefits and savings on household purchases related to a water softener can cover the initial cost of the appliance within five or six years.

1 Exploded view of a water softener, showing the relevant parts, including the resin vessel and salt compartment
2 A typical water softener installation adjoining the kitchen sink, showing the plumbing and wiring connections. Here a tap for unsoftened cold water has been fitted to the sink, although this is optional. If the stand pipe discharges directly into a gully, no 'P' trap is required. Only occasionally will you need to fit a pressure reducer

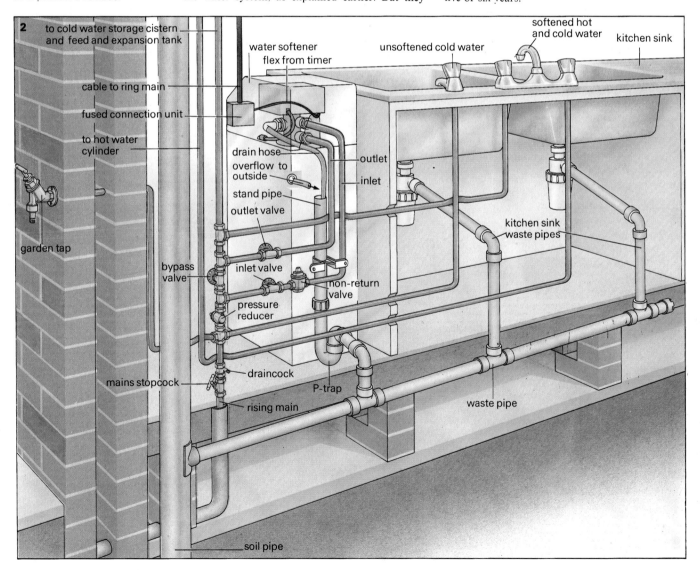

Installing a water softener

Since a water softener is plumbed into the rising main, the positioning of the appliance could be in one of any number of areas in the home. But bear in mind there must be access to an electrical power circuit and a suitable drain outlet. The plumbing in of the average appliance is no more complicated than for a washing machine and is a job which can be tackled by the competent DIY worker, provided the manufacturer's instructions are followed.

Before deciding on the siting of an appliance, remember if you prefer to drink hard water you must leave the kitchen cold tap supplied from the rising main below the water softener – or install a separate tap in this position. If you do keep the kitchen cold tap on hard water supply, you will not prevent the problem of fur in the kettle. Outside taps should remain on the hard water supply.

Plumbing in a softener

Once the water softener has been sited near the rising main and a suitable drain outlet, you will have to alter the existing pipework above the main stopcock. To make any servicing or moving of the appliance easier, you should fit a bypass. Two compression tees and a bypass valve are fitted into the rising main and an inlet and outlet valve suitably positioned in the new pipework so you can isolate the softener from the water supply.

Depending on local regulations, you may also have to fit a non-return/air brake valve assembly between the inlet valve and the appliance. In some areas subject to high water pressure it may be advisable to fit a pressure reducing valve between the main stopcock and the inlet valve to the water softener. This will not only safeguard the appliance, but will also prevent water pressure problems in dishwashers and washing machines.

Waste outlets A water softener has a waste outlet which can be run into any open gully or stack pipe. A standard 32mm (or 1¼in) plastic pipe system is adequate and the fitting arrangement is similar to that required for a washing machine. The hose normally supplied with the appliance for this purpose is cut to length and clipped onto the drain spigot before being inserted into the waste pipe. A second length of hose connected to the overflow spigot must be passed through an outside wall as a warning pipe.

Final connection After checking the new pipework is free from swarf and debris, make the final plumbing connections to the softener and fill it with granular salt to the recommended level.

Wiring up a softener

Most water softeners operate from a 220/240v supply and can be connected through a normal socket outlet. Most manufacturers, however, recommend the appliance is wired to a fused connection unit to prevent you accidentally switching it off. The supply should be fused at 3 amps.

The electrical supply is needed to operate the softener's time clock, on which the regeneration sequence is programmed. This sequence will vary depending on the size of the house and family and the hardness of the water. The programming of the softener is a fairly simple operation described in the manufacturer's instructions.

Operation cycle of a typical domestic water softener: **3a** Service. **3b** Backwash.
3c Brine. **3d** Slow rinse. **3e** Fast rinse.
3f Brine refill

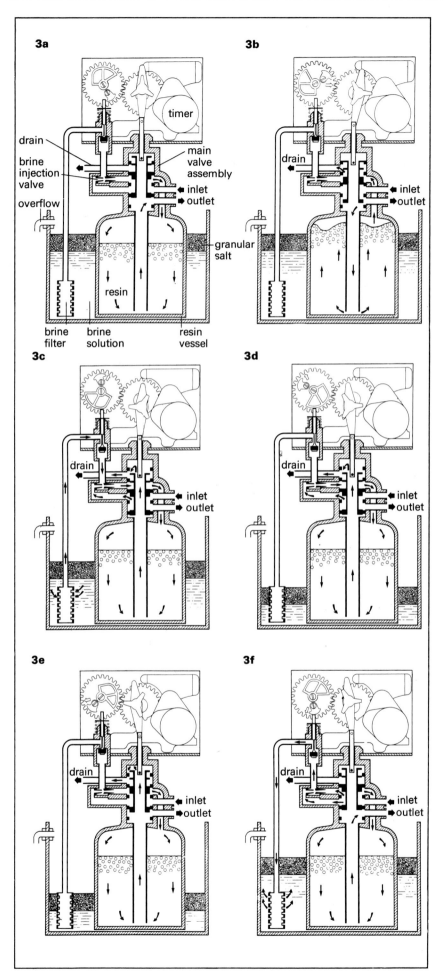

5

HEATING AND INSULATION

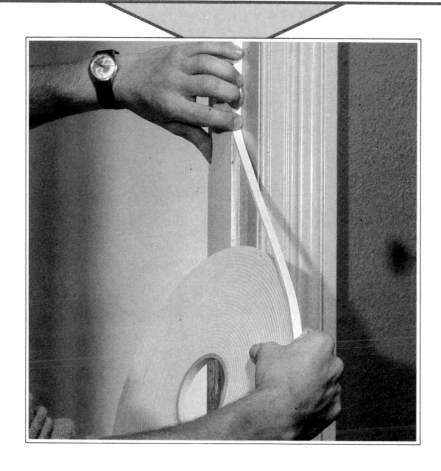

What fuel?

If you are going to install a central heating system, one of the first decisions you will have to make is what fuel to use. This involves a choice between an all-electric system and systems using solid fuel, gas or oil. Each type of fuel has advantages and disadvantages to be considered when you are deciding which system will best suit your requirements. Bear in mind all systems, apart from the solid fuel gravity-fed type, depend on electricity, for example to operate the pump which drives the hot water through the pipes and, in some cases, to power a programming device so appliances are not in operation 24 hours a day; this means they are all susceptible to electrical breakdown and power cuts.

Solid fuel

If you decide to use solid fuel and install an appliance in a fireplace where it can be seen, it provides a source of radiant heat giving physical warmth and a comforting glow with a distinct psychological benefit. Also, modern technology has developed ways of reducing the problems of dirt, smoke and work associated with the use of solid fuel. Some types of solid fuel can be treated to remove some of the volatile matter which makes them burn with a smoky flame; other types such as anthracite are termed smokeless and can be burned in certain appliances without further treatment. A number of appliances can burn a selection of the variety of solid fuels available, so if one fuel is temporarily unavailable another will serve. In some cases, however, selection of the correct fuel is critical if the appliance is to work at maximum efficiency.

There must be adequate space for storing the fuel.

The problem of storage can be considered a chief disadvantage of solid fuel, although once the fuel is delivered and stored you will have the advantage of an independent fuel supply. The more storage space you have the better, so you can buy coal in the summer when it is usually cheaper and store it for use in the winter when it may be in short supply and more expensive. Fuel must be taken from the storage area to the boiler or furnace and ashes must be removed. Appliances with self-feed hoppers cut the need for hand-stoking and eliminate the need to carry fuel through the home; but this does not overcome the problems caused when fuel is delivered, if you do not have a side or back entrance to your house. You will have to remove ashes and clinker, but riddling devices and large ash-pans make this less of a dirty and laborious job.

It is important to ensure the flue is sound before the appliance is installed; if flue defects occur, fumes containing carbon monoxide may enter the room. The flue should be swept at least once a year; but apart from this, if the flue is in good condition and the appliance properly installed, little maintenance is required. Problems may arise where there is an old, oversize chimney flue; in this case a great deal of air is drawn up into the flue causing the loss of useful heat from the room and making draughts likely. With a modern appliance and a standard-sized flue, draughts are minimal and the loss of heat from the room greatly reduced. If there is any doubt about the soundness of the chimney, it would probably be best to choose a gas-fired system since the flue would have to be lined in any case.

Because of the nature of the fuel and the way it

Below left Solid fuel cooker with integral back boiler to provide hot water and heating
Below Pressure jet oil-fired boiler

burns, a solid fuel system cannot operate fully automatically and an element of manual control is needed to adjust flue dampers or temperature regulators. Often the boiler operates for 24 hours since the appliance's response to output demands is too slow to allow programming to take place without overheating; this problem can lead to periods of either over or underheating of the house.

Installation of the appliance itself can be costly in terms of man hours and more difficult when compared with the installation of appliances using other fuels. On the other hand, solid fuel is one of the cheaper fuels.

Gas

This is a clean, economical fuel which does not require storage space on site. Temperature and time control systems are easily applied to gas-fired central heating systems so they will run automatically. The appliances should be serviced regularly; the supply and heat content of the fuel is fully guaranteed by law at certain minimum standards of pressure and quality.

Wherever possible gas appliances with balanced flues should be fitted and these must be installed on an outside wall unless a fan-assisted type is chosen. These can be installed on interior walls, with ducting connecting them to a terminal on an outside wall near by.

When compared with solid fuel appliances balanced flue gas appliances are easier to install. Bear in mind, however, a gas engineer must make the final gas connection and test the system.

Oil

Appliances fuelled by oil have some of the advantages of both gas and solid fuel appliances. For example, once the oil is delivered you will have an independent fuel supply, as with solid fuel. Oil is cleaner in use than solid fuel, but since oil-fired appliances are more difficult to adjust than gas appliances they are not quite as efficient or as clean as gas ones. Balanced flue type appliances are

available and oil is a controllable fuel which can be programmed in the same way as gas.

A large fuel tank is needed to store the oil; this can represent a formidable fire hazard which may affect house insurance premiums. If you are considering an oil-fired system, remember the storage tank must be accessible when deliveries are made.

Setting up an oil-fired system is more difficult than those powered by other fuels. Also, it is advisable – though not legally necessary – to ask a qualified engineer to check your installation before firing the appliance and systems for the first time.

Electricity

This is a clean and efficient fuel and appliances do not require a flue. You do not need space for storage, and time switches and thermostats can be fitted to make a system fully automatic.

Electricity can, however, be an expensive fuel and the running cost may be a disadvantage. Off-peak rates do reduce the cost of operating storage heaters and other forms of electric heating and, if efficiently installed and controlled, an electric system can be competitive to run. Some electric systems can be installed by the home handyman; others require a professional installation.

Top Thermostat for gas-fired wall boiler
Above Control panel for oil-fired boiler
Left Electric storage radiator
Below left Solid fuel gravity feed boiler
Below Gas-fired boiler

Choosing systems and appliances

Having chosen which fuel to use to fire your central heating system, you must decide on the type of system to install and the type of appliance which will be used to fire that system. There are various systems and appliances available which can be fired by solid fuel, oil or gas; there are also various electric systems available.

Warm air systems

Central heating systems can be either dry and based on ducted hot air or wet and based on piped hot water. Warm air systems rely on the distribution of heat using air as a transfer medium which is made to circulate through ducts of an appropriate size by a fan enclosed in the appliance. These systems have the advantage that they ensure a quick build-up of desired temperatures since air is forced to circulate and is constantly reheated; also the systems promote air change and thus ventilation. There are no radiators or pipework and significantly, these systems are cheaper to install in a new property than a wet system of comparable size. Warm air systems are also cleaner than their wet-type counterparts in that problems such as wall staining above radiators do not occur.

While warm air systems are very efficient, they are seldom fitted in an existing property because of the difficulties involved in installing them. A major problem is how to conceal the ductwork; it can be hidden behind false walls or under false ceilings, but this reduces room sizes and makes installation very expensive. These systems do not provide radiant heat, which is sometimes regarded as a disadvantage, and an additional appliance must be provided to supply hot water.

Wet systems

Most of the systems installed in existing properties utilize water as a transfer medium with the associated pipes and radiators. Gravity systems do not have a pump, but large diameter pipes are needed to give adequate circulation. Small bore systems never use copper pipe of an outside diameter smaller than 15mm (or $\frac{1}{2}$in) whereas mini or micro bore systems do incorporate pipes of smaller diameters than this for some runs. Some types of system have become quite complicated with regard to electrical control installation; you will find it easier to install a simple small bore system with pumped circulation to the radiators and gravity circulation to the hot water cylinder, since the design criteria and installation techniques demanded by this type of system are less complicated than with a mini bore system. If the system is to be connected to an existing hot water system, it is worth considering using one appliance to heat hot water and the radiators at the same time; make sure the existing pipework system complies with local Water Board requirements and is of the indirect type.

Small bore Where a small bore system is installed with one appliance heating both hot water and the radiators, the radiator circuit utilizes tappings on one side of the boiler while the hot water circuit

Left This unit, used to heat a warm air central heating system, is gas-fuelled; other fuels may also be used to fire this type of unit
1 A typical warm air central heating system. Heated air passes along ducts and is released through registers in the rooms; air returns into the system through grilles to be reheated and recirculated

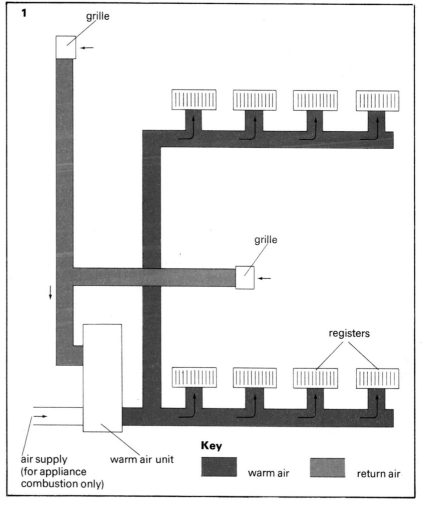

1

grille

grille

registers

air supply (for appliance combustion only)

warm air unit

Key

warm air   return air

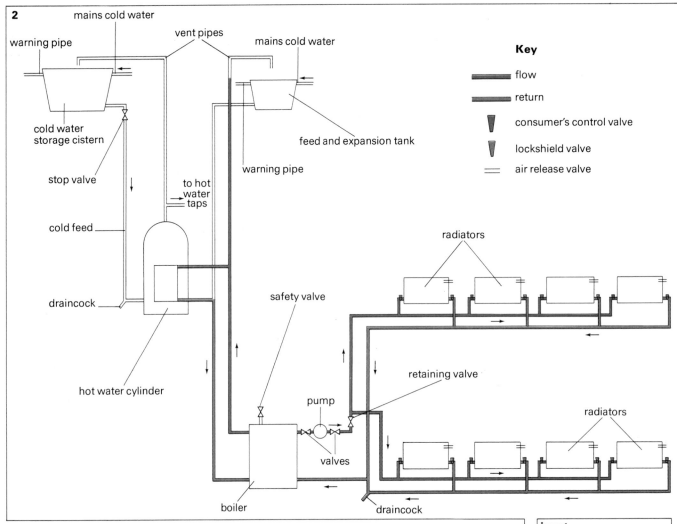

2

mains cold water

warning pipe

vent pipes

mains cold water

cold water storage cistern

stop valve

to hot water taps

feed and expansion tank

warning pipe

cold feed

draincock

safety valve

radiators

retaining valve

radiators

hot water cylinder

pump

valves

boiler

draincock

utilizes other tappings. Some form of temperature control should be fitted to the cylinder to safeguard against overheating of the hot water drawn off at taps, especially if the appliance is gas or oil-fired. If you are intending to utilize the existing hot water system for central heating, you should check the current boiler output; if it is insufficient you will have to replace it with one of the correct size.

If the appliance is to supply central heating only, special attention should be paid to the location of the pump relative to the open vent and cold feed. The open vent must tee-off from the flow pipe before the pump is fitted and the cold feed must be placed in the return pipe as close to the appliance as possible. Where the appliance supplies domestic central heating and hot water, the pump must be located on the flow as close as possible to the appliance before any tees are placed on the flow pipe and must pump water away from the appliance in the direction of the arrow stamped on the pump casing.

A retaining valve, sometimes called a check or non-return valve, should be fitted on all oil and gas-fired installations whether the appliance heats hot water and the radiators or just supplies heating. This is a mechanical weight-loaded non-electrical valve which stops gravity circulation when the pump is not running in the heating circuit.

Extra circuits can be run from the heating flow and return pipes if necessary; but whichever way a system is installed, always make sure it can be totally drained of water to facilitate maintenance.

Mini bore Apart from smaller pipe sizes, this is similar to the small bore system except that the flow and return connections on the radiators are fed with pipes from a manifold. It may be an open system or of a closed type with a sealed expansion tank. The mini bore system has the advantage of less water content than a small bore system and is sometimes cheaper to install. Since the pipe sizes are small a mini bore system is less obtrusive and can be run on top of skirting boards without looking unsightly. The use of copper bending tools is reduced because the pipe is fully annealed and can be bent easily with the fingers; when a system is run under the floorboards, less structural damage is caused to joists since they do not need to be so deeply notched. It is customary to run a manifold tapping to a radiator connection with one piece of 6, 8, 10, or 12mm outside diameter pipe without any joints in it apart from where it joins the manifold and the radiator valve; since there are fewer joints there is less risk of water leakage. Special radiator valves have been designed for mini bore systems.

Types of appliance
Where small and mini bore systems are concerned, appliances can be fired by either gas, oil or solid fuel and can be either free-standing, wall-mounted or back boiler types.

Free-standing boilers, fired by gas, oil or solid fuel, can be conventionally flued or gas and oil-fired types may have a balanced flue. A conventionally flued appliance can be fitted to an existing stack

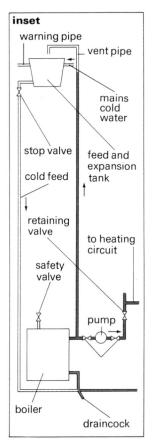

inset

warning pipe

vent pipe

mains cold water

stop valve

cold feed

feed and expansion tank

retaining valve

to heating circuit

safety valve

pump

boiler

draincock

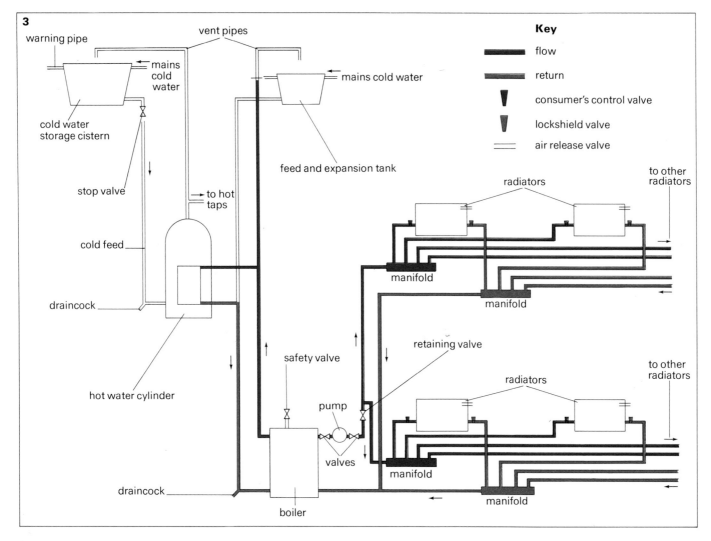

3

warning pipe

vent pipes

mains cold water

cold water storage cistern

mains cold water

Key

flow

return

consumer's control valve

lockshield valve

air release valve

feed and expansion tank

stop valve

to hot taps

cold feed

radiators

to other radiators

draincock

manifold

manifold

retaining valve

hot water cylinder

safety valve

radiators

to other radiators

pump

draincock

valves

manifold

manifold

boiler

2 A typical small bore system. Pipework carries heated water to radiators throughout the home; the boiler heats both the central heating system and the domestic hot water supply. A small bore system can be installed, where the boiler serves the central heating system only (**inset**)

3 A typical open-type mini bore system. Radiator flow and return connections are fed with pipes from manifolds

with a flue liner inserted. Some source of permanent ventilation must be supplied in the room where the appliance is fitted since both the appliance and the flue require adequate fresh air to work efficiently. If possible, it is best to use an appliance with a balanced flue since this results in more efficient running.

Gas or oil-fired wall-mounted boilers with balanced or conventional flues have the advantage that they can be more easily concealed than other types of appliance. Take care when selecting a model of this type since some manufacturers specify complicated pipework systems with the appliance and these are usually too difficult for the average DIY enthusiast to tackle. Also, because this type of appliance is small in size, the output is limited. Oil-fired wall-mounted boilers should be positioned carefully to ensure fumes (which can be more pungent than those from a gas-fired appliance) do not find their way back into the house – for example through a nearby window.

Back boilers have already been covered; oil-fired back boilers for central heating systems are not available.

Which system to choose

Small bore systems are easier to plan and install compared with other types of system. A mini bore closed-type system, for example, is relatively difficult to plan and is best left to the expert, especially since the finished system operates under pressure and this can cause problems at the

planning, installation and running stages.

Selection of appliances depends on personal preference, the position of flues and outside walls, the position of the hot water cylinder and the amount of space available. It is best to avoid the use of existing flues by installing a balanced flue appliance; but if this is not possible, always line the flue irrespective of the fuel. Remember that balanced flue appliances must be fixed to an outside wall. Any hot water vessel fed by gravity circulation must be fixed in relation to the appliance so gravity circulation is not impaired. Sometimes there are occasions when there is only one place where the boiler can be located; if this is the case, normally only one kind of boiler can be selected irrespective of the other factors involved.

Warning Whatever system you decide to install it should always comply with any legal requirements applicable – the Building Regulations and local by-laws, for example – and any instructions given by the manufacturer. Gas equipment and supplies must be finally connected to the gas installation and tested by a qualified gas engineer.

Changes in the Building Regulations have now sanctioned the use of unvented hot water storage systems, subject to changes being made in the water model bye-laws. The layout and arrangement of the distribution pipes for these systems must be discussed and agreed with the local water authority. Proprietary packaged systems of this sort must have British Board of Agrément (BBA) approval.

Designing a small bore system

After you have decided on the fuel and appliance you are going to use to fire your small bore central heating system, you can go ahead with designing the system. Care taken at this stage will prevent disappointment later.

Calculating equipment size

Draw a scale plan of your house showing the construction of exterior walls and their thickness, the area of window space in each room in square metres and whether windows are single or double glazed, the structure of floors and ceilings and the temperatures required in each room. Make heat loss calculations as described earlier; the sum of all the heat losses can be used to estimate the size of the boiler, while the heat losses from individual rooms indicate the size of radiator and the radiator heat output required for each space to be heated.

Radiator size In the example given (**see 1**) radiator A needs an output of 1750 watts to satisfy the heat requirements of the space in which it is fitted. By referring to manufacturers' information sheets on radiator dimensions, the dimensional size of a radiator with an output of 1750 watts can be determined. Remember long low radiators are preferable to high narrow ones since they give a better heat distribution when fitted under a window, which is the best place to locate radiators since they will warm cold down draughts which may enter through a window. Using this method of estimating radiator size means the radiators will be slightly oversize; but an oversize radiator can always be turned down, whereas the additional calculations required to obtain the exact size do not justify the extra benefit derived.

Pipe size Once all the radiator sizes have been estimated you can use calculating tables to work out the pipe sizes needed to connect the radiators to the boiler. You will need to calculate the equivalent heat flow in watts per degree Centigrade. This is obtained by dividing the radiator output by 20 (a standard figure for the temperature difference between the flow and return pipes on the radiator). For example, to work out the size of the pipes needed to supply radiator A (**see 1**) with a heat output of 1750 watts, the equivalent heat flow is $1750 \div 20 = 87.5$ watts/°C; table A indicates 87.5 watts/°C can be served by a 15mm pipe and the water velocity can be kept below 1 metre per second (1m/s) with a pressure loss of 29 Newtons per square metre (29N/sq m). The water velocity must be kept below 1m/s or the noise of water passing through the system would become a nuisance. The pressure loss factor is also important since this is used later to estimate the size of pump required.

Mark the figures you have reached on the plan: the figures in the example given (**see 1**) indicate 15mm copper pipes can be used between radiators A and B upstairs ($3500 \div 20 = 175$ watts/°C). The pipe sizes are best calculated backwards from the furthest radiator in the system to the boiler. The pipe size from the tees at X to radiator C must be large enough to supply the joint outputs of radiators A, B and D: $1750 + 1750 + 2250 = 5750$ watts.

Table A indicates 15mm pipe will be sufficient; but at this stage, at 287.5 watts/°C, the pressure loss will be 230N/sq m.

When estimating the size of pipe from the boiler to upstairs, consider the outputs of all the upstairs radiators (A, B, C and D): $1750 + 1750 + 1750 + 2250 = 7500$ watts. By referring to the nearest value to 375 watts/°C, table A shows 22mm copper pipe is best at a pressure loss of 56N/sq mm.

You can follow the above procedure to calculate the size of all pipes in the circuit except those which supply the hot water storage cylinder; these are sized relative to cylinder capacity as shown in table B. When you are using table B, remember all

1 Typical design for a small bore central heating system in a house with a timber ground floor; if you have a solid ground floor, use a drop pipe system from the first floor

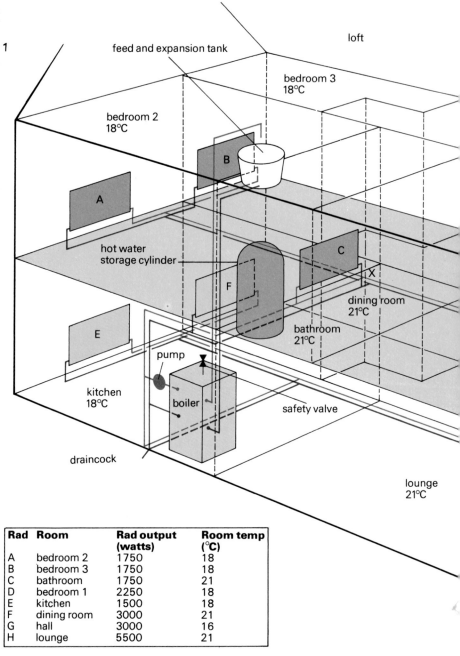

Rad	Room	Rad output (watts)	Room temp (°C)
A	bedroom 2	1750	18
B	bedroom 3	1750	18
C	bathroom	1750	21
D	bedroom 1	2250	18
E	kitchen	1500	18
F	dining room	3000	21
G	hall	3000	16
H	lounge	5500	21

cylinders in central heating systems are of the indirect type.

Once the pipes are sized the type and number of fittings can be estimated by direct reference to the plan; by taking measurements from the plan you can determine the amount and size of copper tube you will require.

Pump size To size the pump you should find the index circuit on the pipe run from the boiler to a radiator which creates the most resistance in N/sq mm to water flow. Use the pressure loss figures marked on the plan to determine this. In the example given (**see 1**) the index circuit runs between the boiler and radiator A; to find the pressure loss in this circuit the pressures indicated on the pipe runs are added together. This figure indicates the size of pump required and should not exceed 350N/sq m; if it does, you will have to use larger diameter pipes on runs with a high pressure drop. Reference is again needed to determine the water flow rate (kg/s) relative to this pressure loss, since pump manufacturers' specification sheets require both factors to be known when selecting the pump.

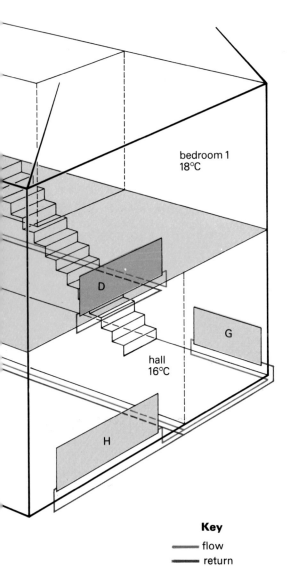

Key

— flow

— return

Table A

Pressure loss in N/sq m per metre run of pipe

flow rate kg/s	equivalent heat flow watts/°C	pipe diameter			
		15mm	22mm	28mm	35mm
0.010	42	9			
0.016	67	18	3		
0.020	84	27	4		
0.025	105	40	6		
0.030	125	54	8	2.5	
0.035	146	71	11	3.5	
0.040	167	90	14	4	
0.045	188	110	17	5	
0.050	209	132	20	6	
0.055	230	155	24	7	
0.060	251	181	28	8	
0.065	272	209	32	9	
0.070	293	237	36	11	
0.075	314	267	41	12	
0.080	334	299	46	14	
0.085	355	335	51	15	5
0.090	376	370	56	16	6
0.095	397	406	62	18	6.5
0.10	418	445	68	19	7
0.11	460	527	80	23	8
0.12	502	*1 m/s* 616	93	27	10
0.13	543	709	107	31	11
0.14	585	808	122	35	13
0.15	627	913	137	40	14
0.16	669	*1.2 m/s* 1025	154	45	16
0.17	711	1140	171	50	18
0.18	752	1263	190	55	19
0.19	794	*1.2 m/s*	210	60	21
0.20	836		230	66	23
0.21	878		250	72	25
0.22	920		271	78	28
0.23	961		294	85	30
0.24	1003		316	91	32
0.25	1045		340	98	35
0.26	1087		362	105	37
0.27	1129		390	113	40
0.28	1170		417	120	42
0.29	1212		443	128	45
0.30	1254		470	135	48
0.31	1296		500	144	51
0.32	1338		528	152	54

Table B

direct cylinder litre/s	indirect cylinder litre/s	pipe size mm
Up to 120	Up to 117	28
144–166	140–162	35
200–255	190–245	42
290–370	280–360	54

Calculating heat loss and boiler size

Heat is a form of energy which always flows from a hot place to a colder one until an even temperature is reached; the greater the difference in temperature, the greater the rate of heat loss. Insulation can slow down the rate of loss, but will never stop it completely; so the lost heat has to be replaced.

In a central heating system the boiler has to provide enough heat to compensate for all the losses. For a hot water cylinder the boiler has to replace the losses and also heat up water which is drawn off for use. It is possible to calculate these heat losses and from there to find the size of boiler necessary for a particular installation.

Calculating boiler size for hot water cylinder

The water in the cylinder is heated by the boiler to a temperature suitable for domestic purposes – usually 60°C. A calculation based simply on this demand would, however, lead to a much larger boiler size than necessary; hot water is rarely drawn off continuously and therefore a heating-up period can be allowed for. A boiler which has twice as long to heat a given amount of water need only be half as powerful – and therefore smaller and less expensive. It is important to strike a balance between usage and heating-up time to avoid having to wait for hot water, but generally a two to three-hour period can be allowed. The total heat requirement is calculated by adding together three factors:

A The heat required to raise the water to the right temperature.
B The heat lost from the pipes.
C The heat lost from the cylinder.

A The heat required to raise the water to the right temperature depends on the quantity of water to be heated and the difference in temperature between the cold water and the desired hot water. For calculations it is expressed in the formula:
$$Q = M \times SH \times (t_h - t_l)$$
where Q is the heat required (in kilojoules), M is the quantity of water to be heated (in litres), SH is the amount of heat required to raise 1kg of water 1°C (known as the specific heat of water – normally 4.2), t_h is the desired temperature of hot water and t_l the temperature of cold water.
B The heat loss from the pipes depends on the length of the pipe run between the cylinder and the boiler and on the temperature difference between the hot water and the air in the surrounding room. This can be estimated from the graph.
C The heat loss from an adequately lagged cylinder can be taken as 145 watts per second.
Example The volume of the cylinder is 400 litres. The cold water is at 10°C and the required temperature of the hot water is 60°C. The total length of 28mm diameter pipe is 20m and the temperature of the room is 10°C. The pipes are painted, but not insulated. (1 litre of water weighs 1kg).
A Using the formula above:
$$Q = 400 \times 4.2 \times (60 - 10) = 84000 \text{ kilojoules}$$
To get the answer in kilowatts (kilojoules/sec) to heat the water in one hour, divide by 3600:
$$Q = \frac{84000}{3600} \text{ kW/hr} = 23.34 \text{kW/hr}.$$
B From the graph (line ABC) the heat loss from the pipes is 62 watts per metre per hour. The total

length of the pipes is 20m, so the total loss is $62 \times 20 = 1240$ watts per hour = 1.24kW/hr.
C The heat loss from the cylinder is 145 watts or 0.145kW. The total heat requirement for the boiler is therefore the sum of A, B and C:
$$23.34 + 1.24 + 0.145 = 24.785 \text{kW/hr}.$$
If the boiler has a two-hour heating-up period, the boiler output needs to be:
$$24.785 \div 2 = 12.39 \text{kW/hr}.$$
If the boiler has a three-hour heating-up period, the boiler output needs to be:
$$24.785 \div 3 = 8.26 \text{kW/hr}.$$
Boiler rating These figures give the output required from the boiler, but unfortunately most manufacturers quote the input figure for the rating. To convert the output rating to the input, an allowance must be made for the boiler efficiency. In addition, an overload factor of 20 percent must be included in the case of any fuel other than gas to allow for

1 Use this graph to estimate how much heat is lost from your pipes: find the temperature difference between the hot water in the pipes and the air in the room (A), draw a line vertically to the curve for the pipe diameter (B), then draw a line horizontally and read off the heat loss (C)

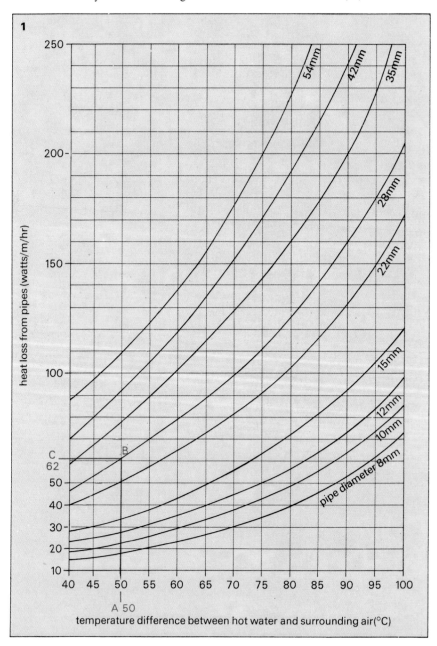

heat loss from pipes (watts/m/hr)

temperature difference between hot water and surrounding air(°C)

variations in output. Therefore the total input rating for a two hour period becomes:

$$12.39 \times \frac{100}{55} \text{ (efficiency)} \times \frac{120}{100} \text{ (overload)}$$
$$= 27.03 \text{kW/hr}.$$

The boiler needed for this installation would therefore be one with an input rating of not less than 27.03kW/hr.

Calculating boiler size for central heating and hot water

To determine the size of boiler required to provide central heating and hot water for a particular property, you must calculate initially the heat loss from the relevant area. Heat is lost in two ways:
A Through the fabric of the building.
B By ventilation.

A The rate of heat loss through the fabric depends on the thermal transmittance (or 'U' value), the area of the surface and the temperature difference between the inside and outside air. The 'U' value is a property of the material – or combination of materials – in the construction and can be found from specially prepared tables (such as in the *Institution of Plumbing: Data* book, which should be available through your local library). An area of different material, such as a window, has a different 'U' value and must be calculated separately from the rest of the wall. For calculations the heat loss through the fabric is expressed in the formula:

$$Q = A \times U \times (t_h - t_l)$$

where Q is the heat loss, A is the area of each separate material, U is the 'U' value of the construction, t_h the desired room temperature and t_l the outside air temperature.

The outside air temperature is taken as $-1°C$ in Britain. For an internal wall of a room, t is taken as the temperature on the other side of the wall; if this is the same as the temperature in the room – or higher – there is no heat loss.
B Heat loss through ventilation depends on the volume of the room, the number of air changes per hour and the difference in temperature between the room air and the outside air. For calculations the heat loss is expressed in the following formula:

$$Q = M \times N \times SH \times (t_h - t_l)$$

where Q is the total heat loss, M is the volume of the room, N is the number of air changes per hour (see table), the specific heat of air (1.21kJ/m³/°C at 16°C). t_h the desired room temperature and t_l the outside air temperature.
Example The dimensions of the room are as shown on the plan. The ceiling height is 2.8m and the window is 2m high and 2.5m wide. The floor is timber on joists, with an airbrick below. The ceiling is plasterboard on joists, with a timber floor above and a temperature of 16°C in the room above. The rooms are of average exposure. Rooms are said to be exposed when the building is on a hillside, at the coast or on the riverside – and when it has an outside wall facing north, north-east or east. The 'U' value tables give two sets of readings – for average and exposed rooms.
A Using the formula above:

$$Q = A \times U \times (t_h - t_l)$$

the heat loss must be calculated for all the surfaces in the room. You must first list the relevant surfaces and work out their areas:
outside wall $A = 4.0 \times 2.8 = 11.2\text{m}^2$
outside wall $B = (3.5 \times 2.8) - (2.5 \times 2) = 4.8\text{m}^2$
window $C = 2.5 \times 2 = 5.0\text{m}^2$

partition wall $E = 4.0 \times 2.8 = 11.2\text{m}^2$
floor $= 3.5 \times 4.0 = 14.0\text{m}^2$
ceiling $= 3.5 \times 4.0 = 14.0\text{m}^2$
The partition wall D is not included in the calculations since the temperature is the same on both sides. The 'U' values for each surface can be found from the specially prepared tables (see above). The room temperature required is 21°C and the outside temperature is $-1°C$. The heat loss for the outside wall A will therefore be:
$$Q = 11.2 \times 1.5 \times [21 - (-1)] = 369.6 \text{ watts}$$
Follow the same procedure for all the surfaces and add the amounts together. The total heat loss for the room will be:
$$369.6 + 158.4 + 473.0 + 98.0 + 187.88 + 119.0$$
$$= 1405.88 \text{ watts}$$
B The volume of the room is 39.2m³ (3.5 × 4.0 × 2.8m³). The number of air changes per hour is taken as 2 (see table). The required room temperature is 21°C and the outside temperature is $-1°C$, as above. The heat loss through ventilation will therefore be:
$$Q = 2 \times 39.2 \times 1.21 \times [21 - (-1)] = 2087.01 \text{kW/sec}$$
or 0.58kW/hr
Therefore the total heat loss from the room is:
1.406kW + 0.58kW = 1.99kW.
The heat losses from each room have to be added together to give the heat loss for the whole house – and hence the boiler output rating. The boiler input rating is derived from this in the same way as for the hot water cylinder.

If there is a combined boiler for central heating and hot water, it is only necessary to calculate the requirements for the central heating and add on an extra 1kW for the hot water, if the hot water cylinder is no larger than 140 litres.

2 This room has been taken as an example from which to work out heat losses through the fabric of the building
3 The recommended number of air changes for particular rooms and the temperatures which should be maintained in those rooms when the outside temperature is $-1°C$

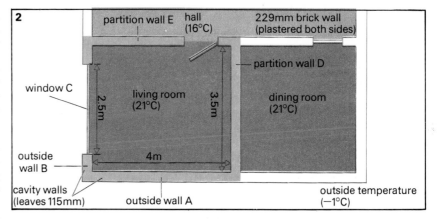

2
partition wall E | hall (16°C) | 229mm brick wall (plastered both sides)
partition wall D
window C
living room (21°C)
dining room (21°C)
2.5m · 3.5m
outside wall B
4m
cavity walls (leaves 115mm)
outside wall A
outside temperature (−1°C)

3 Room	Desired temperature	Air changes/hr
Living room		1½-2
Dining room	21°C	1½-2
Bedsitter		1½-2
Bathroom		2
Hall or landing		2
Toilet	16°C	1½
Bedroom		1
Kitchen	18°C	2

Controlling a small bore system

If you are installing a central heating system yourself, it is likely you will choose a small bore system because this type is less complex and involves a relatively small capital outlay compared with other systems. At the design stage it is essential to consider the type of temperature control which will be used on the system to maintain maximum standards of economy and safety. Most appliances, especially those which are gas or oil-fired, have integral controls fitted to them to ensure minimum standards of safety; but care must be taken when installing the system and wiring up the controls to make sure these inbuilt safety factors do not malfunction or are not overridden.

Types of control

With a system which has gravity circulation to the hot water storage cylinder and pumped water to the radiators and where there is a gas or oil-fired boiler, three factors need to be controlled; the time you want the system functioning, the temperature of the water stored in the hot water storage cylinder and the temperature of the rooms and living spaces in the house. With a solid fuel boiler only two factors need to be controlled: the ambient temperature and the water temperature in the hot water storage cylinder. Time control on a solid fuel appliance is not feasible since the boiler runs continuously. Methods of control can be either mechanical or electrical.

Mechanical controls If you choose a mechanical method, you can control the hot water storage temperature by fitting a thermostatic control on the cylinder or the pipes which run to or from it. Some manual control of room or living space tem-

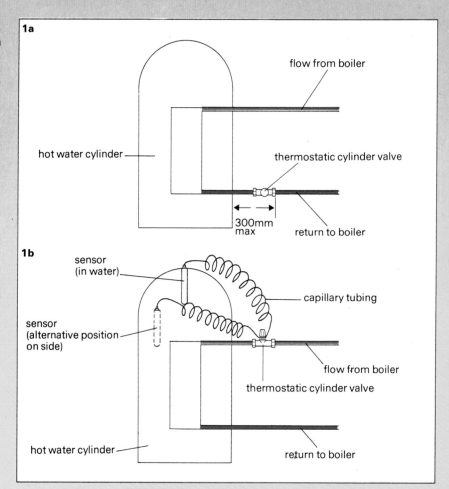

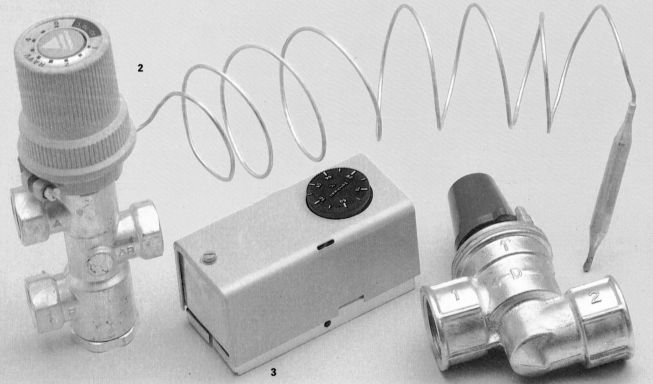

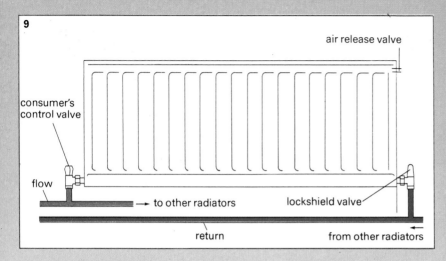

9

air release valve

consumer's control valve

flow

→ to other radiators

return

lockshield valve

from other radiators

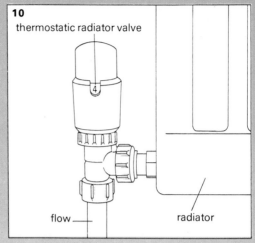

10

thermostatic radiator valve

flow

radiator

perature can be achieved by fitting a consumer's control valve to the flow pipe on each radiator; but this will only turn the radiator on or off. To achieve further control you can fit a thermostatic radiator valve in place of the control valve.

On the return pipe of each radiator there is a lockshield valve which is used by the installer to balance the system along with all the other lockshield valves in the system. An air release valve, which may be an integral part of the radiator or may need to be fitted to the radiator using PTFE tape or hemp, is used to remove air from the radiator, in particular when filling the system.

Electrical controls Systems of electrical control are more complex; but since either the boiler and/or the pump require electricity anyway, it can be more economical and functional to use electricity for control systems in most cases. A basic wiring system involving a boiler with electrical controls and a pump is where the pump and boiler are wired in parallel, usually through a switched fused connection unit. However, this type of system will not operate automatically and this could be inconvenient.

Remember earth connections must be made to all appliances and controls, unless otherwise stated by the manufacturer, to maintain maximum safety.

To provide time control in a simple system a clock can be used to turn a system on or off at pre-arranged times, while there is a separate manual control of the central heating pump. The temperature of the water is determined by the boiler's operational temperature and gravity circulation between the boiler and the hot water storage cylinder.

You can achieve improved control and a reduction in running costs by operating the pump automatically with a room temperature control thermostat. It is also worth fitting a clock with a selector, known as a programmer, which will allow you to choose different programmes related to your hot water and heating requirements. This type of control system provides adequate control of the heating circuit, but still leaves the domestic water supply stored in the cylinder to be heated to the operation temperature of the boiler of say 82°C (or 180°F). A hot water temperature of 60°C (or 140°F) is quite adequate for purposes of household

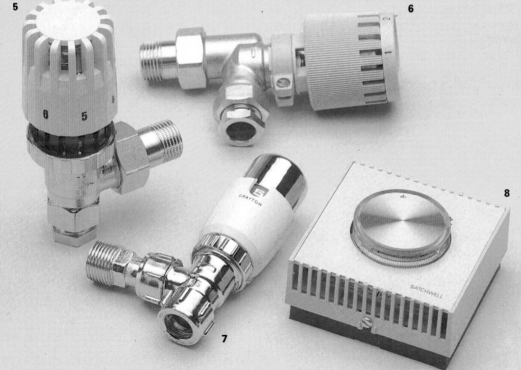

5

6

7

8

1a Thermostatic cylinder valve, with self-contained sensor, fitted on return pipe to boiler within 300mm of hot water cylinder
1b Thermostatic cylinder valve fitted on flow pipe from boiler with remote sensor in cylinder; the valve is pressure operated and has a small by-pass connecting to the indirect vent pipe to prevent pressure build-up when the valve is closed
2 Thermostatic cylinder valve with remote sensor
3 Cylinder thermostat which straps onto the cylinder and should be wired to the boiler
4 Thermostatic cylinder valve with self-contained sensor
5, 6, 7 Thermostatic radiator valves
8 Room thermostat
9 Radiator connections
10 Thermostatic radiator valve with numbered ring fitted instead of consumer control valve

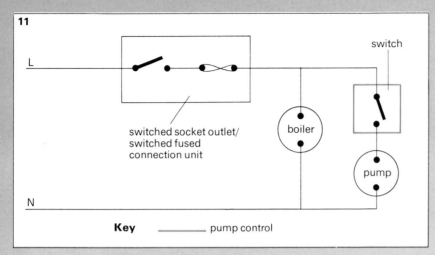

11

L

switch

switched socket outlet/
switched fused
connection unit

boiler

pump

N

Key ———— pump control

use, including general chores such as washing up.

You can partially overcome this problem by fitting a cylinder thermostat on the cylinder. This circuit also prevents the boiler switching on and off to make up its own rate of heat loss; since this is a common source of energy wastage in domestic systems, this addition results in substantial savings in running costs.

You may decide to use a combination of controls; for example, an electrical room thermostat to control the heating and a mechanical temperature control on the cylinder. Most manufacturers of control equipment provide detailed instructions on the application and installation of more elaborate control systems; but it is worth thinking carefully before you contemplate such systems since they may be too complicated for the average home handyman to install safely.

11 Basic wiring system which is operated manually (earth omitted)
12 Wiring system providing automatic time control with manual control of pump (earth omitted)
13 Wiring system with programmer and room thermostat to control the pump and hot water automatically (earth omitted)
14 Cylinder thermostat added to previous system to provide some temperature control for domestic hot water (earth omitted)
15 Time switch
16, 17, 18 Four types of programmer

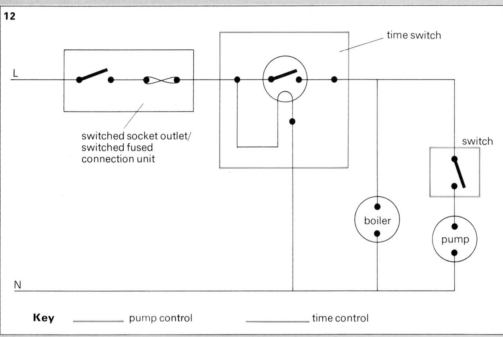

12

L

time switch

switched socket outlet/
switched fused
connection unit

switch

boiler

pump

N

Key ———— pump control   ———— time control

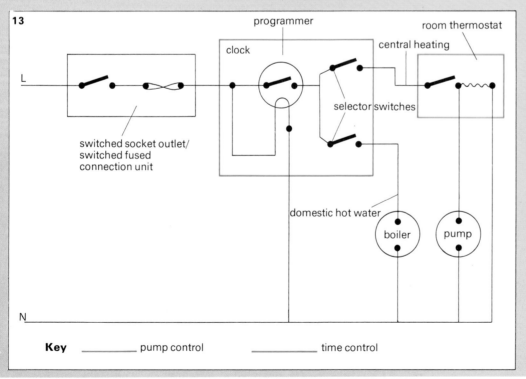

13

L

programmer

clock

room thermostat

central heating

switched socket outlet/
switched fused
connection unit

selector switches

domestic hot water

boiler

pump

N

Key ———— pump control   ———— time control

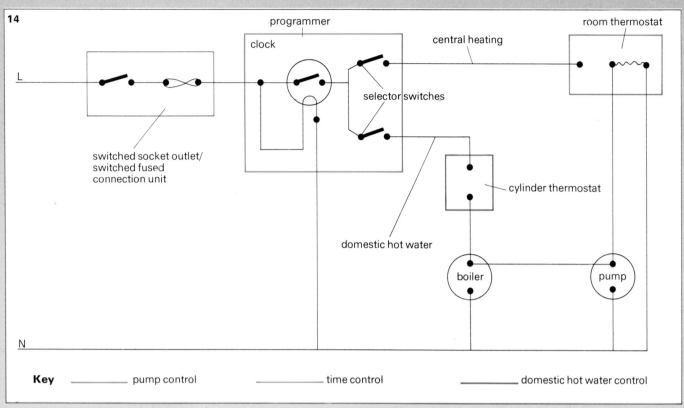

14

programmer

clock

central heating

room thermostat

L

switched socket outlet/
switched fused
connection unit

selector switches

cylinder thermostat

domestic hot water

boiler

pump

N

Key ——— pump control   ——— time control   ——— domestic hot water control

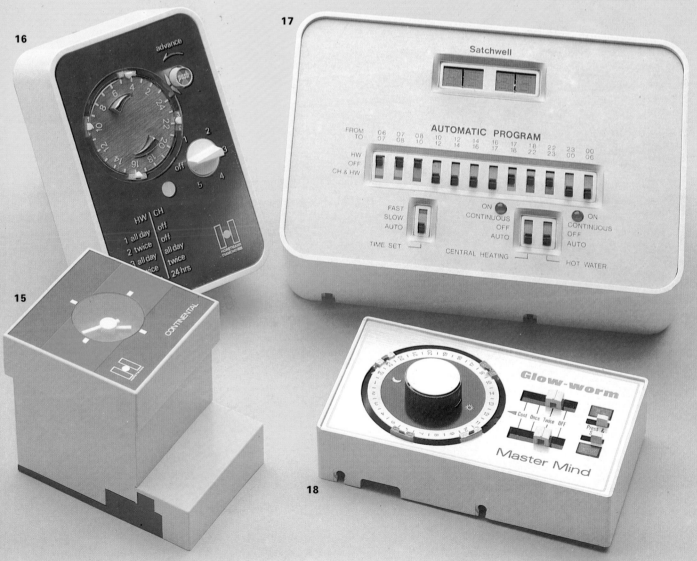

16

17

Satchwell

AUTOMATIC PROGRAM

15

18

Installing a small bore system

When you have bought all the equipment for your central heating system, lay it out so you can easily identify the parts – particularly such fittings as tees, elbow joints and valves – when you start work.

Fittings Either soldered capillary or compression joint fittings can be used to make pipework connections. The soldered type is less expensive and neater in appearance; but it is advisable to fit compression type fittings on any part of the installation which may need to be periodically disconnected or removed for servicing, such as the boiler, pump, retaining valve or radiators.

Installing radiators

Place the radiators in position to check they will fit the space allocated. Usually they are secured to the wall with brackets held in position by screws and wall plugs; it is best to use No 14 screws and plugs even with small radiators since they will be reasonably heavy when filled with water. Wherever possible, fit the bottom of the radiator level with the top of the skirting board; try also to place the radiator in the centre of the space under a window so cold down draughts from the window are heated before they can circulate round the room.

To determine the position of the wall brackets, hold the radiator up to the wall with its weight resting on the floor; lean it slightly away from the wall and mark the bracket positions with vertical lines on the wall. Remove the radiator, place a bracket on it and measure the distance between the base of the radiator and the base of the bracket;

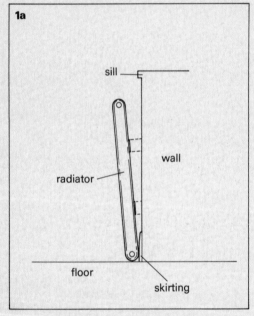

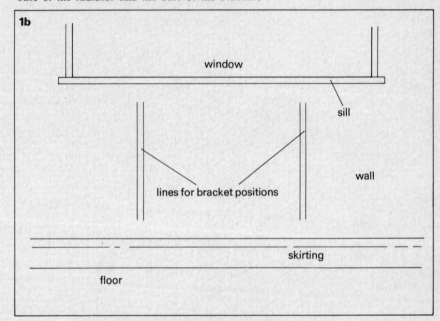

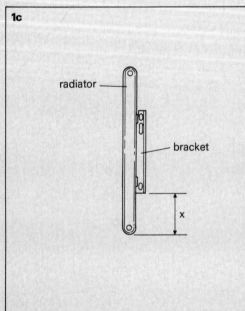

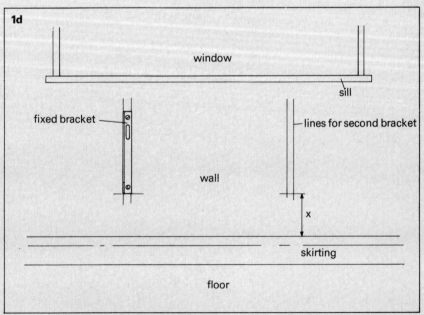

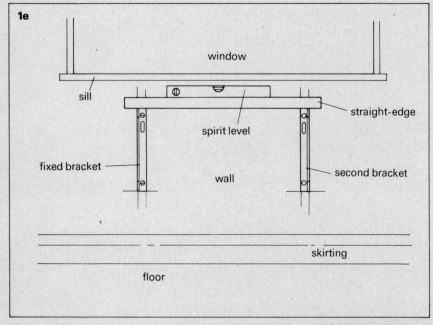

1e

window

sill

spirit level

straight-edge

fixed bracket

wall

second bracket

skirting

floor

1a To find the position for the radiator brackets, rest the radiator on the floor so it leans slightly away from the wall; mark the position of the radiator bracket slots on the wall
1b Draw vertical lines on the wall to indicate the position of the brackets; if under a window, the radiator should be fitted centrally
1c Place a bracket on the radiator and measure the distance x between the base of the radiator and the base of the bracket.
1d Mark the distance x on the vertical lines on the wall and place the bottom of the bracket on the mark; fix the bracket in place
1e Follow the same procedure for the second bracket; before fixing it in place use a spirit level and a straight-edge to ensure it is level with the first
2 If you have a solid floor, you can channel out grooves in the surface to take the pipework (here connecting a heated towel rail)
3 Alternatively the pipes connecting up the radiator can be run along the wall
4 Use clips to hold pipes firmly in place

mark this distance on the vertical line on the wall, measuring from the top of the skirting. Place the bottom of the bracket on this mark and mark the position of the fixing holes; drill the holes and fix the bracket. Follow the same procedure for the second bracket, using a spirit level and straight-edge to ensure it is level with the first before finally fixing it in place.

Before finally hanging the radiator in position, fit the tails of the radiator valves in the radiators and fit the necessary air release valves. With the most common type of radiator valve the tail connection into the radiator should be made using PTFE tape or boss white and hemp.

While the compression nut and olive are put onto the copper pipe in the normal way, the nut tightens onto the main body of the valve and a water-tight joint is made via a ground seating on the valve and the boss.

Installing boiler and cylinder
You should now install the boiler and cylinder and carry out any work which needs to be done in the loft. Remember when you are installing the feed and expansion tank in the loft it should be on a firm base and the bottom of the tank should be fitted level with or lower than the base of the main cold water storage cistern. This ensures that, if a leak develops in the indirect hot water cylinder, the direct hot water will flow into the indirect system because of the greater head of pressure; otherwise the direct supply could be contaminated by any additives in the feed and expansion tank. This arrangement also has the effect of causing the feed and expansion tank to overflow through the warning pipe, giving audible and visual indication of a fault.

Take great care when attaching fittings to the cylinder. These must eventually be watertight; but since the walls of the cylinder are thin, force exerted in the wrong direction can easily cause the cylinder to collapse. Also remember cylinders full of water weigh a considerable amount, so they must be fitted on a firm floor or base which can support the weight. Be sure to fit an efficient cylinder jacket to prevent undue heat loss.

Installing the boiler is a relatively difficult part of

5 Any pipes which run under floorboards should be lagged as they are installed
6 With timber floors pipes can be run under the boards and fed up to connect with each radiator
7 Check with our chart to determine the spacing of the clips for the size of pipe you are using

the operation; make sure it is installed strictly according to the manufacturer's instructions. The appliance must be situated on a fireproof base; where there is a timber floor under the boiler, you should place a 25mm (1in) thick sheet of asbestos or similar fireproof material between the boiler and the floor as a safety requirement. Ideally the boiler should be of the balanced flue type and the flue should also be fitted exactly to the manufacturer's specification. Remember when you are positioning the boiler to allow yourself space to carry out any future maintenance work which might be required.

Installing pipework
When the radiators, boiler and cylinder are in place, the pipework to the radiators can be installed. Make sure pipes which are run under boards on the ground floor are lagged as they are installed; you will have to lift the floorboards to run pipes here and usually when installing pipework you will have to make holes in brick walls and ceilings. Where there is a solid ground floor you will have to channel out grooves for the pipes or lay them on top of the floor.

It is advisable first to lay out the fittings for a particular pipe run on the floor; this will help you to decide whether any fittings are missing and also to remember to fit items such as tees where they are required. When installing pipework, try to eliminate the use of fittings; these not only increase the cost of the installation, but also restrict the flow of water round the system.

Once you have decided on a pipe run, you can prepare the route. Lift any floorboards where necessary, make holes through walls and ceilings and channel out the tops of joists to take the pipes. Check the pipes can be run where you want them to go; if any obstacles are met which would prevent the chosen route being followed, select a new route to avoid wasting material, labour and time.

Checking system
Once all the pipework, including any safety valves, pumps or water controls, is installed, you should fill the system with water and check for leaks. If the system is watertight, empty it and repeat the filling and emptying process at least three times to remove any foreign matter which may be in the pipes or ancillary fittings. You can then finally fill the system with water and make the necessary electrical connections. Then fit the fuel supply; remember if the appliance is gas-fired, this work must be carried out by a qualified gas engineer.

It is worth leaving the initial commissioning and testing of the system to a professional heating engineer; heating systems are fairly complex and a professional will be able to detect any faults and set up the system for efficient operation quite quickly. Also remember to retain any technical information which applies to your system, since you will probably need this to sort out any future problems which may arise; it should also be passed on to the next owner should you decide to sell the property.

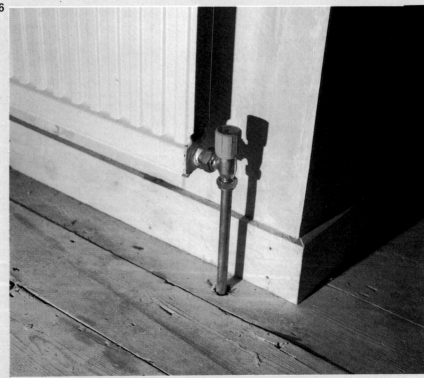

Spacings for copper pipe clips

Size of pipe (mm)	Intervals for vertical runs (m)	Intervals for horizontal runs (m)
15	1.9	1.3
22	2.5	1.9
28	2.5	1.9
35	2.8	2.5
42	2.8	2.5

Fitting a gas or solid fuel back boiler

Although the installation of back boilers and room heaters involves a considerable amount of work, there is no reason why a competent DIY worker should not tackle it provided the proper tools are available and certain essential factors are considered. There are three types of appliance generally installed in the home – the solid fuel-fired back boiler, the solid fuel room heater and the combined gas-fired space heater and back boiler unit.

Solid fuel back boiler This appliance utilizes the surplus heat from an open fire. One type basically supplies domestic hot water since its heat output is insufficient to supply radiators with adequate heat to guarantee room temperatures. A second type, which has side cheeks, has a high output and will supply radiators as well in an average size house.

Solid fuel room heater This is an extremely popular appliance with householders who wish to use solid fuel to supply their total hot water requirements, since it has a high enough output to provide full central heating and hot water for an average size house.

Combined gas-fired space heater/back boiler This type of appliance is also extremely popular since gas is a cleaner fuel than coal; it is capable of providing an inexhaustible supply of hot water for washing, cooking and central heating. The gas space heater provides a source of heat which can be operated independently of the back boiler unit. This means it can be used to heat a single room when the weather is not so cold and full central

heating is unnecessary. However the back boiler unit will have to be used if hot water is required. Normally, when the appliance is used for central heating, the hot water is automatically supplied to the cylinder via gravity circulation.

Checking the chimney

It is imperative the chimney is swept before the boiler is installed, since a blocked chimney will cause fumes to come into the room. If you decide to sweep the chimney yourself, lay down plenty of dust sheets to avoid damage to furnishings. Although you can easily hire the necessary equipment, the cost of employing a sweep is comparatively low and this is a job which might be best left to the professional. Even if the chimney is clear, you must test it to ensure there is a good updraught for fumes to clear properly. The chimney is best tested with the fire surround in position as follows:

● Cover the fireplace opening with a damp sheet of newspaper.

● Make a small hole, not larger than 50mm (2in) in diameter, in the centre of the sheet.

● Close all doors and windows in the room where the fireplace is situated and in any adjoining rooms.

● Light a match and place it in front of the hole, taking care not to set the paper alight. If the flame is drawn towards the opening, the chimney is clear. But if the flame remains upright or blows into the room, the chimney is defective or inadequately cleaned; any faults must be rectified before any

Below Solid fuel back boiler
Bottom left Inset room heater
Bottom Gas-fired heater with back boiler

1 Before installation, check for correct updraught in the chimney so fumes will clear properly
2a Minimum depth of recess required for most appliances
2b The recess can be deepened by using a hollow surround
2c With a shallow recess, or where you do not wish to remove the existing fireback, use a free-standing heater
3 Where a back boiler is to supply central heating, it must be connected to an indirect hot water system; all pipe dimensions given here are minimum sizes

415

appliances are fitted. If the flue is in poor condition, you can line it; but for solid fuel installations the job should be done by a professional.

Checking the water system

Once the chimney has been checked it is advisable to examine the existing water system; it must conform to water board regulations with regard to pipe size and methods of connection. Remember back boilers must be connected to an indirect water system if needed to supply a central heating system. If you need to purchase a new cylinder, it might be worth considering one with a special boss so an immersion heater can be fitted in the system at the same time as the other appliances. This will be a useful standby for providing hot water should the main appliance be shut down for any reason.

Estimating boiler size

To determine what size boiler you need to fit, you must assess the total heat loss of the area the boiler is intended to supply. Relative heat loss is easily measured by checking with the manufacturer as to the output of each radiator. The outputs are added together, with an additional 1–2kW to compensate for hot water requirements, to give you the total output.

If you have no radiators, you must use a more

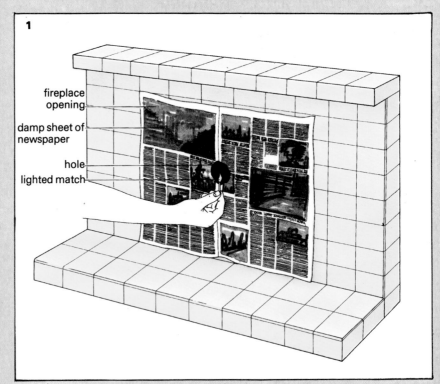

1

fireplace opening
damp sheet of newspaper
hole
lighted match

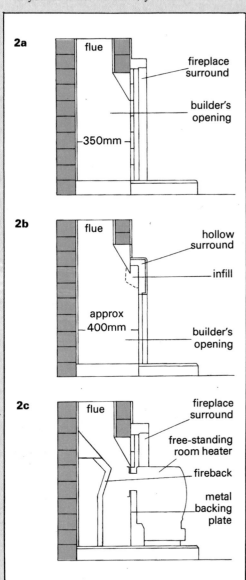

2a

flue
fireplace surround
builder's opening
350mm

2b

flue
hollow surround
infill
approx 400mm
builder's opening

2c

flue
fireplace surround
free-standing room heater
fireback
metal backing plate

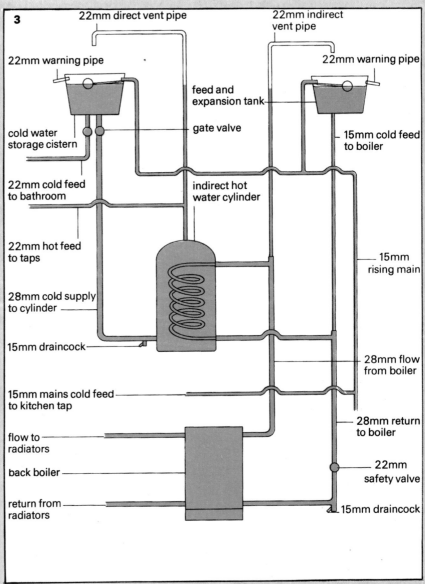

3

22mm direct vent pipe
22mm indirect vent pipe
22mm warning pipe
22mm warning pipe
feed and expansion tank
gate valve
cold water storage cistern
15mm cold feed to boiler
22mm cold feed to bathroom
indirect hot water cylinder
22mm hot feed to taps
15mm rising main
28mm cold supply to cylinder
15mm draincock
28mm flow from boiler
15mm mains cold feed to kitchen tap
28mm return to boiler
flow to radiators
back boiler
22mm safety valve
return from radiators
15mm draincock

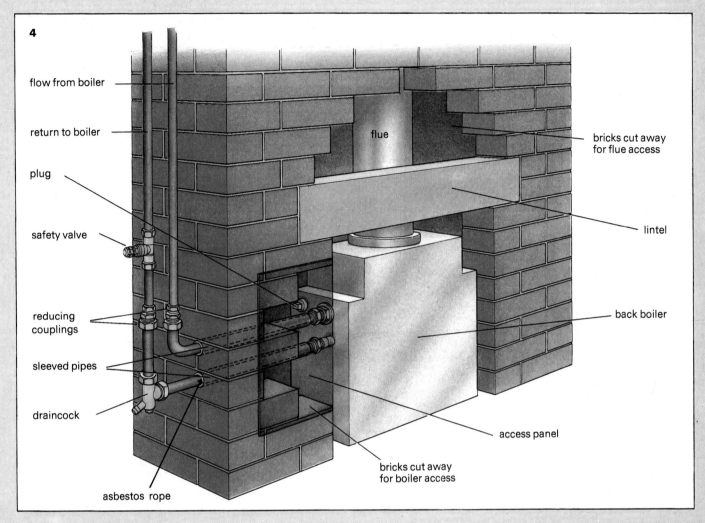

4

flow from boiler

return to boiler

plug

safety valve

reducing
couplings

sleeved pipes

draincock

asbestos rope

flue

bricks cut away
for flue access

lintel

back boiler

access panel

bricks cut away
for boiler access

elaborate method of calculating heat loss. This involves a sound knowledge of basic mathematics, since you have to calculate the number of air changes per room or space and the heat loss that ensues, as well as the heat loss through the structure from each room or space. This will be covered on pages 105 and 106.

Since appliances are not 100 percent efficient, care must be taken to ensure a boiler with the correct input is installed to provide a sufficient output of heat to supply the system. As a rough guide, most modern gas-fired and high output solid fuel boilers are over 70 percent efficient, whereas solid fuel boilers supplying just hot water are only 45–50 percent efficient. If the size of the back boiler needed to heat a particular area is too large for the fireplace, another type such as the free-standing model is available. Installing an undersized boiler with insufficient output is bad economics.

Preparing the fireplace
You may need to remove the fire surround, in which case take care not to damage it if you intend to replace it. Each individual surround has to be treated differently since there are various types with a variety of fixing points. They are usually quite simple to remove and it is worth considering selling the surround to a second-hand furniture shop.

Once the surround has been removed, the fabric of the old existing fireback should be cleared away. (With some room heaters this is not necessary.) Break the firebrick with a club hammer and clear away all the backfill material to reveal a clean

builder's opening of square brickwork. The builder's opening is the structure that is left after the fire surround, the fire bricks and all the builder's rubble have been removed from the fireplace.

Since this operation will be very dusty, lay plenty of dust sheets around the fireplace and wear a protective mask. Check there is sufficient room in the builder's opening to take the boiler. The depth of the recess should be at least 350mm (14in), although some boilers require more space than this. If this is the case, a different type of fire surround can be fitted to increase the overall depth of the fireplace opening; where the space is still too small, a free-standing room heater may be fitted.

Connecting the water supply
Apart from slight variations in the positions of the tappings in the boiler, the method of connecting any boiler to the water supply is the same. Connections to the boiler itself should always be made with compression type fittings, since these are easy to disconnect should the need ever arise. The external thread on the fitting must be screwed into the internal thread on the boiler, using hemp and jointing compound to ensure a sound, watertight joint. PTFE tape should not be used since boiler tappings usually have deep thread forms which are not easy to seal.

The boiler tapping determines the size of pipes which must pass through the chimney-breast; you must sleeve these pipes by running them through a pipe one size larger than that being used and insulate between the two with asbestos rope. If the pipe

4 The connections for the water supply to the boiler. The pipes which pass through the chimney-breast must be sleeved in pipes one size larger and asbestos rope should be placed between the two. Where pipes must be reduced, this should be done on vertical runs by using reducing couplings. A draincock should be fitted on the lowest part of the system and a safety valve incorporated in the return pipe to the boiler. A removable panel will make access easier for maintenance of the installation later

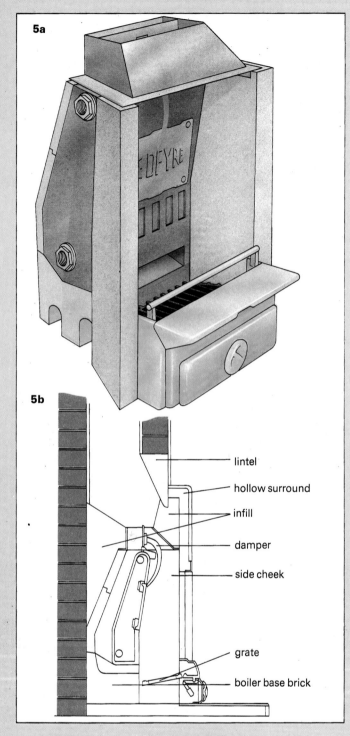

5a

5b

lintel

hollow surround

infill

damper

side cheek

grate

boiler base brick

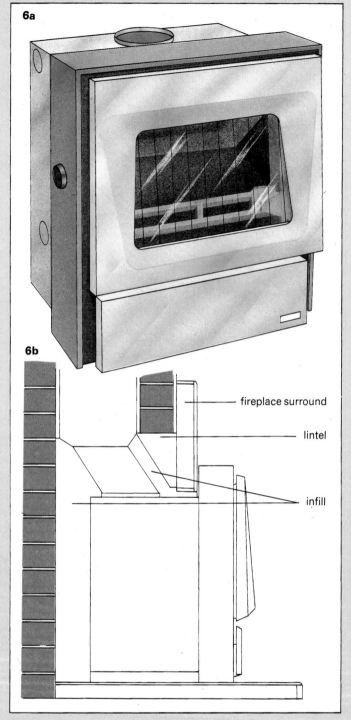

6a

6b

fireplace surround

lintel

infill

size needs reducing, this should be done on a vertical piece of pipe, since this aids circulation.

To gain access to the pipework connections during installation, it may be necessary to cut away some of the chimney-breast. Once the water connections are made, any opening can either be bricked up or covered with a temporary panel which can be removed should inspection or maintenance be necessary. Do not forget to install a draincock in the system so it can be drained when necessary; this should be fitted onto the lowest part of the system. Fit a safety valve on the return to the boiler in a position which can be easily reached when carrying out maintenance.

Existing pipes should be connected with either compression or soldered capillary fittings, whichever is easier, although the latter are generally

cheaper to buy. Any tappings that are not used can be blocked off with brass plugs if a direct cylinder is used; with an indirect cylinder black iron plugs, commonly called gas plugs, should be used. Galvanized plugs should never be used.

Once the connections are made they must be tested by filling the system and any radiators with water and flushing through to ensure all pipes are clear. Failure to test the system at this stage may lead to difficulties later should the joints prove unsound. It is advisable to flush the system again after about six months.

Installing a solid fuel back boiler
Most modern back boilers take the place of the firebrick back. The boiler is usually supplied in parts and consists of a back, side cheeks and a flue

5a Solid fuel back boiler for use with open fires
5b Section through the installation
6a Inset room heater with back boiler
6b Section through the installation

damper assembly; all these must be assembled on site. Once assembled and correctly positioned, the water connections (as described above) can be made.

Once the water connections have been checked, fill in the space between the opening and the back of the boiler with infill (six parts vermiculite to one part lime) and refix the fire surround close up to the back boiler cheeks.

Warning When the fire is first lit, run the system at a low heat for at least 24 hours to allow the installation to expand and settle down slowly.

Installing a solid fuel room heater

There are two types of room heater available, one free-standing and the other inset. Both are available with or without a boiler attached. The inset type, although more difficult to fit, does not project as far into the room as the free-standing type and is therefore more likely to comply with Building Regulations.

Since the inset appliance is mostly hidden, the opening needs to be exposed by removing the fire surround, while part of the chimney breast at the side will need to be cut away to gain access to the pipework and flue connections, as described above.

Once the builder's opening has been cleared and the brickwork exposed, you can replace the surround. It is essential the surround is replaced perfectly level and upright in relation to the hearth, which must also be level, otherwise the appliance will be poorly sealed; this will affect both the performance and the efficiency of the appliance.

Ease the appliance into position and secure it to the hearth with screws; make sure the wall plugs you use are non-combustible. Fixing points vary

7a Free-standing room heater with back boiler
7b Section through the installation and detail of the flue connection (**inset**)
8a Gas-fired space heater and back boiler
8b Section through the installation
9a Ventilation for a gas-fired appliance may be provided by metal ducting under the floor; the ducting should lead from the side of the chimney-breast to an airbrick in an outside wall
9b Alternatively ventilation may be provided by an

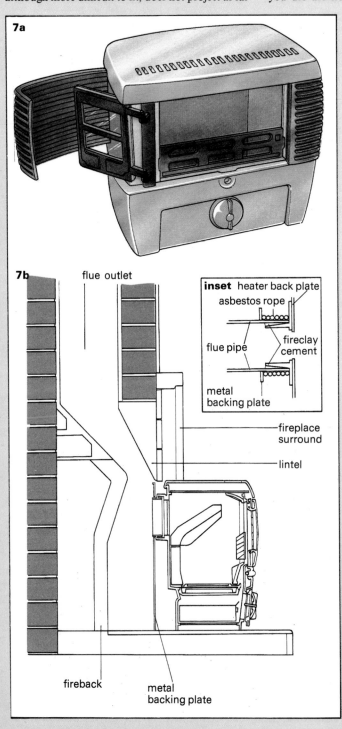

7a

7b
flue outlet

inset heater back plate
asbestos rope
flue pipe
fireclay cement
metal backing plate
fireplace surround
lintel
fireback
metal backing plate

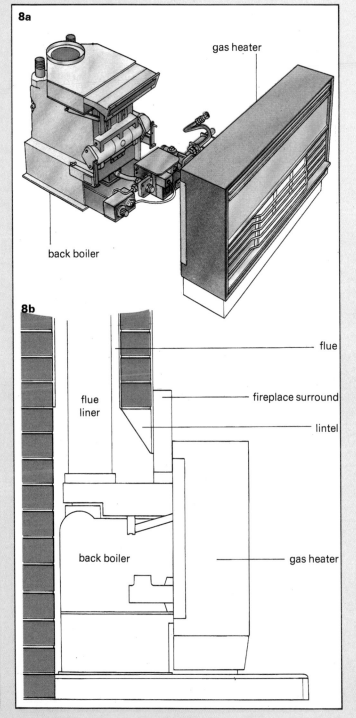

8a
gas heater
back boiler

8b
flue
fireplace surround
lintel
flue liner
back boiler
gas heater

airbrick set into the chimney-breast and covered with a fixed grille

10a Before fitting a flue liner, measure the length required by lowering a piece of weighted string down the chimney; the liner must protrude 150mm above the chimney

10b Pass the liner down the flue

10c At the top of the stack; clamp the liner into position and fit a cowl terminal; at the bottom, fit the liner onto the flue spigot of the boiler

from one appliance to another, but the manufacturer's instruction sheet should clarify the method of fixing. Connect up the pipes and test, as described above.

Appliances are available with either a back or top flue socket which is also the flue outlet. Top outlets are usually more suitable and certainly easier to attach to the main flue, although the type best suited to any particular situation will depend on the way in which the main flue is constructed. The top outlet on the boiler is extended into the main chimney stack; a piece of cast iron or mild steel can be used for this. The flue extension must be sealed to the main stack and the flue outlet on the appliance. The gap between the appliance and the builder's opening should now be filled after a final check for water leaks. Finally, fill the opening at the side of the chimney-breast.

Installing gas-fired space heater/back boiler

The installation of this type of appliance involves the following sequence of work: installing the flue liner, positioning the boiler, connecting the water supply, wiring, making the final gas connection and testing the installation.

Flue liner A gas appliance produces carbon dioxide and water vapour. Both are harmless provided the appliance is adequately ventilated and care is taken to prevent condensation occurring in the flue. The question of ventilation is most important and provided it is adequate no problems will arise; your local gas board will tell you how much you need. Condensation, however, will occur if a flue liner is not placed in the chimney.

The flue liner is installed in two stages: the liner is first passed down the flue from the roof, before the boiler is positioned; then the final sealing and

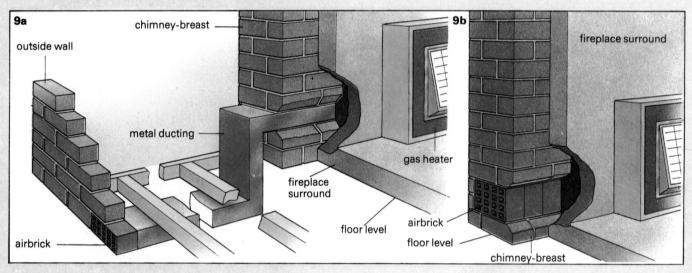

9a — outside wall, chimney-breast, metal ducting, fireplace surround, floor level, airbrick, gas heater

9b — fireplace surround, airbrick, floor level, chimney-breast

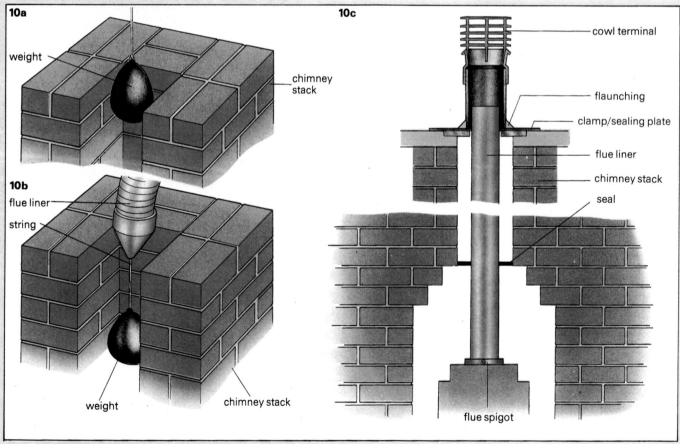

10a — weight, chimney stack

10b — flue liner, string, weight, chimney stack

10c — cowl terminal, flaunching, clamp/sealing plate, flue liner, chimney stack, seal, flue spigot

connection to the boiler is made, when the boiler is positioned and connected to the water supply. Before inserting the flue liner, remove the chimney pot and make sure the flue is clear. Lower a weighted piece of string down the chimney in order to measure the exact length of the flue liner required, bearing in mind the flue liner must protrude 150mm (6in) above the chimney at the top and must fit onto the flue spigot of the boiler at the bottom. Pass the liner down the chimney, using the string as a guide and preferably having someone at the bottom to hold it. When connecting the flue liner to the boiler it is essential all the air seals are maintained since these prevent condensation.

Positioning boiler Once the flue liner is in its approximate position, the boiler can be placed in the fire opening. Whether or not the surround needs to be removed depends upon the make of boiler being fitted; whatever the type, however, it is necessary to remove the fire bricks and clear the builder's opening, since this facilitates the connection to the water supply which is installed in the same way as for the solid fuel appliances. Once the appliance has been tested for water leaks, the flue liner can be attached to the appliance and the installation of the flue completed at roof level.

Wiring The use of electrical controls on gas appliances is now universal and it is impossible to buy a domestic gas fired boiler without them. The method of wiring up a system depends on the make of boiler and the type and number of controls incorporated in the system. It is therefore essential to examine thoroughly the maker's data sheets on the boiler and any controls used to determine how the system is wired. The installation must be wired in accordance with IEE regulations, using heat resistant cable of the correct loading. The cable must not touch any hot surfaces or pipes and all controls – including the boiler – must be earthed to the common earthing point provided by the local Electricity Board.

Making final gas connection Under the 1972 Gas Regulations Act it is illegal for anybody other than a qualified gas engineer to interfere with or fix any part of a gas installation. Severe penalties are imposed for contravention, including imprisonment. Therefore at this stage of the installation it is essential you contact a qualified gas engineer to run the gas supply, make the final gas connections to the boiler and space heater, check the installation and test it for correct operation. Under no circumstances tackle this part of the work yourself.

You will have to replace the fire surround before the space heater is finally fixed.

Following regulations

All the installations described must be carried out in accordance with the relevant section of the Building Regulations and must also comply with Gas, Electricity and Water Board regulations where applicable. The manufacturer's instructions should be strictly adhered to at all times.

11 The wiring from the mains to a gas boiler via a froststat, time clock/programmer and room thermostat
12 The minimum dimensions for fireplaces stipulated by the Building Regulations

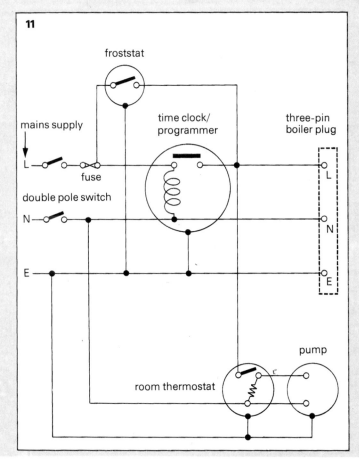

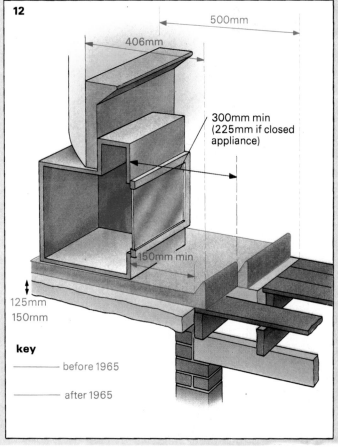

Guarding against corrosion

Some plumbing fittings are subject to corrosion. When this occurs, they are weakened and eventually leaks develop. There are several ways of preventing this happening in your system.

Modern galvanized steel water storage cisterns frequently show signs of rust within a few months of being installed. Older plumbing systems, which were constructed entirely of lead or galvanized steel, could generally be expected to last, without this kind of deterioration, for 50 years or more. In modern systems the use of copper, which itself virtually never corrodes, has greatly increased the risk of corrosion to any galvanized iron or steel fittings incorporated in the system.

The process which gives rise to this corrosion is known as electrolytic action. This is the same principle on which the simple electric battery cell is based; where rods of zinc and copper are in electrical contact with each other and are immersed in a weak acid solution which is able to conduct an electric current (an electrolyte), electricity will pass between the rods, bubbles of oxygen will be produced and the zinc rod will slowly dissolve away. A plumbing system in which copper water supply and distribution pipes are connected to a galvanized steel cold water storage cistern or hot water storage tank, may reproduce these conditions; the copper tubing and the zinc coating of the galvanized steel are in direct contact and the water in the cistern or tank, if very mildly acidic, will act as an electrolyte. This results in rapid failure of the protective galvanized coating, allowing aerated water to penetrate to the vulnerable steel underneath; eventually rust will form.

A particular form of electrolytic corrosion may result in damage to brass plumbing fittings, such as compression joints and stop valves. Brass is an alloy of copper and zinc; electrolytic action may result in the zinc in the fittings dissolving away to leave them unchanged in appearance but totally without structural strength. Where these fittings in your plumbing system are showing signs of leakage, it would be worth checking with a local plumber if the type of water in your area is likely to create a situation favourable to electrolytic corrosion. If so, you should replace brass fittings with those made of a special alloy classed as 'dezincification resistant'. The fittings are marked with a special symbol – CR. Although these fittings are more expensive, you should use them where this problem of corrosion exists.

Warning Corrosion as a result of electrolytic action is also likely to occur in pipework if a new length of copper tubing is fitted into an existing galvanized steel hot or cold water system. Always use stainless steel tubing instead – this is not liable to the same risk.

Protecting cisterns and tanks
There are steps you can take to prevent corrosion in galvanized steel cisterns and tanks. For example, when you are installing a new cistern or tank, it is important to make sure you remove every trace of metal dust or shaving resulting from drilling holes

for tappings. The least fragment remaining will become a focus for corrosion.

One way of protecting a cold water storage cistern is to ensure the metal of the cistern does not come into direct contact with the water it contains. This can be done by painting the internal surfaces with two coats of a taste and odour-free bituminous paint using an old 50mm paint brush. Before applying this treatment to a new tank, cut holes for the pipe connections; when you are painting, pay particular attention to the areas in the immediate vicinity of these holes.

Warning Galvanized steel hot water storage tanks, which can still be found in many older homes, cannot be protected by this paint treatment.

Cathodic protection A sacrificial magnesium anode which dissolves instead of the zinc coating will

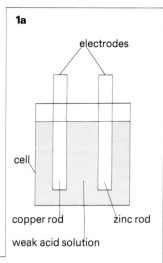

1a

electrodes

cell

copper rod zinc rod

weak acid solution

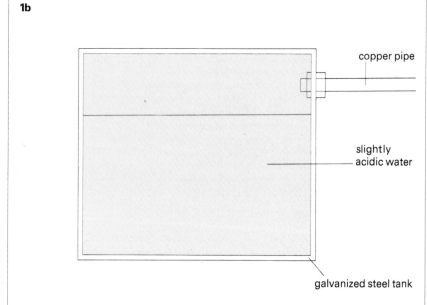

1b

copper pipe

slightly acidic water

galvanized steel tank

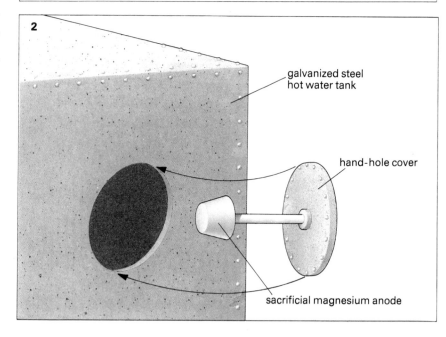

2

galvanized steel hot water tank

hand-hole cover

sacrificial magnesium anode

1a & b The process which causes corrosion in plumbing systems with copper and galvanized iron or steel fittings is principally the same as the process which takes place in a battery cell
2 Fit a sacrificial magnesium anode into a galvanized steel hot water tank to prevent corrosion
3 When venting a radiator check for the presence of hydrogen – which indicates internal corrosion – by holding a lighted taper to the escaping air
To remove magnetite sludge from a central heating system, drain the system (**4a**) and introduce a special solvent into the feed and expansion tank (**4b**)

protect both galvanized steel cold water storage cisterns and hot water tanks. The procedure for a hot water tank involves fitting the anode to the hand-hole cover of the tank. Turn off the water supply and drain the system from the draincock beside the boiler; unscrew the bolts retaining the hand-hole cover and remove it. Drill a hole in the centre of the cover, use abrasive paper to rub down the area of metal around the hole and screw in the anode before replacing the cover.

Protecting central heating systems

A form of electrolytic corrosion can take place in a central heating system where copper tubing is used in conjunction with pressed steel radiators. Some air – a prerequisite of corrosion – will always be present in the system; it dissolves into the surface of the water in the feed and expansion tank and may also enter through minute leaks too small to permit water to escape.

Electrolytic corrosion within a central heating system results in the formation of black iron oxide sludge (magnetite) and hydrogen gas. This leads to

impeded water flow and radiators will need continual venting to release airlocks to keep up the required heat level. The iron oxide sludge is drawn towards the magnetic field of the circulating pump and its abrasive qualities contribute towards early pump failure. Also the metal of the radiators, from which the magnetite and hydrogen are produced, becomes thinner until leaks eventually develop in the radiators.

Removing airlocks by venting the radiator is a simple process. A key supplied for this purpose is inserted in the radiator when the water is warm and turned anti-clockwise to open the vent valve. Hold a container underneath the key since some water may escape when the valve is opened. Air will come out of the radiator – when it stops doing so and water begins to flow you should tighten the valve. If a radiator in your heating system needs to be continually vented, it is worth testing for internal corrosion while you are carrying out this operation. Apply a lighted taper to the gas escaping from the radiator; hydrogen gas burns with a blue flame and indicates the presence of corrosion.

Protection treatment A chemical corrosion-proofer can be introduced into the feed and expansion tank to protect the system against corrosion. It is best to do this when the system is first installed, but it can be carried out with an existing system; it will not, however, undo damage already done. Before introducing a corrosion-proofer into an existing system you should get rid of any magnetite sludge with a special solvent. Like the corrosion-proofer, this is introduced into the feed and expansion tank and you should drain the system first. Disconnect the fuel supply to the boiler and switch off the ignition system several hours before draining to give the water time to cool. Tie up the ball float arm of the feed and expansion tank and fit a hose to the draincock near the boiler, running the hose to a drain outside. Undo the draincock, empty the system and, when you have closed the draincock, free the ball float arm in the feed and expansion tank. Allow the system to refill, introducing the solvent at the same time. Follow the manufacturer's instructions for the length of time you should allow for the solvent to complete its work before carrying out treatment with the corrosion-proofer.

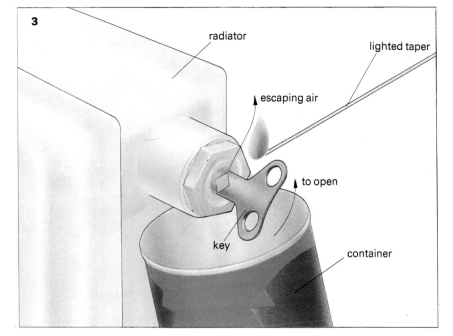

3
radiator
lighted taper
escaping air
to open
key
container

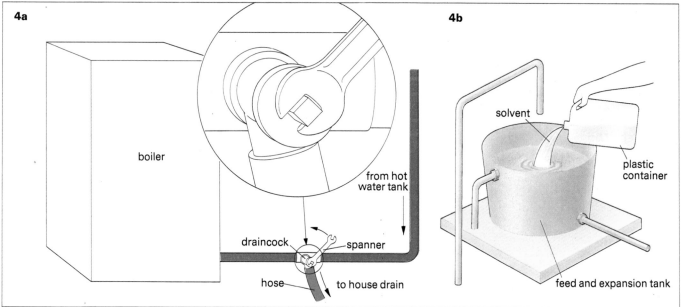

4a
boiler
from hot water tank
draincock
spanner
hose
to house drain

4b
solvent
plastic container
feed and expansion tank

Cold weather protection

If the plumbing system in your home is not adequately protected, severe weather can cause water to freeze in the pipes, producing blockages and burst pipes. You can deal with these yourself, but it is better to prevent any damage by checking your anti-frost defences every autumn.

Protecting plumbing

Frost protection is built into the structure of a well-designed, modern home and the important design points are explained below.

Service pipe This pipe conveys water from the water authority's communication pipe to the house and should be covered by at least 750mm (or 30in) of earth throughout its length. If it enters the house by a hollow, boarded floor, it should be thoroughly protected from draughts. The pipe should be taken up into the roof space – to supply the cold water storage cistern – against an internal wall.

Storage cistern The cold water storage cistern is best situated against a flue which is in constant use.

To prevent icy draughts blowing up the warning pipe leading from the cistern, you can fit a hinged copper flap over the outlet; there is, however, a risk that this will jam in the open or closed position. A better method is to extend the pipe within the cistern and bend it over so its outlet is about 38mm (1½in) below the surface of the water. There are gadgets, such as the frostguard, which make it easy to extend internally the warning pipe from a storage or flushing cistern.

The boiler, hot water storage cylinder and cold water storage cistern are best installed in a vertical column so the vulnerable cold water cistern receives the benefit of the rising warm air.

All lengths of water pipe within the roof space should be kept short and well away from the eaves.

Lagging Efficient lagging of storage tanks and pipes reduces the rate at which water loses its warmth and protects pipes exposed to cold air; but it cannot make up for a bad plumbing design and it will not add heat to the system.

Pipes to lag are those against external walls, under the ground floor and in the roof space. Don't omit the vent pipe of the hot water system since the water in this pipe is not as hot as that in the rest of the system and, if it freezes, it can create a vacuum which could damage the cylinder.

There are several types of pipe lagging available and it is best to use inorganic materials. These include wrap-round glass fibre; moulded polystyrene (which comes in rigid sections which fit round the pipe) and flexible moulded foam plastic (which you split open to fit round the pipe). Polystyrene is rather awkward to use, but is good for underground pipes since it does not absorb water. The moulded types of lagging come in a variety of sizes to fit different pipes, so make sure you buy the appropriate size.

Whichever type you use, make sure you lag behind pipes against external walls to protect them from the cold wall. Cover the tails of ball valves and all but the handles of stopcocks and gate valves; if you are using rigid lagging sections, you will need some of the wrap-round type for these areas.

Bind wrap-round insulation round the pipe like a bandage, overlapping it to prevent gaps, and secure it with string or adhesive tape. Where a pipe joins a cistern, make a full turn and tie it to hold the end in place. When joining two lengths overlap them and tie securely.

Secure moulded sections with plastic adhesive tape, starting at the cistern. Where the sections join along a length of pipe, seal the joint with tape. Open up flexible moulding along one side, slip it round the pipe and seal the opening with adhesive tape, taking particular care at any elbows. If you lag the pipes before fitting them, there is of course no need to slit the lagging; you can slide the pipe length through it. Where pipes go through a wall, make sure the insulation goes right up to the wall.

You also need to protect the cold water cistern. The easiest way to cover a square cistern is to use expanded polystyrene slabs. For a circular cistern use glass fibre tank wrap. If you have insulating material between the floor joists in the loft, make sure the area immediately below the tank is left uncovered so warm air is allowed to reach the tank.

Dealing with frozen pipes

If, in spite of your precautions, a freeze-up does occur, it is essential to deal with it immediately. If there is any delay the plug of ice will spread along the pipe and increase the risk of damage.

You can gauge the position of the freeze-up from the situation of the plumbing fittings which have stopped working. If, for instance, water is not flowing into the main cold water storage cistern but is running from the cold tap over the kitchen sink, the plug of ice must be in the rising main between the branch to the kitchen sink and the cistern.

Strip off the lagging from the affected pipe and apply heat – either with cloths soaked in hot water and wrung dry or a filled hot water bottle. If a pipe is inaccessible, direct a jet of warm air towards it from a hair dryer or the outlet of a vacuum cleaner. Fortunately modern copper tubing conducts very well and a small plug of ice can often be melted by applying heat to the pipe about a metre from the actual location of the ice.

Burst pipe If the freeze-up results in a burst pipe the first indication will probably be water dripping through a ceiling, since pipes in the loft are most likely to burst; wherever the leak, immediate action is vital. Turn off the main stopcock and open up every tap in the house. This will drain the cistern and pipes and reduce the damage. When the system is completely drained, find the position of the leak.

Damaged copper piping If you have copper piping, you will probably find a compression or soldered capillary joint will have been forced open by the expansion of ice. All you need to do in this case is fit a new joint. Copper piping does sometimes split under pressure. If that happens, you will have to cut out the defective length and insert a new length. An easy way of doing this is to insert a repair coupling.

Cut out the damaged section of pipe with a fine tooth hacksaw, leaving a gap of not more than 89mm (3½in) between the pipe ends. Remove the burr from the tube ends with a small file. One end of the coupling has a tube stop, the other is free to

Right Efficient lagging will protect pipes against freezing conditions

424

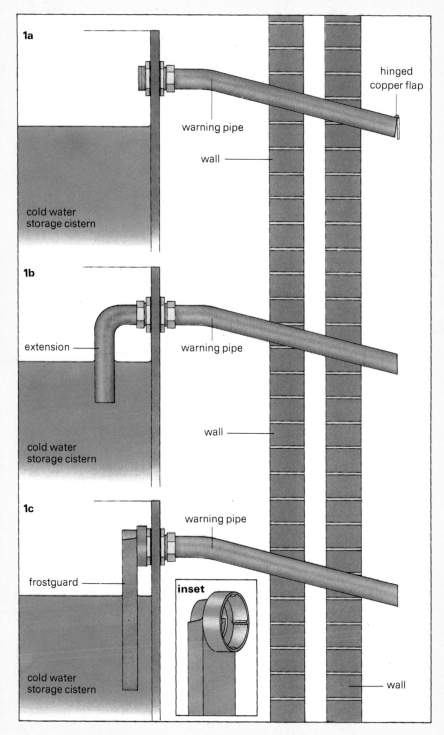

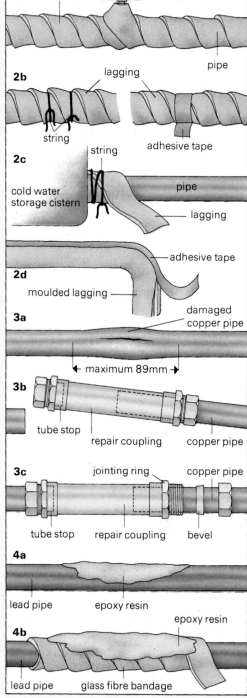

1a

warning pipe

wall

hinged copper flap

cold water storage cistern

1b

extension

warning pipe

wall

cold water storage cistern

1c

warning pipe

frostguard

inset

cold water storage cistern

wall

2a lagging — stopcock

pipe

2b lagging

string

adhesive tape

2c string

cold water storage cistern

pipe

lagging

adhesive tape

2d moulded lagging

damaged copper pipe

3a

← maximum 89mm →

3b

tube stop

repair coupling

copper pipe

3c jointing ring — copper pipe

tube stop

repair coupling

bevel

4a

lead pipe

epoxy resin

4b

epoxy resin

lead pipe

glass fibre bandage

1a-c Ways of protecting cold water cistern from severe external conditions. **2a** Lagging pipe but leaving handle of stopcock clear; **2b** Secure lagging with tape or string; **2c** Where pipe meets cistern, make full turn and bind lagging firmly; **2d** Cut moulded lagging along one side, place round pipe and seal join with tape. **3a-c** Removing damaged section of copper pipe and fitting repair coupling. **4a-b** Making temporary repair to lead pipe with epoxy resin and bandage

slide along the pipe. Slacken the nuts of the coupling, spring one end of the pipe out just enough to allow you to slide the repair coupling over it. Line it up with the other pipe end and push the coupling on to it until the tube stop is reached. Unscrew the nuts and slide them and the copper jointing rings along the pipe. Apply jointing compound or gloss paint into the bevels of the fitting and around the leading edge of the jointing rings. Tighten the nuts with a spanner so the tube is lightly gripped; make another turn, or a turn and a quarter, making sure you do not overtighten.

Burst lead pipe The orthodox and approved method of repairing a burst lead pipe is to cut out the affected length and replace it with a new length of pipe; this job is best left to an expert.

You can, however, make a temporary repair with

one of the epoxy resin repair kits available. Dry the affected length of pipe thoroughly and knock the edges of the split together with a hammer. Rub down with abrasive paper. Make up the resin filler according to the manufacturer's instructions and apply it round the pipe to cover the split and the surrounding area. While the filler is still plastic, bind round it with a glass fibre bandage and 'butter' a further layer of resin filler over the bandage. When thoroughly set, rub down with abrasive paper to make an unobtrusive joint. You will be able to use the pipe again within a few hours.

Frost and the hot water system

A well designed hot water cylinder storage system provides any home with its best insurance against the risk of frost damage. No matter how effectively a cylinder is lagged, some warmth will always be conducted along the pipework and rise up into the roof space, giving a measure of protection to the cold water storage cistern. This again emphasizes the importance of having the cold water storage cistern sited directly above the hot water cylinder – and not insulating the area immediately below the cistern.

A packaged plumbing system, in which the storage cistern and hot water cylinder are combined in one unit, gives virtually total protection to the cistern and the pipes in the immediate vicinity as long as the water in the cylinder is hot.

Boiler explosion

One of the great fears, particularly where water is heated by means of a boiler, is still that of a boiler explosion – and people often worry a great deal more about their hot water system during cold spells than they do about the cold water supply pipes. However, if you can understand the cause of boiler explosions and take simple and straightforward precautions to avoid them, you need never have a moment's anxiety over this happening.

A cylinder hot water system is, in effect, a large 'U' shape tube with the boiler at its base and the vent pipe and open storage cistern providing the two open ends. Provided the pipe run between the boiler and the vent pipe – or the boiler and the cold water storage cistern – is not obstructed, there can be no dangerous build-up of pressure. A spring-loaded safety valve, positioned on either the flow or return pipe in the immediate vicinity of the boiler, provides a final line of defence.

Boiler explosions usually take place when a house is reoccupied after having been empty during a prolonged spell of severe weather. The existence of the normal protective measure – lagging – will not add warmth to the plumbing system; all it can do is slow down the rate of heat loss. While the house is occupied, this is all that is needed; the fabric of the house is warm and water is constantly being drawn off and replaced. When the house is empty, however, the fabric chills off and water stagnates in the supply and distribution pipes. If a spell of cold weather intervenes, a severe freeze-up is inevitable. Plugs of ice will form in the upper part of the vent pipe and in the cold water supply pipe from the cistern to the cylinder. Ice may even form in the boiler itself and in the pipes between the boiler and the cylinder.

The real danger comes if, under these circumstances, the boiler fire is lit. Water in the boiler will heat up, but it will not be able to circulate or expand. Internal pressure will build up until, ultimately, something gives and releases it. In an instant the superheated water in the boiler will turn into steam, with many thousand times the volume of the water from which it was formed, and the boiler will explode like a bomb – with equally devastating results.

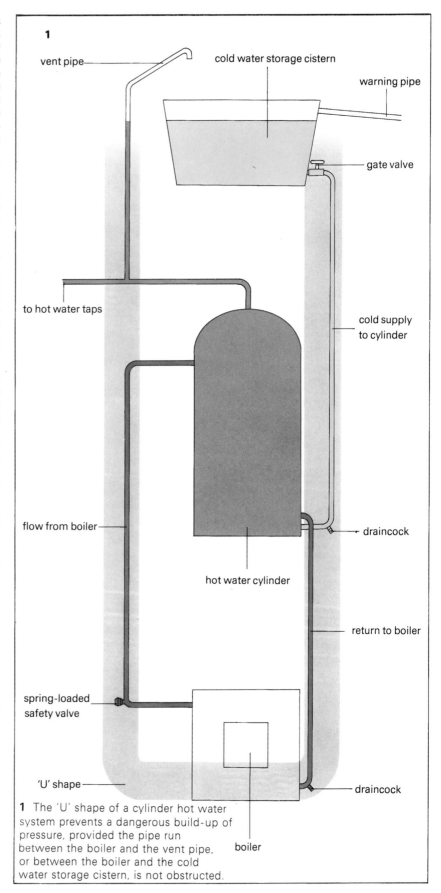

1 The 'U' shape of a cylinder hot water system prevents a dangerous build-up of pressure, provided the pipe run between the boiler and the vent pipe, or between the boiler and the cold water storage cistern, is not obstructed.

Cylinder implosion

Boiler explosions are, happily, an extremely rare occurrence. Cylinder implosion – or collapse – is rather more common in frosty weather; this is particularly likely to occur when the boiler is allowed to go out at night. Small plugs of ice form in the upper part of the vent pipe and in the upper part of the cold water supply pipe to the cylinder. The warm water in the cylinder and boiler cools and contracts, producing a partial vacuum. Cylinders are not constructed to withstand external pressure and, when this occurs, the storage cylinder will collapse like a paper bag under the weight of atmospheric pressure.

The way to avoid either cylinder collapse or boiler explosion is to keep the boiler fire alight and the house warm during cold weather, although this may be difficult if you have to go away for any length of time.

Useful precautions

If you have a reliable automatic central heating system, the best precaution is to leave it turned on at a low setting or under the control of a 'frost-stat'. Keep internal doors open to allow warm air to circulate through the house and partially remove the flap to the loft space to permit some warmth to penetrate to this area as well.

You may not be able to control your central heating system in this way; but both it and the primary circuit of your indirect hot water system can be protected by the addition of a proprietary anti-freeze solution. Don't, however, be tempted to use the same anti-freeze you put in your car radiator, since it is quite unsuitable for central heating systems.

The only other really safe precaution is to drain the domestic hot and cold water systems. Turn off the main stopcock (located where the mains water enters the house) and empty the system by opening the draincock immediately above it if there is one. Remember to attach a length of hose and run it to the sink or outside, otherwise you will flood the room. Open all the taps as well until water stops running. The hot water storage cylinder and – with a direct hot water system – the boiler will still be filled with water. With a direct system this can be drained by connecting one end of a length of hose to the draincock beside the boiler and taking the other end to the sink (if nearby) or outside. Open the draincock and wait while the boiler empties. If you have an indirect hot water system – or a direct system heated only by an immersion heater – the appropriate draincock will be located by the cylinder, probably at the base of the cold water supply pipe which feeds it.

When you return home, remember the system is empty – and make sure you refill it before lighting the boiler fire. To reduce the risk of air locks forming as you do this, connect one end of a length of hose to the cold tap over the kitchen sink and the other end to the boiler draincock. Open up the tap and the draincock and the system will fill upwards, driving air before it.

2 A spring-loaded safety valve will give extra protection to your hot water system. If pressure builds up, the safety valve opens and relieves pressure in the pipes. Before fitting a safety valve, bind it with PTFE thread sealing tape

3 Wiring a frost-stat into an automatic central heating system. For a programmer with separate hot water and central heating settings, you will need a double pole frost-stat as shown in the diagram. The programmer selector should be set to 'Off' when the frost-stat is to be used

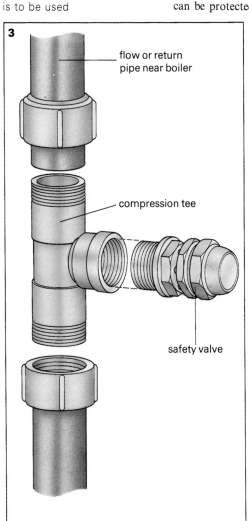

3

flow or return pipe near boiler

compression tee

safety valve

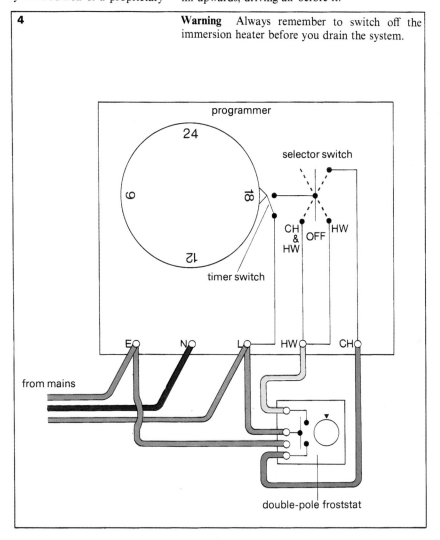

4

Warning Always remember to switch off the immersion heater before you drain the system.

programmer

24

9

18

12

selector switch

CH & HW   OFF   HW

timer switch

E   N   L   HW   CH

from mains

double-pole frostat

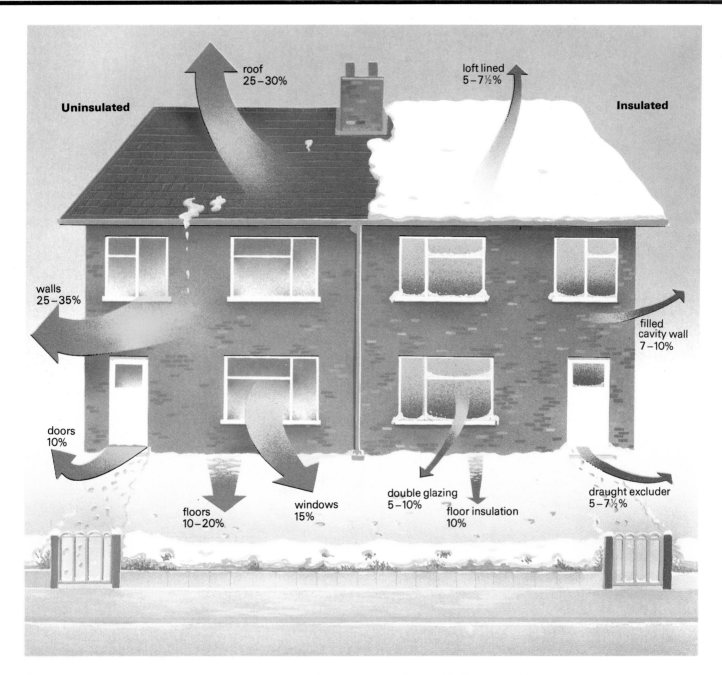

Uninsulated

roof
25–30%

loft lined
5–7½%

Insulated

walls
25–35%

filled
cavity wall
7–10%

doors
10%

floors
10–20%

windows
15%

double glazing
5–10%

floor insulation
10%

draught excluder
5–7⅓%

Reducing heat loss in the home

Many houses fall well below the minimum thermal insulation standards set under building regulations. Although some forms of insulation should be carried out by a professional, there is still much that can be done by the home handyman. Before you begin the process of keeping heat inside where it belongs, it is useful to understand the ways in which heat is lost from a house. The amount of heat lost does depend on the nature of

the building, its aspect and exposure to winds – and figures vary from house to house.

In a typical uninsulated house approximately one-quarter is lost through the roof, one-third through the walls, one-tenth through the doors, one-fifth through the windows and one-sixth through the floors. After insulation these losses can be cut down to approximately one-twentieth, one-tenth, one-twentieth, one-ninth and

one-tenth respectively. So although insulation does not prevent all the heat escaping, it substantially reduces the amount of loss and correspondingly diminishes the size of your heating bills. It shortens the time it takes to heat a room and enables you to keep down the number and size of radiators and the size of the boiler – or to install a less powerful and therefore less expensive central heating

system around the home. Forms of insulation vary from the simple rubber strip draught excluder on your door to insulating boards lining the walls. What you decide to do will depend on the amount of time and money you have available; but the more thoroughly you carry out the job, the greater the rewards will be in terms of comfort and eventual savings, which will well repay the initial expense and effort.

Insulating the loft

Heating costs rise with the warm air if heat is allowed to escape through the roof. By insulating the loft area you can keep down the bills and hold heat where it belongs – in the house. This is a job well within the scope of the handyman, requiring no special techniques. The materials are all readily available.

A loft that has no insulation will account for a heat loss of about 25 per cent in the average size house. Several forms of insulation are available and fall into two categories: loose-fill materials such as vermiculite granules, and the blanket type made from glass fibre or mineral wool. The materials we mention are all resistant to fire and you must check on the fire-resistance of any alternative product you consider buying. As a precaution, first treat all timber for woodworm.

joists in most houses, and can be cut quite easily with a large pair of scissors or a sharp knife. Even handled carefully, glass fibre can irritate the skin, so always wear gloves when working with it.

Mineral wool Another blanket insulation material, this is made from spun molten rock and is handled in the same way as glass fibre.

Laying rolls Place the roll of material between the joists and tuck the end under the eaves. Working backwards, unroll the material until you reach the other end of the roof. Cut it and tuck the end under the eaves as before. Lay the strip flat between the joists or, if it is a little wider, turn the sides up against the sides of the joists. Continue in this way until the whole loft area has been covered. If you have to join two strips in the middle of the roof, overlap them by about 75mm (3in).

Below left To lay granules, pour them between joists and level them with T-shaped piece of timber
Below If your insulating roll is wider than space between joists, turn up each side against joists
Below centre Don't lay insulation under cold water cistern; leave area uncovered so warm air from below can stop water freezing
Bottom Use latex adhesive to glue piece of glass fibre on loft flap

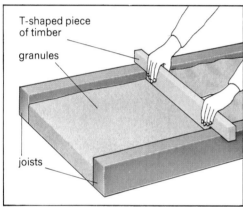

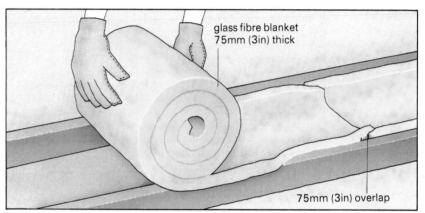

glass fibre blanket 75mm (3in) thick

75mm (3in) overlap

Granule insulation
One advantage of using granules to insulate your loft is that they flow easily and smoothly and will fill any awkward spaces. They are also safe to handle since they do not contain any splinters or loose fibres.

Vermiculite Expanded mica in granule form, this is supplied in easy-to-handle bags. The manufacturer's instructions will give you a guide to the number of bags needed for specific areas.

You should wear a mask and some form of eye protection when using vermiculite since it is a dusty material that easily gets into the atmosphere.

Laying granules Pour vermiculite between the joists to a depth of about 125mm (5in), which will bring it almost level with the top of the joists in most lofts. Level the granules by drawing a piece of timber along the top edges of the joists. If the joists are significantly deeper than 125mm, level the granules to the required depth by dragging a T-shaped spreader along the top of the joists. Make this from any piece of scrap wood a little longer than the joist separation, and notch its corners so the base of the T will fit between the joists.

Blanket insulation
This form of insulation does not need to be laid as thickly as granules and should be used in lofts where there are gaps around the eaves, since wind might blow the granules about.

Glass fibre The most economical form of blanket insulation for loft spaces. It comes in 100 or 150mm (4 or 6in) thick rolls and is available in 400mm (16in) widths, equivalent to the space between roof

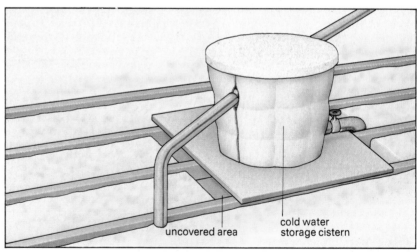

uncovered area

cold water storage cistern

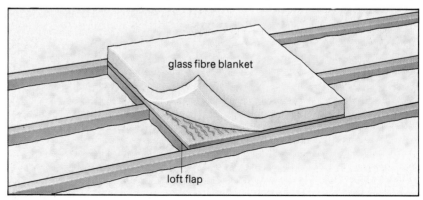

glass fibre blanket

loft flap

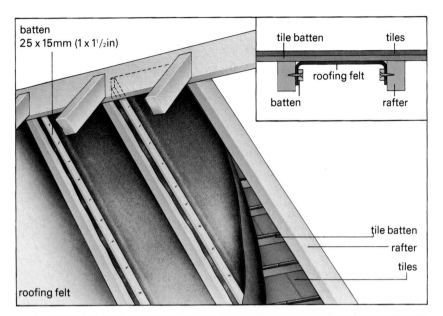

batten
25 x 15mm (1 x 1½in)

tile batten   tiles

roofing felt

batten   rafter

roofing felt

tile batten
rafter
tiles

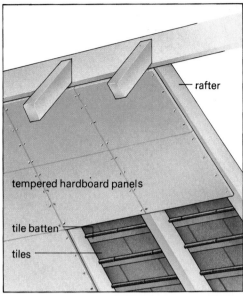

rafter

tempered hardboard panels

tile batten

tiles

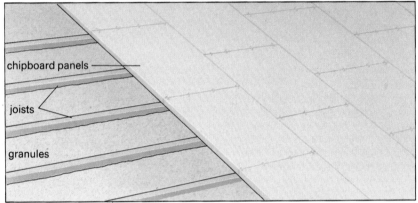

chipboard panels

joists

granules

Top When fixing felt between rafters, allow enough width to turn onto rafters and hold felt in place by screwing through battens and felt into rafters. **Inset** Cross-section of felt and batten fixing
Top right When insulating with tempered hardboard, butt-join panels and fix to rafters with countersunk screws
Above Improve insulation by laying floor using chipboard panels, staggering joins and screwing through sides of each panel into joists. Cut panels so they butt-join each other in middle of each joist

Insulating awkward areas You will find it easier to cover awkwardly shaped or inaccessible areas with granules. A 125mm (5in) thickness of granules is roughly equivalent to 100mm (4in) of blanket material in terms of insulation efficiency.
Warning Whichever method of insulation you use, don't insulate under the cold water tank. You must allow a warm air current to flow from below to prevent the tank from freezing in cold weather. But don't forget to insulate the loft flap or cover. Cut a piece of blanket material to the size of the cover and stick it down with a latex adhesive. And when working in the loft, remember to tread only on the joists or on a board placed across them.

Other forms of insulation
Even more insulation can be provided if you make a floor to the loft by fixing panels of chipboard or planks of timber to the joists above the insulating material. This will also give you extra storage space, but you may have to strengthen the joists by spanning the load-bearing walls with large timbers before laying the floor if you want to put heavy items on it. Seek advice from a builder or your local authority.

Heat loss through the roof space can be further reduced by lining the ceilings immediately below the loft with an insulating-type material such as expanded polystyrene or acoustic tiles. It should be emphasized, however, that this is not a substitute for loft insulation.

Effective insulation of the floor will make the loft colder, so it is vitally important to ensure the

cold water tank (except beneath it) and all pipes are thoroughly protected, otherwise they will be susceptible to frost damage.

Protection from frost
The type of loft most likely to suffer from frost damage is one with an unboarded tile-hung roof. If your roof has no close-boarding or roofing felt – as is the case with many older houses – it is worth insulating it.

Cut lengths of roofing felt about 200mm (8in) wider than the distance between the rafters. Lay one long edge onto the inside edge of one rafter, lay a 25×15mm ($1 \times \frac{1}{2}$in) batten onto the felt and screw through the batten and felt into the rafter. Use No 8 countersunk screws 25mm long, spacing them at 300–380mm (12–15in) intervals. Don't use nails as the vibration from hammering could dislodge and break the roof tiles. Stretch the roof felt across to the next rafter and fix the other edge onto the edge of that rafter, again screwing through a batten. Leave a space between the roof and the felt to allow air to circulate, otherwise you may find rot will form on the rafters.

An alternative to roofing felt is tempered hardboard: butt-joint each panel of hardboard to the next by screwing it to the centre of each rafter with No 8 countersunk screws 25mm long. You may have to trim your cut panels so they fit neatly in the middle of each rafter.

All this work can be done in easy stages; when you have finished, the roof space will certainly remain warmer in winter and will also be much cleaner – an important consideration if you are using the loft for storage.

Cutting sheets to size
Boards are available in 2440×1830mm (8×6ft) and 1830×1220mm (6×4ft) sheets. You need 25mm (1in) thick flooring grade chipboard or 6mm ($\frac{1}{4}$in) thick hardboard. Cut the larger sheet into six convenient 1830×407mm (6ft × 1ft 4in) panels, or the smaller one into three panels of the same size. If the loft opening space allows, cut the larger sheet into three 1830×813mm (6ft × 2ft 8in) panels, or the smaller sheet into one similar size panel and one 1830×407mm (6ft × 1ft 4in) panel.

Door, floor and window insulation

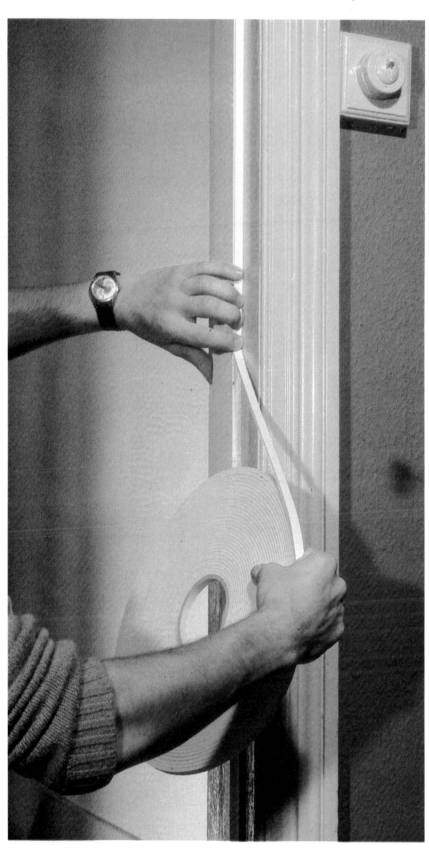

Cold air leaking in through gaps around doors and windows or through floorboards can account for up to ten per cent of the heat lost from a house. Eliminating the worst effects of draughts through doors, floors and windows is quite a simple task for the handyman, giving immediate financial returns which quickly pay for the inexpensive materials. Your winters will also be considerably more comfortable in a draught-free home. One solution to prevent draughts and help keep up the inside heat is to fit an excluder.

Draught excluders
One of the cheapest draught excluders is the plastic foam strip with an adhesive backing which you peel off as you apply the strip to a clean surface and cut to length with scissors. Although this is simple to use, it is less durable than other types and has to be replaced each year. It is effective if the gaps are not too wide and two strips can be used, for instance, on doors and door jambs or windows and frames so they come together when the door or window is closed.

Two more permanent draught excluders are the plastic (polypropylene) strip and the sprung metal strip. Both of these have ready-punched clearance holes, usually at about 25mm (1in) intervals, are tacked round the door or window rebate and are not visible when the door is closed. Because closing the door puts the strip under tension, however, it can cause the door to stick.

When using aluminium or phosphor bronze strips, position them with care and make sure there are no kinks when nailing them into place. For metal windows you should use an aluminium strip with a special groove to fit the window frame. Clean the frame with a stiff wire brush to remove rust and dirt and fill pit holes with plastic filler before applying the strip. If you clean right down to the bare metal you will have to apply a coat of metal primer after filling holes and leave it to dry before fixing the strip. With wire cutters or scissors, cut the strip in sections to the size of the frame sides and mitre across the width at the ends of each section. Fitting the top piece first and then the sides and bottom, push the groove of the strip over the outside lip of the frame. Push the corner clip tongues over the strip junctions and then turn the tongues of the clips over the flanges to secure the strip.

Under-door draughts
To eliminate draughts under doors, you can nail or screw a piece of 6mm ($\frac{1}{4}$in) thick timber batten at regular intervals, say two nails or screws per floorboard, across the threshold to form an effective seal. A carpet of the same thickness placed either side of the batten will stop people tripping

Foam tape seal, impregnated with adhesive, comes in 5 or 20m (16 or 65ft) long rolls. Easy to apply, it can be painted; and because it is very flexible you do not have to mitre the corners

431

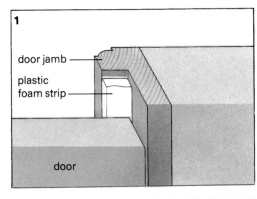

1

door jamb
plastic
foam strip

door

2

door jamb
plastic or
spring metal
strip

door

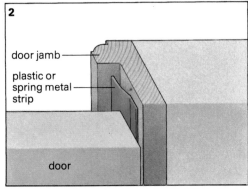

3

fixed
frame

glass

corner
clip tongue

putty
flange
groove

opening frame

aluminium strip

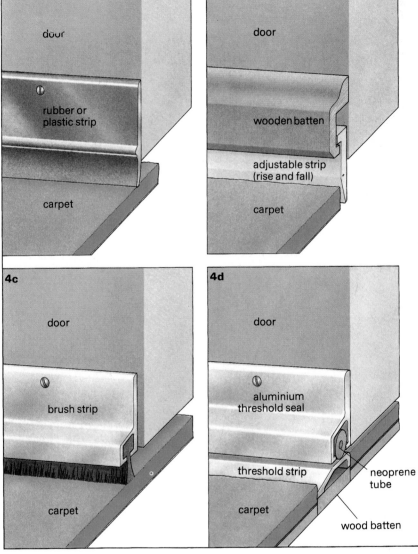

4a

door

rubber or
plastic strip

carpet

4b

door

wooden batten

adjustable strip
(rise and fall)

carpet

4c

door

brush strip

carpet

4d

door

aluminium
threshold seal

threshold strip

carpet

neoprene
tube

wood batten

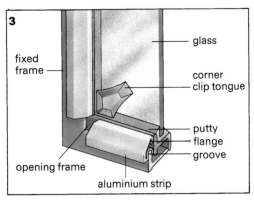

For doors and windows
excluder (of type required)
tacks, nails, screws, adhesive (as needed)
wire-cutters or tin snips
scissors
hammer
hacksaw (for aluminium)
panel saw (for wood)
screwdriver
plane (as needed)
wire brush (as needed)
plastic filler (as needed)
metal primer (as needed)

For floors
papier mâché or wood filler
22mm ($\frac{7}{8}$in) quadrant or scotia moulding
32mm ($1\frac{1}{4}$in) oval wire nails
paper-faced glass fibre flanged
    building roll
knife
staple gun
staples
hammer
filling knife

equipment

over it. Alternatively, bevel the edges of the batten with a plane to make a less sharp rise from the floor.

Other excluders are made of rubber mouldings, aluminium sections or a combination of metal and plastic, so you must choose the most effective for the job in hand.

Warning You may have to take the door off its hinges and trim the bottom so the door opens and shuts freely. Otherwise, fix excluders when the door is in place.

A simple type of excluder for interior doors is a flexible plastic or rubber strip which you screw or stick to the bottom of the door so it brushes over the floor covering. Measure carefully so you do not fix this too high to be effective or too low so as to put too much wear on the floor covering. If the door has to clear a mat, a rise and fall type excluder is available. Here a flexible strip is forced, by moving over the floor covering, to ride up into a hollow wood moulding fitted to the bottom of the door and drops back into place when the door is shut. A brush strip excluder and aluminium threshold seal are also designed to ride over carpets. For exterior doors some draught excluder threshold strips come in two halves – one is fixed to the threshold and the other to the door. The two halves interlock when the door is closed.

1 Plastic foam strip attached to door jamb
2 Plastic or sprung metal strip fixed to door jamb
3 Aluminium strip around window frame
4a Flexible rubber or plastic strip on bottom of door
4b Rise and fall strip
4c Brush strip attached to metal plate at bottom of door to ride over carpet
4d Aluminium threshold seal with threshold strip raised to clear carpet

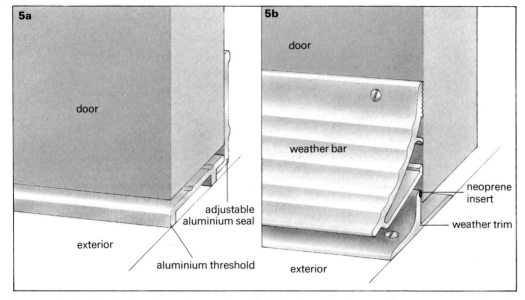

5a Aluminium door strip in two halves which interlock
5b Weatherproof threshold excluder

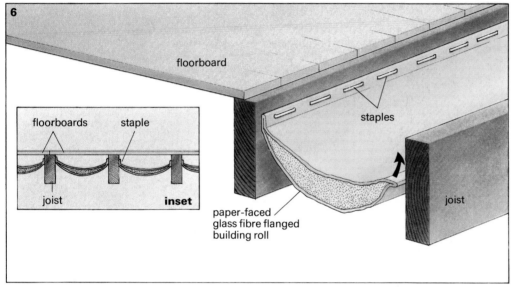

6 Paper-faced glass fibre flanged building roll stapled between joists. **Inset** Staple to each joist in turn to insulate complete floor

A badly-fitting letter-box can be very draughty. Inexpensive draught excluders are made specifically to overcome this problem.

Floor draughts

Having prevented draughts around doors and windows, the problem may still not have been entirely solved. Floorboards may have gaps which you should plug with papier-mâché or wood filler. You can also nail down strips of quadrant or scotia moulding to the floor to cover gaps between the floor and the skirting. Covering the floor with either vinyl or carpet afterwards makes an even better job.

If the boards are badly worn and damaged, and there are a lot of gaps between them, it is best to relay the floor. If it is a ground-floor room this is a good opportunity to install underfloor insulation.
Underfloor insulation A very simple method is to staple paper-faced, glass-fibre, flanged building roll under the floorboards. Rolls are available in a range of widths to fit exactly between the joists.

Using a staple gun or hammer and staples, fix one flange of the roll to a joist. The staples should be about 100mm (4in) apart. Then staple the flange on the other side of the roll to the next joist and repeat the process for the other joists to complete the insulation.

Checking for draughts

It is best to work systematically around the house so no likely areas are missed. Eliminate the worst draughts first. To find out where door and window draughts are coming from, check paintwork which has not been washed down for some time. Draughts bring with them a considerable amount of dirt, so a build-up of dirt around the edges of doors and windows and their frames indicates some form of excluder is needed. Another way is to hold a lighted candle a safe distance away from the edges of doors and windows and move it gently along the line of the edge. Any sudden flickering of the flame indicates a draught. Don't get too close to any soft furnishings when using this method.

Double-glazing

Undoubtedly, this is the best answer to a draughty window and double-glazing will be covered in detail later on in the book. A well-fitting system will completely seal off the sources of entry of cold air. Although this is certainly an expensive undertaking solely to overcome draughts, remember that not only will sound insulation be substantially increased, but additionally a quite considerable saving on fuel bills will result after the initial outlay.

Wall insulation

Heat loss through walls can be reduced in a number of ways. Apart from one specialist method, there are three simple jobs you can tackle yourself – lining walls with plasterboard laminate, expanded polystyrene or foil.

Heat produced in a house eventually escapes to the outside via draughts and through the roof, walls and windows. The nature of the building affects the rate of loss and the path it takes. A bungalow loses more heat through the roof, while a two-storey detached house loses more through the walls. After thermal insulation there will still be heat losses, but the warmth will be dissipated at a much slower rate and heat can therefore be replaced at an equally slower rate. If your heating system is inadequate, insulation can at least ensure more effective use of the heat before it escapes.

Besides comfort from warmth, another reason for insulation is to reduce condensation. The warmer the air in a heated room, the more water vapour it can contain. When the air cools, as it does when it meets a colder wall or window, the water turns into droplets known as condensation. Insulating the walls results in these internal surfaces being kept warmer and the heat in the room being retained longer, so there is not such a dramatic contrast between the temperature of the air and the surfaces on which condensation forms. So condensation is eliminated or at least reduced. Also, insulation means that heating levels can be kept lower and, when desirable, temperatures can be boosted more effectively.

Cavity walls

Insulation of cavity walls is not a job for the home handyman – it should be carried out only by an approved contractor. The material generally used for cavity filling is urea formaldehyde foam which is injected into the cavity under pressure through holes drilled in the outer wall. There it sets, trapping millions of tiny air pockets which act as a barrier against escaping heat.

Other materials used are mineral wool fibre blown into the cavity in a similar way to urea

To insulate cavity walls, small holes are drilled in the mortar courses (below), the foam is pumped into the cavity (top) and the holes made good (above)

formaldehyde foam, and glass fibre panels placed in the cavity at the time the wall is built.

Warning Installing cavity wall insulation requires Building Regulations approval from your local authority. The materials and methods used must be approved, especially if urea-formaldehyde foam types are being installed.

Solid walls

There are a number of ways to insulate solid walls. The method you choose will depend on the lengths you wish to go to and the time and money you have available.

Lining with boards

One of the most common and effective methods of insulating solid walls is to line the inside of exterior walls with insulating board. Good results can be obtained with ordinary fibre insulating panels, but greater savings in heat loss can be gained by using plasterboard laminate, which is an extremely bad conductor of heat. This material consists of rigid urethane foam (polyurethane having a very low level of thermal conductivity) with a tough waterproof backing, a vapour barrier and a layer of plasterboard with a paper backing. When used on ceilings in particular, this board not only reduces heat losses and gives a surface which warms up rapidly but, when bonded to the ceiling with adhesive and finished with gypsum plaster or texturing compound, it minimises the risk of condensation and is especially valuable in combating persistent condensation. For use on walls, the total thickness of board should be 21mm (or $\frac{7}{8}$in). It is most effective when fixed to a timber batten framework and used with other insulating material such as mineral wool quilting.

Fixing First remove all electrical fittings (after isolating the supply at the mains), cove, window and door surrounds and skirting. Cut the boards to shape by slicing through the waterproof backing and foam with a sharp knife or fine tooth saw, before snapping the board and cutting through the facing paper. It is important to cut away the foam at the joins so plasterboard edges will butt together to give a continuous surface. With screws and wall plugs, fix a timber batten framework (treated with wood preservative) to the wall. The main framework is made of 50×25mm (2×1in) timber and the inside supporting pieces of 38×25mm ($1\frac{1}{2} \times 1$in) timber. Ensure the timber framework is 25mm (1in) thick overall. Apply impact adhesive to the wall and loosely fix strips of mineral wool quilting between the battens. Then apply impact adhesive to the battens in strips and in a corresponding position on the boards so the strips match up when the two surfaces are joined. Fix the boards in place, taking care to position them accurately since they cannot easily be moved once contact has been made. For a smooth finish, fill any gaps between the boards with cellulose filler reinforced with plasterboard joint tape.

You will have to remount electrical fittings and refix ceiling cover door and window surrounds and skirting to bring these to the new level. If desirable, window sills can be tiled to raise their level using extra tiles positioned on top of the existing sill so they project slightly in front of the face of the plasterboard.

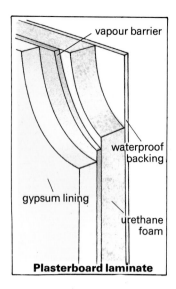

Plasterboard laminate

Above The composition of plasterboard laminate – an extremely effective insulating material

Below left To fix the boards, screw a timber framework to the walls and apply mineral wool quilting between the battens

Below Spread impact adhesive on the boards and the battens and position the boards accurately on the framework

Fixing mineral wool between battens

mineral wool

adhesive

batten

wall

skirting

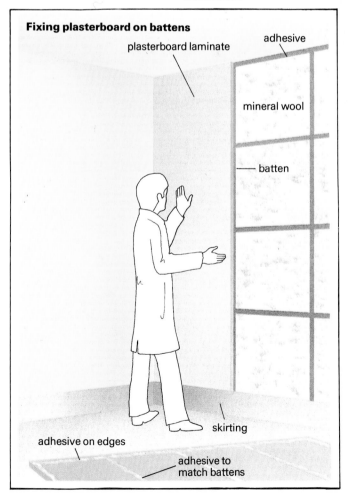

Fixing plasterboard on battens

plasterboard laminate

adhesive

mineral wool

batten

skirting

adhesive on edges

adhesive to match battens

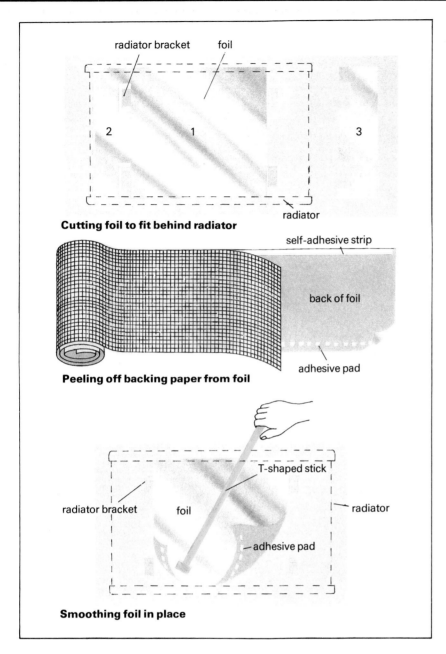

radiator bracket   foil

2   1   3

radiator

Cutting foil to fit behind radiator

self-adhesive strip

back of foil

adhesive pad

Peeling off backing paper from foil

T-shaped stick

radiator bracket   foil   radiator

adhesive pad

Smoothing foil in place

Both types of foil are easier to fix than the frequently-used aluminium kitchen foil, which tears easily during fixing. Applying any foil is obviously considerably simplified if access to the wall is improved by removal of the radiator from its wall brackets. If the radiators are positioned below a window, make sure no damp is penetrating the wall around the window frame before fixing foil, as the drying effect will be reduced.

Lining with expanded polystyrene
A simple, inexpensive way of reducing condensation on cold exterior walls is to line them with expanded polystyrene veneer before papering or decorating. However, these veneers are not thick enough to cut down significantly on heat losses.

This lining is available in 2–5mm (or $\frac{1}{12}$ – $\frac{3}{16}$ in) thicknesses and is supplied in rolls. Apply it in the same way as wallpaper. Make sure walls are clean and dry then spread a heavy duty fungicidal wallpaper adhesive or polystyrene adhesive onto the wall and apply the lining. At joins allow 13mm ($\frac{1}{2}$in) overlap, cut the overlap with a sharp knife, remove the waste edges, apply more adhesive and lightly roll the edges. If you intend to decorate with a heavy wallpaper, it is advisable to apply a lining paper over the polystyrene lining before fixing the wallpaper.

Expanded polystyrene panels or tiles can be used instead. Use the tile-fixing adhesive recommended by the manufacturer. If you decide to paint the tiles or panels, remember to use a fire-retardant paint. Check with your supplier which paint is suitable.

Warning Never paint expanded polystyrene with gloss paint, since this can dangerously increase the rate of surface spread of flame in a fire.

Lining with plasterboard laminate
21mm (or $\frac{7}{8}$in) thick plasterboard
 laminate insulating boards
50 × 25mm (2 × 1in) timber batten
38 × 25mm (1$\frac{1}{2}$×1in) timber batten
wood preservative
No 10 countersunk screws 63mm (2$\frac{1}{2}$in)
 long, wall plugs 38mm (1$\frac{1}{2}$in) long
mineral wool quilting
 additional tiles for sill (if needed)
trimming knife or fine tooth saw
hand or electric drill, 5mm ($\frac{3}{16}$ in) twist
 drill and masonry bits,
 countersink bit
impact adhesive
hammer, screwdriver
cellulose filler, plasterboard joint tape

Lining with expanded polystyrene
expanded polystyrene veneer
heavy duty fungicidal wallpaper
 adhesive or polystyrene adhesive
brush, knife, boxwood roller
lining paper (if needed)
expanded polystyrene panels or tiles,
 tile adhesive (for ceiling)

Lining behind radiators
self-adhesive heat reflecting radiator
 foil with applicator, or foil with
 self-adhesive pads and tape
scissors

equipment

Above Use heat-reflecting foil behind radiators. Cut the foil into three, trimming it to fit round the radiator brackets. Peel off the paper backing, position the foil behind the radiator and smooth it into place

Lining behind radiators
It is also worthwhile lining the wall behind radiators with self-adhesive heat reflecting foil. This is reinforced with glass fibre and plastic-coated (to prevent tarnishing for several years).

Turn off the radiators and make sure the wall behind them is cool and clean before applying the foil. Cut the foil to a size slightly smaller than the radiator so it will not protrude when in position. For easy application, cut it into three pieces with slots in the end sections cut to fit round the radiator brackets. Remove the backing of the centre piece, place it in position against the wall and smooth it down with the applicator which is supplied with the foil. Repeat for the end pieces.

Another type of foil is available which allows more flexibility when positioning, where there is very limited space between the radiator and wall. It is fixed by an adhesive tape at the top and self-adhesive pads at the bottom. Hang the foil behind the radiator and, when it is in the correct position, press along the top to seal the tape to the wall. Then press the pads at the bottom into place to complete this very simple process for reducing heat wastage.

Insulating with boards

Hardboards and insulating boards are made from wood: the natural timber is reduced to fibres which are then reassembled to form large sheets. There is no grain, there are no knots and the surface is smooth and even every time. Wood fibre boards provide insulation where it's needed – on the warm side – to reduce heat loss through walls, ceilings and floors.

Types of board
The range of special types for a great variety of commercial uses is considerable, but for the home handyman the ones most readily available – apart from insulating board – are standard, tempered, medium and decorated hardboard.

Insulating board is non-compressed, lightweight and porous and is used for heat insulation, particularly on ceilings and walls. It is available in 13, 19 and 25mm ($\frac{1}{2}$, $\frac{3}{4}$ and 1in) thicknesses and also comes in the form of planks or tiles. Decorated insulating board is most commonly found in the form of ceiling tiles.

Conditioning Wood fibre boards may take up moisture from the surrounding air, causing them to expand, so it is always best to condition the boards before fixing. The treatment varies with the type of board so always check first with your supplier.

All these materials are relatively easy to handle and will cover large areas quickly. The following suggestions will give you ideas for using boards, planks and tiles.

Insulating walls
Hardboard and insulating boards can provide effective insulation if used on the inside of external walls. In houses with solid walls – as is the case with more than half of Britain's homes – this is almost the only way of providing insulation.

Where the board is unlikely to suffer rough treatment (in bedrooms, for example) and the walls are sound and flat, decorated insulating board may be stuck direct with impact adhesive. Denser standard or medium hardboards should be used if walls are likely to suffer at the hands of children. These provide heat insulation when mounted on a batten framework by creating an air gap. Lining the cavity with aluminium foil will also help.

Direct gluing Prepare painted walls by washing with household detergent or a solution of water and sugar soap. Glasspaper down to remove any flaking paint and to provide a key for the adhesive. Wallpapered areas must be completely stripped and glasspapered down.

Above Boards finished with hessian provide an attractive wall covering as well as insulation against heat loss. Fix the boards quickly by gluing them direct to the wall with impact adhesive **(inset)**

Fixing to battens (wall)

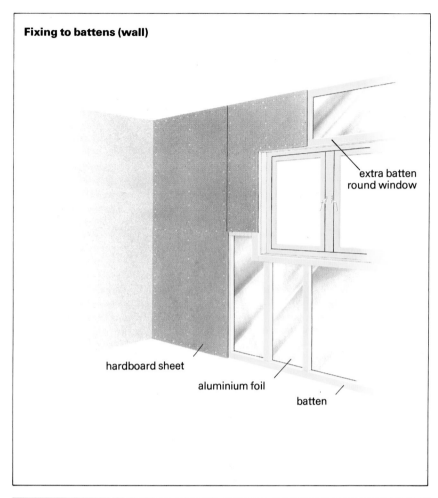

extra batten round window

hardboard sheet

aluminium foil

batten

Order of tiling unsquare ceiling

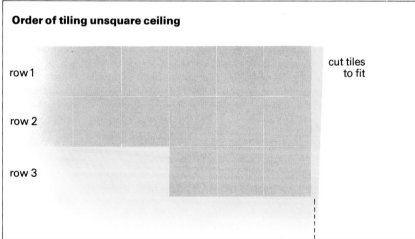

row 1

row 2

row 3

cut tiles to fit

Fixing the boards If desired, tape sheets of aluminium foil into place between the battens. Fix decorated boards to the framework with impact adhesive to avoid damaging the finish and work from the centre of the board, upwards and downwards, to prevent the board bulging in the middle.

Other types of board should be fixed with rust-resistant round head nails or hardboard pins. Fix the top of the board to the battens about 13mm ($\frac{1}{2}$in) in from the edge at 100mm (4in) intervals, working outwards from the centre. Then fix the board to the vertical battens at 150mm (6in) intervals, working upwards and downwards from the centre. Finally secure the other edges at 100mm (4in) intervals, 12mm ($\frac{1}{2}$in) in from the edge.

Finishing off For an attractive finish you can use either emulsion paint or wallpaper. Before painting, use glasspaper to round off the board edges and key the surface for the paint. Prime the boards with special hardboard primer or diluted emulsion paint (one part water to four parts paint) before giving the finishing coats. If using wallpaper, first seal the boards with a coat of hardboard primer.

Insulating ceilings

In the average house most heat is lost through the roof and it has been estimated that more than a quarter of the homes in Britain have either no lofts or no access to loft space. In such cases insulating the underside of the upstairs ceiling is the only effective answer. Fixing 13mm ($\frac{1}{2}$in) fibre insulating board tiles to the ceiling will reduce the heat loss from the house in winter by about ten per cent; the time it takes to heat up a room is also reduced. Using decorated tiles ensures an attractive finish. from the house in winter by about ten per cent; the

Planning and fixing

First decide on the method of fixing. If the ceiling can be easily cleaned and is reasonably flat, fixing the tiles direct to the ceiling with acoustic tile adhesive is the easiest and most economical way. If the ceiling is loose, badly cracked or very uneven, it will be necessary to screw wood battens through the ceiling to the timbers above.

Measure the ceiling and other surfaces to be tiled. For a symmetrical job, with equal margins of cut tiles at opposite sides of the room, it is worthwhile drawing the areas to be tiled on a planning grid. This will not only act as a guide to the number of tiles required but will also help in determining the positions, lengths and number of battens, if these are to be used, and amount of adhesive needed.

Insulating board tiles usually come in 305 × 305mm (12 × 12in) sizes in cartons of 30, 60 or 100. Adhesive manufacturers also normally state the covering capacity of their products – for example, 1 litre for 2sq m (or 2pt for 22sq ft) of tile area.

Direct gluing First wash down the ceiling with household detergent or a solution of water and sugar soap and scrape away any stubborn flaking paint. Check the corners are square by drawing a line at right-angles to the longer wall. Plan to start fixing in a corner with the first row of tiles against the longer wall.

With a putty knife apply 25mm (1in) diameter blobs of acoustic tile adhesive to the back of the tiles at each corner. Press the tiles into place on the ceiling, ensuring each tile lines up with the one before. Adhesive can be applied to a number of tiles at a time and the tiles fixed one after the other.

Tiles which fit together with tongues and grooves

Spread impact adhesive in strips on both the wall and the insulating boards. Start fixing at the corner of the wall, as far as possible pressing each board onto the wall from the centre, upwards and downwards, to prevent bulging. Butt-join the boards, taking care not to damage the edges.

Fixing to battens Construct the framework from 50 × 25mm (2 × 1in) timber battens. Drill holes in the horizontal battens at about 400mm (16in) intervals for standard hardboards and 610mm (24in) intervals for thicker ones. Drill holes in the vertical battens at 1200mm (48in) intervals. Now drill corresponding holes in the wall, insert wall fixings and screw the battens into position. Make sure the battens are level, packing low areas with hardboard offcuts if necessary.

Fixing tongued and grooved tiles

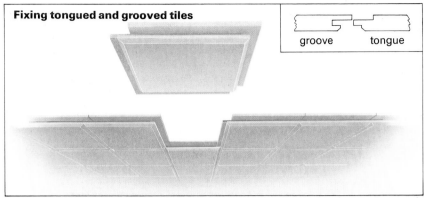

groove   tongue

Fixing to battens (ceiling)

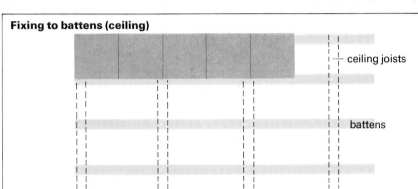

ceiling joists

battens

Section of finished surface

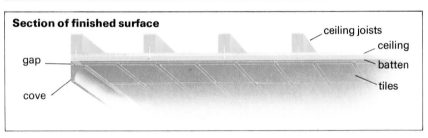

gap

cove

ceiling joists

ceiling

batten

tiles

Order of nailing hardboard to floorboards

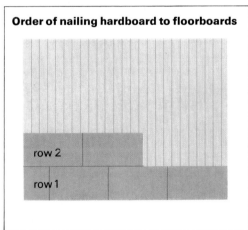

row 2

row 1

Fixing hardboard to panelled door

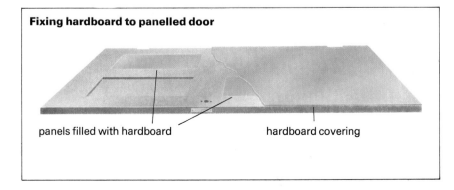

panels filled with hardboard

hardboard covering

Concealed fixing method

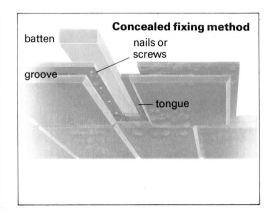

batten

nails or
screws

groove

tongue

are easier to use and give a more level finish. For
the first row, however, remember to cut off one of
the tongues on each tile so the plain edges go next
to the wall, allowing a small gap for expansion.

Fixing to battens First establish by trial and error
the position and direction of the roof timbers by
knocking nails through the ceiling. Once you have
located one or two timbers the rest will be easy to
locate since they run parallel to, and are equidistant from, each other. Since the ceiling will later
be covered, a few holes will not matter.

Cut $50 \times 25mm$ ($2 \times 1in$) timber battens to run
across the line of the timbers and screw them to the
timbers at 305mm (12in) intervals. Make sure the
undersides of the battens are level with one another,
packing them if necessary with offcuts of hardboard.

Fix the tiles to the battens with staples or round
head nails. With tongued and grooved tiles the
fixings are concealed by the tongue of the next tile.

Finishing For the best finish fix cove to cover the
join between the tiles and the walls.

Insulating floors

Standard hardboards are used to improve both
timber and concrete floors. On suspended timber
floors you can eliminate draughts and so reduce
heat loss by nailing hardboard to the floor, making
sure the joins in the hardboard and the floor do
not coincide. Hardboard applied to plain-edged
floorboards above lath and plaster ceilings provides the minimum fire resistance required by
current building regulations. Again, the joins in the
hardboard and the floor must not coincide.

Heat insulation on concrete floors is improved
by bonding sheets of insulation board in place with
bituminous adhesive. Cover this with carpeting or,
if you intend to place heavy items on the floor, use
a harder-surfaced insulating board.

Never put down hardboard or insulating board
on a concrete floor where damp is suspected. Treatment for this situation has already been described –
see page 62 onwards.

Insulating doors

You can improve the fire resistance of old panelled
doors by fixing on hardboard. To do this you will
have to remove the door and take off the fitments.
Glue medium board into the existing panels and
cover the whole door with 3mm ($\frac{1}{8}$in) standard
hardboard, nailed into place. The extra thickness of
hardboard on the door may mean you have to re-
hang the door further away from the closure bead
(by extending the hinge recesses in the door frame)
or move the closure bead further away.

Double glazing

While heat losses vary depending on the nature of a building and its aspect, in a typical uninsulated house about 15 percent of house heat is lost through the windows. If all the windows in such a house are double-glazed, this heat loss will be halved to give a seven and a half percent saving on fuel bills. There are many factors which can affect this figure – for example, the type of system used and how well it is fitted. Installing double glazing in an old cottage with just a few small windows would not obtain this saving, whereas there will be higher savings in a modern 'goldfish bowl' type of property.

Double glazing is not a money saver on the scale of other forms of insulation such as glass fibre laid in the loft or cavity wall infill; however, there are a number of reasons why you will find the necessary expenditure worthwhile to add to the comfort of your home. An efficient system will eliminate cold, draughty areas round windows, making the whole floor area of a room usable on cold days, and rooms will seem larger without the need for occupants to cluster round the fire or radiators.

Preventing condensation
When rooms are properly heated and ventilated, condensation will be reduced and possibly eliminated by double-glazed windows, since the inner panes of glass will be warmer and less susceptible to misting. With some double glazing systems, interpane misting may occur; this is usually slight and can be wiped away provided the new window is hinged or sliding. Alternatively you can place silica gel crystals between the panes of glass; these absorb moisture and, when saturated, should be temporarily removed and dried in a warm oven.

Misting on the room side of the window indicates the temperature of the glass is too low, given the water content of the room's atmosphere; by a process of trial and error, you should carry out adjustment until there is a proper balance between heat and ventilation in the room.

Condensation on the cavity surface of the outer glass is usually a sign that moist air is leaking into the cavity from the room. Make the seal round the new double glazing as airtight as possible, using a

1 Sachets of silica gel crystals placed between the two panes of glass can help reduce interpane misting; when saturated, the sachets should be removed, dried in a warm oven and replaced
2 To cure condensation on the cavity surface of the outer glass, drill ventilation holes right through the primary frame
3 Drill the ventilation holes 10mm deep and pack them with glass fibre to act as a filter

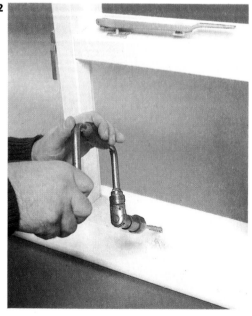

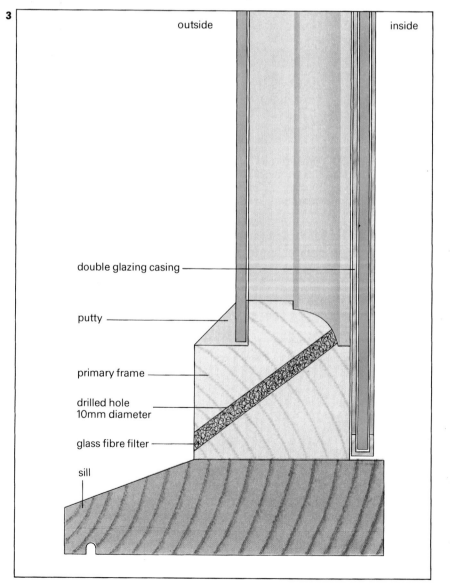

outside   inside

double glazing casing

putty

primary frame

drilled hole 10mm diameter

glass fibre filter

sill

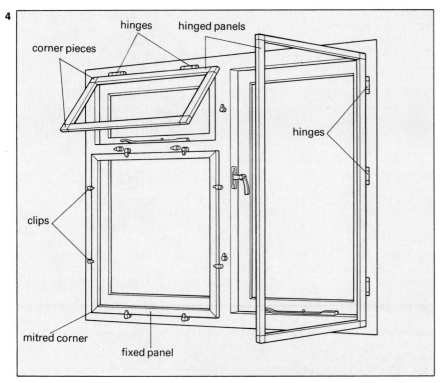

4

5

4 Installing fixed or hinged double glazing. The new panes are fitted in aluminium or plastic U-shaped channel, joined at the corners by mitring or by using special corner pieces; use hinges to fix the panels to opening windows and clips for fixed windows

5 Using plastic film as double glazing; cut the film to size and fix it to the frame with double-sided adhesive tape

noise permeating through windows from typical town traffic or a local playground. However, if your noise problem is more acute, noise prevention is a more extensive technical matter – the actual source of the noise, the location of the house, the type of glass thickness needed, the distance the two panes are set apart and any additional insulation around windows or between the double glazing should all be considered before you buy any expensive system to solve the problem.

Remember Government grants to install double glazing can be given to people living in certain heavy traffic areas or where there is an airport nearby. Your local authority will be able to supply details and advice.

In normal noise level situations the two sheets of glass in a double glazing system should be at least 100mm (or 4in) apart to provide adequate sound insulation. To provide effective thermal insulation, the optimum gap should be of 19mm ($\frac{3}{4}$in). If you want both sound and thermal insulation, you should select a wider gap of up to 200mm (or 8in); you will find thermal insulation is not greatly reduced in this case.

Buying double glazing

Certain double glazing firms do not cater for the DIY market, others cater for both professional and DIY work and some solely for the DIY market. If you choose a professional installation, a representative from the company will call on you, discuss your requirements, measure up and arrange for the work to be carried out by company operatives. If you choose to install double glazing yourself, you will find local retail outlets stock at least one kind of kit for the framework. Measure up your requirements and buy the correct size; then read the instructions carefully to find out the thickness of glass required – 3 or 4mm (or $\frac{1}{8}$ or $\frac{1}{6}$ in) – and the height and width of glass. Glass can vary in price, so it is well worth shopping around.

One or two companies offer a mail order service whereby you measure up, send the firm the dimensions and they return a kit – in one case at least the glass also is supplied. At least one company offers the best of both worlds – a company representative will call and measure up and you will then receive a tailor-made kit complete with glass. The advantage of this method of buying double glazing is the company takes responsibility for any errors in measuring and making the framework; also, since you are dealing directly with a company and not through a middle man, this system is often less expensive than other systems.

Costs Depending on the house style and the system chosen, to double glaze all the windows in a house could be a costly business. You could reduce the amount by completing only selected windows – perhaps those in the living room, hall and landing or a particularly draughty bedroom. A little-used dining room or spare bedroom might not be worth the expense; it would probably be better to keep the doors of these rooms closed and well sealed in cold weather to prevent the house heat drifting into them. When they are in use, heavy curtains pulled across would be as effective as double glazing, as long as the windows have been effectively draught-proofed.

Factors which can drastically affect the price of double glazing one window, let alone all the windows in the house, are obviously the cost of the

tape form of draught excluder, and seal any gaps in the joints of a timber framework with a matching wood filler, making sure the filler penetrates through the full depth of the joint.

If this fails to cure the problem, drill ventilation holes through the primary frame to the drier air outside. In a 1m (39in) wide window, two 10mm (or $\frac{3}{8}$in) diameter holes set 500mm (or 20in) apart should be sufficient. More will be needed for larger windows; you can decide the exact number by a process of trial and error – drilling an extra hole and waiting to see if this cures the problem. Pack the holes with glass fibre to act as an air filter.

With hermetically sealed units (see below) the air in the cavity is dried, so condensation between the panes is not possible as long as the seals remain sound; failure of the seals is a rare occurrence, but reputable manufacturers give long-term guarantees to cover the possibility.

Sound insulation
Installing a good quality double glazing system will give a substantial reduction in the decibel level of

glass and the retail price of the kit you choose, which again can differ from shop to shop.

Types of double glazing

There are four types of double glazing in common use: insulating glass, secondary sashes, coupled windows and plastic film.

Insulating (hermetically sealed) glass These units look like a single pane of glass and consist of two pieces of glass joined together and hermetically sealed in the factory – a process in which the air space between the panes is dried to prevent misting when installed. The pieces of glass are sealed with edge spacers of metal, alloy or plastic. The units are tailor-made and replace a single pane, enabling a window to open and close normally.

There are two types – standard and stepped. The stepped units are ideal where there are shallow rebates since installation can be carried out without having to alter the existing frame to accept the new units. The existing frame must be well fitting and sound enough to take the extra weight which will be imposed by the units.

Secondary sashes This is the most popular DIY method of installing double glazing. A second pane of glass in its own frame is secured to the existing frame or to the inner or outer sill and reveal; in some circumstances it is possible to fit the new window outside the existing frame. The existing window remains unaltered to form the other half of the double glazing. Manufacturers supply frames of aluminium or plastic; other types consist of plastic extrusions which are cut to length and joined with corner fittings to enable a frame for the glass to be made up. Hinges or clips are then used to secure the secondary sash to the existing window. The secondary sash is movable for cleaning, ventilation or summer storage and can be fixed, hinged or sliding.

Coupled windows These are usually specified only for new buildings or where entire frames are being replaced during conversion. One single-glazed window has an auxiliary window coupled to it, allowing both to move together. They are fitted with hinges and fasteners so the frames can be separated for cleaning purposes.

Plastic film This is a low-cost one-season option which can be a very effective form of double glazing for fixed windows. Plastic film is cut to size and applied to the window frame with double-sided adhesive tape. If you use this method, make sure that where windows are to be opened they are double-glazed separately from fixed panes; if a complete film was stretched across the entire window it would not be possible to open the window without first removing the film.

If you are restricted to a very small budget, you can use kitchen self-clinging plastic to make a form of double glazing for small panes. For larger panes, you will have to break up the pane space with a thin timber framework to create the effect of smaller panes and fix the film inside these smaller areas.

Installing double glazing

If you are going to install your own double glazing, it is likely you will choose a secondary sash type since kits for these are widely available and are relatively easy to install.

There are, however, a number of problems you may come across when fitting them. For example,

they can be fitted to existing timber or metal window frames; but if metal frames are fixed directly into masonry, you will have to drill and tap the frame to provide screw-fixing points or fit a secondary timber frame to accept the double glazing, particularly if the frame is too narrow. However, most metal windows are set in a timber surround and this can be treated as the window.

If you want to fix the double glazing frame to the reveal, you may come across the problem of an out-of-square reveal; to deal with this you will have to pack the out-of-square area with timber wedges or choose a system which fits directly to the window. Again, certain types of kit require the channels in which the new glazing is fitted to be mitred at the corners and joined. If you think you will find this too much of a problem, choose a type which is supplied with corner pieces. Remember to cut the channel lengths squarely at the ends or you will find it difficult to fit on the corner pieces and the final appearance of the glazing will be marred. Also, don't expect the glass to be a push-fit into the channel; it might slide in, but often you will need to encourage this by tapping gently with a mallet or with a hammer and a block of wood placed to protect the glass.

Warning If you are going to double glaze bay windows, remember to treat each window as a separate unit.

There are many makes of secondary sash double glazing available and the manufacturers supply

6 Fitting sliding secondary sashes; this type may be fixed to the face of the window or to the reveal

7 Fitting shatterproof panels into self-adhesive plastic track; mark the sill trim where it reaches the edge of the frame

8 Cut the side channel to length, remove the adhesive backing and press the strip onto the wall

9 Fit the top channel along the top of the frame

10 To shape the panels, score with a sharp knife and break over the edge of a firm surface

11 Fit the first panel, slit the top channel at the end of the panel and clip in place

12 Fix a panel divider and continue fitting the panels

13 Fit the final panel, ensuring the side channel is pressed firmly along its length

14 The finished installation; separate panels can be removed by opening the channel at the top and side

6

7

8

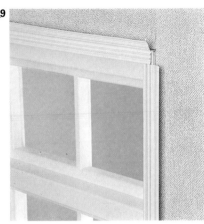
9

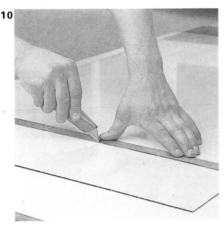
10

11

12

13

14

detailed instructions for installation. There are, however, three basic types of system: plastic channel, fixed or hinged, and sliding secondary sashes.

Plastic channel With this type, each pane of glass is fitted into a frame made by cutting lengths of U-shaped plastic channel to size; remove any sharp edges from the glass with a carborundum stone. The corners of the channel have to be mitred. Using a sharp knife and a mitre guide, cut the first mitre corner and then fit the channel to the glass to determine the position of the second corner. Remove the channel and mitre-cut at this position; repeat this process until all four corners have been cut. Secure the channel to the glass; some kits require the use of adhesive to form a rigid frame. Hold this assembly up to the window and fix it in place on the frame with the plastic clips supplied with the kit.

With this type of double glazing, out-of-square reveals will not cause problems since the channel is always fixed to the frame.

Fixed or hinged Usually this type consists of plastic or aluminium channel cut to shape and joined at the corners by mitring or by using special corner pieces. Fixing is either by clips to non-opening windows or by hinges to opening windows (the new windows can be hinged to open sideways or upwards). You could, of course, use hinges with fixed windows to make them easier to clean. This type of double glazing will, if correctly assembled, eliminate draughts and the new windows can be removed for summer storage.

Before you buy this type of system, read the manufacturer's instructions carefully to check the frame around your window is wide enough to take the double glazing and that it is made of the right material to take this particular system. With some systems the manufacturer recommends fixing only to wood rather than metal frames. Again, your existing window catches or handles may protrude in such a way they will interfere with the installation of the new system. You can usually solve these problems by fitting a secondary timber frame to take the double glazing; butt-join the corners of the frame, fill in any gaps with wood filler and apply a wood primer followed by two coats of paint, allowing the first coat to dry before applying the second.

There is one system which uses PVC shatterproof panels instead of glass. These are fitted into self-adhesive plastic tracks which are cut and pressed into place to the wall outside the reveal. The panels can be easily removed, but you may consider this too much trouble with opening windows.

Sliding Usually this type is fitted in the reveal. An outer frame is fixed in the reveal to square up the opening; use pieces of wood as packing if necessary. The glass is fixed in a separate frame which is fitted inside the outer frame to enable the glass and its separate frame to slide. The framed glass is removable and horizontal and vertical sliders are available. Depending on the size of the window, two or more sliding panels will be needed.

One system can be fixed to the face of the window frame so you will avoid the problems of squaring up a reveal, although it can be reveal-fixed as well. In this case the company offers a kit specially designed to suit your windows; it comprises plastic channelling cut to size and ready to be joined on site so no cutting or mitring is required. The glass comes complete in its tailor-made frame ready to be installed in the channelling.

Coping with condensation

For most people condensation conjures up pictures of bathroom walls running with moisture, windows steamed up and water on the window sills. These more easily recognizable forms of condensation can be temporarily cleared up with a little time and effort devoted to mopping up. But there are ways of helping to prevent condensation forming in the first place.

Condensation is caused when moisture in warm air comes into contact with a cold surface and turns to water. Kitchens and bathrooms are the obvious places to suffer, but condensation will often occur in patches on walls or ceilings in living areas too.

Windows

Single glass windows are undoubtedly one of the worst offenders in causing condensation. In damp winter conditions few homes escape the problem – and bedrooms in particular suffer from its effects. This is the result of lower night temperatures reacting with the warm air we breathe out or warm air circulated by heating equipment.

The problem is made worse by the introduction of new moist air into a room by cooking, using hand basins or running baths. Probably the worst effect of condensation is the damage it can do in a short time to window frames and paintwork. Even when frames are correctly painted 3mm ($\frac{1}{8}$in) in on the glass pane, the lower beading quickly breaks down

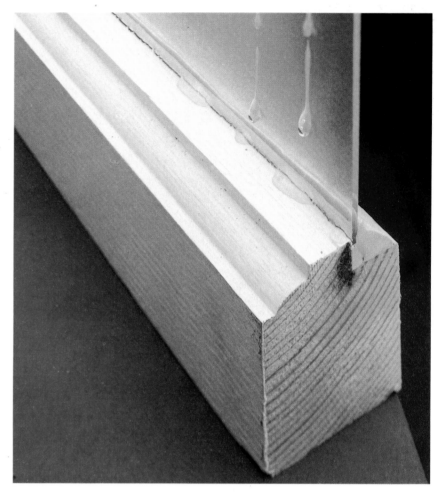

Above Condensation on window will break down paint surface and attack wood or metal frame

Far left When lining walls with expanded polystyrene, hang first length and over-lap second length by about 13mm ($\frac{1}{2}$in). Check with your supplier on suitable adhesive
Left Trim halfway across overlap through both thicknesses of polystyrene

Far left Peel away both trimmed edges
Left Stick back edges, having applied more adhesive to wall, to give flush finish to join

To test for damp floor, place piece of glass on ring of Plasticine over affected area
Right Moisture on underside of glass indicates penetrating damp
Below right Moisture forming on top of glass indicates condensation present

and allows moisture to attack the timber or metal beneath.

One remedy is the installation of good quality double-glazing. Although condensation may not be completely eliminated, the build-up is reduced sufficiently to prevent moisture being a problem.

Bathrooms

Decorative materials with cold surfaces, such as ceramic tiles, are renowned for the rapid formation of condensation. The build-up can be quickly dispersed by opening the windows. An extractor fan set into the window or mounted on (or ducted to) an exterior wall will also help remove vapour quickly. You can reduce condensation in cold bathrooms by heating the room for a short time before running the bath water. But remember you must use wall or ceiling-mounted heaters of the type recommended for bathrooms. Try running a little cold water into the bath before you turn on the hot tap, as this will also help reduce condensation.

Other wall surfaces

The real problem areas are patches of condensation which sometimes appear in odd corners of the home. Often these go unnoticed until a patch of mould appears. Poor circulation of air is one of the prime causes and on a damp day a short burst of warm air from a fan heater, or a hair dryer, will help to check condensation.

If mould persists – and the surface is not wallpapered – rinse the wall with a strong solution of bleach. If the surface is wallpapered you will have to remove the paper and line the wall with rolls of expanded polystyrene which you can then wallpaper over or paint with emulsion. In severe cases this may not be completely successful and a painted wall, which can be treated with bleach from time to time, is preferable.

Penetrating damp

Patchy wall condensation is often confused with penetrating damp. Removal of a small area of plaster should tell you which it is. If it is condensation, the brick area behind will be perfectly dry; if it is damp, try to find the cause. At ground floor level it could be a faulty damp proof course; upstairs it may be a faulty gutter or down pipe or driving rain on porous solid brickwork might be the reason. Try to increase the circulation by warm, dry air in the affected area, but remedy the cause of the problem as soon as possible otherwise the trouble will recur.

Ceilings

Those with a high gloss finish are most susceptible to condensation and covering the area with expanded polystyrene, cork or fibre tiles will help solve the problem.

Damp floors

These are often caused by damp from the outside and not by condensation. You can make a simple test to see which condition is present with a piece of glass on a ring of Plasticine, as shown above.

Condensation on floors usually occurs with cold-surfaced materials on concrete, such as tiles in the kitchen. The most effective remedy is to substitute cork or a similar warm-surfaced flooring.

INDEX